Contents

KU-775-934

Introduction

Brussels is not a city that sets out to make you love it. Paris lifts its skirts in an ooh-la-la attempt to be admired; London gives you a hearty back-slap to keep you on your toes; Rome injects you with an adrenaline rush. But Brussels simply sits back and waits. It's up to you to do the wooing.

The city's spiritual and architectural heart is without doubt the Grand'Place, so awe-inspiring and perfect you could be forgiven for believing the façades are a façade, a romantic film-set. The Gothic square typifies much of what Brussels stands for; a series of set pieces with, in between, life as it is lived. Arrive at the Gare du Midi and you may wonder what you have let yourself in for; a fairly desolate area with never-ending building works and a taxi rank reminiscent of a Middle-East bazaar. Walk through downtown Brussels admiring the architecture, turn a corner and gasp at a tatty street with washing hanging from balconies. Stand looking at the splendid royal opera house, turn round and see your reflection in the monstrous shopping centre which is now its neighbour. And wonder why the architects of the '60s and '70s had not equally reflected on their actions.

But buildings are merely objects of desire or distaste. To start a romance with Brussels, you need to get beneath its skin, not to fight, just to go with the flow. There is a defiance in Brussels that needs to be understood. It is the capital of Flanders and is set firmly in that viciously proud part of Belgium. As the capital of Belgium, it is officially bilingual, though French speakers make up over 90 per cent of the population. This francophone island is surrounded by the Flemish belt, *communes* that fiercely protect their language and culture. Add African colonial influences, the significant North-African and Middle-Eastern communities, the burgeoning (and soon-to-increase) EU and NATO workforce and all the service industries surrounding that – and you have a city that is constantly finding its way. What is so remarkable is that it succeeds.

Over the past two years, Brussels has been giving itself a face-lift to make itself more of a catch. It has three potential lovers and must preen suitably for all of them; residents, visitors and the international political community. Swaths of residential Brussels have gone under the surgeon's knife to smooth out the wrinkles, making inner-city life more attractive, encouraging the young and entrepreneurial to set up home. This is mostly evident in the Ste-Catherine area opposite the Bourse. Trendy Flemish designers, single Eurocrats and pink Euro gays have moved in and live happily alongside old brown bars and working-class rooming houses.

The legacy of Brussels 2000 renovation projects is a new homogeny, with its railway-green signposts, maps and flagstaffs pinpointing sites of interest. Buildings have been cleaned, pavements scrubbed and vistas reopened for the photo opportunity. Walking is the best way to get around and feel the spirit of the place. Look up, architectural gems sit above the ground-level shopfronts. Then look down – the poodle is a sacred animal and is allowed to leave its offerings wherever it deems appropriate.

An undeniable part of Brussels' make-up is the European Quarter, a city within a city, a glass and steel metropolis where life is lived differently, and often with little regard for the traditions of the locals. It has its own attraction, even if only to see the gold-star flag of DG-Agri to understand it is this building that explains the high price of your beef. Brussels is in a conundrum. With 13 countries waiting to join the EU, where to put them? The message from locals is loud and clear: not on our patch.

And of course, it is on their patch that you should be spending most of your time; this guide attempts to point you in local directions as well as on the tourist trail. Smoky bars, superb restaurants, museums full of the old masters, art nouveau architecture, the finest antiques or the most house-cleared of rubbish. There is a nightlife that routinely moves into day, a café culture ranging from muttering old men to hyper-cool young dudes in black, and an Antwerp-inspired fashion industry that is second to none. There are more green spaces than any other European city, a transport system that is clean, efficient and cheap, and an air of laissez-faire that means you can be what you want, whenever you want. It is this final attribute that may finally make you fall for Brussels. It is a real, living, breathing – yes – great city and, with a little attention, it will slowly extend a hand of friendship and finally embrace you.

Brussels

Antwerp, Ghent & Bruges

timeout.com/brussels

Penguin Books

PENGUIN BOOKS

Published by the Penguin Group
Penguin Books Ltd, 80 Strand, London WC2R ORL, England
Penguin Books USA Inc., 375 Hudson Street, New York, New York 10014, USA
Penguin Books Australia Ltd, 250 Camberwell Road, Camberwell, Victoria 3124, Australia
Penguin Books Canada Ltd, 10 Alcorn Avenue, Toronto, Ontario, Canada M4V 3B2
Penguin Books (NZ) Ltd, cnr Rosedale and Airborne Roads, Albany, Auckland, New Zealand

Penguin Books Ltd, Registered Offices: Harmondsworth, Middlesex, England

First published 1996
Second edition 1998
Third edition 2000
Fourth edition 2002
10 9 8 7 6 5 4 3 2 1

Colour reprographics by Icon, Crowne House, 56-58 Southwark Street, London SE1 1UN
Printed and bound by Cayfosa-Quebecor, Ctra. de Caldes, Km 3 08 130 Sta, Perpètua de Mogoda, Barcelona, Spain

Edited and designed by
Time Out Guides Limited
Universal House
251 Tottenham Court Road
London W1T 7AB
Tel + 44 (0)20 7813 3000
Fax + 44 (0)20 7813 6001
Email guides@timeout.com
www.timeout.com

Editorial

Editor Peterjon Cresswell
Deputy Editor Cath Phillips
Consultant Editor Gary Hills
Listings Researchers Wim Verhaeghe, Yvan Vonck,
Charlie Royall
Proofreader Marion Moisy
Indexer Selena Cox

Editorial Director Peter Fiennes
Series Editor Ruth Jarvis
Deputy Series Editor Jonathan Cox
Guides Co-ordinator Anna Norman

Design

Group Art Director John Oakey
Art Director Mandy Martin
Art Editor Scott Moore
Designers Benjamin de Lotz, Lucy Grant, Sarah Edwards
Scanning/Imaging Dan Conway
Ad Make-up Glen Impey
Picture Editor Kerri Littlefield
Deputy Picture Editor Kit Burnet
Picture Librarian Sarah Roberts

Advertising

Group Commercial Director Lesley Gill
Sales Director Mark Phillips
International Sales Co-ordinator Ross Canadé
Advertisement Sales (Brussels) TKR
Advertising Assistant Sabrina Ancilleri

Administration

Chairman Tony Elliott
Managing Director Mike Hardwick
Group Financial Director Kevin Ellis
Marketing Director Christine Cort
Marketing Manager Mandy Martinez
US Publicity & Marketing Associate Rosella Albanese
Group General Manager Nichola Coulthard
Production Manager Mark Lamond
Production Controller Samantha Furniss
Accountant Sarah Bostock

Features in this guide were written and researched by: Introduction Gary Hills. **History** Gary Hills, Sarah Burnett (*Guilds, Waterloo* Jonathan Cox; *Heart of darkness* Dave Rimmer). **Brussels Today** Gareth Harding. **Architecture, Art Nouveau** Bridget Hourican, Renee Cordes. **Accommodation** Alix Leveugle. **Sightseeing** Peterjon Cresswell (*Strip search* Jon Eldridge; *By tram 1* Sharon Riggle; *African Brussels* Gareth Harding; *Green Brussels* Sarah Wolff; *Brew, Troubadour* Jeremy Duns). **Restaurants** Gary Hills, Gareth Harding, Alix Leveugle (*No Macs* Jeremy Duns; *Veggie options* Alix Leveugle; all other boxes by Gary Hills). **Bars** Gary Hills, Peterjon Cresswell, Tony Mallett, Alix Leveugle (*Grand' Place, Charbon, Beers* Gary Hills; *Late haunts, EU* Alix Leveugle; *Bar life 1* Leo Cendrowicz; *Bar life 2* Gary Hills, Jeremy Duns). **Shops & Services** Alix Leveugle, Sarah Wolff (*Galeries* Sarah Wolff; *Dressing* Sarah Wolff, Alix Leveugle; *Chocolate, Trading places* Alix Leveugle). **By Season** Gary Hills (*Royal* Gary Hills; *Christmas* Peterjon Cresswell). **Children** Sarah Wolff. **Clubs** Nico Deckmyns. **Film** Gareth Harding (*Belgian Bert* Gareth Harding). **Galleries** Hugo Martin. **Gay & Lesbian** Gary Hills. **Music: Classical & Opera** Julius Stenzel (*Festival fever 1* Gary Hills). **Rock:** Dave Cronin, Jon Eldridge (*Festival fever 2* Gary Hills; *The best ...* Dave Cronin, K). **Sport & Fitness** Leo Cendrowicz (*Complementary* Leo Cendrowicz). **Theatre & Dance** Gary Hills. **Trips Out Of Town** Sarah Wolff, Jeremy Duns, Jonathan Cox (*Panamarenko* Cath Phillips; *Clubs* Nico Deckmyns; *Culture city* Gary Hills; *Party* Nico Favoreel; all other boxes Jeremy Duns). **Directory** Gary Hills, Jeremy Duns, Nico Favoreel (*Poste, Cards* Sharon Riggle).

The Editor wishes to thank: Pauline, Monica and Cormac Doyle; Sue Heady (Tourist Office of Brussels and Wallonia); Anne Reynens (Brussels Tourist Office); Alexander Corne (Tourist Office of Brussels and Flanders); estimé Philippe G, sa famille et ses amis; Walter De Weerdt; Isabelle Lousberg; Paul O'Donnell; Susanna (Pisa) and Luigi (Roma); Erik Stock et Sophie; Yvan, Hugo, Bridget, Sarah, JD, Gareth, Alix (for duty above and beyond the call of recompense); Ted Milton; Nico Favoreel; Wim Verhaeghe; Bones, Pen, The Mogul and Doris; Catheroo; Haddies; Chrissie Feltham. And especially Gary Hills. Drinks wonderfully provided by Nico, barman extraordinaire, Gare Centrale.
Alix wishes to thank Ralf; Hadley wishes to thank Debbie, P2, François and Jean-Luc; Gary wishes to thank Philip Sheppard.

Maps by Mapworld, 71 Blandy Road, Henley on Thames, Oxon RG9 1QB, and JS Graphics, john@jsgraphics.co.uk.

Photography by Hadley Kincade except: pages 63, 95, 223, 238, 239, 244, 245, 246, 255, 256, 260, 264, 265, 267, 268, 272, 273, 275, 276, 277, 279, 282 and 283 Tourism Flanders; page 255 Corbis; pages 228, 232, 233, 235, 237, 241 and 257 Sarah Blee; page 205 PA Photos/EPA; page 209 AP Photo/Steve Holland; pages 6, 8, 11, 13, 17 and 22 AKG London; pages 23 and 24 Hulton Archive; pages 187, 227 and 249 Art Archive.

The following pictures were provided by the featured establishments/artists: pages 33, 92, 183, 197, 202, 211, 215, 217, 236, 251 and 271.

ABOUT TIME OUT GUIDES

This is the fourth edition of the *Time Out Brussels Guide*, one of the expanding series of *Time Out* guides produced by the people behind London and New York's definitive listings magazines. It paints a detailed picture of the *carrefour de l'Europe*, the crossroads of Europe. This edition has been completely updated and all listings checked by a team of Brussels-based writers and experts. Some chapters have been rewritten, others have been revised and brought up to date. Many more restaurants and bars have been included.

THE LIE OF THE LAND

Brussels is a sprawling and confusing city. Its centre is essentially defined by a pentagonal series of linked major roads known as the Petit Ring. In the centre of this ring, in the Lower Town is the Grand' Place, the undisputed centre of the city. East of the Grand' Place the ground rises up to the logically named and grander Upper Town. Outside the Petit Ring to the east is the rather characterless EU area and the formal Parc du Cinquantenaire. To the south, around the posh-shopping mecca of avenue Louise stretches the lively Ixelles district. West of here is St-Gilles and its art nouveau gems. West of the Petit Ring is Anderlecht, famous for its football club and beer museum. To the north of the Petit Ring is Laeken, home to the royal family and the Atomium. Further out are the wide green spaces of the Bois de la Cambre and the Fôret de Soignes.

This guide also includes sizeable chapters on three of Flanders' most beautiful and exciting cities, Antwerp, Bruges and Ghent, and we also have a number of suggestions for rewarding day trips from Brussels: Liège, Ostend, Leuven, Mechelen, Namur, Tournai and the Ardennes.

ESSENTIAL INFORMATION

For all the practical information you might need for visiting the area – including local transport systems, emergency numbers and useful websites – turn to the Directory chapter at the back of this guide. It starts on page 286.

THE LOWDOWN ON THE LISTINGS

We have tried to make this book as easy to use and practically useful as possible. Addresses, phone numbers, transport information, opening times and admission prices are all included. However, owners and managers can change their arrangements at any time. Before you go out of your way, we'd strongly advise you to

phone ahead to check opening times and other particulars. While every effort and care has been made to ensure the accuracy of the information contained in this guide, the publishers cannot accept responsibility for any errors it may contain.

PRICES & PAYMENT

In the listings, we have noted which of the following credit cards are accepted: American Express (AmEx), Diners Club (DC), MasterCard (MC) and Visa (V). Other cards may be taken.

For every restaurant we have given the price range for main courses, and set menus where relevant. The prices we've supplied should be treated as guidelines, not gospel. If prices vary wildly from those we've quoted, ask whether there's a good reason. If not, go elsewhere. Then please let us know. We aim to give the best and most up-to-date advice, so we want to know if you've been badly treated or overcharged.

TELEPHONE NUMBERS

To phone Brussels from outside Belgium, first dial the international code 00, followed by 32 (the code for Belgium), then 2 (the code for Brussels) and finally the seven-digit number. When within Belgium, all telephone numbers now require that the area code is dialled as part of the number, whether you are within the relevant area or not.

MAPS

At the back of this guide (and within the Trips Out of Town chapter) you'll find a series of maps of Brussels, Antwerp, Ghent and Bruges. Map references are given after each listing that includes an address. Every place listed in this guide which falls within these maps will have a map reference against it to aid location.

LET US KNOW WHAT YOU THINK

We hope you enjoy the *Time Out Brussels Guide*, and we'd like to know what you think of it. We welcome your tips for places to include in future editions and take notice of your criticism of our choices. There's a reader's reply card at the back of this book – or you can email us on brusselsguide@timeout.com.

Advertisers

We would like to stress that no establishment has been included in this guide because it has advertised in any of our publications and no payment of any kind has influenced any review. The opinions given in this book are those of *Time Out* writers and entirely independent.

There is an online version of this guide, as well as weekly events listings for 33 international cities, at **www.timeout.com**

In Context

Battle of the Golden Spurs, 1302. *See p7.*

History

Invasions, revolutions, wars, language disputes: the past has been a turbulent time for Belgium and its capital.

Early & medieval history

When Julius Caesar embarked on the Gallic Wars in 57 BC, most of the tribes in what is now Belgium were Celtic. The Romans called them the Belgae and Caesar complained that of all the peoples in Gaul, they were the toughest. He attributed this to the fact that they were the tribes furthest from the Mediterranean and had missed out on the civilising influence of visiting merchants. Nevertheless, they were not too tough to be cooks; even in these early years, the Belgae enjoyed a gastronomic reputation, and the Flemish coast had become famous for its exported fish sauces.

Despite the toughness of the Belgae, Caesar's armies conquered the region. In 15 BC it became the Roman province of Gallia Belgica, and was later divided into administrative districts called *civitates*. The area was thinly populated and undeveloped, and was not as economically important for the Romans as other towns in

Gaul. Even so, the districts paid taxes and provided troops to the Romans, who built a network of roads and army camps. Tournai (then Turnacum) in south-west Belgium became an important quarrying town, as well as an early centre of Christianity. Salt was refined from sea water along the coast, there was an ironworks near Ghent, and wool was also produced.

The Roman empire in the north began to founder in the third century, when Germanic tribes attacked the northern borders of Gallia Belgica. Excavations of Roman camps show that massive destruction took place in the third century. Severe flooding, a problem that recurred throughout the history of the Low Countries and often caused huge loss of life, also weakened the empire, and Roman Gaul collapsed in the fifth century. The Germanic invasions of the third to fifth centuries were the first stage in the process that was to lead to the linguistic division of present-day Belgium. The northern areas slowly became German-speaking, while the southern part of the country continued to speak Latin-based languages. The division was by no means crystallised at this time, and it is premature to refer to a clear split before the tenth century, but its roots can be clearly traced. No records relate to Brussels from this period.

THE FRANKS

The Romans' successors were the Franks, and Gallia Belgica formed the northern border of their authority. They in turn were succeeded by Charlemagne, who ruled from 768 to 814 and built a vast empire from Denmark to southern Italy, from the Atlantic to the River Danube. When Charlemagne died in 814, his sons and grandsons went to war over their inheritance. Eventually, in 843, the kingdom was split between his three grandsons following the Treaty of Verdun: Louis the German received East Francia, which roughly corresponds to Germany; Charles the Bald was given West Francia, which roughly equates to France plus Flanders; and Lothair received Middle Francia, or the Middle Kingdom. This was a thin strip comprising the land between the River Scheldt and Germany in the north, and stretching down to the Mediterranean. It would continue to be a source of contention between France and Germany right into the 20th century.

> **'Even in Roman times, the Belgae enjoyed a gastronomic reputation, and the Flemish coast became famous for its exported fish sauces.'**

The grandsons of Charlemagne were not the only ones fighting over the region in the Dark Ages. Throughout the ninth and tenth centuries, the old Frankish kingdoms were subject to regular invasions by the Vikings, who took advantage of the power vacuum. There was a gradual disintegration of coherent central power and a rise of feudal domains. Flanders became one of the most powerful of all, and although it was theoretically ruled by the kings of France, the Flemish counts were virtually autonomous. Other fiefdoms to emerge from the ninth to the 11th centuries were Liège, Hainaut, Namur, Luxembourg and Brabant.

Brussels was in Brabant. The first extant documented reference to Brussels (Brocsella or Bruocsella, meaning 'village in the marshes') dates from 695, when it was a stopping point on the trade route from Cologne to Bruges

and Ghent. However, the city was not officially founded until 979, when Charles of France built a fortress on the island of St-Géry.

FLANDERS, ENGLAND AND FRANCE

The history of the fiefdoms of northern Europe is a complex series of wars, shifting boundaries, trade disputes and intermarriages. One of the Flemish counts, Baldwin II, married the daughter of England's King Alfred the Great, while William the Conqueror married the daughter of Baldwin V. The Flemish were trading far beyond their own borders. Flanders was already exporting cloth to England in the tenth century and there is evidence of a slave trade between the two. By the 12th century, Flemish cloth was being sold in France, Italy and England. The economic health of Flanders depended not only on the state of its relations with England and English wool imports, but also on Anglo-French relations, with Flanders often suffering from English reprisals against the French. Despite the fact that the Flemish counts were vassals of the French kings, the Flemish were often hostile to the French.

On 11 July 1302, at the Battle of the Golden Spurs (Gulden Sporen in Dutch; Eperons d'Or in French), the French knights suffered a shock defeat, the victorious Flemish collecting 700 pairs of spurs from the fleeing Frenchmen. It was a milestone in Flemish resistance to the French. Consequently, the victory was hugely important in Flemish and Belgian consciousness (11 July is still a holiday in Flanders). The balance of the England-France-Flanders triangle became even more fragile in 1337 when the Hundred Years' War began. At the start of the war, a Flemish landowner called Jacob van Artevelde led a rebellion in Ghent against the pro-French counts of Flanders, who fled to France. Flanders had been officially neutral, but van Artevelde actively allied it with the English.

Further problems arose in the 13th and 14th centuries because of unrest in Flanders, Liège and Brabant. Townspeople and merchants demanded new powers from their rulers, who in the past had relied on French backing to quell disorder. Guild power increased and the towns gained a share of the government. The new rights given to townspeople and the growth of trade caused cultural and economic disparities between the towns and the surrounding countryside. Ghent, Bruges, Ypres, Brussels, Leuven, Antwerp and Mechelen all became wealthier and more powerful and, by 1340, Ghent was the largest city in Europe after Paris.

The growth of Brussels had started in the 11th century, when it spread out from the marshy valley of the River Senne into the hills and plateaux around it. The forests around the

Guild power

When Louis XIV of France ordered Marshal de Villeroy to have his troops bombard Brussels in 1695, it took three days and three nights for them to reduce some 4,000 houses and 16 churches to tinder and rubble. Medieval Brussels was destroyed. Somehow the Hôtel de Ville survived – the rest of the Grand' Place, the site of magnificent pageants and tournaments for 300 years, was razed to the ground (*pictured above*).

It is testament to the power, riches and guile of the local guilds that it took them only five years to rebuild the 39 wonderful guildhouses you see today (*pictured right*), all in beautiful baroque style, resulting in one the finest central squares in all Europe.

When the Grand' Place was a humble Lower Market – Nedermerct – in the early 1300s, the guilds were far more than bodies of

skilled craftsmen. Mercantile and artisan guilds had started out as occupational organisations, set up to help people trading outside their home town. Later, guild statutes regulated hours and conditions of work, conditions of mastership, entry fees and the length of apprenticeships. Some had courts to levy fines for breach of these statutes, and most guilds were rigorous about restricting entry. The majority started excluding women in the 14th century, although some still allowed them to work as journeymen. A closed shop, if you like. They also developed social and charitable roles. In Ghent, six guilds had almshouses, and most others gave charity to members who needed it.

But more than anything, the guilds, run by wealthy families, exerted political influence on the authorities of the day to further their own

town provided materials for construction and fuel. They also provided hunting grounds for the Dukes of Brabant, who built a palace in 1041 on higher ground at Coudenburg. Wool was the most important trade from the 13th to 15th centuries, along with metalwork.

The Dukes of Burgundy

A process of great cultural change began in the 1360s when Margaret of Male, daughter of the Count of Flanders, married Philip the Bold

(Philippe le Hardi), Duke of Burgundy. When Margaret's father died in 1384, Flanders and, later, other provinces came together in a loose union under the authority of the Dukes of Burgundy. The key figure in the rise of the Dukes of Burgundy was Philip the Good (Philippe le Bon), grandson of Margaret and Philip the Bold. Having inherited Flanders, Burgundy, Artois and other provinces, he then acquired Brabant, Holland, Hainaut, Namur and Luxembourg through a combination of politics, purchase and military action. Nevertheless,

economic interests. The guilds, therefore, ever swift to rise to the cause of Brabant, were the only viable counterbalance to the aristocracy. Guild militias took part in the great Flemish victory over the French at the Battle of the Golden Spurs in 1302 (*see p7*). The powerful textile guilds, in particular, were the most frequent instigators of urban unrest – followed by the smiths, brewers, butchers and carpenters. Headquarters were built, on the main squares of Brussels and Antwerp, stark evidence of the guilds' influential role in daily life.

As the textile industry declined, some guilds became more political than occupational. Men were often masters in more than one guild, or changed affiliations from one year to the next. By the 16th century they were chiefly occupied with lawsuits and disputes among themselves, helplessly watching the rise of new non-guild industries such as cotton and coal. The era of the guilds was over.

the Low Countries were by no means a country as such, merely a group of territories under the control of one family. Although the Dukes of Burgundy ruled for less than a century, the cultural changes during this period were significant. In addition to their ducal palace in Dijon, they had important residences in Lille, Bruges and Brussels. The court moved regularly between them, although from 1459 it was based mainly in Brussels. Keen to be viewed as the equals of the French court, the

Dukes of Burgundy initiated their own court culture in the Netherlands, and were active patrons of the arts.

A FLEMISH CULTURAL GOLDEN AGE

Parades, tournaments, jousting and pageants were a major part of city and court life under the Dukes, as a means of displaying their power and wealth. This was also apparent in the great building works which took place. The first university in the Low Countries was founded in Leuven (Louvain) in Brabant in 1425; work on Brussels' town hall, the dominant feature of the Grand' Place, began in 1402 and was completed in 1455; and the awesome tower of Mechelen Cathedral was begun in 1452.

In the arts, the best-known evidence of the Dukes' patronage is in 15th-century art. The Brabant-born painter Jan van Eyck worked in Ghent and Bruges. Rogier van der Weyden worked in Brussels as the city's official painter. German artist Hans Memling settled in Bruges in 1465. Although the Dukes were the most prolific patrons, works were also commissioned by city governments, and by native and Italian merchants in Bruges. Painters had to enrol in guilds in the city where they worked and were regarded as no more than craftsmen. Many of them also painted banners for parades and festivals. In Bruges, sculptors belonged to the carpenters' guild. For more on the guilds, *see p8* **Guild power**.

Although the textile industries were declining in the 14th and 15th centuries, mainly in the face of cheaper English competition, other industries were replacing them. Brussels was producing tapestries, Ghent had a growing leather industry, mainly producing gloves and purses, and the Flanders coastal towns were exporting pickled herring. Meanwhile, new agricultural techniques, particularly the use of the single-handed plough, were boosting production in the countryside. There were repeated uprisings and rebellions in Ghent between 1400 and 1450, primarily because economic power had shifted from Flanders to Brabant. Not only were Brussels' industries more prosperous than Ghent's but Bruges's access to the sea had silted up and it had been superseded by Antwerp as a port and a centre of trade.

The Spanish Netherlands

With the death of Philip the Good in 1467, the end of the rule of the Dukes of Burgundy was in sight. Philip was succeeded by his son Charles the Rash (Charles le Téméraire), whose attempts at modernisation were unpopular, and there was no great grief when he was killed at the Battle of Nancy in 1477. He was succeeded by his daughter Mary whose death five years later left the Netherlands in disarray. Mary had married Maximilian von Habsburg of Austria, and their son Philip was only four when she died, so the Low Countries were ruled by Maximilian for the next ten years, making them part of the Habsburg empire.

'After an extraordinary series of deaths and childless marriages, Emperor Charles V had inherited most of Europe by the time he was 20.'

Like his father-in-law Charles, Maximilian was unpopular in the Netherlands, and unrest in the provinces developed into civil wars in Holland and Utrecht, although he did eventually restore order.

EMPEROR CHARLES V

Maximilian's son Philip married Juana the Mad, the daughter of King Ferdinand and Queen Isabella of Spain. Their son Charles was born in Ghent in 1500, and after an extraordinary series of premature deaths and childless marriages among the ruling families of Europe he had inherited most of Europe by the time he was 20. He became Lord of the Netherlands in 1506 and King of Spain in 1516, and was made Emperor Charles V of Germany when his grandfather Maximilian died in 1519. In this way, a native of Ghent came to rule the Netherlands, Austria, the Tyrol, Spain, Mexico, Peru, the Caribbean, Sicily, Naples and the German empire. Charles spent much of his earlier reign in Brussels and spoke Dutch as his first language. Between 1506 and 1555 he enlarged the territory of the Netherlands, adding Tournai, Friesland and Utrecht.

When Charles inherited the Low Countries, the province of Brabant had eclipsed Flanders. Brussels had its new town hall with a 90-metre (300-foot) tower, and the Dukes of Brabant and other nobles had built palaces on the higher ground. The Netherlands were still booming culturally, and among Charles's advisers during his late teens was the theologian and humanist Erasmus. The first regular international mail service was set up in Brussels in 1520 by Jean-Baptiste de Tour et Taxis.

Antwerp, also in Brabant, was even more prosperous than Brussels, because it was the crossroads of the trading routes between Spain, Portugal, Russia and the Baltic. Each day, as many as 5,000 merchants gathered in the exchange, while up to 500 ships came and

went from the port. So euphoric was one Victorian historian about this golden age that he described the population of the Netherlands as 'three millions of people, the most industrious, the most prosperous, perhaps the most intelligent under the sun'.

THE REFORMATION

But Charles' rule over the Netherlands and the other parts of his empire was far from trouble-free. Outside Brabant, provinces were drifting into poverty because of flooding, high taxes and racing inflation. Far more serious was the fact that his reign saw the beginning of the Reformation, which had devastating consequences for the whole of Europe. Lutherans from Germany extended their influence westwards into the Netherlands, while Calvinism spread northwards from Geneva. Although Charles was prepared to negotiate with Luther and his followers, he also dealt harshly with Protestants (or heretics as many preferred to label them). The first Lutheran martyrs were burned in Brussels in 1523, and in 1550 Charles passed the Edict of Blood, which demanded the death penalty for all those convicted of heresy.

Charles abdicated in 1555, in a tearful ceremony at Brussels, and handed over the reins of the Netherlands to his son Philip. He had already abdicated in Austria in 1521, and three months after the Brussels ceremony, he abdicated in Spain, again in favour of his son, who became Philip II. Like his father, Philip inherited a collection of provinces in the Low Countries, rather than a nation. There was no common ancestry or language among the 17 provinces, and the French and Dutch language split was already evident. However, there was some administrative unity: provincial assemblies, the States, sent delegates to the central States General, and the rulers had personal representatives (*stadtholders*) in each state or group of states.

The problems afflicting the Netherlands during Philip's rule were similar to those suffered under Charles: heavy taxation and the spread of Protestantism. But whereas Charles had remained popular, Philip was never liked. He was Spanish by birth and sentiment, and had little affection for his subjects in the Low Countries. He was also more hardline in his defence of Catholicism than his father. In this he was aided by the Inquisition. Although the Spanish achieved the greatest infamy, their colleagues in northern Europe were hardly soft. One man in Bruges who trampled on a consecrated wafer had his hand and foot wrenched off by red-hot irons and his tongue ripped out, before being roasted over a fire.

Emperor Charles V, aged 12. *See p10.*

THE DUTCH REVOLT

Philip's troubles in the Netherlands started fairly quickly. He appointed his half-sister Margaret of Parma as regent, but power was mainly in the hands of two hated pro-Spanish councillors, Cardinal Granvelle and Count Berlaymont. Equally unpopular were Philip's attempts to reorganise the bishoprics, especially among the clerics and nobles who saw a threat to their power and wealth. Philip's most prominent opponents were Prince William of Orange, Count Egmont and Count Hoorn.

In 1565, a group of nobles opposed to Philip formed the League of Nobles. Berlaymont referred to them disparagingly as *ces gueux* ('those beggars') and *Vivent les Gueux* became their rallying cry. They objected to Philip's refusal to tolerate Protestantism, his attempt to centralise power, the heavy taxes imposed on the provinces, and the presence of Spanish troops in the Netherlands.

The spread of Protestantism was not confined to the League of Nobles. It burgeoned among the poor in the towns of Flanders, Brabant, Holland and Zeeland. In the 1560s, Calvinist 'field preachers' attracted huge crowds, and part of their attraction to the poor was that the preachers railed against the wealth of the Catholic Church. The preachers also criticised the imagery and art in the Catholic churches. In the Iconoclastic Riots of 1566, Calvinist mobs destroyed Catholic churches all over the Netherlands. In Antwerp, crowds attacked the cathedral with axes: they hacked up the Madonna, pulled down the statue of Christ at the altar, destroyed the chapels, drank the communion wine, burned manuscripts and rubbed the sacred oil on their shoes. They then did the same to 30 other churches in the city.

In 1567, Philip appointed the Duke of Alva as new governor in the Seventeen Provinces, and he arrived with an army of 10,000. He called the Netherlanders 'men of butter' and said he had come to tame them. One of his first acts was to set up the 'Council of Blood' (officially the Council of Troubles or Tumults). On 4 January 1568 alone, he had 84 people executed on the scaffold. In March of that year, there were 1,500 arrests, 800 of them in one day, and in June Count Egmont and Count Hoorn were beheaded in the Grand' Place in Brussels. Their deaths marked the start of a full-scale revolt in the Netherlands that would last for 80 years.

A major turning point was the Spanish Fury of 1576. A financial crisis in Spain meant that the troops had not been paid for three years, and Spanish soldiers in the Antwerp garrison went on the rampage, setting fire to almost a thousand buildings in the wealthiest quarter of Antwerp. Their behaviour strengthened the resolve of potential rebels. But from 1578, when Philip sent Alexander Farnese to govern in the Netherlands, the Spanish began to regain control over the southern Netherlands.

Although Calvinism had first taken hold in the south, the southern provinces were now coming under the influence of the Counter-Reformation, and in 1579 the ten southern provinces formed the Union of Arras, accepting the authority of Philip, and Catholicism. The north's response was the 1581 Union of Utrecht, which was essentially a declaration that the seven northern provinces no longer recognised Philip's authority. The boundaries were not yet fixed, however, and Parma reconquered Bruges, Ghent and, later, Antwerp. By the end of the century, the northern provinces had formed the Republic of the United Netherlands, also known as the United Provinces, while the southern provinces were known as the Spanish Netherlands.

Although the rebels were hostile to Philip and the Spanish and many of them were anti-Catholic, their aim was not to achieve independence but merely to gain greater autonomy and religious freedom and to get Spanish troops out of the Low Countries. But the split became irreversible, particularly since continuing revolt unified the different classes and interests in the new republic in the north.

The Battle of Waterloo

The rolling green fields of the battle of Borodino (1812), west of Moscow, are spotted with small obelisks marking the units fallen in the name of Napoleonic France and Tsarist Russia; Nelson's victory at Cape Trafalgar (1805), by the strait of Gibraltar, is fiercely celebrated on the rock every year; the battlefield of Waterloo (1815), which you pass on any train heading south from Brussels, is marked with a motorway.

There is a definite initial sense of disappointment if you stop at Waterloo. But walk 15 minutes up to the old Bodenghien Inn, and all will be revealed. For this was Wellington's quarters; now it's the **Musée Wellington**, where history is brought to life. Original documents, plans and models illustrate what was going on in Wellington's mind that muddy June of 1815. The tourist office is next door.

The previous February, Napoleon and a few hundred loyal troops had escaped from exile on the Mediterranean island of Elba and landed near Cannes. Despite the defeats at Trafalgar, the retreat from Moscow and the dismemberment of his empire, Napoleon needed only three weeks to reconquer the hearts and minds of his people. The major European powers duly declared war, and Brussels was chosen as the Allied base. From April troops began to arrive in the city, and there began a frenzied round of officers' balls. Napoleon knew the only way to defeat such a formidable coalition would be to strike quickly and decisively – he had to stop the British and Prussian armies joining together.

On 15 June, his 125,000-strong army crossed the border, took Charleroi and moved north-east towards Brussels. The partying came to a sudden end (although the hardcore allegedly danced all night at the Duchess of Richmond's legendary ball and then rode into battle in their ballroom shoes). The Duke of Wellington, commander of the Anglo-Dutch-German army, knew he had to stop Napoleon before he reached Brussels and chose to defend a ridge to the south of the village of Waterloo, about 18 kilometres (11 miles) south of the capital.

The campaign of Waterloo consisted of three main battles. As Napoleon had only half the forces of his Allied opponents he sought to engage them separately. On 16 June he defeated Marshal Blücher's Prussians at Ligny, but crucially neglected to follow up the victory. Believing the Prussians to be in flight, that same day he challenged Wellington at Quatre Bras, on the Brussels–Charleroi road.

Despite appalling conditions of mud and rain, Wellington's forces reached their allotted positions on a ridge at Mont St-Jean.

Counter-Reformation

In 1598, Philip handed over his remaining territories in the Netherlands to Archduke Albrecht of Austria, husband of his daughter Isabella. Philip hoped this might make reconciliation between north and south possible. However, when Albrecht died without an heir in 1621, the provinces reverted to Spanish rule, although Isabella remained governor until her death in 1633. Isabella and Albrecht maintained a lavish court, the focal point of which was their court painter Pieter Paul Rubens. The political and military achievements of Isabella and Albrecht's rule were less notable.

They negotiated a truce with the Dutch in 1609, but it lasted just 12 years, and the war continued until 1648. During the last half-century of the war, the religious gap between the two sides widened, with the United Provinces becoming more firmly Calvinist and the Spanish Netherlands in the grip of the Catholic Counter-Reformation. The Dutch developed a gruesome literature and art of martyrdom at the hands of the Spanish. This, together with the reams of propaganda issuing from both sides, cemented the differences between north and south. The war ended in 1648 with the Treaty of Münster in which Spain recognised the independence of the north's United Provinces, with the agreed borders corresponding to the present-day Belgian-Dutch border.

One of the terms was that Antwerp's access to the sea was to be cut off by a Dutch blockade of the River Scheldt, rendering it redundant as a port. In the 1660s, Antwerp was allowed a sea outlet via a canal, but this was no substitute. The Scheldt would remain closed for nearly 150 years. During the war, a flood of Calvinist and anti-Spanish merchants, workers and bankers had emigrated from the south to the north, taking with them their skills and wealth.

Napoleon arrived at the Belle Alliance inn, nine kilometres (five miles) south of Waterloo, the evening of Saturday 17 June, before establishing his quarters at Le Caillou dairy farm. The two-storey house is now the **Musée du Caillou,** featuring assorted items of Napoleonic memorabilia. The two armies passed uncomfortable nights in the teeming rain. As day broke the 67,000 Allied soldiers looked across the shallow valley at the 72,000 French troops arrayed just 1,500 metres (one mile) away.

When it came, the battle itself didn't actually take place at Waterloo, but just south of the neighbouring village of Braine l'Alleud. The site became a centre for tourist pilgrimage almost before the last bodies had been carted off the field, and almost two centuries of visitors have resulted in a curious grouping of attractions.

▶

The result was that the north (and Amsterdam in particular) flourished, becoming an affluent maritime and trading power. The south did not. Antwerp had been especially hard hit during the war by the Spanish Fury and the Dutch blockade. Its population fell from 100,000 in 1560 to 42,000 in 1589, and the post-war period brought little recovery.

Things were to become worse for the Spanish Netherlands in the second half of the 17th century. Louis XIV of France had ambitions to dominate Europe at the expense of the Dutch, the English and the Habsburgs, and Spain's power had dwindled so far that it was no longer able to defend its territory. The late 17th century brought a succession of wars – the War of Devolution, the Dutch War, the War of the Grand Alliance – in all of which the Spanish Netherlands were either attacked or occupied. Several of the ensuing peace treaties led to the territory of the Spanish Netherlands being whittled away. For example, France gained Artois and Ypres. Ironically, almost the only protection given to the southern Netherlands at this time came from the Dutch, who wanted a barrier between themselves and the French.

The semi-permanent state of war in the Spanish Netherlands caused serious economic decline in the late 17th and early 18th centuries. The only sector to prosper during those years was agriculture, and there was a shift of population from town to country. But the cities were not bereft of economic activity. Brussels, for example, was still producing a variety of luxury goods, including lace, tapestries and porcelain, both for export and for the nobles and merchants still living in the Spanish Netherlands.

The Austrian Netherlands

When Philip IV of Spain died in 1665, the Spanish throne passed to his sickly and feeble-minded four-year-old son Charles. Despite two marriages, Charles II remained childless and for most of the 1690s seemed to be teetering

▶ The Battle of Waterloo (continued)

The drab modern **Waterloo Visitors' Centre** has a model of the battlefield and an audio-visual display. The most prominent monument is the **Butte du Lion**, outside the centre. Rising 45 metres (147 feet), this impressive mound, topped by a 28-tonne lion, was built ten years after the battle, on the spot where Prince William of Orange fell injured. From the viewing platform, there's a fine panorama of the battlefield, and a plan laying out which army was where as dawn broke on Sunday 18 June 1815.

The waterlogged ground put paid to Napoleon's plan to launch an early attack, and it wasn't until 11.35am that it was deemed dry enough for battle to commence. A massive artillery barrage engulfed the Allied army while Napoleon sent his less than competent brother, Prince Jerome, to take the fortified farm of Hougoumont on the Allied left. This was supposed to be a diversionary tactic to force Wellington to weaken his centre in defence of the stronghold, but the defenders held off the enemy. At 5pm, when the attack was abandoned, more than 3,000 French corpses were piled outside the farm's battered walls. In the meantime, Napoleon had learned that Blücher's troops hadn't been routed and were closing; he sent 14,000 troops from his main army to attempt

to prevent the Prussians reaching the battlefield. To try to force the battle he took the risky step of ordering a huge infantry assault on Wellington's left and the farm of La Haie-Sainte.

The arrival of the Prussians would swing the balance in favour of the Allies. Wellington ordered his troops to pull back slightly from the ridge. Wave after wave of French cavalry attacks wreaked havoc on the Allies, but they refused to crumble. By 6.30pm the French *tricolore* was raised at La Haie-Sainte and the Allied lines were buckling under the pressure. It was then that the first Prussian troops reached the field, and Blücher's forces began making inroads on the French right.

Napoleon threw every resource he had available into the battle in a last desperate attempt to snatch victory. At 7.30pm his beloved Imperial Guard entered the fray, but, bogged down in the mud churned up by their own cavalry, they made easy targets. Onwards they marched, almost as far as Mont St-Jean, before being forced to retreat. By 8.15pm, and the arrival of Blücher's entire army, Wellington rode up and down his lines urging his soldiers into a huge counter-attack. The French confidence evaporated and their troops fled. The battle was over.

on the verge of death. Eager to fill a vacuum, the French, English, Dutch and Austrians manoeuvred over his successor. In 1695, in retaliation for English and Dutch attacks on their ports, the French destroyed medieval Brussels, including the Grand' Place. Miraculously, the Hôtel de Ville survived, and within five years, the guilds had rebuilt their houses in the magnificent style you see today (*see p8* **Guild power**).

By this time Charles II had died, and there were two candidates to succeed him: Archduke Charles of Austria and Philip of Anjou, grandson of Louis XIV of France.

Charles favoured the Frenchman as his heir, partly, it is said, out of dislike for his own German wife, and in 1701 the French Duke of Anjou entered Madrid as King of Spain. Shortly afterwards, the French occupied Dutch-held 'barrier fortresses' in the Spanish Netherlands, and the English and the Dutch declared war on France. The War of the Spanish Succession lasted from 1701 to 1713

and was fought in Germany, the Netherlands, Italy and Spain, as well as at sea. During the war, the Spanish Netherlands were governed by the French and the English. Peace was made at the 1713 Treaty of Utrecht and the 1714 Treaty of Rastatt. Philip of Anjou kept the Spanish throne, but the Austrians came away with the Spanish Netherlands, henceforth known as the Austrian Netherlands.

The Dutch gained the right to keep a line of defensive forts in the Austrian Netherlands, with the cost borne by the Austrian emperors (and indirectly by the taxes of the inhabitants). The main effect felt by the Austrian Netherlands during the first years of the 18th century was peace, for the country was no longer the prey of French armies. Only once during Austrian rule, which lasted until 1794, were the Netherlands invaded by the French, in 1744. Emperor Charles VI of Austria wanted his daughter Maria Theresa to inherit his empire, but the rest of Europe refused to accept this. France invaded and occupied the Austrian

At 9.30pm Wellington and Blücher embraced at the Belle Alliance inn. Wellington's victory despatch was sent from the village and, following the convention of the time, this was the name that was given to the battle. News reached Brussels half an hour later.

'A damned near thing, the nearest run thing you ever saw in your life,' said the Duke of the victory gained at such heavy cost. The suave Irishman was said to have broken down when the casualty list was read to him, his aide-de-camp Sir Alexander Gordon among the 13,000 dead.

Yet Napoleon had been decisively beaten and, on 22 June, he was forced to abdicate to a lonely exile on the remote Atlantic island of St Helena. The map of Europe would be redrawn.

Musée du Caillou

66 chaussée de Bruxelles, Vieux-Genappe (02 384 24 24). **Open** *Apr-Oct* 10am-6.30pm daily. *Nov-Mar* 1-5pm daily. **Admission** €2.

Musée Wellington

147 chaussée de Bruxelles, Waterloo (02 354 78 06). **Open** *Apr-Sept* 9.30am-6.30pm daily. *Oct-Mar* 10.30am-5pm daily. **Admission** €5.

Office de Tourisme de Waterloo

149 chaussée de Bruxelles, Waterloo (02 354 99 10). **Open** *Apr-Sept* 9.30am-6.30pm daily. *Oct-Mar* 10.30am-5pm daily. **Admission** €5; €1-€4 concessions. A package deal for the two museums, the visitor centre, the mound and the panorama costs €12 (€6-€10 concessions).

Waterloo Visitors' Centre

254 route du Lion, Braine l'Alleud (02 385 19 12). **Open** *Apr-Sept* 9.30am-6.30pm daily. *Oct* 9.30am-5pm daily. *Nov-Feb* 10am-4pm daily. *Mar* 10am-5pm daily. **Admission** Centre €4.96; Panorama de la Bataille €2.73; Butte du Lion 99¢; combined ticket €7.44. Concessions available. One-hour walking tours (€3) of the battlefield are held on weekend afternoons in summer. Every five years a major reconstruction of the battle takes place – the next one is due in 2005.

Getting there

Trains for Waterloo leave Brussels about every 20 minutes; journey time is 25 minutes. Bus W links Waterloo with Braine l'Alleud; there is also a frequent train service between Braine l'Alleud and Brussels.

Netherlands until the Treaty of Aix-La-Chapelle restored Austrian rule in 1748 and gave the throne to Maria Theresa's husband, Francis I.

MARIA THERESA AND JOSEPH II

The real force, however, was Maria Theresa. Her rule, lasting until 1780, brought considerable economic renewal in the Austrian Netherlands. This was partly a result of peace, and partly of efforts by her governor, Charles of Lorraine, to build roads and waterways. There were also improvements in agricultural techniques, to the extent that the late 18th century was the only time in Belgium's history when it was self-sufficient in grain. A rural textile industry had grown up, with half the rural population of Flanders making their living spinning flax and weaving linen. There were also new glass, coal and cotton industries, which, unlike the trades that came before, did not revolve around the power of the guilds. Smaller industries such as paper mills, sugar refineries and silk factories also grew.

Cultural life developed, censorship was relaxed, French books circulated freely and bookshops were opened in the towns. There was a growing printing industry too. However, the Austrian Netherlands were scarcely at the fore of the Enlightenment, and rural culture was still traditional, with companies travelling around the countryside performing medieval mystery plays. Brussels also changed under the Austrians. In 1731, the Coudenberg Palace burnt down after a fire in the kitchens. In 1740, work began on a new palace, the Palais Royal, which is now the town residence of the Belgian royal family. The neo-classical place Royale and the Palais de la Nation, the seat of the Belgian parliament, were built in the 1770s and '80s.

Maria Theresa was succeeded by her son Joseph II in 1780. His rule was more zealous and more radical than his mother's. He immediately tried to modernise the country, closing monasteries and seminaries, taxing the Church and reforming the judicial system and government administration. In 1781 he passed the Edict of Toleration, which recognised religious freedoms. He also tried, but failed, to unblock Antwerp's access to the sea.

'Around 100,000 peasants, led by priests, marched through Brussels to protest against the progressives, many of whom were forced to flee to France.'

Joseph was loathed by the conservative Belgians, who saw their traditional privileges and vested interests threatened. The result was the Brabançon Revolution of 1789-90, involving all the provinces except Luxembourg. The rebels, led by a Brussels lawyer, wrote a new constitution inspired by the US Articles of Confederation and formed the Confederation of the United Belgian States. But the revolution collapsed into chaos as a result of the widening split between conservative and progressive rebels. Around 100,000 peasants, led by priests, marched through Brussels to protest against the progressives, many of whom were forced to flee to France. Austrian authority was restored in 1791, and when Joseph II died, he was succeeded by the liberal Leopold I who had less enthusiasm for reform and was preoccupied with events in other parts of his tottering empire.

FRENCH REVOLUTIONARY RULE

In 1792, the French declared war on Austria and Prussia, occupying the Austrian Netherlands and independent Liège. The French armies were initially greeted as liberators, but the welcome quickly faded, and when the French temporarily withdrew from Brussels after a defeat in 1793, the people of Brussels ransacked the houses of pro-French families. When France reoccupied the Austrian Netherlands in 1794, tens of thousands of Belgians emigrated. The French exacted war levies and military requisitions and set up an *agence de commerce* to take anything from cattle to art back to France. Among their booty was Jan van Eyck's *Adoration of the Mystic Lamb*.

Shortly afterwards, in 1795, the French absorbed the former Austrian Netherlands and set up a new administration. They abolished the old provinces and created nine new *départements*. Brussels became a departmental capital answering to Paris. Liège and the Netherlands were united for the first time, and the region was increasingly referred to by the French as Belgique.

The French passed laws suppressing feudalism and the guilds and from 1796 applied French law to Belgium. The Belgians accepted the occupation and annexation passively but unenthusiastically, and the French leaders complained of their apathy. Such protests as did occur were aroused by measures taken against the Catholic Church. In 1796, the French confiscated the property of the monasteries, making 10,000 people homeless. In 1797, they closed the Catholic University of Leuven, and in 1798 some 600 priests were given the death sentence for refusing to swear loyalty to France, although most of them escaped death.

The main opposition to French rule came in 1798, after the French introduced conscription. There were riots in east and west Flanders and about 10,000 peasants formed an army in Brabant. The uprising was crushed brutally and bloodily, and hundreds were executed despite the fact that the peasants had been relatively restrained – they had burnt down pro-French houses and destroyed lists of taxpayers, but had not murdered anyone.

The last five years of the century saw industry in decline, the depopulation of towns, new taxes, economic hardship and organised gangs of robbers roaming the highways. But from 1800, there was an economic resurgence. The French encouraged the growth of industries such as coal and cotton, which benefited from the new markets in France, and Ghent in particular became an important industrial centre. The new industries were capitalist, largely funded by entrepreneurial nobles and traders who had bought former monastery lands cheaply. One of the chief beneficiaries of the French occupation was Antwerp, which regained its access to the sea. Napoleon constructed a new harbour and port, which he described as 'a pistol aimed at the heart of England'. He also made his mark on Brussels, ordering the city's old walls to be demolished and replaced with open boulevards.

French rule of the Netherlands came to an end in 1814, when Napoleon was forced to abdicate as Emperor of France, following his defeat at the Battle of Leipzig. His opponents (Britain, Prussia, Russia, Austria) recaptured Brussels in February and appointed a council of conservatives to govern the city. The council was keen for Belgium to return to Austrian rule. That same year, the Congress of Vienna began its work to break up and redistribute Napoleon's empire.

THE ROAD TO WATERLOO

However, in 1815, there was an interruption, when Napoleon made a final attempt at a comeback – his so-called Hundred Days. In

Riots break out in Brussels in August 1830, heralding the **Belgian Revolution**. *See p20.*

early 1815, Napoleon left his exile on the Mediterranean island of Elba and landed near Cannes with a force of 800. By the time he reached Lyons this had grown to 7,000. Less than three weeks after landing, he triumphantly entered the capital with an army of thousands. Condemning the landing, the Congress of Vienna said that Napoleon had made himself an enemy and disturber of the tranquillity of the world, and had rendered himself liable to public vengeance. Europe prepared for war. The combined armies of the British, Spanish, Prussians, Austrians and Dutch numbered over one million men. Napoleon had gathered about 375,000.

The main Austrian armies massed along the Upper Rhine; the Spaniards were approaching the Pyrenees; the Prussians were in the Netherlands; and the Duke of Wellington, commander-in-chief of the British, Hanoverians and Belgians, established his headquarters in Brussels. Napoleon resolved to attack the Prussians and the British, convinced he had the secret backing of the Belgians and the Belgian army.

The two sides met at Waterloo, about 18 kilometres (11 miles) south of Brussels. The battle lasted ten hours and 50,000 soldiers were killed. Towards the evening the French broke ranks and fled, pursued by Prussian troops. Napoleon himself escaped by coach to Paris, where he eventually abdicated and surrendered to the British. He was banished to the island of St Helena, where he died in 1821. For more on Waterloo, *see p12* **The Battle of Waterloo**.

Unity & revolution

In 1814 and 1815, the Congress of Vienna redrew the map of Europe in the wake of Napoleon's military adventures. One of the dilemmas facing it was the future of the Netherlands. The north had been an independent state since 1648, but the former Spanish and Austrian Netherlands had no tradition of independence and Congress was reluctant to create one. Austria had no desire to recover these provinces, and there was no question of their going to France. So what was to become of them? The Congress of Vienna

Belgium's heart of darkness

In Joseph Conrad's *Heart of Darkness*, the narrator Marlow describes his job interview in Brussels, a city he thinks of as 'a whited sepulchre'. Conrad was in part writing from experience. In 1890 he had himself been interviewed at the headquarters of the Société Anonyme Belge pour le Commerce du Haut-Congo, and ended up with the job on the river that would later inspire this novel. The building, at 13 rue de Brederode, a street behind the Palais Royal that then housed the Congo administration, remains much as Conrad describes it. But 'whited sepulchre' is a reference to Matthew 23: 'Woe unto you, scribes and Pharisees, hypocrites! For ye are like unto whited sepulchres, which indeed appear beautiful outward, but are within full of dead men's bones...'

A city built on bones? The image is far from fanciful. In 1885 Léopold II achieved diplomatic recognition for the Congo state, a territory 86 times the size of Belgium, with himself at its head, saying 'civilisation' would 'pierce the darkness'. By 1908, when he was forced to cede control to the Belgian government, 'civilisation' had reduced the population of the Congo basin by half. Author Adam Hochschild in his *King Leopold's Ghost*,

a brilliant account of what was essentially the first holocaust of the 20th century, estimates that up to ten million Africans were shot, worked to death, starved or died from exposure after being driven off their land.

We'll never know the actual number for sure – Léopold ordered all Congo archives burned before the handover, a job that fired the rue de Brederode furnaces for eight days – but some kind of accounting was kept at the time. In order to keep track of ammunition, real-life counterparts of Conrad's Kurtz ordered company troops to bring back one severed right hand for every bullet fired.

The profits from this savagery were immense. Belgian historian Jules Marchal 'conservatively' estimates that Léopold, running the colony as his personal fiefdom, earned around 220 million francs of the time – over $1 billion in the dollars of today. Most of Brussels' neo-classical landmarks were built on the proceeds, including the Arc de Triomphe and the Parc du Cinquantenaire, extensive renovations to the Palais Royal and the Château Royal at Laeken, and a host of buildings in Tervuren, including the Louis XV-style palace that now houses the Musée Royal de l'Afrique Centrale (*pictured*).

opted to unite the Netherlands and the Austrian Netherlands and form the United Kingdom of the Netherlands, thereby creating a strong buffer between France and Prussia. It was a solution that few inhabitants had asked for, other than a few Belgian entrepreneurs who saw that union with the Dutch might compensate for the loss of markets in France.

The United Kingdom of the Netherlands was created as a constitutional monarchy ruled by William of Orange. He was installed as sovereign prince on 31 July 1814, and declared king in 1815. The new kingdom had 17 provinces and two capitals, the Hague and Brussels. William I was eager to promote prosperity and unity, and although he succeeded in the former, he failed in the latter. The southerners found many reasons to resent the new state. Bread, the main article of the Belgian diet, was heavily taxed, while potatoes, the principal Dutch fare, escaped. The south of the kingdom was already industrialised and had become wealthy as a result. Although Brussels was joint capital, the new country was governed by a Dutch king, Dutch ministers

and Dutch civil servants. Despite being more numerous and prosperous, the Belgians had little political power at the outset and gained little more over time; even 15 years later in 1830, only 18 out of the 119 generals and staff officers in the army were Belgian.

'In 1831, Britain advocated a Belgian state, France and Germany agreed, and Belgium was recognised as an independent and neutral state.'

Many Belgians took refuge in memories of the earlier grandeur of Antwerp and Brussels, regarding the Hague, Amsterdam and the Dutch as upstarts. There was also fury at the government's attempts to introduce Dutch as the standard language. This resentment was not confined to French speakers; those who spoke Flemish dialects also protested against the use of Dutch.

Riots break out in Brussels in August 1830, heralding the **Belgian Revolution**. *See p20.*

This last houses a fusty collection of masks and spears, canoes and costumes, stuffed animals and wooden statues. Among the exotica, plaques commemorate hundreds of white pioneers who died on African soil. But of the millions of Congolese who met an unnatural death, the museum's 20 gloomy galleries contain absolutely no mention at all. This silence, perhaps, is the true heart of darkness. (Though current renovation, due for late 2002, aims to redress the balance.)

When Conrad went upriver in 1890, the trade was mostly in ivory. But after the Dunlop Company began manufacturing pneumatic tyres a few years later, the profits – and the brutality – redoubled as Léopold went all out for rubber. But the horror was not confined to the Congo; Léopold simply had more rubber-producing territory than anyone else. Wild rubber extended into the French territories north and west of the Congo, into Portuguese Angola and the German Cameroons, where similar forced-labour operations produced similarly genocidal consequences.

As Conrad put it: 'All Europe contributed to the making of Kurtz.'

Belgium's Catholics were opposed to the new government because it had declared religious freedom and removed the Catholic bias in the education system. Belgian liberals also opposed the new state, seeking freedom of the press and a less autocratic style of government. In 1828, Catholics and liberals formed an unlikely alliance, demanding that the Belgians, not the Dutch, be the dominant force in the Netherlands. The government made concessions, repealing the language decrees in the south and guaranteeing freedom of education, but it would neither accept Belgian supremacy nor grant freedom of the press.

BELGIAN REVOLUTION

The winter of 1829-30 was severe, and farmers suffered accordingly. In addition, overproduction in the industries of the south had caused wage cuts, bankruptcies and unemployment. Workers in both sectors were mutinous, and there were regular protests and demonstrations in Brussels. On 25 August 1830 (a month after the July 1830 revolution in France), an opera called *La Muette de Portici*, by Daniel Auber, was performed at the Théâtre de la Monnaie in Brussels. Its subject was the Naples rebellion of 1647, and the opera had been banned since being written in 1828. During an aria called 'L'Amour Sacré de la Patrie' ('Sacred Love of the Fatherland'), liberals and students inside the theatre started rioting, and then joined the workers who were protesting in the square outside.

This marked the start of the Belgian Revolution. The Dutch government negotiated with the leaders of the revolution and there seemed a possibility of administrative separation. But William I prevaricated and the impatient and disillusioned rebels decided to go for secession. William sent 10,000 troops into Brussels at the end of September 1830, and while the numbers were insufficient to crush the revolution, they were enough to inflame the southern provinces into joining the uprising. Belgian soldiers deserted their regiments, and William's troops were driven out of Brussels. A new government was rapidly assembled. On 4 October, the rebels declared an independent state and provisional government; on 3 November they held elections for a National Congress. This met for the first time on 10 November and comprised 200 members, most of them intellectuals, lawyers and journalists. There were few men from industry or finance.

On 22 November the new Congress decided on a constitution. Belgium was to be a parliamentary monarchy and unitary state of nine provinces, with freedom of religion, education, assembly, press and language, and

a separate church and state. On 3 March 1831, the Congress passed an electoral law defining the electorate, which consisted of about 46,000 men of the bourgeoisie. This meant that one out of every 95 inhabitants had the vote. At the time, this was a relatively high proportion – in France only one in 160 people could vote.

'French was the language of the dominant class. Dutch was more widely spoken. The majority of the population was governed in an alien language.'

There was rapid recognition of the new nation in the rest of the world, and in January 1831 the Great Powers met in London to discuss the issue. Britain advocated the creation of a Belgian state, France and Germany agreed, and Belgium was duly recognised as an independent and neutral state. The choice of a new king was less easily reached, but eventually Léopold of Saxe-Coburg-Gotha was selected. He was related to the major European royal households, most famously as uncle to both Victoria and Albert. He took an oath to the constitution on 21 July, now Belgium's National Day.

Shortly afterwards, the Dutch invaded Belgium, and this helped prolong a sense of unity among the Catholics and liberals. The Dutch beat the Belgian rebels at Leuven and Hasselt but then retreated on hearing reports of an approaching French army of 50,000. They did not recognise the new country until 1839. Léopold's resolve in the crisis strengthened his popularity, along with his steadfast belief in the new constitution.

Independent Belgium

It was inevitable that the coalition between liberals and Catholics in the new state of Belgium would be neither harmonious nor long-lived. The political history of Belgium in the 19th century consisted of a tug of war between the two sides, the main subjects of contention being education and the language split.

Belgium's history as a nation state began with the Catholics and the French speakers in the ascendant. The new constitution allowed people to use whichever language they preferred, but French was the language of the dominant class and was spoken in the courts, the education system (apart from some primary schools) and the administration. In the country as a whole, Dutch was more widely spoken, with 2.4 million Dutch speakers and 1.8 million French speakers. The majority of the population was governed in an alien language.

Intellectuals in Antwerp and Ghent soon began to resent the prevalence of French. In 1840, they organised a petition demanding the use of Dutch in the administration and law courts of Dutch-speaking provinces. However, this did not generate much popular support, for at this stage the Catholic-liberal split was a far more serious issue.

Initially, the Catholics were dominant at most levels. Membership of monasteries and convents more than doubled during the 1830s and '40s, and in 1834 a new Catholic university was founded at Mechelen, moving to Louvain (Leuven) in 1835. The Catholic Church also controlled much of secondary education. It was not until the 1840s that the Belgian liberals gained any impetus. In 1846, they held a congress in Brussels to clarify a political programme and to plan an election strategy. The sense of focus and organisation they gained from the congress gave them the upper hand over Catholics who did not organise themselves in the same way until the 1860s. Charles Rogier formed a liberal government in 1848, and the liberals governed, with a few gaps, until 1884.

THE INDUSTRIAL REVOLUTION

Although Belgium lost the Dutch East Indies markets when it split from the Netherlands, there was industrial expansion in the 1830s, at a time when much of Europe had falling industrial prices. With its programme of railway construction and large-scale investment in the coal, iron and banking industries, Belgium was the first country in continental Europe to undergo the Industrial Revolution. Nevertheless, there were still economic problems, such as a serious banking crisis in 1838. There was also a crisis in the countryside. The rural linen and flax industries of Flanders were unable to compete with cheaper, more industrialised manufacturers in Britain. Matters weren't helped by a potato famine in Belgium in 1847. In that year 28 per cent of the population of East Flanders received poor relief.

As in the rest of Europe, a growing proletariat nurtured the rise of socialism. The Belgian Workers' Party was founded in 1885, and there were extensive strikes and protests by workers in 1886. Universal male suffrage was introduced in 1893 (although the wealthy had more votes than the poor), and in 1894 the socialists gained their first parliamentary seats.

But the 1880s saw the Catholics regain power in Belgium (with the bulk of their support in Flanders), where they remained until 1917.

By the time the Catholics came to power in 1884, there had already been concessions to Dutch speakers, and the Catholics accelerated the process. In the 1870s and '80s there had been legislation introducing bilingualism in Flanders and strengthening the Dutch position in law and education, but the Flemish were still essentially governed and tried in French. Eventually, in 1898, Dutch was given official equality with French.

Despite constant dispute over particular issues, the Belgians did demonstrate a sense of unity in some areas of public life. Independence led to a building spree in Brussels. Among the earliest additions were the Galeries St-Hubert in the 1840s. These were followed by a spate of official buildings and commemorative projects as Belgium celebrated its own existence, culminating in the construction of the Parc du Cinquantenaire for the 50th anniversary exhibition. The vast Palais de Justice was completed in 1883.

The main town planning feat of the 19th century was covering over the River Senne. At first sight, Brussels appears to be an urban oddity in that it did not grow up around or near a river. In fact it did, but the Senne was slow flowing and narrow, and frequently caused flooding in low areas. It was also seen as a cause of disease and ill-health. So, in 1870, it was covered up, and thereafter Brussels shipping used the Canal de Willebroeck, which joins Brussels to the River Scheldt. A smaller river, the Maelbeek, was covered over in Ixelles.

BELGIUM AS A COLONIAL POWER

The Belgian people expressed little appetite for imperialism or exploration in the 19th century, but Léopold II was eager to gain an empire. He succeeded his father in 1865 and it was clear from the start that his ambitions reached far beyond Belgian borders. As crown prince, he had looked around for suitable territories, and considered British-run Borneo, the Philippines, South Africa and Mozambique. Finally, he decided to grab a piece of the 'magnificent African cake'. Much of central Africa was still unexplored and in 1876 Léopold set up the Association Internationale Africaine with the help of Henry Stanley (of 'Dr Livingstone, I presume?' fame).

Although other European governments and the US expressed qualms about Léopold's activities in Africa, he dismissed them sufficiently for the Berlin Declaration of 1885 to recognise the independent state of the Congo, with Léopold as head of state. He referred to himself as its proprietor. His new territory, over which he had absolute power, was 86 times the size of Belgium. From 1895, when he started exporting wild rubber, it generated massive revenue, much of which was passed back to Belgium and used for massive public works such as the Musée Royal de l'Afrique Centrale at Tervuren.

By the early 20th century, Léopold's policy of extracting maximum profit from the Congo, regardless of ecological and human cost (*see also p18* **Belgium's heart of darkness**), was exposing Belgium to international criticism, particularly from Britain. In 1908, the Belgian government forced Léopold to hand it over to the nation, and it remained a Belgian colony until independence in 1960.

Belgium in the wars

On its creation in 1830, Belgium declared itself perpetually neutral. But on 2 August 1914, Kaiser Wilhelm of Germany demanded that Belgium give German troops free passage on their way to invade France. Belgium had 12 hours to respond to the ultimatum, which it rejected. On 4 August, German

Bemused Germans take Paris, 1914...

troops entered the country, and seven hours later Britain declared war on Germany. By midnight, five different empires were involved in war – and they all thought it would be over by Christmas.

Belgium suffered horribly in World War I. Snipers – known as *franc-tireurs* – shot at the Germans from ditches and outbuildings, and the Germans retaliated brutally. When the Germans were fired on at the village of Hervé, they decided to set an example. Within a few days, only 19 of the 500 houses were still standing, the church was in ruins and the shattered village was littered with corpses. Other massacres occurred elsewhere: the Germans shot 110 people at Andenne, 384 people at Tamines, and 612 people, including a three-week-old baby, at Dinant. Meanwhile, the German newspapers were full of stories about the torture and sadistic acts committed by the Belgian *franc-tireurs* against German troops.

'Germans revealed they were surprised to find themselves in Brussels, having believed they were marching on Paris.'

Belgium fell and the government took refuge in Antwerp. The Germans entered Brussels on 20 August and held a military parade to celebrate. English nurse Edith Cavell, who had stayed on in the city and was later executed by the invaders, said that conversations with the Germans revealed they were surprised to find themselves there, having believed they were marching on Paris.

Antwerp was under siege by the end of September, and fell on 10 October, despite the arrival of British troops, including the poet Rupert Brooke, in a fleet of London buses. About 500,000 refugees left Antwerp, among them thousands of people who had fled there from elsewhere in Belgium. Around 1.5 million had already left Belgium, although many later returned. The government went to Le Havre in France, while King Albert I, who had succeeded to the throne from his uncle Léopold II, took up position with the small Belgian army in the north-west of the country. Known as *le Roi Chevalier* ('the soldier king'), he earned acclaim from his people by fighting with his troops in the deadly Ypres trenches alongside the French and British.

The four-year German occupation of Belgium had terrible consequences for the country. Its total of 44,000 war dead might be dwarfed by the losses of Russia and France, but there

Bemused Germans take Paris, 1914...

was still great suffering. Around 700,000 Belgians were deported to Germany to work on farms and in factories, and the economy was devastated. Belgium had depended on other countries for its raw materials and its export markets, and it lost both. Much of its rail system was destroyed in an attempt to halt the German invasion, agricultural production fell, and there was widespread poverty and hunger.

The situation was prevented from becoming worse by the organisation of committees to provide food and relief. The National Assistance and Nutrition Committee (NHVC) was set up by the Belgians, while in the US Herbert Hoover helped to set up the Commission for the Relief of Belgium. Belgium was liberated in 1918, and until 1921 the main consideration of the post-war governments was how to rebuild the country. It is estimated that its losses represented about one-fifth of its national assets in 1914, and not all of them were recovered in war reparations.

The issues that had preoccupied the country before the war stagnated during and after it. The Flemish cause suffered a sizeable setback during the war; the Germans had been pro-Flemish, and a small group of Flemish politicians had been enthusiastic collaborators. In 1916, the Germans had given the Flemish lobby the prize they had been campaigning for since the turn of the century by declaring the University of Ghent Dutch-speaking. Not surprisingly, the university reverted to French when the Germans were defeated and did not adopt Dutch again until 1930. Having recovered what they had lost during World War I, the Flemish made a series of language gains during the 1930s. In 1932, French and Dutch ceased to have equality in Flanders, where the official language now became Dutch.

BETWEEN THE WARS

The period immediately after World War I had been marked by political unity, as Catholics, liberals and socialists worked together to rebuild the country. The unity quickly dissipated, however, particularly after the introduction of proportional representation. The first universal male suffrage elections without multiple votes for the bourgeoisie were held in 1919, and they resulted in a series of coalition governments. Between 1918 and 1940, Belgium had 18 different administrations. There was some economic recovery in the late 1920s, with Belgium's workers enjoying a standard of living much higher than before the war.

But during the 1930s, Belgium slumped into depression, and its politics show much the same pattern as other European states. There was severe unemployment, social unrest and a move to the right. In the 1936 elections, Flemish nationalist and right-wing parties in Wallonia and Brussels made big gains, blaming the depression on the weak parliament, lack of

Modernisation arrives with the **1958 World Fair** in Brussels. *See p25.*

strong leadership and the unions. Also, the brave Soldier King, Albert I, had died in a rock-climbing accident in 1934 and his son Léopold III lacked the same charisma.

After World War I, the Belgian government tempered its perpetual neutrality with an alliance with France. But towards the end of the 1930s, as Germany flexed its muscles, Belgium returned to its former position, reasserting its neutrality after Germany invaded Poland in 1939.

WORLD WAR II

Once again neutrality did Belgium little good, and on 10 May 1940 Hitler attacked. The Belgian response was different this time; whereas its stand in 1914 had led to international sympathy and admiration for the 'plucky' Belgians, this time there were raised eyebrows. Showing opposite traits to his father, Léopold III surrendered to the Germans after just 18 days. Much of the population supported Léopold's action, but the government itself did not. Believing that Belgium should commit itself to the Allies, it became a government-in-exile in Le Havre and then London.

Despite initially espousing a policy of normalisation in Belgium, the Germans became more authoritarian during the course of the war. As the people became aware of this, there was greater resistance to the occupation. In the end, Belgium suffered many of the same problems as it had in World War I: deportations, forced labour, poverty and food shortages. The fate

of Jews was a particularly dark period for Belgium. From 1 June 1942, Belgian Jews were required to wear the yellow Star of David, which fast became a symbol of repression. The Germans created a deportation centre in Mechelen and, between 1942 and 1944, sent 25,257 people from there to Auschwitz. Two-thirds of them died on arrival. However, an intricate network of Belgian resistance and opposition saved many thousands of others from a similar fate. Belgians from all classes and backgrounds risked their own lives by taking Jewish children into their families and creating new identities for them. The Mechelen Museum of Deportation & the Resistance, located in the old barracks, is now both a memorial and an education centre.

Belgium was liberated in September 1944 and one of the leaders' earliest tasks was to tackle the issue of collaboration. Between 1944 and 1949, the war tribunals considered 405,000 cases, and reached 58,000 guilty verdicts, of which 33,000 were in Flanders. Most importantly, the country had to deal with the behaviour of the king himself. The debate lasted five years, and eventually in 1950 the government held a non-binding referendum on whether Léopold should return. Only 57 per cent voted in his favour (72 per cent in Flanders and 42 per cent in Wallonia), and when he did come back there were serious disturbances. Léopold then stepped aside in favour of his son Baudouin, who was crowned in 1951.

Even in the 1990s, the issue of collaboration was still sensitive. Up to 15,000 Belgians convicted of collaboration still receive reduced pension and property rights. In February 1996, a military court in Brussels reconsidered the case of Irma Laplasse, a Flemish farmer's wife who had betrayed resistance fighters to the Nazis in 1944. She was executed by firing squad in 1948. The court upheld her conviction, but ruled that the death sentence should have been commuted to life imprisonment. The judgement was met by protests from both sides. Concentration camp survivors and former members of the resistance and the Belgian secret army demonstrated outside the Palais de Justice in protest at any moves to rehabilitate collaborators. For their part, members of the far-right Flemish Vlaams Blok party campaign for an amnesty for all those accused of collaborating, insisting that the war tribunals were an attempt to victimise and repress the Flemish.

POST-WAR BELGIUM
World War II had made it clear that Belgium's traditional neutrality was untenable, and even before the war was over the government-in-exile set about rejecting the policy in favour of international alliances. It signed the Benelux Customs Union with Luxembourg and the Netherlands in 1944 (it came into force on 1 January 1948), abolishing all customs tariffs between the three countries and setting a common external tariff. Belgium was also an enthusiastic participant in post-war international relations; partly it realised that as an export-driven economy it needed to belong to the growing international relations superstructure.

'King Baudouin is credited with preventing Belgium from splitting into two countries.'

Belgium was one of the first signatories of the UN Charter in June 1945, it participated in the Marshall Plan and it joined the Organisation for European Economic Co-operation in 1948. It joined the Council of Europe and the European Coal and Steel Community, and became the HQ of the European Economic Community (EEC) when it was set up in 1957. At the same time, the city's hosting of the World Fair of 1958 allowed for rapid modernisation, the ring boulevards becoming a network of highways and tunnels. In 1960, Benelux countries abolished their internal borders. In 1967, Brussels became the headquarters of NATO.

King Baudoin became a respected and beloved monarch during this period, concerning himself with the well-being of his subjects and social issues. A quiet, unassuming man, he is credited with preventing Belgium from splitting into two countries. He reigned until his death in 1993 and, as he was childless, his crown passed to his brother, the present King Albert II.

FLEMISH AND WALLOON TENSION
The other important issue of the post-war years was the worsening of Flemish-Walloon conflict. As in 1918, the debate was initially dampened after the war by the awkward question of Flemish collaboration, but from 1960 onwards the split over language and community deepened. The language barrier between French-speaking Wallonia and Dutch-speaking Flanders was formally created in 1962 (Brussels is officially bilingual). In 1965, the political parties split into Flemish and Walloon wings. With the language question settled, the debate focused on the constitution and the treatment of the Flemish and French communities.

The split between Flanders and Wallonia was exacerbated by economic developments. In the 19th and early 20th centuries, Wallonia was the economic engine of Belgium because of its coal and steel. But these declined after World War I, and unemployment rose. Flanders, meanwhile, developed successful new industries, such as telecommunications, and complained that its wealth was being drained to prop up Wallonia. The Walloons in turn accused the government of economic favouritism towards the Flemish. In the 1971 elections, parties whose main policies centre on language issues, such as Volksunie, Front des Francophones and Rassemblement Wallon, achieved nearly a quarter of the vote.

Since 1970, the Belgian government has made a series of constitutional reforms, granting greater autonomy to the two communities and changing Belgium from a centralised to a federal state. There were prophesies of doom in 1993 when King Baudouin died, for he had been credited with holding the country together. So far, however, the country has not fallen apart and a new constitution was introduced in 1994. This created a new system of elected assemblies and governments representing the three regions of Flanders, Wallonia and Brussels, and the French, Flemish and German language communities. Belgian taxpayers complain bitterly about the cost of supporting these structures in addition to the national government, but at least the system has postponed any further split.

Key events

EARLY AND MEDIEVAL HISTORY

57-51 BC Julius Caesar fights Gallic Wars.
15 BC Foundation of Roman Gallia Belgica.
5th century AD Collapse of Roman rule.
814 Death of Emperor Charlemagne.
843 Charlemagne's kingdom split between his three grandsons.
979 Official founding of Brussels (Bruocsella).
1041 Dukes of Brabant build palace at Coudenburg in today's Upper Town.
1302 Flemish army beats the French at the Battle of the Golden Spurs.
1337 Outbreak of Hundred Years War.
1348-9 Black Death in Flanders.

DUKES OF BURGUNDY

1369 Margaret of Male marries Philip the Bold, Duke of Burgundy; they inherit Flanders, making it part of the Duchy of Burgundy.
1459 Philip the Good's court set in Brussels.
1467 Death of Philip the Good.
1477 Death of Charles the Bold.
1482 Mary of Burgundy dies and her husband Maximilian becomes regent.

THE SPANISH NETHERLANDS

1516 Maximilian's son Charles inherits Spanish throne and becomes Charles I.
1519 Charles inherits the Hapsburg empire and becomes Emperor Charles V.
1555 Abdication of Charles V in the Netherlands in favour of his son Philip.
1565 Nobles in the Netherlands form the League of Nobles, opposing Spanish rule.
1566 Iconoclastic Riots spread from Antwerp.
1568 Execution of Counts Egmont and Hoorn and outbreak of the Revolt of the Netherlands.
1579 Southern provinces form Union of Arras, in support of Philip II and Catholicism.
1581 Northern provinces form Utrecht Union and declare independence from the Spanish.

COUNTER-REFORMATION

1598 Philip hands over the Netherlands to his son-in-law Archduke Albrecht.
1609-21 Twelve Year Truce between the Dutch and the Spanish Netherlands.
1621 Netherlands revert to Spain on Albrecht's death.
1648 Spain recognises Dutch independence in the Treaty of Münster.
1695 The French bombard Brussels.

THE AUSTRIAN NETHERLANDS

1701-13 War of the Spanish Succession.

1713 Spanish Netherlands pass to Austria in the Treaty of Utrecht.
1740-8 War of Austrian Succession.
1780 Joseph II becomes Emperor of Austria.
1789-90 Brabant Revolution against Austria.
1790 Austrian authority restored.
1792 France occupies Austrian Netherlands.
1795 Austrian Netherlands annexed into France and old boundaries abolished.
1798 French introduce conscription and Belgian peasants riot.
1814 Napoleon exiled; Congress of Vienna merges Belgium into the United Kingdom of the Netherlands.

UNITY AND REVOLUTION

1815 Napoleon defeated at Waterloo. William Prince of Orange declared King William I.
1830 Start of the Belgian Revolution.
1831 Belgium recognised as an independent state; Léopold of Saxe-Coburg-Gotha is invited to be king.
1848 First liberal government, after initial political domination by Catholics.
1885 Belgian Socialist Party founded.
1885 Berlin Declaration recognises Léopold II as head of state of the Congo.
1893 Introduction of universal male suffrage.
1898 Dutch given official equality with French.
1908 Léopold hands Congo over to Belgium.

BELGIUM IN THE WARS

1914 Germany invades Belgium.
1918 Belgium liberated by Allies.
1919 First universal male suffrage elections.
1940 Germany invades Belgium; Léopold III surrenders.
1944 Belgium liberated; war tribunals set up.

POST-WAR BELGIUM

1948 Benelux Customs Union established.
1949 Women given the right to vote.
1950 Léopold III returns but stands down due to national unease over role in the war.
1957 Brussels becomes the headquarters of the European Economic Community.
1962 French-Flemish language border set up.
1967 Brussels headquarters of NATO.
1970-94 Constitutional reforms change Belgium from a centralised to a federal state.
1993 Death of Baudouin I; accession of Albert II.
1996 Dutroux paedophile scandal.
1999 Dioxin scandal rocks government; marriage of Prince Philippe and Mathilde.

Brussels Today

The future looks mixed for the capital of Europe.

Bilbao and Barcelona are the two European cities that usually trip off the tongue when talking about urban regeneration at the tail end of the 20th century. Brussels has nothing as flash as the Guggenheim Museum or as ambitious as the Olympic quarter, but over the past decade the city has changed so radically that it deserves to join the Spanish duo on the 'most improved European cities' rostrum.

If this sounds far-fetched, picture the city ten years ago. Property sharks, unscrupulous speculators and laissez-faire town planners conspired to make sure that large chunks of the centre looked like post-war Sarajevo. Houses lay derelict, public squares were little more than traffic islands and pavements were pot-holed, strewn with dog dirt or blocked by parked cars. You could even drive through the Grand' Place: arguably the most beautiful square in the world.

CIVIC REJUVENATION

Things gradually started to improve in the late 1990s. The scaffolding was finally peeled off the 15th-century Hôtel de Ville after almost a decade of sandblasting; clean-up work began on the imposing Palais de Justice; and the stunning Sablon church and run-down areas such as the place St-Géry and the rue du Marché au Charbon were given a makeover.

The impetus for all this was Brussels' stint as one of Europe's nine capitals of culture in 2000. More than 300 architectural, artistic and cultural projects took place under the banner of Brussels 2000, and 100,000 people took part in the festival's opening weekend of fireworks, concerts and street parties. Critics accused the festival's organisers of focusing on obscure artistic fare rather than popular culture, but few would doubt that Brussels 2000 has kickstarted a new feeling of civic pride in the city.

This was reflected in the local elections of 2001. Fed up with decades of mismanagement, voters booted the Liberals out of power in central Brussels and replaced them with a red-green coalition. Greens did spectacularly, the racist Vlaams Blok was routed and long-serving mayors of the centre-right went the way of the dinosaurs. In Belgium, which is not renowned for its radicalism, the result was the equivalent of a political earthquake.

City authorities can take some credit for rejuvenating the centre of Brussels. In recent years trees have been planted, parks have been redesigned, flashy new signposts have been erected, streets have been narrowed, pavements have been widened, recobbled and fenced off by bollards – and public squares such as the place St-Jean have been reclaimed from the car. There are still some blackspots – la place du Grand Sablon is little more than a glorified car park, while the dank and gloomy Gare Centrale is hardly the best welcome for visitors – but there is a mood of confidence in the city that was noticeably absent just three or four years ago.

Nowhere is this truer than around place St-Géry, where trendy restaurants, cafés and clothes shops have sprouted to cater for the increasing numbers of young Flemings and EU professionals making their home in the centre. Showcase events such as Brussels 2000 and the European Football Championships – which Belgium co-hosted with the Netherlands in June 2000 – have certainly raised the international profile of the city. But it is Brussels' unofficial status as the 'capital of the European Union' that keeps it in the headlines.

THE IMPACT OF THE EU

Brussels houses all three major EU institutions: the European Parliament (which also meets in Strasbourg for a week a month); the European Commission (the EU's 'civil service on steroids' as it has been described), and the Council of Ministers. Lesser-known bodies such as the Committee of the Regions and the Economic and Social Committee have also set up shop in the ugly EU Quarter.But this spaghetti soup of organisations is just the tip of the iceberg. Feeding off these institutions are tens of thousands of journalists, lobbyists, translators, interpreters, drivers, security guards, cooks, waiters and members of mankind's oldest profession.

'Pressures are likely to increase as the number of EU member states doubles from 15 to almost 30.'

Brussels now outranks Washington, DC as home to the world's largest international press corps, and the lobbying culture that was once the exclusive preserve of the UK and the US has hit Brussels with a vengeance. There are more than 10,000 lobbyists in the city, ranging from Greenpeace campaigners to the European Chemical Industry Council. So numerous are the associations that there are even associations of associations: the Federation of International

Associations and the Union of International Associations are both based in Brussels. In addition to EU bodies, the city is home to the North Atlantic Treaty Organisation (NATO) and is the European HQ for American multinationals such as Levi's, IBM and Coca-Cola. Three Belgian parliaments – the national, regional and Flemish assemblies – also sit in the 1,000-year old capital.

The presence of so many international organisations has had both positive and negative effects. The institutions have brought in vast amounts of money – statistics show that Brussels is the second richest region in Europe, with a per capita GDP of over twice the EU average. They have also helped to make Brussels one of the world's most cosmopolitan cities. Almost a third of the city's residents are foreign-born – Turks, Moroccans and Congolese make up a large chunk of the recent arrivals – and this is changing the city's eating habits and means of communication. You are just as likely to see diners tucking into Thai, Indian, North African or Middle Eastern food as steak and *frites*. And if you eavesdrop on their conversation, there is as much chance that they will be speaking English as French or Flemish – the city's two official languages.

As befits Europe's self-styled capital, Brussels is also rapidly becoming one of Europe's major transport hubs. Paris is only 80 minutes away by high-speed train; London is two-and-a-half hours under the Chunnel and Amsterdam less than three hours up the line. Despite the collapse of Sabena airlines in late 2001, Brussels airport is also mushrooming. A new terminal is currently under construction to add to the two built in the mid 1990s and it is no coincidence that no-frills airlines Ryanair and Virgin Express chose Brussels as their European hub.

Brussels may be wealthy, but as in inner London this figure masks gross disparities. Walk through the largely immigrant enclaves of Anderlecht and Molenbeek and you don't get the impression of a capital dripping with wealth. The presence of the EU and other international bodies has accentuated the difference between wealthy expats and poor immigrants. Rising property prices have forced many locals out of upcoming suburbs such as Ixelles, Etterbeek and Woluwe-St-Pierre.

But no area has been so profoundly affected by the EU's presence as the 'suitcase quarter' to the east of the Royal Palace. This was once a bohemian area famed for its parks, tree-lined boulevards and grand *maisons de maître*. These days, it is a concrete jungle crammed with office blocks, five-lane freeways, Irish pubs and elegant houses waiting to be bulldozed. The pressures on the area are likely to increase substantially as the number of EU member states doubles from 15 to almost 30. Polish diplomats, Czech translators and Slovenian civil servants will all require office space and living quarters – pushing up rents still further and triggering off a new building boom in a city that already seems to have more cranes than steeples.

A further headache for the city's authorities was created at Nice in December 2000 when European leaders decided that all EU summits should take place in the Belgian capital once the number of Union members tops 18. As this could happen as early as 2004, authorities are currently debating whether these political jamborees – which attract thousands of government officials, journalists and demonstrators – should be held in the EU Quarter or at a more secure out-of-town site.

'Brussels is still a city desperately in need of a PR job.'

The regional government has recently launched an advertising effort to persuade local doubters about the benefits of housing the EU institutions. The billboard campaign features quotes by statesmen such as former European Commission President Jacques Delors, local crooner Jacques Brel and one-time Brussels resident Victor Hugo. But this is unlikely to wash with local residents who have seen traffic and rents increase and whole swaths of the area torn down to create more office space.

IMAGE MATTERS

In the past, Brussels – and Belgium as a whole – would not have felt the need to sell itself or to counter negative publicity. But after the scandals of the 1990s, when the country briefly became better known for its paedophiles and poisoned chickens than its beer and chocolates, the government launched a €2.5 million campaign to improve Belgium's image abroad. A recent advertising campaign called 'Belgium – A State of Mind' urges people to 'be involved, be ambitious, be beautiful, be aware, be small'.

Forty years of Christian Democrat rule left the country morally compromised at home and suffering from a severe lack of confidence abroad. Since taking power in 1999, Prime Minister Guy Verhofstadt's rainbow coalition of Liberals, Socialists and Greens has worked tirelessly to portray Belgium in a different light. In early 2000 it became the first country to demand sanctions against Austria for bringing post-fascists into government, it played a leading role in bringing former Chilean dictator

The EU has a huge impact on the city.

Augusto Pinochet to justice, and it has recently issued a mea culpa for some of its more heinous actions in the Congo. In the latter half of 2001, Belgium held the rotating presidency of the EU for six months and won plaudits for its handling of Europe's response to the September 11 attacks on the United States.

If Belgium has managed to improve its image, Brussels is still a city desperately in need of a PR job. American travel writer Bill Bryson once described the Belgian capital as a 'seriously ugly place, full of wet litter, boulevards like freeways and muddy building sites'. Many still associate the city with sprouts, lace, rain, bloated bureaucracy and barmy laws.

High-speed trains have introduced a younger generation of Brits, Dutch, Germans and French to the epicurean delights of the city – clubbing, dining and all-night drinking – and there is no danger of the city losing its reputation as the beer and chocolate capital of the world. But the charms of Brussels will never be as easy to sell as, say, Paris or Amsterdam. It is too chaotic to be categorised and too self-effacing to indulge in the sort of hype London goes in for. Instead, it is a city that needs to be discovered slowly.

If in any doubt, ask foreigners who came to the city for six months but are still here after 15 years. They will boast of the affordable rents, the ease of travel, the high standard of living and the great restaurants, shops and bars on their doorstep. But don't take their word for it – check out the designer stores on rue Antoine Dansaert, Trappist beers on the terraces of St-Géry or impeccable cuisine right across the city – and then dare mention lace or sprouts.

Architecture

The low-down on Brussels' best buildings.

When Samuel Beckett was casting around for a suitable insult for Vladimir to throw at Estragon, he remembered an argument between a taxi driver and a bus driver in a Brussels street after a close scrape. 'You fool!' said the bus driver. 'You imbecile!' shouted the taxi driver. 'You... you... you ARCHITECT!' triumphed the bus driver.

His insult didn't make the final version of *Waiting for Godot*, but says much about the imbecility of post-war Belgian architects. Or, rather, how between them architects and the authorities carved up the beautiful city of Brussels. Tunnels and dual carriageways sliced through neighbourhoods, and 'town planning' was not even part of the vocabulary until the 1960s. 'Bruxellisation' is still architectural

> ▶ Many of the buildings mentioned here are described in more detail in the **Sightseeing** section.

shorthand the world over for bad urban planning. In the 1960s the Flemish architect Renaat Braems wrote a book entitled *Is Belgium the Ugliest Country in the World?*. Despite excited rebuttals, it shocked people into action.

Focus groups such as ARAU (Atelier de Recherche et d'Action Urbaines – *see p38* **Open house**) were formed in the 1960s to protect the civic heritage. Their complaints first fell on deaf ears, but over the past 15 years the government has been involving them in a concerted effort to list and preserve buildings. Since the late 1980s, masterpieces such as Victor Horta's **Magasins Waucquez** have been saved, renovated and given new functions (it's now the Centre Belge de la Bande Dessinée).

Other buildings, such as the 19th-century meat market, **Halles de St-Géry**, have been profitably turned into bars and restaurants. All this refurbishment culminated in Brussels 2000, involving 120 innovative architectural projects. Most were aimed at renovation and have been largely successful. Paul Saintenoy's art nouveau **Magasins Old England** has been restored as one of the most beautiful buildings in Brussels, and now houses the Musée des Instruments de Musique; the 15th- and 16th-century **Palais du Coudenburg** has been excavated under the place Royale and can now be visited; the **Institut National de Radiodiffusion** in place Flagey is expected to be fully renovated by September 2002. Brussels is enjoying the facelift.

This is all fine, until we come to another gripe: the lack of any first-rate modern architecture. Compared with Paris, London, even Antwerp, Brussels has been timid about welcoming in the new. There just aren't any exciting modern buildings. The most famous since World War II have been the **Atomium** and the EU headquarters, the **Berlaymont** (*see p32* **High jinks at Europe's HQ**). Both have achieved cult status, but nobody could claim either as a modern masterpiece.

Belgium isn't short of good architects; its urban planners need to be more daring. In 1998 Bob Van Reeth (or bOb Van Reeth as he writes it) was appointed the Flemish region's first ever chief architect or *bouwmeester*. Van Reeth is a radical; his black-and-white striped house in Antwerp is among its most famous landmarks. His activities may be oriented towards Flanders (where he's already planned 39 projects), but his appointment is a sign of new architectural direction and risk-taking in Belgium. Hopefully this will include not just renovation, but also creation.

'"Bruxellisation" is still architectural shorthand the world over for bad urban planning.'

First-time visitors to Brussels will probably find it an appealing, if slightly run-down city. Despite the constant renovations it still has a rather shabby air. The cobblestones are uneven, with grass growing through them; notable buildings like the Royal Palace are begrimed. Brussels doesn't enjoy the funding of smarter Antwerp. Another quirk is the eclecticism of Brussels' buildings. No two houses are exactly alike. On any one street, you'll find differing heights and widths, and one house with round windows next to one with the rectangular variety. This is partly due to the fact that Brussels was built mainly by private citizens, without the interference of town councils or building companies. The strict town planning laws that restrict Dutch streets to uniform order do not apply here. Moreover, home façade

competitions in the 19th century prompted a great deal of creativity. Belgium's different architectural styles are also largely a reflection of its many invading rulers: France, Spain, the Netherlands and Austria.

The most immediately striking style is Flemish Renaissance, showcased in the guildhouses of the Grand' Place, one of the most beautiful squares in Europe. To get a feel for the other great Belgian style, art nouveau, wander round the *communes* of Ixelles and St-Gilles and the centre of town. French neo-classicism left its mark on the Royal Quarter; while anything imposing and imperial (Adolph Buyl's broad avenues, Joseph Poelaert's Palais de Justice), is bound to have been ordered by Léopold II. The destruction of hundreds of homes to make way for Poelaert's Law Courts in working-class Marolles allowed a new insult to creep into the rich slang of the area: *architek*.

GOTHIC

A few Gothic buildings are all that remains of medieval Brussels, ruled by the Dukes of Burgundy for more than a century, when the city blossomed into an important centre for trade and culture. Churches are the mainstay of Gothic times, and Brussels' finest examples are **Notre-Dame du Sablon** and the **Cathédrale des Sts Michel et Gudule**. The former, also known as Notre-Dame des Victoires, started out as a chapel built by the archers' guild in the 13th century, but was expanded in the 15th after pilgrims flocked to see a wooden Madonna statue reportedly endowed with healing powers. The twin-towered cathedral, named after Brussels' two patron saints, has undergone numerous facelifts since construction began

Impressive roofline on the **Grand' Place**.

in 1226. Rebuilt after ravages by Protestant iconoclasts in 1579 and the French revolutionaries in 1793, today it is a medley of different architectural styles. The stained-glass windows date from the 16th century and depict King Charles V, his wife Isabella of Portugal, his sister Mary of Hungary and her husband. Remains of the original Romanesque church can be found in the crypt.

The **Hôtel de Ville** (Town Hall), built in the first half of the 15th century, is Brussels' only secular example of this period, and the only building to survive the 1695 French bombardment of the Grand' Place. Its 100-metre (328-foot) tower is topped by St Michel. The right side was started 40 years later than the left, ending up shorter through lack of space.

FLEMISH RENAISSANCE

This is a loose term applied to the Italo-Flemish rococo baroque style of the 17th century, though Renaissance is misleading for such a late period. It's a home-grown style of which the Belgians are very proud. Luc Fayd'herbe, a student of Pieter Paul Rubens, is the name most often connected with this style

in churches, though his best work is elsewhere. In Brussels his masterpiece is the honey-coloured **St-Jean-Baptiste au Béguinage**, once host to Brussels' largest *béguinage*, a community for celibate religious women founded in the 13th century. A fire has substantially damaged the roof and recently it's been occupied by homeless groups.

The most elaborate instances of this style are the ornate **guildhouses** on the Grand' Place, which were built to replace the timber headquarters that had been destroyed in the 1695 bombardment. The guilds used the reconstruction as a demonstration of their power, rebuilding the square in five years, replacing their timber structures with stone ones to create one of the most beautiful squares in Europe. The buildings are adorned with bronze and gold touches, stately columns and symbols of their trade: hop plants on the brewers' headquarters at No.10 and wheelbarrows for the grease-makers at No.2.

But this period was not all serious. Italo-Flemish baroque also influenced sculptures of this period – most notably the **Manneken-Pis**

High jinks at Europe's HQ

Belgium's most famous building, after the Atomium, is the Berlaymont, headquarters of the European Union and the star-shaped symbol of Europe's heartland. It has all the requirements for a landmark building. Vast and distinctive, it was considered at first avant-garde, then a gross eyesore and, finally, a cult symbol. But whatever the image, it's always in the news for the wrong reasons.

A functioning Berlaymont has been a rare sight. For the last third of its 35-year life, it has been vacated. First it was riddled with asbestos, then it was shrouded in white plastic. Now it is being renovated, but is still the butt of bar jokes as costs and completion dates mount. Is this what the EU wants for its most famous landmark?

Designed by architects De Vestel, Jean Gilson and Jean and André Polak, and built on the site of an old convent, the building opened in 1967. Technically bold, it was big, brash and the symbol of a united Europe. Its structure hung from steel braces. Its four wings housed 3,000 officials over 13 floors, while the four underground levels comprised 1,600 parking spaces, conference rooms, a TV studio, restaurants, shops and warehouses, with an underground connection

to the metro. By the 1980s, this once avant-garde design was looking decidedly dated. The media perception of the officials it housed was that they were overpaid, incompetent and corrupt. Brussels' urban action groups, such as ARAU, complained vociferously that the EU had replaced the dynamic, beautiful Quartier Léopold with a soulless Gotham City of steel and glass.

Worse, in 1991 colossal chunks of cancer-causing asbestos were uncovered in the building – and it was evacuated. At this stage there was idle talk of demolishing it and starting afresh, but bolshy locals suddenly grew protective; it was their symbol, their cult building. Moreover, its foundations were embedded in the complicated road and metro network of the Schuman interchange. It would have to be preserved – and renovated.

For years the Berlaymont was shrouded in white plastic while the asbestos was removed. The phrase 'white elephant' seemed embarrassingly appropriate – especially when then Commission President, Romano Prodi, started banging on about 'transparency' in the EU. Yet the renovation plans, currently being undertaken by a group of Brussels-

fountain, though the one on display today is a 19th-century copy of the 1619 bronze original, sculpted by Jérôme Duquesnoy.

NEO-CLASSICISM

This 18th-century style was more grown up than in the previous era, as the Austrians and then the French who ruled Brussels sought to transform it into a city for the aristocracy, one that would rival London and Paris. The **Palais de Charles de Lorraine**, former residence of the governor of the Austrian Netherlands, is an early example of this style, though in many ways it was ahead of its time; its numerous statues, pillars and mouldings are more typical of the end of the century.

The **Palais de la Nation**, now the Belgian Parliament, was designed by Barnabé Guimard, who was also the mastermind behind the elegant **place Royale** on the site of the 15th-century Coudenberg Palace. The church of **St-Jacques sur Coudenberg**, built in 1775, was meant to resemble a Roman temple. The **Galeries Royales de St-Hubert**, designed by Jean-Pierre Cluysenaer, were opened by Léopold I in 1847, and were one of Europe's first covered shopping arcades. Belgian independence in 1831 brought new neo-classical projects to a sudden halt, leading to a dramatic divide between a French aristocratic Upper Town and a Flemish mercantile Lower Town that is still apparent today.

LEOPOLD II

By the middle of the 19th century, Brussels was literally bursting at the seams: its population had exceeded 100,000 for the first time. This prompted a construction boom, the old cleared to make way for the new.

Following outbreaks of cholera the Senne river was silted up and added to the city sewage system. The city had lost more than a body of water. From 1867 to 1871, much of the historical heart of the city disappeared; more than a thousand houses were demolished. In their place, straight avenues were constructed, connecting the Gare du Nord to the Gare du Midi, divided by several squares. Few gardens were left intact.

If Brussels has some of the imperial feel of Paris and London, it is thanks to Léopold II, who took the throne in 1865 and used the riches

based architects and engineers under the title Berlaymont 2000, are spectacular. When it reopens the Berlaymont will be a showcase environmental building. Nearly all its waste water will be recycled, it will have its own generator and it will be self-cooling through its own iceberg frozen in the basement. Specially angled glass panels will deflect and trap sunlight depending on the weather. Even the press will get a new media centre.

Fine. But when?

In 1997, Berlaymont 2000 estimated that renovation would take 28 months and €327 million. That was a pipe dream. By February 2002 costs were being estimated at €1.36 billion and the first renovation phase put back to August 2003. Not all of this has been borne by the EU. The Berlaymont belongs to the Belgian government and they paid for the asbestos removal. The EU agreed to pay some renovation costs and to buy the building when – if? – it's completed. But currently under discussion is just who will bear the huge extra costs. And what happens when the EU expands again? It looks like this one will run and run.

exploited from the Congo to finance projects around Brussels. Everything monumental and imposing in the city can be credited to him. The **Parc du Cinquantenaire** with its regal **Arc de Triomphe** is typical of this era, as is the massive **Palais de Justice**. The **Musée Royal de l'Afrique Centrale** in the Parc de Tervuren was designed by French architect Charles Girault, who also designed the Petit Palais in Paris. The **place de Brouckère** was completed in August 1897, its fountain later dismantled to make way for the metro.

While history has shown Léopold II as an arrogant opportunist, and his style of architecture is little admired today, he did set standards for urban planning. He opened up the city with a broad-minded coherence that the 20th-century developers wholly lacked. To see this, you only need trace the remarkable straight line (rue Royal Ste Marie, rue Royale and rue de la Régence) that runs from the railway station in Schaerbeek to the Palais de Justice, past the stunning Schaerbeek town hall, the neo-Byzantine church of Ste-Marie, the lovely glass Jardins Botanique, the colonne du Congrès, the royal palace and place Royale. That's some chain of buildings.

ART NOUVEAU AND ART DECO

At the end of the 19th century, a new style burst on to the scene, one that would change the face of Brussels for good and forever: art nouveau. Inspired by the British Arts and Crafts movement of the 1880s, and incorporating the fluid shapes of flowers and plants into an organic whole, art nouveau was wholeheartedly seized by architects in Brussels, the greatest exponent being Victor Horta. For more on Horta and Brussels' very own version of art nouveau, *see chapter* **Art Nouveau**.

After World War I and a long *séjour* in the US, Horta became disenchanted with art nouveau and moved to a cooler, more sober style known as art deco. His greatest achievement during this era was the **Palais des Beaux-Arts**, completed in 1928. This was the world's first multi-purpose entertainment centre, comprising a concert hall, theatre, cinema, exhibition spaces, shops and cafés all under one roof. The building was part of a larger urban development plan called the Quartier Ravenstein, but Horta died before seeing the end of the project – including the **Gare Centrale**, which he also designed.

Another stunning example of the period is the 11-storey **Résidence**. Built as an apartment block for the haute bourgeoisie in the 1920s, it predates New York's Rockefeller Center, which it closely resembles. Equipped with a luxurious swimming pool, theatre, shops and a roof garden, the building has been immaculately restored and now provides pleasant office space for journalists in the heart of the EU Quarter. In 1938 the **Institut National de Radiodiffusion** in Ixelles was constructed; at the time it was the most advanced communications building in the world.

The two main innovations between the wars were apartment blocks and *cité-jardins*. Blocks of rather stolid, geometrical buildings were designed to flank a small garden square, and this became a feature of Brussels. The Tintin illustrations of the period reflect this development: well-brushed paving stones, straight buildings and a certain calm.

POST-WAR

The post-war period was not the best for Brussels architecture. Tunnels and dual carriageways sliced through neighbourhoods, and the once lively **Quartier Léopold** was torn down and replaced with glass and steel complexes to suit the EU bureaucracy. Horta's masterpiece, the **Maison du Peuple**, was pulled down in 1964, despite numerous protests to leave it standing. One post-war building does stand out: the 102-metre (335-foot) **Atomium**, built in the shape of a steel molecule for the World Fair of 1958. Brussels' iconic structure now houses a shabby science museum, but, again, restoration is under way.

TODAY AND TOMORROW

To preserve the city's architectural heritage, a number of interest groups were founded: **ARAU** in 1969 and, seven years later, the **Fondation Roi Baudoin**. The latter organisation was the force behind the Brussels 2000 renovation campaign.

Yet the main story remains the same: how much of the Quartier Léopold can be saved from EU development? ARAU and other groups have been protesting about the demolition of this once lively neighbourhood for years, but to little avail. The EU just keeps expanding. Beside the Berlaymont (the giant European Parliament) and the sprawling Council of Ministers, there are countless glass, steel and concrete office blocks to house the enormous bureaucracy of the current 15-nation EU. And it is only getting bigger. Parliament plans two more buildings in the place du Luxembourg; probably only the façade of the now disused Gare du Luxembourg will remain as a reminder of what this square used to look like. Meanwhile, the area has to prepare for the onslaught of the extra countries that are part of the enlargement process. Where will a Europe of 25 nations be housed? And what will it mean for the architectural future of Brussels?

Maison de St-Cyr. *See p38.*

Art Nouveau

The jewel in Brussels' architectural crown.

Many of Brussels' most spectacular houses and shops were built in the art nouveau style that flourished at the end of the 19th century and start of the 20th. Today it is one of the main draws for tourists. The most famous and prolific architect of the time was **Victor Horta**, who set new standards for modern architecture that still hold up today. Along with **Henri van de Velde**, **Paul Hankar**, **Ernest Blérot**, **Gustave Serurrier-Boyvy**, **Octave van Rysselberghe**, **Paul Cauchie** and a host of others, he turned Brussels into the capital of the art nouveau world – albeit for just a brief period. Sadly, their creations have not always received the respect and dignity they deserve, and some were even ruthlessly torn down or neglected for long periods. However, over the past couple of decades, many have been lovingly restored, including Horta's own home, now the Musée Horta.

THE BIRTH OF ART NOUVEAU

Art nouveau originated in England around 1890 and spread quickly to the European continent, where it was known as Jugendstil in Germany, Modernista or Modernismo in Spain, Stile Floreale in Italy and Sezessionstil in Austria. There is some debate as to the precise origin of the term art nouveau, but most sources trace it to an interior design gallery that opened in Paris in 1896, la Maison de l'Art Nouveau. The phrase was also used in numerous articles published at the time in the Belgian avant-garde publication *Art Moderne*.

Art nouveau combined the linear patterns of the English-inspired Arts and Crafts movement with the curves of plants and flowers into what Horta dubbed 'maximum fluidity': the intertwining of all elements into an organic whole. It also borrowed heavily from Japanese wood prints, which blended angular shapes with the movement of flowing kimonos and trees. Marrying traditional craftsmanship with contemporary style, art nouveau architects created a design all their own, pouring their all into every detail, right down to the last doorknob and window pane. Their hallmarks were sinuous lines, ornate cast ironwork, rounded windows, tiled floors, stained glass, winding staircases, and sgraffito (a mural design technique in which the top layer of glaze, plaster and other materials is cut to reveal what is underneath).

'Art nouveau was the preferred medium of free-thinkers and Socialists, while Catholics condemned it as a godless extravagance.'

In Brussels, art nouveau was embraced by a new emerging middle class eager to break with old traditions and find a style of its own. About 30,000 houses were built at the end of the 19th century. Men such as Ernest Solvay and Edmond van Eetvelde, industrialists and engineers who got rich in the Congo Free State, built themselves great houses with no regard for expense. Although the architects generally had free rein to do what they wanted, good taste always seemed to prevail; they took great pains to tailor each house to the owner's own lifestyle and needs, turning each creation into a unique work of art, while keeping it practical at the same time.

The lovely **Maison de Cauchie**. *See p38.*

Although patronised by the phenomenally wealthy, many art nouveau architects were in fact Socialists and more interested in building for the people than the elite. The Belgian Workers' Party gave its approval to the new style. Art nouveau was therefore the preferred medium of free-thinkers and Socialists, while Catholics condemned it as a godless extravagance and turned to neo-Renaissance for their houses. Louis Bertrand, mayor of the fast-growing *commune* of Schaerbeek, decreed that all public buildings should be in the new style.

Art nouveau is generally concentrated in four areas in Brussels: **St-Gilles**, including Horta's own house; the **Ixelles** lakes; the centre of town including **avenue Louise**; and **Schaerbeek**, including square Ambiorix. Outside Brussels, head to Antwerp's Cogels-Osylei district. Of course, there are houses elsewhere, but if you want to see it all in one go, it's best to concentrate your tour. The tourist office, TIB (*see p303*), sells maps for self-guided tours. Sadly, not many of Brussels' 2,000 art nouveau buildings are open to the public; for the best of those that are, *see p37* **Top ten art nouveau**. You could also sign up for a trip organised by ARAU (*see p38* **Open house**), which takes you into private homes not usually open to visitors.

VICTOR HORTA
Born in Ghent in 1861, Horta is the father of art nouveau in Belgium. After studying drawing, textiles and architecture at the Ghent Académie des Beaux-Arts, he worked in Paris. He then returned to Belgium to work for classical architect Alphonse Balat – who designed the Serres de Laeken for Leopold II – before opening his own practice. Horta's big break came in 1889 when he was commissioned to design a monument to house a sculpture by Jef Lambeaux, depicting the pleasures and misfortunes of unbridled humanity. Horta said that designing the **Pavillion des passions humaines** in the Parc Cinquantenaire excited his enthusiasm for beautiful architecture. Unfortunately, he never got to finish the project, and Lambeaux's creation inside was closed after three days because it was considered too racy. It remains closed to this day.

In 1893 a lawyer, Eugène Autrique, asked Horta to design his house at **266 chaussée de Haecht** in Schaerbeek. He accepted immediately and refused a commission, on the condition that the money be spent instead on white stone for the façade. The house, located in an otherwise drab neighbourhood, has remained empty for many years, but is currently being restored as part of the Brussels 2000 project. The same year Horta built a house in Ixelles for industrialist Emile Tassel,

Top ten
Art nouveau

Brussels' proudest architectural heritage is mainly tucked away on quiet streets, behind marvellous façades closed to the public. Fortunately some masterpieces are open to all: here are five museums and five bars.

Keep an eye out too for the **Maison Autrique** (266 chaussée de Haecht) in Schaerbeek, the first house that Victor Horta built in Brussels. Its renovation is part of the Brussels 2000 project; work has been delayed, but completion is expected in summer 2002.

Musée Horta
The family home of the greatest architect of them all, designed 1898-1901. *See p88.*

Centre Belge de la Bande Dessinée
This Horta building (1906), designed as a fabric warehouse, became the Grand Magasin Waucquez before being rescued from demolition in the late 1980s. It now showcases Belgium's great comic book tradition. *See p63* **Strip search**.

Musée des Instruments de Musique
The former Magasins Old England department store, designed by Paul Saintenoy in 1899, now houses 6,000 musical instruments. *See p73.*

Hôtel Hannon
Jules Brunfaut's house for the photographer Hannon (*pictured*), built in 1902 and restored in 1985, is currently a contemporary photography museum, Contretype. *See p88.*

Maison de Cauchie
The family home of architect-painter Paul Cauchie, built in 1905 and recently entirely refurbished, is open on the first weekend of every month. *See p83.*

Hôtel Métropole
A luxurious café in a grand hotel, designed by Alban Chambon in 1894. *See p41 & p122.*

Le Falstaff
An institution, vast and famous. Art nouveau and art deco features, designed by Horta disciple Houbion in 1903. *See p123.*

De Ultieme Hallucinatie
The most beautiful of the art nouveau pubs, in shabby Schaerbeek. *See p137.*

Le Perroquet
Off Sablon, a resto-bar with an authentic art nouveau interior. *See p133.*

La Porteuse d'Eau
Another art nouveau gem, a St-Gilles café. *See p136.*

a bachelor who lived with his grandmother. Tassel, an engineer and university professor who liked to entertain, asked Horta to build something 'a bit new', a place where friends would feel welcome. The façade features stones of different colours, cast-iron railings, curved windows, stained glass and five small glass columns. Tassel was an amateur photographer, so Horta bathed the interior in light. **Hôtel Tassel** (6 rue Paul-Emile Janson), soon became famous as the world's first art nouveau edifice. Sadly, it's not open to the public.

Horta put just as much effort into building his own home and offices on rue Américaine; the renovated building now houses the **Musée Horta** (*see p88*). Behind the plain exterior is a stunning place adorned with mosaic tiled floors, Asian tapestries and elaborate staircases. The place is kept in immaculate condition and even on the gloomiest of days is cheerfully bathed in light. Horta's final art nouveau commission before wartime exile in the US was the Grand Magasin Waucquez, a fabric warehouse, later department store – and now the **Centre Belge**

Open house

In 1969 a group of concerned citizens, stung by the relentless bureaucratisation – *bruxellisation* – of their city, and the callous neglect of architectural masterpieces, formed the Atelier de Recherche et d'Action Urbaines: ARAU. Its immediate aims were to save and renovate listed buildings and put them to new uses. Long-term, ARAU has breathed new life into deserted or overly commercial and administrative areas. They are currently trying to salvage what they can of the residential Quartier Léopold from the EU. The recent renovation programme, Brussels 2000, owes much to ARAU and the other architectural organisation, Fondation Roi Baudouin.

Since 1975 ARAU have been running tours to raise public awareness of the city's treasures. The weekend tours, from March to mid December, concentrate mainly on art nouveau and art deco. Each tour lasts about two to three hours, Sunday walking ones (€10) included. The Saturday stop-off ones by coach (€12-€15) expertly guide visitors around fabulous art nouveau interiors otherwise closed to the public. Although wonderful examples of art nouveau can be seen at various restaurants and museums in town (*see p37* **Top ten art nouveau**), the real eye-openers are around Ixelles, Schaerbeek and St-Gilles, full of ornate private houses whose sheer opulence beggars belief. Don't miss your chance to see them.

Tours are usually in French, though regular English ones are scheduled. It's best to book ahead; tickets are available from TIB (*see p303*) or direct from ARAU.

ARAU

55 boulevard Adolphe Max, 1000 Brussels (02 219 33 45/fax 02 219 86 75/ www.arau.org). **Open** 9am-5pm Mon-Fri.

---

de la Bande Dessinée (*see p63* **Strip search**). The modern Brasserie Horta in the main entrance is done out in art nouveau style.

The greatest tragedy befell Horta's famous **Maison du Peuple**, built at the height of the art nouveau era in Sablon for the Société Coopérative. One of Horta's finest buildings, the place was a stunning glass and cast-iron palace with an auditorium, café and numerous shops for the locals. But in 1964 it no longer suited the needs of the cooperative, who ignored

numerous protests and had the building demolished. Some of the balustrades are on display at Horta metro station.

PAUL HANKAR & OTHERS

The other great name in Belgian art nouveau is Paul Hankar. To view his masterpieces go to **rue Defacqz** in Ixelles, which could easy be renamed rue Hankar. He built his own home at No.71, whose façade was an exquisite contrast of textures and colours; the sgfraffiti tiles were the work of Adolphe Crespin. Hankar was strongly influenced by Henri Beyaert, for whom he worked at the start of his career. Just down the street at No.48 is the house he designed for Symbolist painter Albert Ciamberlani. No.50 is also Hankar-built, for the painter Jansens, though it is less striking. Hankar also designed numerous shopfronts, the only surviving one being at **13 rue Royale**. Once a flower shop, the place has been deserted for some time.

The most striking example of an abandoned art nouveau masterpiece being transformed by modern use is the **Musée des Instruments de Musique** (*see p73*), formerly the Old England department store. Designed by Paul Saintenoy in 1899, this magnificent structure of glass and swirls of wrought iron stood empty for years before extensive renovation a century after its inauguration.

Unfortunately, the art nouveau tale is one of demolition. As well as Hankar's shops, Alban Chaubon's theatres were demolished, as was Ernest Blérot's own house. By the beginning of the 20th century, interest in art nouveau was already fading, but it would not make a quiet exit. Vertical and angular buildings were in, and some of the most stunning works were produced during this time. The 1905 **Maison de Cauchie** (*see p83*) on rue des Francs shows the influence of the Vienna Sezession with its geometric shapes. The gilded mural of lovely maidens in long gowns is reminiscent of Gustav Klimt and was meant to be an advertisement for Cauchie's art.

The five-storey **Maison de St-Cyr** in square Ambiorix (1905), designed by 22-year-old **Gustave Strauven**, is stunningly photogenic. Perhaps Brussels' narrowest façade, the brick house has ornate ironwork, intricate railings and a round loggia at the top. At the time of writing it was still up for sale, though any new owner would undoubtedly have to abide by very strict occupancy rules.

The last significant year for art nouveau in Brussels was 1905. Horta soon abandoned the style for the static, geometric art deco. It had been an incredibly brief flowering, just 12 years from 1893, but it transformed the city of Brussels forever.

Accommodation

Accommodation **40**

Features

Accommodation

Business hotels predominate, but there are plenty of other sleeping options.

By virtue of its status as EU capital, Brussels boasts far more hotels than other cities its size. By the same token, these tend to cater more for the business stopover than the lingering private visit. Since a good three-quarters of hotel clientele are business folk, the emphasis is usually placed on cleanliness, efficiency and functionality, meaning that individual character and charm tend to take a back seat. This is something the new five-star Mondiale, a stylish art deco hotel and apartment complex sited prominently in rue Léopold and due to be completed in 2004, will hope to address. More and more hotels have begun to prioritise individuality and distinctiveness.

The **Belgian Tourist Reservation Office** (02 513 74 84/fax 02 513 92 77) offers a free accommodation booking service; it's got a comprehensive list of hotels and quotes discounts, which can be 50 per cent or more. If you prefer to book yourself, you can obtain the hotel list from the Tourist Information Office (02 504 03 90/fax 02 504 02 70).

STAR RATINGS

The state awards star ratings by the quantity and type of services a hotel offers, rather than by the innate quality of the establishment. A nondescript hotel with a slew of services will have more stars than a characterful first-rate one that doesn't see the need for trouser presses and 24-hour room service.

ALL SHAPES AND SIZES

Rooms vary from the minuscule to the massive, but you're unlikely to find many of the latter at the lower end of the price scale. Many of the smaller hotels occupy converted townhouses (*maisons de maître*), tall, narrow buildings mostly dating from the early 20th century. Usually they have high ceilings and windows, which make the rooms feel more spacious, and there are often curvy wrought-iron balconies and other pretty art nouveau detailing.

PRICES AND CLASSIFICATION

All prices quoted below apply to rooms with a toilet and a shower or bath and include breakfast, unless otherwise stated. Cheaper hotels can offer communal facilities, a boon if you're on a tight budget. If you are going the bargain route, make sure that you specify if you want en suite facilities when booking.

A side effect of the primacy of business in Brussels is that hotels are much busier in the week, and most therefore offer drastically reduced rates at the weekend. Even when not specifically mentioned below, this is generally the case, especially for pricier hotels. Consult websites for off-peak deals (which may vary during the year). Although some hotels may appear to be outside your budget, weekend and seasonal bargains can produce pleasant surprises. The time of year also plays a major role in fixing rates: in Brussels, the low season covers July and August, a bargain time to visit.

We have classified hotels by the cost of their cheapest double room: **Deluxe** (over €273), **Expensive** (€161-€273), **Moderate** (€87-€161) and **Cheap** (up to €87). We also list the best B&Bs and hostels. Most hotels below will have no trouble with enquiries in English.

Grand' Place & around

Deluxe

Amigo

1-3 rue de l'Amigo, 1000 Brussels (02 547 47 47/ fax 02 513 52 77/www.hotelamigo.com). Pré-métro Bourse. **Rates** single €400-€490; double €430-€520; suite €990-€2,350; weekend rates on request. Breakfast (not incl) €15-€25. **Credit** AmEx, DC, MC, V. **Map** p317 B3.

Another chapter has been added to the history of this listed building, which has given its name to this narrow cobbled street off the Grand' Place. A dwelling under various guises since the 16th century (when it was a prison), it was turned into a hotel for the 1958 World Fair. Taken over by Rocco Forte in 2000, it is now once more reborn as one of the city's most prestigious hotels. The Amigo breaks the mould of the typical (19th-century Anglo-inspired) design of upmarket Brussels hotels: behind the Spanish Renaissance-style red-brick façade is a very modern design, although the hotel still retains many of its famed period pieces (from medieval flagstones to Flemish paintings by Courtens and Bastien). Sober without being bland, its elegant and ultra-comfortable rooms are quite a treat for the eyes, and to the touch. An excellent location tops it all off. **Hotel services** *Bar. Business services. Conference facilities. Disabled: adapted rooms (1). Fax. Gym. Laundry. Lift. Parking. No-smoking rooms. Restaurant.* **Room services** *Dataport. Hairdryer. Minibar. Room service (24hr). Safe. Telephone. TV: satellite.*

Métropole

31 place de Brouckère, 1000 Brussels (02 217 23 00/ fax 02 218 02 20/www.metropolehotel.com). Métro/ Pré-métro De Brouckère. **Rates** *Mon-Thur* single €275-€375; double €325-€424. *Fri-Sun* single/ double €115. Suite €450-€999. **Credit** AmEx, DC, MC, V. **Map** p317 C2.

Opened in 1895, this grande dame of the Brussels hotel scene was an afterthought of the Wielemans, the brewing family who set up the adjoining café five years earlier to promote their beers – and who still own the Métropole. It continues to command attention and respect, as a luxury hotel and as part of the capital's architectural heritage. The French Renaissance main entrance leads into one of the city's loftiest hotel interiors. The Empire-style reception hall, with its gilt flourishes and columns, features the impressive stained-glass windows that were to become characteristic of art nouveau. The lift is original, and the rooms – whether in the original building or in the extension purchased in 1925, with mainly art deco fittings – are simply splendid.

Hotel services *Babysitting. Bar. Beauty salon. Business services. Conference facilities. Fax. Gym. Laundry. Lift. No-smoking rooms (70). Restaurant. Safe.* **Room services** *Dataport. Hairdryer. Minibar. PlayStation. Radio. Room service (24hr). Safe. Telephone. TV: satellite.*

Le Plaza

118 boulevard Adolphe Max, 1000 Brussels (02 227 67 00/fax 02 227 67 20/www.leplaza-brussels.be). Métro/Pré-métro Rogier or De Brouckère. **Rates** *Mon-Thur* double €400-€450. *Fri-Sun* double €125. Suite €620-€870. Breakfast (not incl) €18/€27. **Credit** AmEx, DC, MC, V. **Map** p319 C2.

The distinctive old-world appeal of this magnificent hotel is no artificial construct. Nearly half a century after it opened in 1930, the Plaza was forced to close, but made a comeback in 1996 under the ownership of Baron van Gysel de Meiser. It remains a distinguished presence (despite its location on a drab central boulevard), successfully marrying authenticity and tradition with the most up-to-date comforts and services. As headquarters of the Nazis and then the Allied Forces during World War II, the building (now listed) was largely spared the bomb blasts. The winter garden, which did suffer, has been faithfully rebuilt and houses the restaurant. The rest of the building, replete with original fittings (amethyst crystal chandeliers, Gobelins tapestry, marble bas-reliefs), has been restored to former glory. The sumptuous rooms contain fabrics and fittings hand-picked by the baroness on her travels; usually in fairly neutral creams, beiges and ochre hues. The hotel's jewel in the crown is the ornate theatre of Hispanic-Moorish design, now used as a multi-functional event room.

Hotel services *Bar. Business services. Conference facilities. Fax. Gym. Laundry. Lift. No-smoking rooms. Parking. Restaurant.* **Room services** *Dataport. Fax. Hairdryer. Minibar. Room service (24hr). Safe. Telephone. TV: cable.*

Radisson SAS

47 rue du Fossé aux Loups, 1000 Brussels (02 219 28 28/reservations 02 227 31 33/fax 02 219 62 62/ www.radissonsas.com). Métro/Pré-métro De Brouckère. **Rates** *Mon-Thur* single €290-€340; double €290-€365. *Fri-Sun* single €125-€175; double €150-€200. Breakfast (not incl in standard room Mon-Thur) €25. **Credit** AmEx, DC, MC, V. **Map** p317 C2.

Plenty of space to share with friends at **Amigo**. *See p40.*

This joint Scandinavian and American venture is an exercise in crisply efficient sophistication and service. Choose from four different styles of room (Classical, Scandinavian, Oriental and Royal Club), but don't expect an original look; these are essentially standard luxury rooms. The Scandinavian rooms have 'allergy-aware' teak floors, but the Oriental theme is limited to the odd decorative touch. Royal Club rooms are a tad classier and include extra services. A top-class business hotel.
Hotel services *Babysitting. Bar. Business services. Conference facilties. Disabled: adapted rooms (3). Fax. Gym. Laundry. Lift. Parking. No-smoking rooms. Restaurants (2). Safe. Sauna. Solarium.* **Room services** *Dataport. Hairdryer. Minibar. Radio. Room service (24hr). Telephone. TV: satellite.*

Moderate

Arlequin

17-19 rue de la Fourche, 1000 Brussels (02 514 16 15/fax 02 514 22 02/www.arlequin.be). Métro/Pré-métro De Brouckère. **Rates** single €77; double €97-€115; triple €110; duplex €105-€150. **Credit** AmEx, DC, MC, V. **Map** p317 C3.
It's a surprise to find such a large (92-room), modern and inexpensive hotel tucked away in one of the little cobbled streets near the Grand' Place. The neutral rooms vary in size, but are uniformly comfortable, bright and clean. A top-floor breakfast room offers panoramic vistas of the capital's rooftops.
Hotel services *Bar. Conference facilities. Fax. Internet. Laundry. Lift. Safe.* **Room services** *Hairdryer. Room service (24hr). Telephone. TV: cable.*

La Madeleine

20-22 rue de la Montagne, 1000 Brussels (02 513 29 73/fax 02 502 13 50/www.hotel-la-madeleine.be). Métro Gare Centrale. **Rates** single with sink €46; single with shower €65; single with bath €85; double with bath €93; executive single €98; executive double €106; executive triple €120. **Credit** AmEx, DC, MC, V. **Map** p317 C3.
A no-frills hotel in a brilliant location. The rooms are rudimentary, the furniture and plumbing laughably basic and the singles downright poky – but they are clean enough, and the staff are friendly. Perhaps pricey for something so basic, but one of the cheapest hotels close to the Grand'Place, and the choice of shared bathroom facilities makes La Madeleine a good option for sightseeing on a budget.
Hotel services *Fax. Laundry. Lift. Safe.* **Room services** *Telephone. TV: cable.*

Mozart

23 rue du Marché aux Fromages, 1000 Brussels (02 502 66 61/fax 02 502 77 58/www.hotel-mozart.be). Métro Gare Centrale. **Rates** single €70; double €88; triple €113; quadruple €138. **Credit** AmEx, DC, MC, V. **Map** p317 C3.
This labyrinthine hotel is a mixed bag, its rooms varying in size, light and decor. None are especially spacious, some even dark and cramped. Decorated in a pervasive mock antique style (gilt, brocade,

chintz), the Mozart smacks of inadvertent kitsch, perhaps mildly refreshing after another neutral hotel room. It's brilliantly central, by the Grand' Place – but on a noisy street full of kebab shops.
Hotel services *Fax. Laundry. Lift. Safe.* **Room services** *Hairdryer. Refrigerator. Telephone. TV: cable.*

Saint-Michel

15 Grand' Place, 1000 Brussels (02 511 09 56/fax 02 511 46 00/hotelsaintmichel@hotmail.com). Pré-métro Bourse. **Rates** single with view €109-€116; single back room €62-€82; double with view €129-€136; double back room €98; extra bed €22. **Credit** AmEx, DC, MC, V. **Map** p317 C3.
Situated behind a picturesque façade on the main square, this is a great hotel for sightseeing. The rooms are a bit musty and dated, with weary-looking trappings. Still, they are in the process of being renovated, and all the beds are new. The larger front rooms provide a splendid view, but can be on the noisy side – there is no double-glazing.
Hotel services *Bar. Fax. Lift. Restaurant. Safe.* **Room services** *Hairdryer. Minibar. Room service (noon-11pm). Telephone. TV: cable.*

Cheap

À la Grande Cloche

10 place Rouppe, 1000 Brussels (02 512 61 40/fax 02 512 65 91/www.hotelgrandecloche.com). Pré-métro Anneessens. **Rates** single/double with shower €60; single/double with bath €73-€90. **Credit** AmEx, MC, V. **Map** p320 B4.
If the fashion police raided hotels, this would be one of its first ports of call. Unappealing fittings include green carpets and marble-effect wallpaper, but the rooms are clean and quite comfy. Windows are on the small side, but double-glazing guarantees peace. Queen beds lie in store for all: roomy for one, but a bit of a squeeze for two (the twin-bed rooms avoid the problem and are usually spacious). The cheaper rooms tend to have only a small shower room. The location is fairly central, towards Midi station.
Hotel services *Fax. Lift.* **Room services** *Hairdryer. Safe. Telephone. TV: cable.*

La Légende

35 rue du Lombard, 1000 Brussels (02 512 82 90/fax 02 512 34 93/www.hotellalegende.com). Métro Gare Centrale. **Rates** *Mon-Thur* single €71-€104; double €79-€113; triple €123; quadruple €132. *Fri-Sun* single €65-€98; double €73-€107; triple €117; quadruple €126. **Credit** AmEx, DC, MC, V. **Map** p317 B3.
This 26-room, family-run hotel boasts a great location near the Grand' Place. The recently renovated rooms are functional, more than adequate and all have parquet floors. They come in all sizes, some very generous, notably the family rooms. Others look on to an inner courtyard, so you can snatch a few moments' peace within the city centre.
Hotel services *Fax. Lift. No-smoking rooms. Safe.* **Room services** *Dataport. Telephone. TV: cable.*

Accommodation

The best Hotels

For sightseeing
You can't get more convenient than the **Saint-Michel** (*see p43*), slap bang on the Grand' Place. Or the **Jolly Hotel** (*see p45*) on the pretty, antique-laden, upmarket place du Grand Sablon.

For history
Grace Kelly occupied the wedding suite at the belle époque **Crowne Plaza** (*see p49*); and the Nazis, and then the Allies, occupied **Le Plaza** (*see p41*).

For interior design
Try the grander-than-grand **Métropole** (*see p41*) or the sassily opulent **Barsey** (*see p51*). Lovers of the kitsch or eccentric should opt for the **Mozart** (*see p43*), the **Noga** (*see right*), **Les Bluets** (*see p52*) or the bizarrely original **Comfort Art Hotel Siru** (*see p49*).

For value
Plenty of choice: the cheap and cheerful **Galia** (*see p45*), the centrally located **George V** (*see below right*) or the beautiful B&Bs **Chambres en ville** (*see p53*) and **Phileas Fogg** (*see p53*).

For business
The **Radisson SAS** (*see p41*) offers Scandinavian touches and super-efficiency. The EU-themed **Dorint** (*see p50*) is ideal for EU execs and secs.

For breakfast
Enjoy a view with your croissants at the **Arlequin** (*see p43 – pictured*) or sunbathe on the terrace at the **Du Congrès** (*see p47*).

Ste-Catherine & St-Géry

Expensive

Atlas
30 rue du Vieux Marché aux Grains, 1000 Brussels (02 502 60 06/fax 02 502 69 35/www.atlas.be). Pré-métro Bourse or Métro Ste-Catherine. **Rates** single €145; double €168; weekend and off-peak rates on request. **Credit** AmEx, DC, MC, V. **Map** p318 B3.
What lies outside the Atlas is more exciting than what lies within. Off trendy rue Antoine Dansaert, near the bars of St-Géry, the hotel scores highly for its location. The rooms teeter on the edge of sterility, but are generally acceptable. Half look on to an inner courtyard, and are relatively peaceful. The five duplex (split-level) rooms sleep up to four people. Service is up to standard, but you're paying for the location, not comfort.
Hotel services *Conference facilities. Disabled: adapted rooms (1). Fax. Laundry. Lift. Parking. Safe.* **Room services** *Dataport. Hairdryer. Minibar. Room service (7am-4pm). Telephone. TV: cable.*

Moderate

Noga
38 rue du Béguinage, 1000 Brussels (02 218 67 63/ fax 02 218 16 03/www.nogahotel.com). Métro Ste-Catherine. **Rates** *Mon-Thur, Sun* single €75-€80; double €95; triple €125; quadruple €150. *Fri,Sat* single €65; double €75; triple €100; quadruple €125. **Credit** AmEx, DC, MC, V. **Map** p318 B2.
A friendly and delightfully kitsch-tastic hotel on a charming little Ste-Catherine street. Nautical-themed knick-knacks jostle for space with pictures of past royals and assorted bric-a-brac. The bar and billiard room (complete with *trompe-l'oeil* bookcase) are equally busy. The rooms are a tad more restrained, but each is quite individual in its colour scheme and fittings. As a rule, they are brightly hued, spotless and comfy. Warm service and fair prices.
Hotel services *Bar. Bicycle rental. Billiard room. Fax. Garden. Internet. Laundry. Lift. Parking (€10). Safe.* **Room services** *Dataport. Hairdryer. Minibar. Telephone. TV: cable.*

Cheap

George V
23 rue 't Kint, 1000 Brussels (02 513 50 93/fax 02 513 44 93/www.george5.com). Pré-métro Bourse. **Rates** single €59; double €69; triple €79; quadruple €89. **Credit** AmEx, MC, V. **Map** p318 A3.
It's pot luck in this slightly tatty but clean hotel, its rooms either bright or morose. The tiny bathrooms in the single rooms are for acrobatic limbo dancers only. But it's pretty central, and the option of triples and quads makes it a good deal for weekend parties.
Hotel services *Bar. Fax. Laundry. Lift.* **Room services** *Dataport. Telephone. TV: cable.*

Noga: nautical but nice. *See p44.*

Pacific Sleeping
57 rue Antoine Dansaert, 1000 Brussels (02 511 84 59). Pré-métro Bourse. **Rates** single €33; double €50-€55; triple €75. **No credit cards. Map** p318 B3.

'Safe, clean and cheap' is the motto – and it doesn't come much cheaper than this frankly ramshackle hotel on the trendiest street in town. If you can get past the bathmats as rugs, occasional plastic garden furniture and often dire need for refurbishment, you might appreciate the appeal of this century-old venue, summed up by the period breakfast room and the original sinks in the rooms. Eclectic artwork in the corridors records the appreciation of former guests. No en suite bathrooms.
Hotel services *Lift. No-smoking rooms (all). Safe.*

Welcome
1-5 rue du Peuplier, 1000 Brussels (02 219 95 46/fax 02 217 18 87/www.hotelwelcome.com). Métro Ste-Catherine. **Rates** single €65-€120; double €70-€120; suite €160; extra bed €13. Breakfast (not incl) €8. **Credit** AmEx, DC, MC, V. **Map** p318 B2.

This tiny hotel's main attribute used to be the warmth of its service, thankfully still with us. But after recent expansion and renovation, it also offers individually decorated rooms catering for myriad tastes. Lavish Indian and Moorish rooms, sober and minimalist Chinese and Japanese rooms, more home-spun North Sea and Provençal rooms – all fulfil the hotel's credo of stamping out standardisation and anonymity. For masses of space, go for the more conventional 'Simon' room, with a view over the pretty square and its fish restaurants. Mr and Mrs Smeesters also run a restaurant on the ground floor.
Hotel services *Bar. Fax. Laundry. Lift. Parking (€8). No-smoking rooms. Restaurant. Safe.*
Room services *Dataport. Hairdryer. Room service (6am-1am). Safe. Telephone. TV: cable.*

Marolles & Gare du Midi

Moderate

Agenda Midi
11 boulevard Jamar, 1060 Brussels (02 520 00 10/ fax 02 520 00 20/www.hotel-agenda.com). Métro/ Pré-metro Midi. **Rates** single €84; double €97; suite €112; extra bed €12. **Credit** AmEx, DC, MC. **Map** p320 A4.

CS Lewis observed that a city always shows its worst face to the railway. If you need to stay in the rather insalubrious neighbourhood of Midi station, look out for this bright yellow façade peeping out among the seedy hotels and sex shops. It's a cut above the rest. The standard rooms aren't huge or especially spectacular, but a real effort has been made to make them bright and cosy. A pseudo-Mediterranean look combines yellow and orange hues with blue, and there are pretty, mosaic-tiled bathrooms. It's handy for the Eurostar and the colourful market on a Sunday. The town centre is reasonably close on foot or by metro.
Hotel services *Fax. Laundry. Lift. No-smoking rooms. Safe.* **Room services** *Hairdryer. Minibar. Telephone. TV: cable.*

Cheap

Galia
15-16 place du Jeu de Balle, 1000 Brussels (02 502 42 43/fax 02 502 76 19/www.hotelgalia.com). Métro Porte de Hal. **Rates** single €55; double €62; triple €81; quadruple €99. **Credit** AmEx, DC, MC, V. **Map** p320 B5.

A simple but good-value little hotel. Cheerfully and unobtrusively decorated in a quintessentially Belgian comic strip theme, rooms are basic but clean and pleasant; the three- and four-person rooms are fairly large. Some have phones. New bathrooms as small and spotless as an aeroplane toilet. The lighter front rooms, with triple-glazing, look on to the daily flea market and surrounding bars. Also nearby in this poor area is Belgium's most hyped club, the Fuse. A 15-minute walk to the Grand' Place.
Hotel services *Bar. Fax. Lift. No-smoking rooms (all).* **Room services** *TV: cable.*

Upper Town

Deluxe

Jolly Hotel du Grand Sablon
2-4 rue Bodenbroek, 1000 Brussels (02 518 11 00/ fax 02 512 67 66/www.jollyhotels.it). Tram 91, 92, 93, 94/bus 95, 96. **Rates** single €289-€380; double €310-€380; suite €470-€620; weekend and off-peak rates on request. **Credit** AmEx, DC, MC, V. **Map** p317 C4.

Location, location, location. The Italian hotel chain prides itself on the whereabouts of its handful of establishments in Europe. This one is ideally set on

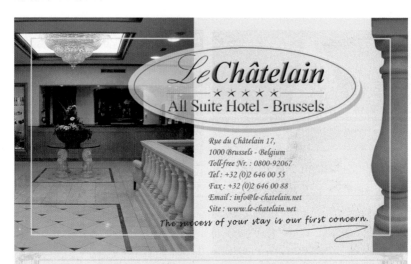
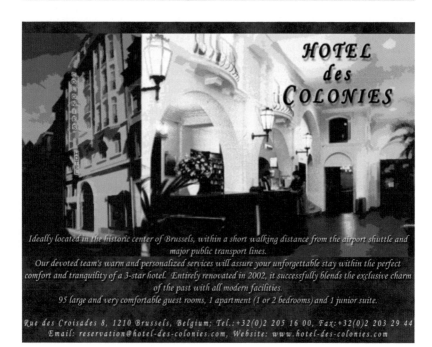

a pretty square, with terrace cafés, antiquarian shops and a weekend antiques market. The rooms are also of a high calibre, although they vary in size. The decor of the suites is warmer than the fussy grey and white look of the standard rooms, but equally traditional and favouring flowery and gilt detail. Stylish without being especially characterful, this is still a deserving member of the Brussels hotel scene's glitterati, in a star spot.
Hotel services *Bar. Business services. Conference facilities. Disabled: adapted rooms (2). Fax. Laundry. Lift. Parking. No-smoking rooms. Restaurant.* **Room services** *Dataport. Hairdryer. Minibar. Room service (6am-noon). Safe. Telephone. TV: cable.*

Stanhope Hotel

9 rue du Commerce, 1000 Brussels (02 506 91 11/ fax 02 512 17 08/www.stanhope.be). Métro Trône. **Rates** *Mon-Thur, Sun* single €295; double €395; suite from €615. *Fri, Sat* single €150; double €195; suite from €255. Breakfast (not incl Mon-Thur, Sun) €21.50. **Credit** AmEx, DC, MC, V. **Map** p324 E4.
An atmosphere of calm and intimacy pervades the elegantly converted townhouses that make up this impeccable hotel. Fairly centrally located not far from the Royal Palace and easily accessible from the Upper and the Lower Town, it evokes an idealised 19th-century English country home. The ultra-comfy rooms are individual in decor and layout, but certain themes run throughout, such as the Ming vases and bookcases. The restaurant is inspired by the interior of the Brighton Pavilion. The slightly effete charm is, of course, entirely contrived, but the Stanhope is exemplary in its discreet sophistication and attention to detail. If money is no object, check into one of the split-level junior suites.
Hotel services *Bar. Business services. Conference facilities. Fax. Garden. Gym. Laundry. Lift. Parking. No-smoking rooms. Restaurant. Sauna.* **Room services** *Dataport. Hairdryer. Minibar. Room service (24hr). Telephone. TV: cable.*

Expensive

Astoria

103 rue Royale, 1000 Brussels (02 227 05 05/ fax 02 217 11 50/www.sofitel.com). Métro Botanique/tram 92, 93, 94. **Rates** single/double €170-€250; suite €460-€575. Breakfast (not incl) €23. **Credit** AmEx, DC, MC, V. **Map** p319 D2.
In its heyday, the Astoria was a luxury palace hotel, and many illustrious elements remain. Now a listed building, it has wonderful high ceilings, stained-glass windows and a stunning glass roof in the ostentatious turquoise and gold lobby. But the rooms seem faded and may not attain the level of comfort the standard rates might suggest. Still, a splendid edifice with peaceful soundproofed rooms, and ten minutes' walk from the centre. It regularly hosts classical and jazz concerts.

Hotel services *Bar. Business services. Conference facilities. Fax. Gym. Laundry. Lift. No-smoking rooms. Restaurant. Safe.* **Room services** *Dataport. Hairdryer. Minibar. Room service (24hr). Telephone. TV: cable.*

Moderate

Du Congrès

42-44 rue du Congrès, 1000 Brussels (02 217 18 90/ fax 02 217 18 97/www.hotelducongres.com). Métro Madou. **Rates** single €110; double €125; triple €140; quadruple €155. **Credit** AmEx, DC, MC, V. **Map** p319 D2.
The renovated Du Congrès achieves a successful marriage of a sleek, neutral, minimalist, modern design with original turn-of-the-century features of the four converted townhouses that make up the hotel. Simple lines, plenty of creams and unfussy flower arrangements complement ornately carved wood panelling and gilt. Rooms may be on the small side, but are light and fairly attractive, especially if you chance on one with original features. The back garden and split-level terraces provide a peaceful enclave where breakfast may be taken, and some rooms open out on to it. A 15-minute walk into town.
Hotel services *Bar. Business services. Conference facilities. Fax. Garden. Laundry. Lift. No-smoking rooms. Safe.* **Room services** *Dataport. Hairdryer. Telephone. TV: cable.*

Welcome: it's aptly named. *See p45.*

Stairway to heaven

If you've got the urge to splurge, indulge it at Le Dixseptième. Set along the faceless façade of rue de la Madeleine, which steeply and sleepily connects Gare Centrale with the Grand' Place down below, its plain front door gives nothing away. A ring of the bell, the door opens, and a further pair of electronic doors – zzzzzhhhh – ushers the uninitiated into the lap of luxury.

The threshold crossed, Louis XVI panelling, crystal chandeliers and hands-off attentive service await at reception. Next door is a lovely period breakfast salon looking out on to a verdant inner courtyard. None of this is suitable preparation for the individually designed rooms, 24 in all, in classic and contemporary styles. Elegance, light and space have been used with rich abandon. You have indeed died and gone to... the 17th century, in fact.

For the truly heavenly Le Dixseptième has been restored to the 17th-century grandeur it once knew, when it was home to the ambassador of Spain. Then Brussels was also rebuilding itself, after the French bombardment of 1695, and this street – the first in Brussels to be paved – was considered prestigious. *El embajador* soon built a magnificent oak staircase and marble fireplaces.

The 1990 restoration added the rest, including the unusual twist of naming each room after a Belgian or Flemish artist, their

work and style subtly imprinted on the decor. The most outrageous examples are the walking stick and *trompe-l'oeil* paintings in the toilet of the Magritte room, one of the 12 more modern studios in the old stables, across the courtyard at the back. The most luxurious is the dreamy Jordaens, with its own four-poster bed. Many are done out in Louis XVI or French Renaissance style, with their own sitting room housing stunning collectibles. Most are suites, some with a balcony or a mezzanine. All have a marble bathroom, a free internet connection and perfect soundproofing from the busy city – you're four minutes from the Grand' Place.

Wave the magic wand at the CD player, open the minibar and order up the champagne. The 21st century may never be this gorgeous again.

Le Dixseptième

25 rue de la Madeleine, 1000 Brussels (02 517 17 17/fax 02 502 64 24/ www.ledixseptieme. be). Métro Gare Centrale. **Rates** single €170-€390; double €190-€420; extra bed €25. **Credit** AmEx, DC, MC, V. **Map** p317 C4.
Hotel services *Bar. Business services. Fax. Laundry. Lift. No-smoking rooms.*
Room services *Dataport. Hairdryer. Minibar. Radio. Room service (24hr, drinks only). Safe. Stereo. Telephone. TV: cable.*

Cheap

Madou

45 rue du Congrès, 1000 Brussels (02 217 18 90/ fax 02 217 18 97/www.hotelducongres.com). Métro Madou. **Rates** single €58; double €72; triple €88. **Credit** AmEx, DC, MC, V. **Map** p319 D2.

This one-star hotel is the poor relation of the classier three-star Du Congrès opposite (*see p47*), and accordingly inherits its hand-me-down furniture and fittings. The rooms are also more basic, with less attention paid to their aesthetics, but they are clean and decently sized – and guests have access to the reception and breakfast room across the road. **Hotel services** *Bar. Business services. Conference facilities. Fax. Garden. Laundry. No-smoking rooms. Safe.* **Room services** *Telephone. TV: cable.*

Sabina

78 rue du Nord, 1000 Brussels (02 218 26 37/fax 02 219 32 39/www.hotelsabina.be). Métro Madou. **Rates** single €61; double €73; suite €83; extra bed €20. **Credit** AmEx, DC, MC, V. **Map** p322 E3.

This slightly downbeat hotel's 24 rooms are modest, but bright and spotless. In fact, they're way above adequate and of a higher standard than you'll find in many other similarly priced hotels. Sadly, the only element of this converted early 1900s townhouse to have survived intact is the period breakfast room, with its dark wood panelling, beams and intricate painted ceiling *à la française*. The area is not the liveliest, being mainly taken up by offices, but it's only a ten- to 15-minute walk to the city centre. **Hotel services** *Fax. Lift. Parking. Safe.* **Room services** *Hairdryer. Telephone. TV: cable.*

Deluxe

Crowne Plaza

3 rue Gineste, 1000 Brussels (02 203 62 00/ fax 02 203 55 55/www.crowneplaza.com). Métro/ Pré-métro Rogier. **Rates** *Mon-Thur* single €297; double €322; club single/double €347. *Fri-Sun* single/double €124; club single/double €397. Breakfast (not incl Mon-Thur) €23.50. **Credit** AmEx, DC, MC, V. **Map** p319 D2.

The 1930s were the golden era of this belle époque palace hotel, and its historical background remains of utmost importance: its pride and joy is Grace Kelly's original wedding tour suite. When the hotel was renovated in 1998, great effort went into preserving its architectural heritage while also guaranteeing up-to-date comfort and services. Sadly, the lobby still feels a teeny Disneyish. Many of the slightly diminutive rooms (compared with other hotels in this class) are partly original, partly imitation art deco. It's worth asking for an original room, as there's a whiff of the chain hotel about the others. On the other hand, some of the original ones may seem a little dated for those used to contemporary

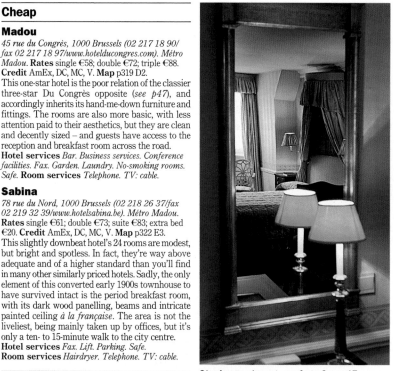

Stanhope: elegant comfort. *See p47.*

luxuries, and most have twin beds, in accordance with the mores of the era. Just off the place Rogier, the hotel is centrally situated between the Lower Town and the Gare du Nord.

Hotel services *Babysitting. Bar. Business services. Disabled: adapted rooms (15). Gym. Lift. No-smoking rooms. Restaurant. Sauna.* **Room services** *Dataport. Fax. Minibar. PlayStation. Room service (24hr). Telephone. TV: cable.*

Expensive

Comfort Art Hotel Siru

1 place Rogier, 1000 Brussels (02 203 35 80/ fax 02 203 33 03/www.comforthotelsiru.com). Métro/Pré-métro Rogier. **Rates** *Mon-Thur* single €165; double €185. *Fri-Sun* single/double €100. **Credit** AmEx, DC, MC, V. **Map** p319 C1.

It is strange that a hotel that sells itself as an 'art hotel' should demonstrate such a lack of aesthetic sensitivity in terms of the basic decor of its rooms, which, without the original artworks by around 130 contemporary artists, would be quite unremarkable. At least the Siru doesn't suffer from the plague of standardisation that affects its more expensive neighbours, nestled as it is among the big-bucks hotels on place Rogier. It wins top marks for the sheer originality of the sometimes subtle, sometimes outrageous works of art: fake rocks hang from the ceiling (*Still Life* by William Sweetlove) and bright, coloured nudes arch over the bedhead (*Discoveries of the Night* by Roger Somville).

Hotel services *Business services. Conference facilities. Fax. Internet. Laundry. Lift. No-smoking rooms. Restaurant.* **Room services** *Dataport. Hairdryer. Minibar. Safe. Telephone. TV: cable.*

Sheraton Brussels Hotel & Towers

3 place Rogier, 1000 Brussels (02 224 31 11/ fax 02 224 34 56/www.sheratonbrussels.be). Métro/Pré-métro Rogier. **Rates** standard double €212-€325; club/smart double €287-€400; suite €412-€650. Breakfast (not incl in standard room) €21/€24. **Credit** AmEx, DC, MC, V. **Map** p319 C1.

Size matters at the Sheraton. The biggest hotel in Belgium boasts 30 floors (but no 13th, in case you're superstitious) of spacious and elegant rooms with lavishly sized beds and all the other standardised comforts and services we have come to expect from the American giant. Nothing new there, but then that's the point. Constant modernisation does mean a newly renovated lounge bar and 'smart rooms', an added perk for high-powered business types, on top of the long-established private tower reception area. Wonderful panoramic vistas of the city from the rooms and the top-floor pool.

Hotel services *Bar. Business services. Children's room. Disabled: adapted rooms (30). Gym. Lift. No-smoking rooms. Pool. Restaurant.* **Room services** *Dataport. Minibar. PlayStation. Room service (24hr). TV: cable.*

EU Quarter & Montgomery

Deluxe

Dorint

11-19 boulevard Charlemagne, 1000 Brussels (02 231 09 09/fax 02 230 33 71/www.dorint.com). Métro Schuman. **Rates** Mon-Thur double €325-€360. Fri-Sun €99. Suite €460. Breakfast (not incl Mon-Thur) €9/€22. **Credit** AmEx, DC, MC, V. **Map** p325 F4.

Situated in the heart of the EU district, the Dorint is ultimately a business hotel, modern and sleek in both design and services. While the rooms verge on the sterile, with severely elegant black leather armchairs and blue furnishings, the hotel contrives to make a distinctive aesthetic statement, and does so beautifully. Belgian architect Serge Roose has used plenty of glass and metal, but softened some of the harshness with curves, wood and natural light. Photography is integrated everywhere, from the shows in the recently opened gallery to the original prints in each room and the prints on the unique (and periodically replaced) plates in its stylish restaurant. The EU itself has a presence, in works by artists from member states, and in the production of the restaurant's menu. All this creates an appealing air of efficiency and understated sophistication.

Hotel services *Art gallery. Babysitting. Bar. Business services. Disabled: adapted rooms (1). Gym. Laundry. Lift. No-smoking rooms. Parking. Restaurant. Sauna. Solarium. Turkish baths.* **Room services** *Dataport. Minibar. Room service (24hr). Telephone. TV: cable.*

Montgomery Hotel Brussels

134 avenue de Tervueren, 1150 Brussels (02 741 85 11/fax 02 741 85 00/www.hotelmontgomery.be). Métro Montgomery. **Rates** Mon-Thur, Sun single €320; double €360. Fri, Sat single €160; double €180. Suite €505. Breakfast (not incl Mon-Thur, Sun) €20. **Credit** AmEx, DC, MC, V.

A high-class hotel set apart from the rest by its location in a residential area (on a busy roundabout, a short metro ride from the city centre), and its small size: 63 spacious rooms. All this helps create the impression of calm and intimacy, underscored by a soupçon of personalised service. This is a finely tuned machine of an establishment that nevertheless exudes effortless calm. Lilting classical music plays even in the fitness centre. Books (in a multitude of languages, and on loan during your stay) line the bookcase of the bar and each room. Rooms are decorated in three different styles – 'marine' (dark blue and mahogany), 'romantic' (flowery red and green) and 'Oriental' (chintzy light blue and white) – but are all predictably classical. Originality is not the hotel's forte. Instead, it pulls off the painstaking creation of a sanctuary of traditional luxury with the unaffected grace of a true professional.

Hotel services *Bar. Conference facilities. Gym. Lift. Laundry. Parking. No-smoking rooms. Restaurant. Sauna.* **Room services** *Dataport. Fax. Hairdryer. Minibar. Room service (24hr). Safe. Telephone. TV: cable.*

Ixelles

Deluxe

Conrad Brussels

71 avenue Louise, 1050 Brussels (02 542 42 42/ fax 02 542 42 00/www.brussels.conradinternational. com). Métro Louise. **Rates** deluxe €495; executive €545; suite from €1,150; extra bed €25. Breakfast (not incl) €29. **Credit** AmEx, DC, MC, V. **Map** p321 C5.

An ultra-deluxe hotel with the appropriate trappings and service, and matching attitude. At the apex of the capital's upmarket hotels (in price terms, at least), it is a tad overbearing in its swanky opulence and glamour, and soulless in its pursuit of the image of time-honoured sophistication. A luxury stopoff for royals, politicians and celebrities, it boasts the plushest of facilities and fittings. Luxurious it most certainly is, prestigious it may be, but understated, tasteful and welcoming it is not. The Conrad is aptly located in Brussels' most upmarket area, near all the designer boutiques.

Hotel services *Bars (2). Beauty salon.
Business services. Conference facilities. Disabled:
adapted rooms (2). Fax. Gym. Laundry. Lift.
Parking. Pool. No-smoking rooms. Restaurants
(2).* **Room services** *Dataport. Hairdryer.
Minibar. Room service (24hr). Safe. Telephone.
TV: satellite.*

Hotel Bristol Stéphanie

*91-93 avenue Louise, 1050 Brussels (02 543 33 11/
fax 02 538 03 07/www.bristol.be). Métro Louise.*
Rates *Mon-Thur, Sun* single €300-€340; double
€325-€365. Fri, Sat single €110-€150; double;
€130-€170. Breakfast (not incl Mon-Thur, Sun)
€22. **Credit** AmEx, DC, MC, V. **Map** p321 C5.
This Norwegian-owned hotel, located on avenue
Louise – Brussels' Fifth Avenue – has some of the
most spacious standard rooms in the city, but retains
an intimate feel. This is immediately apparent in the
lobby, all brocade upholstery, deep blues, reds and
gold – the inspiration for the unadventurous (19th-
century English) decor. Resolutely Scandinavian, it
quietly exudes an atmosphere of efficiency and
prides itself on its clichéd national characteristics,
even incorporating these into its suites. There's one
done out in chalet style; another skirts the cutesy in
its nautical theme and boasts a balcony and sauna.
Hotel services *Bar. Business services.
Conference facilities. Disabled: adapted rooms
(2). Fax. Gym. Laundry. Lift. No-smoking rooms.
Pool. Restaurant. Safe. Sauna.* **Room services**
*Minibar. Room service (24hr). Telephone.
TV: cable.*

Hyatt Regency Brussels – Barsey

*381 avenue Louise, 1050 Brussels (02 649 98 00/
fax 02 640 17 64/www.brussels.hyatt.com). Métro
Louise, then tram 93, 94.* **Rates** *Mon-Thur* single
€325-€353; double €353-€380. Fri-Sun single/
double €114. Suites €489-€1,009. Breakfast (not incl)
€22. **Credit** AmEx, DC, MC, V.
Since its complete overhaul in 2000, the Barsey has
joined the ranks of the world's 'boutique hotels'. Its
aesthetics were masterminded by (*Elle*-celebrated)
Jacques Garcia, of Paris's Hôtel de Costes fame. The
entrance hall sets the tone, with its deep crimson
(Garcia's signature colour) Napoleon III-style furnishings and 18th-century paintings from the
Château de Chenonceaux. There is an abundance of
neo-classical-inspired statues on the terrace, and
nestling amid an orgy of rich velvets, satin-finished
wood, tassels and gilt in the intimately lit restaurant.
The rooms live up to this promise of sassy opulence.
Decor varies, but is always wilfully baroque, as well
as incorporating top-of-the-range comforts, while the
top-floor jacuzzi, set in turquoise and gold paintwork and with a panoramic view of the city, nearly
steals the show. The Barsey treads a fine line
between kitsch and opulence, and may not suit more
understated tastes, but its unique brand of sophistication is quite a head-turner. It's located at the
leafier end of the avenue Louise (quite a hike from
the centre), near the Bois de la Cambre and not too
far from Brussels' luxury shopping district.

Hotel services *Bar. Conference facilities. Fax.
Garden. Gym. Internet. Laundry. Lift. No-smoking
rooms. Parking. Restaurant. Sauna. Solarium.*
Room services *Dataport. Hairdryer. Minibar.
Room service (24hr). Safe. Telephone. TV: satellite.*

Manos Premier

*100-106 chaussée de Charleroi, 1060 Brussels
(02 537 96 82/fax 02 539 36 55/www.manoshotel.
com). Métro Louise, then tram 91, 92.* **Rates**
single €285; double €310; suite €460; extra bed
€25; weekend and summer rates on request. **Credit**
AmEx, DC, MC, V. **Map** p321 C6.
Run by a Greek family for the past three decades,
this converted townhouse provides an impressive
setting – Louis XVI-style decor, lots of antiques – as
well as a degree of intimacy (there are only 50
rooms). While the rooms are very comfortable and
elegantly fitted, the highlights lie elsewhere: lunch
or dinner in the Kolya restaurant; drinks in the
trendy, African-themed bar (think striped carpets,
curvy velvet armchairs and leopard skin); a few
moments of peace and quiet in the beautiful, vast,
split-level garden and terraces; or a session in the
exercise complex, comprising a fully equipped gym
and, the icing on the cake, a superb, Moorish-styled
hammam, with a jacuzzi and sauna.

Top B&B **Chambres en ville.** *See p53.*

Branch: **Manos Stéphanie** 28 chaussée de
Charleroi, 1060 Brussels (02 539 02 50/fax 02 537
57 29/www.manoshotel.com).
Hotel services *Babysitting. Bar. Conference
facilities. Fax. Garden. Gym. Laundry. Lift. Parking
(€7). No-smoking rooms. Restaurant. Safe. Sauna.
Solarium.* **Room services** *Dataport. Hairdryer.
Minibar. Room service (6am-11pm). Safe.
Telephone. TV: cable.*

Moderate

Agenda Louise

*6-8 rue de Florence, 1000 Brussels (02 539 00 31/
fax 02 539 00 63/www.hotel-agenda.com). Métro
Louise, then tram 93, 94.* **Rates** single €104;
triple €128; extra bed €12. **Credit**
AmEx, DC, MC, V. **Map** p321 C6.
A jolly little hotel on a quiet street, the Agenda
Louise offers up-to-date comforts and services. It
manages to narrowly avoid sterility by veering
towards a kind of uniform cosiness in its relatively
bright and spacious rooms. Most have kitchenettes.
Hotel services *Fax. Garden. Laundry. Lift.
No-smoking rooms. Parking. Safe.* **Room services**
Dataport. Hairdryer. Minibar. Telephone. TV: cable.

Argus

*6 rue Capitaine Crespel, 1050 Brussels (02 514 07
70/fax 02 514 12 22/www.hotel-argus.be). Métro
Louise.* **Rates** *Mon-Thur, Sun* single €90; double
€102. *Fri, Sat* single €75; double €85. Extra bed
€15. **Credit** AmEx, DC, MC, V. **Map** p321 C5.
The recently renovated, functional grey rooms here
are nothing to write home about, but at this price
and in this upmarket neighbourhood, you could do
a lot worse. Located just off the avenues de la
Toison d'Or and Louise, and a few steps from the
metro, the Argus is a pleasant and modern if unex-
citing hotel. Oodles of space and character are not
on offer, but relative comfort, cleanliness and
friendly, professional service are.
Hotel services *Internet. Fax. Laundry. Lift. Parking.
Safe.* **Room services** *Dataport. Hairdryer. Minibar.
Room service (7am-2pm). Telephone. TV: cable.*

Cheap

Les Bluets

*124 rue Berckmans, 1060 Brussels (02 534 39 83/
fax 02 543 09 70/bluets@swing.be). Métro Hôtel
des Monnaies.* **Rates** single €44-€57; double €52-
€81; extra bed €23. **Credit** AmEx, DC, MC, V.
Map p320 C6.
Les Bluets' premises and rather eccentric live-in
landlady have got so much character it might be a
bit much for some. Plants and flowers spill out from
balconies and bathrooms, birds tweet merrily in the
breakfast room, furnishings range from antique to
jumble sale, and the whole house is jam-packed with
knick-knacks and pictures. Nothing is standard,
from the decor to the services, the amenities (specify
if you want an en suite toilet) and the size of the

rooms. Bear in mind that you will be under the
landlady's beady eye. Noise, smokers and young
people are not welcome. Check-in is 10pm at the
very latest. Cash payments preferred.
Hotel services *Fax. Garden. Internet. Laundry.
No-smoking rooms (all).* **Room services** *Telephone.
TV: cable.*

Rembrandt

*42 rue de la Concorde, 1050 Brussels (02 512 71 39/
fax 02 511 71 36/rembrandt@brutele.be). Métro
Louise, then tram 93, 94.* **Rates** single with shower
€37; double with shower €60; single with shower
& toilet €50-€54; double with shower & toilet
€68-€75; suite with bath & toilet €60-€83. **Credit**
AmEx, DC, MC, V. **Map** p321 D6.
A séjour in this good-value, 13-room hotel just off
upmarket avenue Louise may be akin to staying
with an elderly relative. Not only does the reception
close at 9.30pm, but the lobby and breakfast room
are chock-a-block with twee china ornaments and
gilt-framed still lifes. The rooms then follow suit
with flowery wallpaper, heavy old wooden furniture
and other elements of grannyish decor – but at least
provides a homey feel. Not all rooms have en suite
facilities, and those that do are often separated by
only a flimsy partition, but the prices are excellent.
It may be worth splashing out on the top-floor suite,
which was designed as a private apartment and is
very popular with regulars.
Hotel services *Fax. Lift.* **Room services**
Dataport. Telephone.

Uccle

Moderate

Les Tourelles

*135 avenue Winston Churchill, 1180 Brussels
(02 344 02 84/fax 02 346 42 70/www.lestourelles.be).
Tram 23, 90/bus 60.* **Rates** single €83; double €94;
suites €104-€117. **Credit** AmEx, MC, V.
The twin turrets of this dusty establishment have
graced the leafy and desirable residential area of
Uccle for seven decades. It retains the feel of an
old-fashioned retreat at a distinguished, if a little
down-at-heel, country home. It might be a bit staid
for some. The city centre is a good 30 minutes
away by public transport.
Hotel services *Bar. Conference facilities.
Garden. Laundry. No-smoking rooms. Parking.
Safe.* **Room services** *Dataport. Room service
(6am-11.30pm). Telephone. TV: cable.*

B&Bs

B&Bs in Brussels (sometimes known as
maisons/chambres d'hôtes) are in no way
equivalent to a cheap hotel; they involve
staying in someone's house. This not only
entails the need to respect that person or
family's requirements (usually peace and quiet,

Sleep Well Youth Hostel: cheap 'n' cheerful – and very colourful. *See p54.*

sometimes an aversion to smoking), but also the lack of hotel-style services. So don't expect to necessarily find locks on doors or a phone in your room. They are often run by people with an eye for interior design or architecture, and you may in part be paying for that element of originality. Their appeal lies in this, and in the more personalised service available to the less frantic traveller – B&Bs are not recommended for boozy weekenders. This said, your privacy will be respected and certain standards should, of course, be expected.

Bed & Brussels

02 646 07 37/fax 02 644 01 14/www.BnB-Brussels.be. **Rates** *Per night* single €35-€68; double €53-€91. *Per week* single €196-€389; double €302-€524. *Per month* single €442-€972; double €680-€1,313.
Book B&Bs throughout Brussels with this friendly (but sometimes a little flustered) agency. Rates vary from hospitable accommodation with shared bathroom facilities to luxurious, en suite places. For a one-night stay you pay a 13% supplement.

Bed and Breakfast Belgium

*02 217 83 38/fax 02 223 17 62/
www.bedandbreakfastbelgium.com.*
A newcomer to the scene, this Internet service (run by Karin Dhadamus from Phileas Fogg – *see below*) is available in English, French, Dutch, Spanish and German. It lists B&Bs throughout Belgium, with rates, vacancies, contact details, directions, descriptions, photos and local restaurant tips from the B&B owners. You can book online.

Chambres en ville (Philippe Guilmin)

19 rue de Londres, 1050 Brussels (02 512 92 90/fax 02 502 41 01/www.chez.com/chambreenville). Métro Trône. **Rates** single €57; double €77; supplement for 1-night stay €13. **No credit cards. Map** p324 E5.
A very attractive and good-value option lies behind an ordinary front door. Rather than give up their lovely townhouse, the sympathetic and erudite Philippe Guilmin and his two grown-up children have set aside four rooms, all with spacious en suite bathrooms and individually decorated. Think stone or stripped wooden floors, high ceilings and windows (so plenty of light), and little touches like fresh flowers and wall hangings. It's on a quiet street by a pretty square, close to the metro, the shops and restaurants of Ixelles, and the palaces of the Royal Quarter. Calm and privacy assured, thanks to a cosmopolitan and friendly clientele – many stay here on the basis of a friend's recommendation.

Phileas Fogg

6 rue van Bemmel, 1210 Brussels (02 217 83 38/ 0495 22 09 85/fax 02 223 17 62/http://users. skynet.be/bnb.phileasfogg). Métro Botanique or Madou. **Rates** single €80; double €85-€100; suite (2 people) €85; suite (4 people) €120. **Credit** AmEx, MC, V. **Map** p322 E2.

Karin Dhadamus, a seasoned traveller who speaks seven languages, has an instinctive feel for imaginative design. In her lovely townhouse, you'll find three large double rooms – two with a shower actually in the room, one with an en suite bathroom – and one less remarkable basement suite. Asian antiques and wall hangings bring warmth, unusual lamps (by artists from Ghent and Bruges) add a delightfully quirky touch, and there are fluffy Chinese feathers, swirly wrought iron, fairy lights and other weird and wonderful designs throughout. A particular favourite is the blue and gold room, which has its own balcony overlooking the garden, and a romantic-cum-minimalist urban feel, with its big mirror, frothy curtains and futon with metal-and-rock detail. Dog-phobic people should abstain (there's an on-site pooch). Apartments cost €620-€745 per month.

Services Fax. Garden. Internet. Laundry. No-smoking rooms (all).

Youth hostels

Not all the hostels below are members of Youth Hostelling International, but they are all non-profit-making organisations (ASBL in French, VZW in Flemish). Non-YHI hostels call themselves 'youth hotels' and have slightly different policies, such as an upper age limit (35). All tend to have a maximum stay (usually a week), but this is sometimes negotiable.

You can book online for any YHI hostel through www.hostelbooking.com. This is encouraged, and often guarantees your bed will be kept for longer than usual (so you can arrive later in the day.) YHI hostels also require you to have a membership card, which can only be purchased in your country of residence. If you don't have one, as a rule you will be charged a supplement of around €3.50-€4 per night. The use of bedsheets is compulsory, but some hostels will allow you to bring your own or use your sleeping bag. Prices quoted are per person and they include breakfast.

Centre Vincent Van Gogh (CHAB)
8 rue Traversière, 1210 Brussels (02 217 01 58/ fax 02 219 79 95/chab@ping.be). Métro Botanique. **Rates** single €21; double €15.50; 4-person room €13; 6/8-person room €11.50; 10-person room €9; sheet rental (optional) €3.50. **Credit** AmEx, DC, MC, V. **Map** p322 E2.
The largest hostel in town, the Van Gogh is about a 15-minute walk from the centre, and a two-minute walk from the metro. Housed in two buildings, it has clean, bright and modern rooms, including a few split-level rooms with en suite bathrooms. The veranda-style lobby and the garden, open 24 hours, are not bad places to hang out in, and the staff are young, friendly and helpful. The newly renovated bathrooms and reception area should be operational from mid 2002.

Hostel services Bar. Billiards. Fax. Garden. Internet. Kitchen. Laundry. Luggage storage. No-smoking rooms (all). Safe. TV. 24hr access. VCR.

Jacques Brel (YHI)
30 rue de la Sablonnière, 1000 Brussels (02 218 01 87/fax 02 217 20 05/www.laj.be/en/hostels/ brussels_brel.htm). Métro Botanique. **Rates** (incl sheet rental) single €22.50; double €17.50; 3-4-person room €14.50; 6-14-person room €12.50. **Credit** MC, V. **Map** p319 D2.
A cheerful hostel, with some light and airy rooms, each with an en suite shower (doubles also have a toilet). The newly renovated ones are particularly bright and fresh. Murals are dotted about and art exhibitions are held, and there's a roof terrace for the summer. You can't get into rooms until 3.30pm, but shower facilities (for which you have to pay) are available beforehand. This hostel caters more for individuals and small groups (although there are a couple of dorms). It's a 15-minute walk to the Grand' Place and right next to a metro stop.

Hostel services Bar. Cafeteria. Internet. Lift. Luggage storage. No-smoking rooms (all). Table tennis. Tourist info & events (summer only). 24hr access.

Jeugdherberg Bruegel (YHI)
2 rue du St-Esprit, 1000 Brussels (02 511 04 36/ fax 02 512 07 11/www.vjh.be). Métro Gare Centrale. **Rates** (incl sheet rental) single €22.50; double €17.50; 4-person room €14.50; 12-person room €12.50. **Credit** MC, V. **Map** p317 C4.
A little bleaker and shabbier than its counterparts, this Flemish hostel boasts the best location, on a pleasant church square near the genteel Sablon area and its resident antiquarians, bars and restaurants. It's also close to the Grand' Place, and 300m from the central station. On the downside, this is the only Brussels hostel to impose a curfew: 1am.

Hostel services Bar. Disabled: adapted rooms (10). Internet. Lift. Lounge. Luggage storage. No-smoking rooms (all). Parking. Safe. TV. VCR.

Sleep Well Youth Hotel
23 rue du Damier, 1000 Brussels (02 218 50 50/fax 02 218 13 13/www.sleepwell.be). Métro/Pré-métro Rogier or De Brouckère. **Rates** €9.30 (8-bed room)-€20.95 (single); sheet rental (obligatory for 1st night) €3.50. **Credit** AmEx, DC, MC, V. **Map** p319 C2.
The least institutional of the hostels, this is a kind of 'youth hotel', complete with muzak, armchairs in the communal areas and plants and comic strip murals in the lobby (it's part of the official 'comic strip tour' of the city). But the basic formula is still bunk beds in bare rooms, all adapted for disabled use. It also scores highly in terms of facilities as well as location – it's pretty central, off the downtown shopping street rue Neuve – and has an on-site tourism adviser and guide.

Hostel services Bar. Billiards. Disabled: adapted rooms (all). Internet. Lift. Lounge. No-smoking rooms (all). Restaurant. Tourist info & guided tours. TV: cable. 24hr reception.

Sightseeing

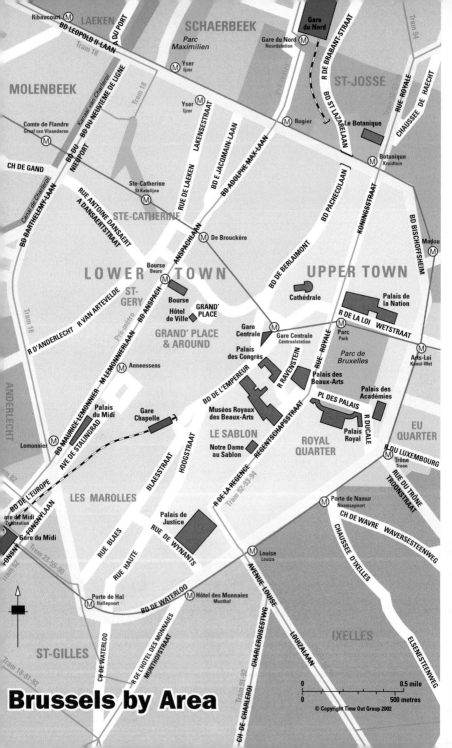

Brussels by Area

Introduction

Before you start, get your bearings here.

'City of contrasts', spiels the tourist brochure blurb for many a destination. 'Frankfurt, city of contrasts', 'Birmingham, city of contrasts', 'Malmo, city of contrasts'. For this, read: 'We don't have very much else to say about it'.

But Brussels really is.

Strictly divided geographically, its Upper and Lower Towns faultlined by a major boulevard, historically and linguistically, Brussels beckons the discerning traveller.

Why do so many come away boasting about their weekend without being able to put their finger on why?

Without being able to tumble out a list of sights (there's only one true one, the **Grand' Place**, the stunning old town square; and one false one, the **Manneken-Pis**, the urinating urchin), or eulogise a once-in-a-lifetime museum (many of the city's artistic treasures are spread quite thinly around town, bar interiors included) – boast they surely do. Why?

Often grey by day, always neonlit by night, more than anything Brussels is different. It has a refreshing lack of national flags and an annoying absence of cashpoints. It chews baguettes stuffed with chips but eschews McDonald's (*see p111* **No Macs please**). It's human-sized, with a pleasantly walkable centre and good, if at first confusing, transport links (*see p74* **Brussels by metro**). It can be shabby, it can be grand – when Victor Hugo, Baudelaire, Verlaine and Rimbaud hung out in exile here it became known as 'La Lune de Paris'. It feels like a port but has no river; the Senne was built over in the 19th century. It's got more green space than any other capital in Europe (*see p90* **Green Brussels**), Kiev excepted. It's a drinker's paradise. It's a diner's delight. It's a child's playground. Cartoon characters cover its walls (*see p63* **Strip search**). On its day, or rather on its night, it can be totally, utterly, magic.

Neighbourhood watch

Greater Brussels is comprised of 19 municipalities, or *communes*. Seven (listed clockwise from the north) border le Petit Ring, the ring road that follows the medieval walls, enclosing the clearly divided **Upper** and **Lower Towns** of central Brussels. See also the **Brussels by Area map** on p56.

Schaerbeek
The other side of the Ring from Ste-Catherine, stretching out into the city's far northern wastelands. Despite vestiges of imperial grandeur – churches, mansions and art nouveau gems – it's dark and shambolic.

St-Josse
A tiny district hugging the north-west corner, site of Turkish restaurants, cheaper expat housing and the odd must-see venue, such as the Botanique and De Ultieme Hallucinatie.

EU Quarter
The old Léopold quarter – once grand and green – fades amid the faceless steel and glass of the European Parliament and other institutes. Euro expansion set for 2004.

Ixelles
Neatly divided east–west by avenue Louise, the eastern half extends way south to the Ixelles lakes, taking in the city's African quarter, Matongé; the elegant western sector is grand if somewhat bland.

St-Gilles
This is a laid-back, scruffy bohemian village, scattered with plenty of greenery and the occasional art nouveau gem.

Anderlecht
A former riverside industrial district now quietly sleeping, with a couple of worthwhile museums tucked away.

Molenbeek
Of similar character to Anderlecht, with no worthwhile museums. Neighbouring **Jette** is even blander, the very reason why Magritte chose to live there. Further north rolls leafy **Laeken**, home to the royal family, also including the Heysel estate, site of the Atomium, the Stade Roi Baudouin and the Bruparck entertainment complex.

A rare glimpse of Brussels' cityscape, towards the Lower Town.

So where's the bland Euroland?

Let us first find the faultlines. As a village, then as a grand medieval stronghold built by the guilds, and then used as a handkerchief blown into by every major European power bar England (who, according to De Gaulle, 'invented Belgium just to annoy the French'), Brussels sympathetically grew around its historic heart of **St-Géry**, **Grand' Place** and quayside **Ste-Catherine**. By the modern era, after King Léopold II's grandiose ideas of a great empire-building capital, a bloody great fissure was knocked into it, the north–south railway line providing three linked main train stations, carving through the heart of the city. Certainly the Marolles quarter, while today still earning the regular epithet 'earthy', was devastated. A distinct east–west divide appeared, of a grand east **Upper Town** of parks, hotels and palaces, and a workmanlike **Lower Town** of shops, offices and bars. Elegance and decadence. The dividing boulevards de l'Empereur, de l'Impératrice, de Berlaimont and Pacheco, do a marking job as efficient as the Berlin Wall's.

Around the Lower and Upper Towns, **Marolles** and the **Royal Quarter** is a ring road. Around the ring road, seven quarters of distinct character (*see p57* **Neighbourhood watch**). On the horizon, forest. To the east, grafted on, the bland Euroland of legend, the **EU Quarter**, with a life all of its own. You can live and work in the steel-and-glass no-man's-land around Schuman and never need or notice the goings-on in the city centre – and vice versa, thank you very much.

Then there's the Belgians. Of Brussels' one million inhabitants, a quarter are foreigners. That means that, apart from the fashionable few, three-quarters have goofy teeth, scarecrow hair, round shoulders, a bad gait and, doubtless, a worse anorak. Handlebar moustaches, coke bottle-bottom glasses, yappy dogs wrapped in red plastic. And they insist, no absolutely insist, on offering the brief foreign guest a drink and a chat. The most mocked, maligned and put-upon people in Europe, Poles included. Invaded, stamped upon and generally bullied, squeezed between France, Germany and the deep North Sea, Belgium has been a convenient, nay convivial, rendezvous for wars, many a faultline running in and around Brussels. (Nothing is ever far away in Belgium.) Waterloo, Ypres, Flanders fields; a tiny new country cornered into heroism by historical coincidence. Brussels saw the destruction of its finest treasure, the Grand' Place, by French bombardment, the Duchess of Richmond's Waterloo ball and the march-in of spiky-hatted Germans in 1914.

These last atrocities nurtured a subliminal reaction: Surrealism. Brussels, residence of Magritte, Delvaux and Scutenaire, was its spiritual home. Just as art nouveau blossomed around Léopold's pomposity, so Surrealism bloomed here, authentic traces of each providing reason enough to visit.

Finally, the linguistic divide that runs right through Belgium cuts deepest in Brussels. Capital of Flanders, Belgium and Europe, this fractured city is swaddled in the warm glove of Francophonia, with fingers – fashion, clubbing, commerce – of overt Flemish influence. Covertly, the construction digging up half the city right now is mainly being carried out with Flemish money, the hand of Flanders grabbing pieces of the capital cake it cannot otherwise scoff by political manoeuvering alone. And why not? It's their capital, too. The Flemings won't speak French – the traditional language of law, education and perceived day-to-day order – and the French can't speak Flemish. Like Athens (Greek and English), all the street signs are in two languages, so simple Tree Street becomes rue de l'Arbre Boomstraat. Athens is easier, actually. Imagine the bureaucracy.

Bref, kortom, in short, Brussels has contrast in spades.

And what about the sights? Brussels has a museum for everything (see p79 **Top ten curios**). Chocolate, comic strips, sewage; you name it, it's housed and documented. No Prado or Louvre, it's true, but the contrasting **Musées Royaux des Beaux-Arts** has enough Flemish old masters and artistic icons of the modern era to satisfy most cultural appetites. Failing that, there's always a thousand and one ways to sculpt a saxophone (Adolphe Sax was Belgian) at the beautifully renovated **Musée des Instruments de Musique** – or art nouveau master Victor Horta's truly fantastic **Palais des Beaux-Arts** and his own house, now a museum in St-Gilles, an area stuffed to the gills with masterpieces of a similar architectural vein. Add an **Atomium**, secret shrines to high and low culture and Magritte's own Museum chez René himself – et voilà!

Interested? Convinced even?

Then where do I start? The Grand' Place. That's a very good place to start.

Guided tours

Brussels has tours to suit most interests. Information on the following, and specialised ones run by TIB itself, should be available from the tourist office (see p303).

ARAU
Highly recommended architectural tours of the city, offering access to private houses otherwise closed to the public. See p38 **Open house**.

Arcadia
02 534 38 19. **Tickets** walking tours €8.25; coach tours €12.5. **No credit cards. Map** p320 B6. Arcadia provides several specialised walking and coach tours in various areas of the city. Three-hour

English-language walking tours generally take place at 4pm on Sundays from June to October, but phone for details. Pick-up points vary.

De Boeck's Sightseeing Tours
02 513 77 44/www.brussels-city-tours.com. **Tickets** €19. **Credit** AmEx, DC, MC, V. **Map** p317 C3. Three-hour coach tours in English – usually three a day – covering the main sights, with a short walk at the Grand' Place, Laeken, Sablon and the EU Quarter. Pick-up is from the Grand' Place.

Top ten Sights

Atomium
Spectacular load of balls, with a great view from the uppermost one. See p93.

Cathédrale des Sts Michel et Gudule
Marvellously restored to its medieval Gothic glory. See p71.

Centre Belge de la Bande Dessinée
Tintin and peers in a peerless, Horta-designed department store. See p63.

Fondation Internationale Jacques Brel
See and hear the old troubadour trot out the classics. See p96.

Grand' Place
As good as it gets, Brussels' premier landmark. See p61.

Musée Bruxellois de la Gueuze
Spontaneous fermentation in action at the last of Brussels' working gueuze breweries. See p94.

Musée Horta
At home with art nouveau's chief architect. See p88.

Musée Magritte
Bowler hat, fireplace and all, chez René. See p94.

Musées Royaux des Beaux-Arts
Top Benelux art from Flemish mastery to modern classics. See p72.

Palais des Beaux-Arts
The world's first entertainment complex, a Horta-conceived art deco masterpiece. See p71.

DISCOVER EUROPE'S NICEST PLACES

MINI-EUROPE

Europe in a few hours... A unique experience !
Mini-Europe is above all an "invitation to travel". The chimes of Big Ben welcome you to the heart of London, while gondolas and mandolins reveal the charms of Venice, and much more... A tour of 350 monuments and miniature working models that you will find nowhere else !

All kinds of working models.
Be surprised by the eruption of Vesuvius or the fall of the Berlin wall. Cheer on the matador at the Corrida in Seville, watch the launch of Ariane V, follow the Thalys from Paris to the other end of France and marvel at many other working models, for both young and old.

The best miniature park in Europe.
All the monuments have been recreated down to the smallest detail. Big Ben is 4 m high. With its height of 13 m, the Eiffel tower projects above a 3-storey building ! And yet all the buildings are on a scale of 1 to 25. The town hall of Brussels is decorated with 294 hand-carved statues. All against a backdrop of miniature gardens with an area of 2.5 hectares.

Get to know the European Union better
The catalogue - bursting with anecdotes - is designed for the adults. Each region and building visited is described in a commentary which will show you a different view of the EU. The special brochure on European issues and the European area will fascinate the more curious ones among you.

MINI-EUROPE... a visit not to be missed !
Open from 23/03/2002 to 05/01/2003

Mini-Europe, Bruparck, 1020 Brussels
Tel. : 02/478.05.50 - Fax: 02 478.26.75
http://www.minieurope.com

The Lower Town

The beating heart of Brussels: churches, shops and some dazzling architecture.

The splendid **Maison du Roi** on the Grand' Place, home of the city museum. *See p64.*

The Lower Town is where the day-to-day business of Brussels takes place. It can be divided into three areas: the **Grand' Place & around** (the tourist showcase, with a scruffy commercial zone to the north, and to the south, meandering streets of quirky boutiques and bars); **Ste-Catherine** and **St-Géry**, dilapidated downtown districts undergoing renovation, dotted with chic bars, designer stores and not a few churches; and the **Marolles**, the shabby working-class area stretching from the slopes of upmarket Upper Town Sablon to the seedy estuary of Midi railway station.

Grand' Place & around

Maps p317, p318 & p319

One of the most beautiful squares in the world, the Grand' Place is Brussels' magnificent showcase centrepiece. Mercifully traffic-free, and without its own metro stop – it's between the Bourse and Gare Centrale – the Grand' Place is the perfect pivotal point for any pedestrian tour of the town centre. But first, you'd want

to spend a while here. Swamped with tourists all year round, changing character according to season (decked with flowers in summer, lit up at Christmas, pageanted and paraded upon – but always best at night), the Grand' Place is a triumph of gilded façades and dazzling baroque.

The guilds rebuilt almost all of it in under five years, after the French bombardment of 1695. Ironically, the main target, the immense focal **Hôtel de Ville** (Town Hall) survived. This magnificent Gothic structure, adorned with numerous sculptures, was begun in 1402 and completed in 1448. The architect, Jan van Ruysbroeck, then added the splendid 96-metre (315-foot) tower, which upon its completion seemed to de-centre the rest of the building. Legend has it that, in despair, the architect climbed to the top of his masterpiece and threw himself from it. You can't climb the wonderful tower, alas, but a series of elegant official rooms can be perused on the guided tour. The most flamboyant of them is the 18th-century Council Chamber, awash with gilt, tapestries, mirrors and ceiling paintings.

Crowded around the Town Hall, composing the rest of the square, are the **guildhouses**. Each guild left individual markings on its house and gave it a distinctive name (although some actually predate the guilds and their activities). Looking at the array of ornate splendour, it is as well to reflect that its origins are neither royal nor aristocratic, but firmly and proudly mercantile. The following are among the most spectacular of the guildhouses:

Nos.1-2 **Au Roi d'Espagne** (on the north side of the square, on the corner with rue au Beurre) – also the bakers' guild, now a pub (*see p123* **Brussels by bar crawl: Grand' Place**). The Spanish king in question is Charles II, ruler of Brussels when the house was rebuilt.

No.3 **La Brouette** (the wheelbarrow) – tallow merchants' guild.

No.4 **Le Sac** (the sack) – joiners' and coopers' guild.

No.5 **La Louve** (the she-wolf) – archers' guild.

No.6 **Le Cornet** (the horn) – boatmen's guild. Perhaps the best of Antoon Pastorana's numerous contributions to the Grand' Place.

No.7 **Le Renard** (the fox) – haberdashers' guild.

No.9 **Le Cygne** (the swan) – butchers' guild. Marx and Engels used to meet in a bar here; they wrote the Communist Manifesto in Brussels.

No.10 **L'Arbre d'Or** (the golden tree) – brewers' guild. The only building still owned by the original guild.

Nos.24-25 **La Chaloupe d'Or** (the golden galleon) or **La Maison des Tailleurs** (the tailors' house) – the tailors' guild.

No.26 **Le Pigeon** (the pigeon) – artists' guild. Victor Hugo stayed here in exile in 1852. Alongside No.8 **L'Etoile** (the star) is a much-caressed recumbent figure of Everard 't Serclaes, the guild leader who fought off a Flemish attack on Brussels in 1356. Some 30 years later he was captured by soldiers from Gaasbeek who tore his tongue out, prompting the enraged Bruxellois to extract revenge by destroying Gaasbeek castle. Stroking his much-worn limbs is meant to bring good luck.

The patron saint of merchants is **St Nicolas**, whose church – the oldest in Brussels – stands off the Place from the Roi d'Espagne on rue au Beurre. Founded in the 11th century, this calm model of medieval sanctity also survived the 1695 bombardment. Its slightly curved shape follows the old line of the River Senne.

Diagonally opposite is the **Bourse**, the old Stock Exchange. This grand, neo-classical building boasts a decorative frieze by Carrier-Belleuse and statues by Rodin adorning the top. Underneath, in the metro stop, is the hands-on **Scientastic Museum** (*see p174*), bringing science alive for children. Above roars spinal boulevard Anspach, across which stand the quarters of Ste-Catherine and St-Géry. Flanking the Bourse are two classic old-style cafés, the **Falstaff** (*see p123*) and the **Cirio** (*see p122*).

Detail of the ornate **guildhouses** around the Grand' Place.

Strip search

The French name streets after their poets and philosophers. In Madrid, great explorers are honoured with a metro station. The Belgians deck out their capital in cartoons.

Murals of comic strip heroes are splashed all over central Brussels, 20 and counting, excluding the decorated wall of many an underground station (see p74 **Brussels by metro**). A statue of Franquin's Gaston Lagaffe, and a nearby museum dedicated to what Belgians term the 'Ninth Art', complete the picture and provide the introduction to a six-kilometre (3.7-mile) downtown comic strip walking tour, which can be followed with a route map (€1.25) available from the tourist office (see p303).

Turning the corner into rue des Sables from accident-prone Gaston on the corner of boulevard de Pacheco, the **Centre Belge de la Bande Dessinée** (Belgian Comic Strip Centre) tells the story of the comic cultural phenomenon on three floors of a beautiful Horta-designed former department store.

Comic strips were popularised in the US in the late 19th century. One particular such strip, Windsor McCay's flamboyant *Little Nemo*, was taken to Belgian hearts at the height of the craze for art nouveau. At the same time, in 1907, Georges Remi was born. Hergé, as he became known, began by drawing for boy scout and Catholic journals before *Tintin in the Land of the Soviets* was published in 1929. Hergé had never been to Russia, nor would he go to the Congo, Tibet or the moon, places visited by his intrepid reporter, dog Snowy and trusty companion Captain Haddock. The museum shows the kind of research material Hergé used to create the storyline for Tintin's adventures. As iconic as Mickey Mouse, Tintin took off to global acclaim.

His success saw the launch of comic strip journal *Spirou* in 1938, where many of Belgium's best-loved characters first appeared. Spirou and Tintin's own *Journal* then inspired a post-war boom that became a national industry. Brussels boasts 42 comic shops, and three institutes instruct visiting French cartoonists in the Ninth Art.

The best Belgian exponents have their works displayed elsewhere in the museum and on the murals of the tour. (Beware, though, that modern, more erotic works such as *A Suivre*, are featured on the museum's third floor). *Spirou*'s own artists developed as part of the so-called Marcinelle School, as eccentric, anarchic and surreal as any great Belgian art of the 20th century.

The route runs from the museum to Willy Vandersteen's Bob and Bobette, on the corner of rue de Laeken and rue du Pont-Neuf. Suske and Wiske, as they are known in their original Flemish, became the biggest post-war smash after Tintin.

The walk then takes us into the heavily muralled Ste-Catherine and St-Géry quarters, passing such characters as L'Archange (Yslaire, rue des Chartreux) and Lucky Luke (rue de la Buanderie), before heading, via Edgar P Jacobs' Yellow M on rue du Petit Rampart, to a myriad of murals on and off rue Marché aux Charbon. Clock, for example, Frank Pé's Broussaille at the top of the street. The trail then winds through Marolles (Hergé's Quick et Flupke on rue Haute keeping in character with the area) down to the Gare du Midi.

Here you are bid farewell on to the Eurostar by Philippe Geluck's Le Chat and, fittingly, the figures of Tintin and Snowy on top of the Lombard Publications building.

Centre Belge de la Bande Dessinée

20 rue des Sables (02 219 19 80/ www.brusselsbdtour.com/cbbd.htm). Métro Botanique or Métro/Pré-métro De Brouckère. **Open** 10am-6pm Tue-Sun. **Admission** €6.20; €2.50-€5 concessions. **No credit cards. Map** p319 D2.

Sightseeing

Back on the Grand' Place, facing the Town Hall is the **Maison du Roi**, which now houses the **Musée de la Ville de Bruxelles**. Built in the 13th century, and thrice rebuilt, it is known in Dutch as the Broodhuis – a more accurate title since it was owned by the bakers' guild and never by a king. The museum is a rather dowdy affair, containing paintings, photographs, documents, tapestries and models chronicling the history of Brussels. There are enlightening sections on the bombardment of 1695 and Léopold II's ambitious building programme, but the dizzying impression is one of constant foreign invasion.

The museum also contains the vast wardrobe of the Manneken-Pis (amounting to some 600 costumes, with 200 on permanent display) and, less tackily, examples of the art – including Pieter Bruegel the Elder's *Wedding Procession* – and stonework by produced local artists and craftsmen.

The **TIB** tourist office (*see p303*) is located in the Hôtel de Ville, and there are two museums in the square's southern corner devoted to oral pleasure: **Musée du Cacao et du Chocolat** (Museum of Cocoa and Chocolate) and the **Musée de la Brasserie** (Brewery Museum). The former is a mildly diverting three-floor celebration of the making

and history of the sweet stuff, samples and all; the latter, in the brewers' guildhouse, is a dull trudge through the brewing process. You'd be better heading to the superior **Musée Bruxellois de la Gueuze** (*see p94* **Strange brew**) in Anderlecht.

Hôtel de Ville
Grand' Place (02 279 22 11/tourist information 02 513 89 40). Pré-métro Bourse or Métro Gare Centrale. **Open** *Guided tours* (in English) 11.30am, 3.15pm Tue; 3.15pm Wed. *Apr-Sept* also 12.15pm Sun. **Admission** €2.50. **No credit cards.** **Map** p317 C3.

Musée de la Brasserie
10 Grand' Place (02 511 49 87). Pré-métro Bourse or Métro Gare Centrale. **Open** 10am-5pm daily. **Admission** €3. **No credit cards.** **Map** p317 C3.

Musée du Cacao et du Chocolat
13 Grand' Place (02 514 20 48). Pré-métro Bourse or Métro Gare Centrale. **Open** 10am-5pm Tue-Sun. **Admission** €5; €4 concessions; free under-12s. **No credit cards.** **Map** p317 C3.

Musée de la Ville de Bruxelles
10 Grand' Place (02 279 43 50). Pré-métro Bourse or Métro Gare Centrale. **Open** 10am-5pm Tue-Fri; 10am-1pm Sat, Sun. **Admission** €2.48; €1.24-€1.98 concessions; free under-6s. **No credit cards.** **Map** p317 C3.

St-Nicolas
1 rue au Beurre (02 513 80 22). Pré-métro Bourse. **Open** 7.30am-6.30pm Mon-Fri; 9am-6pm Sat, Sun. **Services** 11am, 6pm Mon-Fri; 11am, 5pm Sat; 10am (English), 11.30am, 5pm, 6.30pm Sun. **Map** p317 C3.

The Ilot Sacré

Immediately north of the Grand' Place is the **Ilot Sacré** (Holy Isle), restored by the local authority in 1960, and now one of the Lower Town's liveliest areas. It's an evocative medieval tangle of small streets, devoted almost entirely to restaurants, many of which entice tourists with stupendous displays of fish and seafood reclining on mountains of ice. Rue des Bouchers is the classic example, although its somewhat tacky tone is offset by the renowned **Théâtre du Toone** (*see p215*), a puppet theatre and café in an alley off adjoining petite rue des Bouchers. Even the street names are appetising, with the likes of rue des Harengs (herrings) and rue du Marché aux Herbes. In the Middle Ages each street had its speciality and, despite the contemporary glut of tourists, it's not difficult to imagine the similar bustle of medieval markets.

Here, too, is a shining modern-day example of the area's commerce, the lovely glass-covered **Galeries St-Hubert**. Europe's oldest glass

The spire of the **Hôtel de Ville**. See p61.

Manneken-Pis: national symbol. *See p67.*

COLLECTING THE STARS

WALLONIA. ENJOY A WARM-HEARTED WELCOME.
WWW.WALLONIA-TOURISM.BE

arcade was designed by JP Cluysenaer and opened by Léopold I in 1847 and still sparkles, matching the glitter of the jewellery shops that line it (*see also p144* **Galeries galore**). Also here is the **Arenberg Galeries** cinema (*see p181*), which shows erudite films; and the **Théâtre Royal des Galeries** (*see p215*).

By the southern entrance to the Galeries stands busy place d'Espagne, known to locals as place d'Agora, an oasis of waiting taxi cabs.

South of the Grand' Place

The south side of the Grand' Place is quieter, characterised by idiosyncratic shops and odd vendors of strange plastic figures. During the day, only at the corner of rue de l'Etuve will you find a crowd, camera-clickers thronging around the **Manneken-Pis**. Famous as a national symbol but eternally disappointing as a tourist spectacle, the tiny bronze statuette is set on a stone façade while pissing cheerfully down. Little is known of its origins. The current statue was made in the 17th century by Jérôme Duquesnoy. Stolen by the British in 1745, then again by the French in 1777, it was smashed by a French ex-con in 1817, who got a life sentence for doing so. Stuck back together again, now

the Manneken dresses to suit the occasion: love hearts for Valentine's Day, a condom on World AIDS Day, and so on.

Rue de l'Etuve borders the main gay quarter (*see p190*), particularly parallel rue du Marché au Charbon. By night, this snaking street becomes Brussels' main thoroughfare for bars (*see p135* **Brussels by bar crawl: Charbon**), with one in almost every building.

Perhaps the loveliest of the Lower Town's half-dozen churches also stands here: **Notre Dame de Bon Secours**. Built in the late 17th century, this delightful baroque masterpiece, designed by Willem de Bruyn, is a fine example of Flemish Renaissance style. On the other side of the Manneken-Pis, off place St-Jean, is the **Fondation Internationale Jacques Brel** (*see p96* **The troubadour returns**), dedicated to Brussels' prodigal singing iconoclast.

Around rue Neuve

The area between the Grand' Place and the Gare du Nord has a different atmosphere. Around formerly distinguished De Brouckère – once site of a lovely fountain, still home to the classy **Hotel** and **Café Métropole** (*see p41* and *p122*) – charmless commerce reigns. The awful **Centre Monnaie** mall now overshadows

The baroque tower of **Notre Dame du Finistère** on rue Neuve. *See p68.*

Sightseeing

the neo-classical opera house, **Théâtre de la Monnaie**, built in 1819. This was the site of the uprising of August 1830 that sparked the Belgian revolution. During a performance of François-Esprit Auber's *La Muette de Portici*, the duet 'Sacred Love of the Fatherland' so inspired the audience they rushed outside to join protesting workers. In a rare moment of class unity, together they attacked the Dutch garrison and raised the flag of Brabant. Within a year, Belgium had achieved its independence. As well as its historical importance, the venue is worth visiting for its ornate interior.

Sprawling north from the square is gaudy rue Neuve. It could be any high street in any town, a crowded, pedestrianised stretch of brand names blending into one ugly shopping centre, **City2**. It's hard to believe that here was the site of the Duchess of Richmond's famous ball on the eve of Waterloo, although the airy **Notre Dame du Finistère** church does give some architectural relief. Largely built in the early 18th century, its baroque interior features a stupendously over-the-top pulpit.

Nearby, **place des Martyrs**, with its monument dedicated to the 445 revolutionaries who gave their lives for their country in 1830, is lined with fine neo-classical buildings. espite its grandeur and patriotic associations, the square fell into decay and is under renovation.

Around the corner is one of Brussels' most popular museums, the **Centre Belge de la Bande Dessinée** (*see p63* **Strip search**). Housed in a beautifully restored Victor Horta building, you can admire it from its café without having to enter the museum.

Notre Dame du Finistère

rue Neuve (02 217 52 52). Métro/Pré-métro De Brouckère or Rogier. **Open** 8am-5.45pm Mon-Sat; 8am-noon Sun. *Services* 9.15am, 12.10pm, 5pm Mon-Fri; 4.30pm, 6pm Sat; 9am, 11am Sun. **Map** p319 C2.

Ste-Catherine & St-Géry

Map p317 & p318

Bars and churches are the key features of former quayside Ste-Catherine and sassy St-Géry, two small, self-contained quarters the others side of boulevard Anspach from the Bourse. Their shoddy bohemian feel is a refreshing discovery in the heart of Europe's capital, although frantic construction – including a new Hotel Marriott right opposite the Bourse – is changing this fast. There's still an appealing mix of scruffiness and ultra-chic, worth catching before the neighbourhood goes.

St-Géry is really centred on the square of the same name, composed of a slew of designer bars built around refurbished **Halles St-Géry**, (*see p129*), a former covered market now a large bar and nightclub. St-Géry was revived by entertainment mogul Fred Nicolay, who set up a string of trendy cafés and spread word of a scene. **Zebra** (*see p130*) and **Mappa Mundo** (*see p129*) are typical of the genre. Although lively on summer evenings, when terraces throng with café life, it is doubtful whether any will last as long as classic establishments such as the nearby **Greenwich** (*see p129*), former chess-playing haunt of René Magritte.

It is no surprise that Nicolay chose St-Géry to set up his empire, for it borders the genuinely groundbreaking **rue Antoine Dansaert**. Known as Little Antwerp, this is the city's fashion centre, which sprung to life when little-known designers from Antwerp had their works displayed in **Stijl** (*see p148*), then in neighbouring chic designer clothes shops in the mid 1980s.

A drab downtown street was transformed. Ru Dansaert, aided and abetted by the ever fashionable late-night bar **Archiduc** (*see p127*), became a byword for cool. The lingua franca on the street was Flemish – although now Brussels-based designers are beginning to establish themselves here (*see p150* **Dressing for success**).

Bohos, media types and the gay community flocked to Ste-Catherine in droves, setting up chichi shops and cafés, pushing up ground rents. Local investment boomed, huge yellow construction cranes loomed over modern shopfronts, while stretches of streets fell under the jackhammer for months at a time, or stood grey and neglected. The whole scene resembles an occasionally glamorous array of gold teeth in a crumbling set still in need of dentistry.

Ste-Catherine, meanwhile, has somehow not lost its charm – or its churches. Based around the quays of the old harbour, where a thriving traffic of fishing boats was grounded with the filling in of the River Senne in 1870, Ste-Catherine still feels like a port. Fountains and paved walkways now cover what locals (but not maps) refer to as the Marché aux Poissons, the Fish Market, either side of the metro stop. Hosting, indeed, a fish market once a week, lined with fish restaurants lit up with vast red neon lobsters – and turned into a giant outdoor skating rink over the Christmas period (*see p179* **Do they know it's Christmas?**) – Ste-Catherine is dominated by its namesake church.

Almost as unkempt as its surroundings (and with a pissoir built between the buttresses), **Ste-Catherine** was designed in 1854 in neo-Gothic style by Joseph Poelaert, architect of the Palais de Justice, and almost became the

Mourning angels in **place des Martyrs**, currently under renovation. *See p68.*

city's stock exchange before finally opening as a church in 1867. Fortunately, the interior is arched and graceful, clean-lined and cathedral-like in its proportions, with pretty blue and yellow glass windows. One of its treasures is a 15th-century statue of a Black Madonna and child, supposedly rescued from the Senne after being chucked in by rampaging Protestants. The belfry of an earlier (13th-century) Ste-Catherine is nearby.

Also nearby are two more churches: **Notre Dame aux Riches Claires** and **St-Jean-Baptiste au Béguinage**. Notre Dame, in the street of the same name, is a charming asymmetrical building built in 1665, probably the work of Rubens' pupil, Luc Fayd'herbe. It reopened in 2000 after extensive renovation. Just to its north on place du Béguinage is one of the best examples of Flemish baroque architecture in the city, St-Jean-Baptiste. This large church, also possibly designed by Luc Fayd'herbe, has a wonderfully fluid, honey-coloured façade. Its light-filled interior has a beautiful pulpit and paintings by the 17th-century Brussels painter Van Loon. The church was once the centre of Brussels' largest *béguinage*, a charitable community for single women, founded in the 13th century.

Despite the fish market and restaurants, all that really remains of the river is the Canal de Charleroi, a thin stretch of water running north–south along the western edge of town. Here, along bankside boulevard Barthélémy, the thriving art gallery complexes of **Kanal 11** and **Kanal 20** (*see p187*) could help boost an urban revival in this forgotten quarter too.

Notre Dame aux Riches Claires
21 rue des Riches Claires (02 511 09 37/02 511 50 99). Pré-métro Bourse. **Open** phone for details. *Services* 10am, 11.15am Mon, Tue, Thur-Sun; 10am, 11.15am, 6.30pm Wed. **Map** p318 B3.

Ste-Catherine
place Ste-Catherine (02 513 34 81). Métro Ste-Catherine/tram 23, 52, 55, 56, 81. **Open** 8.30am-5pm (summer until 6pm) Mon-Sat; 9am-noon Sun. *Services* 8am (chapel), 10am (church) Sun. **Map** p317 B2.

St-Jean-Baptiste au Béguinage
place du Béguinage (02 217 87 42). Métro Ste-Catherine/tram 23, 52, 55, 56, 81. **Open** 10am-5pm Tue; 9am-5pm Wed-Fri; 10am-5pm 1st, 3rd & 5th Sat of the mth; 9.30am-noon Sun. *Services* 5pm Sat; 10am, 8pm Sun. **Map** p318 B2.

Marolles & Gare du Midi

Map p320
The Marolles is the nearest Brussels gets to Marseilles. Poverty and fierce local pride fester and flourish under washing lines strung between dilapidated buildings, tatty but

There are shops of all sorts around the Grand' Place, from the trendy to the quirky.

durable resistance to urban expansion and standardisation. The area stretches haphazardly from the slopes of the imposing Palais de Justice down to the estuary of the Gare du Midi, immediately adjoining lofty Sablon to the east. At its epicentre is **place du Jeu de Balle**, where a daily **flea market** (*see p163* **Trading places**) is surrounded by downmarket bars and cafés. Leading north are the quarter's two vertebrae, rue Blaes and rue Haute, feeding into place de la Chapelle at Marolles' northern edge.

With Chapelle railway station overhead – part of the north–south axis connecting Midi, Centrale and Nord – the underpass shelters the **Recyclart** bar and arts venue (*see p132*). Outdoor concerts liven the drab, graffitied concrete. On the square itself stands **Notre Dame de la Chapelle**, the local church built in an interesting mix of styles. Part of the chapel dates from the 12th century, the transepts are Romanesque and the nave 15th century Gothic. Most of the paintings date from the 19th century, although Notre Dame is best known as the burial place of Pieter Bruegel the Elder. In fact, he is buried elsewhere, but there's a memorial plaque made by his son in the fourth chapel. The house where Bruegel lived is nearby at 132 rue Haute, the 16th-century **Maison de Bruegel**. Although it doesn't contain any of the great artist's works or artefacts, it's open to groups by written request.

The Marolles' association with poverty and persecution date back to the Middle Ages, when a leprosy centre was founded here. By Bruegel's time, it was slowly becoming a thriving area populated by artisans who worked at the

mansions of Sablon above. The artist would have drawn inspiration for his great peasant feasts and skating crowds from the energy around him. The short, narrow streets of Marolles proclaim their roots: rue des Orfèvres (Goldsmiths' Street); rue des Tonneliers (Barrelmakers' Street), and rue des Ramoneurs (Chimney-Sweeps' Street). The burial of the River Senne saw much industry move out of the centre, and the Marolles was left to rot. Thousands of homes were destroyed to make way for the railway and vast Palais de Justice.

As if to reverse a downward trend, a free public lift is being installed to transport locals from Marolles to the Upper Town, its terminus next to the Palais entrance, and is expected to be open by the summer of 2002.

Although the district is an incongruous mix of shabby shops and gentrified boutiques, immigrants and deep-rooted locals who speak Brusselse Sproek, the fantastically rude Flemish dialect local to Marolles, it has a certain energy few other ones can muster. Later on, as corner bars still serve up chips and beer to nightshifters off to work, clubbers swarm to the **Fuse** (*see p177*), the top techno club in town.

Marolles' seedy character spills over to the area immediately north of Midi station, shabby by day, dodgy by night, but blessed with a cheap North African **market** on Sunday mornings (*see p163* **Trading places**).

Notre Dame de la Chapelle

place de la Chapelle (02 512 07 37). Métro Gare Centrale or Pré-métro Anneessens. **Open** *June-Sept* 9am-4pm daily. *Oct-May* noon-4pm daily. *Services* 4pm Sat; 8am, 9.30am, 10.30am, 4.30pm, 6.30pm Sun. **Map** p317 B/C4.

Sightseeing

The Upper Town

The royal area, home to palaces, the cathedral and the major museums.

The ruling class have always surveyed their subjects from the heights of the Upper Town, ever since the Dukes of Burgundy settled in the area in the 14th century. The parks, mansions and palaces are mercifully well preserved, and this is still the **Royal Quarter**, although power is no longer concentrated here. Amid the grand, neo-classical edifices and landscaped greenery stand the city's most important museums, especially the **Musées Royaux des Beaux-Arts**, the finest fine art collection in all Belgium. In step with the grandeur gleams the tiny chic enclave of **Sablon**, nestled around the church of the same name.

The Royal Quarter

Maps p317 & p319

Five minutes' walk uphill from the Grand' Place stands the **Cathédrale de Sts Michel et Gudule**, rather isolated from the city by the modern buildings crowding around it, but shining and pristine after a lengthy restoration. It's dedicated to the male and female patron saints of Brussels (the former, an archangel, is better known than the latter, an obscure figure who died in 712 after an appropriate 'life of great holiness at home' – she's often portrayed in art holding a lantern). The current Brabant Gothic building (replacing the Romanesque original) was started in the early 13th century and completed by the end of the 15th.

The cathedral weathered the ravages of Protestant iconoclasts and French revolutionary armies, and a lengthy restoration of the exterior and interior was completed in time for the royal marriage of the heir apparent Prince Philippe and Princess Mathilde in 1999. As the scaffolding came down, the façade and towers (by top 15th-century builder Jan van Ruysbroeck of Hôtel de Ville fame) emerged gleaming. The interior is splendidly proportioned and contains a feast of treasures. Most impressive are Bernard van Orley's wonderful 16th-century pictorial stained-glass windows in the transepts, and the 13th-century choir. The altar is surprisingly modern, unlike the crazy baroque oak pulpit.

Continuing uphill you hit the long, straight rue Royale, alongside which lies the focal point of the Upper Town: the 18th-century **Parc de Bruxelles**. Crossed by numerous avenues, and

punctuated by fountains, it was once a chic strolling ground. In the Belgian Revolution of 1830, its avenues ran with blood. Today, the park provides a prime spot for office workers on their lunch break and a gorgeous setting for the **Théâtre Royal du Parc** (*see p215*).

At the park's northern end stands the Belgian parliament building, the **Palais de la Nation**, graced by a lovely 18th-century façade by Guimard. The park's south-east and south-west corners are occupied, respectively, by the **Palais des Académies** and the Horta-designed **Palais des Beaux-Arts** (*see also p195*). Built in 1928, the Beaux-Arts was the great architectural feat of its time – the first building in the world to put concert halls, exhibition spaces, theatres, cinemas, shops and restaurants under one roof.

The recently restored **Cathédrale**.

High art from the Low Countries

The **Musées Royaux des Beaux-Arts** combines two museums: the **Musée d'Art Ancien** and the **Musée d'Art Moderne**. For lovers of 15th- to 17th-century Flemish painting in particular, the former is a treat. There are typically lucid pieces by **Rogier van der Weyden**, Brussels' official city painter in the mid-15th century; radiant portraits by **Hans Memling**; a superb triptych by **Quentin Matsys**; and, most impressively, a room devoted to Brussels resident **Pieter Bruegel the Elder** and the work of his sons and disciples, including *The Census at Bethlehem* and the astonishing Bosch-inspired monster-mongous *Fall of the Rebel Angels*.

The 17th-century section is dominated by a number of astonishingly versatile pieces by Antwerp's most famous son, **Pieter Paul Rubens**, and the work of his talented pupils **Anthony Van Dyck** and **Jacob Jordaens**. Frenchmen Géricault, Delacroix and David get a look in the 18th- and 19th-century rooms; the latter most notably with his famous painting of the revolutionary Marat assassinated in his bath. It's also worth glancing at Belgium's contributions to Impressionism (including Théo van Rysselberghe and Henri Everpoel), and the fascinatingly bizarre work of the fascinatingly bizarre pre-Expressionist **James Ensor**.

Since the museum is so large (and also contains some mediocre works – mawkish 19th-century depictions of dogs and children,

anyone?), it is best to focus your attention. One good strategy is to follow the museum's blue (15th-16th centuries), brown (17th-18th) or yellow (19th) routes.

The museum is connected to the Musée d'Art Moderne by an underground passage. Space problems dictated subterranean solutions for this absorbing journey through 20th-century art. Although international big cheeses – including Dufy, Picasso, Ernst, Dalí, Bacon and Matisse – are represented in the museum's eight underground levels, it's no surprise that it's the Belgians, and particularly Surrealist maestros **René Magritte**, **Paul Delvaux** and **James Ensor**, who take centre stage. Take the time, though, to check out their less famous compatriots, such as **Pol Bury** and his moving sculptures, and the Fauvists **Léon Spilliaert** and **Rik Wouters**. There's also a good number of works by the influential post-World War II **Cobra** (Copenhagen, Brussels, Amsterdam) **Group**. The signposting can occasionally be confusing, but crowds are rare and the atmosphere is restful.

Musées Royaux des Beaux-Arts

3 rue de la Régence (02 508 32 11/ www.fine-arts-museum.be). Métro Gare Centrale or Parc/tram 92, 93, 94. **Open** 10am-5pm Tue-Sun. **Admission** €5; €2-€3.50 concessions. **Credit** AmEx, MC, V. **Map** p317 C4.

Stripped of his fanciful art nouveau whirlings and reduced to clean art deco lines, Horta made his swansong a spacious, functional municipal building that gracefully combined its separate elements. In 1996, the entire hall was finally renovated. Eleven interlinked hexagonal and circular rooms ensure that there is space for even the largest sculptures – you can get lost wandering round a show. The Palais also hosts the regular Europalia festival, which focuses on a different theme each year, and serves as an information point about other exhibitions in the city.

Along the south side of the Parc de Bruxelles stands the king's imposing official residence, the **Palais Royal**. The old seat of the Dukes of Brabant was destroyed by fire in 1731; the current, charmless building dates largely from the 19th century. Only in late summer can you look inside the state rooms and see the tapestries designed by Goya. Changing of the guard occurs daily at 2.30pm. The flag flies on the rare occasions when the monarch is home.

At the western end of the palace is the **Musée de la Dynastie**, where memorabilia, documents and photographs chronicle the short history of the Belgian monarchy since 1831. The museum has become of wider interest since the Fondation Baudouin installed an exhibition on the life of the popular last king, Baudouin, including his office and relics of his childhood. It's all rather voyeuristic, which makes it bizarrely irresistible.

Directly behind the palace is the narrow rue Brederode, where Joseph Conrad visited the Congo Trading Company in 1889, just as creepy today as when described in his *Heart of Darkness*. See also *p18* **Belgium's heart of darkness**.

West of the Palais Royal lies the graceful **place Royale**, on the site of the 15th-century Coudenberg Palace; its name is remembered in the church of **St-Jacques-sur-Coudenberg** at the top of the square. The church was built in 1775 to resemble a Roman temple (although an incongruous belltower was added in the 19th century) and has none of the Gothic piety exuded by most of the city's churches. The interior is just as imposing as the outside and one can easily imagine that it served perfectly as a temple of reason and then as a temple of law when Brussels was under the sway of revolutionary France, before being returned to Catholicism in 1802.

The **Palais Coudenberg**, one-time home of the Dukes of Burgundy, burned down in 1731 and was subsequently built over and forgotten. In the 1930s its location was rediscovered but it is only since 2000 that the public has been able to view the excavations. The most impressive

Musée des Instruments de Musique.

sight is the Aula Magna, a huge reception chamber with a capacity of 1,400 people, once used by Charles V. There's also a chapel and the rue d'Isabelle, an underground street.

In the square's centre stands Eugène Simonis' vigorous and triumphant figure of Godfrey de Bouillon, one of the leaders of the successful first Crusade in the 11th century. Abutting the western corner of the place Royale are Brussels' two major art galleries, the **Musée d'Art Ancien** and the **Musée d'Art Moderne** – collectively, the **Musées Royaux des Beaux-Arts**; for both, *see p72* **High art from the Low Countries**. They focus primarily on the art of the Low Countries over the past six centuries, from masterworks by Rogier van der Weyden, Hans Memling and Pieter Bruegel the Elder to a great spread of Belgian Surrealist work.

Downhill from the place Royale on rue Montagne de la Cour are a couple of architectural gems. The first is one of the great triumphs of art nouveau in the city: the shining black Magasins Old England, long shuttered up but open from 2000 as the **Musée des Instruments de Musique**. Designed by Paul Saintenoy in 1899, with its curving black wrought ironwork framing large windows, this is one of the most distinctive and best-known buildings in Brussels. The 6,000-strong

Sightseeing

instruments collection is one of the world's most important – around 1,500 instruments are on display at any one time. Look out for the various combinations of saxophone dreamed up by Adolphe Sax, the instrument's inventor. There are concerts on Thursday evenings in the 200-seater hall from October to May, and the top-floor café offers excellent panoramic views of the city.

Further down the street, as it sweeps right into rue Ravenstein, is the red-brick, gabled **Hôtel Ravenstein**. This 15th-century building, the only significant survivor from the old Coudenberg quarter, was the birthplace of the ill-fated Anne of Cleves, fourth wife of Henry VIII. Descending Ravenstein, to the left, in between occasional snatches of fabulous cityscape, is the classic shopping arcade **Galerie Ravenstein** (*see p144* **Galeries galore**); to the right, on rue Baron Horta, is the **Musée du Cinema** (*see p182*). This modest but fascinating museum traces the early days of cinema, particularly the main inventions that led to the discovery of cinematography by the Lumière brothers. The two projection rooms show classic films from the pre-war era, silent ones accompanied by a pianist.

From here, you can climb the steps back up to rue Royale, or take the steep descent down Ravenstein to the Mont des Arts, a

Brussels by metro

Bruxelles Gare Centrale. Commuters and tourists rush down the staircase past a fearsome statue dedicated to railway workers fallen in two world wars. Underground, a little wooden metro bar quietly goes about its business: beers freshly served, friendly banter in two languages, the clientele surrounded by paraphernalia from an era when Belgium was at the cutting, not rusty, edge of continental rail travel, a century before Magritte drove trains out of fireplaces. Brussels starts here. One stop west, under **De Brouckère**, shines a 1960s' brown bar of rare authenticity.

One metro stop east gleams **Parc** station, giving access to the royal palaces and prestigious museums of the Upper Town. But in the station, on the walls, shines a striking Pop Art construction by Marc Mendelson, one of the oldest of an extensive citywide series of contemporary art, embellishing the system since the 1970s. Delvaux, Hergé, Horta; they're all here.

There's a world going on underground. A maddeningly poorly signposted and wonderfully primitively pictographed system, with trains similar to Bucharest's, Brussels by metro can be an art in itself. You'll get surprisingly lost amid the two-and-a-half criss-crossing lines – although on most platforms your mobile will work if you need to call for help. To compensate, quality art and quasi-troglodyte bars. You won't go thirsty, or hungry for culture.

Some of the art can be quite poignant. Sketches for the huge frescoes decorating **Stockel** metro – featuring nearly 150 characters from Tintin's adventures – were drawn by Hergé shortly before his death. Renowned cartoonist François Schuiten (responsible for *Brüsel*, a nightmare journey through the urban jungle) gives a similar *Metropolis* tone on two levels of **Porte de Hal** station.

Paul Delvaux's *Nos Vieux Trams Bruxellois* in **Bourse** Pré-métro station is a melancholic 13-metre (43-foot) mural in praise of the urban transport of his childhood. Even Horta gets a look-in, **Parvis de St-Gilles** station (*pictured*) featuring fragments of his art nouveau buildings since demolished. A complete list of underground art can be found at **www.art-public.com/caid**.

Meanwhile, underground sources of beer crop up where least expected. Below the bland Euroland of **Schuman** station, the Brasserie de l'Europe surprisingly turns up an utterly tacky pinball bingo bar that could thrive nowhere else but Belgium. **Botanique**'s is busy, while **Midi** has a myriad of oases before the métro, pré-métro, train, Thalys or Eurostar journey to Lemonnier or London. Why hurry?

staircased piazza that joins the Upper and Lower Towns. It's flanked on one side by the **Palais du Congrès**, on the other by the **Royal Library**, and on both by skateboarding teenagers.

The library owns the neighbouring 18th-century **Palais de Charles de Lorraine**, which in 2000 opened to the public for the first time and contains art, furniture and documents from the time when he was governor-general of the Austrian Netherlands.

Cathédrale des Sts Michel et Gudule
place Ste Gudule (02 217 83 45). Métro Gare Centrale or Parc/tram 92, 93, 94. **Open** 8am-6pm daily. *Services* 7.30am, 8am, 12.30pm Mon-Fri; 4pm, 5.30pm Sat; 10am., 11.30am, 12.30pm Sun. **Admission** crypt €2.50. **No credit cards.** **Map** p319 D3.

Musée du Cinéma
rue Baron Horta 9 (02 507 83 70). **Open** 5.30-10.30pm daily. **Admission** €2. **No credit cards** **Map** p317 C4.

Musée de la Dynastie
7 place des Palais (02 511 55 78). Métro Gare Centrale or Parc/tram 92, 93, 94. **Open** 10am-4pm Tue-Sun. **Admission** €6.20; €4-€5 concessions. **Map** p321 D4.

Musée des Instruments de Musique
2 rue Montagne de la Cour (02 545 01 30). Métro Gare Centrale or Parc/tram 92, 93, 94. **Open** 9.30am-5pm Tue, Wed, Fri; 9.30am-8pm Thur; 10am-5pm Sat, Sun. **Admission** €9; €4-€7 concessions; free after 1pm on 1st Wed of month. **No credit cards. Map** p317 C4.

Palais des Beaux-Arts
23 rue Ravenstein (02 507 84 86). Métro Gare Centrale or Parc/tram 92, 93, 94. **Open** 10am-6pm Mon-Thur, Sat, Sun; 10am-8pm Fri. **Admission** €9; €4-€7 concessions. **No credit cards. Map** p319 C/D4.

Palais de Charles de Lorraine
1 place du Musée (02 519 57 86). Métro Gare Centrale or Parc/tram 92, 93, 94. **Admission** €3. **Open** 1-5pm Mon-Fri; 10am-5pm Sat. **Map** p317 C4.

Palais Coudenberg
Entrance through Musée Bellevue, place des Palais (02 512 28 21). **Open** 10am-5pm Tue-Sun. **Admission** €4; €3 concessions; free under-12s. **Credit** V. **Map** p317 D4.

Palais Royal
Place des Palais (02 551 20 20). Métro Gare Centrale or Parc/tram 92, 93, 94. **Open** *Late July-early Sept* usually daily; phone for details. Closed early Sept-late July. **Admission** free. **Map** p321 D4.

Palais des Beaux-Arts: unique. *See p71.*

St-Jacques-sur-Coudenberg

1 impasse Borgendael, place Royale (02 511 78 36/ 02 502 18 25). Métro Gare Centrale or Parc/ tram 92, 93, 94. **Open** 10am-5.45pm daily. *Services* 5.15pm Mon-Fri; 9am, 11am Sun. **Map** p321 D4.

Sablon

Maps p317 & p321

South-west of the Royal Quarter, and equally grand, is the elegant enclave of Sablon. This comprises the lovely **place du Grand Sablon** – lined with lively bars and pricey antique shops – and the equally charming **place du Petit Sablon**.

Upmarket antique and crafts stalls invade the area every Saturday. Between the two squares is **Notre Dame au Sablon**, probably the loveliest Gothic church in Brussels. It was built in the 15th and 16th centuries; the interior,

with its 14-metre (46-foot) high exquisite stained-glass windows, is especially stunning. Across the busy rue de la Régence from the church is place du Petit Sablon. The centre is taken up by a small park, designed in 1890 by Henri Beyaert. Its railings, by nouveau architect Paul Hankar, are divided by 48 columns, each topped by a statuette representing one of the ancient guilds of Brussels. Inside the park are statues of various little-known Belgian worthies (although anyone who's ever looked at a map of the world will be familiar with the projection devised by Gérard Mercator), but its chief dedicatees are the 16th-century counts Egmont and Hoorn, who dared to join the rebellion against Philip II and were rewarded with martyrdom in the Grand' Place in 1568.

At the top end of the square stands the **Palais d'Egmont**. Begun in the 16th century, it was enlarged in the 18th century and had to

Brussels by tram 1: The royal ride

You almost feel like giving the royal wave from the window. Trams 92, 93 and 94 run regally down **rue Royale**, past the main sights of Royal Brussels – it's like having your own guided tour, without having to be talked down to in eight languages. This is a trip run by locals for locals – and you can stop off for a drink at any number of pit-stops. Once stamped, your €1.40 ticket is valid for one hour, enough for a few gawps and gulps en route.

Tram 94 sets off from Jette cemetery, 92 and 93 from Schaerbeek station; all converge on the first main sight, the neo-Byzantine church of **Ste-Marie** on place de la Reine at the northern tip of rue Royale (*pictured*). Almost immediately, there's a pit-stop, attractive enough to make an early jump-off point: the classic art nouveau café-restaurant **De Ultieme Hallucinatie** (*see p118*). The stop also allows for a longer look around the 19th-century glasshouse and statued gardens of the nearby **Le Botanique** cultural centre (*see p199*).

Once back on the tram, **place du Congrès**, with its memorial column and eternal flame, will soon appear on your right, as will a fabulous view over the lower Old Town. Should you wish to disembark here, just across from the square is the famous chocolatier **Mary**, purveyors of fine chocolate to the royals. Suitably sweetened, after passing the city's cathedral, **Sts Michel et Gudule**, in the

distance on your right, the royal park, **Parc de Bruxelles**, soon comes into view on your left. Surrounding it are grand buildings of state: the **Palais de la Nation**, the Flemish and French-speaking parliaments, and, at the far southern end, the **Palais Royal**, the king's official residence. This rather unremarkable façade hides the royal family from view – when they're not up in Laeken. They do come out and wave from the grand balcony on Belgian National Day, 21 July. At the western end of the palace is the **Musée de la Dynastie**, documenting the brief history of the Belgian monarchy since 1831.

As the tram approaches **place Royale**, passing Horta's magnificent **Palais des Beaux-Arts** on the right and the statue of great crusader Godfrey of Bouillon in the middle, the church of **St-Jacques-sur-Coudenberg** appears at the top of the square, a reminder of the 15th-century royal palace that once stood here. Remains of the residence of the Dukes of Burgundy can be accessed from 10 place Royale. **Les Musées Royaux des Beaux-Arts** on the south side of the square complete the grand vista. Behind them, the newly opened **Palais de Charles de Lorraine** shows off the royal collection of the governor-general of the Austrian Netherlands.

The tram then trundles through Sablon, past its stunning church **Notre Dame au Sablon**, on the right and, on the left, the **Palais d'Egmont**, named after the count

be rebuilt at the beginning of the 20th following a fire. The palace is now used for receptions by the Minister for Foreign Affairs, and it was here that Britain, Ireland and Denmark signed the Treaty of Accession to the EEC in 1972. The rooms are magnificent, but only the gardens are open to the public (and only part of these).

After dark, with its lively restaurants and bars, Sablon feels more like the bright lights of Paris than Brussels. This is all the more incongruous considering it borders shabby Marolles down below. Between the two stands the execrable (unless, of course, imperial bombast is your thing) **Palais de Justice**. The biggest building in Europe when it was completed in 1883, it is Joseph Poelaert's masterpiece – and was literally the death of him, reducing the architect to insanity and an early end in a mental asylum before it was finished. Its heaviness of style is not widely admired, but by sheer dint of size it cannot fail to impress. The interior is equally imposing and equally good at overawing luckless criminals, with giant magisterial statues of Demosthenes and Cicero, and the echoing Salle des Pas Perdus (waiting room). By the summer of 2002, a public lift will link the entrance to Marolles down below. There's a fine view of northern Brussels from the terrace at the front – try the telescopes.

Notre Dame au Sablon

3B rue de la Régence (02 511 57 41). Métro Porte de Namur/tram 92, 93, 94. **Open** 9am-6pm Mon-Fri; 10am-6pm Sat, Sun. *Services* 6pm Mon-Sat; 11am, 12.15pm, 6pm Sun. **Admission** free; guided tours on request. **Map** p321 C4.

Palais de Justice

place Poelaert (02 508 65 78). Métro Louise/tram 92, 93, 94. **Open** 8am-5pm Mon-Fri. **Admission** free. **Map** p320 B/C5.

beheaded by the Habsburgs in 1568. Severe justice has also been meted out at the grotesque **Palais de Justice**, whose vast goulish mouth appears ahead in the distance. In front of it is **place Poelaert**, named after the architect made mad designing it, which offers a wonderful sweep of cityscape below.

The bright shops of places Louise and Stéphanie complete the royal tour. Then the routes divide: the 93 and 94 head towards the university and Bois de la Cambre, while the 92 takes in a few bars on the Ixelles/St-Gilles border before its verdant terminus at Fort Jaco, Uccle.

EU Quarter & Around

Green spaces offset the soulless high-rises of the capital of Europe.

Sightseeing

The vast sweep of Brussels from the east side of the Petit Ring to the Fôret de Soignes contains treasures and horrors aplenty. There's the unattractive but not uninteresting centre of bureaucratic Brussels in the old **Quartier Léopold** and the **EU Quarter**, as well as some surprisingly graceful squares and art nouveau buildings. Overlooking this district is the stately **Parc du Cinquantenaire**, containing a clutch of worthwhile museums. Further out, on the way from **Montgomery** to **Tervuren**, are large swaths of greenery, offering great walking opportunities and a glimpse of a Brussels few visitors ever see.

Quartier Léopold & the EU Quarter

Maps p322 & p324

This is Gotham City, Belgian-style. Take the métro to Schuman, come up for air at the Rond-Point – and suddenly you're out of grey, shabby

The **EU Parliament** above Léopold station.

Brussels and in steel-and-glass Euroland. Walk south along rue Froissart and you'll see the EU institutions spread out below you. To the right is the distinctive four-pronged **Berlaymont**, the Commission headquarters (*see also p32* **High jinks at Europe's HQ**). Built in 1967, vacated since 1991 (owing to the obscene amounts of asbestos within), the Berlaymont has been slated for an expensive overhaul since the mid 1990s. For now, the vast edifice is still a sorry symbol of bureaucratic waste.

Alongside it is Justus Lipsius' 1995 **Council of Ministers** building, sprawling across a huge area in peach granite. Away to the left, just visible through the trees of the **Parc Léopold**, is the **European Parliament** (opened in 1998), shining blue-green in the distance. Check out the odd, covered, geometric bridge on rue Belliard by which EU officials walk from one building to another. And look for the large, elegant, honey-coloured shape of the **Résidence**, Brussels' finest art deco building, built as a luxury apartment block in the 1920s, and mercifully preserved – a rare survival from the pre-EU days. Take in the panoramic view but don't necessarily go down and walk among the buildings – it's pretty encroaching at street level. But make your way to the open-air platform of Schuman railway station for another fine view – the incongruous juxtaposition of the grandiose buildings and the railway lines. The area is crying out for a great chase movie to be shot here.

The EU area has a great many detractors, not least among heritage action groups. People will refer nostalgically to pre-EU days when it was the lively Quartier Léopold, with plentiful local bars and beautiful houses. There are those who are still enraged at the way this area was picked off to make way for Europe. Perhaps it's a casualty of progress, but it's certainly Europe now, not a Brussels *commune*. The thing to be grateful for is that the 1970s are over and the 1990s had some architectural style, so those heavy grey office blocks that line the streets may one day be replaced by more daring buildings with glass curves, like the undulating European Parliament.

Three long, narrow roads cut through the area: rue de la Loi, rue Joseph II and rue Belliard. It's no fun walking along these traffic-heavy thoroughfares between the concrete blocks and expansive panes of glass humming quietly with the sense of mighty goings-on within. Only at lunchtime and between 6pm and 8pm could the area be described as bustling; at weekends it becomes a ghost town, the only people on view being security guards. At night there is some activity in a few places, namely the Irish pubs full of networking EU employees: *see p130* **Brussels by bar crawl: EU Quarter**.

Not far from the western end of rue Joseph II is a welcome escape from the monotony of the office blocks: the **Musée Charlier**. Guillaume Charlier was an active figure in the artistic world of Brussels in the early 1900s. Trained at the Beaux-Arts in Brussels, he was taken under the wing of Henri van Cutsem, a collector and patron of the arts. Charlier actually moved into van Cutsem's house, the site of this museum, where he organised concerts and salon discussions for the city's intellectual and artistic circles. The fin-de-siècle house is crammed with beautiful tapestries, furniture, silverware, and works by Ensor, Meunier and Charlier himself. Concerts are still held in the concert hall; contact the museum for a full programme.

As soon as you move away from these three main streets, you are almost immediately back in cobbled enclaves familiar from central Brussels. North of Berlaymont, at the end of rue Archimède, are the twin squares of Ambiorix and Marie-Louise, both of them small and graceful and lined with beautiful listed houses (if, unfortunately, victim to the national mania for trellised trees). Don't miss **11 place Ambiorix**. Long and thin, with its spidery balconies and bronzed, rounded façade, it stands out like a fairy-tale home of a captive princess. North-east of the square is the sloping rue des Confédérés. Here, in a red-brick house at No.83, WH Auden spent five months in the late 1930s 'bathing and café-crawling'. His poems, 'Musée des Beaux-Arts' and 'Brussels in Winter', contain his impressions of the city.

Back in the south of the EU area, **place de Luxembourg** is a square of great charm, numerous bars – and the Quartier Léopold railway station. With the European Parliament looming over it, this romantic, if tatty old station became a cause célèbre in 2001 when it was occupied by squatters protesting its demolition. Although the old booking hall has been spared, many of the original features – ceilings, iron columns – have been destroyed. The station will become the terminus of an underground shuttle service between the airport and Parliament – even the booking hall is slated to be an EU Information Centre.

Behind the Parliament, on the other side of the rail tracks, lies **Parc Léopold**, a modest, steeply sloped smear of green with a lake and

Top ten Curios

The Little Brussels Museum of Nests & Feeding Troughs
17 rue L Lumière, Forest (02 376 52 97).
Build and recognise the nests of birds.

National Museum of Historical Figurines
14 rue J Tiebackx, Jette (02 479 00 52).
The complete history of mankind shown with lead, tin and plastic models.

Sewers Museum
porte d'Anderlecht, Lower Town (02 513 85 87). **Map** p317 B3.
An insight into the city's 300km (186 miles) of sewage ducts.

Private Museum of Fairground Organs
104 rue Waelham, Schaerbeek (02 241 27 91).
Plus music boxes through the ages.

Witloof Museum
29 rue Leekaerts, Evere (02 216 10 59).
Open-air and indoor museum dedicated to chicory, or Belgian endive.

Belgian Elevator Museum
15 rue de la Source, St-Gilles (02 525 82 11). **Map** p320 B6.
Ride high to view *le plat pays*.

Album
25 rue des Chartreux, Lower Town (02 511 90 55). **Map** p318 B3.
Annually themed museum of advertising.

Museum of Pharmacognosis
Campus de la Plaine, Université Libre de Bruxelles, Ixelles (02 650 52 79).
Retraces the history of herbal plants and their use through the ages. No samples.

Boyadjian Museum of the Heart
Musée Royal d'Art et d'Histoire, 3 parc du Cinquantenaire, EU Quarter (02 741 72 11). **Map** p325 H5.
Dedicated by a cardiologist who collected hearts in all forms, down the ages.

Ch Debeur Museum of Fencing
373 avenue de la Couronne, Ixelles (02 648 69 32). **Map** p324 F6.
The world's only museum solely dedicated to the Olympic sport of sword fighting.

Brussels by tram 2: A trip to Tervuren

Of Brussels' 17 tram routes, the most haunting is the 44. Gliding under the leafy bowers of the Forêt de Soignes, from Montgomery metro station to the outlying village of Tervuren, ten kilometres (six miles) east of town, the 44 would be worth the ticket alone even if there weren't an eerie, controversial museum at the end of it.

Its terminus, in picturesque Tervuren, provides a glimpse into the heart of darkness, for a short stroll from the tram stop is the imposing **Musée Royal de l'Afrique Centrale** (*pictured*). Opened in 1897, at present the museum displays only a fraction of the vast booty collected by Belgium during King Léopold II's appalling exploitation of the Congo (*see p18* **Belgium's heart of darkness**). The museum's renovation – and redirection – has been a source of dispute thanks to bitter examinations of Belgium's colonial past.

Little prepares the first-time visitor for the dark, gruesome tour of plunder – certainly not the merry little 44 tram that sets off from the underground level of Montgomery metro. A jaunty statue of Monty himself stands above the tunnel facing Le Cinquantenaire, reminding motorists that the field marshal marched along here from France, up the German right flank.

The tram emerges into the beautiful, wide, tree-lined avenue de Tervuren. It's best to sit on the right-hand side; then you get a good view of the brilliantly geometric **Palais Stocklet** at No.281 (on the edge of the oval-shaped square Léopold II), built between 1906 and 1911 by Austrian Josef Hoffman in deliberate opposition to the lavishness of art nouveau. In its sparseness and purity it is quite modern, but, alas, closed to the public. Just beyond the palace, you come to the lovely hills and lakes of

Parc de Woluwe (blissfully free of the stuffy flowerbeds and straitjacketed layouts of the city's more formal parks) and, further on, you can glimpse the grand embassy houses through the trees.

Across avenue de Tervuren from the park is the **Musée du Transport Urbain Bruxellois**, packed with beautifully restored trams and memorabilia. In summer, the old trams trundle out and head south through the immense beech woodland of the **Forêt des Soignes** (*see p90* **Green Brussels**).

Although the forest has reduced by two-thirds since its heyday, it's still impressive to see primeval woodland so close to a built-up capital. The forest includes the **Tervuren Arboretum** (02 769 20 81), full of old and new forest flora; the **Groenendaal Arboretum** (02 657 03 86), which contains about 500 exotic plant species, as well as a forest museum and a high-class restaurant in what used to be an abbey; and the **Jean Massart Experimental Garden** (02 673 84 06), a research centre with some 5,600 species.

At the edge of the forest is Quatre Bras, where the elegant Hussar regiment met Napoleon's troops in 1815 and fled right back to town.

Back at Tervuren, a statue of an elephant on a roundabout announces the Royal Central Africa Museum. Purpose-built by Léopold, the grand building houses a bizarre collection of stuffed animals, African tools, clothes and masks, plus, in room 7, relics from the travels of explorers Henry Stanley (such as his suitcase) and David Livingstone (such as, says the label, the 'small block of wood of the Livingstone tree under which the heart of Livingstone was buried when he died on the first day of May 1873 at Ilala in Central Africa').

small playground (*see also p90* **Green Brussels**). Overlooking the park from the south is a recommended stop for families: the **Institut Royal des Sciences Naturelles** (Natural History Museum). Of primary interest is the evocatively lit dinosaur department, which contains the skeletons of 29 iguanadons discovered in a Belgian coal mine at the end of the 19th century. Thanks to the robotic wonders of 'dinamation', you can also watch full- and half-scale dinosaurs blink, wriggle and snarl. Look out, too, for the cutest animatronic baby

mammoth, the whale room (with 18 whale skeletons), the representations of Arctic and Antarctic habitats on either side of a tunnel, and the insect department, with its 5,000 butterflies and beetles.

Across the street is the **Musée Wiertz**. The paintings of Belgian Antoine Wiertz are chiefly known nowadays for their size (some peak at around 11 metres/36 feet) and often gruesome themes. His chief inspiration was biblical and mythical scenes, particularly those involving people being shot, crushed, impaled, ravaged,

Guido Gyseels, director of this most decrepit of museums, has plans for audio-visual exhibition halls and rotating shows. Astonishingly, more than 95 per cent of the museum's archive is still under lock and key, including 70,000 maps, 8,000 musical instruments and the largest collection of preserved African fish in the world. The first major exhibition, set for 2004, should be controversial, as it coincides with the centenary of Stanley's death.

The lovely grounds around the museum originally belonged to a palace and there are still remains of 18th-century stables and the Renaissance Chapelle St-Hubert. Around these is the large and attractive **Parc de Tervuren**, with its series of canals and woods.

Dutch-speaking Tervuren village itself is cobbled and pretty, its main square featuring the 18th-century church of St-Jan, surrounded by fine houses, home to many a Eurocrat.

Musée Royal de l'Afrique Centrale

13 chaussée de Louvain, Tervuren (02 769 52 11). Tram 44. **Open** 10am-5pm Tue-Fri; 10am-6pm Sat, Sun. **Admission** €2. **No credit cards.**

Musée du Transport Urbain Bruxellois

364 avenue de Tervuren, Woluwe-St-Pierre (02 515 31 08). Tram 39, 44/bus 36, 42. **Open** Apr-Oct 1.30-7pm Sat, Sun. Closed Nov-Mar. **Admission** (includes 2 tram tickets) €5.50; €3.72 concessions. **No credit cards.**

stabbed and generally roughed up, preferably with some gratuitious titillation thrown in. *Le Souflet d'une Dame Belge* depicts a woman so outraged with the unwelcome attentions of a French soldier she blows his brains out with a pistol. Other titles include: *Thoughts and Visions of a Decapitated Head, The Suicide, The Burned Child*, etc. Well regarded in his time (not least by himself – he saw himself on a par with Rubens and Michelangelo), Wiertz managed to persuade the state to buy him this house and studio, where he died in 1865. Characteristically,

he insisted on full ancient Egyptian burial rites; his heart was embalmed separately and sent back to his home town of Dinant in a lead-lined box for display in the town hall. The museum contains some 160 Wiertz works and makes for an amusing hour's diversion.

Institut Royal des Sciences Naturelles

29 rue Vautier (02 627 42 38). Métro Trône/bus 34, 80. **Open** 9.30am-4.45pm Tue-Fri; 10am-6pm Sat, Sun. **Admission** €4; €1.50-€3 concessions; free under-5s. **No credit cards. Map** p324 F5.

Sightseeing

Among the sights in the **Parc du Cinquantenaire** are the imposing **Arc de Triomphe** ...

Musée Charlier

*16 avenue des Arts (02 218 53 82). Métro Arts-Loi
or Madou/bus 29, 63, 65, 66.* **Open** 10am-5pm Mon;
1.30-5pm Tue-Thur; 1.30-4.30pm Fri. **Admission**
€2.48. **No credit cards.** **Map** p322 E3.

Musée Wiertz

*62 rue Vautier (02 648 17 18). Métro Trône/
bus 34, 59, 80.* **Open** 10am-noon, 1-5pm Tue-Fri,
every 2nd Sat, Sun. **Admission** free. **Map** p324 F5.

Parc du Cinquantenaire

Map p325

Compared to the ugly EU Quarter, far more
rewarding strolling can be had by heading
east from Rond-Point Schuman towards an
earlier attempt to stamp a grandiose dignity
on the area: the **Parc du Cinquantenaire**.
If it's overblown and neo-classical in Brussels,
it's probably the work of Léopold II, and so
is the case with the largest, most impressive
and best-known of the city parks (*see also p90*
Green Brussels). The king had 300 labourers
working day and night to finish it in time
for Belgium's 50th anniversary (hence
Cinquantenaire) in 1880. It has all the trappings
of an imperial park. At its eastern end,
colonnades swing round from the central
Arc de Triomphe to link the museums of
the two wings of Le Cinquantenaire.

On the north side is the **Musée Royal de
l'Armée et d'Histoire Militaire** (Royal
Museum of the Army and Military History),
an enjoyable retro journey for military buffs.
Guns, swords, cannons, grenades, uniforms
and artillery are arranged in somewhat
haphazard displays, with special emphasis on
the Belgian army. There's an interesting section
on the 1830 Belgian Revolution. Of wider appeal

is the aviation section's enormous hangar,
housing 130 aircraft from World War I to the
present, with a special focus on World War II
planes used by the Allies and the Luftwaffe.
Also included are MiG fighter jets, Douglas
Dakotas and Sikorski helicopters. Not all
sections of the museum are always open.

Two, very different, museums share the
south wing. The self-explanatory **Autoworld**
contains one of the world's most prestigious
collections of motor vehicles. Starting
from 1886, it traces the development of the
automobile through hundreds of incarnations,
including the glamorous 1928 Bentley and the
1930 Bugatti. There is a sad display of pre-
World War II cars produced by Belgium's now-
defunct car industry, and also cars driven by
various members of the Belgian royal family.

Sharing the south wing with Autoworld is
the **Musées Royaux d'Art et d'Histoire**
(Royal Museums of Art and History). This vast
museum has one of the world's largest antiquity
departments, with a huge collection of artefacts
from the ancient worlds of Egypt, Greece,
the Near and Far East, and pre-Columbian
America. Items of interest include the Roman
Apamea mosaic, discovered in Syria in the
1930s by a team of Belgian archaeologists, and
the amazing feather cloak (and other feather
art) made by Amazon Indians in the early 17th
century. Other collections include European
art from the Middle Ages, art deco glass and
metalwork, lace and 18th-century carriages.
Inevitably with a museum of this size, it's vital
to focus your interests on a few areas to avoid
glazed eyes and aching feet.

It's also worth heading to the north-west
corner of the park, where the unexpectedly
neo-classical **Pavillon Horta** is an early piece

(1889) by the architect who was to become synonymous with art nouveau in Brussels. The real interest, though, is Jef Lambeaux's luxuriant reliefs *Les Passions Humaines* inside. Unfortunately, partly for reasons of economy and partly out of respect for the neighbouring mosque, the pavilion is kept locked (although it may be worth enquiring at the Musées Royaux d'Art et d'Histoire about their occasional tours). A tantalising peephole allows a glimpse of creamy thigh or breast.

Beside the pavilion is a **monument** to the Belgian soldiers who 'freed' the Congo: it shows Africans in attitudes of ecstatic gratitude to the soldiers, and is wisely being allowed to decay quietly. Aside from these sights, the park's long, rather unkempt avenues are pleasant for a leisurely walk. By day there's a regular squeak of feral parakeets; by night it takes on a rather sinister edge.

On the south side of the park, on avenue des Nerviens, is the **Centre d'art contemporain** (*see p189*), an information centre for modern Wallonian art that organises themed shows of (often young) Belgian and European artists. Nearby, on rue des Francs, is the **Maison de Cauchie**, home of painter and architect Paul Cauchie, built in 1905 in the twilight of Brussels' art nouveau period. It's not, in fact, typically Belgian – but it's one of the finest examples of sgraffiti (designs scratched through plaster to reveal different colours underneath) in the city, and, like the Palais Stoclet, was much influenced by the Viennese Sezession movement.

Autoworld

11 parc du Cinquantenaire (02 736 41 65). Métro Mérode or Schuman/tram 81, 82/bus 20, 28, 38, 67, 80. **Open** *Apr-Oct* 10am-6pm daily. *Nov-Mar* 10am-5pm daily. **Admission** €5; €2-€4 concessions. **No credit cards. Map** p325 H4.

Maison de Cauchie

5 rue des Francs (02 673 15 06). Métro Mérode/ tram 81, 82/bus 20, 22, 80. **Open** 11am-1pm, 2-6pm 1st weekend of the mth, and by appointment. **Admission** €4. **No credit cards. Map** p325 H5.

Musée Royal de l'Armée et d'Histoire Militaire

3 parc du Cinquantenaire (02 737 78 11/www.klm- mra.be). Métro Mérode or Schuman/tram 81, 82/ bus 20, 28, 36, 67, 80. **Open** 9am-noon, 1-4.30pm Tue-Sun. **Admission** free. **Map** p325 H4.

Musées Royaux d'Art et d'Histoire

10 parc du Cinquantenaire (02 741 72 11/ www.kmkg-mrah.be). Métro Mérode or Schuman/ tram 81, 82/bus 20, 28, 36, 67, 80. **Open** 9.30am- 5pm Tue-Fri; 10am-5pm Sat, Sun. **Admission** €3.72; €1.24-€2.48 concessions; free 1st Wed of the mth. **No credit cards. Map** p325 H5.

... austere **Pavillon Horta** ...

... and the crumbling **Congo Monument.**

Ixelles & St-Gilles

Discover art nouveau treasures, African shops and plenty of open green space.

Perhaps Brussels' two most attractive neighbourhoods fan out south from the Petit Ring: **Ixelles** and **St-Gilles**. Each *commune* has its fair share of art nouveau treasures, each has plenty of bars and restaurants, each extends southwards to leafy expanses (*see p90* **Green Brussels**). And each is a desirable place to live – with occasional grim exceptions.

Avenue Louise divides Ixelles between the glitzy west and the earthy east; between Versace and the vibrant market stalls of the Matongé quarter (*see p87* **African Brussels**); between elegant bistros and the eclectic ethnic boozing dens of rue Longue Vie. St-Gilles is also equally divided. Grey and deprived at its northernmost point by Gare du Midi, it becomes increasingly appealing as it stretches east. At its best, it's a friendly community in leafy surroundings interspersed with some stunning architecture.

Ixelles

Map p321 & p324

In 1864, land was sliced from Ixelles and St-Gilles so that a suitably magnificent avenue could tie the centre of town to the pleasant grounds of the Bois de la Cambre. Behind the plan was Léopold II, who named this imperial boulevard after his eldest daughter Louise.

The more earthy swaths of Ixelles stretch around **avenue Louise**, although the Gucci, Versace and Chanel boutiques on it lend a certain glitz to the immediate surroundings. From **place Louise** at the Petit Ring, you can see the dome of the Palais de Justice, then as you proceed down the avenue there are small pedestrianised streets sloping off to the right, where cafés put their tables out on the street, giving the area a relaxed, Mediterranean feel.

However, as soon as you hit place Stéphanie, you are into avenue Louise proper and you understand why it generally fails to arouse enthusiasm (apart from the well-heeled sex-shoppers who target a small upmarket red-light area at this part of the street). Pedestrians feel very humble indeed.

Avenue Louise is very long and wide, with six lanes of traffic, its buildings are tall and its shops out of any decent price range. Young execs and middle-aged wives of the rich abound. Variety, however, does not. For this you need to head a few blocks east to the twin

In the south of Ixelles lie the pretty, duck-friendly **Etangs d'Ixelles**. *See p85.*

roads that run south from the Petit ring: the chaussées d'Ixelles and de Wavre. The lavishly named **Galeries de la Toison d'Or** (Golden Fleece Galleries) not only separates the chaussée d'Ixelles from the avenue Louise; it also sets the tone for the mix of shops – and clientele – to be found once you venture off avenue Louise into Ixelles itself. Louise-style designer shops stand alongside more downmarket brand names; and then, from lively Porte de Namur, and a short distance down the twin chaussées, there's the **Matongé**. This area, so close to avenue Louise, could hardly be more different. The population is predominantly Congolese, but there are Indians and North Africans, and the quarter is a welcome change from the bland neon of Louise.

Away from the Petit Ring, if Louise has a centre, then it's place du Châtelain just off it, a pleasant square of bars, cafés and a Wednesday afternoon market. The rest of the avenue is parcelled up between travel agencies, hotels, large companies, haute couturiers and interior decorators. The only worthy sight is the Horta-designed **Hôtel Solvay** at No.224, built for the son of an enlightened industrialist. A 33-year-old Horta was given free rein to produce a work of fluid, intricate, symmetrical lines, with gigantic windows and imaginative use of stone.

At the heart of the Matongé, meanwhile, is rue Longue Vie, a lively pedestrianised strip of bars and restaurants. Almost too conveniently, Longue Vie runs into the lively nightlife haunts around place St-Boniface, which throngs with attractive bars and restaurants – **L'Ultime Atome** (*see p135*) is one of many. (Round the corner, almost incongruously, is the blackened, sinister, turreted church of St-Boniface itself, strangely attached to the houses on either side.)

Further south, halfway down chaussée d'Ixelles, the uneven square of place Fernand Cocq is as lively as anywhere in town. The resto-bar **L'Amour Fou** (*see p133*) is the best example, but there are half-a-dozen others. In summer, when customers sip their drinks outside, the square becomes a Mediterranean terrace, offset by the **Maison Communale** at the far end. Surrounded by gardens, this large, pleasant building formerly belonged to the violinist Bériot and his Spanish wife, the singer La Malibran, who bought the house as an inspired monument to their newly wed love.

As it slowly meanders southwards, chaussée d'Ixelles has little to commend it apart from the occasional bar and ubiquitous middle- and low-range retail names. Near the end, up steep rue Van Volsem, is Ixelles' art gallery, the **Musée Communal d'Ixelles**. This excellent little museum, founded in 1892, is housed in a former abattoir and is well known in Brussels

Union St-Gilloise supporter. *See p90.*

for its exhibitions of mainly modern art. It also has a good permanent collection, including works by Belgian artists Magritte, Delvaux, Spilliaert, de Smet and Van Rysselberghe, and original posters by Toulouse-Lautrec. It also has Picasso's *Guitar and Fruit Bowl*, which was stolen a few years ago but later recovered. A new wing blends perfectly with the older part to create a well-lit and interesting space for the paintings. Off the usual tourist track, the museum is rarely crowded.

The chaussée ends at the **Etangs d'Ixelles** (Ixelles Ponds), pretty in spring and summer when there are ducks and fishermen. At the edge of the lake is a large, rather ugly, mustard-coloured building in the shape of a boat: the **Institut National de Radiodiffusion**. Constructed in 1938 by Joseph Diongré, it was the largest, most advanced communications building in the world. Its vast Studio Four is still reckoned to be one of the best anywhere, and its 19 studios are so well insulated that recording goes on absolutely undisturbed. Neglected for years, its renovation and conversion into a concert hall – slated for December 2001 – is now scheduled for completion in September 2002.

Near the southern end of the ponds is the wonderful, intelligent **Musée des Enfants** (*see p173*). The guiding principle here is hands-on. There are cooking, painting, modelling and puppet workshops, and the displays and activities are completely rearranged every three years so that children don't tire of the place. Labelling is in French and Dutch only.

The imposing 14th-century **Porte de Hal** in St-Gilles. *See p88.*

East of here is the bilingual **university**, the French side being the ULB and the Flemish the VUB. They are both enclosed by boulevard du Triomphe within a pleasant campus. This is a very lively area, with a swath of bars and restaurants along the chaussée de Boondael, between the university and the Abbaye de la Cambre, particularly near Ixelles cemetery. **Le Tavernier** (*see p134*) and, round the corner, **L'Atelier** (*see p133*), are two fine examples. Also around place de la Petite Suisse are several good, reasonably priced Vietnamese restaurants.

To the west of the ponds and the university, at the end of avenue Louise, the **Bois de la Cambre** is a treat (*see p90* **Green Brussels**). This used to be part of the old Forêt de Soignes and was the favoured strolling spot of the well-to-do. It retains some of the rarefied atmosphere of avenue Louise, with its restaurants, tearooms and boating on the lake. The peripheries tend to be used as through roads, so you have to penetrate quite far in for tranquillity. It's a good size at 124 hectares (50 acres), and has plenty of handsome old trees – the beeches are especially beautiful. The avant-garde **Théâtre de Poche** (*see p215*) is situated inside the park, and it's bordered by the magnificent, embassy-lined avenue Franklin Roosevelt.

Just north of the park is the **Abbaye de la Cambre**. Founded in the 12th century by a noblewoman called Gisèle for the Cîteaux

Order, the abbey was badly damaged during the Wars of Religion and was rebuilt in the 16th and 18th centuries, although the 14th-century church attached to the abbey survives. The buildings are set in elegant French gardens and now house the National Geographical Institution and an art exhibition centre.

There are two worthwhile sightseeing stops just off avenue Louise. About halfway down the street on its east side is the **Fondation pour l'Architecture**, a converted pumping house that holds good exhibitions on Brussels' architectural heritage. Displays are varied and well put together, with models, photos, videos and furniture, and the interpretation of architecture is not too restrictive.

On the avenue's west side, not far from the Abbaye de la Cambre, is the **Musée Constantin Meunier**. The former home and studio of the 19th-century Belgian sculptor and painter, it contains more than 170 sculptures and 120 paintings (of his 800-works lifetime output), the best known of which are the bronze figures of industrial workers. Meunier began his artistic career painting religious scenes, but changed tack in his 50s, turning to sculpture and inspired by social realism. His later works feature farmers, miners and industrial workers labouring heroically in fairly grim surroundings. Although much of his work appears rather worthy and monumental, his figures do convey a sense of dignity and suffering, and can be moving in small doses.

African Brussels

After the independence of the former Belgian colony of the Congo in 1960, waves of African students came to Brussels to study. Many stayed and set up shop near Porte de Namur, an area which became popularly known as **Matongé**, after a suburb of the Congolese capital Kinshasa.

The heart of the district developed around the **Galerie d'Ixelles**, the shopping gallery that links chaussée de Wavre with chaussée d'Ixelles. The gallery's two sides also took their names from Kinshasa, from its main streets of Inzia and Kanda-Kanda. Inzia is filled with snack bars and cafés, while the Kanda-Kanda side is awash with hair product shops. Stores of every description sprung up around, most of them selling food, clothes and cosmetics. Great bunches of tiny bananas spill on to the street, alongside mangoes and guavas. You'll find smoked fish, locusts and caterpillars, hairdressers-cum-social centres, telephone booths offering cut-price calls to Kin' and shipping agents bundling up boxes destined for the homeland.

Hanging in windows and clothing passers-by are richly patterned dresses and traditional Zairean menswear. Scattered about are hairdressing salons advertising dreadlocks and displaying additional tresses. In the Galerie d'Ixelles is **Musicanova**, a record shop that has its own label and helps to promote new African artists.

Although a bustling market by day, Matongé really comes to life at night. The main drag is **rue Longue Vie**, a pedestrianised section of street between chaussée de Wavre and rue de la Paix, crammed full of raucous bars and restaurants. Most are Central African, interspersed with a few Portuguese, Latin American and Indian venues. All offer chilled beers, spicy meats and loud music, and most open late. Round the corner in rue de la Paix, the trendier venues of **Dada** (No.24) and **Tanganyika** opposite offer a more subtle alternative. You may not get a better night in Brussels than this. Cameroonian **Le Makossa** at No.18 serves a delicious *moambé* (chicken in palm oil sauce), and the chicken wings marinated in lime and *pilli pilli* are divine. More variety is available on the Wavre/Trône intersection, such as the fish stew and chicken in peanut sauce at **L'Horloge du Sud**.

All is not finger lickin' sweetness and light, however. Although it's a safe neighbourhood, drug trafficking and tension between rival gangs of youths has increased. With the bar and restaurant boom, rents have increased dramatically, so many students have had to move to cheaper Schaerbeek and St-Josse, although the scene there is more North African and Turkish than Congolese. Regular police checks for work and residence permits also add to an occasional air of frustration and tension.

For the curious visitor, however, you couldn't dream of a more vibrant alternative to the superficial gloss of avenue Louise than the Central African community on its doorstep.

Abbaye de la Cambre

*11 avenue Emile Duray (02 648 11 21). Tram 23,
90, 94.* **Open** 9am-noon, 3-6pm Mon-Fri; 3-6pm Sat;
8am-12.30pm, 3-6pm Sun; 9am-noon Catholic feast
days. **Admission** free.

Fondation pour l'Architecture

*55 rue de l'Ermitage (02 642 24 80). Tram 81, 82,
93, 94/bus 54, 38, 60, 71.* **Open** 10.30am-6.30pm
Tue-Sun. **Admission** €6.20; €3.70 concessions.
No credit cards. Map p321 D7.

Musée Communal d'Ixelles

*71 rue Van Volsem, Ixelles (02 515 64 21). Bus
38, 54, 60, 71.* **Open** 1-6.30pm Tue-Fri; 10am-5pm
Sat, Sun. **Admission** €5-€6.20. **Credit** MC, V.
Map p324 E6.

Musée Constantin Meunier

*59 rue de l'Abbaye (02 648 44 49). Tram 93, 94/
bus 38, 60.* **Open** 10am-noon, 1-5pm Tue-Sun.
Closed every other Sat & Sun (phone to check).
Admission free.

St-Gilles

Map p320

Parts of St-Gilles merit inclusion on any list
of Brussels' most beautiful spaces – although
its run-down north-western corner, around the
Gare du Midi and the **Porte de Hal**, is not
the best introduction to the area. The latter is
a 14th-century tower, embellished in the 19th
century, giving it something of a fairy-tale
appearance. It's been a prison, a toll house,
a grain store, a repository for archives and
latterly (although currently closed) a museum
of folklore. The shops around are humdrum, the
restaurants – mostly Mediterranean – are cheap.

The rest of St-Gilles is an area of uneven
squares and gentle angles; the short, wide
streets lead to small squares or charming
crossroads. It is as if the *commune* were
designed around the principle of 'pause and
contemplate'. Everything is brought to a
considered conclusion, whether it is the Barrière
de St-Gilles at the centre, where the main
avenues converge and slope off down hills, or
a smaller square such as parvis de la Trinité,
where graceful houses face the lovely church,
which looks as if it might belong in Latin
America. If you avoid the main thoroughfares
(chaussées de Waterloo and de Charleroi), you
can remain among quiet, composed streets
where almost every corner has a bar and the
small shops are discreetly interesting and
expensive. Even the main square, the **parvis
St-Gilles**, is contemplative, except for the
bustling market on Sunday mornings.

St-Gilles is largely residential, and the main
reason why people visit is its unequalled
number of art nouveau houses. It has always

been a rich *commune* and all the houses are
elegant, but at the turn of the 19th century a
few wealthy men commissioned fabulous art
nouveau residences. With their swirling, daring
lines and elaborate friezes, the houses appear
flamboyant and insouciant beside their more
stalwart neighbours. Most of these are to be
found in the area between rue Defacqz and the
prison – and most are closed to the public.

One rare exception is Victor Horta's house,
known as **Musée Horta**, at the heart of the
art nouveau area in rue Américaine. Horta
was one of the founders of art nouveau, a new
architectural language that combined glass,
iron, wood and organic shapes to create airy,
fluid and rhythmic spaces. He was responsible
for some of the finest art nouveau architecture
in Brussels, although some of his most famous
buildings were demolished – his Maison du
Peuple, for example, was torn down in 1965
during Brussels' wrecking ball period.

Horta built the house in 1899-1901 as his
home and studio. The exterior is plain enough,
and is nothing compared with the Hankar-
designed house round the corner in rue Defacqz.
This external reticence is fairly typical of an
architect who was Belgian enough to want to
keep his delights hidden away indoors. The
interior is astonishingly light, flowing, graceful
and harmonious. It's clearly a place to live in;
there's no attempt to dazzle, startle or disturb,
as there is in art nouveau elsewhere.

The attention to detail is astonishing and
every functional element, down to the last door
handle, is designed in a fluid, sensuous style.
The staircase and stairwell are particularly
breathtaking: an extravaganza of wrought
iron, mirrors and floral designs, topped by a
stained-glass canopy. The museum often gets
very crowded, and even the wonderful staircase
loses its appeal when you have to queue for ten
minutes to climb it. Try to visit on a weekday.

There are more art nouveau houses further
south towards the prison. The prison seems to
have been integrated to avoid disturbing the
harmony around it, with fairly low walls and
the pleasant avenue de la Jonction dissecting it.

At the beginning of the avenue is the classic
art nouveau **Hôtel Hannon** – now called
the photography gallery **Contretype** –
thankfully open on a daily basis. The great
breadth of the interior hints at what we are
missing in the other houses. It's all staircase
and light and lofty salons, even if, stripped of
its original furniture, the house has the echoing
impersonality of a grand showpiece studio.
The immense fresco decorating the staircase
(by PA Baudouin) is particularly arresting.
Jules Brunfaut built the house in 1902 for the
industrialist Edouard Hannon, who was also

Among the area's art nouveau gems is **Hôtel Solvay** (above and top right). *See p85.*

a keen amateur photographer. His photos are displayed, alongside other classically lovely works. No gritty urban realism here.

North of the prison towards the Barrière, occupying a commanding position, is St-Gilles' **Town Hall,** an impressive 19th-century building in French Renaissance style. Designed by Albert Dumont in 1900-4, the most arresting features are its frescoes, on the ceiling above the main staircase and in the Marriage Room.

To the west of the prison are the **Parc de Forest** and **Parc Duden**. The latter is the more attractive and was once famously elegant, although both are now rather ramshackle. It used to be part of the Forêt de Soignes, and was where Emperor Charles V went hunting. You are now in the *commune* of **Forest** and you can feel the difference. (Ironically, proud local football team Union St-Gilloise are based here – *see p206*). The houses are less graceful and the shops cheaper.

South of here, in the sedate, suburban streets of the neighbouring *commune* of **Uccle** is, unexpectedly, one of the most remarkable museums in Brussels. The house at 41 avenue Léo Errera was built in 1928 for David Van Buuren, a wealthy Dutch banker who became enamoured of the art deco style. Opened as the **Musée David et Alice Van Buuren** in 1973, it is at once a museum of art, architecture and landscaping. Every single object in the house conforms to the strict, polished lines of the art deco movement (the custom-made piano is of particular note). The art collection is remarkable; there is a version of Bruegel's *Landscape with the Fall of Icarus*, as well as works by Ensor, Wouters and Gustave van de Woestyne (a friend of the Van Buurens'), plus a Braque, a Van Gogh and a Patenier. A framed letter from David Ben Gurion shows the Van Buurens' dedication to the Zionist cause. Outside, the garden is laid out in a maze by the Belgian landscape architect René Péchere.

Surrounding Uccle boasts plenty of greenery. Perhaps the most charming of its parks is the **Parc de Wolvendael**, which was owned by successive royals through the centuries.

Contretype

1 avenue de la Jonction (02 538 42 20). Tram 90, 92. **Open** 1-6pm Tue-Sun. **Admission** €2.50. **No credit cards**.

Musée David et Alice Van Buuren

41 avenue Léo Errera (02 343 48 51). Tram 23, 90/bus 60. **Open** 2-6pm Mon; 1-6pm Sun. *Garden* 2-6pm daily. **Admission** €7.50; €5 concessions.

Musée Horta

25 rue Américaine (02 537 16 92). Tram 81, 82, 91, 92/bus 37, 38, 54, 60. **Open** 2-5.30pm daily. **Admission** €5. **No credit cards**.

Green Brussels

Brussels, spotted by parks and surrounded by woods, is the greenest city in Europe after Kiev. Nearly 15 per cent of the capital is occupied by green space and all of it is easily accessible from the centre, adding a breath of fresh air to a morning's shopping or sightseeing. Not too far beyond stand acres of woods and fabulous *châteaux* with landscaped grounds.

Inner-city parks

Bois de la Cambre

Entrances on avenue Louise & chaussée de Waterloo, Ixelles. Tram 23, 90, 93/ bus 38. **Open** 24hrs daily.
Brussels' answer to Central Park. On Sundays some of the inner roads are closed to traffic, making it an ideal jogging, rollerblading or biking circuit. Otherwise, it is a vast wooded park that formed the northern tip of the Forêt de Soignes until the city took it over in 1842. Great for picnicking and feeding the ducks. Dogs are given a free leash, so watch where you sit.

Jardin d'Egmont

Entrances on boulevard de Waterloo & place du Petit Sablon, Upper Town. Métro Louise/tram 92, 93, 94. **Open** 7am-dusk daily. **Map** p321 C5.
A smallish patch of green sandwiched between boulevard de Waterloo and the Sablon makes for an excellent shortcut between the Upper and Lower Towns. The gardens afford a great view of the Palais d'Egmont, which now houses the Ministry of Foreign Affairs. Don't miss the cute statue of Peter Pan.

Parc de Bruxelles

Entrances on rue Royale, rue Ducale & place des Palais, Upper Town. Métro Parc. **Open** 6am-9pm daily. **Map** p319 D3/4.
Once the shooting and hunting ground of the Dukes of Brabant, the park (pictured) was transformed into French-style formal gardens in 1835.

Parc du Cinquantenaire

Entrances on avenue de la Renaissance & avenue des Nerviens, EU Quarter. Métro Mérode or Schuman. **Open** 24hrs daily. **Map** p325 G/H 4/5.

This stately park was laid out in 1880 to coincide with Belgium's 50th anniversary celebrations. It contains a scattering of statues and a string of worthy museums connected by a grand Arc de Triomphe. Can get somewhat dodgy after dark.

Parc de Laeken
Entrances on avenue du Parc Royal, Laeken. Métro Stuyvenbergh/tram 94. **Open** *8am-8.30pm daily.* **Map** *p326.*
Léopold II's grand pretensions arguably reached their zenith here with his creation of a Japanese tower and Chinese pavilion. Nearby, on the grounds of the royal residence, are the Royal Greenhouses, open to the public in summer (*see p168* **Royal Brussels**).

Parc Léopold
Entrances on chaussée de Wavre, chaussée d'Etterbeek & rue Belliard, EU Quarter. Métro Schuman or Trône. **Open** *24hrs daily.* **Map** *p324 F5.*
This is the local lunchtime haunt of staff at the nearby European Institutes and picnicking parties of schoolchildren who have come to visit the Natural History Museum. The hilly landscaped gardens are lovely, and there are plenty of secluded benches and a small lake.

Parc Tenbosch
Entrances on chaussée de Vleurgat & square Henri Michaux, Ixelles. Tram 60, 93, 94. **Open** *7am-dusk daily.*
Closer to town than Cambre, Tenbosch is a handy place to placate young kids. It features manicured lawns with rose beds, a lily pond

full of terrapins and an enclosed play area with swings. It's also one of the few parks where dog owners have to abide by the rules, on account of a resident warden.

Greater Brussels

Château de la Hulpe
Entrances on chaussée de Bruxelles, at chaussé de la Hulpe. Bus 48. **Open** *Summer 8am-9pm daily. Winter 9am-6pm daily.*
Outdoor classical concerts are held in summer on the grounds of the Loire-style *château*; there's also a lake to walk around, formal gardens to admire and tracks to cycle. The estate was the folly of the Marquis de Béthune, laid out in the mid 1800s, and we have him to thank for the exotic trees and hilltop summerhouse.

Forêt de Soignes
Entrances on chaussée de la Hulpe. Tram 92/Métro Montgomery, then tram 44. **Open** *24hrs daily.*
A must in autumn for the beech trees, and in spring for the wild flowers. Only five kilometres (three miles) south-east of town, this primeval beech forest stretches 12 kilometres (7.5 miles) from the Bois de la Cambre to Waterloo and the same from La Hulpe to Tervuren. Once the hunting ground for the Dukes of Brabant, at the time of Napoleon the forest covered 12,000 hectares (29,650 acres). Now it's only a third of that, but a treat for hikers, cyclists, horse-riders and anglers.

Anderlecht & Laeken

Head further afield for the famous Atomium and an unusual beer museum.

The scruffy, run-down district of **Anderlecht**, west of the centre, is an unlikely but rewarding destination for the more adventurous visitor, while the sanitised big sights (including the Atomium) and parks of **Laeken**, a good few kilometres north of the Petit Ring, are on more conventional itineraries.

Anderlecht

Map p320

A couple of kilometres west of the Gare du Midi, Anderlecht is a poor *commune* with a growing immigrant community. It's a large district, with small, haphazardly arranged houses – there are no high-rises – and, although, on the surface, much of it doesn't look appealing, it is frequently invaded by visitors drawn by a happy juxtaposition of highbrow and lowbrow culture. 'Anderlecht' is roughly translated as 'love of Erasmus' and the house where the great humanist lived is here. The district is also home to the most popular football team in the country, RSC Anderlecht.

Most of the interesting bits – including the Parc Astrid where RSCA play – are around the St-Guidon metro station. On emerging from the station, the first thing you see, standing gracefully aloof from the standard-issue shopping arcade, is the beautiful **Collégiale des Sts Pierre et Guidon**. The architecture

is late 15th-century Gothic, and inside is a long altar illuminated by light filtering through the stained glass above. Behind it is the 17th-century *béguinage*, now a museum. (*Béguinages* were lay sisterhoods whose members lived in religious communities but were not bound by nuns' vows. Often widows or spinsters, they did charity work and existed in large numbers in the Low Countries. There are still some *béguinages* in Flanders.) Running up one side of the church is a charming lane, rue Porselein, lined with cottage-style houses, climbing plants and Jacques Prévert poems written on the wall beside Miró drawings. It ends at a good local bar, the high-windowed **Le Porcelain**.

The atmosphere of quiet sanctity is also present in the **Maison d'Erasmus** around the corner – a small, well-preserved, red-brick seat of learning set in a shady garden. Erasmus only spent five months here in 1521, but there is an impressive collection of documents, including first editions of *In Praise of Folly* and *Adages*, and letters from Charles V and Francis I. The house itself, with its Renaissance furnishings, is well worth seeing. There are portraits of Erasmus by Dürer and Holbein, and a medal by Cellini.

Five minutes' walk south-west from the church in the pleasant and hilly **Parc Astrid**, announced by its proud purple-and-white flag, is the **Stade Constant Vanden Stock**,

The Grand Palais in the **Parc des Expositions**. See p93.

home of Anderlecht football club (*see p206*). The football bars lining avenue Théo Verbeeck are packed on match days.

Back east, towards the seedy Gare du Midi area, there are other pockets of interest: a canal (with occasional urban boat excursions) and industrial-looking 19th-century abattoirs and markets. *See also p163* **Trading places**. South of here, off rue Emile Carpentier, is the moving **Monument aux Martyrs Juifs**; on its side are imprinted the names of 23,838 men, women and children who were taken from Mechelen between August 1942 and July 1944 and sent to concentration camps. Not one survived.

Finally, Anderlecht boasts a couple of good museums. On dreary rue Gheude is the great **Musée Bruxellois de la Gueuze** (*see p94* **Strange brew**), the last Bruxellois brewer of the naturally fermented beer. A five-minute walk away is the small **Musée de la Résistance**, presenting some of the secret history of Belgium's World War II experience.

Collégiale des Sts Pierre et Guidon

place de la Vaillance (02 523 02 20). Métro St-Guidon/tram 56/bus 47, 49. **Open** 2-5pm Mon-Fri; by appointment Sat. **Admission** free.

Maison d'Erasmus

11 rue de Chapitre (02 521 13 83). Métro St-Guidon/ tram 56/bus 47, 49. **Open** 10am-noon, 2-5pm Mon, Wed, Thur, Sat, Sun. **Admission** €1.30. **No credit cards.**

Musée de la Résistance

14 rue Van Lint (02 522 40 41). Métro Clemenceau or Gare du Midi/tram 56/bus 47. **Open** 9am-noon, 1-4pm Mon, Tue, Thur-Fri. **Admission** free.

Laeken

Map p326

In many ways Laeken, stretching over a huge area some distance north of the centre, should be a major stop on any tourist itinerary. Yet it always seems like an unreal, artificial city hovering outside Brussels proper. Its giant amusement park, brimming with treasures that are constantly updated and expanded, efficiently streamlines the populace's leisure time. But it's like a bland committee's idea of what humans require for time out. It's easy to resent the efficiency of the Kinepolis's endless screens (*see p183* **Belgian Bert's Hollywood smash**) and the tackiness of the miniature village of **Mini-Europe**.

Still, it's not without a certain fascination. Take the metro or, better, the 18, 19, 81 or 91 tram, to Heysel. Here you'll find the infamous stadium, renamed the **Stade Roi Baudouin** (*see p204*), where 39 people died in 1985 before the Liverpool vs Juventus European Cup Final

A street corner in **Anderlecht**.

when violence led to the collapse of a wall. Next door is the immense **Parc des Expositions**. Eleven palaces were built here, the first in 1935 to commemorate a century of Belgian independence. They offer a suitable venue for trade fairs – Brussels is a major conference city. The largest, the Grand Palais built by Van Neck, is a triangular composition with ever-decreasing pavilions flanking the imposing, four-columned centre building.

Directly down the wide boulevard du Centenaire from here is the iconic **Atomium**. From the outside it certainly impresses; it's a 102-metre (335-foot) representation of the nine atoms of a molecule in steel and aluminium. Designed by André Waterkeyn for the 1958 International Exhibition, it has a certain dated space-age feel to it. The trouble is, much like space, there's not much to do once you're up there. A lift takes you the 92 metres (302 feet) to the top for somewhat murky views through the often rather grubby windows. You then descend to the middle sphere where there are occasional exhibitions. Escalators bring you back down to earth via the Atomium's spokes, seemingly plastered with bacofoil.

Close to the foot is the purpose-built entertainment complex known as **Bruparck** (*see p173*). It's all rather tacky but can be fun for families. Kitsch **Mini-Europe** shows famous buildings from member countries over 2.5 hectares (six acres). The models are exact copies, on a scale of 1:25, and include household names such as the Acropolis, the Brandenburg Gate and, er, the church at Ootmarsum in the Netherlands. Similarly shrunk cars, buses and trains speed along the roads and under the tunnels. Press a button to hear the relevant national anthem, or to make Vesuvius erupt and the ground shake. It's all a bit lame, but can make for some quirky holiday snaps.

More fun is the neighbouring **Océade** water park with its pools, slides and other aquatic attractions. On fine summer days it can get uncomfortably packed. The complex also features the **Kinepolis** multi-screen cinema (*see p182*).

If you're pining for attractions of a rather less relentless man-made nature, head south to the huge **Parc du Laeken**. The centrepiece of the park is the **Château Royal**, the favoured residence of the Belgian royal family. It was built in 1782-4, though subsequently rebuilt with neo-classical façades. It was here that Napoleon started planning his catastrophic invasion of Russia. The public are granted periodic admittance (*see p168* **Royal Brussels**) to the **Serres Royales**, north of the palace. This magnificent sequence of 11 linked greenhouses was built on the orders of Léopold II by Balat and the young Victor Horta in the 1870s.

Just north of here are a couple of other, unexpectedly oriental, attractions. The fanciful red tower of the **Tour Japonaise** and, across avenue Jules Van Praet, the **Pavillon Chinois**, were designed by Marcel for Léopold II, after an inspirational visit to the 1900 Paris Exhibition. They were respectively made by carpenters from Yokohama and Shanghai; the tower was an important landmark in the early days of aviation. Standing incongruously but graciously between solid Belgian trees, each is now fully restored and open to public scrutiny.

Ten minutes' walk south of the Château Royal is **Notre Dame de Laeken**, the burial place of Belgium's kings and queens. Although opening times are severely restricted, the huge, neo-Gothic exterior, designed by Poelaert in 1851, is worth a look. In the cemetery behind are tombs of important Belgians – including Poelaert himself – and a cast of Rodin's sculpture *The Thinker*. There are also a couple of incongruities: a mosque and an Egyptian temple. Look out also for the wonderful 13th-century madonna on the altar.

Atomium

boulevard du Centenaire, Laeken (02 474 89 77/ www.atomium.be). Métro Heysel/tram 23, 81/bus 84, 89. **Open** *Apr-Aug* 9am-8pm daily. *Sept-Mar* 10am-6pm daily. **Admission** €5.45; €3.97 concessions. **Credit** AmEx, MC, V. **Map** p326 B2.

Notre Dame de Laeken

parvis Notre Dame (02 478 20 95). Tram 81/ bus 53. **Open** 2-5pm Tue-Sun. **Admission** free. **Map** p326 E3.

Pavillon Chinois

44 avenue Jules Van Praet (02 268 16 08). Tram 23, 52, 92. **Open** 10am-4.45pm Tue-Sun. **Admission** €2; €3 combined tour with Tour Japonaise. **No credit cards. Map** p326 D1.

Tour Japonaise

44 avenue Jules Van Praet (02 268 16 08). Tram 23, 52, 92. **Open** 10am-4.45pm Tue-Sun. **Admission** €2; €3 combined tour with Pavillon Chinois. **No credit cards. Map** p326 D1.

Strange brew

Walking around sombre Anderlecht, you may wonder: what, football club arguably excepted, does this area have to offer humanity?

Your answer, my friend, is indeed blowing in the wind. For the air of Anderlecht is responsible for the most mysterious and natural of all of Belgium's myriad beers: *gueuze*. Gueuze is the world's only spontaneously fermented beer. And its acme, its Dom Pérignon, its Château Latour Pauillac Impérial, is Gueuze Cantillon. Like many Belgian specialities, Cantillon Gueuze is better appreciated elsewhere. In Brussels, eight bars stock this authentic brew. In Helsinki, there are 12.

A hundred years ago, Brussels boasted some 80 *gueuze* breweries. Now, fittingly, the last surviving one in the capital, Cantillon, festers away in Anderlecht. Fittingly, because the brewery only makes *gueuze* between October and May, picking around a dozen days when they feel the fermentation has a chance of working well. Anderlecht's settled but gloomy climate suits the fermentation process perfectly.

It starts with the grinding of 1,450 kilograms of wheat and 850 kilograms of barley. This is mixed with 10,500 kilograms of water and heated to 72°C for two and a half hours, after which it is drained. It is then boiled so that the water evaporates, and is left to cool in a wide, shallow copper container, allowing a large surface area to be exposed to the air. The liquid is emptied into oak barrels, which have been cleaned in a way that manages to preserve the organic particles. With any luck, after three days the liquid starts to

Jette & Koekelberg

The large, anonymous *commune* of Jette borders Laeken to the west. Its very anonymity made it the perfect home for that most respectable and bourgeois of Surrealists, René Magritte. The house where he lived with his wife and muse Georgette between 1930 and 1954 opened as the **Musée Magritte** in 1999, and is an essential stop for anyone with more than a passing interest in the artist (*see p186* **Hats off to Brussels**). The Magrittes lived only on the ground floor (although they also used the garret; the first and second floors were occupied by others),

react to microbes – from the barrels, the brewery's wooden beams and the Anderlecht air that is deliberately let in through vents in the roof – and ferment. The result of this is a *lambic*, a flat beer that can be drunk young or old – many village cafés in the Pajottenland area west of Brussels serve it.

But the best is yet to come. A couple of months later, the *lambic* starts to foam. And a couple of years after that, the master brewer will blend together *lambics* from a selection of barrels – each brew creates a slightly different tasting *lambic* – to create a *gueuze*. There is no recipe for it: he just uses his instincts and experience, assessing the appointed hour with a wettened finger in the open air. It's not just a long process – it's also risky. Unlike most beers, *gueuze* has no sugar and no added yeast. 'We could

add yeast like the other brewers do,' says Jacques Vanhaerbeke, who gives guided tours of Cantillon Brewery. 'That way, the fermentation process will be guaranteed to work. But we do it naturally.'

Attached to the brewery is a museum, where you can have a tasting after your tour. So what's it like? Sweet, sour, a little metallic, almost like fizzy cider... 'Not everyone likes it,' Vanhaerbeke says, 'but those who do, love it.' Cantillon's staff are passionate about their slice of heritage. Keeping the building from falling into irreversible disrepair is a costly business, but the company refuses to modernise. 'If we did that,' says Vanhaerbeke, 'we'd be just like all the others.' Plus, as Vanhaerbeke will well know, you should never keep a Finn thirsty.

The following Brussels bars stock Cantillon *gueuze*: **Chez Marcel**, 20 place du Jeu de Balle, Marolles (02 511 13 75); **L'Etoile d'Or**, 30 rue des Foulons, Lower Town (02 502 60 48); **In 't Spinnekopke** (*see p105*); **Toone** (*see p127*); **Poechenelle Kelder**, 5 rue du Chêne, Lower Town (02 511 92 62); **De Ultieme Hallucinatie** (*see p137*); **La Villette**, 3 rue du Vieux Marché aux Grains, Lower Town (02 512 75 50); **Zageman**, 116 avenue de Laeken, Jette (02 219 50 65).

Cantillon Brewery & Musée Bruxellois de la Gueuze

56 rue Gheude, Anderlecht (02 521 49 28/ www.cantillon.be). Métro Clemenceau or Gare du Midi/tram 18, 23, 52, 55, 56, 81, 82, 90/bus 20, 47, 49, 50. **Open** 9am-5pm Mon-Fri; 10am-5pm Sat. Last entry 4pm. **Admission** €5; €2.50 concessions. **No credit cards. Map** p320 A4.

and it has been restored to as authentic a condition as possible. The window and fireplace in the front room appear in numerous Magritte paintings, but perhaps the most surprising discovery is the tiny back living room where the painter entertained and executed hundreds of his works, despite the lack of light due to the tall wall outside the window. Magritte did actually build himself a studio in the garden but never used it, preferring the comfort of the house. The first and second floors are now taken up with an excellent display of letters, photos and other personal artefacts, together with a smattering of original works by Magritte and his circle.

The tiny bordering *commune* of Koekelberg houses Brussels' most bizarre and overblown church: the **Basilique du Sacré Coeur**. Commissioned by Léopold II in 1905, this vast structure, an ugly mix of Gothic and art deco with a lit-up cherry-coloured crucifix on top, took nearly seven decades to finish. Fantastic panoramic view from the dome, though.

Basilique du Sacré Coeur

1 parvis de la Basilique (02 425 88 22). Métro Simonis then tram 19. **Open** *Church: Summer* 8am-6pm daily. *Winter* 10am-5pm daily. *Dome: Summer* 9am-5pm daily. *Winter* 9am-4pm daily. **Admission** *Church* free. *Dome* €2.48. **No credit cards.**

St-Josse & Schaerbeek

There are a few gems to seek out in the poorer northern *communes*.

Sightseeing

The huge grey expanse of **Schaerbeek** stretches across northern Brussels, its southern edge bordering the tiny *commune* of **St-Josse**, which hugs the north-east portion of the Petit Ring. Only a small sign tells you that you have officially crossed from one district to the other. Apart from a few sights, neither are on the tourist trail, but each has its own attractions.

Schaerbeek

Map p322

Before the construction of the Gare du Nord in 1841, Schaerbeek was a bucolic idyll of cherry orchards, family-run bakeries and breweries. The *commune* grew with the new Belgian state. At independence in 1830 there were 1,600 people living here; by 1900 there were 65,000, travelling to work down busy boulevards, with trams rattling past grand houses, many built in art nouveau style for the new bourgeoisie. Such visible grandeur had faded to blandness by the time the prodigal son of Schaerbeek, *chanteur* **Jacques Brel** (*see below* **The troubadour returns**), grew up there.

Modern times have left Schaerbeek behind. The population is now for the most part North African and Turkish. The area on the west of rue Royale, around the Gare du Nord, once infamous as Brussels' red-light district, now contains high-rise office blocks. Without its own metro station, Schaerbeek is a visibly poor *commune* – bad street lighting, erratic refuse collection and no glamorous shops – but don't let that put you off. It's a vast *commune* but you don't have to see all of it. Jump on the 92 or 93 tram and make for the Hôtel Communal in place Colignon (alight at rue Verwée).

This is the heart of Schaerbeek. It is all built on a rather grandiose scale, with long avenues sweeping down to monumental buildings and churches overlooking the city. The **Hôtel Communal** itself is a mighty work, inaugurated in 1887 by Léopold II. Badly damaged by fire at the beginning of the century, the Flemish Renaissance-style building is constructed from red brick, with numerous towers and windows.

Place Colignon was constructed around the Hôtel, its houses equally grand, with gables, turrets and flagpoles. Down rue Royale Ste-Marie from the square is the large, beautiful,

The troubadour returns

Gloomy singing star Jacques Brel is one of the most famous French pop icons of the post-war era. After rising to stardom in Paris in the late 1950s, his great hits – including the all-time weepie 'Ne Me Quitte Pas' and the sordid Amsterdam – were covered by artists across the French-speaking world. David Bowie even tried one. In his own way, Brel was as big as Gainsbourg. He toured the globe as a French singer, called his daughter France, and died outside Paris in 1978.

But Brel was a Bruxellois. And 25 years after his death, and the hitherto underwhelming local acknowledgement of his achievements – a desolate metro station and a small foundation tucked in behind place St-Jean – Brussels wants him back. As if raised from the dead, the prodigal son will return – reinstated and rehabilitated. Come 2003, you won't be able to walk around

Brussels without Brel. Guided tours, open-air screenings of old concert footage, posters, exhibitions, the works. 2003 will be the Year of Brel. It's official. Check out **www. brel-2003.be** if you don't believe us.

Jacques Brel was born to Flemish-speaking parents in 1929 in Schaerbeek, at 138 avenue du Diamant, where a poetic plaque now stands. '*Il a chanté le plat pays…*' it begins, recounting Brel's bitter-sweet homage to his flat homeland of Belgium. His parents, Romain and Lisette, moved Jacques and brother Pierre in rented accommodation across the grey north of the city while his father climbed the ladder to eventual ownership of a cardboard factory. Another bitter-sweet Brel work, 'Les Vieux', relates parental lives and sacrifices. Eventually, in 1942, the Brels moved from 26 boulevard Belgica to their own place (with garage and

The lovely **Botanique**: originally a greenhouse, now a thriving cultural centre. *See p98*.

Sightseeing

if decaying church of **St-Servais**. It holds services in Spanish and Italian, and has a commanding view over avenue Louis Bertrand. This once grand street, its modest Saturday flea market complemented by the quaint **Musée de la Bière**, leads east to pretty Parc Josaphat.

Here you'll find ponds, an animal reserve, a sculpture museum, various sporting facilities and free concerts on summer Sundays.

Near St-Servais stand the **Halles de Schaerbeek**. A rare example of 19th-century industrial architecture, the Halles (there is a

garden!) at 7 rue Jacques Manne in sombre Anderlecht. His parents would stay in Anderlecht until their death in 1964.

Meanwhile their son had other ideas. He had begun to write songs, poignant ones, angry ones, tender ones, trying them out to modest audiences shortly after the war. In Brussels he received polite applause. In Flanders they pelted him with tomatoes. He would work in Brussels. Hanging out at all the right places – classy haunts such as **Restaurant Vincent** (*see p103*), **A La Mort Subite** (*see p124*), the **Café Métropole** (*see p122*) – he landed a prime spot at the Rose Noire cabaret, by the restaurant **Aux Armes de Bruxelles** (*see p103*), in 1952. It proved his big break.

A year later, he left for Paris, planning to make his name as a songwriter. However, it was his own performances that caught the French public's imagination, and within

►

Grande and a Petite Halle) are also a rare example of a Brussels renovation success story. Millions were spent on converting this former meat and vegetable market into a fully functioning theatre and concert hall. They were built in 1865, burned down in 1898 and then reconstructed according to the original design.

South from St-Servais, the neo-Byzantine church of **Ste-Marie** marks the border with the *commune* of St-Josse. This mosque-like building, curvaceous and arched, with an octagonal dome, looks down over Schaerbeek.

Musée de la Bière
33-35 avenue de Louis Bertrand (02 216 59 70). Tram 90, 92. **Open** 2-6pm Wed, Sat. **Admission** (with drink) €2. **No credit cards.**

St-Josse

Almost completely North African and Turkish in character, St-Josse is full of fruit shops and tiny ethnic eateries. Situated near the Petit Ring, the small community lacks the dark, seedy edge of surrounding Schaerbeek. Its main attractions are worth crossing town for: the classic art nouveau café-restaurant **De Ultieme Hallucinatie** (*see p118 and p137*) and, slightly further down rue Royale, the **Botanique** (*see p199*), an inspired mixture of neo-classicism, glass and iron, built in 1826. Formerly the city's greenhouse, it is now the cultural centre for the francophone community – with a cinema, theatre and exhibition halls – that maintains a hothouse atmosphere.

The small and sweet **Museé de la Bière**.

▶ ## The troubadour returns (continued)

a couple of years he was a star. Brel's lyrics painted vivid pictures of politics, working-class life – and the country he had left behind. In Bruxelles, he sang of men and women dancing in the city's squares: place de Brouckère and place Ste-Catherine are both name-checked, as is place St-Justine. But don't bother searching for the latter – Brel made it up to fit the rhyme. The bourgeoisie also came in for a terrible time from Brel's bitter – that word again – pen.

Occasionally, in between tours – Europe, the US, the USSR – Brel would pop back to Brussels but, ever the troubadour, would soon hotfoot it back to his cherished France. And there he died. Although he never denied his Bruxellois roots – 'everyone has to come from somewhere,' he would grunt – he hardly eulogised them either.

After years of inertia, and the growth of a cult following in the UK, his daughter France set up the **Fondation Internationale Jacques Brel**, a small museum archive, telling Brel's life story in film, photographs and jukebox bar form, on a mock stage. The metro stop nearest his parents' house, in a faceless bourgeois area of Brussels, was renamed Jacques Brel.

Brel, meanwhile, spent his last years neither in Paris nor Anderlecht, but aboard a yacht in the middle of the Pacific Ocean.

Fondation Internationale Jacques Brel
11 place de la Vieille Halle aux Blés, Lower Town (02 511 10 20/www.jacquesbrel.be). **Open** 11am-6pm Tue-Sat. **Admission** €5. **No credit cards. Map** p317 C4.

Eat, Drink, Shop

Restaurants

Belgians love their food, and it shows in the capital's excellent dining scene.

It is said that Belgians eat out more per capita than any other people else in the world. Whether or not this is true is not the point; it's the fact that locals are seen in restaurants everywhere and at any time of the day. Try to get into a popular restaurant at *midi* (the generic term for lunchtime) and a waiter's shrug of the shoulders will suggest you should have reserved. No language problems there.

This is because eating out is a national pastime. Every Belgian will rattle off four or five favourite eating places, be it a tiny *friterie* or a swanky restaurant weighed down with medals. Snob value is minimal, with the regular diner searching for honest, well-cooked food in the simplest of ambiences. If the food is good, the talk is good, and it's the buzz of contentment that creates the atmosphere. The consistently best restaurants in Brussels are those with wood-panelled walls, globe lights, rickety furniture and tiled floors. More upmarket variations on the theme

Head to **rue des Bouchers** for seafood.

may include original art nouveau or deco fittings or perhaps cloths on the table rather than paper. They come complete with swiftly efficient and sometimes brusque service. No harm is meant by this; it is a reflection of the democracy of eating, the great leveller, and even the most demanding diners will be put in their place by a steaming plate of turbot sauce mousseline.

Restaurants are everywhere in Brussels, and it is difficult to find a street in the centre without one. The restaurants around the **Grand' Place** attract tourists, sure, but this does not make them average or avoidable, and you are just as likely to find Belgians tucking in. The **rue des Bouchers** area between the Place and the covered galleries is atmospheric and attractive with its displays of seafood and candlelit terraces. Just a little warning – it is not as cheap as it seems and once lured in you may be disappointed. You will not find the Bruxellois here. If they want fish, they walk over to the **Ste-Catherine** area where the restaurants are more geared to their needs. Near place **St-Géry** is a Chinatown of sorts, with Vietnamese, Thai and Chinese restaurants.

Outside of the centre, the **European Quarter**, **Ixelles** and parts of **St-Gilles** are the hotspots for fantastic family-run restaurants and their trendier cousins. The **Châtelain area**, **place Jourdan** and **chaussée de Charleroi** are alive and quite overflowing with places to eat.

PRACTICAL TIPS

Brussels is not a particularly cheap place to eat and does not adhere to the French set menu system, though some places volunteer to do so. The best bargains are at *midi*, when the majority of restaurants offer a *plat du jour*. The restaurants below are listed by area and then by cuisine. We've listed the average price of main courses and, when applicable, the cost of set menus. It's also worth bearing in mind that house wines are usually more than acceptable, although wine prices are not extortionate in European terms.

Almost all restaurants now accept credit cards, with the exception of some particularly enigmatic types who still need to feel the cash in their hands to be sure they've been paid. Bills come with service included, so there is no obligation to tip; the usual practice is to round

Comme Chez Soi: top-class chefs and three (count 'em) Michelin stars.

up or to tip if you feel you've been particularly well looked after. The top-notch lot will expect around ten per cent.

Website **www.resto.be** is the most wide-reaching in Belgium, providing details of almost every restaurant in the country. It also has links to the home pages of those restaurants that have their own websites. The search engine works in French, Dutch and English.

Grand' Place & around

Belgian & French

Les 4 Saisons

Royal Windsor Hotel, 2 rue de l'Homme Chrétien (02 505 51 00). Métro Gare Centrale. **Open** 11.30am-2.30pm, 7-10.30pm Mon-Fri. **Main courses** €30. **Credit** AmEx, DC, MC, V. **Map** p317 C3.
As the flagship restaurant of the Royal Windsor, the 4 Saisons has established itself as an important ingredient in Brussels dining circles. Evidence of this is in the clientele, a mix of hotel guests and well-heeled Belgians. It's a favourite for quiet business lunches, and the menu is affordable and well structured. The room features stained-glass panels, and it's easy to forget you're in a modern hotel building. It also has its own street entrance. But this is no corporate fix; it's luxurious, yes, but it's also top-quality French cooking and manageably elegant.

Chez Léon

18 rue des Bouchers (02 511 14 15/www.chezleon. be). Métro Gare Centrale or Pré-métro Bourse. **Open** noon-11pm daily. **Main courses** €17. **Credit** AmEx, DC, MC, V. **Map** p317 C3.

It's brash, it's busy, it's popular – but it's not particularly liked by the locals. Put it down to snobbishness, as this restaurant chain has a formulaic fast-food look and feel to it and has extended its brand across the border, particularly into France. The menu is big on mussels and has photos of what you're ordering: perfect for kids and the linguistically challenged. You won't be pampered, but the food is always high quality. And whatever the locals may think, Léon has become an important part of the Belgian food scene.

Comme Chez Soi

23 place Rouppe (02 512 29 21/www.commechez soi.be). Pré-métro Anneessens. **Open** noon-1.30pm, 7-9.15pm Tue-Sat. **Main courses** €50. **Set menu** €62-€138. **Credit** AmEx, DC, MC, V. **Map** p320 B4.
This is the top stratum of heady haute cuisine and chef Pierre Wynants is a national hero, being one of Europe's top chefs. The family has won every accolade going, including three stars from the picky Michelin people, and the food is the absolute best, of course, with such delights as pigeon stuffed with truffles. The changing set menu can make the bill a little more bearable. A veritable temple to the art of fine dining, this art nouveau-inspired townhouse is nigh on impossible to get into unless you book many weeks ahead. But that's the price you pay for eating at the top restaurant in Brussels, and arguably in Belgium.

La Maison du Cygne

9 Grand' Place, entrance at 2 rue Charles Buyl (02 511 82 44). Pré-métro Bourse. **Open** 12.30-2.30pm, 7.15-10.15pm Mon-Fri; 7.15-10pm Sat. **Main courses** €35. **Set menu** €40-€70. **Credit** AmEx, DC, MC, V. **Map** p317 C3.

Belgian cuisine

It is a predictable cliché to say that the food scene in Brussels is one great melting pot of influences and traditions. But there's no other way to describe the sheer variety of world cuisine that is available in the city, from North African kebab stalls to the finest French restaurants. Yet running through this mix is the determined and unassailable flavour of Belgium. Belgian cuisine is at the heart of it all in a way that few other countries can match.

So what exactly is Belgian food? And why is it the great pride of a tiny country? Answering the second question first, it unifies the nation. It doesn't matter whether you come from Flanders or Wallonia, the provinces of Luxembourg or the German hinterland. Appreciation of food in all its forms has been a preoccupation of the people of this corner of Europe for centuries. This is evident in Breughel's great peasant banqueting scenes, in tapestries of overflowing tables and in modern-day recipes, unchanged over the years and often using for flavouring beers that were first brewed hundreds of years ago.

Human endeavour is not the only influence. Geographical location has played its part too. The forests of the Ardennes produce the venison and boar so popular today in the *chasse* season (October to December), along with wild mushrooms such as girolles and chanterelles. The plentiful farmland sustains

husbanded meat; the famous Blanc-Bleu Belge cattle, the free-range chickens, the rabbit, chicory and asparagus, all of which form the base of Belgian cooking. Then there's the North Sea, its icy coldness just perfect for the tiny shrimps (*crevettes grises*), sole and, of course the famous oysters and mussels of Zeeland.

The former are cheap and plentiful while the latter have become ubiquitous and are freely associated with Belgium, particularly in Brussels restaurants, where they are

There can surely be no grander building or location in which to eat. Sitting right on the Grand' Place, the house has associations with Karl Marx and now wafts an authoritative, distinctly capitalist air across the square. It has the feel of a gentlemen's club, and the rich French food, liberally sprinkled with truffles and caviar, costs an arm and a leg. Only the proletariat with expense accounts can afford to visit, though the set menus make it more acceptable. For a celebration meal or an impulsive treat, it's perfect and you won't begrudge a cent once you see the view and experience the cushioned luxury that's on offer.

L'Ogenblik

1 galerie des Princes (02 511 61 51). Métro Gare Centrale. **Open** noon-2.30pm, 7pm-midnight Mon-Sat. **Main courses** €25. **Set menu** €50. **Credit** AmEx, DC, MC, V. **Map** p317 C3.
Set in the glamorous covered galerie des Princes, this has fast become one of the top trendy places. The interior is nothing new – natural materials mixed with industrial lighting – while the menu is classic

French with a modern twist. And fantastically worthwhile it is too, though the restaurant's name lives up to its promise by emptying your wallet in the blink of an eye.

La Roue d'Or

26 rue des Chapeliers (02 514 25 54). Pré-métro Bourse. **Open** noon-12.30am daily. **Main courses** €17. **Credit** AmEx, DC, MC, V. **Map** p317 C3.
The Golden Wheel takes its name from the gold motif at the heart of a wide stained-glass window above the kitchen. Despite being one minute from the touristy Grand' Place, this brasserie has won the hearts of Belgians for its absolutely authentic food at authentic prices. The menu is not recommended for vegetarians. There is no political correctness about this Magritte-inspired place. Lamb's tongue, pig's trotter and chitterling sausage sit comfortably with oysters and finely prepared fish. And if all this makes you a little nervous, this is one of the few Belgian restaurants where you can ask for a menu in English. Just to be sure.

served in steaming cauldrons with a bowl of *frites* and chunks of bread to mop up the juices. Other world-famous dishes such as *carbonnades* of beef cooked in dark Belgian beer remain part of the culture of childhood memory, along with *stoemp*, the bubble-and-squeak-like mixture of mashed potato and vegetables served with sausage or slabs of hot ham (for this and other quintessential examples of Belgian food, *see p114* **Top ten local dishes**).

Street food is endemic in Brussels. People eat in public with no concern for the safety of others. Sandwiches on the metro, waffles on the high street or boiled whelks from Chez Jef & Fils on the square opposite the Bourse. Madame will serve you in her house coat and be happy that you are happy.

French influences have inevitably crept to Brussels, though the connoisseurs will be quick to tell you that it's just that, an influence; a mere variation on the much-loved theme of home cooking. The French begrudgingly admit that Belgian food is almost as good as theirs. But Belgium believes otherwise. This from an official tourist authority guide for American visitors: 'All Belgian food is, of course, delicious and portions are huge, so try to save room for dessert. After all, you can always go on a diet in Paris.'

'T Kelderkerke

15 Grand' Place (02 513 73 44). Pré-métro Bourse. **Open** noon-2am daily. **Main courses** €11. **Credit** AmEx, DC, MC, V. **Map** p317 C3.
If you like buzz, if you like brushing elbows with your neighbours, if you don't mind smoke swirling around, you'll love this Grand' Place restaurant. It's located in a basement, down a steep set of stairs from the square; once in, you will be in a surprisingly Belgian environment for such a touristy area. This is reflected in the menu as well as the decor, with tables ranged in long rows. Honest Belgian food at honest prices, smack in the centre of town. What more could you ask for?

La Taverne du Passage

30 galerie de la Reine (02 512 37 32/www.tavernedu passage.com). Métro Gare Centrale. **Open** noon-midnight daily. **Main courses** €18. **Credit** AmEx, DC, MC, V. **Map** p317 C3.
Think time warp for this restaurant. It's a perfectly preserved reminder of the 1920s where the gold-epauletted, white-jacketed waiters serve traditional

Belgian food with a traditional efficient brusqueness in a room reeking of red. All the classic dishes are here; if you want to try a slice of real Bruxellois dining, this is the place. Since it is in the covered galleries the 'outside' terrace keeps you protected come rain or shine.

Fish & seafood

Aux Armes de Bruxelles

13 rue des Bouchers (02 511 21 18/www.arme brux.be). Métro Gare Centrale or Pré-métro Bourse. **Open** noon-11.15pm Tue-Sun. **Main courses** €20. **Set menus** €28.50-€33. **Credit** AmEx, DC, MC, V. **Map** p317 C3.
Sitting rather grandly in the theme park of fish restaurants near the Grand' Place, Aux Armes is a veritable institution beloved by business folk and middle-aged, middle-class Belgians. It's got a wide range of classics on the menu, and is renowned for its perfect mussels and chips. With its art deco interior, busy clatter of plates and buzzy talk, you could be forgiven for thinking you were in a Parisian brasserie. You'll pay a little more, but you pay for quality and a slice of the good life. Booking essential.

Restaurant Vincent

8-10 rue des Dominicains (02 511 26 07/ www.restaurantvincent.com). Métro/Pré-métro De Brouckère. **Open** noon-2.45pm, 6.30-11.30pm Mon-Fri; noon-3pm, 6.30-10.30pm Sat, Sun. **Main courses** €19. **Credit** AmEx, DC, MC, V. **Map** p317 C3.
You would usually be advised to avoid the formula restaurants in the rue des Bouchers area, but Vincent, founded in 1905, is something different. For a start, you make your entrance through the bustling kitchen. The brigade of waiters, all men, all dressed in white and gold braid, treat you with professional respect. The main room (ask for the *salle carellée*) is exquisitely tiled, with tables shaped like fishing smacks. But this is no theme restaurant; it offers serious Brussels cuisine and is as close as you can get to the traditional Bruxellois experience.

Sea Grill

Radisson SAS Hotel, 47 rue du Fossé aux Loups (02 227 31 20). Métro/Pré-métro De Brouckère. **Open** noon-2pm, 7-10pm Mon-Fri; 7-10pm Sat. **Main courses** €40. **Set menus** €49-€72. **Credit** AmEx, DC, MC, V. **Map** p317 C2.
Regarded by many as the top seafood restaurant in Belgium and as such is suitably expensive. Chef Yves Mattagne has won a chestful of gongs for his innovative style, which uses traditional French preparation in an utterly modern way. The restaurant is buried deep inside a five-star hotel (*see p41*), so the entrance to it is rather corporate. Once inside, however, you sit in pure luxury, surrounded by specially commissioned panels with etched glass designs of fjords. Also look out for the 40kg lobster press designed by Christoffle, one of only three in the world. Watching it in action may make you decide to have the bisque. Or not.

Eat, Drink, Shop

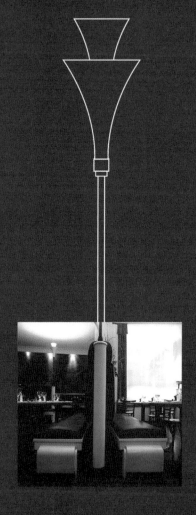

LE FILS DE JULES
RÉSOLUMENT BASQUE ET LANDAIS

Italian

Rugantino

184 boulevard Anspach (02 511 21 95). Pré-métro Bourse. **Open** noon-3pm, 6.30pm-midnight Mon-Fri; 6.30pm-midnight Sat. **Main courses** €10. **Credit** AmEx, MC, V. **Map** p317 B3.

An art deco emporium of traditional Italian food, right in the centre of Brussels' nightlife district. There's a safe menu of pastas, pizzas and meats – but this is the kind of place you go to because you know exactly what you want and what you'll get, so there's rarely disappointment. The waiters dash around amiably, though they get more serious as it fills up – and fill it does, thanks to the keen prices and the fact that it's become one of the great early-evening meeting places.

Japanese

Samourai

28 rue du Fossé aux Loups (02 217 56 39). Métro/ Pré-métro De Brouckère. **Open** noon-2pm, 7-9pm Mon, Wed-Sat; 7-9pm Sun. **Main courses** €35. **Credit** AmEx, DC, MC, V. **Map** p317 C2.

It's not easy to find this place; it's not directly on the street and you need to enter a quiet arcade to find the front door. The first room is tiny, with a bar jammed into it, but small stairs lead up through the labyrinth of rooms, all stacked higgledy-piggledy together. For lovers of Japanese food, you can do no better. This is the most serious of serious, with fully trained Japanese chefs to do your bidding on the sushi and sashimi. So renowned is it that Japanese tourists come here by the busload. The wines are incomprehensibly expensive, so stick to the sake.

Ste-Catherine & St-Géry

Belgian & French

L'Achepot

1 place Ste-Catherine (02 511 62 21). Métro Ste-Catherine. **Open** 11am-midnight Mon-Sat. *Food served* noon-3pm, 6.30-10.30pm Mon-Sat. **Main courses** €12. **No credit cards**. **Map** p317 B2.

A distinctive little diner with a tiny downstairs room and plate-glass frontage. Always busy, it serves a modest range of skilfully cooked pastas and Belgian favourites, including perfectly pink lamb kidneys in mustard and braised chicory, all caramelised and sticky. It's a decent little bar too, and a great place to drop in for a beer. In summer it joins with its neighbours and has a terrace at the front, which is big on atmosphere but small on size and packed solid, so arrive early.

In 't Spinnekopke

1 place du Jardin aux Fleurs (02 511 86 95). Pré-métro Bourse. **Open** noon-3pm, 6-11pm Mon-Thur; noon-3pm, 6pm-midnight Fri; 6pm-

Aux Armes de Bruxelles. *See p103.*

midnight Sat. **Main courses** €20. **Credit** AmEx, DC, MC, V. **Map** p318 B3.

The first thing that strikes you about this Flemish restaurant is the charm of the building itself. It's a gem of a 17th-century cottage, which would look more at home in a country lane rather than the centre of a bustling city. It also gives a clue to how the *quartier* would have looked in another age. Still, the square has been sympathetically refurbished, making the outside terrace a more appealing prospect. Classic rich food, such as rabbit in sour fruit beer, gives the place a seductive, heavy-portioned edge. The name means spider's head, by the way.

Eastern European

Les Ateliers de la Grande Ile

33 rue de la Grande Ile (02 512 81 90). Pré-métro Bourse. **Open** 8pm-1.30am Tue-Sat. **Main courses** €15-€25 **Credit** AmEx, DC, V. **Map** p318 B3.

Raucous Russian restaurant set in a 19th-century foundry, on a narrow street leading off place St-Géry. In operation since 1985, Les Ateliers features small ramshackle rooms connecting with one another, which fill with the frantic communal squeek of Gypsy and Slav violinists on a Saturday night. Hearty Russian fare – blinis, chicken shashlik, borscht – is complemented by a dangerously expansive choice of vodkas. Quiet conversation a no go.

Eat, Drink, Shop

L'Achepot: good food, nice bar. *See p105.*

Fish & seafood

Bij den Boer
60 quai aux Briques (02 512 61 22). Métro Ste-Catherine. **Open** noon-2.30pm, 6-10.30pm Mon-Sat. **Main courses** €12-€15. **Set menu** €20. **Credit** AmEx, DC, MC, V. **Map** p318 B2.
Located in the heart of the fish restaurant district, this typical bistro is always packed with customers of all ages and backgrounds. No pretension, no skimping on portions and no-nonsense service make this a great experience. It's famous for its mussels and bouillabaisse, and prices are reasonable, with a great-value four-course menu. Don't confuse informality with rudeness. You may think the food is thrown at you; rather it is placed unceremoniously on the table so you can heartily tuck in. Stay with the ethos, make no fuss and enjoy.

Jacques
44 quai au Briques (02 513 27 62). Métro Ste-Catherine. **Open** noon-2.30pm, 6.30-10.30pm Mon-Sat. **Main courses** €20. **Credit** AmEx, DC, MC, V. **Map** p318 B2.
A real favourite with locals, Jacques oozes traditional Belgian charm, especially in summer when the huge windows are open and the restaurant meets the street. An old-fashioned, wood-panelled interior and tiled floors give the place its atmosphere, along with the diners who tuck in happily. Try a simple sole fried in butter or a thick slice of

turbot with mousseline sauce. Wines can be pricey, but the house white is a perfectly decent Alsace. Booking is essential.

Le Loup-Galant
4 quai aux Barques (02 219 99 88). Métro Ste-Catherine. **Open** noon-2.30pm, 6.30-10.30pm Tue-Fri; 6.30-10.30pm Sat. **Main courses** €20. **Credit** AmEx, DC, MC, V. **Map** p318 B2.
Tucked at the end of the swath of fish restaurants in Ste-Catherine, this smart little restaurant sits in an original 17th-century house. There's plenty of space for the large tables, while in summer a brick-walled terrace makes for perfect outdoor eating. The menu is short, but full of imaginative fish and seafood based along traditional French lines. The bouillabaisse is the star turn, coming as it does in two portions, each with different varieties of fish. It's a little on the expensive side, but this restaurant is perfect for a tête-à-tête about business or love.

Le Pré Salé
20 rue de Flandre (02 513 65 45). Métro Ste-Catherine. **Open** noon-2pm, 7-10.30pm Wed-Sun. **Main courses** €18. **Credit** AmEx, MC, V. **Map** p318 A/B2.
For a flavour of Brussels at flavoursome prices, Le Pré Salé is a perfect choice. This family-run restaurant has a dedicated crowd of diners, mainly Belgian, who come here for the freshest fish, golden mussels and great chunks of meat. The white-tiled dining room leads directly to the open kitchen, where you can see *madame* preparing your food to order. Friday nights become a bit of a party once the service is finished and the staff join their customers and friends for a French *chanson*, some holiday camp entertainment and a bit of '70s disco.

Vismet
23 place Ste-Catherine (02 218 85 45). Métro Ste-Catherine. **Open** noon-2.30pm, 7-11.30pm Tue-Sat. **Main courses** €15. **Credit** AmEx, MC, V. **Map** p317 B1.
This relative newcomer to Ste-Catherine has provided fresh competition for some of its stuffier neighbours. For a start, the design is industrial minimalist, which sits rather well in the red-brick 17th-century house. Then there's the chef, Tom Decroos, who received his training under Mattagne at the award-winning Sea Grill (*see p103*). An open kitchen allows you to see the work at hand; what comes out of it is fish prepared à la chic bistro, stylish, modern and fresh from Brittany twice weekly. Vismet attracts a young professional crowd who know exactly what they want. Service can be slow.

Le Vistro
16 quai aux Briques (02 512 41 81). Métro Ste-Catherine. **Open** noon-2.30pm, 6.30pm-midnight Mon-Fri; 6.30pm-midnight Sat. **Main courses** €25. **Credit** AmEx, DC, MC, V. **Map** p318 B2.
Blink and you'll miss it. Le Vistro is a tiny restaurant among a terrace of bigger neighbours. Inside it's cosy, all raw brick, wooden tables and chairs; in

summer, there's a canopied al fresco area across the road. What makes this different from the rest of the Ste-Catherine set is its lack of lobster and its abundance of seafood platters. Come here if you want to sit around a vast tray of oysters, mussels, prawns, crab and all those little seafoody things you need a pin for. It's all opened fresh, so be prepared to wait. Wine can be served by the *pot*, a Lyonnaise-style bottle filled from the tap.

Greek

Strofilia
11 rue du Marché aux Porcs (02 512 32 93).
Métro Ste-Catherine. **Open** 7pm-midnight Mon-Thur; 7pm-1am Fri, Sat. **Main courses** €15.
Credit AmEx, DC, MC, V. **Map** p318 B2
The location of this Greek restaurant is stunning, in an old converted warehouse-cum-market. The soaring ceilings and distressed walls give the feel of a New York loft. Downstairs, an arched and vaulted brick cellar, now a bar, offers romantic candlelight and overstuffed sofas; it's here that the fine selection of Greek wine is stored behind iron gates. Strofilia is a caring place that appeals to a varied clientele, from young and hip to older and ambassadorial.

Indian

Shamrock
27 rue Jules van Praet (02 511 49 89). Pré-métro
Bourse. **Open** 7-10.30pm Tue-Sun. **Main courses**
€9. **No credit cards.** **Map** p317 B3.
You could be forgiven for walking past this dingy-looking place, especially as it's lodged among the gaudy bright lights of the St-Géry Chinatown. The interior is no more inspiring, but the Shamrock's draw is the authentic Indian food (despite the name!) and the friendly atmosphere created by the family

who runs it. Each dish on the extensive menu can be ordered to your preferred chilli quotient. Prices are pleasingly low, but the portions tend to be small, so order well. The boss man sits behind the bar smoking, the sons cook in the back, the wives and daughters serve up front and in among it all are the kids with their toys. Go with the flow.

Middle Eastern & North African

Kasbah
20 rue Antoine Dansaert (02 502 40 26). Pré-métro
Bourse. **Open** noon-2.30pm, 7-11pm Mon-Fri; 7-11pm
Sat. **Main courses** €20. **Credit** AmEx, MC, V.
Map p318 B3.
Another Fred Nicolay success story, this Middle Eastern restaurant hits you between the eyes even before you enter. From the street, barrow-loads of oranges are arranged in the window and, beyond, a sea of Moroccan lanterns hangs from the ceiling in multicoloured waves. The experience continues with the food; couscous and tagines are just a sample of the wide range on offer, with ample mezes for starters or to share with friends as a main course. It's always busy, so make sure you book.

Modern European

Bonsoir Clara
22-26 rue Antoine Dansaert (02 502 09 90).
Pré-métro Bourse. **Open** noon-2.30pm, 7-11.30pm
Mon-Thur; noon-2.30pm, 7pm-midnight Fri;
7pm-midnight Sat. **Main courses** €15. **Credit**
AmEx, MC, V. **Map** p318 B3.
This is the restaurant that started it all off for entrepeneur Fred Nicolay, who now owns a large chunk of bars and restaurants around Antoine Dansaert. Zinc table tops, bare brick and theatrical lighting make this a place to see and be seen. The menu is

The chefs work their magic at Flemish specialist **In 't Spinnekopke**. *See p105*.

Eat, Drink, Shop

Lunch 3 services : 19 €
Menus surprises - 3 à 6 choix : de 24.66 à 49.55 €

Restaurant **Tour D'y Voir** *- Place du Grand Sablon, 8/9 bte 6*
Bruxelles 1000 - Tél: 02/511.40.43 - Fax: 02/511.00.78
tourdyvoir@skynet.be - www.tourdyvoir.com - 90 couverts - Fermé le lundi.

modern European with lots of carpaccio of this and griddled that, all topped with lashings of first-press virgin olive oil. There's a reasonable choice for vegetarians. Clara is one of Brussels' trendy institutions, and will satisfy even the fussiest diner. Do make sure you wear this year's black.

Vietnamese

Da Kao
38 rue Antoine Dansaert (02 512 67 16). *Pré-métro Bourse.* **Open** noon-3pm, 6pm-midnight daily. **Main courses** €5-€10. **No credit cards.** **Map** p318 B3.
Looking a little out of place on this designer-boutique-strewn street in the city centre (and right next door to the rather plush Bonsoir Clara – *see p107*), this Vietnamese restaurant is a treat: great food at some of the city's lowest prices. It's so cheap that many people make the mistake of ordering multiple dishes, but one is more than enough (especially if it's a noodle dish). Don't expect to be treated with kid gloves, nor to have a long and leisurely meal – there are plenty of others waiting to take your place.

Thiên
12 rue Van Artevelde (02 511 34 80). Pré-metro Bourse. **Open** noon-3pm, 6-11pm Mon, Tue, Thur-Sun. **Main courses** €10. **Credit** AmEx, MC, V. **Map** p318 B3.
First impression of this Vietnamese restaurant is that it's a wooden-tabled caff incongruously set in a jungle of kitsch artefacts from the Far East, including the obligatory fluoro waterfall and red-tasselled lanterns. Despite this outlandish decoration, it is too self-effacing for its own good. It calls itself a snack-resto, but is so much more than that. Great steaming bowls of hot chilli soup, lacquered duck, and scrunchy stir-fried vegetables sum up one of the longest menus this side of Hanoi. The food is sublime, the portions huge, concocted by the smallest chef you'll ever see. If you can – her white bobbing hat is all you glimpse above the counter-top as she shakes the wok and feeds an eager crowd single-handedly.

Marolles

Belgian & French

La Grande Porte
9 rue Notre-Seigneur (02 512 89 98). Bus 95, 96. **Open** noon-3pm, 6pm-midnight Mon-Fri; 6pm-midnight Sat. **Main courses** €12. **Credit** MC, V. **Map** p320 B4.
Walk though the big door and find yourself in a cosy room reminiscent of a Dutch brown café, with an old bar running along one wall. Turn the corner and you could be in a different country. This restaurant seems to have been stitched together from two different patterns, the modern addition being rather soulless compared with the buzz of the main room.

The best Restaurants

Best terrace
Les Petits Oignons. A lantern-lit jungle in a 17th-century walled garden. But remember, this is rainy Belgium, so the terrace is only open about two nights a year. Take the mosquito repellent. *See p110.*

Best entertainment
Le Pré Salé. On Friday nights only, they lock the kitchen, erect a stage in front of the kitchen and entertain the punters with bad drag and a disco in the old style – aka Village People. *See p106.*

Best carvery
Roue D'or. This award goes to the restaurant with the meatiest menu. Knuckles, knee-joints and feet; tongue, brain and brawn; steak, which even when ordered *bien cuît* looks like Freddie Kruger rustled it up. *See p102.*

Best fish
Jacques (*see p106*). This place must surely have someone fishing out the back. The fish sparkles on the plate and even summons up a wink before you tuck in. The **Sea Grill** (*see p103*) also qualifies, but arrange a bank loan in advance.

Best dressed
Les Salons de l'Atalaïde. An amusing pastiche or a Gothic nightmare, you decide. OTT, ostentatious and unashamedly in-yer-face. Shades of Miss Haversham before she was stood up. *See p115.*

Best buffet
Anarkali. All-Indian food and all-in wrestling as punters fight for a table. Among the best and cheapest buffet spreads this side of the subcontinent. *See p116.*

Best unpretentious
Bij den Boer. You wanna eat? Sit there. You want a menu? *Voilà.* You want the mussels? Plonk, clunk, clatter. You want the bill? Thanks, bye. Brilliant food though. *See p106.*

Wherever you sit, though, this place is great for late-night eats, with food served until the early hours. It's classic Belgian food: mussels, steaks with sauce, *stoemp, waterzooi,* all served with deep bowls of fresh *frites.* It attracts artists, actors, musicians and groups of chums who just don't want to go home.

Fast, flavoursome and fairly priced Vietnamese nosh at **Da Kao**. *See p109.*

L'Idiot du Village
19 rue Notre-Seigneur (02 502 55 82). Bus 20, 48.
Open noon-2pm, 7.15-11pm Mon-Fri. **Main courses**
€16. **Set menu** €14. **Credit** AmEx, DC, MC, V.
Map p320 B4.
A small and very popular two-room bistro, hidden
away in a side street off rue Blaes. Done out in midnight blue, the dried flowers, chandeliers and kitsch
furniture could put you off – but, along with the
wafts of herbs and garlic from chef Alain Gascoin's
kitchen, the result is endearing. An eclectic menu
also helps. Reservations essential.

Les Petits Oignons
13 rue Notre-Seigneur (02 512 47 38). Bus 95, 96.
Open noon-2.30pm, 7-11pm Mon-Sat. **Main courses**
€16. **Credit** AmEx, DC, MC, V. **Map** p320 B4.
From the outside this delicate 1600s house looks as
if it could have starred in a Bruegel painting.
Walking in, you feel warm and welcomed, though
there is a strange 1970s air to it. In winter there's a
blazing log fire; in summer, a green and lantern-lit
terrace at the back. The food is unfussy French/
Belgian but cooked with finesse, arriving at the table
in invigorating portions. They sometimes ask you
to order dessert at the beginning of the meal to allow
time for preparation, which is difficult for purists,
but only goes to show that this is a restaurant that
likes to get things right.

Au Stekerlaplatte
*4 rue des Prêtres (02 512 86 81). Métro Hôtel
des Monnaies.* **Open** 7pm-1am Tue-Sun. **Main
courses** €15.50. **Set menus** €35-€42. **Credit**
MC, V. **Map** p320 B5.
This is renowned as one of Brussels' late-night
restaurants, where you can get traditional no-nonsense food at no-nonsense prices. At first glance, you

may think it full and turn to leave, but it's a warren
of rooms and corridors and there's always a table
somewhere. It's a friendly place despite its darkness
and offbeat location, though it is becoming a little
more desirable. Whatever, you'll be among a crowd
who are in the know.

Global

Bazaar
63 rue des Capucins (02 511 26 00). Bus 20, 48.
Open 7.30pm-11.30pm. **Main courses** €12-€15.
Credit DC, MC, V. **Map** p320 B5.
The most striking thing about this former monastery,
now a Moroccan/Modern European restaurant, is the
decor. After walking through an unpromising
entrance and up a shabby flight of stairs, you're faced
with a James Bond set: high ceiling, grand mirrors,
drapes and a hot-air balloon above the bar. That said,
the food's pretty seductive, too: wallow in the old
sofas as you polish off meze, couscous or ostrich
steaks. The basement bar becomes a laid-back club
on the weekends, playing reasonable dance music
until long after the kitchen closes.

Thai

Les Larmes du Tigre
*21 rue Wynants (02 512 18 77). Métro Hôtel des
Monnaies.* **Open** noon-2.30pm, 7-10.30pm Mon-
Thur; noon-2.30pm, 7-11pm Fri; 7-10.30pm Sat;
noon-3pm, 7-10pm Sun. **Main courses** €12-€20.
Credit AmEx, DC, MC, V. **Map** p320 B5.
This Thai restaurant hidden behind the Palais de
Justice is a favourite spot for political players to meet
discreetly. The bright red, black and white decor

(complete with parasols hanging from the ceiling) is a little at odds with the food on offer, which is understated – and exquisite. Despite the waitresses' occasional brusqueness, this is one of the best Asian restaurants in town.

Upper Town

Belgian & French

Le Cap Sablon

75 rue Lebeau (02 512 01 70). Métro Gare Centrale. **Open** noon-midnight daily. **Main courses** €10.50. **Set menus** €12-€17. **Credit** DC, MC, V. **Map** p317 C4.

A candlelit bistro with a slightly minimalist take on the art deco interior. Although it's located on the road leading up to chic place du Sablon, with a clientele to match, this is among the cheapest dining options in the vicinity. The menu is packed with enticing items such as salmon in lime and acacia honey. If you're here on the summer, make sure you ask for a table on the terrace.

Lola

33 place du Grand Sablon (02 514 24 60). Tram 92, 93, 94. **Open** noon-3pm, 6.30-11.30pm daily. **Main courses** €14-€22. **Credit** AmEx, MC, V. **Map** p317 C4.

Imaginative in decor and menu, Lola is also blessed with a fab location, slap among the bright lights of Sablon. Diners – professional, trendy, chatty gay/straight mix – are ushered to a swish holding bar or a long row of dark leather seating and tables. The menu offers classic French cooking with a contemporary twist. *Pomme de terre farci au canard confit*, potato stuffed with preserved duck, and *céleri rave et croquant au parmesan*, celeriac with a parmesan gallette, spring to mind as examples, the majority kind to vegetarians and indulgent to carnivores. Desserts are similarly enticing. Recommended – as is a table reservation.

Maison du Boeuf

Hotel Hilton, 38 boulevard de Waterloo (02 504 13 34). Métro Louise. **Open** 11.30am-2.30pm, 7-10.30pm daily. **Main courses** €35. **Credit** AmEx, DC, MC, V. **Map** p321 C5.

Eat, Drink, Shop

No Macs please, we're Belgian

For many of us, paradise must be Pyongyang, a city bereft of the Golden Arches. Ronald has not stamped his red-booted authority on the North Koreans, who are unaware of his authoritarian presence across the globe. To Pyongyong we can add the Philippines and, closer to home, we can at least pencil in Brussels.

One of the things that the first-time visitor often notices is the remarkable lack of MacDonalds. The main branch opposite the Bourse was burned down in strange circumstances in 2001. A polite announcement was then posted up – the kind of notice you'd read on the door of an antiquarian bookseller's – advising loyal customers to try the other two smaller branches on rue Neuve and at the Porte de Namur. True, the branch is slated to reopen in summer 2002 as part of the new Marriott Hotel building; but all the same, one big branch for a metropolitan city of one million is almost reason alone to visit.

The reason for the Macs' absence is two-fold. First, the native chip cornered the fast-food market decades ago. No anaemic floppy white fries here, no sir. The Belgians' secret is that they fry the potatoes twice, once for about five minutes at around 160°C and then, half-an-hour later, at 180°C for two minutes. This creates golden brown *frites*, crispy on the outside and soft in the middle. Belgium boasts more than 6,000 chip stands, ranging from portacabins to elaborate brick huts. The most famous in Brussels is the Maison Antoine in place Jourdan, which has been run by the DeSmet family in the same spot since 1949. An elaborate range of sauces accompanies each cone: garlic, pepper, ketchup, herbs and spices, and the omnipresent mayonnaise. But that's not all. Chips also find themselves in a variety of meats-in-baguettes: *boulettes* (random balls of meat), *brochettes*, shish kebabs and, ultimately, the *mitraillette*, the machine-gun, 30 centimetres of baguette stuffed to bursting with hamburger patties, mayonnaise, salad and onions, topped with fries.

Secondly, Belgium has its own hamburger chain, thank you very much: Quick. From their foundation in a supermarket car park outside Waterloo in 1971, Quick have gone global, despite a laughably lame red-and-white logo. There are more than 400 branches worldwide, with franchises in France (where they bought Burger King in 1997), Hungary, Slovenia and far-flung parts of the francophone world including Andorra, Guadeloupe and Réunion Island. With more vegetarian options than the *MacDo*, Quicks touch the Belgian public in a way that *MacDos* don't. *Allez les Belges!*

Deciphering the menu

Virtually all menus in Brussels are written in French, though some restaurants in the centre also have versions in Dutch and English (and even German, Italian and Spanish).

Meat (viande)

agneau lamb; **andouillette** chitterling sausage of offal; **biche** venison (doe); **bœuf** beef; **boudin noir/boudin blanc** black or white pudding; **caille** quail; **canard** duck; **confit de canard** preserved duck leg; **magret de canard** duck breast; **caneton** duckling; **cerf** venison (stag); **cervelle** brain; **cheval** horse; **chevreuil** venison; **dinde** turkey; **escargot** snail; **faisan** pheasant; **foie** liver; **gésier** gizzard; **gibier** game; **(cuisses de) grenouille** frog's legs; **jambon** ham; **jambonneau** ham (normally knuckle) on the bone; **langue** tongue; **lapin** rabbit; **lard** bacon; **lardon** small cube of bacon; **lièvre** hare; **oie** goose; **perdreau** young partridge; **perdrix** partridge; **pied** foot/trotter; **pintade/pintadeau** guinea fowl; **porc** pork; **poulet** chicken; **ris** sweetbreads; **rognon** kidney; **sanglier** boar; **saucisse** sausage; **tripes** tripe; **veau** veal; **volaille** poultry/chicken; **suprême de volaille** chicken breast. *Meat cooking terms* **bleu** all but raw; **saignant** rare (**rosé** pink, for lamb, duck, liver and kidneys); **à point** medium rare, **bien cuit** well done.

Fish & seafood (poisson & fruits de mer)

crustacé shellfish; **anguille** eel; **bar** similar to sea bass; **barbue** brill; **brochet** pike; **cabillaud** cod; **carrelet** plaice; **coquille Saint Jacques** scallop; **colin** hake; **crevette** shrimp; **crevettes grises** tiny sweet shrimps; **daurade** sea bream; **écrevisse** crayfish (freshwater); **eglefin** haddock; **espadon** swordfish; **flétan** halibut; **hareng** herring; **homard** lobster; **huître** oyster; **langoustine** Dublin Bay prawn/scampi; **limande** lemon sole; **lotte** monkfish; **loup de mer** similar to sea bass; **maquereau** mackerel; **merlin** whiting; **merlu** hake; **morue** dried salt cod; **moule** mussel; **palourde** clam; **plie** plaice; **poulpe** octopus; **raie** skate; **rouget** red mullet; **roussette** rock salmon/dogfish; **St Pierre** John Dory; **sandre** pike-perch; **saumon** salmon; **scampi** prawn; **seîche** squid; **thon** tuna; **truite** trout.

Vegetables (légumes)

ail garlic; **artichaut** artichoke; **asperge** asparagus; **aubergine** aubergine/eggplant; **betterave** beetroot; **céleri** celery; **céleri rave**
celeriac; **cèpe** cep mushroom; **champignon** mushroom; **chicon** chicory/Belgian endive; **chou** cabbage; **choucroute** sauerkraut; **chou-fleur** cauliflower; **cresson** watercress; **échalote** shallot; **épinards** spinach; **fève** broad bean/fava bean; **frisée** curly endive; **girolle** pale wild mushroom; **haricot** bean; **haricot vert** French bean; **morille** morel mushroom; **navet** turnip; **oignon** onion; **pleurotte** oyster mushroom; **poireau** leek; **poivron vert/rouge** green/red pepper/bell pepper; **pomme de terre** potato; **truffe** truffle.

Fruit (fruits)

ananas pineapple; **banane** banana; **cassis** blackcurrant; **cerise** cherry; **citron** lemon; **citron vert** lime; **fraise** strawberry; **framboise** raspberry; **griotte** morello cherry; **groseille** redcurrant; **groseille à maquereau** gooseberry; **marron** chestnut; **mûre** blackberry; **myrtille** blueberry/bilberry; **pamplemousse** grapefruit; **pêche** peach; **poire** pear; **pomme** apple; **prune** plum; **pruneau** prune; **raisin** grape.

Desserts (desserts)

chantilly whipped cream; **crème anglaise** custard; **Dame Blanche** vanilla ice-cream with hot chocolate sauce; **feuilleté** layers of puff pastry; **gâteau** cake; **glace** ice-cream; **glacé** frozen or iced; **île flottante** soft meringue floating on custard sauce; **macédoine de fruits** fruit salad; **massepain** marzipan; **mignardises** small biscuits or cakes to accompany coffee; **soufflé glacé** iced soufflé; **tarte tatin** caramelised upside-down apple cake.

Herbs & spices (herbes & épices)

aneth dill; **basilic** basil; **cannelle** cinnamon; **cerfeuil** chervil; **ciboulette** chive; **citronelle** lemongrass; **estragon** tarragon; **fenouil** fennel; **muscade** nutmeg; **persil** parsley; **romarin** rosemary; **sauge** sage; **thym** thyme.

General

amande almond; **beignet** fritter or doughnut; **beurre** butter; **chaud** warm/hot; **chèvre** goat's cheese; **cru** raw; **farci** stuffed; **frites** chips; **froid** cold; **fromage** cheese; **fumé** smoked; **gaufre** waffle; **gelée** aspic; **haché** minced; **lentille** lentil; **miel** honey; **moutarde** mustard; **noisette** hazelnut; **noix** walnut; **nouilles** noodles; **oeuf** egg; **pain** bread; **pâtes** pasta; **poivre** pepper; **potage** soup; **riz** rice; **sel** salt; **sec/sèche** dry; **sucre** sugar; **thé** tea.

One of Brussels' top restaurants, the Maison du Boeuf sits in the bland tower-block Hilton near avenue Louise. But it's not just hotel guests or business accounts who dine here; locals use it for a treat or to sample the latest expertise from long-time chef Michel Thuerel. Of course, there's more to the restaurant than beef, specialising as it does in the finest French cuisine. The signature dish is a US rib of beef roasted in a salt crust, something for which diners are prepared to travel from afar.

EU Quarter

Belgian & French

Au Charlot

1 rue Froissart (02 230 33 28). Métro Schuman. **Open** noon-7.30pm Mon-Fri. **Main courses** €12. **Set menu** €17. **Credit** AmEx, DC, MC, V. **Map** p324 F5.

The name of this brasserie is in homage to Charlie Chaplin, though, apart from the sign, there's no real hint of him within. The interior has a lived-in, flea-market feel, with wooden tables, and is relaxed and informal, despite the hordes of Euro-workers who use it at lunchtime. Slabs of steak with *sauce à choix*, mussels and great bowls of crunchy chips sum up the kitchen.

Chez Moi

66 rue du Luxembourg (02 280 26 66). Métro Trône. **Open** noon-3pm, 7-11pm Mon-Fri. **Main courses** €10-€20. **Set menus** €15-€22.50. **Credit** AmEx, DC, MC, V. **Map** p324 E5.

A great favourite in the EU Quarter. If you go at lunchtime, you can pretend to be a Eurocrat; it's full of every nationality, with English the common language. The evenings are much quieter. It's not a large restaurant, but is spread over two floors, with dark wood and whitewashed walls. The food is French with some nods in the direction of Belgium. It ranges from lentils, duck and fish steaks to a more cool-café approach, where six seared scallops with balsamic vinegar are served on a monster glass dish. The service is slick and friendly; the atmosphere buzzing with enticing overheard conversations.

Italian

Dieu des Caprices

51 rue Archimède (02 736 41 16). Métro Schuman. **Open** noon-3pm, 6.30-11pm Mon-Sat. **Main courses** €30. **Credit** AmEx, MC, V. **Map** p323 G3.

One of Brussels' oldest Italian restaurants, all muffled waiters and old-fashioned manners and comfort. You can go the whole hog here: antipasta, pasta, main course, dessert. The menu is designed for no-rush eating and encourages you to tackle the food in the French style, rather than pop in for a pizza. There are plenty such options in the area if that's what you want; save this place for a decently decadent meal with a grand choice of wines.

Chic 'n' cheerful **Le Cap Sablon**. *See p111.*

Japanese

Takesushi

21 boulevard Charlemagne (02 230 56 27). Métro Maalbeek. **Open** noon-2.30pm, 7-10.30pm Mon-Fri; 6-10.30pm Sun. **Main courses** €15-€20. **Credit** AmEx, DC, MC, V. **Map** p322 F4.

An inconspicuous restaurant serving traditional Japanese food in quiet, slightly cool surroundings. It doesn't help that there's rarely many people in here, so you feel as if you need to whisper, but the staff are also agonisingly formal. The food, while expensive, is among the best in town, with excellent teriyaki and sashimi menus.

Modern European

Balthazar

63 rue Archimède (02 742 06 00). Métro Schuman. **Open** noon-3pm, 7-10.30pm Mon-Fri; 6-11pm Sat. **Main courses** €18. **Credit** AmEx, DC, MC, V. **Map** p323 G3.

At Balthazar, East meets West via minimalist decor and food fusion. This stylish restaurant serves clean combinations of French classics jazzed up with the likes of ginger and lemongrass, and it wouldn't be out of place in California with its Pacific Rim feel. A loyal EU lunchtime crowd gives way to trendy diners in the evening – whatever, whenever, the place is full of intelligent chat and quiet appreciation of the surprising food, all in a cool and sophisticated atmosphere.

Le Cosmopolite

36 avenue de Cortenberg (02 230 20 95). Métro Schuman. **Open** noon-3pm, 6-11pm Mon-Fri. **Main courses** €25. **Credit** AmEx, MC, V. **Map** p323 G4.

Local dishes

Andouillette
A sausage made from all the leftover bits no one else wants. There is a system of grading the bangers with a capital A, depending on how much offal they contain – if you see AAAA, you're in trouble.

Anguilles au vert
Chunks of stewed eel suspended in a muddy yet vivid sea-green sauce of spinach, sorrel and parsley. Best as a starter; tedious as a main course.

Cervelle de veau/agneau
No other way of putting this: it's brain.

Filet américain
You may think you're ordering a filet steak, or the choicest home-made beefburger. You are; the only difference is, it's raw, indescribably orange/pink and peppered up with spice and mayonnaise. Similar in appearance to cat food.

Fondus au fromage
Deep-fried croquettes filled with a cheese and cream sauce. They're fondus because they've been dropped in hot oil, get it?

Moules parquées
Take your life in your hands and try a plate of sparkling raw mussels. Only for brave souls or those who've had the jab.

Pied de porc
A pig's trotter. There's no attempt to make it look like something else, or even put a paper frill on the end. The split hoof simply stares challengingly at you.

Stoemp
A variation of bubble-and-squeak, this is mashed potato roughly mixed with veg. On top, sausages or hot ham. It's farmer's food that has made it big in the city.

Tête de veau/tête pressée
Literally 'veal's head' or 'pressed head'. It's like brawn and comes with plenty of that jelly substance that you know can only come from an animal's skull.

Waterzooi
Almost every restaurant serves this famous dish from Ghent. A creamy stew with either chicken or fish (sometimes eel). Can be sublime or as dull as dishwater.

A rather trendy white wood and stainless steel place with linen director's chairs, Cosmopolite is a great option for a power lunch or gossip with friends. An extensive menu in the modernist style gives pride of place to salads, and what salads they are. Ranging from giant fresh prawns to foie gras and fig, they are designed to look good and feed well. Being in the heart of the EU Quarter gives you a good idea of the clientele, but this is a melting pot of a place where anyone can feel at home.

Spanish

Le Jardin d'Espagne
65-67 rue Archimède (02 736 34 49). Métro Schuman. **Open** noon-3pm, 7-10pm Mon-Fri; 7-10pm Sat. **Main courses** €25. **Credit** AmEx, DC, MC, V. **Map** p323 G3.
There is mixed feeling about this Spanish restaurant. Some swear by its authenticity, others bemoan an offish, impersonal staff. It's located in a street of quality eateries, but is the only one offering the real McCoy, from tapas to paella and grilled meats and prawns. The chef has been here forever, it seems, and does the deed for the Spanish embassy, so it can't be so bad. Downstairs is a more informal tapas bar, perfect for a glass and a bite.

Ixelles

Belgian & French

Chez Marie
40 rue Alphonse de Witte (02 644 30 31). Tram 81, 82/bus 71. **Open** noon-2.30pm, 7-11pm Mon-Fri; 7-11pm Sat. **Main courses** €22. **Credit** AmEx, DC, MC. V.
The latest star to rise in the Belgian culinary sky. Or the Michelin book to be precise, as French chef Lilian Devaux wins an *étoile* for the little bistro near the Ixelles ponds. The tiny place – around 40 covers – is wood panelled, heavily curtained, warm and cosy. An open kitchen and big old bar give it touches of old world character. Yet the menu is crackingly modern and clean, with a wink to the traditional; Bresse chicken with lobster, or tongue-in-cheek nod to fast food in the shape of a Michelin-star beefburger. A vast wine list is overseen by Canadian sommelier Daniel Marcil, who is only too happy to point you in the right direction. Earning a star means earning a new crowd of eager punters, so advance booking is about to become essential.

Le Fils de Jules
35 rue du Page (02 534 00 57/www.filsdejules.be). Métro Louise, then tram 81, 82, 91, 92. **Open** noon-2.30pm, 7-11pm Mon-Thur, Sun; noon-2.30pm, 7pm-midnight Fri, Sat. **Main courses** €17. **Credit** AmEx, DC, MC, V.
A favourite with the professional chattering classes, who have great difficulty deciding whether to talk to their friends or their mobiles. They come not for

Eat, Drink, Shop

the uninspired decor, but for the fabulous Basque influenced food and informal approach of the good-looking staff. Many dishes – and drinks – have deep-south France spellings, with Xs and Zs scattered around as generously as the foie gras. Sunday evenings have become particularly popular, when the FdeJ is an undeniably exciting place to be.

Ma Folle de Soeur

53 chaussée de Charleroi (02 538 22 39). Métro Louise then tram 91, 92. **Open** noon-2.15pm; 7-10.30pm Mon-Fri. **Main courses** €15. **Credit** AmEx, DC, MC, V. **Map** p321 C6.

Run by two sisters (the name roughly translates to 'My idiot of a sister'), this small restaurant has a huge picture window on to the street and a door that opens directly into the understated and fresh dining room. A huge bar dominates, but is softened by the sun-yellow walls and soft candlelight in the evening. The menu, Belgian in nature with French bistro influences, has flair and a touch of adventure; meat is at the fore but dressed with imaginative sauces. Business folk in suits give way to young lovers and pals in the evening.

Le Garde-Manger

151 rue Washington (02 346 68 29). Métro Louise, then tram 93, 94. **Open** noon-3pm, 6-11pm Mon, Wed-Sat (open daily summer). **Main courses** €13. **Credit** AmEx, DC, MC, V.

This sophisticated, candlelit brasserie is as close as you can get to a true neighbourhood bar-restaurant. Locals drop by for a drink in the front room, or sit at the bar to tuck in when eating alone. The main room and funky downstairs lounge bar are theatrical but calm and original works of art create a slightly bohemian, offbeat world; taupe, aubergine and flickering candle is the name of the game. Irish Brian out front and Belgian Claude in the kitchen couldn't make you feel more welcome. A diverse, homely menu offers some intriguing surprises, such as duck breast in lavender sauce. The busy, buzzy summer terrace will keep you gossiping until dark.

Mange Ta Soupe

7 rue de la Tulipe (02 512 14 12). Bus 54, 71. **Open** 11.30am-3.30pm Mon-Sat. **Main courses** €6. **No credit cards. Map** 321 D6.

An upmarket soup kitchen, and very nice it is too. Opened in 2001, Mange Ta Soupe (its name is a mother's admonishment) is a petite, airy, spruce lunchtime option a few steps from place Fernand Cocq. Hulking great bowls of finely concocted thick soup – mushroom and hazelnut, shrimp bisque, Pekinese broth with Chinese fish ravioli – are dished out in a friendly, elegant fashion to a varied clientele. Cheese and desserts, too – if you have room. Takeaway service available.

La Quincaillerie

45 rue du Page (02 538 25 53/www.quincaillerie.be). Tram 81, 82. **Open** noon-2.30pm, 7pm-midnight Mon-Fri; 7pm-midnight Sat, Sun. **Main courses** €21. **Credit** AmEx, DC, MC, V.

Set in an old ironmonger's shop, La Quincaillerie has become one of Brussels' enduring success stories. Sitting amid the ironwork and sets of drawers that once held screws and coach bolts, you can enjoy the finest brasserie food with an emphasis on seafood and shellfish. Be warned: the service is indifferent, verging on the rude – but it doesn't seem to stop the well-heeled crowd pouring through the shop doors, and it's always great fun playing the 'crack-a-smile' game.

Salons de l'Atalaïde

89 chaussée de Charleroi (02 537 21 54/ www.lessalonsatalaide.be). Tram 91, 92. **Open** noon-3pm, 7pm-midnight daily. **Main courses** €19. **Credit** AmEx, MC, V. **Map** p321 C6.

This old auction house now resembles a film lot as the crazy, eclectic, over-the-top restaurant preens itself in baroque-shelled mirrors. Ornate chandeliers, oversized paintings, gothic candles, ostentatious palms – all combine to give this place a surreal edge. The bistro-style menu is big on choice, and you have to try the *tarte au sucre* for dessert – yes, you read correctly, sugar tart. It's to die for. So is a table, as this is one of Brussels' most popular nightspots. Try not to miss the experience, it's truly unique.

De la Vigne à l'Assiette

51 rue de la Longue Haie (02 647 68 03). Métro Louise then tram 93, 94. **Open** noon-2pm, 7-11pm Tue-Fri; 7-11pm Sat. **Main courses** €20. **Set menu** €35. **Credit** AmEx, DC, MC, V. **Map** p321 D5.

A tiny restaurant tucked on a street corner in a residential area, De la Vigne has established itself with young professional regulars who come here for its youthful style, traditional kitchen and outstanding wine selection. The scrubbed tables, lemon walls and 1930s lamps give it a nonchalant air, which reflects the low-key approach of the young business partners who own it. Eddy Dandimont was number one Belgian sommelier in 1995 and his reasonably priced wine list makes choice difficult. The food is French-based with world influences; spices and herbs combine to give zestful life to sauces, while vegetables such as grilled aubergine with almonds complement the fish and meat dishes in a way that a steamed bean never could.

Fish & seafood

Rouge Tomate

190 avenue Louise (02 647 70 44). Métro Louise, then tram 92, 93. **Open** noon-2.30pm, 6.30-11.30pm daily. **Main courses** €12-€18. **Credit** AmEx, DC, MC, V. **Map** p321 D7.

One of the newest movers and shakers in town, the light, bright Rouge Tomate offers a refreshing take on Belgian cuisine. Fish dominates the menu, with a couple of options for confirmed carnivores as well as some imaginative vegetarian fare (chickpea steak with peppers, four-grain pasta with tomato coulis, for example). Friendly service occasionally pushes

Lovely **De Ultieme Hallucinatie**. *See p119*.

the boundary between leisurely and slow. By no means flawless, Rouge Tomate is at least a lively, sophisticated uptown treat.

La Table d'Abbaye

62 rue de Belle-Vue (02 646 33 95). Métro Louise, then tram 93, 94. **Open** noon-2.30pm, 7-11pm Mon-Fri; 7-11pm Sat, Sun. **Main courses** €27. **Set menu** €45. **Credit** AmEx, DC, MC, V.
This attractive restaurant is set in a fine old Brussels townhouse just off avenue Louise. The fresh yellow and blue interior is fluffy but unpretentious, classic yet relaxed. In summer the back garden is dressed in cloudy cream gauze and candlelight and makes for a dreamy evening under the stars. The menu is pretty good too, concentrating on fish with classic French sauces *au beurre*. Enticing set menu options can make the prices reasonable, though keep an eye on your booze bill.

Greek

L'Ouzerie

235 chaussée d'Ixelles (02 646 44 49). Bus 71. **Open** 7pm-midnight Mon-Thur; 7pm-1am Fri, Sat. **Main courses** €25. **Credit** AmEx, DC, V. **Map** p324 D6.
No plate smashing, moussaka or waiters in national costumes in this warm and cosy joint. Instead, diners are confronted by a long meze list in Greek, French

and English. Choose two or three dishes each and watch your table fill up with fried squid, grilled octopus, sardines, *saganaki* sausage and bean salads. Save some room for the trademark dessert: Greek yoghurt with nuts and honey.

Indian

Anarkali

33 rue de Longue Vie (02 513 02 05). Métro Porte de Namur/bus 54, 71. **Open** noon-2.30pm, 6pm-midnight daily. **Main courses** €8. **Set menu** €10.50. **Credit** AmEx, DC, V. **Map** p321 D5.
Ever since the Pakistani owners ripped up the menus and introduced an 'all you can eat' buffet, it's been hard to get a table in Anarkali. For €13 you get to choose from a half a dozen or so starters and at least ten expertly cooked main dishes, including fish curry, mixed vegetables, lamb biryani and vindaloo chicken. Plus rice, naan, side salads and finger food thrown in along with a dessert and coffee. At the end you're left wondering how the owners can possibly make a profit – until you see the next group eagerly waiting for your table.

Italian

Cose Cosi

16 chaussée de Wavre (02 512 11 71). Métro Porte de Namur. **Open** noon-3pm, 6pm-midnight daily. **Main courses** €23. **Credit** AmEx, MC, V. **Map** p321 D5.
It takes a while to latch on to what's happening in this restaurant. From the outside it's clearly Italian, but once in, zebra skins, antelope heads and other African artefacts stare you in the face. You sit in a colonial-style room with painted shutters and tropical plants and choose from a typically Italian menu. Just when you thought it was safe, a chef emerges from the kitchen and joins the pianist in a serenade. Bizarre but great fun – and the food is well worth the confusion.

Vini e Antipasti

28 rue du Berger (0477 26 14 87). Métro Porte de Namur. **Open** noon-7pm Mon-Wed; noon-midnight Thur, Fri; 7pm-midnight Sat. **Main courses** €7-€11. **No credit cards**. **Map** p321 D5.
At first glance, the tiny black triangular frontage of this Italian *enoteca* looks like a wine merchant's. The right-hand wall is constructed entirely of a soaring wine rack and an aged oak barrel hangs from the ceiling. It's a good introduction to one of Brussels' tiniest restaurants, which serves exquisite Italian snacks and pasta dishes. A sign of its popularity is the clientele; this is one of those places where off-duty chefs come to eat, as much for the buzz and loud laughter as for the olive oil-rich food and wild boar sausage. One can also imagine secret, lodge-like activities – such as white Umbrian truffles changing hands in crumpled brown packages. Booking is essential as it's the size of a cupboard.

Japanese

Yamayu Santatsu

*141 chaussée d'Ixelles (02 513 53 12). Métro
Porte de Namur.* **Open** noon-2pm, 7-10pm Tue-Sat;
7-10pm Sun. **Main courses** €15-€20. **Credit**
AmEx, MC, V. **Map** p321 D5.

Lively, straightforward restaurant that attracts a
loyal Japanese clientele. On one of the city's busier
streets with a large cinema nearby, so it means that
it's usually very busy. It's wise to book ahead, but
once you're in, expect a lively atmosphere. Great
sushi, sashimi and tempura, as well as takesushi and
sukiyaki menus too.

Middle Eastern & North African

Mont Liban

*30-32 rue Livourne (02 537 71 31). Métro Louise,
then tram 91, 92, 93, 94.* **Open** noon-3pm, 7pm-
midnight Mon-Sat. **Main courses** €15-€20. **Set
menu** €25. **Credit** AmEx, DC, V. **Map** p321 C6.

A new Lebanese joint just off avenue Louise, Mont
Liban has rapidly established itself as one of the
finest Middle Eastern eateries south of the centre.
Just take a look around – the place is packed with
expat Lebanese leisurely enjoying a four- or five-
course meal. It's best to order the meze menu; dish
after dish of houmous, falafel and grilled sausage
will be plonked on your table. For traditionalists,
they even have belly-dancing at the weekend.

Vie Sauvage

*12 rue de Naples (02 513 68 85). Métro Porte
de Namur.* **Open** noon-2pm, 7-11pm Tue-Fri;
7-11pm Sat. **Main courses** €18. **Credit** AmEx,
DC, MC, V. **Map** p321 D5.

One of Brussels' best-kept secrets – until now – Vie
Sauvage is tucked away down a side street just off
Porte de Namur. Once you enter this Aladdin's cave
of a restaurant, you'll soon forget the drab surroundings. Exquisite Moroccan pottery hangs from
the ochre coloured walls, but there is nothing kitsch
about this refined restaurant. The speciality is *pastil-
la*: a flaky pastry chicken or pigeon pie topped with
honey and cinnamon. If you don't fancy waiting for
this to be prepared, try the tagines and couscous,
both served in authentic pots.

Oriental

Ô Chinoise-Riz

*94 rue de l'Aqueduc (02 534 91 08). Métro Louise
then tram 91, 92.* **Open** noon-2.30pm, 6-11pm
Mon-Fri. **Main courses** €12-€15. **Set menu** €16.
Credit MC, V.

Just off place Châtelain, this is one of Brussels' better
Chinese restaurants. The open kitchen by the door
serves up mouthwatering traditional fare (Peking
duck, Sichuan beef) to a youngish crowd. It's almost
always packed, and the pink walls and narrow
entrance give proceedings an intimate air.

Veggie options

Brussels is no longer carnivore central –
but the choice for vegetarians is still often
between a mainstream restaurant, with
one unimaginative meat-free option, or a
totally veggie place whose proselytising
agenda includes a no-smoking diktat.

Among the latter are such old-school
haunts as **Shanti** in the university area (68
avenue Adolphe Buyl; 02 649 40 96) and
Den Teepot (66 rue des Chartreux; 02 511
94 02) in the town centre, which does only
a fixed daily lunch menu. **L'Elément Terre**
(*see p118*) is along similar lines. **Tsampa**
(109 rue de Livourne; 02 647 03 67)
scores highly for general vibe, but **Dolma**
(*see p118*) is the most appealing strictly
vegetarian restaurant in Brussels, for
ambience, decor, food and value.

So, what is there in between the token
omelette and all-out food facism? More
than you might think. Downtown, there's
Arcadi (1B rue d'Arenberg; 02 511 33 43).
It's tiny and very popular – testimony to an
extensive menu of quiches, pastas and
scrumptious cakes. **De Markten** (5 rue du
Vieux Marché aux Grains; 02 514 66 04)
is another lunch pit stop, in a trendy
setting favoured by an arty Flemish crowd.

The Italianate trio of **Chez Martin**
(15 Borgval; 02 513 93 03), **Ricotta &
Parmesan** (31 rue de l'Ecuyer; 02 502 80
82) and **Basta Pasta** (34 rue de la Grande
Ile; 0477 202090) are worth checking out
for their quality veggie pasta dishes at
reasonable prices. Pizzerias of similar ilk
include **Mirante** (13 Plattesteen; 02 511
15 80) and **Rugantino** (*see p105*). Still
downtown, a trendy option is **Totem** (42
rue de la Grande Ile; 02 513 16 40), a
bar-restaurant and art gallery that makes
a point of signalling its veggie options,
while **Raconte-Moi des Salades** (19 place
du Chatelain; 02 534 27 27) is another
vegetarian stand-by, with a lovely garden.

Finally, Brussels is seeing the rise
of a new generation of establishments
at least trying to offer a fusion of
international cooking styles. **Grandeur
Nature** in St-Gilles (296 chaussée de
Waterloo; 02 544 18 23) is one such
place. Its reasonably priced menu is evenly
split between vegetarian dishes, fish and
meat. One day – not quite yet – this will
be the rule rather than the exception.

Eat, Drink, Shop

Le Deuxième Elément

7 rue St-Boniface (02 502 00 28). Métro Porte de Namur. **Open** noon-2.30pm, 7-11.30pm Mon-Fri; 7-11.30pm Sat, Sun. **Main courses** €7-€11.50. **Credits** MC, V. **Map** p321 D5.

If you've come to associate Thai restaurants with soapstone Buddhas and alabaster elephants, prepare for a shock when you walk through the doors of the Deuxième Élément. A giant space-age mural dominates one wall, the lighting is stark and the tables are topped with brushed steel. The food is more traditional than the decor – the red curry is an assault on at least three senses – which probably has something to do with the Thai chefs darting in and out of the kitchens. With friendly service, great grub and wicked flavoured gin shots sold by the metre, you can't go wrong.

Les Perles de Pluie

25 rue du Châtelain (02 649 67 23). Métro Louise then tram 93, 94. **Open** 7-11pm Mon, Sat; noon-3pm, 7-11pm Tue-Fri; noon-3pm, 7-10.30pm Sun. **Main courses** €10-€20. **Credit** MC, V.

An elegant Thai restaurant famed for its Sunday buffet (€27), which is one of those all-you-can-eat deals featuring dishes from across the broad and sophisticated menu – making it an ideal opportunity to sample specialities you might otherwise never try. The decor is traditional Thai with a dash of minimalism; the back room has ground-level wooden tables and cushions. Booking advised.

Vegetarian

Dolma

329 chaussée d'Ixelles (02 649 89 81). Tram 81, 82/bus 71. **Open** noon-2pm, 7-9.30pm Mon-Sat. **Main courses** €5-€7.50. **Set menu** €12-€14. **Credit** AmEx, DC, MC, V. **Map** p324 E6.

Vegetarians don't have to compromise here on decor, choice, flavour or even healthy appetites. They can – and do – eat as much as they like from a varied buffet of salads and quiches, as well as desserts such as the Dolma speciality cake of creamy chocolate and chestnut on a biscuit base. Meanwhile a Tibetan-themed decor provides a simple but stunning backdrop. All round, a strong contender for the title of Brussels' finest veggie restaurant.

L'Elément Terre

465 chaussée de Waterloo (02 649 37 27). Métro Louise, then tram 91, 92. **Open** noon-2.30pm, 7-10.30pm Tue-Fri; 7-10.30pm Sat. **Main courses** €8-€13. **Credit** AmEx, DC, MC, V.

Welcome to full-on veggie territory à la Bruxelloise. This is not the kind of place you come to for a boisterous evening of smoking and drinking (though alcohol is served), but it's a good bet for tasty and creative meat-free cooking. The assiette découverte, a substantial smörgåsbord of different titbits, is a good way of sampling a variety of dishes on the menu, such as pulse-, tofu-, seitan- or quorn-based dishes, and Mediterranean-inspired concoctions.

This place feels like the living room it was once, quiet and intimate, even verging on the stilted. The decor is pleasantly ethnic.

St-Gilles

Middle Eastern & North African

Aux Mille et Une Nuits

7 rue de Moscou (02 537 41 27). Pré-métro Parvis de St-Gilles. **Open** 11.30am-3pm, 6.30-11.30pm Mon-Sat. **Main courses** €11-€15. **Credit** AmEx, DC, MC, V. **Map** p320 B6.

One of half a dozen North African restaurants around the Parvis de St-Gilles square, this Tunisian restaurant stands out thanks to its over-the-top lighting and kitsch decor. It resembles a modern Bedouin tent, with oriental rugs hanging from the walls and thousands of tiny lights sparkling brightly above like stars. And the food is out of this world. For starters, try the harira chickpea soup or honey-soaked chicken in crispy pastry. Then grapple with the eternal dilemma of whether to plump for the tagine or the couscous. There's a huge selection of both, although you can't go far wrong with the caramelised lamb couscous or chicken tagine with grapes and honey. Service is impeccable.

Spanish

El Madrileño

50 chaussée de Waterloo (02 537 69 82). Pré-métro Parvis de St-Gilles. **Open** noon-3pm, 6-11pm Mon, Tue, Fri-Sun; noon-3pm Wed. **Main courses** €10-€15. **No credit cards.** **Map** p320 B6.

In a town riddled with hopelessly naff tapas bars, this is at least authentic. Run by a shuffling old Madrileño – Andrino, his Atleti team photo slapped on the wall – this long-established venue is laid out exactly as you would see in Spain. All is as it should be: the blue-and-white tiling, and the hams hanging over the bar counter where trays of sardines, *patatas bravas* and meatballs enticingly await Andrino's now shaky spoon. Great paella too. On Sundays noisy Spanish families and silent old couples gather in the spacious back area.

St-Josse & Schaerbeek

Belgian & French

La Bonne Humeur

244 chaussée de Louvain (02 230 71 69). Bus 29. **Open** noon-2pm, 6.30-9.30pm Mon, Thur-Sun; 6-11pm Sat. **Main courses** €15. **Credit** MC, V. **Map** p322 F2.

It looks an uninteresting proposition from the outside; an old-style caff on one of Brussels' busiest and most unattractive roads. But this unintentionally retro resto, with its formica tables and chequered floor tiles, is deemed to serve the best mussels and

Blue Elephant: the first and still the best.

chips one could hope for. A family business for decades, it has certainly passed the test of time, and folk come from far and wide to tuck into its totally unpretentious food and atmosphere.

De Ultieme Hallucinatie

316 rue Royale (02 217 06 14). Métro Botanique/ tram 92,. 93, 94. **Open** noon-2.30pm, 7-10.30pm Mon-Fri; 7-10.30pm Sat. **Main courses** €35. **Credit** AmEx, DC, MC, V. **Map** p322 E1.

You may think you're walking into a private home or museum when you enter this Arts and Crafts house. Every detail, down to the skirting boards and window frames, are in this late 19th-century style and there is a real sense of regressing in time. Even the traffic on the busy road seems to disappear. The stylish restaurant at the front, with its Tiffany-style chandeliers and lamps, serves classic French food, with classic service and classic prices – driving some to the safer, blander café at the back (*see p137*).

Global

L'Ecole Buissonière

13 rue Traversière (02 217 01 65). Métro Botanique. **Open** noon-2.30pm, 6.30-10pm Mon-Fri. **Main courses** €10. **Credit** MC, V. **Map** p322 E2.

This cheap and cheerful café-cum-restaurant used to be a student canteen and has certainly not forgotten its roots, partly because it's still attached to a youth hotel. Scrubbed pine tables sit perilously close to each other and there is a distinct feel of camaraderie among the diners as they jostle for places or share a table. It's not just the prices that make this place worthwhile, it's also the outlandish array of international cuisine, from Mexico to Japan: mix and match to your heart's content. Another neat touch is

the wine, which is put on the table by the bottle and charged by the centimetre, the tape measure being the final judge of whether or not you should drive.

Indian

Passage to India

223 chaussée de Louvain (02 735 31 47). Bus 29. **Open** noon-3pm, 6pm-midnight daily. **Main courses** €15. **Set menu** €22. **Credit** AmEx, MC, V. **Map** p322 F2.

There's a run of Indian and Pakistani restaurants along this stretch of road, a little out of the centre of town, but easy enough to get to and well worth the effort. This is one of the best and popular with the expat crowd in search of that British Asian taste. Chicken madras and vindaloo you'll certainly find, but the succulent tandoori dishes are as good as can be, cooked as they are in a traditional clay oven.

Anderlecht

Middle Eastern

Chez Julia et André

6 avenue Clémenceau (02 522 73 01). Métro Gare du Midi. **Open** 9am-5pm Mon-Fri. **Main courses** €10. **Credit** MC, V. **Map** p320 A5.

The area around the Gare du Midi remains on the barren side, despite huge renovations and public works. Yet the side streets are filled with numerous ethnic snack bars and small restaurants. Among these, Chez Julia et André is perfect for a quick bite. Run by a Moroccan couple, it specialises in Jewish and Middle Eastern food such as chopped liver and falafel. The menu varies daily and runs from sandwiches through to steaming main courses. It looks more like a sandwich bar than a restaurant, but it's a pleasant place to sit if waiting for a train.

Uccle

Oriental

Blue Elephant

1120 chaussée de Waterloo (02 374 49 62). Bus 41. **Open** noon-2.30pm, 7-10.30pm Mon-Fri, Sun; 7-11.30pm Sat. **Main courses** €17. **Set menu** (Mon-Fri) €12. **Credit** AmEx, DC, MC, V.

Having successfully established this upmarket Thai eatery in 1980, co-owner Karl Steppe then spread the Blue Elephant brand globally. Now stretched out from Dublin to New Delhi, Blue Elephants comprise staff in traditional Thai costume delivering top-notch Thai cuisine to the background of Thai music. Few Irish or Indian diners are aware of the Belgian provenance. This founding father, in Uccle, also features an indoor garden and enough Thai antiques to make the journey to your table a little hazardous. Once you're there, the beef paneng and Thai-style chicken curry will have made it all worthwhile.

Eat, Drink, Shop

Bars

Let's face it, it's why you came to Brussels. Enjoy.

Step back in time at historical **Café Métropole**. *See p122.*

'*S'il vous plaît!*' With that bizarre Belgian vernacular use ('Your drink!') of the French 'please', the waiter plonks your first beer down in front of you. It could be the colour of autumn leaves, or bananas, or even suntan lotion. It could be bright red. In any case, what it won't be is predictable, and it will be served in the nifty logoed glass of the beer in question, with a mat to match (*see p125* **Beers of Belgium**).

Then look around you. Dutch bars are dreary, German ones plain beery, provincial French ones drab. Mostly, they are average. But Belgian bars are none of these things. Certainly not in central Brussels, where art nouveau, art deco and Surrealism all stopped by for a drink at one point or another. The decor could be ornate, it could be understated, it could be the stuff of wild fantasy. Again, it shouldn't be predictable.

Beginning, inevitably, with the Grand' Place (*see p123* **Brussels by bar crawl: Grand' Place**), lined with imposing, intricate, terraced guildhouse pubs, where aproned waiters also serve hulking great portions of food, a network of bar-starred streets fans out around you. In the immediate vicinity will be ones of great and often unusual tradition (known as *estaminets*) or of gleaming artistic taste. South-west snakes rue du Marché au Charbon (*see p135* **Brussels by bar crawl: Charbon**). If you've only one night in town, drink it here.

On the other side of the Bourse lie Ste-Catherine and St-Géry. The latter, in particular, is the stuff of legend. Glowing descriptions abound, the terms 'happening' and 'cutting-edge' scattered with abandon. Although there are indeed brash new cafés (many established by entertainment guru Fred Nicolay and team) and certainly many good bars, unless it's a balmy summer's eve and the terraces are thronging with bright young things, place St-Géry itself is overrated, really. Centred on the Tardis-like structure of the old covered market, it can feel like that apes-meet-box scene from *2001*. Hacking your way out of it, deep into the night, through the kaleidoscopic bar jungle of retro, deco and downright dippy, can be much more fun.

For all-night Brussels, *see p126* **Brussels by bar crawl: Late haunts**.

True, there is a standard Belgian bar. Some still exist downtown. Generally, they are curious, smoky and brown – before it became the new black. A selection of draught beers (Stella, Maes, Jupiler, Hoegaarden) at €1.50 a glass will be complemented by at least a dozen bottles of dizzying flavours at €2 each. You've just been given the keys to the sweetshop. Behind the bar will be a basket of boiled eggs, a box of Royco cup-a-soups and a promise of cheese on toast. Some may have a lunch menu, most a drinks menu; all serve wine, coffee and tea. Specialities include *genever*, a pure grain spirit, strong, clear and often fruit-flavoured; and *half-en-half*, usually a mixture of white wine and champagne. French jukebox pop will be punctuated by the occasional frap of a bingo machine (*see p128* **Belgian bar life 1: Bingo**) in the corner. Guarding the toilet will be a grumpy crone, armed with a frown and a mop (*see p137* **Belgian bar life 2: Madames Pipis**).

Bars also tend to reflect the area they serve. Sablon's are more glitzy, Marolles' are full of the same odd characters that Breugel watched from his window, while those in St-Gilles have a boho, community feel. Ixelles has a mix of African (rue Longue Vie), student-oriented (near the cemetery) and trendy (around place St-Boniface). Finally, on its own, is the expat drinking-and-networking culture around the EU Quarter and avenue Louise (*see p130* **Brussels by bar crawl: EU Quarter**).

Santé!

Grand' Place & around

A La Bécasse
11 rue de Tabora (02 511 00 06). Pré-métro Bourse. **Open** 10am-1am Mon-Fri; 10am-2am Sat; 11am-midnight Sun. **Credit** MC, V. **Map** p317 C3.
This bar comes as a total surprise. From the street, all that signifies its presence is a red neon light, hinting there's something tacky involved. Not at all. Look down at your feet and see the stone and brass welcome mat fixed to the pavement. Follow the little alleyway through the houses and there you see the Dickensian-style bottle windows. Behind them is an ancient tavern where customers sit at long tables and have their beer poured from jugs by aproned waiters – including draught *lambic*.

Les Brasseurs
24 rue de la Colline (02 511 38 97) Métro Gare Centrale. **Open** 11am-11pm Mon-Thur, Sun; 11am-midnight Fri, Sat. **No credit cards. Map** p317 C3.
Despite its address, this relatively young bar-cum-pub looks right out over the Grand' Place. For years, the house in which it sits lay derelict, its faded cherubs waiting for someone to scoop them up and love them. Now they're surrounded by copper

The best Bars

For variety of beers
More than a thousand types at the **Chez Moeder Lambic** (*see p136*) – with the sideburned hophead as the main type of customer.

For drinking the stuff by the bucketload
La Lunette (*see p124*), where eight on-tap varieties are sold by the Lunette, or litre.

For class in a glass
Archiduc (*see p127*). Part bar, part ocean liner. The *Titanic* sails at dawn…

For nostalgic tunes on crackly vinyl
It's got to be **Goupil le Fol** (*see p123*), home of 3,000 choice records from Aznavour to Brel and back.

For checking out the local football scene
Bright league ladders cover the back wall of the otherwise bohemian **Brasserie Verscheuren** (*see p136*).

For that magical chess moment
Pieces clack and clocks tick-tock at **Le Greenwich** (*see p129*), where Magritte once played the tables.

For the smokiest atmosphere
Everyone brings a smoker's cough and a pack of Bastos to **Chez Martine** (*see p127*).

For authentic art nouveau
Le Falstaff (*see p123*). Don't go changin'…

For authentic Surrealism
The lads all hung out at **La Fleur en Papier Doré** (*see p123*), leaving sketches and doodles to cover their bar bill.

For death-wish drinking at unfeasibly late hours
Can't top the **Celtica** (*see p122*). Head home with a hangover and perhaps worse.

brewing kettles capable of holding 1,000 litres and a somewhat formulaic 'let's pretend we're in a brewery' feel. In truth, you are in a brewery, for this place boldly and audaciously brews its own: three types of beer, hoppy, malty and fresh. Don't be too dismayed by the continental head on it. Fine for a pop-in pint and a taste of something different, but you wouldn't want to spend an entire evening here.

Café Métropole

31 place de Brouckère (02 219 23 84/www.metropole hotel.be). Métro/Pré-métro De Brouckère. **Open** 9am-1am Mon-Sat. **No credit cards. Map** p317 C2.

For a little fin-de-siècle finesse, pop into the café of the grand Hotel Métropole. The atmosphere is nothing special, the prices are steeper than elsewhere, but it is an institution. You needn't walk through the lobby as there is a direct street entrance, but a peek at the Renaissance-inspired interior is irresistible. This place is from a different age: over-burdened chandeliers, mirrored walls, ornate ironwork and a hush that hasn't changed for a century. Sarah Bernhardt stayed here and she is reincarnated in the ladies with hairdos who sit on the terrace in sunglasses and fur coats all year round. It's steeped in history and, while the café won't necessarily make you tingle, the ghosts from the past will.

Café de l'Opéra

4 rue des Princes (02 219 52 96). Métro/Pré-métro De Brouckère. **Open** 9am-midnight Mon-Sat (Sun if there is a performance). **Credit** V. **Map** p317 C3.

As the name suggests, this café sits in the shadow of the opera house and attracts an older, well-heeled clientele. A log fire keeps the place warm and cosy and the dark wood-panelled walls contribute to the feel-good factor, though it is often accused of being a little overbearing – especially the strict waiters,

Join the puppets at **Toone**. *See p127.*

who you know just want to slap the back of your hand and tell you to be quiet. In summer, the terrace is huge and spills across the square. And if you wonder why it suddenly fills for 20 minutes and empties again, it's used as the main bar for the opera. Interval bells ring to get the punters back in for act two. Or three, or four…

Celtica

55 rue du Marché aux Poulets (02 514 22 69). Métro/Pré-métro De Brouckère or Pré-métro Bourse. **Open** 1pm-6am Mon-Thur; 1pm-8am Fri, Sat. **Credit** AmEx, DC, MC, V. **Map** p317 B3.

Some visit the Celtica for its punchy live blues and rock music of a Saturday eve. During the week, friendly students like to meet others of similar ilk in the reasonably sympathetic surroundings. But there are those doomed creatures who use it as a trough to wallow in sin at ungodly hours of the night, festering in alcohol, driven by all kinds of warped desire. Don't be surprised if you wind up sharing breakfast with a complete stranger, somewhere around dinner time.

Le Cercueil

10-12 rue des Harengs (02 512 30 77). Pré-métro Bourse. **Open** 11am-2am Mon-Thur; 11am-4am Fri, Sat. **No credit cards. Map** p317 C3.

If you don't know what the name of this bar means, you soon will as you put your glass down and realise your beer is sitting on a coffin. Just off the Grand' Place, Le Cercueil is typical of the darker side of Belgian humour and looks grimly unwelcoming from the outside. It may seem theme-parkish with its black light and spooky music, but it's always busy with a mix of amused tourists and serious young partygoers. It's worth popping in for an (expensive) drink, but it's doubtful you'd want to spend a night here. Besides, the coffin lids open at midnight as the living dead head into town for a spot of bloodlust boogying.

Cirio

18-20 rue de la Bourse (02 512 13 95). Pré-métro Bourse. **Open** 10am-late daily. **No credit cards. Map** p317 B3.

Take a few steps out of the Grand' Place and into the 19th century in this time-capsule of a bar. It still has its original embossed wallpaper, its original lights and, it seems, its original waiters. Service on the summer street terrace can be a little slow, but this is a no-rush place. It has its loyal customers: silver-permed ladies with similarly permed poodles in the morning, sipping *half-en-half* (half sparkling, half still wine), and a younger student crowd in the evening. It has a great selection of Belgian beers and offers good-value food at lunchtime. The toilets were renovated in the 1920s, so are relatively new.

Le Corbeau

18-20 rue St-Michel (02 219 52 46). Métro/Pré-métro De Brouckère. **Open** 10am-midnight Mon-Thur; 10am-3am Fri, Sat. **Credit** DC, MC, V. **Map** p317 C2.

Brussels by bar crawl: Grand' Place

'Don't drink on the Grand' Place, it's too expensive' is an oft-heard cry. Why the hell not, should be the stern reply. Sure, the bars are more expensive than elsewhere, but elsewhere doesn't offer the free spectacle and sheer beauty of what is arguably Europe's most perfect square. Nor will you be seriously ripped off. The bars are, without exception, located in the fine merchant and guildhouses; you can sit inside in the glow of a log fire or, in summer, outside on the terraces, taking in the atmosphere. There's not much to distinguish between them; all have a similar range of beers and serve lunch, and most serve supper.

Stand with your back to the Hôtel de Ville. To your left is **Le Roi d'Espagne** (see p126), housed in one of the most stunning of the guildhouses. The waiters here wear Trappist monk aprons, but it doesn't make them move any faster. Just take your time and enjoy the Bruxellois puppets and pig bladders hanging

from the ceiling, or move upstairs where tiny windows give a great view of the square. From here, move round clockwise until you hit **Le Paon de Pauw** (35 Grand' Place; 02 513 35 82), a tiny bar with one of the busiest terraces. Look for the golden peacock above the door and you know you've got the right place. To the right of the museum is **La Chaloupe d'Or** (No.24; 02 511 41 61), regarded as one of the best, and popular with locals. The food is finer than most, something reflected in the prices. Continue to the right and you will see the latest addition to the family. **Les Brasseurs** (see p121) is different in that it brews its own beer, ranging from a standard pils to blow-your-head-off stuff. The interior is a stunning blend of cherry wood and copper vats and well worth a look. Over your right shoulder, on the same side as the town hall, is **La Rose Blanche** (No.11; 02 513 64 79) with its beautiful carved and painted ceiling, extensive beer list and traditional Belgian food.

You could walk straight past Le Courbeau without spotting it. The unnoticeable outside leads to an unremarkable inside, just like scores of other neighbourhood bars. But this is in the centre of town and thus makes the clients a little more mixed. Quiet by day, with good-value food, the bar gets louder as time passes, and by the evening there is a real party atmosphere. Especially on Saturdays, when the pop music takes over and everyone joins in the singing, dances on the tables, does Donna Summer impersonations and uses a rolled-up newspaper as a microphone. Really.

Le Falstaff

19-25 rue Henri Maus (02 511 87 89). Pré-métro Bourse. **Open** 10am-3am daily. **Credit** AmEx, DC, MC, V. **Map** p317 B3.

One of the most imposing art nouveau bar-cafés in Brussels. Once part of a sweeping terrace of majestic townhouses, now its red awnings bring cheer to an uncared-for street smack in the centre of town. It's a true oasis; from the outside the organic nouveau windows give a glimpse of the classic interior with its mix of clientele, young and old, local and visitor. The Falstaff is big on menus, both Belgian beer and food; the former exciting and enticing, the latter predictable but honest. The heated terrace is

open most of the year and creates an ambience all of its own. The Falstaff is open from early to late and is the perfect place to grab the Brussels equivalent of a pie and a pint at any time.

La Fleur en Papier Doré

55 rue des Alexiens (02 511 16 59). Pré-métro Anneessens. **Open** 11am-1am daily. **No credit cards. Map** p317 B4.

This is an odd place, but so was the group of Surrealists and Dadaists who used it in the 1920s, Magritte and Delvaux included. Among the flea-market artefacts and the huge stove are doodles and sketches from the artists themselves, so much so it's rather like sitting in a dusty museum that is forever on the fade. It's visited by milky-eyed, diehard locals and over-enthusiastic tourists; its past glory and total eccentricity are its charm.

Goupil le Fol

22 rue de la Violette (02 511 13 96). Pré-métro Bourse. **Open** 8pm-5am daily. **No credit cards. Map** p317 C3.

What can we say about Goupil that won't upset le Fol that runs it? Well, for a start, we should say Goupil is a kooky labyrinthine junk-shop of a bar, where all trace of time can be lost thanks to a jukebox of nearly 3,000 choice pieces of vinyl and the house selection of home-made fruit wines and cognacs. Intimacy is all. Goupil himself – the stocky, grey-haired gent handing out sweets by the front door by the end of the night – says his original intention three decades ago was 'to change the world with togetherness, music and fruit wine'. Indeed. It's eccentric, velvety and nostalgic; check out the beads and neon. If you're on the pull and have made it as far as Goupil's, there is no finer springboard.

A L'Imaige Nostre-Dame
8 rue du Marché aux Herbes (02 219 42 49).
Pré-métro Bourse. **Open** noon-midnight Mon, Tue,
Thur, Fri; noon-8pm Wed, 2.30pm-1am Sat; 4pm-1am
Sun. **Credit** AmEx, MC, V. **Map** p317 C3.
An old inn owned by the same people as A La Bécasse (*see p121*), Nostre-Dame is of similar heritage feel and also hidden down an alleyway, its interior filled with long wooden benches and assorted neo-medieval tat. The pub food is acceptable without bursting the taste buds, but the range of beers is substantial. Mainly an older clientele, many scribbling postcards or swapping stories of their day spent looking for something to write about.

Loplop Café Expression
29 rue de l'Ecuyer (02 512 18 89). Métro/
Pré-métro De Brouckère. **Open** 9am-4am Mon-
Sat; 11am-4am Sun. **Credit** AmEx, DC, MC, V.
Map p317 C3.
The first thing you notice as you approach this corner bar is the display of national flags. This seems part of the magnetic attraction to the generations past and present of international youth who pack out the top floor on weekend nights. Downstairs is a more mature affair, full of boozy regulars and piano tunes. Under British ownership and, loosely speaking, anglophone, it can be a comforting discovery for groups of Brits who want to soak up a cosmopolitan vibe without being too disoriented. It's a mystery exactly why (the 100 beers on offer?), but the Loplop is one of the most popular bars around, with a mixed and often loyal clientele. Integral to Brussels nightlife for over a decade now, it's at its most pleasant during the day or on a quiet night, when it feels more like a reassuringly scruffy local than a heaving youth hostel foyer. There's change on the cards for the night-time mood: an 18 age restriction and a DJ upstairs. Many will mourn the end of a golden era.

La Lunette
3 place de la Monnaie (02 218 03 78). Métro/
Pré-métro De Brouckère. **Open** 9am-1am Mon-
Thur; 9am-2am Fri, Sat; 10am-1am Sun. **No credit**
cards. Map p317 C3.
This has become a bit of an institution, partly because of its location, near the main pedestrian shopping street, and partly because of its beer list, with eight on-tap varieties. Measures come in a standard glass or a Lunette, which is like a magnum champagne glass. That's a polite way of putting it;

Lose yourself in **Goupil le Fol**. *See p123*.

a Lunette is a bucket. The interior is nothing to write home about, being the suburban side of the 1970s, but the atmosphere is exactly what you expect from a continental café, full of shoppers, drifters and folk waiting for a film to start.

Mokafé
9 galerie du Roi (02 511 78 70). Métro Gare
Centrale. **Open** 7am-midnight daily. **Credit**
AmEx, DC, MC, V. **Map** p317 C3.
This is an arty types favourite as it's close to the opera and immediately opposite Brussels' best classical music shop. Being in the covered galleries means you can sit outside all year round, and watch the rich waft by. It's good for lunch, with reasonably priced Belgian café food and pasta. On Sunday mornings, locals bring their newspapers and sit for hours with coffee, croissant and a West Highland terrier. Everyone pretends to be in their own little world, but just watch eyes dart and ears prick when a newcomer takes a table; knowing nods to regulars and faux-disinterest at strangers.

A La Mort Subite
7 rue des Montagnes aux Herbes Potagères (02 513
13 18). Métro Gare Centrale. **Open** 11am-1.30am
Mon-Sat; 11am-midnight Sun. **No credit cards.**
Map p317 C3.
If you're looking for a real slice of Brussels, join the crowds at the wooden tables at A La Mort Subite. Hardly touched for a century, the bar is cavernous, loud and brash. The waiters chat and puff away at their cigarettes in the self-imposed pauses between serving, and there are times when you feel you may be an inconvenience to them. But underneath it all, they are loveable rogues and you can play the

Eat, Drink, Shop

Beers of Belgium

Belgium has some of the most challenging and important beers in the world. Passing over the dull lager mega-brands of Jupiler, Maes and Stella Artois, more substantial amber beers such as **Leffe**, **Grimbergen** or **Duvel** blonde deliver taste and strength. Many of these beers hint at monastic origins, but only five have truly seen the hand of God: **Orval**, **Chimay**, **Rochefort**, **Westmalle** and the lesser-known **Westvleteren**. These are the Trappist beers and are seriously good, if deep brown and creamy is your thing. For deep brown and creamy with a kick, select the *dubbel* or *tripel* versions delivering up to 9% ABV. Pale, unclassifiable Orval is the tricky Trappist exception.

Summer days lead the trendy and thirsty to things white. The *blanche* or *witte* beers are traditionally brewed with malted wheat, and deliver a capacity to quench thirst, which a lager never quite achieves. Try the ubiquitous **Hoegaarden** or regional **Brugs** and **Limburgse** versions. Like gin, they come iced with lemon.

And then there's the challenging *lambics*. *Lambics* are fermented with natural air-borne yeasts and have a decidedly acidic twang. Young *lambics* are called *faro*, while *lambic* itself is aged for a year or more to let the bacteria get to it. Blend young and old and you get *gueuze*, tasting like tinned cider to

the novice and like nectar to those who acquire the taste. In Brussels, only one working *gueuze* brewery remains, the **Musée Bruxellois de la Gueuze** in gloomy rue Gheude, where bacteria in the grimy air of Anderlecht helps the natural fermenting process. Masking the taste of *lambics* with cherries (to produce *kriek*) or raspberries (to produce *framboise*) starts to make them approachable again. Drink well chilled on hot days. And once you've drank the above, remember there's another 600 to go, including speciality Christmas beers, honey beers and small-production artisanal beers.

When in a bar, the menu will show what is available on draught (*au fût/van 't vat*). Unlike many other parts of Europe, drinking bottled beer in Belgium is never a second choice, and the bottles will form the larger part of the menu. Bars will always give you the correct glass for the beer, and most breweries produce their own shape and size to match the beer's character. Beer mats are always used and, in the more traditional bars, can become a receipt if you really need one. Beer drinking is partaken by all, male and female, young and old alike. There's even *bières de table* for weaning children. Only in Belgium could beer match mother's milk.

Eat, Drink, Shop

crack-a-smile game. This is a place to go with the flow. It is an important meeting place and, virulent anti-smokers apart, people love it. The beer list is surprisingly short for a traditional Belgian bar, but you'll find enough on draught to keep you happy, including various flavours of *gueuze*, the famous sour fruit beers.

O'Reilly's

1 place de la Bourse (02 552 04 80). Pré-métro Bourse. **Open** 11am-2am Mon-Thur, Sun; 11am-4am Fri, Sat. **Credit** AmEx, DC, MC, V. **Map** p317 B3.

Just one of the many Irish pubs in Brussels, though none are more central – it's directly opposite the Bourse. It gets packed and noisy and is a magnet for football fans when the big matches are on. In spring 2002, it took over the nearby Wilde Bar Lounge (77 boulevard Anspach; 02 513 44 59), a venue attracting a younger type of expat.

Plattesteen

41 rue du Marché au Charbon (02 512 82 03). Pré-métro Bourse. **Open** 11am-midnight Mon-Sat. **Credit** AmEx, DC, MC, V. **Map** p317 B3.

This traditional Belgian bar-café is truly multifunctional. It acts as a neighbourhood bar, as an inexpensive restaurant and as a place for ladies with poodles, ladies with men and men with men. It's a great melting pot on the corner of the street, joining shopping Brussels to gay Brussels and the trendy rue du Marché au Charbon. Thus it is a great meeting place, especially in summer when you can sit on the terrace and watch the world cruise by arm-in-arm. It's one of the great Brussels contradictions; homely and unexceptional decor slap in the middle of the new trendsville.

Le Roi d'Espagne

1 Grand' Place (02 513 08 07). Pré-métro Bourse. **Open** 10am-1am daily. **Credit** AmEx, DC, MC, V. **Map** p317 C3.

It might look a bit of a theme bar at first, with the puppets and pigs' bladders hanging from the ceiling, the open log fire, and waiters dressed as Trappist monks. But le Roi, a prime spot in one of the grandest guildhouses on the square (it was the HQ of the bakers' guild) has been like this forever. Inevitably full of tourists (plenty of Belgian ones, too), upstairs le Roi is like a labyrinth with endless rooms, dark corners and window tables overlooking the square – though many a diplomatic incident has been caused in grabbing one. Sadly, there's no terrace – the staff are hard pushed to cope as it is.

Brussels by bar crawl: Late haunts

Drinking Brussels-style? Let's get one thing straight. Closing time – pah! Forget frenzied last orders and getting them in quick. Brussels' bar culture encompasses an appreciation of the consummate art of getting slowly and gradually shitfaced.

While some bars do have an official closing time, it is enforced with varying degrees of exactitude. More often than not, bar closure depends on the number of customers and the barman's mood and patience. Most self-respecting Belgian bartenders would baulk at ringing a bell or demanding you down your drink and clear off. This unspoken understanding works both ways. You take the hint and finish up when the staff are busy cleaning up. If you're among the lingerers, you won't be hurried away too unceremoniously.

During the week, you should have little trouble finding places open until around 1am. On Friday and Saturdays, you can stretch it until two, even three. After that hazily defined crossover point, accommodating watering holes are a bit thinner on the ground. But if you know where to look, and you're not too fussy, Brussels is a city in which you can drink around the clock.

Downtown is where you'll find a plentiful selection of late-night bars in which to flout the dawn chorus. For some lively background tunes, **Pablo Disco Bar** (60 rue du Marché au Charbon; 02 514 51 49) spins house grooves in a small colourful clubby interior. Neighbouring Brazilian bar **Canoa Quebrada** (53 rue du Marché au Charbon; 02 511 13 54) is invariably pumping with a lively atmosphere of a weekend. Nearby **Dali's Bar** (35 rue des Bouchers; 02 511 54 67) pounds out dance tunes to a young crowd. **Coaster** (*pictured – see p128*), well known among night owls for potent shots and

Toone

21 petite rue des Bouchers (02 513 54 86).
Pré-métro Bourse. **Open** noon-midnight daily.
No credit cards. Map p317 C3
The narrow paved path leading off from the Grand'
Place – where the Toone is signposted by the Musée
de la Ville de Bruxelles – is well trampled with
tourist tracks. Although the puppet theatre (*see
p215*) is a rare treat for kids, its bar is a frequent
haunt for adults. Despite its popularity, the Toone
– built in 1835 in medieval style – is a pleasant pit-
stop, composed of two cosy rooms decorated in old
posters and filled with sturdy wooden furniture. A
full range of beers accompanies the modest menu of
salads, sandwiches and light lunches.

Ste-Catherine & around

Chez Martine

*37 rue de Flandre (02 512 43 23). Métro
Ste-Catherine.* **Open** noon-1am Tue-Fri; 4pm-
1am Sat. **No credit cards. Map** p318 B2.
Also known as Chez Haesendonck or Le Daringman,
Chez Martine is a wantonly retro bar that attracts
the lower echelons of Flemish bohemia. The lush in
the straw hat, the actor between jobs, the chain-

shakers plus a mean table football, only
really starts to fill up at around midnight.
Goupil le Fol (*see p123*) is intimate and
bonkers. The resolutely bohemian
Archiduc (*see right*) has the added
enticement of a doorbell to be rung.

As alcohol consumption begins to cloud
your better judgement, you may end up in
the **Celtica** (*see p122*), where the average
age hovers around 16. Some customers
are as slimy as the beer-covered tables
and floor, but most are just plainly off their
tits. In the same vein, the dregs of the
evening are confined to a drunken stupor
at **TJ's** (43 rue de la Fourche; 0479 484
260), a seedy den of contemporary R'n'B,
for which there may be a nominal door
charge. If you're still on your feet, so is
La Faim de Nuit (1 rue Van Artevelde; 02
513 77 38), which never seems to close.
You'd be best advised to stay clear of the
food, but you could avail yourself of their
extensive range of vodka shots.

And, as you emerge blinking in the
morning light, remember that **Falstaff**
(*see p123*) opens at 10am for breakfast,
coffee and cognac, thus starting the whole
cycle over again. Ding, ding, round two.

smoking Kerouackette, hey ho, the gang's all here.
Jumble sale shots of Elvis, Ella and others contrast
with the subtle wood panelling and iconic Stella
sign. CM also adheres to the every-bar-should-have-
one rule for house plants, c1955. Smoky, so smoky
(send for the ALF!), and often impossibly crowded
around the pokey bar counter, but all in all a most
wonderful antidote to neighbouring Trendonia
down rue Antoine Dansaert.

Kafka

*6 rue de la Vierge Noire (02 513 54 89). Métro/
Pré-métro De Brouckère.* **Open** 4pm-1am Mon-Sat;
5pm-2am Sun. **No credit cards. Map** p317 B3.
If it's late and you're lashing back the vodkas,
chances are you're in the Kafka. Not that you might
remember this the next day, but the Kafka boasts a
directory of vodkas, *genevers* and other assorted
white spirits, plus all the usual beers to chase the
chasers with. You may remember the clientele –
downtown flotsam and jetsam, eccentric chess-
playing intellectuals – but not the decor, brown and
bare tiles. Deliberately dressed down, and open till
far past your bedtime, the Kafka is not the pretentious poserie you were afraid it might be.

La Tentation

*28 rue de Laeken (02 223 22 75/www.latentation.
org). Métro/Pré-métro De Brouckère.* **Open**
4pm-2/3am Fri, Sat; noon-6pm Sun. **Credit** V.
Map p318 B/C2.
An urban-chic converted drapery warehouse with
huge windows, brick walls and effective low lighting, with a stylish and civilised vibe. A good spot to
start the evening or for a quiet drink. It's run by
Brussels' Galician community, but this is only really
apparent in the menu (Spanish liqueurs, tapas,
cheese and cold meats), the (re)lax(ed) staff, and the
odd folk music night (*see p200*). It cannot always be
banked on to be doing business as usual. When it
does, it's a hit with all age groups and types, and
suits tête-à-têtes and large gatherings.

St-Géry

Archiduc

*6 rue Antoine Dansaert (02 512 06 52). Pré-métro
Bourse.* **Open** 4pm-dawn daily. **Credit** AmEx, MC,
V. **Map** p318 B3.
The classic of all classics. Renovated in time to be
part of the cultural wave that swept down rue
Antoine Dansaert and washed over the rest of
Brussels in the mid 1980s, the Archiduc is a small,
cosy, two-floor art deco bar with a certain cocktail
feel about it. It's on the smart side, certainly, though
you could be sitting next to a trannie as much as a
couple just back from the opera. It's known as a
piano bar and sometimes there's a little jazz, but this
needn't spoil the mood. It's a fine place for an early
evening drink, an even better one towards sun up.
This gives it an enticing demi-monde feel as morning approaches, as does the doorbell to gain
entrance. It really doesn't get any better than this.

Eat, Drink, Shop

Le Booze 'n' Blues

20 rue des Riches Claires (02 513 93 33). Pré-métro Bourse. **Open** 5pm-2am Mon-Thur; 5pm-5am Fri, Sat. **Credit** AmEx, DC, MC, V. **Map** p318 B3.

This slightly seedy bar is an antidote to the nearby trendy cafés of place St-Géry – and it has one of the best jukeboxes in Brussels. Sit sipping locally brewed *gueuze* while listening to Otis Redding's *Dock of the Bay* belting out from the ancient Rock-Ola in the corner. Occasional live blues too. Atmospheric, if you're in that kind of mood.

Coaster

28 rue des Riches Claires (02 512 08 47). Pré-métro Bourse. **Open** 8pm-late Mon-Sat. **No credit cards. Map** p318 B3.

Set in a tiny red-brick house, this bar gets packed to its 17th-century beams, especially at weekends. Its small room traps the atmosphere and also the volume of the music. It's popular with a young crowd who stand on the chairs to party, and there's an outsize video screen and the biggest industrial bar

light you'll ever see. The candles are a nice touch, though they scream to be knocked over. This is one of the better music bars in St-Géry, but if you're to enjoy it, you should feel comfortable with busy, confined spaces. If the hedonism gets too much, there's plenty of choice in the area for moving on. Stays open until the wee hours.

Le Coq

14 rue Auguste Orts (02 514 24 14). Pré-métro Bourse. **Open** 9am-late daily. **No credit cards. Map** p317 B3.

Where do you go when you tire of all the trendies hanging around neighbouring place St-Géry? Le Coq. Where do all the trendies go when they tire of all the trendies hanging around St-Géry? Le Coq. The perfect antidote to the brash Nicolay-branded bars nearby, Le Coq may feature reluctant hints of hip – scattered flyers, occasionally tastefully behatted clientele – but in essence it's just a bar. Inside are two straight lines of brown chairs, beers signs neoned in kind yellow, pleasingly incongruous chandeliers,

Belgian bar life 1: Bingo

Schuman, Europe's capital. Faceless steel and glass, faceless bars and cafés, pit-stops for EU employees to quickly refuel. Brasserie de l'Europe, *par exemple*. Could be Brussels, could be Birmingham. Dive into one. A dozen tongues order the same standard Eurodrinks. Look in the corner. Flashing lights, a splash of primary colours, a mass of seemingly unrelated numbers. It's as if they asked a design team from Planet Zarg to invent a pinball machine. But it's not pinball, it's bingo. A Belgian bingo machine. You've found that little corner of Europe that is forever Belgium.

It may be primitive to the Playstation generation, but this hopelessly, unfashionably low-tech pastime is a staple of Belgian bar culture. Puzzled, uninitiated strangers blithely describe bingo machine as Belgian pinball. There is the same tilted table, the same shiny steel balls catapulted beneath the glass cover, the same buzzing and flashing upright display, the same gaudy neon. But clearly, it's not pinball. It has no flippers. The balls do not whizz satisfyingly from one spring to another. And there is no castle trapdoor jealously guarded by a plastic troll.

No, in bingo machines, the balls float down lazily to any of up to 25 holes, and there they stay. Indeed, it is quite common for addicts to get hooked on this sedentary diversion. The spectacle of the steel balls tumbling into the

holes is said to be profoundly soothing, and players spend hours at it, drowning out their worries in a stupor of sound and lights.

There is, of course, the same random element involved as paper bingo, but with six different 'cards' or number grids to deal with, it becomes more complex. Only true devotees are up to the task. Players are allowed to gently tip the machine to help direct the balls, as far as the anti-tilt mechanism will allow. And there are more devious ways to cheat. Desperadoes have been known to drill holes in the wood just under the glass and poke a metal rod inside to guide the balls into the right spot.

The vogue for bingo machines came and went in the US in the 1950s, a bizarre and brief counterpoint to the chrome and macho imagery of the era. But the machines survived – nay, flourished – in Belgium, one of the few corners of the world that could possibly see bingo as quirkily cool. Here it can be an addiction. Only recently the government set a number of strict laws to limit the game: only two machines per venue and a maximum payout from a single €6.25 stake of €500. The laws came into force after the arrest of 'Bingo King' Willy Michiels in 1999, who made national headlines by staking his all on these wonderful machines – to the point of bribing a high-ranking government official prior to the new gaming act.

Whatever you do, don't miss the wonderful **Archiduc**. *See p127.*

and a corner counter inevitably featuring a snoozing tabby curled up in a beer tray, next to which a chubby, grey-stubbled barman indolently shoots pinball when not shouting up for beers ('*Cadets!*, *Cadets!*'). Three mock cocks over the counter give a vague nod in the direction of theme. All is otherwise swamped in French jukebox pop. *Vive Le Coq!* (Unless the demolition ball encroaches any further along rue Orts.)

Fin de Siècle

9 rue des Chartreux (02 513 51 23). Pré-métro Bourse. **Open** 6pm-1am Tue-Sun. **Credit** MC, V. **Map** p317 B3.
This bar-restaurant has become a favourite with trendy twenty- to thirtysomethings who come here for the laid-back atmosphere and hearty, good-value food. Deliberately distressed, the long old room has no pretensions, though the terracotta walls are hung with a changing display of for-sale art. There is a lethal ironwork spiral staircase leading to the loos. This is one of the few central places where you can guarantee good food after midnight; pastas and salads sit alongside traditional Belgian, and the portions are huge. It gets packed, but you can usually find a space. The owner and staff are as friendly as anything, despite being run off their feet.

Le Greenwich

7 rue des Chartreux (02 511 41 67). Pré-métro Bourse. **Open** 11am-1am Mon-Thur; 11am-2am Fri, Sat. **No credit cards. Map** p317 B3.

Sitting in one of Brussels' trendiest streets, this bar simply refuses to change. Just as well. It is famed as Magritte's bar, where he tried to sell his pictures in the 1920s when everyone thought of him as a bizarre local who might go away if ignored. He didn't, nor did Le Greenwich. It's an oasis of calm, where people come to read, work and, most importantly, play chess. Conversations hush as the chess pieces clack. No music, no fuss and – please – no mobile phones. Make sure you take a look at the art nouveau door canopy; it's a little gem in need of a nice compliment.

Halles St-Géry

place St-Géry (02 502 44 24). Pré-métro Bourse. **Open** 10am-11pm daily. **No credit cards. Map** p318 B3.
This imposing red-brick building gives the whole *quartier* its character. A market until the 1970s, it was refurbished and now lends a trendy, laid-back air to eating and drinking. The lofty space with its intricate ironwork and odd Hawksmoor-like obelisk is used as a café-cum-exhibition space. In the cellar is a separate Latino dance club, and the pavements outside fill with bright wicker chairs in summer.

Mappa Mundo

2-6 rue du Pont de la Carpe (02 514 35 55). Pré-métro Bourse. **Open** 10am-3am daily. **No credit cards. Map** p318 B3.
This is one of the many bars and restaurants owned by young entrepreneur Fred Nicolay. Stand in the middle of place St-Géry and on each corner you will

find one of his establishments – the tell-tale sign is the job lot of uncomfortable wooden chairs on the terraces. Mappa looks as if it's been here forever. It hasn't, but it has created a 17th-century feel and could be termed a trendy local pub. The music is cool and the staff are ultra-cool, but be prepared to wait; they're always busy and there should be more of them. This is a warren of a place so if you think it's full, just keep climbing those stairs.

De Markten
5 rue Vieux Marché aux Grains (02 512 34 25). Métro Ste-Catherine or Pré-métro Bourse. **Open** 9am-8pm Mon-Thur; 9am-5pm Fri. **No credit cards. Map** p318 B3.
Before you step into this ground floor café, take a step back and look at the magnificent building. It's part of a cultural centre, and as such attracts young arty types from the Flemish school of thought. The style is postmodernist industrial chic. OK – it looks like a school canteen. But its minimalism is just what these possessions-are-capitalist folk want. A terrace in the summer looks on to the square which is filled with café tables. All very continental.

Le Roi des Belges
35 rue Jules van Praet (02 503 43 00). Pré-métro Bourse. **Open** 11am-1am Mon-Thur, Sun; 10am-2.30am Fri, Sat. **Credit** V. **Map** p318 B3.
Immediately opposite Mappa: same chairs, different mood. This bar is quieter, more determined than its sister and attracts a crowd of solo dreamers and intelligent couples. Upstairs is what in Belgium is

known as an alcohol bar – which means spirits rather than beer – furnished in a comfortable retro-lounge style. Service can be exasperatingly slow, especially on the terrace; it's quicker to go to the bar yourself. The food is good and it gets busy at lunchtime, but you should always be able to find a table in one of the two big rooms.

Zebra
33 place St-Géry (02 511 09 01). Pré-métro Bourse. **Open** noon-2am daily. **Credit** MC, V. **Map** p318 B3.
On another St-Géry corner, Zebra is the grand-daddy of them all, being the bar-café that started the whole thing off and helped give the square its hip appeal. This is poserville par excellence, with loyal regulars using it as a meeting place or to spend an evening on the busy terrace. Finding a table is almost impossible, though you'll have better luck earlier in the day. Because of its pedigree and the shortage of chairs, its clientele tends to cock a snoot at all the other pretender bars, even though they are of the same family.

Marolles & Midi station

Café de la Place
29 place du Jeu de Balle (no phone). Métro Porte de Hal/bus 20, 48. **Open** 5am-4pm daily. **No credit cards. Map** p320 B5.
Jeu de Balles, the flea-market square, is surrounded by cafés in the more traditional style. This one is no better, no worse than the others, but it gets a vote

Brussels by bar crawl: EU Quarter

Pseudo-Celtic hostelries are, sadly, by no means exclusive to Brussels. Yet the role the Irish pub plays on the social scene of Europe's capital is somewhat different. For two score years and more, the neighbourhood housing the main European institutions, centred on place Schuman, has sprouted a network of Irish and assorted anglophone pubs that have been treated as locals by homesick employees.

Schuman is where the pan-European EU workforce drinks itself silly. None are more up for it than the rampaging *stagiaires*, twentysomethings of either but determinate sex, from a cross-section of member states on a six-month internship at the EU. Think *It's A Knockout* on a binge. Their entertainment committee organises regular nights of alcohol-fuelled partying in Schuman's pubs from Monday to Thursday (on weekends they take to the centre of town, mob-handed). Each weekday night sees a different pub

hosting a frenzied session. They follow a standard fail-proof recipe: hordes of young European revellers, lashings of loud cheesy music, doused in copious quantities of alcohol on special offer. Leave to marinate and raucous, multilingual, heavy-handed flirting soon ensues. (Routes vary with the bi-annual arrival of fresh European blood.) Whether you're looking to link up or sidestep them, the *stagiaires* are hard to miss.

Before you set off in earnest, the **Old Hack** (176 rue Joseph II; 02 230 07 95), a peaceful little corner pub, is handy for a spot of well-priced lunch. Down the road, the **Wild Geese** (*pictured* – 2 avenue Livingstone; 02 230 19 90) is a shining example of the manufactured Irish pub. This is where Ryanair Charleroi airport buses wait. Incoming visitors are either happy or horrified to be eased into Belgium via this harp-o-rama. The meat market is usually on Thursday nights, when *stagiaires* descend en masse.

Eat, Drink, Shop

You can eat, drink and catch up on the news at **L'Amour Fou**. *See p133*.

for its vast windows on to the square, which means you can sit and enjoy the free spectacle of folk wading through unfathomable junk.

A la Clef d'Or

1 place du Jeu de Balle (02 511 97 62). Métro Porte de Hal/bus 20, 48. **Open** 4.30am-5pm daily. **No credit cards. Map** p320 B5.
This large loud caff is a fave with locals, so it can be a squeeze for the casual visitor. Sunday mornings are the best and busiest, partly because of the live accordionist and party atmosphere. Unintentionally retro, it sports vinyl chairs and pink neon advertising signs. The food is of the *croque monsieur* and fried-egg variety. Madame skates around in her mules and black leggings, while monsieur stands at the coffee-machine barking orders to the overworked staff. Oh, he's also in charge of the *soupe du jour* pot, which means he lifts the occasional ladle.

Indigo

160 rue Blaes (02 511 38 97). Métro Porte de Hal/bus 20, 48. **Open** varies. **No credit cards. Map** p320 B5.

For something a mite more civilised and less contrived, walk back up the hill to **Kitty O'Shea's** (boulevard Charlemagne; 02 230 78 75), a snug and lower-key Irish haunt favoured by middle-aged Commission workers. From there, you could venture across the roundabout to the **Sin é** (50 rue Breydel; 02 230 36 56). Beware though – there might be Irish music. Back to the main drag, where the small dark interior of **O'Dwyers** (55 rue Archimède; 02 735 10 09) is a stopoff for sports fans. Before attempting the ascent of the next hill, you might want to pop into the **Hairy Canary** (12 rue Archimède; 02 280 05 09) for a quick one. It's English-themed rather than Irish, hence the carpets and Walker's crisps. The **Old Oak** (26 rue Franklin; 02 735 75 44) is your best bet for Irish sports.

Make it to the top of rue Franklin hill, and you'll be rewarded by the most idiosyncratic of the neighbourhood's anglophone bars. The **Bok & Dragon** (189 rue du Noyer; 02 733 39 66), run by Pat and Steve, a South African and Welsh combo, is a curious hybrid of a sleepy little Belgian local and rowdy expat bar. Wind things up by heading back down the hill to the **James Joyce** (34 rue Archimède; 02 230 98 94), one of Brussels' most long-established Irish pubs. Celtic-themed but not nauseatingly so, it's the place to head to when everywhere else has closed for the night. Even an Irish pub looks welcoming at 6am on a weekend morning.

This is so trendy it hurts. Hand-painted walls in primary colours, broken-glass mosaics, white wooden garden furniture and candles by daylight. Get the picture? Sit and enjoy great frothy coffees and a slice of quiche or a fried egg, all presented on flea-market crockery. It gets busy, especially on Sunday mornings, but patience is a virtue and the friendly staff will squeeze you in somewhere.

Le Laboreur
3 place de la Constitution (02 520 18 59). Métro/ Pré-métro Gare du Midi. **Open** 9am-10pm Mon-Fri, Sun. **No credit cards. Map** p320 A5.
Somewhere in Brussels it is forever 1957. Le Laboreur is part of that somewhere. Just round the corner from Midi station, the Lab is a perfectly preserved slice of time, its long walls lined with colourful stained-glass tableaux of happy farm workers. Underneath, mirrors, strip lights, and bar snacks frequently boasted of by name ('Croque Divers! Croissants!'). A vast old table football and pool table (ping-pong is also promised) nestle among the three straight rows of marble tables, which lead to a bar serving, among other ales, draught *lambic*, another rare find. A lovely old pentagonal door frame completes the picture.

Recyclart
Gare de la Chapelle, 25 rue des Ursulines (02 502 57 34/café 02 289 00 59/www.recyclart.be). Métro Gare Centrale. **Open** *Café* 11am-5pm Tue-Fri & 1hr before events. **No credit cards. Map** p317 B4.

Zebra: perfect for canoodling. *See p130.*

Daytime café and club venue run by a non-profit arts group that focuses on the recycling of materials and the urban landscape itself, starting – in 1997 – with the rehabilitation of the disused train station that houses it. Recyclart runs art workshops for children, young artists and craftspeople, training schemes for the unemployed and holds an annual street art festival. It also hosts some excellent club nights (with room for 450 people) – more affordable (around 7.50) and less mainstream than a lot of the overtly trendy clubs; check the website for details. Recently awarded a generous sum by the Ministry of Culture, and a with good track record, it's a space to watch for art, cultural events and stomping tunes.

Het Warm Water
25 rue des Renards (02 513 91 59). Métro Porte de Hal/bus 20, 48. **Open** 8am-7pm Mon, Tue, Thur-Sun. **No credit cards. Map** p320 B5.
This café is located on a steep little hill leading up from the flea market. The street is filled with eclectic second-hand and antique shops, so the place is often busy and caters to both browsers and traders. Its flavour is firmly Dutch, both in look and menu, and the green awning and cream walls make it an inviting place. It specialises in breakfast and brunch, with daily specials chalked up outside.

Upper Town

Le Bier Circus
89 rue de l'Enseignement (02 218 00 34). Tram 92, 93, 94. **Open** noon-2.30pm, 6pm-midnight Mon-Fri; 6pm-midnight Sat. **No credit cards. Map** p319 D3.
Rue de l'Enseignement is not a bad place to start your education, beer-wise. There's a huge list of brews at this traditional Belgian bar, including plenty of *gueuze*, Trappist, organic and wheat beers. Cartoon characters line the walls, the staff know their onions, and you'll graduate after this immersion course somewhat wiser and not too much out of pocket.

Le Grain de Sable
15 place du Grand Sablon (02 514 05 83). Tram 92, 93, 94. **Open** 8.30am-late daily. **Credit** MC, V. **Map** p317 C4.
An at-first-glance understated bar on Brussels' poshest squares. Although surrounded by the big and blousy, there is no fear of le Grain suffering from an inferiority complex. For a start, the pavement terrace snakes its way around a corner, and in the warm weather becomes a right-angle of bright buzz and respectable reunion. Inside, the tiny ground-floor bar plays funky Latin-jazz with the flickering candles seemingly finding their own bossa rhythm. The clientele tend toward the vodka-Schweppes rather than the beer bottle. No startling effects here, just a modest room filled with beautiful people and the friendliest of muscular staff. It's as if this tiny 17th-century house never closes. Doesn't it do well considering its age?

Bustling **Brasserie Verscheuren**. *See p136.*

Le Perroquet
31 rue Watteau (02 512 99 22). Tram 92, 93, 94. **Open** 10am-1am daily. **No credit cards.** **Map** p317 C4.
Authentic art nouveau bar close to the Sablon that features mirrors a-plenty plus stained glass, a striking black and white tiled floor and a summer terrace. There's a modest menu of salads and pitta sandwiches. A few too many keen young expats, perhaps, but not a bad atmosphere for all that.

La Pirogue
18 rue St-Anne (02 511 35 25). Tram 92, 93, 94. **Open** 11.30am-2am daily. **Credit** AmEx, DC, MC, V. **Map** p317 C4.
A small Senegalese resto-bar, La Pirogue is run by a Polish-Belgian named Serge. He's an ex-legionnaire with a taste for home-made ginger beer, now a house speciality. Other specials include African beer Mongozo (7%) – traditionally drunk from the bowl-shaped shell of a fruit somewhat akin to a yellow coconut – and the owner's peppered vodka (oof!). Exotic food too, mainly Congolese and Senegalese, with some European dishes.

EU Quarter & Etterbeek

Chez Bernard
47 place Jourdan (02 230 2238). Métro Trône then bus 34, 80. **Open** 7am-2am daily. **No credit cards.** **Map** p325 F5.
Sitting unfazed amid the mock-nouveau wine bars and brasseries on this busiest of squares, Bernard's Place remains rock-solid traditional. A long mirrored room leads to an unlikely glass conservatory at the back, giving the impression that a tearoom has been stuck on the back of a beer hall. Madame spots you

at table, takes a drag on the fag that could be her last, then clacks over to take your order, greeting you with the friendliest of *s'il vous plaîts* you could hope to hear. It also greets the Eurocrats feeling good about mixing with locals, locals feeling indifferent about mixing with Eurocrats, Sunday morning shoppers and diners from Maison Antoine, the famous *frites* stall opposite. *See also p111* **No Macs please.** Yep, you can buy your chips, bring them here and they'll offer you a napkin and a beer list.

Fat Boy's
6 place du Luxembourg (02 511 32 66/ www.fat-boys.com). Métro Trône. **Open** 11am-late daily. **Credit** MC, V. **Map** p324 E5.
Opened in early 2000, Fat Boy's is the latest temple to be erected in the honour of the great god football. With its nine screens, lesser sports can even get a look-in. There's a buzzing terrace in summer and US-style burgers. Live music most Friday nights.

Ixelles

L'Amour Fou
185 chaussée d'Ixelles (02 514 27 09). Métro Porte de Namur/bus 54, 71. **Open** 9am-3am Mon-Thur; 10am-2am Fri-Sun. **Credit** AmEx, DC, MC, V. **Map** p321 D6.
A hip resto/bar opposite the Maison Communale, where canoodling customers can retreat to comfy sofas at the back for candlelit snuggles away from prying eyes. Eye-catching art on the walls and multilingual newspapers make it easy to pass a couple of hours, even if you're alone. Look out for the chandelier made from wine glasses. The food – salads, croques, veg and meaty mains – is recommended, though the waitresses are standoffish.

L'Atelier
77 rue Elise (02 649 19 53). Métro Louise then tram 93, 94/bus 71. **Open** 6pm-3am daily. **No credit cards.**
Yes, we know, it's absolutely miles from anywhere, but, believe us, it's worth every click of the taxi meter. This is a cosy, wood-and-brick candlelit scout hut of a bar, with a counter separating a conspiratorial backroom from the front of house. Behind the dividing line, a vast fridge of bottled beers, meticulously labelled. Draught options – Kriek, Barbar, Chouffe, Pecheresse et al – are chalked up, as are *genevers* and wines. Also displayed is a league table in honour of the diversity of Belgium's national drink, many examples of which are happily available. You'll come again. Just you see.

Grain d'Orge
142 chaussée de Wavre (02 511 26 47). Métro Porte de Namur. **Open** 11am-3am Mon-Fri; 6pm-3am Sat-Sun. **No credit cards.** **Map** p321 E5.
The Grain is where the guitar is still god, and where its pot-bellied followers wallow in its Friday night malprachice (eg Fried Bourbon) surrounded by pinball and posters of past protagonists (eg the Who).

Eat, Drink, Shop

On the six nights of the week when not assailed by barking four-piece combos, barmen with tattooed palms serve a range of beers in this spit-and-saw-dust saloon to an audience of apparently hardy parole jumpers. Some bring forgiving lady friends. After they argue, you'll find the men in the Tulipe diagonally opposite, a mosaic-tiled hospice for unshaven losers extracting cheer from 75¢ beer.

Luigi's

253 boulevard Général Jacques (02 646 92 96). Tram 23. **Open** noon-late Mon-Fri; noon-5pm Sat, Sun. **Credit** MC.

This café-bar is a kicking little Flemish place. Run by the eponymous Luigi, it's a fave late-night haunt of students and has table football (beware making bets). Huge crowds descend when Anderlecht appear on TV; those wearing other team colours should don a jacket. At other times, watch out for guitar-playing *gendarmes* (really!). Atmospheric and refreshingly cheap.

Monkey Business

30 rue Defacqz (02 538 69 34). Métro Louise then tram 93, 94. **Open** 11.30am-3am Mon-Fri, Sun; 6pm-late Sat. **Credit** AmEx, DC, MC, V. **Map** p321 D7.

This American sports bar, recently taken over by a basketball player, serves diner food and is usually pretty busy. Refurbished at the end of 2001, it attracts a lot of Americans, but not exclusively so. The Thursday karaoke sessions are famous.

Le Pantin

355 chaussée d'Ixelles (02 640 80 91). Bus 71. **Open** 11am-2am Mon-Sat; 5pm-2am Sun. **No credit cards. Map** p324 E7.

Le Pantin has the potential to provide the backdrop for one of Guinness' philosophical ads, its creaky wooden furniture keeping regulars deep in thought and in suitable discomfort. Here older world-weary students dedicate their existence (existence? Pah!) over smoking, sipping, chess-playing and whispered conversation. As if to spite them, a coquettish black cat enjoys the run of an eclectic dislocation of objects – puppets, playthings, pinball – while a sober bar staff provide a reluctant nod toward normality.

Rick's Bar

334 avenue Louise (02 647 75 30). Métro Louise then tram 93, 94. **Open** 10.30am-midnight daily. **Credit** AmEx, DC, MC, V.

Around for some 20 years, Rick's is by far and away the best-known American bar in Brussels. Housed in a magnificent three-storey building on avenue Louise, it's swish, chic and, yes, expensive – but serves arguably the best bar brunch in town. Frequented by suits, it's a busy after-office haunt, and the rear terrace is glorious in summer.

Le Stoemelings

7 place de Londres (02 512 43 74). Métro Trône. **Open** 11am-2am Mon-Fri; 5pm-2am Sat, Sun. **No credit cards. Map** p324 E5.

Hipper-than-hip **L'Ultime Atome**. *See p135.*

The tatty review from *After Dark* proudly curling its corners on the front door glass dates from 1991, but the same adjectives still apply: traditional, cosy and hearty. Since then, all that has changed at le Stoemelings has been the unwise substitution of its lovely pub cat for a menacing Rottweiler, although puss is still revered with pictures by the two prime window seats. Otherwise, it's the same lived-in feel, Belgian bar fare and friendly service. Beautiful bar counter too, proper for propping up. Perhaps not the stuff of revolution, but in 1991, apparently, le Stoemelings helped relaunch wheat beer back into Brussels' bar life: 'The Blanche Revolution starts here!'. Well I do declare!

Le Tavernier

445 chaussée de Boondael (02 640 71 91). Bus 95, 96. **Open** 11am-3am Mon-Thur, Sun; 11am-5am Fri, Sat. **No credit cards.**

St-Géry bar guru Fred Nicolay gets smart. Having established a host of cutting-edge bars in the centre of town, Nicolay has wisely plonked a hunk of Hoxton into the university quarter of Brussels, deep into Ixelles by the cemetery. After all, who better to exploit than students? Wantonly metallic, with zinc and brick touches, and obligatory low brown furniture, le Tavernier consists of one main room with a long bar counter, a separate side bar with a DJ deck in the corner, and two courtyards, a leafy outer one and a heated inner one. You'll find the usual beers and bar snacks, with unusually good music most of the time. Look out for the big red Duvel sign, the beer company that has helped bankroll Nicolay's little empire.

Au Trappiste

3 avenue de la Toison d'Or (02 511 79 27). Métro Porte de Namur or Louise. **Open** 9.30am-midnight Mon-Thur, Sun; 9.30am-1am Fri, Sat. **Credit** AmEx, DC, MC, V. **Map** p321 C5.

This turn-of-the-century Belgian brasserie is highly recommended for a summer evening, as much for for its terrace and trendy location as for its fine beers. The food's not bad either, with plenty of hearty Belgian specialities.

L'Ultime Atome

14 rue St-Boniface (02 511 13 67). Métro Porte de Namur. **Open** 8.30am-midnight Mon-Thur; 9am-1am Fri, Sat. **Credit** MC, V. **Map** p321 D5.

Art deco bumps unceremoniously into Conran in this vast corner bar, which attracts every luvvie you could hope to meet in a lifetime. Impossibly thin waiters, all low-slung hips and trainers, gel back their hair to stop it getting in the way of the air

kisses they dish out to seemingly every person who drops by. Cuisine non-stop, around 50 beers on offer and a background thump of ambient electronica gives the Atome an air of smug self-satisfaction. Daytime shopaholics give way to Trendsville City in the evening; designer carrier bags making room for the slick and willowy, their labels worn on the outside. Yet it's still basically Belgian; a lone formica table and metal locker outside the loo by day suggests the presence of a Madame Pipi in the evening to relieve the trendy things of their 50¢ pieces.

St-Gilles

Brasserie de l'Union

55 parvis de St-Gilles (02 538 15 79). Pré-métro Parvis de St-Gilles. **Open** 7.30am-1am daily. **No credit cards. Map** p320 B6.

Proudly propping up one corner of St-Gilles' main square, the Union's amiable nature allows three communities to mingle in one large bar-room. Most prominent are the beer-swilling arty bohos, by day surrounded by cigarette smoke, by late night

Brussels by bar crawl: Charbon

The rue du Marché au Charbon is one of the main arteries of the late-night bar scene in central Brussels. It begins as a tiny street with a cluster of gay bars (*see chapter* **Gay & Lesbian**), then continues after crossing a main road. The street has a character all of its own: narrow and in the original old-town style, and filled with characteristic houses, many of which have been converted into stylish (and sometimes kitsch) bars. It's a perfect place to bar-hop and build up the evening over time depending on mood. Even though there may be dancing, these are bars not clubs, and the lack of entrance fees means you can come and go as you please.

The first port of call, on the right, is the inspirational **Canoa Quebrada** (No.53; 02 511 13 54), a strange name for a bar that plays funky, Latin-inspired sounds. The decor is mysterious and dark, with its UV light and white canopies. Next door, a beautiful Gothic arched tunnel leads to the **Rock Classic Bar** (No.55; 02 512 15 47), a tiny place that plays hefty rock music until 6am daily. Opposite, you can't miss the traffic lights of the **Pablo Disco Bar** (No.60; 02 514 51 49), one of Brussels' diehards, much loved for its stylish interior and speciality Shakers – cocktails served in the shaker with accompanying shot glasses. If you feel

peckish, drop into **La Guantanameca** (No.57) a Spanish bar where you can take wine by the glass and choose any tapas at €5; it's a nicely old-fashioned place offering a welcome change of mood.

The strap-line of **Cartagena** (No.70; 02 502 59 08) is 'dance first, drink later'. You may feel you're entering a time warp as you catch sight of the bubbling lava-lamp pillars holding up the bar and the orange glow of the main room. Next door, the **Da Caro** (No.72) offers retro of a different type with its 1950s-inspired interior, though it's the real thing and no theme room. Sit and stare at the ultraviolet mountains at the back as you work your way through a staggering range of South American cocktails.

Once you hit **Au Soleil** (No.86; 02 513 34 30), the street has become pedestrianised and in summer is full of tables and late-night buzz. Housed in an old tailor's shop, as the original advertising plates bear witness, the bar is a favourite of artists, musicians and a slightly bohemian crowd. Just past the church, **Fontainas** (No.91) follows this theme in a 1950s milk bar way, with its wooden floor, globe lights and kitchen diner chairs. Ultimately trendy, it has regular DJ evenings to make the place swing, but is also hyper-cool to return to for your first Sunday morning coffee with the newspapers.

Football fans unite at eccentric **Brasserie de l'Union**. *See p135*.

pleasantly totalled. (On market Sundays they bring improbably named offspring to be entertained by a frantic accordionist.) Then come the Union football faithful, their meeting place decorated with fringes of yellow and blue, a poster for the nearby home match or away trip religiously taped to the huge windows, and sepia team shots expressing a fierce if dated pride. In between are locals, true locals, over-lipsticked locals, dog-cursing locals, thirsty locals. Overseeing the whole show scowls a framed Screamin' Jay Hawkins, still casting spells on the poor mortals down below. Welcome to St-Gilles.

Brasserie Verscheuren

11-13 parvis de St-Gilles (02 539 40 68). Pré-métro Parvis de St-Gilles. **Open** 8am-1am Mon-Thur, Sun; 8am-2am Fri, Sat. **No credit cards**. **Map** p320 B7.
Mercifully renovated in the late summer of 2001, in the shadow of St-Gilles church, on the far corner of the main square, Verscheuren is as valuable to the village-like quality of community life here as the market in front of it. With its lovely art deco interior, light fittings more befitting an ocean liner than a humble local, and a vast clock worthy of Grand Central, the V offers class behind delicate panels of stained glass. The back wall is a boy's own wonder, seven league tables stretching down to lowly Promotion D, each team delineated in bright Subbuteo colours. Good selection of beers too. Hectic of a lunchtime, when the dim but fanciable staff seem to lose the plot and the fine soup too, but laid-back later on, when the outdoor tables perfectly catch the last rays of a summer's evening.

Chez Moeder Lambic

68 rue de Savoie (02 539 14 19). Pré-métro Horta/tram 18. **Open** 4pm-4am daily. **No credit cards**.
The BBC would love it. Sweedlepipe or Fezziwig would be perfectly at home among the hand-hewn wooden benches, the cobwebbed rows of bottled beer, the dusty, smoke-stained walls. No further set-dressing needed in this brownest of brown bars. Dwarfed by the soaring St-Gilles town hall, the beer-labelled windows declare brews such as Silly Saison and Pee Klak, the beer list (almost 1,000 on offer) is as long as Micawber's debts, and the well-thumbed comic-strip books are stacked in bins like Gradgrind's ledgers. Yet the clientele is 20th-century eclectic, real ale, Pink Floyd types with a smattering of grunge. They tend to hang around inside, fearing the daylight offered by the summer terrace.

La Porteuse d'Eau

48 avenue Jean Volders (02 537 66 46). Métro Porte de Hal. **Open** 10am-midnight daily. **No credit cards**. **Map** p320 B6.
Lovely art nouveau café, all dinky and curlicued, the perfect spot to launch an illicit affair. A grand entrance guarded by a pair of vast, green curtains ushers you into an extravagant, perhaps effete interior. A swirl of bar counter is offset by bundles of green plants and a spiral staircase leading to an atrium themed with friezes of water women. Toasts, sandwiches and, incongruously, tagliatelle, compose a food menu available till 11pm. Tea is as widely sipped as wine or beer, but then you're always out to impress on the first pick up.

Tierra del Fuego
4 rue Berckmans (02 537 42 72). Métro Louise then tram 91, 92. **Open** *Bar* 5pm-12.30am Mon-Thur, Sun; 5pm-2am Fri, Sat. *Food served* 7-11pm Mon-Thur, Sun; 7pm-midnight Fri, Sat. **Credit** AmEx, DC, MC, V. **Map** p321 C6.
This Latin American bar and restaurant, located just off chaussée de Charleroi, is one of the city's best-kept secrets – and has one of the nicest beer gardens. Cross the little footbridge to the high-walled court-yard to sip a Cuba Libre surrounded by exquisite tiling, greenery and a heady, intimate atmosphere.

St-Josse & Schaerbeek

Makin' Whoopie
65 rue Royale Ste-Marie (02 215 30 39). Tram 92, 93, 94. **Open** 7pm-late Mon-Thur, Sun; 8pm-late Fri, Sat. **No credit cards. Map** p319 E1.
Not as bad as its name would have you believe, this is a typically raucous Flemish bar, opposite the Halles de Schaerbeek, with a youngish clientele of the mainly rock fraternity. If you're of the same persuasion, it's a good place to pick up on what's happening on the local live music scene, try some unusual brews from the extensive selection, and listen to a few old tunes. It comes into its own late at night, much like its regular clientele.

De Ultieme Hallucinatie
316 rue Royale (02 217 06 14). Métro Botanique/ tram 92, 93, 94. **Open** 11am-2am Mon-Fri; 4pm-2am Sat. *Food served* noon-2.30pm, 7-10.30pm Mon-Fri; 7-10.30pm Sat. **Credit** AmEx, DC, MC, V. **Map** p322 E1.
Famously lavish art nouveau café-restaurant (*see p119*) hidden behind a dingy exterior on a dingy stretch of the rue Royale. A fine choice of beers match the surroundings, the back bar area done out like a train from the grand era of travel. The build-ing dates back to the turn of the century, and a tasty range of snacks are best taken in the pleasant back garden. As good as it gets in grey old Schaerbeek.

Woluwe-St-Pierre

Schievelavabo
52 rue du Collège St-Michel (02 779 87 07). Métro Montgomery. **Open** noon-2pm, 7pm-1am Mon-Fri; 7pm-1am Sat, Sun. **Credit** V.
You can't go wrong with the bistro cooking in most of Brussels' neighbourhood cafés, and this is a prime example, a short stroll from the EU Quarter. Hefty and tasty portions of Belgian classics, pastas and salads will set you back around €10. Brick walls covered in retro ads, and a boat suspended behind the bar give it a polished 'junk store' feel.
Branch: 20 rue Egide van Ophem, Uccle (02 332 20 91).

Eat, Drink, Shop

Belgian bar life 2: Madames Pipis

Theirs is a strange, windowless, twilight world. Perhaps it's the lack of daylight that deprives them not only of colour, but of humour. While you're gleefully guzzling huge amounts of Belgian beer, the bar's toilets are being jealously guarded by a matron of a certain age and ilk. For les Madames Pipis are invariably strong, forceful scary types.

Spookily, the urinals they guard are often in full view of the Madame and the passing world, with no distinction between men's and ladies'. There is no escape. Cough up or cross your legs. Although they feign complete

disinterest, the Madames' eyes and ears are razor-honed; they know exactly who is in, how long they've been in and what for. Pricier *cabine* users beware. They are rabid ready-reckoners, who can keep up to 20 visitors in their heads at once and have total recall on who paid on going in – a 25¢ pee toll has replaced the former ten-franc piece – and who still owes on leaving. They got the hang of the euro a nanosecond after midnight on 01.01.02.

Technically, the fee is a tip for keeping the toilets clean. For Madames Pipis, this is often their only means of support. They do not, as is assumed, receive a salary from the bars they work in – in fact, they usually have to pay rent, as well as providing equipment. It doesn't leave them much over for fags.

Usually you'll find them in white backless mules, occasionally in slippers. Always in an apron. Tools of the trade: metal bucket and string mop; Mr Propre cleaning fluid; greyish cloth for wiping down mirrors; white saucer for the money; handwritten price sign, usually in black felt-tip on a bit of card; flea-market vase with fluorescent plastic or silk flowers; ashtray; tablecloth; wooden chair. Beware.

Shops & Services

A capital collection of retail outlets – plus, of course, plenty of shops selling chocolate, comics and Belgian beer.

Brussels' main shopping areas are the **Lower Town**, **Upper Town**, **avenue Louise** and **Ixelles**, but each of the city's 19 *communes* has retained its local shopping area. These are usually self-sustaining, and typically include food shops, cobblers, dry-cleaners, boutiques and chains such as Di (a kind of second-class Boots without the pharmaceuticals) and also, of course, reflect the social and ethnic make-up of the neighbourhood's inhabitants.

Galeries, fairly common in Brussels and found throughout the city centre in particular, are shopping arcades (either single passageways or clusters, some built in the 19th century, others modern structures) housing a diversity of businesses. They sometimes act as the last bastion of resistance of old-fashioned specialist shops, such as milliners or glovers. *See also p144* **Galeries galore**.

Overall, Brussels has everything you would find in most other major cities, but you should certainly not overlook Antwerp (*see p221*). Just a 25- to 45-minute train journey away, it is trendier and livelier, and many big names have chosen to open there rather than in conservative Brussels. Although it's true that the Flemish are in the vanguard of fashion, now that Brussels has begun to support its own fashion industry and has its own prominent art colleges and plenty of fresh local talent, it looks like the capital's fashion scene is diversifying and being given a new lease of life. One day Brussels may rival Antwerp's status as the country's undisputed mecca for fashion junkies. For the moment, however, it is safe to say that Antwerp still holds the title.

Historically sales have been strictly regulated in Belgium, like everything else. However, new Europe-wide legislation is on the cards (and may come into force at any time from 2003), which will effectively liberalise sales, leaving shopkeepers free to offer discounts at any time of the year. In any case, resourceful Belgian shopkeepers have always managed to work their way round the law, which allows sales to be held before renovations of the shop floor, for instance, or specific discounts (promotions) usually coinciding with seasonal events, such as discounts on perfume and chocolate around Valentine's Day.

LOWER TOWN AND UPPER TOWN

Around the **Grand' Place** and particularly near the Manneken-Pis are the tourist-dependent chocolate, lace and European merchandise shops. While some respected big names and reputable smaller ones do join the fray, you would be wise to avoid many of the tourist-traps, either (often in the case of beer and chocolate) because you can get better value not much further afield, or because Brussels really has more to offer than a corkscrew shaped like a small urinating boy or an umbrella featuring the European flag.

Rue des Eperonniers (south-east of the Grand' Place) groups together quirky old-fashioned gift shops (La Courte Echelle at No.12 sells doll's houses and other miniatures; Mata Hari at No.6 specialises in antique jewellery, clothing and perfume bottles) and random clothes stores selling new and second-hand fashionable garments (Peau d'Ane at No.37 sells its own funky designs, and will alter them to measure).

To find the **Galeries Agora**, home to a few good streetwear shops, but otherwise a hellhole of tacky stores selling hippy dippy grunge, trashy boots and cheap piercing and jewellery, follow the smell of incense.

Infinitely more appealing are the architecturally stunning **Galeries St-Hubert** (north-east of the Grand' Place), which opened in 1847. Divided into the galerie du Roi, de la Reine and du Prince, they now house expensive, old-fashioned boutiques selling lace, gloves, hats, bags and jewellery (Patrick Anciaux, at 7-9 galerie de la Reine, has antique items along with new designs), as well as some modern design stores (such as Ligne, at 12 galerie de la Reine), card shops (Flammarion at 4 galerie du Roi) and the odd café (La Taverne du Passage at 30 galerie du Roi is a slice of Brussels history; La Vache Qui Regarde Passer Les Trains at No.29 is a recent newcomer). Chocolate fixes can be satisfied courtesy of Neuhaus (25 galerie de la Reine) and Corné (24 galerie du Roi).

Despite a relatively recent facelift, **rue Neuve** (running from place de la Monnaie, north of the Grand' Place, up to Rogier metro station) remains a lacklustre shopping street, which verges on the hellish on Saturday

Rue Neuve: packed with high-street stores and shoppers galore.

afternoons, when the multifaceted population of Brussels descends en masse. It houses branches of many international high-street stores, such as Morgan, Esprit, H&M and Benetton. Among these, Sisley and Mango are worth a peek. Things continue in the same vein as you reach the northern end of the largely pedestrian-dominated street and the **City 2** mall. Low ceilings, depressing lighting and an unexceptional range of consumer traps make this an even less attractive consumer option, though, to its credit, you will find the large record and bookstore Fnac here. South of the place de la Monnaie is **rue des Fripiers** and, running east of the latter, **rue du Marché aux Herbes**, both of which have a more bearable selection of generic stores.

Ste-Catherine (west of the Grand' Place and boulevard Anspach) has been an up-and-coming area for years now. Frequented by a heterogeneous crowd of art students and a largely immigrant population, it is also home to luxury food shops, such as the Maison du Caviar on quai des Usines. Towards boulevard d'Ypres are shops supplying North African cooking essentials.

The neighbourhood around **place St-Géry** has an interesting mix. Around here you'll find the two streets that make up Brussels' modest

version of Chinatown, a few trendy streetwear and record stores and, on **rue Antoine Dansaert**, clothes by up-and-coming and established Belgian designers.

South-west of the Grand' Place, running down towards the Gare du Midi, **rue du Midi** offers a worthwhile wander, with stamp, coin, camera and art shops. **Boulevard Maurice Lemmonier** (which runs parallel) has comics shops, second-hand book and record stores and an assortment of dusty little businesses. Scattered about a few streets perpendicular to the rue du Midi, such as **rue des Pierres, rue du Marché au Charbon** and **rue Plattesteen**, are a host of trendy vintage clothes shops and other boutiques, interspersed with various bars.

If antiques are your thing, then the Sablon area (between the Lower Town and Upper Town) is the place to head. Upmarket shops line the **place du Grand Sablon**, and the antiques trail continues (descending slowly from chic to more scruffy) along **rue des Minimes** and **rue des Petites Minimes**, and on to **rue Blaes** and rue Haute. These two streets and the **place du Jeu de Balle**, the heart of the Marolles neighbourhood, have an eclectic mix, combining trendy clothing, retro furniture and gift shops with local bakeries and grocers.

AVENUE LOUISE AND IXELLES

Avenue Louise and **boulevard de
Waterloo** are the closest Brussels gets to
London's Knightsbridge and New York's Fifth
Avenue. Foreign business money and Belgian
inheritances are spent in the boutiques of
Chanel, Gucci, Cacharel, Versace, Louis Vuitton
and Cartier – just a sprinkling of the big names
dotted along the two wide, tree-lined streets.

Avenue de la Toison d'Or (parallel to
boulevard de Waterloo, stretching between
Louise and Porte de Namur metro stations) is
a little more mid-range, with its selection of
mainstream gift shops and high-street clothing
shops such as Springfield and ProMod (which
are usually better appointed than many less
well situated branches). Shops such as Bouvy,
at No.52, sell a selection of designer labels,
thus continuing the undistinctive but upmarket
designer theme. **Galeries de la Toison d'Or**
and **Louise** (running off avenue de la Toison
d'Or) are indoor shopping complexes featuring
a similar mélange of middle-of-the-road
boutiques and label emporiums. They make a
good target for shoe shopping, containing a
plethora of footwear shops in close proximity
to each other, and they are handy to duck into
when the Belgian weather begins to take its toll.

About halfway up avenue Louise, running
west, is **rue du Bailli**. Concentrated here and
radiating out to surrounding streets, you'll
find a selection of gift shops and clothing
boutiques (Mademoiselle Lucien, at 48 rue
Armand Campenhout, has original designer
clothes for women). It makes a pleasant location
for wandering, being quieter and housing more
unusual and individual stores than the rest of
this part of town. There is also an abundance
of relatively chic cafés and restaurants,
converging around **place du Chatelain**.

Parallel with avenue Louise and by Porte de
Namur metro station are **chaussée d'Ixelles**
and **chaussée de Wavre**. The former has
most of the main high-street shops; its more
interesting boutiques and gift shops are found
on side streets (such as Sol Luna at 20 rue St
Boniface, which has lots of silver jewellery)
and around **place Fernand Cocq**.

All the shops listed below are closed on
Sundays unless otherwise indicated. Many
smaller shops also close on Mondays.

TAX-FREE SHOPPING

Prices include sales tax of up to 21 per cent
(rates vary depending on the item). In many
shops non-EU residents can request a Tax-Free
Cheque on purchases of more than €145, which
can be cashed at customs when leaving the EU
to reclaim VAT. Savings Shops in the scheme
have a 'Tax-Free Shopping' sticker on their door.

Bookshops & newsagents

For gay and lesbian bookshops, *see p193*.

L'Ame des Rues – Librairie de Cinéma

*49 boulevard Anspach, Lower Town (02 217 59 47/
www.belgianmovieposters.be). Métro/Pré-métro
De Brouckère.* **Open** noon-6pm Mon-Sat. **Credit**
AmEx, DC, MC, V. **Map** p317 B3.
A mecca for film buffs, packed with film stills,
posters and postcards, as well as television- and
film-related books and memorabilia.

Anticyclone des Açores

*34 rue Fossé aux Loups, Lower Town (02 217
52 46/www.anticyclonedesacores.com). Métro/
Pré-métro De Brouckère.* **Open** 10.30am-6.30pm
Mon-Sat. **Credit** AmEx, MC, V. **Map** p317 C2.
A well-stocked travel bookshop for those with itchy
feet or a wishful imagination. Maps, guidebooks,
reference books and attractive coffee table material
on Brussels, Europe and beyond, in French, Dutch
and English. Topics also include geography, astron-
omy, and outdoor sports.

Fnac

*City 2, rue Neuve, Lower Town (02 275 11 11/
www.fnac.be). Métro/Pré-métro Rogier.* **Open**
10am-7pm Mon-Thur, Sat; 10am-8pm Fri. **Credit** V.
Map p319 C2.
Head to the top of the City 2 shopping centre to find
this ever-dependable mammoth store that sells all
kind of media. The book stock is excellent in all languages (the French section is particularly strong)
and disciplines, and the prices aren't bad. There are
also CDs, videos, DVDs, computer games and
assorted audio-visual and computer equipment.

Librairie de Rome

*50B avenue Louise, Ixelles (02 511 79 37).
Métro Louise/tram 91, 92, 93, 94.* **Open** 8am-9pm
Mon-Sat; 8am-8pm Sun. **Credit** AmEx, DC, MC, V.
Map p321 C6.
The best place to get international fashion and spe-
cial interest mags and papers. It's open all day
Sunday, which is a bonus in Brussels.

Peinture Fraîche

*10 rue du Tabellion, Ixelles (02 537 11 05).
Tram 81, 82/bus 54.* **Open** 11am-7pm Tue-Sat.
Credit AmEx, DC, MC, V.
A specialist art bookshop with books in French and
English. It has a particularly good line in architec-
ture and interior design, and also stocks plenty of
tomes on fine art, art theory and photography, and
a selection of art magazines.

Sterling

*38 rue du Fossé aux Loups, Lower Town
(02 223 62 23/www.sterling-books.be). Métro/
Pré-métro De Brouckère.* **Open** 10am-7pm Mon-
Sat; noon-6.30pm Sun. **Credit** AmEx, MC, V.
Map p317 C2.

Eat, Drink, Shop

The most recent major addition to the English-language literary scene operates an interesting system whereby books are sold at the sterling cover price at that day's exchange rate, plus 6% VAT. The ground-floor fiction section has an excellent range of contemporary fiction, including fringe publishers. There's also kids' books, computer, travel and English-language magazines and newspapers.

Waterstone's

71-75 boulevard Adolphe Max, Lower Town (02 219 27 08/www.waterstones.co.uk). Métro/Pré-métro Rogier. **Open** 9.30am-6.30pm Mon; 9am-7pm Tue-Sat; noon-5.30pm Sun. **Credit** AmEx, MC, V. **Map** p319 C2.

One of Brussels' most long-established purveyors of English-language reading materials has a fine selection spread over two floors, but the prices can leave you stunned. The ground floor has a good travel section and an excellent choice of newspapers and magazines, which staff allow you to skim.

Comics

La Boutique Tintin

13 rue de la Colline, Lower Town (02 514 45 50). Métro/Pré-métro De Brouckère or Métro Gare Centrale. **Open** 10am-6pm daily. **Credit** AmEx, DC, MC, V. **Map** p317 C3.

All kinds of Tintin memorabilia can be found in this flagship store, just off the Grand' Place. Tintin albums and other Hergé creations are also on sale.

Brüsel

100 boulevard Anspach, Lower Town (02 502 35 52/www.brusel.com). Pré-métro Bourse. **Open** 10.30am-6.30pm Mon-Sat; noon-6.30pm Sun. **Credit** AmEx, DC, MC, V. **Map** p317 B3.

One of the best shops in its genre, its wealth of choice includes perennial Belgian favourites from Le Chat to Tintin, as well as more recent and/or obscure publications and some foreign elements such as manga and Calvin and Hobbes. Upstairs you'll find a gallery of posters taken from a variety of comic strips and a framing service.

Le Dépôt

108 rue du Midi, Lower Town (02 513 04 84). Pré-métro Anneessens. **Open** 10am-6.30pm Mon-Sat. **Credit** MC, V. **Map** p318 B4.

This store buys and sells all types of new and old comic strips, and also stocks a few matching accessories (socks, ties, mugs and watches).

Forbidden Zone

25 rue de Tamines, St-Gilles (02 538 85 78/www.forbiddenzone.net). Tram 81, 82/bus 54. **Open** 12.30-7pm Mon-Sat.

Masses of potential for comic aficionados in the form of three floors crammed with comics in French and English, old and new, as well as collectibles, trading cards and other paraphernalia.

Utopia

39 rue du Midi, Lower Town (02 514 08 26). Pré-métro Bourse. **Open** 11am-6.30pm Mon-Fri; 11am-7pm Sat. **Credit** MC, V. **Map** p317 B3.

La Boutique Tintin: for Hergé fans.

Something of a specialist in American comics, this den of comic book addicts also sells cartoon, TV and film merchandise.

Second-hand

Nijinski
15-17 rue du Page, Ixelles (02 539 20 28). Tram 81, 82, 91, 92/bus 54. **Open** 11am-7pm Mon-Sat. **No credit cards.**
An impressive array of books is packed into this airy shop. Have a seat, leave the kids in the play area and peruse to a background of lilting classical music. Staff are relaxed and friendly, and the eclectic English-language section is larger than most. It's particularly good for art books and fashion catalogues. Prices are OK – paperbacks sell for anything from €1.70 upwards.

Pêle-Mêle
55 boulevard Maurice Lemonnier, Lower Town (02 548 78 00/www.occases.com). Pré-métro Anneessens. **Open** 10am-6.30pm Mon-Sat. **No credit cards. Map** p318 B4.
Brussels' cheapest second-hand outlet buys and sells books, comics, magazines, CDs, records, videos, DVDs and computer games. Books are mainly in French; Dutch gets short shrift as usual. There is also a decent English section of mainly crime fiction with a few classics. The place is hectic and tatty, but patient delving usually proves rewarding.

De Slegte
17 rue des Grandes Carmes, Lower Town (02 511 61 40/www.deslegte.com). Pré-métro Bourse. **Open** 9.30am-6pm Mon-Sat. **Credit** AmEx, DC, MC, V. **Map** p317 B3.
Probably the largest choice of second-hand books in Belgium: five floors of mainly Dutch, but also French, English and German books make up an extraordinarily diverse collection, with works on myriad topics, from astrology to zoology. Lots of new books, particularly art books, at discount prices.

Cameras & electronics

Ali Photo Video
150 rue du Midi, Lower Town (02 511 71 65). Pré-métro Anneessens. **Open** 9am-6pm Mon-Fri; 10am-6pm Sat. **Credit** AmEx, MC, V. **Map** p317 B4.
Just one of the various photo-video shops along this road, which sells mainly new cameras of all makes. They also buy, sell and exchange second-hand cameras, develop photos and are slide specialists.

Michel Campion
13 & 15 rue St-Boniface, Ixelles (02 512 17 21). Métro Porte de Namur. **Open** *No.13* 9am-6.30pm Mon-Sat. *No.15* 10am-1pm, 2-6.30pm Wed-Sat. **Credit** AmEx, DC, MC, V. **Map** p321 D5.
A shop each for new (No.15) and second-hand (No.13) photography equipment, with far more choice and variety in the latter.

Comics emporium **Brüsel**. *See p142.*

Technoland
22-24 rue Haute, Upper Town (02 511 51 04/ www.technoland.be). Bus 48, 20. **Open** noon-7pm Tue-Sat. **Credit** MC, V. **Map** p317 C4.
Come here for second-hand, high-end audio-visual equipment and computers, usually in good condition and at interesting prices.

Department stores

Hema
117 rue Neuve, Lower Town (02 227 52 11). Métro/Pré-métro Rogier. **Open** 9.30am-6.30pm Mon-Sat. **Credit** MC, V. **Map** p317 C2.
Hardly the most glamorous of stores, but it has two floors unceremoniously filled with absolute basics at often ludicrously cheap prices: candles, hosiery, underwear, chinaware, kitchenware, stationery and other random goods. Don't expect much in terms of style and you won't be disappointed. Quality varies, but zealous rummaging may leave you triumphant.

Inno
111 rue Neuve, Lower Town (02 211 21 11/ www.inno.be). Métro/Pré-métro Rogier. **Open** 9.30am-7pm Mon-Thur, Sat; 9.30am-8pm Fri. **Credit** AmEx, DC, MC, V. **Map** p317 C2.
Inno now holds the monopoly as the only large department store in Brussels. The five floors feature miscellaneous merchandise from cheap to chic. Although none of it will blow your mind, men's, women's and children's apparel and underwear, shoes, bedlinen, bath towels, luggage, toys, crystal, silver, stationery, home furnishings and a hairdresser are all represented.

De Geest

41 rue de l'Hôpital, Lower Town (02 512 59 78).
Métro Gare Centrale. **Open** 8am-7pm Mon-Fri;
8am-6.30pm Sat. **No credit cards. Map** p317 C4.
For those precious items that you can't quite bear to
take to your local bog-standard dry cleaners. Fur,
leather, suede and upholstery are well cared for here.
There's a pick-up and delivery service.

Autour du Monde (Bensimon Collection)

70 rue de Namur, Upper Town (02 503 55 92).
Métro Porte de Namur. **Open** 10.30am-7pm Mon-
Sat. **Credit** AmEx, DC, MC, V. **Map** p321 D5.
A one-off store for Brussels, this branch of a Parisian
'concept' boutique sticks to much the same formula:
a coordinated mix of ready-to-wear, toiletries, home

Galeries galore

When King Léopold I inaugurated Europe's
first shopping arcade, the **Royales Galeries
St-Hubert** (*pictured*), in 1847, it was a
glamorous social occasion. Stretching out
before the conservative German monarch lay
three arcades, la Galerie de la Reine, du Roi
and des Princes, all gleaming iron and glass,
embellished with marble columns, lamps
and statues. Nicknamed 'le Parapluie de
Bruxelles', a reference to the vaulted roof,
the 'umbrella' soon became the fashionable
haunt of 19th-century literary society. Victor
Hugo's literary circle would meet here;
Baudelaire was carried dead drunk from
one of its cafés. There were restaurants, a
theatre – Offenbach wrote *Orpheus in the
Underworld* here – and a dance hall.

But the shops were the prime attraction.
Townfolk would spend entire afternoons
gawping at the glittering windows and
luxurious interiors. Window shopping was
a thing of wonder. It still is – and they still
come in droves. A major renovation in 2000
saw St-Hubert restored to its glory, a neo-
classical mall, site of the **Théâtre Royal des
Galeries** (*see p215*), museum and meeting
place, all just north-east of the Grand' Place.

Its success spawned others: its
contemporary **Galerie Bortier** (17-19 rue de
la Madeleine), designed, like the Galeries
St-Hubert, by JP Cluysenaer, a wrought-iron
and glass arcade now lined with book and
map shops; the **Galerie Ravenstein**, built in
1958, a classic of its time, leading from the
Lower Town to the Royal Quarter; and, in a
fashionable stretch of Ixelles, **Galeries de
la Toison d'Or** and neighbouring **Louise**, back-
to-back blocks of designer shops.

These in turn spawned dreadful modern-
day malls, crowded **City 2** in rue Neuve being
the grim example. Nowadays, charm and
commerce no longer match.

furnishings, stationery and accessories using blocks of primary colours and bold prints, teamed with classic designs. It is a good supplier of smart leather jackets and coats (€300 upwards), basic tops and jumpers (€90-€120) and roomy bags.

Cinq Six Mouches

8 rue de la Grande Ile, Lower Town (02 511 87 57). Pré-métro Bourse. **Open** 11am-6.30pm Tue-Fri; 11am-7pm Sat. **Credit** AmEx, DC, MC, V. **Map** p318 B3.
Originally and colourfully stylish adults' and kids' clothes. The French designer often favours a bias cut, and likes sewing different fabrics and patterns together in a kind of contemporary patchwork of flannels, corduroys, wools, velvets, stripes, animal prints and even PVC. There are cute and practical items for children, such as hats (€15), dresses and jackets (€50-€80); adult equivalents are equally quirky and cosy, if not always slinky or elegant.

Isabelle Baines

48 rue du Pépin, Upper Town (02 502 13 73). Métro Porte de Namur. **Open** 2-6pm Mon; 10.30am-6pm Tue-Sat. **Credit** MC, V. **Map** p321 D5.
Baines' hand-finished and machine-knitted jumpers, and *gilets* (wool for winter, cotton for summer) are top quality and long-lasting. Each season she adapts her designs for men, women and kids to take in fashionable colours and lengths. Nothing outlandish, but classic designs with a modern twist.

Kaat Tilley

4 galerie du Roi, Lower Town (02 514 07 63). Métro Gare Centrale. **Open** 10am-6pm Mon; 10am-6.30pm Tue-Sat; 1-6pm Sun. **Credit** AmEx, DC, MC, V. **Map** p317 C3.
Tilley's store is as whimsical and fairy-like as some of her designs, with twinkling lights and hanging branches. Her womenswear is rather ingeniously constructed out of delicate materials, with wafting layers and sweeping lines. She also designs beautiful, antique-looking wedding dresses.

Maison Degand

415 avenue Louise, Ixelles (02 649 00 73). Métro Louise then tram 93, 94. **Open** 10am-7pm Mon-Sat. **Credit** AmEx, DC, MC, V.
Located in a fin-de-siècle mansion with most of the original interior preserved. Maison Degand creates luxury apparel for men and women, as well as cufflinks with semi-precious stones, cravats, cigar cutters and hip flasks.

Ming Tsy

24 rue du Page, Ixelles (02 424 29 68). Métro Louise, then tram 91, 92, 93, 94. **Open** 10am-6pm Tue-Sat. **No credit cards.**
This Taiwanese designer's shop is almost as beautiful as the items in it. Ming Tsy uses oriental fabrics to create stunning clothes (mainly flattering simply cut dresses and smart fitted jackets), scarves and bags; she will make to measure providing you give her input in the design. She has launched a line of lovely understated wedding dresses, and also sews

together cotton-based paper to make pretty stationery sets. Clothes start at €200, a small price to pay for such uniquely exquisite items.

Nina Meert

1 rue St-Boniface, Ixelles (02 514 22 63). Métro Porte de Namur. **Open** 1.30-6.30pm Mon; 10.30am-6.30pm Tue-Sat. **Credit** MC, V. **Map** p321 D5.
For a dressy one-off, for evening or daywear, Meert can make to measure or, if time is of the essence, there are ready-to-wear garments and beautiful accessories. Styles are classic with a modern twist and would suit the thirtysomething woman. Bridal wear can also be made to order.

Prototype

13 rue du Pont de la Carpe, Lower Town (02 511 61 43). Pré-métro Bourse. **Open** 11am-6.30pm Mon-Sat. **No credit cards. Map** p318 B3.
The small range of smart-casual wear for men and women is predominantly sober in style, but often with a slight twist. A limited number of exclusive designs are stocked at any one time, but each come in a variety of colours and fabrics. Hats and jumpers for men are unique. Prices start at €60 or so.

Ramona

21 rue de la Grande Ile, Lower Town (02 503 47 44). Pré-métro Bourse. **Open** noon-6.30pm Tue-Thur; noon-7pm Fri, Sat. **Credit** AmEx, DC, MC, V. **Map** p318 B3.
Chilean Ramona Hernández Collao designs and makes knitwear for the adventurous. Nothing is out of the orbit of her needles – not just jumpers, but trousers, coats, dresses and tops come in a variety of colours and textures, from chunky to slinky, and from plain to patterned. She'll also make to measure. Sweaters start at around €175.

Chain stores

You'll find popular low- to mid-range Spanish chain **Zara** at 30 rue Neuve (02 250 07 80/ www.zara.com) and throughout the city.

César et Rosalie

14 rue Antoine Dansaert, Lower Town (02 513 05 41). Pré-métro Bourse. **Open** 10.30am-6.30pm Mon-Sat. **Credit** AmEx, DC, MC, V. **Map** p318 B3.
Home-grown nationwide store with its flagship in the centre of Brussels. Great clothes for thirtysomethings, with original accessories and a smattering of choice homewares.

Chine

2 rue van Artevelde, Lower Town (02 503 14 99). Pré-métro Bourse. **Open** 11am-6.30pm Mon-Sat. **Credit** AmEx, DC, MC, V. **Map** p318 B3.
An upmarket Belgian chain with the emphasis on fine fabrics sourced from the Far East in an overtly feminine style. Clothes are designed by Guillaume Thys, who divides his time between Hong Kong and Brussels. A flagship store is planned on avenue Louise for summer 2002.

Eat, Drink, Shop

timeout.com

The online guide to the world's greatest cities

Massimo Dutti

22 avenue de la Toison d'Or, Upper Town (02 289 10 50/www.massimodutti.com). Métro Porte de Namur. **Open** 10am-6.30pm Mon-Sat. **Credit** AmEx, DC, MC, V. **Map** p321 D5.

Smart, conservative clothes for men and women from the sister company of Zara. The elegant and practical attire is of dependable quality if not always breathtakingly exciting.

Rue Blanche

35-39 rue Antoine Dansaert, Lower Town (02 512 03 14). Pré-métro Bourse. **Open** 11am-6.30pm Mon-Sat. **Credit** AmEx, DC, MC, V. **Map** p318 B3.

Timeless basics for women in gorgeous fabrics spiced up with more unusual items, plus a selection of minimalist household objects.
Branches: throughout the city.

Children

Baby 2000

35F Weiveldlaan, Zaventem-Zuid (02 725 20 13). Bus 358. **Open** 10am-7pm Mon-Fri; 10am-6pm Sat. **Credit** AmEx, DC, MC, V.

A vast store near IKEA selling clothes and toys, plus a huge array of prams, pushchairs, car seats, high chairs and bath paraphernalia. There's equipment from all major European manufacturers, so if it's choice you want, this is your place. Brusque service.

Histoire de pieds

34 rue de Namur, Upper Town (02 502 15 50). Métro Porte de Namur. **Open** 10am-6pm Mon-Sat. **Credit** AmEx, DC, MC, V. **Map** p321 D5.

A wide selection of good quality kids' shoes, with styles ranging from conservative to fashionable. Prices start at around €50.

Kat en Muis

32 rue Antoine Dansaert, Lower Town (02 514 32 34). Pré-métro Bourse. **Open** 10.30am-6.30pm Mon-Sat. **Credit** AmEx, DC, MC, V. **Map** p318 B3.

Pricey designer clothes for kids. It's the sister shop of cutting-edge fashion store Stijl for adults in the same street.

Primprenelle

40 rue du Midi, Lower Town (02 513 05 28). Pré-métro Bourse. **Open** 11am-6pm Mon-Sat. **Credit** AmEx, DC, MC, V. **Map** p317 B2.

This little boutique has plenty of options for getting away from the conservative look prevalent in local children's fashion. No frills or ribbons, but lots of bright colours and animal prints – lively and fun, but still practical. Most of stock is shoes, but there are clothes for newborns to 12-year-olds.

Designer

The home-grown fashion scene in Brussels has grown apace in recent years; for the names to look out for, *see p150* **Dressing for success**.

Francis Ferent

19 avenue de la Toison d'Or, Ixelles (02 512 17 60). Métro Porte de Namur. **Open** 10am-6.30pm Sat. **Credit** AmEx, DC, MC, V. **Map** p321 D5.

A fashion emporium housing labels such as DKNY, D&G, Calvin Klein, Sonia Rykiel, Miu Miu and Prada. Clothes for men and children can be found down the road in the galerie Louise, along with footwear by a host of designers. A new store is to open on avenue Louise in summer 2002.
Branches: throughout the city.

Kwasi

18 place St-Géry, Lower Town (02 511 85 89). Pré-métro Bourse. **Open** 11am-6.30pm Mon-Fri; 10am-6.30pm Sat. **Credit** AmEx, DC, MC, V. **Map** p318 B3.

A men's shop run by a Belgo-Scotsman specialising in a little known German label for thirtysomething professionals. Shoes by Olivier Strelli and Kenzo.

Martin Margiela

114 rue de Flandre, Lower Town (02 223 75 20). Métro Ste-Catherine/tram 18. **Open** 3-7pm Mon, Tue; 11am-7pm Wed-Sat. **Credit** AmEx, DC, MC, V. **Map** p318 B2.

The celebrated Paris-based Flemish designer's first shop in Belgium opened early in 2002. Modelled on the world's first Margiela boutique in Tokyo, it is run by Sonia Noël, owner of the Stijl designer emporium and renowned fashion connoisseur. Unlabelled, like the men's and women's clothes, the all-white store is a short walk from Dansaert's main drag, a lustrous enclave of style on an otherwise shabby street. A fitting boutique for the most enigmatic of the famous Antwerp Six designers.

Natan

158 avenue Louise, Ixelles (02 647 10 01/www.natan.be). Métro Louise then tram 93, 94. **Open** 10am-6.30pm Mon-Sat. **Credit** AmEx, DC, MC, V. **Map** p321 D7.

Belgian designer Edouard Vermeulen has many strings to his bow. There's this couture house on avenue Louise where he designs made-to-measure outfits for the well-heeled (domestic and foreign royals included). He also has several ready-to-wear boutiques across Belgium, offering mid-range clothes for women, and more recently he opened Natan Ph, with cutting-edge wear for men.
Branch: 78 rue de Namur, Upper Town (02 512 75 00).

Nicole Cadine

28 rue Antoine Dansaert, Lower Town (02 503 48 26). Pré-métro Bourse. **Open** 10am-6.30pm Mon-Sat. **Credit** AmEx, DC, MC, V. **Map** p318 B3.

French-born, Antwerp-based designer Nicole Cadine favours luxury fabrics and ultra-feminine styles with an emphasis on evening wear.

Olivier Strelli

72 avenue Louise, Ixelles (02 512 56 07/www.strelli.be). Métro Louise then tram 93, 94. **Open** 10am-6.30pm Mon-Sat. **Credit** AmEx, DC, MC, V. **Map** p321 C6.

A stalwart of the Belgian fashion industry for two decades, Strelli is said to take his inspiration and predilection for vibrant colours from his birthplace, Zaire. Audacious hues are teamed with an abundance of blacks and greys, as well as with simple designs, to create contemporary classics for men and women. There's also a lower-cost line of leisurewear for women called 22 Octobre.

Branch: 41 rue Antoine Dansaert, Lower Town (02 512 09 42).

Smadja Men

21 avenue Lepoutre, Ixelles (02 346 50 13). Tram 91, 92/bus 60. **Open** 11am-6.30pm Mon-Sat. **Credit** AmEx, DC, V.

Jacques Smadja, a tailor by trade, was one of the first in Belgium to stock Paul Smith. He still does, along with Joseph and choice items by Japanese designers. His women's shop in nearby place Brugmann sells labels Whistles, Joseph and Walter Lecompte.

Branch: 16 place Brugmann, Ixelles (02 347 66 70).

Stijl

74 rue Antoine Dansaert, Lower Town (02 512 03 13). Pré-métro Bourse. **Open** 10.30am-6.30pm Mon-Sat. **Credit** AmEx, DC, MC, V. **Map** p318 B3.

Owner Sonia Noel has a knack for spotting home-grown talent. Having signed up first-time collections several decades ago from Ann Demeulemeester, Dries Van Noten and Martin Margiela (all three are members of the Antwerp Six), she keeps on picking winners – such as Raf Simons, Jurgi Persoons, Olivier Theyskens, Xavier Delcour and, more recently, Nicolas Dehon. She was also the first to open a cutting-edge fashion shop in rue Antoine Dansaert in the early 1980s, when this area of the city was considered run-down.

Via della Spiga

42 rue Antoine Dansaert, Lower Town (02 502 20 97). Pré-métro Bourse. **Open** 11am-7pm Mon-Sat. **Credit** AmEx, DC, MC, V. **Map** p318 B3.

Another downtown hotspot in which a variety of big names are represented, including Balenciaga, Vivienne Westwood, Alexander McQueen, Jean Colonna, Bernhard Willheim and Martine Sitbon.

Formal & party hire

Amandine

150 rue Defacqz, St-Gilles (02 539 17 93). Métro Louise then tram 91, 92. **Open** 10am-6pm Mon-Sat. **No credit cards. Map** p321 C7.

If you've nothing to wear for that special occasion, head for Amandine. For hire are little black numbers, gowns and a complete range of accessories.

John Kennis

8 rue du Parnasse, Ixelles (02 513 23 03). Métro Trône. **Open** 9.30am-1pm, 2.30-6.30pm Mon-Fri; 10am-1pm, 2.30-5pm Sat. **Credit** AmEx, DC, MC, V. **Map** p324 E5.

Men's formal attire for hire, with all the trimmings.

Maghet

41 rue St-Ghislain, Lower Town (02 514 08 58). Bus 20, 48. **Open** 10am-6pm Mon-Fri; 11am-5pm Sat. **Credit** MC, V. **Map** p320 B5.

A wonderful costume hire store run by a former film costume bod who has made many of the Manneken-Pis costumes. State your preferred period from medieval to the '70s and staff will dress you accordingly. Plenty of furry animal costumes and *Star Wars* headgear, but outfits for kids are limited.

Olivier Strelli. See p147.

Trendy smalls at **Stijl Underwear**.

Picard

71-75 rue du Lombard, Lower Town (02 513 07 90).
Métro Gare Centrale. **Open** 9am-6pm Mon-Sat.
Credit AmEx, DC, MC, V. **Map** p317 B3.
For carnival all year round, try this large jam-packed
shop, whose colourful window display is hard to
miss. The stock spills over like Mardi Gras with
boas, masks, costumes, hats and wigs. There is an
excellent stage make-up counter and an extensive
range of practical jokes and magic tricks. Opposite
is the Palais de Cotillons, which sells much of the
same and some alternative jokes.

Lingerie

Stijl Underwear

*47 rue Antoine Dansaert, Lower Town (02 514 27
31). Pré-métro Bourse.* **Open** 10.30am-6.30pm Mon-
Sat. **Credit** AmEx, DC, MC, V. **Map** p318 B3.
Men's and women's undergarments, nightwear and
beachwear by Helmut Lang, John Smedley and Paul
Smith, among others. They deserve a peek if you're
willing to pay the price for style.

Women'Secret

*2 rue Neuve, Lower Town (02 217 10 28/www.
womensecret.com). Métro/pré-métro De Brouckère.*
Open 10am-6.30pm Mon-Thur; 10am-7pm Fri, Sat.
Credit AmEx, DC, MC, V. **Map** p317 C2.
Launched on the Belgian market in 2001, this
women's high-street retailer should become as popular as it is back home in Spain. An excellent selection includes lingerie, nightwear, beachwear, some
maternity wear and a range of comfortable clothes
for lounging around the home.
Branches: Woluwe Shopping Centre, Woluwe-
St-Lambert (02 772 20 04); 43 avenue de la Toison
d'Or, Upper Town (02 503 58 16).

Second-hand, vintage & discount

Bernard Gavilan pour L'Homme Chrétien

27 rue des Pierres, Lower Town (02 502 01 28).
Pré-métro Bourse. **Open** 11am-7pm Mon-Sat.
No credit cards. **Map** p317 B3.
Bernard is not just an inspired collector of second-
hand goods, he is a creative transformer with an eye
for retro-fashion. He sells a mix of second-hand and
customised vintage clothes, the result of strategic
raids on warehouses. His kitschtastic, showroom-
like shop is heaven for retro-addicts, who can spend
hours browsing through his extensive collection,
with masses of original accessories. The back of the
shop is filled with 1950s, '60s and '70s furniture, also
for sale. Bernard does a couple of extravagant fashion shows a year and has some of the most flam-
boyantly stylish window displays in town.

Dod

16 chaussée de Louvain, St-Josse (02 218 11 61).
Métro Madou. **Open** 10am-6.30pm Mon-Sat.
Credit AmEx, DC, MC, V. **Map** p322 E3.
Dod was one of the first stores to take a warehouse
approach to selling designer fashion at discount
prices. No longer remarkable, the three stores – there
are women's and children's branches in the same
street – are still a good place to rummage for bargains.
You'll find mostly last year's stock, end of series or
clothes from liquidations.
Branches: 44 chaussée de Louvain, St-Josse
(02 218 73 63); 41 chaussée de Louvain, St-Josse
(02 217 52 08).

Les Enfants d'Edouard

175-177 avenue Louise, Ixelles (02 640 42 45).
Métro Louise then tram 93, 94. **Open** 10am-
6.30pm Mon-Sat. **Credit** AmEx, MC, V.
Map p321 D6.
Swanky store that specialises in designer label cast-
offs and end-of-line stock, all in excellent condition
but not always at excellent prices. In spite of the
name, kids' clothes are at the Ixelles branch.
Branch: 40 rue Darwin, Ixelles (02 344 95 45).

Gabriele

14 rue des Chartreux, Lower Town (02 512 67 43).
Pré-métro Bourse. **Open** noon-6pm Tue-Fri; 1-7pm
Sat. **No credit cards.** **Map** p317 B3.
Gabriele Wolf, owner of this pleasantly crammed
vintage clothing boutique, collected period hats from
her work in the theatre. Her collection became so
vast that she opened this shop to sell it off. Mint condition 1920s fare sits alongside modern items.

Idiz Bogam

*76 rue Antoine Dansaert, Lower Town (02 512 10
32). Pré-métro Bourse.* **Open** noon-7pm Mon-Sat.
Credit MC, V. **Map** p318 B3.
This spacious boutique sells pricey second-hand and
vintage clothing from London, New York and Paris.
Some of the stock is updated with sequins, ruffs and

Eat, Drink, Shop

the like, and there are also some wacky wedding dresses plus a good assortment of shoes, hats and retro furniture. Definitely worth a look.

Nicolas Woit

80 rue Antoine Dansaert, Lower Town (02 503 48 31). Pré-métro Bourse. **Open** phone for details. **No credit cards**. **Map** p318 B3.

After studying fashion in Paris, Woit opened his Brussels store in 1998 – and it remains a Dansaert highlight. His fascination with period fabrics and predilection for 1930s and '50s styles are translated into garments with a bold, girly and light-heartedly glamorous feel, cut from luxuriant materials, often with a floral or oriental motif. Accessories are integral to the outfit: cloche hats, scarves, quirky bags and antique-looking jewellery. The look is the antithesis of the sleek minimalism currently in favour. Feminine retro sophistication meets contemporary chic – sassy, not sugar sweet.

Ramon & Valy

19 rue des Teinturiers, Lower Town (02 511 05 10). Pré-métro Bourse. **Open** 11am-7pm Mon-Sat. **Credit** AmEx, DC, MC, V. **Map** p317 B3.

Fashion junkies cannot go wrong here, providing they're willing to spend a little bit. There's a good selection of retro clothes and vintage shoes, plus

Dressing for success

Antwerp – home of the Antwerp Six, a group of graduates who took London and Paris Fashion Weeks by storm in 1987 – is still the fashion centre of Belgium (*see p236* **Antwerp: fashion capital**). Many of its designers set up shop in downtown Brussels, in rue Antoine Dansaert, by the Grand' Place. This became a chic enclave of Flemish style, 'Little Antwerp', its lingua franca Flemish, gabbled in the designer boutiques and label emporiums along this unusual shopping route.

However, Brussels-based designers are now fighting back. Although the capital only began actively supporting its fashion industry ten years after the Antwerp explosion, it has its own prominent design schools, and graduates are increasingly choosing to set up shop in the city. High-profile names, such as Olivier Theyskens and Nicolas Dehon, learned their trade in Brussels, and a new generation of Belgian talent includes several Brussels-based designers: we list the best below.

At grass-roots level, non-profit group **Modo Bruxellae** (02 213 37 42/www.modo bruxellae.be) was set up in 1993 by local government to promote the fashion industry. Modo organises experimental fashion shows, including one held in the Bourse metro station in 2001 and the Transit show of 2002, which turned part of downtown Brussels into a catwalk. The annual Parcours des Stylistes, in which designers exhibit their creations across the city, culminates in the Modo fashion awards. Useful websites include **www.belgianfashion.be** (Belgian clothing federation) and **www.bff.be** (Brussels fashion fairs).

Annemie Verbeke

64 rue Antoine Dansaert, Lower Town (02 511 21 71). Pré-métro Bourse. **Open** 11am-6.30pm Mon, Wed-Sat. **Credit** AmEx, DC, MC, V. **Map** p318 B3.

Annemie's smart, feminine clothes are infinitely wearable, and delicately quirky without appearing outrageous. She seems just as happy to tap into and customise prevailing trends as she is to develop her own softly distinctive look. Knitwear is always pretty and innovative; skirts and dresses combine simple designs (A-lines and baby dolls) and novel fabrics.

Azniv Afsar

28 rue Léon Lepage, Lower Town (02 512 30 96). Pré-métro Bourse. **Open** 1-6.30pm Mon-Wed; 10.30am-6.30pm Thur-Sat. **Credit** AmEx, DC, MC, V. **Map** p318 B2.

Sharp tailoring from this artistic entrepreneur of Armenian origin, who trained at Brussels' St-Luc college. Her womenswear deftly blends extremes of sobriety and frivolity, of fabrics, styles and colours typically associated with either sex. Slate grey flannel is combined with shiny organza or sequin details; pinstripes and fur or feathers lie side by side. Asymmetrical collars add a wacky touch to smart understated suits. The detail is paramount but sparing, with strategically placed stitching and trimmings.

Christa Reniers

29 rue Antoine Dansaert, Lower Town (02 510 06 60/www.christareniers.com). Pré-métro Bourse. **Open** 10.30am-1pm, 2-6.30pm Mon-Sat. **Credit** AmEx, DC, MC, V. **Map** p318 B3.

An exceptionally talented Belgian jeweller whose works complement the clothes at many an international fashion show. She prefers working with silver and platinum,

accessories, mainly for girls. The stock manages to keep up with trends while at the same time providing ample scope for individuality and innovation.

Streetwear

Hype

4 rue des Riches Claires, Lower Town (02 502 88 70). Pré-métro Bourse. **Open** 10am-7pm Mon-Sat. **Credit** MC, V. **Map** p318 B3.

Located right where Brussels' streetwear culture first evolved – and continues to house a choice group of boutiques – Hype is a stylish purveyor of mod-

ern skate fashion for men (including brands such as Diesel, Clarks, Etnies and Carhartt), as well as trainers and streetwear for both sexes.

On

134-138 rue Neuve, Lower Town (02 241 41 66). Métro/Pré-métro Rogier. **Open** 10am-7pm Mon-Sat. **Credit** AmEx, DC, MC, V. **Map** p319 C2.

Similarly responsible for the rise of streetwear in Brussels, this vast shop (under the same management as Prive Joke – *see p152*) features a floor each for girls and boys. A wide selection of streetwear labels accompanies a fine pick of good-looking clothes, shoes and bags at relatively high prices.

bases most of her designs on organic forms such as plants and flowers, and makes all the pieces in the atelier above her shop.

Christophe Coppens – Le Shop

2 rue Léon Lepage, Lower Town (02 512 77 97). Pré-métro Bourse. **Open** 11am-6.30pm Tue-Sat. **Credit** AmEx, DC, MC, V. **Map** p318 B3.

Not content with designing his own range of extravagant headgear, Coppens moved on to scarves and then set about decorating the home as well as the person. His decorative items echo the elaborate craftsmanship and wackiness of his hats; life-size dummies in teddy-bear fabric and doll's head candles are his design, though he uses skilled craftsmen to create them. Scarves (from €100) and hats (from €165) are all entirely handmade, only partly justifying escalating prices.

Johanne Riss

35 place du Nouveau Marché aux Grains, Lower Town (02 513 09 00). Pré-métro Bourse. **Open** 10.30am-6.30pm Mon-Sat. **Credit** AmEx, DC, MC, V. **Map** p318 B2.

Sleek, simple lines make for streamlined silhouettes and high prices. Frothy sheers and diaphanous layers add a hint of frivolity to blocks of plain colour and minimalist purity.

Jonathan Bernard

53 rue du Midi, Lower Town (02 503 10 52). Pré-métro Bourse. **Open** phone for details. **Credit** MC, V. **Map** p317 B3.

Jonathan has been big on Brussels' club scene for years. Often revealing clubwear for women treads a fine line between kinky and tacky, building on nightlife-inspired staples of black, leather, studs and animal prints. Reasonably priced casual daywear is equally glam, but steers a subtler course.

Van V

10 rue Léon Lepage, Lower Town (02 513 01 80/www.van-v.be). Pré-métro Bourse. **Open** 10.30-6.30pm Tue-Sat. **Credit** AmEx, DC, MC, V. **Map** p318 B2.

Loralie Van Leeuw (who worked with Kaat Tilley, Johanne Risse and Nicole Cadine) and Tanguy Vuylsteke (a graduate of the Atelier Lannaux who worked under British jeweller and designer Tomasz Starzewski in London) formed Van V (*pictured*) in 1999. Together, using silks, satins, soft cottons and dry wools, they create stylish workwear or party clothes, making only ten copies per design.

of the design. Modern takes are not as conservative; Walter Van Beirendonck has even created a fluoro yellow version. Many other handmade leather goods, scarves and desk accessories are also available – at a price.

Branch: 31 galerie de la Reine, Lower Town (02 512 71 98).

Les Précieuses

83 rue Antoine Dansaert, Lower Town (02 503 28 98). Pré-métro Bourse. **Open** 11am-6.30pm Thur-Sat. **Credit** V. **Map** p318 B3.

Pili Collado's almost baroque jewellery, with fine strands, velvet ribbons and clusters of polished chunky stones, sits alongside pretty, pricey creations by other designers: Jamin Puech's sequined and embroidered evening bags or flamenco-inspired shawls, jumpers by Isabelle Baines and Olivia Hainaut's corsages and rose-themed jewellery.

Tarlatane

22 rue Ernest Solvay, Ixelles (02 502 79 29). Métro Porte de Namur. **Open** 11am-6.30pm Tue-Sat. **Credit** MC, V. **Map** p321 D5.

Valérie Janssens' accessories all stay on the fringe of trends, not restricting you to the colours and styles *du jour*. There's quite a girly feel to the bags (small silk evening bags can be made to order in the colour of your choice), jewellery (sparkly cut-glass and simple silver designs) and scarves (cut from novel fabrics). The assorted hats include lots of cloches and berets. Roses are a favourite theme.

Lip-smacking **Le Pain Quotidien**. *See p153.*

Prive Joke

12 rue des Riches Claires, Lower Town (02 502 63 67). Pré-métro Bourse. **Open** 10.30am-7pm Mon-Sat. **Credit** AmEx, DC, MC, V. **Map** p318 B3.

One of Brussels' original streetwear boutiques now devotes itself entirely to girls' clothing, with a select range of stylish bits and pieces by the usual suspects. Carhartt, E-pure, Fiorucci, Boxfresh and Lady Soul clothes, accessories by Paul Frank and others, and the latest in the re-invention of brand images, vests and basic T-shirts by Petit Bateau.

Fashion accessories

Arcane

54 rue du Midi, Lower Town (02 511 91 42). Pré-métro Bourse. **Open** 11am-6.30pm Mon-Sat. **Credit** AmEx, DC, MC, V. **Map** p317 B3.

A wide choice of beautiful silver jewellery at affordable prices; classic, simple designs sit alongside more unusual ones, and prices range from €5 to €500. Items hail from India, Mexico, Thailand and Israel, and are hand-picked by the owner.

L'Atelier

99 rue de l'Aqueduc, Ixelles (02 534 88 28). Métro Louise then tram 91, 92. **Open** 11.30am-6.30pm Wed-Sat. **Credit** AmEx, DC, MC, V.

Leatherwear by Micheline and Marc Rochet is sleek and contemporary in design. Bags may dent your budget (from €170); purses, wallets and belts (€8.50-€40) are more whimsical purchases.

Delvaux

27 boulevard de Waterloo, Upper Town (02 513 05 02). Métro Louise. **Open** 10am-6.30pm Mon-Sat. **Credit** AmEx, DC, MC, V. **Map** p321 C5.

The Delvaux 'brilliant' was the old label's classic design first unveiled at the 1958 World Fair: an expensive, trapezium-shaped leather handbag with a handle and removable shoulder strap. The tell-tale 'D' is still there, evidence of the continual revamping

Milliners

Elvis Pompilio

60 rue du Midi, Lower Town (02 511 11 88). Pré-métro Bourse. **Open** 10.30am-6.30pm Mon-Sat. **Credit** AmEx, DC, MC, V. **Map** p317 B4.

Elvis is the proverbial Mad Hatter, a darling of the local fashion industry. His whimsical creations, entirely handmade, come in all shapes, forms and colours. Often not for the shrinking violet, they combine elegance and a touch of humour, as well as accessible prices (for designer goods – women's hats average €125). You'll find plenty of feathers, nets, flowers and felt. The men's collection next door, with permutations of such classics as caps, trilbies, Stetsons and woolly hats, can take a similarly extravagant turn, but are generally streetsmart and wearable. There's also a collection for children, plus bags, umbrellas and frilly parasols (around €75).

Gillis

17 rue du Lombard, Lower Town (02 512 09 26). Métro Gare Centrale. **Open** 10am-6pm Mon-Sat. **Credit** DC, MC, V. **Map** p317 B3.

Less flamboyant (and cheaper) than Pompilio, this small boutique on rue du Lombard offers plenty of advice, styles and personal service. Designs tend to border on the traditional, but it is possible to have the chosen hat dyed to match your dress fabric or made to measure from scratch.

Shoes

US retailer of trainers and sports clothing
Footlocker has long been a high-street staple
in Brussels. Outlets include one on rue Neuve
(No.31-33; 02 217 51 03/www.footlocker.com).

Hatshoe
*89 rue Antoine Dansaert, Lower Town (02 513 80
90). Pré-métro Bourse.* **Open** 11am-6.30pm Mon-Fri;
10.30am-6.30pm Sat. **Credit** AmEx, DC, MC, V.
Map p318 B3.
Exclusively designer footwear that walks a fine line
between trendy and traditional. A limited collection
of hats and scarves by designer Cécile Bertrand
brightens things up.

People Shoes Design
*15-17 rue des Teinturiers, Lower Town (02 502 17
64). Pré-métro Bourse.* **Open** 11am-7pm Mon-Sat.
Credit AmEx, MC, V. **Map** p317 B3.
A shop for men and women full of designer-trendy
urban foot fashion. It always comes up with the
goods, but at prices commandeered by the names
accommodated: Camper, Diesel and Converse, plus
the latest home-grown addition, W&LT, by
acclaimed Antwerp-based designer Walter Van
Beirendonck. A small selection of clothes and bags
is also on offer.

Virgin
*10 rue Antoine Dansaert, Lower Town (02 511
46 03). Pré-métro Bourse.* **Open** 11am-12.30pm,
1.30-6.30pm Mon-Sat. **Credit** AmEx, DC, MC, V.
Map p318 B3.
Fairly formal yet funky footwear purveyor. The
men's collection is larger and more unusual than the
women's, although women will find some trendy
and appealing foot fashion, particularly boots. Prices
start at around €125. This branch has smarter and
more upmarket stock, while the other is more
diverse, clubby and casual.
Branch: 13 rue des Eperonniers, Lower Town
(02 513 14 56).

Y-Enzo
*42 avenue de la Toison d'Or, Ixelles (02 514 45 47).
Métro Louise.* **Open** 10am-7pm Mon-Sat. **Credit**
AmEx, DC, MC, V. **Map** p321 C5.
Ultra upmarket footwear shop selling top designer
labels such as Prada. Service is refreshingly unsniffy
considering the stock.

Flowers

There's also a daily flower market on the
Grand' Place; *see p163* **Trading places.**

Fleurop-Interflora
0800 99669/0800 17007/www.interflora.com.
Open 24hrs daily. **Credit** AmEx, DC, MC, V.
For those who want to say it with flowers, orders
can be placed with this outfit 24 hours a day by
phone or on the internet.

Het Witte Gras
*7 rue Plétinckx, Lower Town (02 502 05 29).
Pré-métro Bourse or Anneessens.* **Open** 9am-6pm
Mon-Sat. **Credit** AmEx, DC, V. **Map** p318 B3.
Het Witte Gras is a pretty corner shop with plants
and flowers spilling out on to the pavement, and an
abundance of attractive vases and pots to display
and grow them in.

Food & drink

Bakeries & patisseries

AM Sweet
*4 rue des Chartreux, Lower Town (02 513 51 31).
Pré-métro Bourse.* **Open** 9am-6.30pm Tue-Sat.
No credit cards. Map p318 B3.
AM Sweet is a gold-mine for anyone with a sweet
tooth. Biscuits, chocolate, cakes, sweets, teas and
coffees come from various manufacturers and alternate between traditional recipes (such as *pain
d'épices* and baked marzipan) and innovative concoctions. Particularly intriguing among all these
goodies are the 'Shanghai oranges' (subtly candied
kumquats lightly covered in bitter dark chocolate).
The shop is attached to a tearoom.

Dandoy
*31 rue au Beurre, Lower Town (02 511 03 26).
Pré-métro Bourse.* **Open** 8.30am-6.30pm Mon-
Sat; 10.30am-6.30pm Sun. **Credit** MC, V.
Map p317 C3.
You'll find the best melt-in-your-mouth *speculoos*
(traditional Belgian ginger biscuits baked in wooden
moulds), *pains d'amande* (wafer-thin biscuits), *pain
d'épices* and *pains à la grecque* in town in this delicious-smelling, long-standing institution. There is
also a tearoom at 14 rue Charles Buls.

Le Pain Quotidien
*16 rue Antoine Dansaert, Lower Town (02 502 23
61). Pré-métro Bourse.* **Open** 7.30am-7.30pm daily.
No credit cards. Map p318 B3.
A successful Belgian chain of tearoom/bakeries
with an airy, pseudo-rustic decor and a large common dining table. It's a good place for lunch, with
tasty salads and sandwiches. It's hard to choose
between delicacies such as raspberry clafoutis, tarte
au citron, moist brownies and the intensely rich
chocolate bomb cake.
Branches: throught the city.

Wittamer
*6 & 12 place du Grand Sablon, Upper Town
(02 512 37 42/www.wittamer.com). Tram 92,
93, 94.* **Open** 10am-6pm Mon; 7am-7pm Tue-Sat.
Credit AmEx, DC, MC, V. **Map** p317 C4.
This family-owned patisserie has been around for
100 years or so, and enjoys a widespread reputation
as one of the city's finest, particularly famed for its
Samba, a double-layered chocolate cake. It is also a
renowned chocolatier, although a separate shop
only opened in 1988.

Chocolate

See also p158 **Belgian chocolate: a user's guide.**

Corné Port-Royal
9 rue de la Madeleine, Lower Town (02 512 43 14).
Métro Gare Centrale. **Open** 10am-8pm daily. **Credit** AmEx, DC, MC, V. **Map** p317 C3/4.
A mid-range chocolatier (classed with Neuhaus and Godiva) with more affordable fare than the city's premium names, and more palatable creations than the more downmarket tourist traps and the likes of Léonidas.

Mary's
73 rue Royale, Upper Town (02 217 45 00).
Tram 92, 93, 94. **Open** 9.30am-6pm Mon-Sat.
Credit MC, V. **Map** p319 C/D2.
Delectable pralines from the *crème de la crème* of Brussels' purveyors of fine chocolates are sold from one exclusive boutique. Concoctions with different types of dark chocolate mousse and fresh cream are specialities. Fine presentation is de rigueur.

Pierre Marcolini
39 place du Grand Sablon, Upper Town (02 514 12 06). Tram 92, 93, 94. **Open** 10am-7pm Mon-Thur; 10am-9pm Fri; 9am-9pm Sat; 9am-7pm Sun. **Credit** AmEx, DC, MC, V. **Map** p317 C4.
One of Belgian chocolate's bright young sparks has seen a meteoric rise to stardom in the past few years. His patisseries, sugar and chocolate sculptures and pralines have earned him various awards and distinctions. Exceptional pralines combine traditional recipes and innovative touches. Particularly sumptuous are the *ganaches* fillings subtly flavoured with tea and spices, such as jasmine and cinnamon.
Branches: 75 avenue Louise, Ixelles (02 538 42 24); 1302 chaussée de Waterloo, Uccle (02 372 15 11);.

Planète Chocolat
24 rue du Lombard, Lower Town (02 511 07 55).
Métro Gare Centrale. **Open** 10am-6.30pm Tue-Sat; 4-10pm Sun. **Credit** DC, MC, V. **Map** p317 B3/C4.
This traditional craft chocolatier is perhaps the funkiest in town, in terms of the look of its creations (chocolate lips are a speciality), packaging (bouquets of chocs, for example) and its separate tearoom (a few doors down).

Delis & health food

Au Suisse
73-75 boulevard Anspach, Lower Town (02 512 95 89/www.ausuisse.be). Pré-métro Bourse. **Open** 10am-8pm Mon, Wed-Fri; 10am-7.30pm Tue; 10am-7pm Sat; 7-9pm Sun. **No credit cards. Map** p317 B3.
There's nothing Swiss about the place, despite the name and flags. A quintessential Brussels institution since 1876, this is the place to nip into for real Belgian fare, to take out or eat in. The deli has two long counters, serving a selection of salads, cheeses,

cold meats, *maatjes* (herring), *tête pressée* (brawn), *filet américain* (a raw minced beef concoction), and other sandwich fillings. The other counter serves hot and cold drinks. The adjacent store serves pretty much the same, with a wide range of cheeses.

Biodrome
76-78 rue du Marché au Charbon, Lower Town (02 502 12 10/www.biodrome.net). Pré-métro Bourse. **Open** 10am-7pm Mon, Wed, Fri; 10am-10pm Tue, Thur, Sat. **Credit** AmEx, DC, MC, V. **Map** p317 B3.
This polished (if a tad pretentious) store is a glowing endorsement of the pro-organic and health food trend. It stocks a wide range of branded foodstuffs, some fresh produce, its own selection of home-made delicacies, plus toiletries, cotton clothing and wooden toys. There's also a café-cum-'tasting-room' at the back, an auditorium for workshops and lectures, and a massage room.

Claire Fontaine
3 rue Ernest Allard, Upper Town (02 512 24 10).
Métro Gare Centrale/tram 92, 93, 94. **Open** 10am-6.30pm Tue-Sat. **No credit cards.**
Map p320/321 C4/5.
Gorgeous goodies aplenty are packed into this little shop off the Sablon. As well as sandwiches, quiches, soups and pastries to take away, you'll find a host of international gastronomical delights such as foie gras, lobster soup, olives, dry goods (risotto rice, pasta, Puy lentils), and a wide range of teas and tisanes. Those with a craving for the out-of-the-ordinary may enjoy delicacies like green tomato and lemon or courgette and orange conserves, and rose and violet cordials. Refined taste buds can put a strain on the wallet, though.

Le Tartisan
4 rue St-Boniface, Ixelles (02 503 36 00/ www.tartisan.be). Métro Porte de Namur. **Open** 10am-7pm Mon-Sat. **Credit** MC, V. **Map** p321 D5.
The speciality of this small, delicious-smelling deli is, as the name suggests, tarts – sweet and savoury, in three different sizes, and astonishingly light, they are all made on site according to traditional recipes. Veggies and carnivores are both catered for. Prices range from just under €4 for smaller and less elaborate versions (broccoli, onion, leek) to €15 for the largest (smoked salmon and leek). Those with a sweet tooth will happily fork out for lemon, walnut and chocolate or frangipane.

Drink

Beer Mania
174-178 chaussée de Wavre, Ixelles (02 512 17 88/ www.beermania.be). Métro Porte de Namur. **Open** 11am-7pm Mon-Sat; Dec open daily. **Credit** AmEx, DC, MC, V. **Map** p324 E5.
More than 400 beers on offer, along with matching glasses, gift packages and accessories. Visit the website for more information on the store and to

Bust out at **Maison d'Art**. *See p157.*

place an order for home delivery (you can also place orders by phone). They deliver internationally – €37 per 48 bottles is added to the basic price for shipping to the UK. New next door is a *salon de dégustation* in which to sample beers, cheeses and beer-based dishes.

De Boe
*36 rue de Flandre, Lower Town (02 511 13 73).
Métro Ste-Catherine.* **Open** 9am-6pm Tue-Sat.
Credit AmEx, DC, MC, V. **Map** p318 A2/B2.
De Boe has been selling coffee (both new blends and traditional favourites such as arabica) and teas from around the world for more than 100 years now. This upmarket shop also offers a decent range of fine wines and liqueurs, dried and candied fruits, chocolates and other refined sweetmeats and deli goodies.

Délices et Caprices
*51 rue des Pierres, Lower Town (02 512 14 51/
02 512 18 83). Métro Gare Centrale.* **Open**
6-10pm Tue-Fri; 2-7pm Sat. **Credit** MC, V.
Map p317 B3.
This little shop off the Grand' Place (which has rather erratic opening hours) offers an excellent selection of the finest Belgian beers. The knowledgeable owner strives to bring in new and diverse brews and will happily advise. Glasses, books and other paraphernalia are sold, plus select quality products such as wines, *genevers* and cheeses. Tastings are held on site.

Mig's World Wines
*43 chaussée de Charleroi, St-Gilles (02 534 77 03/
www.migsworldwines.be). Métro Louise/tram 91,
92, 93, 94.* **Open** 11am-7pm Mon-Sat. **Credit**
AmEx, DC, MC, V. **Map** p321 C6.
A thoroughly appealing and idiosyncratic store all round, from its urban chic decor to its merchandise (accessories as well as the *cuvées* themselves), good prices, website and unobtrusively helpful staff. Australian Miguel Saelens breaks the mould of the city's wine purveyors with a choice pick of wines from all over the world. Most of the stock is from Australia, New Zealand and the Americas, but there are also contributions from the Lebanon and Morocco, and Europe is well represented. Mig himself is friendly and often on hand with advice; he organises tasting sessions on Saturdays.

Le Palais des Thés
*45 place de la Vieille Halle aux Blés, Lower Town
(02 502 45 59/www.palaisdesthes.com). Métro Gare
Centrale.* **Open** 10.30am-6.30pm Tue-Sat; 11am-6pm
Sun. **Credit** AmEx, DC, MC, V. **Map** p317 C4.
While coffee went hip in the anglophone world, tea underwent a similar image revolution in continental Europe. This French chain added a new Brussels shop to its French and Japanese outlets at the end of 2001. Stylishly displayed in matte silver-coloured canisters are around 250 varieties, arranged according to each of the 30 countries in five continents the company exports from; and everyday you can sample two different teas for free. There are also delicacies made with tea, containers, gift packages and even books, tips and courses on the art of tea-making and its cultural background.

Wine Not
*55 rue St-Ghislain, Lower Town (02 513 47 74/
www.wine-not.be). Métro Porte de Hal.* **Open** *Shop*
1.30-7pm Thur, Fri; 10.30am-7pm Sat; 10.30am-5pm
Sun. *Wine bar* noon-4pm Sun. **Credit** AmEx, DC,
MC, V. **Map** p320 B5.
A tiny wine shop-cum-wine bar on a small side street in the Marolles. You can taste a fine assortment of wines on the spot and sample some snacks, or place an order on the web. Select accessories are on sale, including some simple glass decanters.

International

African Asian Foods
*25 chaussée de Wavre, Ixelles (no phone).
Métro Porte de Namur.* **Open** 9am-8pm Mon-Sat.
No credit cards. Map p321 D5.
Located in the heart of the African quarter of Matongé, AAF is just one of the area's many grocers selling exotic produce.

La Ferme Landaise
*41-43 place Ste-Catherine, Lower Town (02 512 95
39). Métro Ste-Catherine.* **Open** 9am-6pm Mon-Sat;
closed Mon in June, Aug. **Credit** AmEx, DC, MC, V.
Map p317 B2.

Eat, Drink, Shop

Foie gras, Sauternes, truffles and rich pre-prepared specialities from the south of France. Special orders are also made up as gifts.

Gallaecia

6 rue Charles Martel, EU Quarter (02 230 33 56). Métro Maalbeek. **Open** 11am-7pm Mon-Fri; 11am-3.30pm Sat. **No credit cards. Map** p322 F3.
Quality Spanish produce: olive oil, Manchego cheese, Serrano ham, biscuits, tinned fish and preserves. It also sells sandwiches and home-made *empanadas*. Local Spaniards head here for *turrones* and *polvorones* (Christmas sweets), and the excellent selection of fine wines, cava and liqueurs.

MNS

25-27 boulevard d'Ypres, Lower Town (02 217 71 49). Métro Yser. **Open** 7am-6.30pm Mon-Thur, Sat, Sun. **No credit cards. Map** p318 B1.
The warehouse for the neighbourhood's former 'morning market', MNS sells a variety of North African fresh herbs, spices and other ingredients.

Tagawa Superstore

119 chaussée de Vleurgat, Ixelles (02 648 59 11). Tram 81, 82, 93, 94/bus 38, 60. **Open** 10am-7pm Mon-Sat. **No credit cards. Map** p324 E7.
Japanese expats and Japanophiles congregate in this upmarket supermarket: two floors of food, including fresh and frozen fish and Japanese cookies.

Thai Supermarket

3-9 rue Ste-Catherine, Lower Town (02 502 40 32). Pré-métro Bourse or Métro/Pré-métro De Brouckère. **Open** 9am-6.30pm Mon-Sat; 10am-3.30pm Sun. **No credit cards. Map** p317 B3.
Next door to Brussels' vast Chinese supermarket this more compact and manageable venue, full of exotic fresh and dry produce. Staff are helpful and usually speak English.

Gifts

Au Grand Rasoir – Maison Jamart

7 rue de l'Hôpital, Lower Town (02 512 49 62). Métro Gare Centrale. **Open** 9.30am-6.30pm Mon-Sat. **Credit** AmEx, DC, MC, V. **Map** p317 C4.
The purveyor to the Court of Belgium has a real old-world feel (unsurprisingly, since it has existed since 1821), with excellent service and a window display filled with quality razors and knives of every variety. Staff will also carry out repairs, sharpening and silver-plating.

Bali-Africa

154-156 rue Blaes, Lower Town (02 514 47 92). Métro Porte de Hal. **Open** 9am-6pm Tue-Sat; 9am-4pm Sun. **Credit** AmEx, DC, MC, V. **Map** p320 B5.
This labyrinthine shop is crammed full of a bewildering array of items, mainly from Africa and Asia (statuettes, masks, bongos, furniture), roughly arranged according to their country of origin. The owners have wisely signposted the rooms and provided a painted yellow line on the floor and stairs to help you find your way from one room to another, from Indonesia to Zimbabwe, via Latin America.

Dukah

8 rue des Chartreux, Lower Town (02 502 69 30/ www.dukah.com). Pré-métro Bourse or Métro/Pré-métro De Brouckère. **Open** 11.30am-6.30pm Tue-Sat. **Credit** AmEx, DC, MC, V. **Map** p318 B3.
A simple shop selling mostly handmade wooden items designed by the owners (a Brit, a Kenyan and a Cypriot) and made in partnership with a team of wood carvers in Kenya. The emphasis is on fair trade and environment-friendly sources. Items include bowls (€7-€87), vases and picture frames, plus brightly coloured fabrics, such as the checked Kikoï cloth worn by Kenyan fishermen.

Bali-Africa.

Luxiol

221 chaussée d'Ixelles, Ixelles (02 648 77 14).
Bus 54, 71. **Open** 11am-7pm Tue-Sat. **Credit**
AmEx, DC, MC, V. **Map** p324 E6.
Ethnic furnishings, ornaments and silver jewellery,
along with wooden toys and games to amuse all
ages and a small selection of juggling equipment.

Ma Maison de Papier

6 galerie de Ruysbroek, Upper Town (02 512 22 49).
Bus 34, 48, 95, 96. **Open** 1-7pm Wed-Fri; 3-7pm Sat;
and by appointment. **No credit cards. Map** p317 C4.
This feels like a store of treasures waiting to be
unearthed, with its drawers of prints, plaques and
posters of art exhibits and adverts from the late
1800s to the present.

Maison d'Art G Arekens

15 rue du Midi, Lower Town (02 511 48 08).
Pré-métro Bourse. **Open** 10am-1pm, 2-6pm Mon-Sat.
Credit V. **Map** p317 B3.
A haven for collectors of kitsch, with a variety of
religious icons such as crucifixes and triptychs, plus
a few Buddhas to make up the balance. There are
also lots of small plaster-cast reproductions of non-
religious statues, but the shop's real strength is its
55,000 postcards and reproduction etchings.

La Maison du Miel

121 rue du Midi, Lower Town (02 512 32 50).
Pré-métro Anneessens. **Open** 9.15am-6pm Mon-Sat.
No credit cards. Map p317 B4.
All things honey-themed, scented and flavoured,
from edible goodies to toiletries and homoeopathic
remedies. Make a beeline for the tiny original shop
on rue du Midi, which is well over 100 years old.
Branches: 11 rue Marché aux Herbes, Lower Town
(02 513 57 50).

Mes Sorcières Bien-Aimées

46 rue des Pierres, Lower Town (02 503 51 76).
Métro Gare Centrale. **Open** 12.30-6pm Mon-Fri;
noon-7pm Sat. **No credit cards. Map** p317 B3.
A commercial take on herbal medicine, lore and any
other esoteric practice you could think of. White
witchcraft rubs shoulders with astrology, feng shui,
numerology and yoga. Fortune telling and tarot
reading is €45 per hour. A little fake pond provides
a setting for ornamental frogs and lily pads.

Plaizier

50 rue des Eperonniers, Lower Town (02 513 47 30).
Métro Gare Centrale. **Open** 11am-1pm, 2-6pm
Tue-Fri; 11am-6pm Sat. **Credit** AmEx, MC, V.
Map p317 C3.
A bit different from your average cardshop, with an
artsy Flemish twist. There's a good selection of
beautiful novelty postcards by photographers, as
well as some slightly alternative views of Brussels
and other original designs. Posters are also stocked.

Rêves d'Art et de l'Orient

146 rue Blaes, Lower Town (02 514 31 40). Métro
Porte de Hal. **Open** 9am-6pm Tue-Sat; 9am-3pm Sun.
Credit AmEx, DC, MC, V. **Map** p320 B5.

Gifts galore at **100% Design**. *See p161.*

An evocative outpost of Far and Middle Eastern
decorative objects, from Persian carpets to ornate
Indian carvings. Enriched with Buddha figures,
modern and antique, as well as collectibles such as
netsukes (old Japanese kimono buttons), the display
makes for varied perusal, and purchase at a price.

Rosalie Pompon

1 rue de l'Hôpital, Lower Town (02 512 35 93). Métro
Gare Centrale. **Open** 2-6.30pm Mon; 10.30am-6.30pm
Tue-Sun. **Credit** AmEx, DC, MC, V. **Map** p317 C4.
A mix of kooky interior decor, toys, trinkets and
jewellery makes up the precariously strewn clutter
that is aimed at the child in you. Large papier mâché
giraffes and elephants jostle for space with flower-
adorned wellies, colourful fairy lights, wacky lamps
and clocks and old-fashioned-style puppets.

Yannart-Remacle

11 rue du Marché au Charbon, Lower Town (02 512
12 26). Pré-métro Bourse. **Open** 9.30am-noon, 2-5pm
Mon-Fri. **No credit cards. Map** p317 B3.
An old-fashioned shop with all sorts of supplies for
jewellers, featuring walls of little drawers full of
crystals and semi-precious stones. Staff also do
engravings and settings.

Z'art

223 chaussée d'Ixelles, Ixelles (02 649 06 53).
Bus 54, 71. **Open** 11am-7pm Tue-Sat. **Credit**
AmEx, DC, MC, V. **Map** p324 D6.
This cheerful shop's credo is to sell novelty or design
items with a function. Think slick little radios and

Eat, Drink, Shop

alarm clocks, octopus salt shakers, snail-shaped Sellotape dispensers and cow-adorned toilet roll holders and you get an idea of the countless items on offer. Fun browsing guaranteed.
Branch: 40 rue des Pierres, Lower Town (02 502 61 21).

Health & beauty

Cosmetics & perfume

Planet Parfum (Cloquet)
56-62 rue Neuve, Lower Town (02 219 38 28). Métro/Pré-métro De Brouckère. **Open** 9.30am-6.45pm Mon-Sat. **Credit** AmEx, DC, MC, V **Map** p317 C2.
Ubiquitous fragrance supermarket. A wide selection of perfumes and some cosmetics.
Branches: throughout the city.

Make-Up Forever
62 rue du Midi, Lower Town (02 512 10 80). Pré-métro Bourse. **Open** 9.30am-7pm Mon-Sat. **Credit** AmEx, DC, MC, V. **Map** p317 B3.
A professional make-up supplier and beauty institute that offers facials, massages, manicures and pedicures, as well as permanent make-up and false nails. It also runs courses on applying make-up, both on oneself and as a professional make-up artist.

Hairdressers

Apart from each area's local coiffeurs, Brussels is home to a host of major chain hairdressers, including **Olivier Dachkin**, **Jean-Claude Biguine** and **Jacques Dessange**. They offer speedy, efficient but unimaginative service with a kind of conveyor-belt feel.

Belgian chocolate: a user's guide

What is chocolate?
A controversial issue. Belgian chocolate is a mixture of cocoa paste, sugar and cocoa butter in varying proportions according to the type of chocolate. Dark or plain chocolate, containing the highest proportion of cocoa (up to 70 per cent at its most bitter), is made from full-fat cocoa paste, cocoa butter and sugar. Milk chocolate is a mixture of cocoa paste, sugar and a high proportion of milk, while white chocolate retains only the butter from the cocoa, mixed with sugar and milk.

Arguments over the EU's definition of chocolate (which permits the use of up to 5 per cent vegetable fats other than cocoa butter and allows products containing less than 35 per cent cocoa to be labelled 'milk chocolate') led the Belgian state to introduce its own quality-control trademark, AMBAO. Nit-picking aside, the taste test is the crucial one: once you've tasted Belgian chocolate, you won't be impressed by Cadbury's ever again. Annual consumption of chocolate products in Belgium totalled 82,480 tonnes in 1999, amounting to a whopping 16.77kg per head.

Apart from the standard chocolate bar, you may come across chocolate powder, spread, sauces, pastries, biscuits, liqueurs, ice-creams, seasonal novelties such as Easter eggs and St Nicholas hollow figures... and much more. The most refined form is the praline, a mouthful-sized moulded chocolate, a national institution in its own right. The Neuhaus chocolate house prides itself on inventing the praline in 1912, when the founder's grandson perfected the technique of putting a filling inside a chocolate shell.

Who?
There are around 500 producers of handmade and factory-made chocolate items in Belgium. **Côte d'Or** and **Callebaut** are the market leaders in terms of basic *couverture* chocolate (standard bars). **Galler** is another major player, specialising in the development of innovative flavours and concepts – at their shop on the Grand' Place, you can sample over 23 original flavours in 70g bars. The international praline market is dominated by a handful of big names, such as the now US-owned **Godiva**.

Guylian – best known for its seashell-shaped chocolates – is the country's leading producer of boxed chocolates, and an export star. Mid-range **Neuhaus**, with its signature gold and green livery, is much in evidence, as is **Léonidas**, the most downmarket of the praline producers. **Corné** is another popular mid-range praline producer, while **Café-Tasse** specialises in Neapolitans in a range of flavours. **Wittamer** is a celebrated chocolatier, and **Mary's** and **Pierre Marcolini** are probably the two finest around. Diehard chocaholics should also not miss a visit to the **Musée du Cacao et du Chocolat**, right on the Grand' Place.

How?
You walk into a chocolate shop, to be confronted by rows and rows of pralines. The shop assistant awaits, gloved hand at the ready, to pluck the pralines you want and place them in a *ballotin* (a special box with flaps, available in different sizes, usually

Burlesque
64 rue du Midi, Lower Town (02 513 01 22).
Pré-métro Bourse. **Open** 10am-6.30pm Tue-Sat.
No credit cards. Map p317 B3.
Hairdresser Laurence B wields a pair of scissors and
a bottle of hair dye dexterously to produce trendy
cuts and flamboyant colouring, and he will create
extravagant coiffures for the adventurous. With his
international, multilingual touch he has built up a
faithful (if at times over-credulous) clientele.

Nicole & Jocelyn
*37 chaussée de Wavre, Ixelles (02 511 28 74). Métro
Porte de Namur.* **Open** 9.30am-7pm Mon, Wed-Fri;
10.30am-7pm Sat. **No credit cards. Map** p321 D5.
This is one of the largest and most popular (though
by no means the only) hairdresser in the area that
specialises in Afro hair. Men, women and children
are all catered for.

Tattooists & piercers

European Tattoo Academy
*23 boulevard Maurice Lemonnier, Lower Town
(02 502 43 52/www.europeantattooacademy.com).
Pré-métro Anneessens.* **Open** 2-10pm Mon-Sat.
No credit cards. Map p320 A/B4.
The environment in this tattoo surgery is sterile and
reassuringly antiseptic. Ring to enter and browse
through the catalogues or bring your own design.
They also do henna tattoos, permanent make-up and
some piercing. Prices are high.

Piercing Arkel
*16 passage St-Honoré, Lower Town (02 223 02 94/
www.arkel.be). Pré-métro Bourse or Métro/Pré-métro
De Brouckère.* **Open** 1-6.30pm Mon; 11am-6.30pm
Tue-Sat. **Credit** MC, V. **Map** p317 C3.

125g, 250g, 350g, 500g and 750g). You can
either ask for a (sometimes pre-packaged)
selection of different varieties or request
specific types – if you have a preference for,
say, white chocolate, marzipan or fresh cream.

ABC of pralines
Each shop usually creates its own special
pralines, but there are certain standard types
and fillings. New varieties include sugar-free
(suitable for diabetics) and organic chocolate.
Bestsellers include milk chocolate and praliné,
dark chocolate and marzipan or butter cream,
manons and truffles.
crème fraîche light fresh cream, slightly
sweetened or refined with chocolate.
ganache a filling made from a mixture of
chocolate with fresh cream, sometimes
combined with a variety of flavours (coffee,
tea, spices).
gianduja a filling or a praline in its own right:
a smooth, creamy paste made from
emulsified hazelnuts or almonds, cocoa
butter and sugar.
manon large pralines, usually white
chocolate, filled with fresh or butter cream
and a halved walnut.
nougatine a caramelised sugar mixture,
with roasted, chopped or flaked almonds,
sometimes combined with praliné. Bears little
resemblance to nougat.
praliné a mixture of nuts and sugar to which
chocolate is then added. Not to be confused
with the praline itself.
truffe (aka truffle). Ganache rolled in cocoa
powder, coating or icing sugar.

Practical tips
It is inadvisable to refrigerate chocolate
(unless it contains fresh cream). Store properly
wrapped in a dry, well-ventilated and dark
place, at a temperature of 15-18°C (59-64°F).
Eat within three months of manufacture.

*Thanks to the Belgian Foreign Trade Board's
Special Report on Chocolate, January 2001.*

Le Chien du Chien Vert for fab fabrics.

A full-on professional piercing parlour with a vast choice of jewellery, plenty of advice and files of photos and piercing literature to flick through. It can handle all types of piercing, for €25 upwards, plus the price of the jewellery.

Hobbies, arts & crafts

De Banier
85 rue du Marché au Charbon, Lower Town (02 511 44 31/www.debanier.be). Pré-métro Bourse. **Open** 10am-1pm, 2-6pm Mon-Fri; 10am-1pm, 2-5pm Sat. **No credit cards. Map** p317 B3.
A quiet little shop, neatly packed with an extensive selection of arts and crafts supplies, from wicker, wood, all kinds of paints and dyes, to beads and plenty more. There are also 'how to' books and magazines, mainly in Dutch and French.

Le Chien du Chien Vert
50 quai des Charbonnages, Molenbeek (02 414 84 00/www.chienvert.com). Métro Comte de Flandre. **Open** 10am-6pm Mon-Sat. **Credit** AmEx, MC, V. **Map** p318 A2.
This huge branch of the reliable textile supplier is a feat of interior design as much as anything else. Old boats, canoes, cars, rickshaws and circus lights make up the eclectic decor; there are snooker tables on which to cut the material, while ripples emanate from fountains and fish ponds. You could not ask for a quirkier or more refreshing shopping experience. This is the more specialised outlet, including furnishing fabrics, silks and leathers, and a bargain section of remnants. Up the road is a slightly less recherché 'general' store.
Branch: Tissus du Chien Vert 2 rue du Chien Vert, Molenbeek (02 412 54 39).

Nénuph'art
147A chaussée de Wavre, Ixelles (02 512 11 39). Bus 54, 71. **Open** 10.15am-6pm Mon, Tue, Thur-Sat. **Credit** AmEx, DC, V. **Map** p321 D5.
Not only are there about six tonnes of beads on offer in every shape, size and colour imaginable, but this specialist shop runs courses on beadwork, and on-the-spot advice and repairs. If you want to browse on your own, there's plenty of scope in the form of strategically arranged baskets and drawers.

Schleiper
151 chaussée de Charleroi, St-Gilles (02 538 60 50). Tram 91, 92. **Open** *Supplies* 8.30am-6.15pm Mon-Fri; 9.30am-6.15pm Sat. *Framing* 9.30am-6.15pm Mon-Sat. **Credit** AmEx, DC, MC, V. **Map** p321 C6.
A mammoth art shop with an excellent choice of all types of art supplies organised on several floors, and an efficient framing service. Prices are not low, but goods are cheaper than in many art shops, and the store operates a loyalty card system.

Home furnishings

Compagnie de l'Orient et de la Chine
1A place Stéphanie, Upper Town (02 511 43 82). Métro Louise/tram 91, 92, 93, 94. **Open** 10am-6.30pm Mon-Sat. **Credit** AmEx, DC, MC, V. **Map** p321 C6.
Next door to the clothing outlet of the same shop is this retailer of decorative and practical objects for the home, all oriental in origin. If you can get past the feeling that it's all a touch contrived – or at least overpriced – you'll welcome the ample selection of attractive kitchenware and tableware (bowls and chopsticks, ahoy), wicker and bamboo goods and smaller, less costly items such as lampshades, bags and stationery materials.

Dille & Kamille
16 rue Jean Stas, St-Gilles (02 538 81 25).
Métro Louise/tram 91, 92, 93, 94. **Open** 9.30am-
6.30pm Mon-Sat. **Credit** MC, V. **Map** p321 C6.
Dille & Kamille provides attractive household basics
galore, and all at decent prices. Glassware, chinaware, baskets, flowerpots, cutlery and baskets are
complemented by cookbooks in various languages,
and select foodstuffs such as teas, oils, herbs and
sugar-free jams.

Espace Bizarre
19 rue des Chartreux, Lower Town (02 514 52 56/
www.espacebizarre.be). *Pré-métro Bourse.* **Open**
10am-7pm Mon-Sat. **Credit** AmEx, DC, MC, V.
Map p318 B3.
There's a notable Japanese influence to the home
furnishings at Espace Bizarre. Futons and tatami
mats share the space with low tables and chairs,
bowls and chopsticks, slippers and kimonos. This
minimalist look is teamed with a more flamboyant,
but equally groovy one. Funky lamps and lampshades, brightly coloured, retro-inspired sofas,
fluffy cushions and a few Alessi and Philippe Starck
items liven it all up.

Max
90-101 rue Antoine Dansaert, Lower Town
(02 514 23 27). *Pré-métro Bourse.* **Open** 11am-
1pm, 2-6.30pm Tue-Fri; 11am-6pm Sat. **Credit**
AmEx, DC, MC, V. **Map** p318 A2/B2.
The designer furniture on show tends be largely
minimalist in look, but there are some more wacky
items too. Curvy armchairs and rather wacky sofas
are almost cartoonish; you'll find plenty of leather
and chrome, and some retro designs. Prices are usually reasonably steep.

New De Wolf
91 rue Haute/40 rue Blaes, Upper Town (02 511
10 18/02 512 96 48). *Tram 92, 93, 94/bus 95, 96.*
Open 10am-6.30pm Mon-Sat; 10am-3pm Sun. **Credit**
AmEx, DC, MC, V. **Map** p317 B/C4.
A bewildering hotchpotch of eclectic and inexpensive home decor and furnishings, from the downright tacky to the sporadically tasteful, is spread
over two enormous floors. During the festive season,
its massive range of Christmas decorations draws
hordes of shoppers. Quite a few bargains can invariably be unearthed.

100% Design
30 boulevard Anspach, Lower Town (02 219 61 98).
Métro/Pré-métro De Brouckère. **Open** noon-6.30pm
Mon; 10am-6.30pm Tue-Sat. **Credit** AmEx, DC, MC,
V. **Map** p317 B3.
Welcome to plastic fantastic: inflatable everything
(well, almost), lava lamps, household knick-knacks
in lurid hues, fluffy cushions and so on. The new
shop opposite (02 223 40 62) is a slightly more
mature and sober version, focusing on more substantial items such as furniture, glassware, lamps
and luggage – all with that ultra-contemporary look
that's increasingly popular.

La Vaisselle au Kilo
8A rue Bodenbroek, Upper Town (02 513 49 84).
Tram 92, 93, 94/bus 20, 34, 48, 95, 96.
Open 10am-6pm Mon-Sat; 10am-5.30pm Sun.
Credit MC, V. **Map** p317 C4.
A bull in this china shop would have to be careful,
as it's chock-full. Inexpensive crockery and glassware are mostly priced by the kilo, but items in some
ranges can be bought singly.

Music & video

Fnac (*see p141*) also stocks music.

Arlequin
7 rue du Chêne, Lower Town (02 514 54 28/
www.arlequin.net). *Métro Gare Centrale.*
Open 11am-7pm Mon-Sat; 2-7pm Sun. **Credit** MC,
V. **Map** p317 B4.
Well-stocked second-hand music shop. This branch
is open on Sunday afternoons and sells a mix of
genres, but focuses on rock, punk, import and jazz;
the other two specialise in soul, funk, jazz, rap, reggae, classical and world music.
Branches: 7 & 8 rue de l'Athenée, Ixelles
(02 512 15 86/02 514 30 64).

BCM
6 Plattesteen, Lower Town (02 502 09 72).
Pré-métro Bourse. **Open** 11am-6.30pm Mon-Sat.
No credit cards. **Map** p317 B3.
A fine selection of dance music on vinyl: techno,
house and drum 'n' bass. The staff are more than
helpful and knowledgeable, and it's a good source
of information for prospective clubbers.

Le Bonheur, Epicerie Audiovisuelle
53 rue des Eperonniers, Lower Town (02 511 64 14/
www.lebonheur.net). *Métro Gare Centrale.* **Open**
noon-7pm Wed-Sat; 2-7pm Sun. **Credit** AmEx, DC,
V. **Map** p317 C3.
A most curious mélange of non-mainstream music,
videos and DVDs, plus posh trendy 'groceries' such
as chocolate, tea, soap, perfumes and incense. The
modest but attractive selection of art-house movies
is eclectic and international.

Caroline Music
20 passage St-Honoré, Lower Town (02 217 07 31).
Métro/Pré-métro De Brouckère. **Open** 10am-6pm
Mon; 9.30am-6.30pm Tue-Sat. **Credit** MC, V.
Map p317 C3.
This retailer of a varied and extensive range of CDs
continues to resist the invasion of the megastores.
Huge sections are devoted to indie and French
music. A good source of gig tickets.

Free Record Shop
Anspach Centre, off boulevard Anspach,
Lower Town (02 219 90 04/www.freerecord
shop.be). *Métro/Pré-métro De Brouckère.* **Open**
10am-7pm daily. **Credit** AmEx, DC, MC, V.
Map p317 C3.

Eat, Drink, Shop

Having ousted Virgin from its pitch in downtown Brussels, the FRS is now the biggest music store in town (with the exception of the more wide-ranging Fnac). As well as CDs, it stocks videos, DVDs and computer games. Its one floor is a rather downbeat affair with vaguely unpleasant lighting and layout. **Branches:** 18 rue Fossé aux Loups, Lower Town (02 217 88 99); 42 chaussée d'Ixelles, Ixelles (02 512 13 54).

Médiathèque

Passage 44, 44 boulevard du Jardin Botanique, Lower Town (02 218 26 35/www.lamediatheque.be). Métro/Pré-métro Rogier. **Open** 10am-6pm Tue-Thur, Sat; 10am-8pm Fri. **No credit cards. Map** p319 D2.
This large, dark institution rents out all media, with an extensive and eclectic selection of CDs and videos. The *version originale* section is quite small, but more art-house than the average local video shop. To use the Médiathèque, you have to confront Belgian bureaucracy in its full glory: you must be a Belgian resident and be in possession of your Belgian ID card, and there's the inevitable paperwork. A fee is charged for membership, on top of rental costs. Passage 44 runs from boulevard du Jardin Botanique to boulevard Pacheco.

Music Mania

4 rue de la Fourche, Lower Town (02 217 53 69/ www.musicmaniarecords.com). Métro/Pré-métro De Brouckère. **Open** 11am-6pm Mon-Sat. **Credit** MC, V. **Map** p317 C3.
One of the best independent music shops in town, selling vinyl and CDs. You can spend hours sorting through records and listening to them at the decks at the counter; both staff and customers seem to be vastly knowledgeable.

Musical instruments & equipment

Azzato

42 rue de la Violette, Lower Town (02 512 37 52/ www.azzato-music.com). Métro Gare Centrale. **Open** 9.30am-6pm Mon-Sat. **Credit** AmEx, DC, MC, V. **Map** p317 C3.
Ethnic instruments from all over the world.

Bigsby (Music Office)

156 rue du Midi, Lower Town (02 502 38 70). Pré-métro Anneessens. **Open** 10.30am-7pm Mon-Sat. **Credit** AmEx, DC, MC, V. **Map** p318 B4.
Musical instruments and recording equipment.

Hills

37-39 rue du Marché au Charbon, Lower Town (02 512 77 71/www.hillsmusic.be). Métro Gare Centrale. **Open** 9.30am-12.30pm, 1.30-6pm Mon-Sat. **Credit** AmEx, MC, V. **Map** p317 B3.
This reputed shop specialises in quality acoustic string instruments.

Opticians

Theo

81 rue Antoine Dansaert, Lower Town (02 511 04 47). Pré-métro Bourse or Métro/Pré-métro De Brouckère. **Open** 10.30am-6.30pm Mon, Wed-Sat. **Credit** AmEx, DC, MC, V. **Map** p318 B3.
These trendy specs have a very distinctive look, often with thick, brightly coloured frames. The Flemish designer successfully marketed them in the world's fashion capitals before setting up on his home turf's own little avant-garde fashion centre.

Top-class toy shop **Serneels**. *See p164.*

Trading places

Markets are part of daily life for most inhabitants of Brussels; each *commune* has a local market of some description. They are usually of two kinds: *brocante* or *rommelmarkt*, selling bric-a-brac, ranging from junk to collector's items; and markets that sell food, plants, clothes or other items, sometimes with *brocante*.

The following are some of the most popular markets in the city. Note that credit cards are rarely accepted.

Agora

Métro Gare Centrale. **Open** 10am-6pm Sat, Sun. **Map** p317 C3.
The square often marked on maps as place de l'Espagne, but known to residents as place de l'Agora, just off the Grand' Place, hosts a kind of art and crafts market on weekends. A handful of stalls sell gifts, jewellery, perfume, toys and useless novelty items such as your name on a grain of rice.

Anderlecht

Métro Clémenceau. **Open** 6/7am-2pm Sun.
Across the road from the metro station, in and around the abattoirs' covered market area, Brussels' largest and most diverse market is held every Sunday morning (don't worry – the slaughterhouses are quite separate). You can get hold of just about anything, from food to home furnishings, music to pets and, above all, bric-a-brac. The surrounding cafés and bars buzz with activity.

Gare du Midi

Métro Gare du Midi. **Open** from 6am Sun. **Map** p320 A5.
The Marché du Midi is another of the largest markets around, and has a distinctly North African and Mediterranean flavour. Stalls selling fresh and dried fruit, veg, meat, fish and dairy products set up on disused train tracks, under flyovers and spill over into parking lots adjacent to the station. There are also cleaning products, pots and pans, cheap toys and clothes, rai music, bread, biscuits and sweets, plants and flowers. It's all very cheap and many of the stallholders speak very good English.

Grand' Place

Métro Gare Centrale or Pré-métro Bourse. **Open** 8am-6pm daily. **Map** p317 C3.
Brussels' main square is the site of a lovely, medium-sized flower market.

Marolles

Métro Porte de Hal. **Open** 7am-2pm daily. **Map** p320 B5.
The flea market (*pictured above*) in the cobblestoned place du Jeu de Balle features a lot of junk unattractively dumped in old cardboard boxes or on blankets. Costume jewellery, clothes, old vinyl, electronic equipment, furniture and home accessories make up the bulk of goods. It's good fun even if you're not planning to buy anything. Prices have been known to suddenly increase on weekends. Go early to get the best bargains.

Place du Châtelain

Tram 81, 82, 93, 94/bus 54. **Open** 2-7pm Wed.
A cluster of stalls assembles on pretty place du Châtelain in Ixelles to sell traditional craft food products, such as cheeses and savoury *tourtes.* Foodie heaven.

Sablon

Tram 92, 93, 94/bus 95, 96. **Open** 9am-6pm Sat; 9am-2pm Sun. **Map** p317 C4.
The place du Grand Sablon and the surrounding area is where money changes hands over antiques, art and home furnishings. A more modest market featuring coins, stamps, china and similar collectibles is held on Saturdays and Sundays.

Eat, Drink, Shop

Pharmacies

Chemists have a monopoly on pharmaceuticals – even aspirin cannot be bought anywhere else. Look for the green cross to find your nearest. Phone 0900 10500 for the closest chemist on night and weekend duty.

Sport

Entre Terre et Ciel

20 place Stéphanie, Ixelles (02 502 42 41). Métro Louise, then tram 91, 92, 93, 94. **Open** 10.30am-6.30pm Mon-Sat. **Credit** DC, MC, V. **Map** p321 C6.
Something of a luxury megastore for outdoor pursuits. An extensive range of kit includes equipment for skiing, snowboarding, sailing, camping and mountaineering, plus scouting accessories.

Go Sport

City 2, rue Neuve, Lower Town (02 217 46 23/ www.go-sport.com). Métro/Pré-métro Rogier. **Open** 10am-7pm Mon-Thur, Sat; 10am-7.30pm Fri. **Credit** AmEx, MC, V. **Map** p319 C2.
Generic store selling sports equipment and clothing for a multitude of disciplines.
Branches: Woluwe Shopping Centre, 200 rue St-Lambert, Woluwe-St-Lambert (02 762 16 38); Westland Shopping Centre, 481 boulevard Sylvain Dupuis, Anderlecht (02 521 53 68).

Ride All Day

39 rue St-Jean, Lower Town (02 512 89 22). Métro Gare Centrale. **Open** noon-6.30pm Mon-Sat. **No credit cards. Map** p317 C4.
One of the original skate shops – selling boards, shoes and clothing – caters for fanatics, who tend to congregate around the skate hotspot that is the neighbouring Mont des Arts. The staff (all die-hard skaters) are happy to offer tips and advice.

Velodroom

41 rue van Artevelde, Lower Town (02 513 81 99). Pré-métro Bourse. **Open** 10am-6.30pm Mon-Sat. **Credit** DC, MC, V. **Map** p318 B3.
This shop specialises in city bikes. It's run by a non-profit organisation that promotes cycling in Brussels as an environmentally friendly alternative to cars.

Toys & magic

A&T Lewis Magic Circus Shop

45 rue Van Artevelde, Lower Town (02 511 24 07). Pré-métro Bourse. **Open** 10am-6.30pm Mon-Fri; 10.30am-6.30pm Sat. **Credit** V. **Map** p318 B3.
A full-on magic store – with a cordoned-off section that is out of bounds to non-magicians – as well as some costumes and masks.

Christiansen

City 2, rue de la Blanchisserie, Lower Town (02 218 09 28). Métro/Pré-métro Rogier. **Open** 10am-6.30pm Mon-Sat. **Credit** AmEx, DC, V. **Map** p319 C2.

Belgium's largest toy shop chain sells everything from Lego to Barbie, and Playdoh to Nintendo. It's all a bit mass-produced, but the choice is good.
Branches: throughout the city.

The Grasshopper

39 rue du Marché aux Herbes, Lower Town (02 511 96 22). Métro Gare Centrale. **Open** 10am-7pm daily. **Credit** AmEx, DC, MC, V. **Map** p317 C3.
Downstairs is chock-a-block with trinkets and small playthings with stocking-filler potential, plenty of timeless classics (yoyos, kaleidoscopes), novelty lamps, adorable but fairly pricey cuddly toys and plenty more. Upstairs there's a wide selection of puzzles, educational and craft-based games, and larger items such as rocking horses. Pretty window displays, a medley of old favourites and contemporary crowd-pleasers, as well as a central location ensure that it attracts shoppers of all ages. ·

La Maison du Bridge

61 rue du Bailli, Ixelles (02 537 43 85). Métro Louise then tram 93, 94/tram 81, 82. **Open** 10am-6pm Mon-Sat. **Credit** V. **Map** p321 D7.
The name is a bit misleading: bridge represents only one aspect of this shop. You'll find a wide selection of different board games, along with larger table games. There's also paraphernalia such as card mats and gambling mats, deluxe chess and backgammon sets and books on games-associated topics.

Serneels

69 avenue Louise, Ixelles (02 538 30 66/ www.serneels.be). **Open** 9.30am-6.30pm Mon-Sat. **Credit** AmEx, DC, MC, V. **Map** p321 C6.
Deluxe toy store with high-flying prices, which stocks just about everything a little heart could desire, from the hi-tech to the traditional, with beautiful-looking puppets, rocking horses, doll's houses and enormous cuddly toys all getting a look-in, as well as the usual plastic and electronic favourites. A whole section is devoted to an impressive collection of board games and puzzles, all of the elegant, luxury variety and safely on display in glass cases.

Travel agents

For some of the best-priced flights in town (especially for students and under-26s) to destinations worldwide, and last-minute deals, try **Airstop** on www.airstop.be/070 233 188.

Connections

19 rue du Midi, Lower Town (02 550 01 00). Pré-métro Bourse. **Open** 9.30am-6.30pm Mon-Fri; 10am-4pm Sat. **Credit** DC, MC, V. **Map** p317 B3.
Trilingual service, offering cheap deals for students as well as over-26s. Staff can book for buses, planes, boats and accommodation; they also sell ISIC cards. Info by phone can vary in reliability and accuracy, and it may well be worth paying a visit in person.
Branch: 78 avenue Adolphe Buyl, Ixelles (02 647 06 05).

Arts & Entertainment

By Season

Enjoy fairs, festivals, fireworks and fun all year round.

Most of Brussels' seasonal festivals and activities take place in spring and summer – not surprisingly, given the dampness at other times of the year. But if you can brave the cold in winter, there are good Christmas markets and festivities in December, and some fascinating carnivals and festivals at the start of Lent, usually in towns outside Brussels (*see p224* **Beer, bears and bathtubs**). There are also numerous festivals of music (classical to rock), dance and theatre throughout Belgium, mainly in summer. For more info, *see p196* **Festival fever 1**, *p201* **Festival fever 2** and *p218* **Festival fever 3**.

The Belgians take a huge and uncynical delight in tradition and folklore, and it is quite common to come across an unexplained procession of giants or a marching band as you walk around Brussels at the weekend. Another Belgian obsession is the *brocante* and

the *braderie*, where a whole square or neighbourhood becomes a flea market for a weekend. Most Brussels *communes* hold at least one such event every spring or summer; of course, there are always scores of food and drink stalls alongside the old clothes and junk. Keep your eyes open for posters.

For general information on seasonal events and festivals – either in advance or while you are in Belgium – **TIB** is a good source. For information about events further afield, contact the **Belgian Tourist Information Office** (for details of both, *see p303*).

For information on the seasons and weather in Belgium, *see p304*. For the dates of public holidays, *see p304*.

Spring

Brussels International Festival of Fantasy, Thriller & Science Fiction Films

02 201 17 13/www.bifff.org. **Date** Mar.
A two-week festival of more than 150 films that is essential viewing for the horror/sci-fi addict and easily missable by everyone else. Films shown include previews as well as classics, and there are also workshops and seminars, plus make-up and body-painting competitions and a Vampires' Ball (at the Halles de Schaerbeek), which takes place at the end of the festival. People-watchers beware: only those in costume will be allowed to attend.

Ars Musica

02 219 40 44/www.arsmusica.be. **Date** mid Mar-early Apr.
This festival of contemporary classical music is becoming one of the most important annual arts events, with concerts taking place in venues across the city. The 2002 festival included works by Péter Eötvös, including his Japanese-inspired opera of *The Three Sisters*, and by 93-year old American composer Elliott Carter.

Brussels International Film Festival

02 227 3989/www.brusselsfilmfest.be. **Date** Apr.
Brussels' most important film festival. Held in cinemas around the city, it often features a number of themes, with Belgian films running alongside shorts and other European and US mainstream and art-house pictures. A few big names usually visit, and though it's not as glamorous as Cannes or Berlin, nor as varied as London, it is a good chance

Manneken-Pis Festival. *See p171*.

Arts & Entertainment

Raid the dressing-up box for **Ommegang**. *See p168.*

to catch previews of some of the forthcoming year's films. Owing to venue problems, the festival could not be held in 2002 but it should return in 2003 to a new site, the renovated Institut National de Radiodiffuson on place Flagey, and in a new month, April (rather than January).

Dring Dring Bike Festival

Parc du Cinquantenaire, EU Quarter (02 502 73 55/ www.provelo.org). Métro Merode. **Admission** free. **Map** p325 G4. **Date** Sun in early May.

A major bike festival centred in the Parc du Cinquantenaire, with bikes for hire (from €3 per hour), guided bike tours all around Brussels and its outskirts, and bike-riding and maintenance classes. Even better, the busy avenue du Tervuren is closed to traffic, making cycling a much more pleasant experience than usual. Organiser Pro-Vélo also hires bikes outside of the festival.

Kunsten Festival des Arts

02 219 07 07/tickets 070 22 21 99/www.kunsten festivaldesarts.be. **Tickets** phone for details. **Box office** *Mar, Apr* 11am-7pm Tue-Fri; 11am-5pm Sat. *May* 11am-10pm daily. **Credit** MC, V. **Date** May.

One particularly refreshing aspect of this major arts festival is that it is non-sectarian: it features works in French, Flemish and, increasingly, English. Established in 1994 by Brussels arts supremo Frie Leysen, the three-week event features dance, theatre and opera, and attracts important international names in all these fields. The venues include large

theatres like the Kaaitheater and the Théâtre de la Monnaie, as well as less establishment venues such as the Halles de Schaerbeek.

Jazz Marathon

02 456 04 86/http://jazz.chello.be. **Tickets** 3-day pass €10 in advance; €11.50 on the day. **Date** last weekend of May.

For three days (virtually non-stop), jazz lovers can hear live music in bars, clubs and restaurants all over Brussels. Most musicians/bands are local amateurs, but there are usually a few bigger names on show, and there's often a free concert in the Grand' Place. A three-day pass buys you access to all the venues, and beer is often at reduced prices. The Jazzbus is a free shuttle service between venues. Tickets are available from Fnac (*see p141*), TIB (*see p303*) and participating venues.

Brussels 20km Run

02 511 90 00/www.sibp.be/20km/intro_fr.html. **Date** last Sun in May.

Belgium's biggest track and field event starts and finishes in the Parc du Cinquantenaire, passing through the Bois de la Cambre and the avenue Louise. Now an established part of the Brussels calendar, it attracts about 20,000 runners, mainly amateurs (entrance fee €10-€12.50). Not necessarily an unmissable event for the weekend tourist – unless you have friends taking part – but it's worth knowing the date, so you can be forewarned about half of Brussels grinding to a halt as the runners pass.

Arts & Entertainment

Concours Musical International Reine Elisabeth de Belgique

Palais des Beaux-Arts, 23 rue Ravenstein, Upper Town (box office 02 507 82 00/www.concours-reine-elisabeth.be). *Métro Gare Centrale or Parc.* **Tickets** €10-€60. **Map** p319 C/D4. **Date** May-mid June.
Young musicians from all over the world take part in this competition, founded more than 40 years ago by Belgium's former Queen Elizabeth, a keen violin player. The competition alternates between three categories – piano (next in 2003), singing (2004) and violin (2005) – with the final featuring 12 competitors. Many of the concerts are shown on national TV.

Summer

Flanders Festival

09 243 94 94/www.festival-van-vlaanderen.be. **Date** May-Nov.
Belgium's biggest classical musical festival, with more than 350 concerts staged in 80 towns throughout Flanders, including Brussels. World music, dance and theatre performances are also included. Most events take place from August to October.

Battle of Waterloo

Waterloo Tourist Information Centre, 149 chaussée de Bruxelles, Waterloo (02 354 99 10). **Date** every 5yrs in mid June.
A large-scale re-enactment of the 1815 Battle of Waterloo, one of the most significant battles in history, usually takes place every five years in the Brussels suburb – the next one is due in 2006. It's a spectacular event: about 2,000 men don period uniforms, wield vintage guns and play war; some represent the troops of the Duke of Wellington and Prussia's Marshall Blücher, while others act as French soldiers fighting under Napoleon. *See also p12* **The Battle of Waterloo**.

Festival de Wallonie

081 73 37 81/www.festivaldewallonie.com. **Date** June-Oct.
The French community's equivalent of the Flanders Festival (*see above*). International and Belgian orchestras, chamber groups and soloists perform at castles, abbeys and churches in the French-speaking part of Belgium. The music is usually of good quality, and many concerts are worth attending for the beauty of the venue.

Ommegang

Grand' Place, Lower Town (TIB 02 513 89 40/ tickets 02 512 19 61 or 02 548 04 54/www. ommegang-brussels.be). *Métro Gare Centrale or Pré-métro Bourse.* **Tickets** Grand' Place performance €28-€68. **Map** p317 C3. **Date** 1st Thur, Fri, Sat in July.
A popular medieval pageant held over three days, in which hundreds of Belgians satisfy their lust for dressing up and processing. A huge parade of people dressed as nobles, guildsmen, soldiers, jesters and peasants marches from the Sablon to the Grand' Place, some on horseback, others on foot.

Royal Brussels

One of the few things shared by Flanders and Wallonia is a love of the royal family. Apart from the national football team, Albert II and Queen Paola help bind this riven nation. As the monarchy is low-key, the hype surrounding them – and the opportunities for royal-inspired events – are generally kept quietly in the background. Plus there have been only six Belgian kings, so historical input remains thin. The main palace in Brussels is now only used for public affairs, while the family itself lives in the Laeken complex. Once a year, however, the royals throw their doors open to the public, in a display of unity and close contact locals seem to thrive on. Some royal sights – including the **Musée de la Dynastie** (*see p75*) and the new **Palais de Charles de Lorraine** (*see p75*) – open all year round.

Serres Royales

61 avenue du Parc Royal, Laeken (TIB 02 513 89 40). *Métro Heysel.* **Map** p326 D1. **Date** end Apr-early May.

This is a real highlight of the Brussels calendar – with correspondingly long queues. For a few weeks in May (dates vary annually but are given out by the Tourist Information Office from January), the king and queen open the royal hothouses at Laeken to the public. The 11 iron and glass vaulted greenhouses were commissioned by King Léopold II and designed by architect Alphonse Balat, who taught Victor Horta. It's said that Léopold was so taken with the greenhouses that he moved into one of them shortly before his death – but he was a weird old soul by the end, so no one was surprised. The evening visits are particularly stunning, when the tropical foliage and ironwork are lit by magical lights.

Palais Royal Open Days

16 rue Bréderode & place des Palais, Upper Town (02 551 20 20). *Métro Parc or Trône.* **Admission** free. **Map** p321 D4. **Date** late July-early Sept.

The origins of the ceremony are disputed: some say it commemorates the visit of Charles V to Brussels; others claim it dates from the 14th century when a statue of the Virgin Mary was transported from Antwerp to the Grand Sablon. Either way, it all ends up with a horse parade, stilt-fighting and a jousting tournament in the Grand' Place. You can buy seats for the grandstand in the Grand' Place (you usually have to book in early June, at the latest), or sit at a bar in the place du Grand Sablon and watch the start or catch the parade along its route.

Brosella Jazz & Folk Festival

Théâtre de Verdure, Parc d'Osseghem, Laeken (02 270 98 56/www.brosella.be). Métro Heysel. **Admission** free. **Map** p326 B1. **Date** 2nd weekend in July.

Organised by a group of unpaid music lovers, the Brosella festival has been going strong for more than 20 years, despite a shoestring budget. A sampling of jazz and folk from Belgian and international musicians is served up all weekend at the Parc d'Osseghem near the Atomium.

National Day

Parc de Bruxelles, rue Royale & place des Palais, Upper Town. Métro Gare Centrale, Parc or Trône. **Map** p319/321 D4. **Date** 21 July.

National Day is a serious business in Belgium (perhaps because it is a relatively young nation) and an excuse for a public holiday. The focus of the celebrations is a military parade and fly-past, an event

Following the National Day celebrations, the Royal Palace (*pictured*) is opened to the public – and unlike Buckingham Palace, admission is free. As this is not a residential palace, there's nothing much of human interest here, so don't expect to see a fur wrap thrown casually over a Louis XV chair. But it's perfect for a nose and to see the classical interior of this splendid 18th-century palace.

that can leave the foreigner bemused: the regiments march somewhat lackadaisically, the military bands play taped music, and the military vehicles on display include Belgacom (the Belgian telephone service) vans and unidentified civilians driving Renault 5s. Still, there is plenty of flag-waving, and the royals are there to watch it. The celebrations in the royal park afterwards are, by contrast, as festive as anything, with a fairground, beer and fast-food outlets and a major fireworks display.

Foire du Midi

boulevard du Midi, Lower Town (02 279 25 30). Métro Gare du Midi. **Map** p320 A5. **Date** mid July-mid Aug.

Brussels' annual family-oriented fair is one of the largest in Europe, with all the usual rides, games, shooting galleries, dodgems and sticky sweets – as well as more indigenous fast food such as *moules-frites*, *gaufres* (waffles), and lots of beer. There's occasionally talk of banning the fair because of the general disruption to traffic and local life, but so far the event is intact.

Meiboom

rue des Sables & rue du Marais, Lower Town (TIB 02 513 89 40). Metro Gare Centrale. **Map** p319 C/D2. **Date** 9 Aug.

Legend has it that in 1213 a wedding party was celebrating outside the city when they were attacked by a gang from Leuven. The gang was chased out of town and, as a token of appreciation, the local duke allowed the victorious wedding party to plant a maypole on the eve of their patron saint's feast day. Nowadays, it's basically an excuse for the people of Brussels to dress up in medieval costume, stage a parade of giants on stilts and generally have a good time. The procession – complete with tree – leaves from rue des Sables at about 2pm, and marches to the Grand' Place before returning to the corner of the rue des Sables for the planting of the tree, which must take place before 5pm. The celebrations then continue into the night.

Tapis des Fleurs

Grand' Place, Lower Town (TIB 02 513 89 40). Métro Gare Centrale or Pré-métro Bourse. **Map** p317 C3. **Date** mid Aug.

Every year, for two or three days, the Grand' Place is the setting for a huge floral carpet (*tapis*) made of up to a million cut begonias. The flowers are supplied and designed by growers from Ghent, and each year there is a different design – though it's usually a traditional scene, such as St Michael (the patron saint of Brussels) killing a dragon. The balcony of the Hôtel de Ville is open for an aerial view.

Autumn

Journées du Patrimoine

Brussels 02 204 14 20/Flanders 03 212 29 55/ Wallonia 081 332 384. **Admission** free. **Date** 1st, 2nd or 3rd weekend in Sept.

Do they know it's Christmas?

'It's an outrage,' cried one Bruxellois, using a word rarely bestowed upon the season of goodwill to all men: Christmas. 'This just isn't Christmas,' complained one *Le Soir* reader on the letters page. Locals were up in arms in the run-up to 2001's festivities when a local government committee decided to move Christmas, lock, stock and skating rink, from its traditional home on the Grand' Place to nearby Ste-Catherine. And what did they replace it with, at this time of tradition, on Europe's most picturesque square? Flying sheep, starry-hide cows and Day-glo donkeys, a kind of postmodern, life-size manger scene more Pink Floyd than pastoral.

Tourists, perhaps weary of the same nativity scene displayed in countless department store windows back home, loved it, clambering half-cut over the cows and donkeys at three in the morning. But for locals a tradition has been broken – and it seems as if it will stay broken, with Ste-Catherine due to stage Christmas again in 2002.

The move was part-political, part-practical. As well as moving the Marché de Noël, the Christmas market, a few days later so as not to clash with the high-security G7 summit that was taking place in town, the authorities also had to deal with a Grand' Place that was fit to bursting, jam-packed with stalls, skaters, prams and a bloody great Christmas tree.

The bloody great Christmas tree is still there, perhaps somewhat bemused by the Day-glo animals below, but the market stalls now line the streets around Ste-Catherine –

a high-investment inner-city area that local government likes to show off, by the way. In the neighbourhood's main square, the former fish market known by all as place du Marché aux Poissons, against a backdrop of 18th-century townhouses, stands the main skating rink. Fuelled with warming glugs of Scandinavian glög (mulled wine), adults join the screaming fray, while Strauss and Kylie provide more melodic accompaniment. There's also an old-fashioned merry-go-round for the less adventurous.

Traditional Christmas markets are also held in towns all over Belgium, the largest being in Liège, the Cité de Noël, with 120 stalls and outdoor skating rinks on place St-Lambert and place du Marché.

Ice skating

place du Marché aux Poissons, Lower Town (TIB 02 513 89 40). Métro Ste-Catherine. **Date** *mid Dec-6 Jan* noon-10.30pm daily. **Admission** (incl skate hire) €4.46; children €2.97. **Map** p317 B2.
Situated in the shadow of Ste-Catherine church, the rink is surrounded by fairy lights and drink stalls.

Le Marché de Noël

Around place Ste-Catherine, Lower Town (TIB 02 513 89 40). Pré-métro Bourse or Métro Ste-Catherine. **Admission** free. **Date** early Dec-1st wk of Jan. **Map** p318 B3.
Some 150 market stalls set up in rues Auguste Orts, Antoine Dansaert and Vieux Marché aux Grains.

The **Tapis des Fleurs** in the Grand' Place. *See p169.*

Hundreds of public and private buildings are open to the public free of charge on Journées du Patrimoine (Heritage Days) in Brussels, Wallonia and Flanders (since Flanders and Wallonia rarely coincide on anything, their *journées* are usually on different weekends). It's an excellent opportunity to see the bits of churches or other public buildings that are usually marked 'No Entry', or to check out some of Belgium's private art nouveau residences. Buildings change each year, and details are usually given in newspapers and the *Bulletin*.

Manneken-Pis Festival
rue de l'Etuve, Lower Town (TIB 02 513 89 40/ 02 201 14 42). Métro Gare Centrale or Pré-métro Bourse. **Map** p317 B4. **Date** early Sept.
Brussels' favourite statue gains yet another outfit to add to its collection of hundreds of costumes, ranging from kilts to a beekeeper's outfit. The ceremony is accompanied by general celebrating and a parade of giants, and eating and drinking on a large scale.

Les Nuits Botanique
Botanique, 236 rue Royale, St-Josse (02 226 12 17/ www.botanique.be). Métro Botanique/tram 92, 93, 94. **Map** p319 D2. **Date** mid Sept.
An excellent Brussels institution: for a fortnight, several bands play in the various rooms, marquees and gardens at the Botanique cultural centre. Bands come from all over the world and usually include a smattering of good British bands, appearing in the size of venue they would have played several years before they became famous. In the past, big names have included Primal Scream and Asian Dub Foundation, and Björk made a guest appearance in 2001. All the atmosphere of a festival without the mud and the travelling.

Circuses
TIB 02 513 89 40 & posters around Brussels. **Date** Oct, Nov.
A number of circuses visit Brussels each year, usually in October and November, but sometimes the run is extended to Christmas and New Year. Regular ones include the Bouglione circus in place Flagey

and the Florilegio at the Hippodrome de Boitsfort. Shows are traditional and, for many, morally objectionable: there are performing tigers, elephants and dogs and even, on occasion, ducks and geese.

Independent Film Festival
02 649 33 40/http://web.wanadoo.be/fifi. **Date** early Nov.
This week-long international festival of independent film offers a chance for alternative film makers to showcase their work in a supportive, interactive setting. The festival started in 1974 when Super8 reigned supreme. Now incorporating a mix of media, the philosophy remains the same: to allow young directors to find a springboard for their work. In 2002, more than 100 films from 60 countries will be shown, many for the first time.

St Nicholas
Date 6 Dec.
Belgian children receive their main presents on the feast of St Nicholas, rather than at Christmas, so shops are geared up for an earlier date. St Nicholas, accompanied by the threatening figure of Zwarte Piet (Black Peter), distributes gifts and *speculoos* (a ginger biscuit, a Belgian speciality). Christmas itself is a low-key family affair, with another set of pressies for the kids on Christmas Eve.

New Year's Eve
Grand' Place and around. **Date** 31 Dec.
If your idea of fun is to be crammed tight into a Gothic square with bangers cracking around your feet, then this is for you. The Belgians just adore their fireworks at the turn of the year, and let them off without a whiff of concern for the neighbours. But the atmosphere on the streets is good-natured and friendly without the drunkenness associated with cities like London. Once the bells stop ringing, the square starts to clear and waltz music is played over the loudspeakers, encouraging couples to dance. There is usually a city-organised fireworks display in one of the big parks.

Arts & Entertainment

Children

From parks to puppets, there's plenty to keep youngsters amused.

Brussels has much to offer children, including plenty of hands-on-style museums, acres of parkland in the city parks, the more natural woodland such as Bois de la Cambre, and inner-city playgrounds for the very young. There are also some fab daytrips on offer: large-scale theme parks, a sandy coastline, wildlife centres and two state-of-the art science museums.

If you book your stay during the country's month-long carnival season (kick-off Mardi Gras/Shrove Tuesday) or at peak puppet show time (October to May), then a good time for all will be guaranteed. There is an astonishing line-up of distinctly non-PC circuses in the run-up to Christmas: big cat acts pack out the ringside seats.

In general, Brussels is a child-friendly place. Kids are welcomed in some of the city's smartest restaurants – but that's because the Belgians expect their offspring to behave and eat as mini adults (special menus aren't the norm). This is reinforced by the massive selection of shops specialising in precious hand-crafted toys and designer label clothes for tots – not the things for grubbing around in a sand pit. Downsides of the city are that pushchair access is appalling, except in the most modern of buildings, pavements are badly maintained and parking is difficult – which all means that carrying tiny kids is the most sensible option.

Surprisingly, few children's outdoor areas are dog turd-free despite regular promises by the authorities to introduce or tighten rules.

Call **Info Vacances** (0900 10 123) for French-language advice on sports and cultural activities for children. For children's clothes and toys, games and magic shops, *see chapter* **Shops & Services**.

Babysitting

Some of the more upmarket hotels offer babysitting; *see chapter* **Accommodation**.

La Ligue des Familles
127 rue du Trône, 1050 Brussels (0900 273 71/ www.liguedesfamilles.be). **Open** *Phone enquiries noon-2pm daily.*
The leading French-language association for families in Belgium runs a babysitting service. Rates vary, but are no more than €5 per hour. You might need to take out membership first.

Office de la Naissance et de l'Enfance (ONE)
02 542 12 11/www.one.be. **Open** *Phone enquiries 8am-5pm Mon-Fri.*
For longer-term childminding arrangements, the ONE can send you a list of state and private nurseries and crèches, and registered childminders in any district of Brussels.

Mini-Europe, part of the **Bruparck** complex. *See p173.*

Arts & Entertainment

Service des Etudiants de l'ULB

02 650 21 71. **Open** *Phone enquiries* 10am-noon,
2-4pm Mon-Fri.
A babysitting service run by students at the
Université Libre de Bruxelles. If possible, ring the
day before you want a babysitter. Rates cost €3.50-
€5 per hour (€7.50 after midnight).

Entertainment

Brussels has a tradition of puppetry. Two of
the city's best venues are the **Théâtre du
Peruchet** (50 avenue de la Forêt, Ixelles; 02
673 87 30/www.paluche.org/loisirs/peruchet/
home.htm), which also has a little museum, and
the **Théâtre du Ratinet** (44 avenue de Fré,
Uccle; 02 375 15 63). The productions of fairy
tales and fables are usually in French, but that
shouldn't hinder enjoyment. Shows are usually
held mid-afternoon on Wednesday, Saturday
and Sunday, but call for details; tickets cost
around €5. There is also the famous **Théâtre
du Toone** (*see p215*), though its productions
are sometimes aimed more at adults than kids.

Bruparck

*1 avenue du Football, Heysel (Mini-Europe 02 478
05 50/Océade 02 478 49 44/Atomium 02 474
89 77/www.bruparck.com/www.minieurope.com).*
Métro Heysel. **Open** *Mini-Europe: July, Aug,
Oct-early Jan* 9.30am-8pm daily. *Mid Mar-June,
Sept* 9.30am-6pm daily. *Océade: July, Aug* 10am-
10pm daily. *Apr-June* 10am-6pm Tue-Fri; 10am-
10pm Sat, Sun. *Sept-Mar* 10am-6pm Wed-Fri;
10am-10pm Sat, Sun. **Admission** *Mini-Europe*
€11; €8.50 under-12s; free children under 1m 20cm.
Océade €12.50; €10 children up to 1m 30cm;
free children under 1m 15cm. **Credit** *All* AmEx,
DC, MC, V. **Map** p326 A/B2.
A mini theme park at the foot of the Atomium (*see
p93*) with plenty of pursuits to appeal to all age
groups. It includes fairground attractions, the vast
multi-screen Kinepolis cinema complex (*see p182*)
and fast-food outlets of every description. There's
also Mini-Europe, which has miniature replicas of
top sights such as the Eiffel Tower and Big Ben, and
the Océade swimming pool with slides and chutes.
There are special deals on family tickets and tickets
that combine visits to all the attractions.

Museums

Among Brussels' many museums, there are
quite a few that will appeal to children. The
Musée des Instruments de Musique (*see
p73*) is a must for aspiring musicians with its
amazing collection of instruments from the 16th
to 20th century arranged into themes. In most
sections it is possible for children to listen to
different types of music by headphones, and
guided tours and children's workshops can be
booked. The library of comic-strip albums at

Puppets galore at **Théâtre du Toone**.

the **Centre Belge de la Bande Dessinée**
(*see p63* **Strip search**) is guaranteed to appeal
to those aged six or over – though the upper
floor of the museum is not suitable for kids.
Children will also enjoy the Belgian-discovered
iguanodon dinosaurs, life-size automated
replicas and the insect department at the
Institut Royal des Sciences Naturelles
(*see p81*). The **Musée Royal de l'Afrique
Centrale** (*see p81*) is set on the edge of the
Forêt de Soignes with a boating park, cycle
tracks and public footpaths a stone's throw
away. The museum itself is currently being
remodelled; it should reopen in late 2002.

There are also a handful of museums aimed
specifically at children:

Musée des Enfants

*15 rue du Bourgmestre, Ixelles (02 640 01 07/
www.museedesenfants.be). Tram 23, 90, 93, 94/
bus 71.* **Open** 2-5.30pm Wed, Sat, Sun. *Phone*
9.30am-noon Mon-Fri. **Admission** €6.20; ticket
for four €22.50. **No credit cards.**
Fabulous for four- to nine year-olds, this rambling
townhouse has been turned into one large children's
play area, with a drama section, dressing-up clothes,
giant interactive puzzles and educational games, a
kitchen with supervised baking sessions, a domestic
animal enclosure and an outdoor playground.

Musée du Jouet

24 rue de l'Association, Lower Town (02 219 61 68).
Métro Botanique. **Open** 10am-12.30pm, 2-6pm daily.
Admission €2.50-€3.50. **No credit cards.**
Map p319 D2.

Privately owned by an enthusiast and toymaker, the Toy Museum reopened recently after years of renovations. The collection of toys, puzzles and interactive games span many a decade and clockwork demonstrations are given. Suitable for children aged three and upwards.

Scientastic Museum

Level 1, Pré-métro Bourse, boulevard Anspach, Lower Town (02 732 13 36/www.scientastic.com). Pré-métro Bourse. **Open** 12.30-2pm Mon-Fri; 2-5.30pm Sat, Sun, school holidays. Reservations required for other times. **Admission** €4.21; €3.72 under-26s; free under-4s. **Credit** MC, V. **Map** p317 B3.

This child-centred science museum couldn't be more convenient. It's slap in the city centre, below ground in the Bourse pré-métro station. Hundreds of interactive experiments are levelled at all age groups from five upwards, and English-language fact sheets and guided tours are available.

Parks

The **Bois de la Cambre** at the end of avenue Louise (entrances on chaussée de Waterloo and avenues Louise and Roosevelt) is a huge landscaped chunk of the Forêt de Soignes, with a lake and acres of parkland. On Sundays, when its vast inner ring is closed to traffic, it becomes a magnet for cyclists, rollerbladers and toddlers on trucks. There are two playgrounds as well as outdoor cafés (closed in winter). Small **Parc Tenbosch** (entrances on chaussée de Vleurgat and place Tenbosch) in Ixelles has a secure, well-maintained and dog-free playground for the very young, a pond with terrapins, ornamental gardens and a basketball court.

For a leafy retreat not far from the centre of Brussels, head for the park in the middle of **Sauvagère nature reserve** in Uccle (entrance on avenue de la Chenaie). It's ideal for younger children with outdoor playground facilities, a picnic area, basketball court, duck pond and farm animals in enclosures. Also in Uccle, lovely **Parc de Wolvendael** (entrances on avenues de Fré and Paul Stroobant; 02 348 65 47) has sloped banks, an outdoor café, crazy golf and a revamped playground marred only by the fact that dogs are allowed a free rein. **Parc de Woluwe** (entrance on avenue de Tervuren) is a great place in winter for sledging.

Out of town

Children can't fail to adore the sandy Belgian coastline, all 67 kilometres (42 miles) of it. A regular tram service runs the length of it, from De Panne on the French border, to Knokke-Heist by the Dutch, via Ostend. Most resorts (there are 14) have wide promenades for

cycling, scootering, and rollerblading, with hire facilities (take personal ID). Most hire places also have an astonishing line-up of family-style tandems, pedal cars and carts for children aged two to ten with racing car models, animals and cartoon characters. There are also plenty of watersports (surfing, windsailing, water-skiing, jet-skiing), and shrimping is popular too.

Ostend (*see p269*) is the most famous resort and the most accessible, with frequent trains from Brussels. **Blankenberge** has more besides the sea with a Sea Life Centre and Serpentarium. **Knokke-Heist** is one of the poshest resorts and has Het Zwin bird sanctuary and a butterfly park, while **De Haan**, with its belle époque architecture, is less developed. A tram runs along the entire coast and stops at each resort. Contact the individual tourist information boards for the various resorts; details on **www.dekust.be**.

If you're visiting Antwerp, the attractive nearby town of **Mechelen** (*see p276*) has lots of things to do for most ages. There is a well-signposted toy museum, **Speelgoedmuseum** (www.speelgoedmuseum. be), plus the **Planckendael Park & Zoo** and science museum **Technopolis** (for both, *see p175*).

South from Brussels is Waterloo (*see p12* **The Battle of Waterloo**). A climb up the Butte du Lion for a bird's-eye view of the battlefield is a must for the over-sixes, and there's also a small playground and quad bike enclosure. The Panorama, a circular evocation of the battle, built in the 19th century, is kitsch and dusty but fun, and a piece of history in its own right. En route, stop off at **Kid's Factory** (63 chaussée de Bruxelles, Waterloo; 02 351 23 45/www.kidsfactory.be), a private indoor playground for children aged one to 12. It's a good place for letting off steam with its padded mats, inflated bouncy areas, rope ladders and other amusements.

Other options are listed below.

Parc d'Aventures Scientifiques (Pass)

3 rue de Mons, Frameries (070 22 22 52/ www.pass.be). By car E19 towards Paris, exit R5 to Frameries, then N544. By train to Gare de Mons (6km) then bus 1, 2. **Open** *Sept-June* 9am-5pm Mon, Tue, Thur, Fri; 10am-6pm Sat, Sun, school holidays. *July, Aug* 10am-6pm daily. Closed 1wk Sept, 2wks Jan. **Admission** €12.50; €7.50 3-14s. **Credit** MC, V.

An exciting state-of-the-art structure set on the site of a disused mine. The architect was none other than Frenchman Jean Nouvel, whose other projects have included Paris's Institut du Monde Arabe and Musée des Arts Premiers. There's an eclectic selection of interactive exhibits aimed at all age groups, a café and an outdoor area.

Explore the world of comic strips at the **Centre Belge de la Bande Dessinée.** *See p173.*

Parc Paradisio

domaine de Cambron, Cambron-Casteau (068 45 46 53/www.paradisio.be). By car A8/E429 to Tournai, exit 29. By train to Cambron-Casteau. **Open** *Easter-Oct* 10am-6pm daily. Closed Nov-Easter. **Admission** call for details.

An hour's drive south from Brussels, between Mons and Ath, this park is in the grounds of an estate crossed by a river and has lakes, water gardens and ornamental flower beds. It includes the ruins of an ancient abbey (where shows involving birds of prey are held), a giant aviary with birds of paradise, desert creatures including a giant tortoise, and an Antarctic section. There's also an adventure playground with slides and rope bridges, a children's petting farm and much else besides.

Planckendael Park & Zoo

582 Leuvensesteenweg, Muizen (015 41 49 21/ www.planckendael.be). By car E19 towards Antwerp, exit 11. By train to Muizen. **Open** *July, Aug* 9am-6.15pm daily. *mid Mar-June, Sept* 9am-5.45pm daily. *1-15 Mar, 1-15 Oct* 9am-5.15pm daily. *Feb, mid Oct-Nov* 9am-4.45pm daily. *Jan, Dec* 9am-4.30pm daily. **Admission** €13; €8.50 3-11s, concessions. **Credit** AmEx, V.

A perfect fair-weather option, Planckendael is an open-air wildlife park (used to breed animals from and for Antwerp Zoo – *see p230*). It has rhinos, deer and antelope, wolves, an aviary, a colony of cranes, excellent playgrounds and lots of green open space. It's ten minutes by bus from Mechelen train station or a 30-minute ride on a canal boat (possible in summer and signposted from station).

Six Flags Belgium & Aqualibi

9 rue Joseph Dachamps, Wavre (Six Flags 010 42 17 17/010 42 15 00/Aqualibi 010 42 16 00/ www.sixflagseurope.com). By car E411 Brussels-Namur, exit 6. By train to Six Flags-Bierges. **Open** *Six Flags Apr-Oct* 10am-6/7/9/11pm daily. Closed Nov-Mar. **Admission** *Six Flags & Aqualibi* €28.50; €23.50 3-11s. *Aqualibi only* €13.50; €10 6-11s; free under-6s. **Credit** AmEx, V.

This mega-theme park is still referred to as Walibi, although it was bought out some time ago by US leisure giant Six Flags and renamed. The new ownership has led to better maintained and new attractions and rides, including seven rollercoasters. Attached to it is Aqualibi, a huge water park with chutes, wave machines, different pools and hundreds of excited children. You can get a combined ticket for both parks. Closing hours can vary and Six Flags is open only at weekends some months, so it's best to check opening times before heading off. Try to avoid the school holidays, when the queues can be horrendous.

Technopolis

Mechelen (015 34 20 00/www.technopolis.be). By car E19 towards Antwerp, exit 10. By train to Mechelen then bus 282, 283. **Open** 9.30am-5pm daily. **Admission** €7.19; €4.70 3-11s, concessions. **Credit** AmEx, DC, MC, V.

A fantastic hands-on science museum. Young kids will like the water and bubble experiments, while older ones will enjoy the optical and mechanical examples. It has a reasonably good café.

Arts & Entertainment

Clubs

Where to dance till dawn – in the capital and beyond.

Brussels' reputation as a clubbing city is partially based on the standing of one club, the Fuse, whose own rep has been built mainly on the deck of one DJ, Pierre. This is not to say there aren't any other clubs – there are, and some good ones too – but the scene is much more fickle and fragmented than that of Antwerp (*see p235*) and Ghent (*see p263*).

Club culture involves Belgium as a whole, a country compact enough not to need Brussels as its focus. In the time it takes to cross London by taxi, you can get to Ghent for half the price by train. Major annual extravaganzas include **I Love Techno** (www.ilovetechno.be), attracting 35,000 to the Flanders Expo in Ghent; the **City Parade** (www.cityparade.be), a huge street festival involving 100,000 music lovers in Liège in June; the **House-Torhout Festival** (www.housetorhout.be) in July; and any number of events staged by Ghent-based **Kozzmozz** (www.kozzmozz.be). Ghent also puts on Belgium's most prestigious international dance party, **Ten Days Of…**, which attracts the very top names to spin at the town's main festival in July. *See p264* **Party on** for details.

In Brussels, apart from the clubs listed below, watch out for occasional underground events and monthly reggae/ragga Bass Culture Soundsystem nights at the **Recyclart** (*see p132*) and new free parties by **Protesta** (www.futureworldfunk.be). Info on these and other events can be gleaned from flyers and free weekly *Out Soon* from bars such as **Pablo Disco Bar** and **Dalí's Bar** (for both, *see p136* **Brussels by bar crawl: Late haunts**); record shops such as **Music Mania** (*see p162*) and **Dr Vinyl** (1 rue de la Grande Ile; 02 512 73 44); and clothes stores such as **Ramon et Valy** (*see p150*) and **Hype** (*see p151*). Online, try the agenda sections of **www.noctis.com** (for house, electro and funk), **www.boups.com** (for drum 'n' bass) and **www.netevents.be** for general nightlife information.

Some clubs listed below are in dark corners of the city. In a hangover from the old system of tipping, you may cross the doorman's palm with €1 or €2 and ask him to call a taxi. Otherwise, unless you're planning to go back into the club, or you have a particular affinity for bouncers, don't tip. Other rules: no training shoes, certainly not in a mainstream club. And cannabis is not legal in Belgium.

Brussels

Bulex

Hippodrome, Groenendael (infoline 02 534 23 92). By train to Groenendael. **Open** from 10pm 1st Sat of the mth. **Admission** varies. **No credit cards**.
The Bulex has been a nightlife institution since the early 1990s. Formed by a group of hip young things from the media and advertising, it continues to perpetuate a relaxed and rather pop/soul style, attracting regulars once a month to far-flung parts of Brussels, more often than not the Groenendael Hippodrome. Occasionally it moves elsewhere, so always phone for details. More fixed is the bar Bulex in Forest (264 avenue Van Volxem), a couple of stops on the 52 tram south of Midi station. It's held every Thursday from 8pm; expect a good music mix by Lucas Racasse and Ben.

Chez Johnny

24 chaussée de Louvain, St-Josse (02 227 39 99). Métro Madou. **Open** 9pm-5am Fri, Sat. **Admission** €5. **No credit cards**. **Map** p322 E3.
Set in an old ballroom of 60 years' standing, this is Brussels' great big slab of cheese, nightlife-wise (you really should be in a red suit waving maracas at the same time). OK, you may hear Dee-Lite, Barry White and Bob Marley, but you're just as likely to hear Sheila, Régine and Cloclo. Occasionally there's hot-spiced raï and even refined breakbeat sounds, but with a decor taken with a joky holiday resort, you're on a hiding to nothing, really. Towards the end of the night, the Captain asks the crowd – and there will be a crowd – to choose one of the two DJs (Jonathan or Vivian) to win control of the decks.

La Doudingue

5 clos Lamartine, Braine L'Alleud (02 384 02 81/ www.doudingue.com). Phone for directions. **Open** 10pm-6am Fri, Sat. **Admission** 10pm-midnight free; midnight-6am €8. **Credit** MC, V.
Of the mainstream clubs, Doudingue is the best known – and deservedly so. Situated in a comfortable suburb 20km (12 miles) south of Brussels, it offers house and R'n'B in the main room, a separate karaoke club, a grill restaurant and neon bowling. This is complemented by a fashionable young crowd, up for enjoying themselves in pleasant surroundings. It's not going to push the boundaries of music to somewhere beyond the next millennium, but it's a pretty impressive venue nonetheless.

The Food

Lounge Club, 25 rue Henri Maus, Lower Town (infoline 0165 80107/www.foodmaincourse.com).

Go on, show 'em who's who at **Who's Who Land**. *See p180*.

Pré-métro Bourse. **Open** 10pm-late Sat. **Admission** *Women* 10pm-1.30am free; 1.30am-late €8. *Men* €8. **No credit cards**. **Map** p317 B3.

Now *this* is house. And since 1996, via the town of Leuven, owner and manager Frank has taken great care to keep the soul of the place intact. Based on the strong DJ trio of Geoffroy, Raoul and Regis, the Food hosts international deep house guest DJs every fortnight (Luke Solomon, Jori Hulkonnen, Derrick Carter). And the public have stayed faithful – never less than 500, often up to 800. Fine music, good sound quality, minimal lighting, plus the fantastic decoration of the Lounge Club (opulent wood, a stucco ceiling and comfy armchairs) – all that's missing is the strawberry syrup and champagne. The Food is also responsible for Main Course, a big-name dance event at Leuven Brabanthallen every May; check the website for details. The Lounge (02 510 05 52) also opens on Fridays for a more low-key night of similar style.

The Fuse

208 rue Blaes, Lower Town (02 511 97 89/ www.fuse.be). Métro Porte de Hal/bus 20,48. **Open** 10pm-7am Fri, Sat. **Admission** *International DJs* 10-11pm €2.50-€5; after 11pm €10. *Resident DJs* 10-11pm free; after 11pm €7. **Credit** V. **Map** p320 B4/5.

The one Brussels club of international significance, the Fuse has seen the world's best DJs at its decks since it opened in 1994. The current residents – Pierre, Deg and T-Quest – aren't sloppy either. On the first floor, Motion is another dancefloor filled with uplifting UK house and deep house mixed by more experimental jocks. Don't come expecting a massive futuristic superclub: the Fuse is more like a disused Spanish hacienda turned into a crazy music box of two floors of 2,000 people cranked up to the max. The Fuse also hosts La Démence (*see p191*), one of the main gay house clubs in Belgium, held one Sunday a month and occasionally before public holidays; and Respect is Burning (www.respectisburning.com; before midnight €2.50, after midnight €10), a reworking of French house parties, held one Friday a month and featuring the deep house of Dimitri from Paris, DJ Deep and Jef K. Oh, and there are also Ibiza and retro parties courtesy of Claude El Divino.

Louise Gallery

Level 1, galerie Louise, avenue Louise, Ixelles (infoline 0475 490465). Métro Louise. **Open & admission** varies. **Map** p321 C5.

Once upon a time, this was a large ballroom in the basement of an ornate shopping gallery. Built in the early 1950s, Arlequin was a jet set destination before becoming a bog-standard 1980s club, then, with some success, Amnezia, the Studio Gallery and the NY Club. After folding in 1993, a new role was announced at a grand press conference in spring 2002: a select house club on Fridays, a populist one on Saturdays and a stylish gay night, Le Cabaret, on Sundays. Definitely worth checking out. (The name of the club hasn't been announced yet.)

MadeinBrussels

6 place de la Chapelle, Lower Town (no phone/ www.noctis.com/made). Bus 20, 48. **Open** 10pm-5am Fri. **Admission** *International DJs* 10-11pm €5; 10pm-5am €10. *Resident DJs* 10-11pm free; 10pm-5am €8. **No credit cards.** **Map** p317 B4.

Opened in 1999 by DJs and prime movers F-X and Psychogene, MadeinBrussels started quick off the blocks. Pretty soon, Fridays in this ancient, low-ceilinged red-brick cellar became the techno/electro place to be. Since then, some big names have passed through – Dave Angel, Fisherspooner, Electric Indigo and Psychogene himself. Like a Jacques Cousteau docu-film, it's luminous out front, but the deeper you go in, the darker and denser it gets. It attracts a polarised mix of thirtysomething techno-heads and keen teenagers new to the scene.

Mezzanine

51 chaussée de la Hulpe, Uccle (no phone). Bus 41. **Open** from 10pm Thur-Sat. **Admission** free.

Once the loaded young frequented the Jeux d'Hiver – now it's the Mezzanine. It began as a monthly club called Return of the Jeudi, a Thursday special held at Boitsfort Hippodrome, playing the hits of the day. Then someone hit on the bright notion of renovating the two late 19th-century rooms (they are rather splendid) and installing a restaurant. At the end of the dinner, the tables are cleared and the dancing commences. Divine young things jig around to *Papa's got a Brand New Bag*, and it's all very jolly in a totally surreal way. If this sounds like your kind of cocktail, and your face fits, great, you're in, enjoy: admission is free.

Mirano Continental

38 chaussée de Louvain, St-Josse (02 227 39 70). Métro Madou. **Open** from 10pm Fri, Sat. **Admission** 10pm-midnight free; midnight-late €6-€7. **No credit cards.** **Map** p322 E3.

Since the shiny 1980s, the Mirano Continental has attracted many of the main players from Brussels' nightlife. Perhaps now it's lost its sheen, but in the right mood (and in the right clothes) it can still be fun. Converted from a splendid 1940s cinema, the building kept part of its original purpose when it began to be used as a venue for film previews. As for the club, Fridays mean straight youth in straight clothes heading straight for the dancefloor. On Saturdays, it's house, house, house, with Olivier Gosseries, Michel Traxx and Jos. Watch out for Noces Royales nights every two weeks. There's a revolving dancefloor too.

The top DJs' clubs

Olivier Gosseries

Currently resident DJ at Mirano Continental and on Fun Radio Belgium, Olivier Gosseries runs his own record label and has been an essential part of the Belgian nightlife scene since the mid 1980s. He plays mostly New York-oriented happy house.

'Even when I don't work there, I go to softly gay Le Cabaret on Sunday, at the **Louise Gallery**. When I get a free Friday I usually go to **Who's Who's Land**. Although I haven't had the time yet, I urgently want to discover **Culture Club** in Ghent.'

Koenie

Considered to be one of the founders of the Belgian deep house scene in 1991, Koenie has been resident in all major house clubs (Café d'Anvers, first floor of the Fuse, monthly guest at Food) and has always worked in the DJ record shops – mostly USA Import (75 St Jacobsmarkt, Antwerp). He now runs a record label and second-hand record shop for electronic rarities under the name Wally's Groove World (www.wallysgrooveworld.be), housed beneath USA Import.

'**Food** – always! **Club Geluk** – sometimes, depending on who's playing. I'd go to the **Cappuccino Club** (at the Eilandje, Antwerp) almost every day if the weather is OK, because it's indoor and open-air. The **Farine, Food & Future** (40 Vlaamsekaai, Antwerp) is also really a nice place.'

Marko

Spinning since 1989, Marko has been resident DJ at La Rocca near Antwerp every Sunday since 1991. He plays house to psy-trance with a slight touch of techno; you'll see him at all major events and his reputation goes before him.

'I used to go to **Goa** trance parties, and it's still an underground scene. You can only get info from rumours and flyers

Movida Social Club

quai des Péniches, Schaerbeek (infoline 0476 721929/0479 576030/www.movidasocialclub.be). Métro Yser. **Open & admission** varies. **Map** p318 B1.

The Movida Social Club – set up by Damien, Lukas, F-X, Gil, Renaud and a handful of others – has been moving around the city since 1999. They started in

Hands up for the **Fuse**.
See p177.

distributed at other Goa parties. I always feel good at the **Fuse** – and at **La Bush** I love the fact that people let me dance in peace for a couple of hours. Nobody bothers me there. That's nice.'

Pierre

House DJ at Café d'Anvers in 1992, Pierre turned to techno with his residency at the Fuse in 1994. He's a top Belgian name on the techno scene, and appears at all the big electronic festivals or events.

'I go to the **Athanor Studio**, mostly for the Ebony Bliss parties, featuring Ugo, when the place is really pleasant. **Food** is not only a good club, it's *the* DJ club. And there's **Pablo Disco Bar**. Plus Respect Is Burning nights at the **Fuse** – and I'm a regular at **Dalí's Bar**.'

Psychogene

Icon of a certain type of techno freak, Psychogene created the Neuroleptic parties to much public acclaim. Since 2000 he has managed MadeInBrussels, filling the DJ booth with the finest knives in acid techno and

electro. He also produces EPs with N Scaravelli under the name Sharpside.

'**Kozzmozz** and **I Love Techno** are musts. I don't go there to DJ, I go there to party. There's also **Dalí's Bar**. I'd pop into **Le Tavernier** for a drink at the start of a night. I really loved **Café d'Anvers** as a DJ when I played there for Antwerp is Burning one year. Also – the parties by Claude El Divino, Ibiza and retro house parties, mostly at the **Fuse**.

Geoffroy

One of the most regular nighthawks in Belgium since the late 1980s, Geoffroy soon started spinning for radio shows and small parties. Since 1996 he's been resident at the referential **Food** club and now plays at almost every big house event.

'**Pablo Disco Bar, Dalí's Bar**, and the **Lounge Club** on Fridays. **Culture Club** when I'm in Ghent. That's a really nice place; I used to go there before moving anywhere else. Monthly Respect is Burning at the **Fuse** – for Jef K, a friend of mine, for the music and for the guest DJs.'

Arts & Entertainment

a small bar at Alma metro station, then moved on to a barge that soon proved a wee bit too small for the kind of tripped and laughing disco-house-electro nights that were beginning to develop. By then they were attracting some 1,200 people. Since those heady days, they've gone from the Glacières of St-Gilles to the Halles de Schaerbeek, and now they're back on Ric's Boat – and it's always a don't-miss. Movida

Social Club parties mainly appeal to lovers of disco-house and electro-pop – but happily suit anyone who just likes a damn good party.

Los Romanticos

25B boulevard Anspach, Lower Town (02 223 69 04). Métro/Pré-métro De Brouckère. **Open** 8pm-3am daily. **Admission** varies. **No credit cards. Map** p317 B3.

Although Los Romanticos is open to all-comers, the most comfortable visitors are salsa dancers – very good salsa dancers. There's no contest, of course, but it may be better to try a few steps beforehand. Although the place looks somewhat average, on its night Los Romanticos can be a hot ticket – and it's right in the middle of downtown.

Sonik
112 rue du Marché aux Charbon, Lower Town (02 511 99 85/www.sonik.be). Pré-métro Anneessens or Bourse. **Open** 11pm-6am Wed-Sat. **Admission** €2.50. **No credit cards. Map** p318 B3.
Sonik proves that small can be beautiful and, above all, fun. It's a little shelter for some of the greatest local DJs in house, electro or techno, who slip in almost anonymously to play for an appreciative 80 (casual, take a drink at the bar) or wild 200 (wear shorts). DJ Pierre on Thursdays is a great case in point. Erik and Sophie run a sympathetic ship, occasionally blown off course by the mysteriously fickle ways of the crowd.

Who's Who's Land
17 rue du Poinçon, Lower Town (02 512 52 70). Pré-métro Anneessens. **Open** 11pm-4am Fri, Sat. **Admission** €8. **No credit cards. Map** p317 B4.
Just down the street from the Manneken-Pis, Who's Who Land, launched in 1996, was meant to be *the* point of reference for club culture in Brussels. The

Some seriously good DJs spin at **Sonik**.

building was splendid, a 1920s theatre done out like a cyber palace from the 1960s. And for two years, it was brilliant. Thousands flocked for two floors of solid house and R'n'B. Some of the greatest names came to spin the decks, Marshall Jefferson, Tony Humphries, Deep Dish and Felix da Housecat included. Then administrative and renovative closure slowed its heartbeat, and the faithful crowd has been scratching their heads ever since. The formula, however, still works, on Saturdays at least: live jazz-funk, plus quality house DJs Eric Beysens and Junior Jack. There are special events too; Fridays have seen Europop Follies (Kajagoogoo meets Kim Wilde). The place still has potential.

Further afield

As well as the major clubs and festivals in and around Brussels, Ghent and Antwerp, the following are happenings around the Belgian provinces. For more info, check generic sites **www.noctis.be** and **www. netevents.be**.

La Bush
180 route de Tournai, Esquelmes (015 310377/ www.labush.com).
'The Temple of House' offers Saturday nights of trance and house in a 2,000-capacity venue.

Le Complexe Cap'tain
118 chaussée de Montgomery, La Glanerie (069 648580/www.complexecaptain.com).
Friday and Saturday nights of trance, house and pop in a 5,000-capacity venue.

La Goa
94 Wervikstraat, Menen (056 519400/www.lagoa.be).
Saturday-night trance with DJs Frank Biazzi and HS. There's room for about 3,000.

Le Millenium
13D route du Condroz, Boncelles (www.millenium.be).
Trance and hits on Mondays, Fridays and Saturdays.

Le Pure
chaussée de Bruxelles, Barry (www.pureclub.be).
Deep house in a warehouse off the A8 towards Tournai from Brussels. Fridays only; free admission.

La Soundstation
6 rue Pouplin, Liège (04 232 13 21).
Refined house parties are held on most Fridays in a disused railway station in Liège.

La Villa
51 chaussée de Liège, Henri-Chapelle (087 447150/ www.lavilla.be).
Trance and hits on a Friday and Saturday.

Le Zoo
169 route de Tournai, Pecq (069 55 90 10/ www.zooclub.be).
R'n'B and hip hop (Saturdays) and house (Sundays), in a 1,500-capacity venue near Tournai.

Film

Original language films, great cinemas, cheap tickets: what more could you want?

Brussels is something of a mecca for movie buffs. The quality of the screens, seats and sound is usually excellent, films tend to be shown in their original language, prices are reasonable and for a city with just over a million people, the choice is bewildering. For these reasons going to the cinema is a hugely popular pastime and it's best to book in advance if you want to avoid long queues.

American blockbusters dominate the listings and multiplexes swallow up most of the trade, but cosmopolitan Brussels always has the latest flicks from France, Spain, Italy and further afield. Belgium also has its own film industry, a somewhat cultish one. In place of all-action bombast, gritty realism and black humour rule – as wonderfully depicted by the 1999 Cannes Palme d'Or winner *Rosetta* by Luc and Jean-Pierre Dardenne. Emilie Dequenne (winner of the best actress award) played the troubled teenager lost in dismal Liège. Other recent hits have included *Une Liaison Pornographique* by Frédéric Fonteyne, and *C'est arrivé près de chez vous* (aka *Man Bites Dog)* and *Everybody Famous!,* both by Rémy Belvaux, the latter nominated for an Oscar for best foreign-language film in 2001.

There are also numerous annual film festivals, the most notable of which are the International Film Festival in April and the Festival of Fantasy, Thriller & Science Fiction Films in March.

TIMINGS AND TICKETS

Film programmes change on Wednesdays. Listings can be found in most of the French and Flemish daily papers and in the weekly English-language *Bulletin.* The Belgian cinema website – www.cinebel.com – has the times of all major cinemas in the country and also runs an online booking service for some cinemas.

Films tend to be shown four times a day, with evening performances at 7-8pm and 9-10.15pm. Features start 20 minutes after the advertised time. The average ticket price is €6-€7, with reductions for students, senior citizens and the unemployed. Some cinemas also offer reductions to all on Mondays. In some cinemas you might be brow-beaten into tipping the usherettes and the toilet attendants. On the plus side, all the major cinemas are near to public transport and offer reduced fees for car parks.

Abbrevations to look out for are: **EA** (under-16s admitted); **CNA** or **ENA** (under-16s not admitted); **St** (with subtitles); **V angl** (English-language version); **V fr** (French-language version); and **VO** (original version, not dubbed).

Cinemas

Actors' Studio

16 petite rue des Bouchers, Lower Town (0900 29969/02 512 16 96/information 0900 27854). *Métro/Pré-métro De Brouckère*. **No credit cards**. **Map** p317 C3.

Hidden among the fish restaurants and a stone's throw from the Grand' Place is one of Brussels' smallest and most intimate cinemas. The two-screen Actors' Studio is a great place to catch reruns of mainstream movies and films by offbeat directors such as Pedro Almodóvar and Peter Greenaway. It also has a cosy bar.

The elegant **Arenberg Galeries**. *See p182.*

Arenberg Galeries

26 galerie de la Reine, Lower Town (02 512 80 63).
Métro Gare Centrale. **No credit cards. Map** p317 C3.
Situated in the magnificent Galeries St-Hubert, the
Arenberg is Brussels' most elegant art-house cinema. On a typical day its two auditoria show films in
Farsi, Spanish and Serbo-Croat, as well as French
and English. Sometimes it seems as if the converted
art deco cinema goes out of its way to showcase
obscure world fare, but the Écran Total festival in
summer more than makes up for this with its populist selection of cults and classics.

Aventure

17 rue des Fripiers, Lower Town (02 219 17 48).
Métro/Pré-métro De Brouckère or Pré-métro Bourse.
No credit cards. Map p317 C3.
If a film has bombed at the box office or been around
for so long that everyone has bought the DVD, you'll
find it showing at the Aventure, a seedy-looking picture house in a downtown shopping mall. Although
plagued by poor sound and picture quality, the
three-screen cinema is cheap and shows a wide
selection of lesser-known and low-budget features.

Kinepolis

Bruparck, avenue du Centenaire, Laeken (bookings
02 474 26 00/information 0900 00555/
www.kinepolis.com). Métro Heysel. **Credit** V.
Map p326 A/B2.
Northern Europe's biggest multiplex might look like
an aircraft hangar from the outside, but the 28 theatres inside boast some of the most high-tech screens
and sound systems in the business. There's a huge
choice in original language, French and Flemish, but
generally little more than Hollywood blockbuster
fare. Sandwiched between the Atomium and
Belgium's national stadium, the Kinepolis is popular with teenagers and out-of-towners. *See also p183*
Belgian Bert's Hollywood smash.

Movy Club

21 rue des Moines, Forest (02 537 69 54).
Tram 52/ bus 49, 50. **No credit cards.**
Situated in a residential suburb south of the centre,
this art deco jewel is well worth the detour. Run by
an eccentric old cinéaste who tears your ticket stub
and also projects the film, the Movy Club is popular
with students, oddballs and arty locals, and shows
an eclectic mix of reruns, French and American classics and recently released hits. A word of warning:
bring a thick jumper in winter as the cavernous auditorium takes a while to heat up.

Musée du Cinema

Palais des Beaux-Arts, 9 rue Baron Horta, Upper
Town (02 507 83 70). Métro Parc or Gare Centrale/
tram 92, 93, 94. **No credit cards. Map** p319 D4.
A film buff's paradise, the Musée du Cinema has one
of the world's largest film archives, and shows silent
movies to live piano accompaniment every day of
the year. Most months are given over to themes,
ranging from the weird world of Tim Burton to the
grim universe of Ingmar Bergman, but time-tested

classics such as *Battleship Potëmkin* and *The Third*
Man make regular appearances. There's an interactive exhibition on the history of cinema.

Nova

3 rue d'Arenberg, Lower Town (02 511 27 74).
Métro Gare Centrale. **No credit cards. Map** p317 C3.
It's a miracle that this art-house cinema has survived
for as long at it has, housed in a disused theatre
belonging to a giant property firm. This precarious
existence has given the Nova an edgy, noncon-
formist feel that is reflected in the films it shows.
Recent programmes have focused on films from
Lithuania and Morocco, and about the Berlin Wall
and the Beat Generation. Studiously unconventional,
the Nova also hosts monthly 'open screens' when
members of the public can screen short features.

Styx

72 rue de l'Arbre Bénit, Ixelles (02 512 21 02). Métro
Porte de Namur. **No credit cards. Map** p321 D6.
This place might look a bit dilapidated, but don't be
put off by the peeling paintwork or the skeletal staff
because the Styx shows the sort of films that are worth
seeing again and again. Its two tiny screens project
modern classics, recent releases and art-house flicks
at ridiculously low prices and, with the last screening
after midnight, it's also one of the few places you can
catch a movie after eating and drinking.

UGC De Brouckère

38 place de Brouckère, Lower Town (French
information 0900 10440/Flemish information
0900 10450). Métro/Pré-métro De Brouckère.
Credit MC, V. **Map** p317 C2.
If Brussels is a mecca for cinema-goers, then this 12-
screen cinema is its holy shrine. Although most of
the fare has 'Made in Hollywood' stamped all over
it, this downtown multiplex is slick, stylish and
super-efficient. There aren't many cinemas where
you can buy draught beer, sit back in armchair-sized
seats and watch a movie on a 70mm screen surrounded by gold-leaf African frescoes. On weekends
it has midnight screenings of upcoming films.

UGC Toison d'Or

8 avenue de la Toison d'Or, Ixelles (French
information 0900 10440/Flemish information
0900 10450). Métro Porte de Namur. **Credit**
MC, V. **Map** p321 D5.
This uptown multiplex used to be the distinctly
poorer cousin of the UGC De Brouckère complex, but
after a complete facelift in 2000, there is little to distinguish the two. The Toison d'Or (formerly the
Acropole) shows mainly French and American hits
in comfortable theatres with good sound and picture
quality. But beware of arranging to meet anyone
here. There are two entrances – one on the main
boulevard and another in the Toison d'Or shopping
mall – making a rendezvous tricky.

Vendôme

18 chaussée de Wavre, Ixelles (02 502 37 00). Métro
Porte de Namur. **No credit cards. Map** p321 D5.

Belgian Bert's Hollywood smash

Having cornered a strange niche in the world of entertainment – chips, comic strips and saxophones – Belgium now boasts mover-and-shaker status in leisure's biggest blue-chip industry: the multiplex cinema.

Many might think that multiscreened movie houses are an American domain. Wrong. The Belgians got there first. Their Kinepolis (Kinepoli?) are now sprouting all over Europe, modelled on and named after the signature site in the Parc des Expositions, in the shadow of the Belgian national stadium.

This vast global concern owes its existence to a modest picture house in the equally modest town of Harelbeke, near Kortrijk, too modest for any guidebook to the country. Here Albert Bert's father once ran the Majestiek Cinema, the town's only thriving source of entertainment – until the advent of television. To help his father's dwindling income, young Albert installed another theatre under the same roof: Duplex! Duplex begat Trioscoop, which begat the big time: Pentascoop in Kortrijk! Top of the world, ma!

By the late 1970s, le Groupe Bert were setting up multiscreened cinemas throughout Flanders before taking the risk to build one outside town, the Decascoop, off the motorway into Ghent. In 1981, a grand total of one million visitors passed through its doors, some four times the local population. Brussels beckoned.

Ironically, multiplexes were closing small cinemas like Harelbeke's all over Belgium – all over Europe, in fact. Hollywood blockbusters ruled. Art-house European cinema – both the art and its houses – suffered. Nothing could stop Bert, however. Leisure was no longer a luxury, but an affordable family habit. Ticket prices were kept low, sound quality and seat comfort high. In 1988, allied with his sister-in-law, Bert-Claeys collaborated on their masterpiece: the Kinepolis.

For years this imposing building was the world's only megaplex (America's first, in Dallas, opened in 1996). With twenty-four screens and free parking facilities, by 1991 the Kinepolis saw three million annual visitors. Built alongside the Bruparck leisure centre, the Kinepolis was essential to any family weekend.

Centres were built in France, Holland and beyond, 26 at the last count, and a film distribution network duly established between them. In 2001, 26 million Europeans (including 12.4 million Belgians) gawped from 93,804 seats at 323 Kinepolis screens.

The next generation – in Madrid, Milan and Valencia – cements the three elements vital to any family: TLC. Total Leisure Complexes comprise film, games activities, shops and food outlets, a Kinepolis and Bruparck rolled into one. You have been warned.

Although this five-screen cinema is situated in the middle of Matongé – the city's liveliest African quarter – the films on offer are almost exclusively French and American. It has an audacious art deco exterior and the inside has been refurbished to compete with the nearby UGC Toison d'Or. Luckily, the Vendôme doesn't try too hard. It still retains a small-cinema charm and screens more highbrow films than the French chain would dare to show.

Special events

It's worth looking out for various mini-seasons and one-off events. **Matinées Classiques pour Jeunes** are aimed at discerning youngsters keen to explore cinematic history. Held at the Musée du Cinéma (*see p182*) at 3pm on every other Sunday, they tend to veer from vintage Chaplin to such modern milestones as Spielberg's *Close Encounters of the Third Kind*. Old Belgian films, such as the adaptations of the Asterix comics, also figure strongly. Under-16s, though not usually admitted to the film museum for some unfathomable archaic reason, are welcome to attend.

On Fridays and Saturdays in August and September, Nova (*see p182*) presents **Open Air**, outdoor screenings of offbeat movies. Typical fare includes the likes of *The Secret Adventures of Tom Thumb* and Fellini's *La Strada* – and it's a great way to pass a summer's evening.

Summer also sees drive-in movies being screened under the Arc de Triomphe in the **Parc Cinquantenaire**, on Saturday nights in July and August (www.dedi.be). Headphones and receivers are distributed for a nominal fee.

Between September and June, **Sneak Preview** offers the chance to see previews of various films, usually for the purpose of gauging the audience's reaction. Polls are conducted immediately afterwards, sometimes leading to heated debate. The unsuspecting volunteers often have to sit through tortuous art-house films of dubious merit, but the occasional gem can surface. Screenings are held on Thursday evenings at the Arenberg Galeries (*see p181*).

Festivals

The highlight of the Brussels cinema calendar is undoubtedly the **International Film Festival** (02 227 39 89/www.brusselsfilmfest. be – *see p166*). For nearly three decades the IFF has showcased a dizzying array of independent films from around the world, and has attracted stars such as John Malkovich, Oliver Stone and Tim Robbins. The festival couldn't be held in 2002 because of venue problems, but it plans

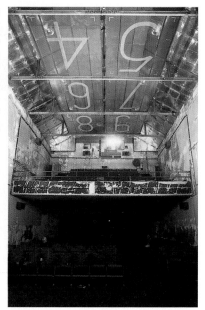

Nova: unconventional art-house. *See p182.*

to return in 2003 at a new site, the renovated Institut National de Radiodiffuson on place Flagey in Ixelles, and in a new month, April.

Less mainstream, but equally popular is the **Brussels International Festival of Fantasy, Thriller & Science Fiction Films** (02 201 17 13/www.bifff.org) in March (*see p166*). Now in its 20th year, the BIFFF not only features some of the spookiest flicks in distribution, but also includes madcap events such as the closing-night Ball of the Vampires and an international body painting competition.

As befits a country steeped in strips, Brussels also hosts the world famous **Cartoon & Animation Festival** (02 503 11 58/www.awn. com/folioscope) every February. The festival attracts the cream of the animated film business, showcasing Hollywood blockbusters such as *Monsters Inc* with more cutting-edge shorts from independent filmmakers. On average, 30,000 people watch a hundred films.

The Arenberg Galeries (*see p181*) hosts the **Écran Total** festival from July to September. Cults and classics are the staple diet of this three-month film extravaganza, but there are also more up-to-date independent films. The **Festival of Spanish & Latin American Film** (02 223 62 60) in November shows new movies, mostly at the Vendôme (*see p182*).

Arts & Entertainment

Galleries

Brussels' internationalism has resulted in a small but thriving art scene.

It is only recently that Belgium has realised its responsibility to its rich artistic heritage. Comprehensive retrospectives in the city's major museums have featured the three great pillars of 20th-century Belgian art: René Magritte, Paul Delvaux and James Ensor. The influential Cobra Group, a post-war artistic collaboration from Copenhagen, Brussels and Amsterdam – the Belgian input coming from Pierre Alechinsky, Christian Dotremont and Serge Vandercam – has also been the subject of several major retrospectives. Sculpture and installation art are other fields where Belgian artists are flourishing to international acclaim.

With this heritage in mind, certain galleries in Brussels are happy to play the patrimonial card, and profit from the avant-gardistes who created this heritage in the first place. Others feel that the Surrealist mother lode is beginning to run out – at least within any reasonable budget – and have since turned towards presenting examples of contemporary works from Belgium, mainly Flanders, and in particular from Antwerp (Panamarenko, Jan Fabre and Marthe Wéry). Most of these should be seen in their international rather than Belgian context, referring to new global trends, especially the current infatuations with photography, video, design and fashion.

Brussels' internationalism is best illustrated by the **Europalia Festival** (02 507 85 50/ www.europalia.be), which has taken place every year since 1969. Concentrating on art, music and theatre from one given country, Europalia offers a major showcase to artists who would find it hard to get a look in elsewhere. The country of choice for three months from October 2002 is Bulgaria.

There are no limitations, then, in the scope of many of Brussels' galleries; on the contrary, by their very involvement in modern-day culture, these galleries provide a great opportunity to feel the pulse of the capital, which has a diverse range of culture at its disposal – even though this may not be part of the image Brussels portrays to the outside world. The lack of great media events and public under-funding of culture are quite indicative; Brussels is, after all, in Belgium, where culture is often the fruit of private initiatives and rarely the subject of patriotic national interest (as it is in France).

Certain areas of town lend themselves to artistic exploration. Clusters of galleries can be found in streets leading off from avenue Louise, Sablon and in particular along the forgotten canal banks at the end of rue Antoine Dansaert, site of 15 exhibition spaces set up in two huge buildings named **Kanal 11** and **Kanal 20**. For less permanent, but perhaps more radical offerings, try the exhibition and sale in **Sablon, Art-Up** (place de la Chapelle, Upper Town; 02 216 88 81), which takes place every third Sunday of the month; or the workshops and graffiti artists at **Recyclart** (*see p132*), under Chapelle railway station. The **BBL Cultural Centre** (6 place Royale, Upper Town; 02 547 22 92) is another space for more off-the-wall exhibitions covering a wide range of artistic disciplines.

The visitor therefore needs a certain curiosity to discover the thriving underground scene – of which only a selection can be listed below. For more information, consult English-language weekly the *Bulletin, Park Mail*, which is handed out in cinemas, and the Wednesday cultural supplement, *MAD*, of French-language *Le Soir*. Useful all-purpose websites include www. trabel.com/brussels.htm and www.idearts.com. You can also find a huge annual exhibition of contemporary Belgian art at www.artexis.com/artbrussels/welcome.shtml.

Commercial galleries

Admission to all the galleries below is free. Most are closed on Mondays, and some on Tuesdays too.

Lower Town

Argos

13 rue du Chantier, Lower Town (02 229 00 03/ www.argosarts.org). Métro Yser. **Open** 2-7pm Wed-Sat. **Map** p318 B1.

Argos is a centre dedicated to audio-visual art, video, documentary, film installations, CD-Roms and so on. As well as organising a large festival and regular exhibitions, Argos also works in the field of distribution, production and conservation. A collection of cassettes, CD-Roms and DVDs can be viewed in the projection room, free of charge but you must make an appointment.

Hats off to Brussels

Magritte is the emblematic figure of a Surrealist movement that has left an indelible mark on the national consciousness, even to the way Belgians perceive reality. What could be more Belgian than one of the major artists of the 20th century spending much of his life in a faceless suburban terrace house (now a museum), who hawked his pictures around Le Greenwich café (*see p129*) and who decorated not churches but the inside of the gaming room of Knokke Casino?

Magritte's signature bowler hat was even used as a logo in a lavish official ceremony on the Grand' Place to promote Belgium's assumption of the EU presidency in July 2001. Surrealism has become the national symbol of Belgium, its fame drawing thousands every year. As many come for Magritte as do for the Mannekin Pis, beer or chocolate; some 65 per cent of all visitors to the **Musée Magritte** are from the English-speaking world.

Much of Magritte's global fame is due to Lolas, an ex-ballet dancer and art dealer, who nurtured his success in the US after the war. Before this, having helped launch the Surrealist movement in Paris in the late 1920s, back in Brussels Magritte was forced to scratch a living from designing wallpaper and advertising hoardings. He and his wife Georgette lived at 135 rue Esseghem in Jette between 1930 and 1954, a terraced house whose very normality inspired the great artist. 'One night in 1936,' he recalled, 'I half-awoke in one of the rooms next to a cage and a sleeping bird. In my drowsy state, I saw the bird replaced by an egg. This was a poetic secret of great astonishment.'

The house itself is almost deliberately plain. Nothing, apart from the board outside during opening hours, would indicate anything out of the ordinary ever took place here. (Consider, in contrast, Dalí's overblown, egg-topped Torre Galatea residence in Figueres, Catalonia.) Enter the front room and you see the window and fireplace (*pictured left*) familiar from many of Magritte's paintings. Through the hallway is the tiny, ill-lit back room where he painted and entertained his circle of literary acquaintances. The upper two floors are full of letters, photographs, drawings and posters, beautifully laid out and clearly documented. Along with a few works in the modern art section of the **Musées Royaux des Beaux-Arts** (*see p72*) and the **Musée Communal d'Ixelles** (*see p85*), Magritte fans rarely leave Brussels disappointed.

Art en Marge

312 rue Haute, Lower Town (02 511 04 11). Métro Porte de Hal/bus 20, 48. **Open** noon-6pm Wed-Fri; 11am-4pm Sat. **Map** p320 B5.
A gallery in Marolles dedicated to works by the mentally challenged. The permanent collection is complemented by a series of temporary exhibitions held throughout the year.

Bastien

61 rue de la Madeleine, Lower Town (02 513 25 63). Métro Gare Centrale. **Open** 11am-6.30pm Tue-Sat; 11am-1pm Sun. **Map** p317 C3.
If you're spending any time in town, you're bound to pass Ms Bastien's beautiful gallery, which is located a few steps down from the Gare Centrale and Albertine Library. As with most of the galleries along this stretch, Bastien is hardly revolutionary, but displays relatively modern works of a certain

value. Among the artists represented are Serge Vandercam, Pierre Alechinsky, Bernard Buffet and Zao Wou Ki. The quality of what's on offer, as the Belgian press is often quick to point out, contrasts with the kitsch conservatism of its neighbours, Horizon and Albert I Bonne, two steps away from the commercial glitz of Sablon.

Galerie P

71 rue des Eperonniers, Lower Town (02 542 11 12/ www.galeriep.be). Métro Gare Centrale. **Open** noon-7pm Wed-Sat. **Map** p317 C3.
Since March 2000, Galerie P, right in the heart of Brussels, has been showing contemporary photography to an extremely favourable response by press and public alike. Meticulously presented, the shows opt for sobriety and professionalism, perfectly suiting a new generation of photographers, Nicolas Dufranne among them.

Yet Belgium's own francophone community, overshadowed by the prestigious museums and galleries of Paris, has been unaware or unappreciative of this artistic heritage. Which other nation would have let a masterpiece such as James Ensor's *Entrance of Christ into Brussels* be sold off to the US in 1949? In June 2001, Magritte's niece Arlette sold eight of her uncle's paintings at Christie's; works – such as *Les Grands Rendezvous* – that had not been seen in public for 50 years.

And the laudable intentions of Magritte's heirs, happy to turn their inheritance over to the public domain, have so often come up against the sheer negligence of the powers that be. After the death of Magritte's widow in 1986, the Belgian state inherited the artist's last home in Schaerbeek – only to unceremoniously offer it up for public sale. Not only the house, but all the objects in it, objects that may well have featured in the kind of work Magritte often produced.

The establishment of the Jette museum is entirely due to the initiative of private collectors. Some of the household items – such as furniture designed by the man himself in the 1920s – were stumbled across by chance in the painter's last residence. Despite its historic value, it is the owners who assume the running costs. In 2001 the museum received a grant of a measly €700, enough to keep the bowler brushed and a few cans of Pledge for good luck.

As opposed to Paris, whose museums are a matter of national pride, if not ego, Belgium continues to underinvest in its own culture.

Magritte's *L'Eureux Donateur*.

Even great federal institutions such as the Musées Royaux des Beaux-Arts, the Palais des Beaux-Arts and others, whose collections are beyond value, suffer from severe financial deficits. Many more artistic treasures are expected to make their way to France and the US before too long.

Musée Magritte

135 rue Essegham, Jette (02 428 26 26). Tram 18, 19, 81, 94. **Open** 10am-6pm Wed-Sun. **Admission** €6; €5 concessions. **No credit cards**.

Kanal 11 & Kanal 20

11 & 20 boulevard Barthélémy, Lower Town (02 735 52 12). Métro Comte de Flandre. **Open** 2-6pm Wed-Sat. **Map** p318 A2.

These two huge buildings overlooking the thin strip of the Canal de Charleroi represent the most exciting artistic development that central Brussels has seen in a long time. And all at the dark end of fashionable rue Antoine Dansaert. There you're greeted by bright, colourful façades (no mean thing in grey old Brussels), behind which some 15 galleries have set up together. The project has brought focus to this rather shady part of town, and also helped galvanise a rather isolated and unconnected local art scene. Although each gallery within the complex has its own autonomy, openings and opening hours are, sensibly, co-ordinated. Among them, it's worth pointing out: **Archétype** (02 514 26 82), in Kanal 11, which presents contemporary artists and tries

to integrate their work in wider enterprises; **Artiscope II** (02 503 17 65/ www.artiscope.be), in Kanal 20, whose exhibitions, either thematic or individual, reflect the most up-to-date trends set by a diverse group of sculptors, painters and photographers (such as Mariani, Paladino, Tricot, Staccioli and De Paris); **Blu Contemporary Art** (0477 205052/www.directions inart.org/blu), in Kanal 20, which focuses on young, experimental artists whose works include video and sculpture; and **Ad!dict Creative Lab** (02 504 00 00/www.addictlab.com), also on Kanal 20, which knows how to bind positive, experimental and creative ties between commercial brands and high art.

Meert Rihoux

13 rue du Canal, Lower Town (02 219 14 22). Métro Ste-Catherine or Yser. **Open** 2.30-6pm Tue-Sat. **Map** p318 B2.

Arts & Entertainment

Dewart Gallery in the **Kanal 11 & Kanal 20** complex. *See p187.*

It's worth making the slight detour to this spacious, third-floor gallery comprising three huge exhibition rooms. The artistic direction is very conceptual, with works by international avant-garde photographers and filmmakers. A recent example is Thomas Struth, but Meert Rihoux also boasts many young Belgians on its roster.

Usage externe

46 rue du Vieux Marché aux Grains, Lower Town (02 502 68 09). Métro Ste-Catherine. **Open** 10am-7pm Mon-Sat. **Map** p318 B3.

While the Flemish community has been supporting video gallery and library resource Argos (*see p185*) over the past three years, the French have at last seen fit to support their own, Usage externe, which opened in November 2001. Its aim is to present and support mainly young, francophone and foreign creators, with a thematic approach (design, fashion and so on), making full use of the three exhibition spaces. Each one will come under the wing of a patron of some renown: François Schuiten or Bob Verschueren, for example. This ambitious project remains very open, if selective, and could be a turning point for young Belgian artists in need of some decent exposure. Watch this space.

Ixelles

Aeroplastics Contemporary

32 rue Blanche, Ixelles (02 537 22 02/ www.aeroplastics.net). Métro Louise, then tram 91, 92. **Open** 2-7pm Wed-Sat. **Map** p321 C6.

Aeroplastics occupies a vast space in a magnificent house on the Ixelles/St-Gilles border – although the choice of art is somewhat incongruous with the grand setting. Contemporary trends are the keynote with featured artists including John Isaacs, John Waters, Anton Corbijn and Daniele Buetti bringing a political dimension to an otherwise energetic and spectacular collection.

Damasquine

62 rue de l'Aurore, Ixelles (02 646 31 53/ www.damasquine.be). Métro Louise, then tram 93, 94. **Open** 1-7pm Wed-Sat.

The scope of this delightful little gallery is generally wide-ranging, featuring young Belgian and European artists, photographers, painters and sculptors, Arnold J Kemp, Antoine d'Agata and Stéphane Mandelbaum among them. Within this, the gallery does concentrate on certain specifics, such as the work of Daniele Buetti, responsible for some quite disturbing reworkings of fashion photography.

Lanzenburg

9 avenue des Klauwaerts, Ixelles (02 647 30 15). Bus 71. **Open** 10am-12.30pm Tue-Sat; 2-7pm Sun.

The Lanzenburg occupies a discreet, intimate space overlooking Ixelles lakes. For nearly 30 years its owner, Fred Lanzenburg, has emphasised contemporary artists for whom the pictorial aspect is all-important. His erudite stance is somewhat out of keeping with current, more radical trends.

Pascal Polar

108 chaussée de Charleroi, Ixelles (02 537 81 36/ www.pascalpolar.be). Métro Louise, then tram 91, 92. **Open** 2-7pm Wed-Sat. **Map** p321 C6.

Pascal Polar has been the domain of rigorously chosen sculptors and installation artists, both Belgian and international, since 1986. Very personal works by Scarpa, Matsutami and Manuel Geerinck are featured, as well as a catalogue boasting Arman, Pol Bury and Alechinsky. Good website too.

Quadri

49 rue Tenbosch, Ixelles (02 640 95 63). Métro Louise, then tram 93, 94. **Open** 2-7pm Tue-Sat.

Just off avenue Louise, this little apartment-gallery is well worth a detour. Quadri comprises a collection of foreign and Belgian artists in an intimate setting, some with a certain predilection for lyrical abstraction. Jean Raine is one of the Belgian artists featured.

Rodolphe Janssen

35 rue de Livourne,. Ixelles (02 538 08 18). Métro Louise, then tram 93, 94. **Open** 2-7pm Tue-Sat. **Map** p321 C6.

One of the main contemporary art galleries, and somewhat comparable to Pascal Polar (*see p188*) in its approach, Janssen features international works with a hint of variety and originality, in disciplines as diverse as photography, sculpture and painting.

Xavier Hufkens

8 rue St-Georges, Ixelles (02 646 63 30/ www.xavierhufkens.com). Métro Louise, then tram 93, 94. **Open** noon-8pm Tue-Sat.

Xavier Hufkens is often associated with photography, but his scope is much wider. Along with Robert Mappelthorpe and Andy Warhol, you'll find Belgian and international names such as Louise Bourgeois, Jan Vercruysse, Adam Fuss and Malcolm Morley. Among the best modern art galleries in Brussels, increasingly concentrated on works of true quality.

Upper Town & St-Gilles

Patrick Derom

1 rue aux Laines, Upper Town (02 514 08 82/ www.patrickderomgallery.com). Tram 92, 93, 94. **Open** 10.30am-6.30pm Tue-Sat. **Map** p321 C5.

Although an openly commercial venture, Patrick Derom's gallery is an enjoyable stopoff on the way to the Musée des Beaux-Arts. The catalogue comprises a large chunk of works by worthy Surrealists, as well as pieces by Belgian Impressionists and Expressionists.

Le Salon d'Art et de Coiffure

81 rue de l'Hôtel des Monnaies, St-Gilles (02 537 65 40). Métro Hôtel des Monnaies. **Open** 9.30am-noon, 2-6.30pm Tue-Sat. **Map** p320 B6.

A combined barber shop, art gallery and antiquarian bookshop, as displayed by the piles of snipped hair, prints and limited editions at the entrance. Jean Marchetti began his business as a hairdresser, then discovered art along the way, but didn't want to abandon his clippers. So in 1976, his salon became a smart, whitewashed gallery, bringing in a daring choice of writers and artists, as well as the likes of Jean-Pierre Maury, Stéphane Mandelbaum and Alechinsky. Marchetti brings out limited editions under three publishing imprints: La Pierre d'Alun, La Petite Pierre and La Haute Pierre, pairing writers with artists, producing works that are equally pieces of art as pieces of text. Fine haircuts too.

Public galleries

The major art galleries and museums with artistic connections are covered in the Sightseeing section of this guide. Of these, the **Palais des Beaux-Arts** (*see p71*) maintains lively programming from the French and Flemish cultural factions in equal measure;

the **Musée Communal d'Ixelles** (*see p85*) often has temporary exhibitions of considerable significance; the **Botanique** (*see p199*) can stage the occasional major avant-gardiste; and retrospective gems can be found at the **Hôtel de Ville** (*see p64*).

Atelier 340

340 drève De Rivieren, Ganshoren (02 424 24 12/ www.atelier340muzeum.be). Métro Simonis, then bus 13. **Open** Tue-Sun 2-7pm.

Non-profit-making, artist-run Atelier 340 is housed in a block of condemned houses in the leafy north-east quarter of Ganshoren, by Jette. Set up by Polish sculptor Wodek Majewski in 1980, it is no surprise that this was one of the principal spaces in the Europalia Polska event that ran throughout 2001.

Centre d'art contemporain

63 avenue des Nerviens, Etterbeek (02 735 05 31). Métro Mérode or Schuman. **Open** 2-5pm Mon-Fri; 1-6pm Sat.

Initially conceived to promote Belgian and European artists and provide a documentary resource, this small space may well be usurped by Usage externe (*see p188*). But it's still one of the rare venues where young artists can get a foot in the door.

Africalia 2003

Oft-neglected African art will at last be given a worthy spotlight in Brussels when the **Africalia Festival** (www.africalia.be) takes place in venues across the city throughout 2003. As well as visual arts, Africalia will feature film, literature, architecture and the performing arts.

Brussels has always been an important crossroads for African artists. It's a major European base where they can get the kind of exposure – and sales – they would find difficult to match at home. Although much of the work winds up in the trendy, commercial boutiques of Sablon, a new vogue is developing for *art sauvage*, contemporary tribal art. One gallery in particular, **Moba**, has a much acclaimed collection of artefacts from a remote tribe in Niger, as well as temporary exhibitions of photos from the region. One of the key Africalia venues, Moba's success will hopefully generate healthy media interest by the time the festival begins.

Moba

29 rue de l'Epargne, Lower Town (02 219 81 82). Métro Yser. **Open** by appointment only. **Map** p319 C2.

Gay & Lesbian

You're guaranteed a good time in friendly, laid-back Brussels.

With so many European hotspots a mere train ride away, Brussels is rarely recognised as a great draw for gays and lesbians. Yet Belgium's liberalism and moral freedoms ensure that the living here is easy, reflected in the relaxed approach to gay lifestyle and entertainment. Gay and lesbian couples can now register their partnerships legally and ongoing legislation is slowly building a society based on equality for all. The attitude here is very laissez-faire, both from outside and within the gay community.

This is reflected in the annual gay pride event (09 223 69 29/www.blgp.be), one of the earliest on the European calendar, held on **Pink Saturday**, the first Saturday in May. What started as a small political march has evolved into a free-spirited carnival that attracts a whole cross-section of the population, both to the parade and to the festivities on place Ste-Catherine. The whole thing is crowned by an energetic, all-night party. Another annual bash with international clout is the **Gay & Lesbian Film Festival** (www.fglb.org), held in January. Organised by **Tels Quels** (*see below*), this is not just a loose collection of films, but a full-on event with live acts and theme nights.

In keeping with most capital cities, the gay quarter is concentrated in the very heart of Brussels, with most bars and clubs in the area surrounding the Bourse. With such a tight-knit city centre and hardly any entrance fees, bar-hopping is an essential pastime. New bars continue to open and flourish, though the commercial scene, as elsewhere, is dominated by clubs for the boys. But this is laid-back Belgium and there is no feeling of ghettoisation; most bars extend a warm embrace to women. From the drag bars in Brussels to the internationally renowned leather bars in Antwerp (*see p235*), gay men, women and their friends enjoy a happy, non-threatening environment in which to party.

Information

For gay and lesbian support groups and helplines, *see p292*.

English-Speaking Gay Group

02 537 47 04. **Open** *Phone enquiries* 8.30am-10pm daily.
Egg, as it is known, has been around since 1987 and continues to hold monthly Sunday afternoon drinks

parties at various venues in Brussels. The parties are often followed by an optional dinner. An easy and relaxed way of meeting new friends.

Tels Quels

81 rue du Marché au Charbon, Lower Town (02 512 45 87/www.telsquels.be). *Pré-métro Bourse*. **Open** 10.30am-5pm Mon-Fri. *Bar* 5pm-2am Mon-Thur; 4pm-4am Fri, Sat; 6am-2am Sun. **Map** p317 B3.
This collective houses the Gay & Lesbian Film Festival, ILGA, Télégal and a wide range of social groups, from parents with gay children to an a capella singing group. The welcoming bar is open to all, and is the only bar in town catering to both lesbians and gay men. A great place to pick up info.

Bars

Le Belgica

32 rue du Marché au Charbon, Lower Town (no phone/http://lebelgica.be). *Pré-métro Bourse*. **Open** 10pm-3am Thur-Sun. **No credit cards**. **Map** p317 B3.
Le Belgica is one of Brussels' must-go bars; a pre-club meeting place filled with gay men and their friends of both sexes. A friendly, international bar decorated in famously distressed chic, it doesn't start buzzing until around 11pm. And then it buzzes. Hefty house music plays to the shoulder-to-shoulder crowd, though there is always room for the ever-energetic Markest to collect glasses. Stars in town often drop by – it's one of Björk's favourite haunts.

Chez Maman

7 rue des Grandes Carmes, Lower Town (02 502 86 96). *Pré-métro Bourse*. **Open** 7pm-2am Wed, Thur; 10pm-late Fri, Sat. **No credit cards**. **Map** p317 B3.
Tiny bar, big reputation. During the week, it's a quiet place for a drink, but at the weekend it becomes a sweat-box as the crowds pile in to see 'Maman' strut her stuff on the bar in her size 11 stilettos. The drag is '70s in style and all mimed, but the guys and gals just love their Maman.

Le Comptoir

26 place de la Vieille Halle au Blés, Lower Town (02 514 05 00). *Métro Gare Centrale*. **Open** *Bar* 7pm-2am daily. *Restaurant* 7pm-midnight Mon, Wed, Thur; 7pm-1pm Fri-Sun. **Main courses** €20. **Credit** MC, V. **Map** p317 C4.
Set in a stunning 17th-century building, Le Comptoir is popular with a well-heeled and slightly holier-than-thou crowd. It's a good place to meet as it's one of the few bars open early evening. The restaurant had a reputation for being average and expensive, though great efforts have been made to change this.

Arts & Entertainment

Le Duquesnoy

*12 rue Duquesnoy, Lower Town (02 502 38 83/
www.duquesnoy.com). Métro Gare Centrale.* **Open**
9pm-3am Mon-Thur; 9pm-5am Fri, Sat; 6pm-3am
Sun. **No credit cards. Map** p317 C4.
An institution. Regarded as Brussels' 'heavy' bar,
the clientele is a mix of leather, denim and skater
boy, and everything in between. It's dark and cruisy,
with porn on the TV and owner Gérard's favourite
tracks on the sound system. The basement and top
floors lead to a labyrinth of darkrooms, but be
warned: the stairs in this old Brussels house are not
for the unfit. Occasional theme nights on Saturdays
and regular Sunday afternoon parties give the place
its fetish edge. And if none of this interests you, the
friendly old Duq is also great for a beer.

Le Gémeau

*12 rue de Laeken, Lower Town (02 219 23 36).
Métro/Pré-métro De Brouckère.* **Open** 10pm-5am
Fri, Sat. **No credit cards. Map** p317 B2.
This bar/disco seems to have been around forever.
Its orange walls, fish tanks and top-hat light shades
speak of a different era. The crowd is a mix of ages
and styles, all out for a good night of dancing. The
music is '70s and '80s classics, in an atmosphere of
package-holiday fun. With down-to-earth bar prices
and a mirror ball to beat them all, it's perfect for a
damn fine time. Get those hands in the air.

L'Homo Erectus

*57 rue des Pierres, Lower Town (02 514 74 93/
www.lhomoerectus.com). Pré-métro Bourse.* **Open**
noon-late daily. **No credit cards. Map** p317 B3.
The name of this relative newcomer really only
works in French, but you probably get the intended
pun. Thirty seconds from the Grand'Place, you can't
miss this tiny bar with its Darwin-esque window of
apes slowly evolving into macho man. It's already a
victim of its own success, and you'll need to evolve
into a snake to be able to squeeze through to the
loo. But L'Homo is great fun, especially when the
chaps start jumping on the bar for a song. If it gets
too much, pop along to the Smart at No.28 for a
blast of pop and house music.

La Reserve

*2A petite rue au Beurre, Lower Town (02 511 66
06). Métro/Pré-métro De Brouckère.* **Open** 11am-
midnight Mon, Thur, Fri; 4-10pm Wed; 3pm-
midnight Sat, Sun. **No credit cards. Map** p317 C3.
Jimmy and Marcel run this bar in a lovely old house
near the Grand'Place. The decor is English country
pub, the atmosphere reminiscent of a gay bar in the
old style, with a mixed clientele who come to chat
with the regulars. The younger boys around town
smirk at its kitsch charm, but everyone goes to La
Reserve at some point, if only because of its user-
friendly opening hours.

The Slave

*7 Plattesteen, Lower Town (02 513 47 46). Pré-
métro Bourse.* **Open** 10pm-4am Mon-Thur, Sun;
10pm-6am Fri, Sat. **No credit cards. Map** p317 B3.

Flex those pecs at **La Démence**.

Despite its name, this is not a specialist masochist
bar. Having said that, it does veer to the sleazier end
of the market with its corrugated iron walls and
ultra-dark basement. But, hey, this is Brussels, and
in the middle of all that macho metal is a roaring
open fire to keep the boys warm. Porn on one video,
cartoons on the other sums up this popular bar. The
good looking staff keep smiling to the early hours.

Clubs

La Démence

*208 rue Blaes, Lower Town (02 511 97 89/
www.lademence.com). Métro Porte de Hal.* **Open**
11pm-late once a mth; check website for dates.
Admission €7 before midnight; €12 after midnight.
Credit MC, V. **Map** p320 B4.
They literally bus the boys in to La Démence – yes,
the organised coach parties come from as far as
Paris and Amsterdam. This is Belgium's biggest
gay party with sounds – and muscles – pumping out
on two floors. From house to techno, the beats keep
a microcosm of the gay world, from moustached
clones to fluoro queens, on the move. And when it's
all too much, there's a chill-out area and a room with
no lights. This place is pure, hard energy released.

Gate

*36 rue du Fossé au Loups, Lower Town (02 223
04 34). Métro/Pré-métro De Brouckère.* **Open** *Bar*

Man to Man: haircuts and gadgets for boys (and bears). *See p193.*

6pm-late Tue-Sun. *Club* 6pm-late Fri (mixed), Sat (women only). **Admission** varies. **No credit cards.** **Map** p317 C2/3.

A friendly, funky place run by Carine de Maesmaker, one of Belgium's renowned DJs on the lesbian circuit. The women-only Saturday nights are packed with up to 300 dancers, making it Belgium's biggest lesbian club. Special theme nights make this a must-go for those who love to dress up and party.

Next

Recyclart, 25 rue des Ursulines, Lower Town (no phone/www.next-party.be). Bus 95, 96. **Open** 10.30pm-late 1st Sat of the mth. **Admission** €6.50; €5 concessions. **No credit cards.** **Map** p317 B4.

Out of the gay pride parties came Different, a Saturday night extravaganza organised by DJs Luuuk and Piiit. So popular was it that a new venue was needed, and it's now located in an exciting and friendly club under the railway lines near the Sablon. Visit the excellent website for party dates and to get a flavour of this alternative gay/lesbian dance fest.

Strong

155 rue de la Loie, EU Quarter (02 539 21 59/ www.strong.be). Métro Maalbeek. **Open** 10pm-6.30am Fri, Sat. **Admission** €12 after 11pm. **No credit cards.** **Map** p324 F4.

Strong has become a big club name in Brussels, both for guys and gals, though it continues to confuse punters by moving location. It currently holds its monthly clubnight in the old art deco theatre of the Residence Palace, an office complex in the EU Quarter. Each Sunday sees a cabaret party, but this is most definitely on the move – check the great website for up-to-the-minute dates and locations.

Why Not

7 rue des Riches Claires, Lower Town (02 512 63 43/ www.welcome.to/whynot). Pré-métro Bourse. **Open** 11pm-late daily. **Admission** free. **No credit cards.** **Map** p318 B3.

This busy and popular dance club draws a crowd as diverse in taste as in age. Pop, house classics, drag, leather, fancy dress – anything can and does happen in this Brussels favourite. Rumours always fly around that the place is closing and will finally die – but they're greatly exaggerated, it would seem.

Restaurants

The Gazebo

5 place du Nouveau Marché aux Grains, Lower Town (02 514 26 96). Métro Ste-Catherine. **Open** 7pm-late Mon, Tue, Thur-Sat. **Main courses** €18. **Credit** AmEx, DC, MC, V. **Map** p318 B2.

Lee Better has been attracting the gay community for some years now in her friendly but unremarkable restaurant. She hit on the notion of holding once-a-month Friday evenings for Brussels Gay Professionals, a loose term with camp dinner party connotations. Of course, you can fib and be any profession you like; whatever, her boys love her.

Lola

33 place du Grand Sablon, Upper Town (02 514 24 60). Bus 95, 96. **Open** noon-3pm, 6.30-11.30pm Mon-Fri; noon-11.30pm Sat, Sun. **Main courses** €10-€25. **Set menu** €40. **Credit** AmEx, DC, MC, V. **Map** p317 C4.

A mixed restaurant that has become a magnet for designer, arty gays, especially the Sablon antique crowd. It's a buzzy, international brasserie with a great menu, and no one will take a second look at any loving glances between you and yours over the crisp linen napkins.

Le Petit Boxeur
3 rue de Borgval, Lower Town (02 511 40 00). Pré-métro Bourse. **Open** 8-11pm Tue-Sat. **Main courses** €15. **Credit** AmEx, DC, MC, V. **Map** p317 B3.
A cosy little restaurant with a posh-camp interior. It draws a mixed, stylish clientele, and is a great place for dinner before hitting the downtown bars. The food is nouvelle Belgian and served with a flourish, though you can spend more than you expect.

Saunas & gyms

Muscle Marys should head to the **Fitness Factory** (114 boulevard Adolphe Max, Lower Town; 02 219 87 19/www.fitnessfactory.be). Admission is €8. **La Griffe** (41-43 rue du Dinant, Lower Town; 02 512 62 51), is the quietest of the city's saunas, but very clean and nicely finished, with a decent bar area.

Macho II
106 rue du Marché au Charbon, Lower Town (02 513 56 67/www.machosauna.com). Pré-métro Anneessens. **Open** noon-2am Mon-Sat; noon-midnight Sun. **Admission** €12.50; €8 concessions. **No credit cards. Map** p317 B3.
The Macho brand is Brussels' most famous, and this place is also good for serious saunas and workouts in the decently equipped fitness room. It's a big, well-kept establishment with friendly and attentive staff. Expect a youngish crowd, particularly later at night. Buy a ticket for repeat access during the same day.

Oasis
10 rue Van Orly, Upper Town (02 218 08 00/www.oasis-sauna.be). Métro Botanique. **Open** noon-1am daily. **Admission** €12.50 Mon, Wed-Sun; €8 Tue; Sun brunch (noon-2.30pm) €2.50. **Credit** AmEx, DC, MC, V. **Map** p319 D2.
Oasis is set in a vast townhouse and the bar area is still very much a *grande salle*, with marble fireplace and cornished ceilings. Some parts are seedier – but they're meant to be. It's clean, it's popular and it has all the facilities one would expect. A downside is the stairs, especially the back ones, which you have to use to reach the top of the house.

Spades 4our
23-25 rue Bodeghem, Lower Town (02 502 07 72/www.saunaspades4.be). Pré-métro Anneessens. **Open** noon-midnight Mon-Thur; noon-2am Fri; 2pm-2am Sat; 2pm-midnight Sun. **Admission** €12.50 Mon, Tue, Thur-Sun; €8 Wed, concessions. **Credit** AmEx, DC, MC, V. **Map** p318 A4.
Brussels' largest and perhaps most exclusive sauna. Its six floors are tastefully designed, with an excellent bar and good food, and helpful staff. Facilities include legitimate massage, an S&M labyrinth, a well-equipped fitness room and a cinema, and many private rooms. Roof terrace in summer.

Shops & services

Books

Artemys
8 galerie Bortier, Lower Town (02 512 0347/www.multimania.com/artemys). Métro Gare Centrale. **Open** noon-6pm Tue-Thur; 10am-7pm Fri; 10am-7pm Sat. **No credit cards. Map** p317 C4.
Belgium's only bookshop catering specifically for lesbians. Set in an arty gallery, the ground floor is mixed while the first floor deals exclusively with books on lesbian and women's issues. A good selection in French, Dutch and English.

Darakan
9 rue du Midi, Lower Town (02 512 20 76). Pré-métro Bourse. **Open** 11am-6.30pm Mon-Sat. **Credit** MC, V. **Map** p317 B3.
Sitting firmly among the more traditional Brussels *bouquinistes*, this bookshop is dedicated to gay and lesbian books, novels and photographs.

Kiosque du Gay délire
13 rue St-Jean, Lower Town (02 511 22 87/www.kiosquegay.com). Métro Gare Centrale. **Open** noon-7.30pm Mon-Thur; noon-9pm Fri; 11am-7.30pm Sat, Sun. **Credit** MC, V. **Map** p317 C4.
A great drop-in place for gay magazines, books, postcards and gizmos that will amaze your friends.

Hairdressers

Man to Man
9 rue des Riches Claires, Lower Town (02 514 02 96). Pré-métro Bourse. **Open** 10am-6.30pm Tue-Fri; 10am-5pm Sat. **No credit cards. Map** p318 B3.
From the outside, more like a serious fetish shop than a coiffeur. Leather undies, handcuffs and other apparatus give it a much harder appearance than its soft inside, where you can get a decent haircut (crops a speciality) and browse at the same time. Men only.

Sex shops

Erot'X Stars
28 rue de Malines, Lower Town (02 217 77 37). Pré-métro Anneessens. **Open** 11am-8pm daily. **No credit cards. Map** p320 A/B4.
Not the most glamorous of places, but there's a huge range of men-to-men videos to buy or rent, which can be sampled in private viewing cabins.

Orly Centre
9 boulevard Jamar, St-Gilles (02 522 10 50). Métro Lemonnier. **Open** 10.30am-midnight Mon-Fri; 12.30pm-midnight Sat; 1pm-12.30am Sun. **Credit** AmEx, DC, MC, V. **Map** p320 A5.
The shop, selling mainly videos, is also a front window for a three-screen cinema complex and a seedy sauna called Club 3000. It's close to the main station, so an alternative waiting room for the Eurostar.

Arts & Entertainment

Music

There's plenty of choice, from Bartók to Björk, in this city of music lovers.

Classical & opera

Music has always held an important place in Brussels' cultural scene. An opera performance at La Monnaie in 1830 precipitated events that led to Belgium's creation as an independent state. The first performances of some major symphonic works by Bartók and Stravinsky took place in Brussels, and students come from all over the world to study at the Conservatoire.

Unfortunately, not all this fine heritage has survived drastic cuts in public funding. Fifteen years ago, the capital was home to the **Théâtre de la Monnaie** (the national opera), several chamber groups and three full-size symphony orchestras: the **National Orchestra** and two radio orchestras, one Flemish, one French. The French orchestra folded in 1991; the Flemish one has been moved somewhat ignominiously to Leuven, a medium-sized town about 35 kilometres (22 miles) east of the capital. Their splendid

former broadcast hall on place Flagey, the **Institut National de Radiodiffusion**, in use since the 1930s, has been undergoing renovation; its long-awaited reopening will be deferred at least until the end of 2002, perhaps longer. Cost overruns and expensive delays are shaking the private consortium whose ambitious plan was to enlarge the world-class broadcasting studios for concerts of symphonic and chamber music and for professional recordings. Even the music and arts-related shops at street level seem to be delayed.

Several other important changes are taking place in 2002. In September, the orchestra of the La Monnaie gets a new conductor, Kazushi Ono, to replace Antonio Pappano, who is headed for London's Covent Garden. Orchestra members say that the new man is a solid craftsman of lucidly classical style, and a contrast to the extroverted Pappano, whose passionate exuberance had charmed musicians and audiences for the past decade. At the National Orchestra, Russian conductor Yuri

Palais des Beaux-Arts: ace acoustics, swanky surroundings. *See p195.*

194 Time Out Brussels Guide

Simonov departs after seven years of steady improvement, leaving a transformed and confident ensemble to Mikko Franck. Only 22 years old, Franck has directed orchestras in his native Finland and guested with major international groups such as the New York Philharmonic and the London Symphony. The word from the players is that he is exceptionally gifted and probably destined for a great career. The orchestra's reputation should continue to rise with his.

The **Musée des Instruments de Musique** (*see p73*), which has been housed in the spectacular art nouveau Magasins Old England since 2000, is increasingly popular. Visitors can take in the occasional concert on period instruments, enjoy a panoramic view of the city from the top-floor restaurant and admire the excellent and well-presented collections. Many of the instruments on display can be heard on earphones, recorded by local specialists.

Brussels has traditionally been a centre of excellence for early music and original-instrument ensembles. Some of the more notable include **La Petite Bande** (one of the pioneering groups), **Philippe Herreweghe** and his orchestra **Chapelle Royale** and chorus **Collegium Vocale**, **Il Fondamento** and **Anima Eterna**. Their concerts often take place in the smaller venues or outlying *communes* of the city. Specialising in accompaniment, the variable-sized **Ensemble Orchestral de Bruxelles** offers young soloists a chance to play and record concertos with a real symphony orchestra.

Some highly original new smaller venues have appeared on private initiatives. Concerts of surprisingly good quality can happen in unexpected places. Belgian concert-goers are often keen amateur musicians; besides its six conservatories, Belgium has an extensive network of preparatory academies where anyone can learn an instrument for a modest fee. Graduates unable to find professional work often end up in the many amateur orchestras and choirs.

This may explain the excitement generated every May by the world-class **Concours Musical International Reine Elisabeth de Belgique** (*see p168*), the royal international music competition, which changes focus each year between violin, piano and voice. Founded by the great Belgian violinist Eugène Ysaÿe in collaboration with the then Queen Elizabeth (herself an amateur violinist), the contest's first winner was David Oistrakh in 1937. The level of virtuosity has remained very high. The final-round gala concerts – always sold out – are broadcast live on both French- and Dutch-speaking TV.

Contemporary music fans should check out the yearly **Ars Musica** festival (*see p166*), which stages events throughout Brussels, featuring Belgian and international performers. Recent years have seen the flourishing of several fine local groups specialising in new music, including **Ictus Ensemble**, **Oxalys** and **Musique Nouvelle**.

INFORMATION AND TICKETS

Details of all concerts can be found in *What's On*, a supplement to the *Bulletin*, which is also distributed free in many hotels and tourist spots. The Philharmonic Society (02 507 84 30), which organises the bulk of big-name concerts throughout Brussels, puts out a glossy brochure of its events, which include many foreign orchestras, soloists and chamber groups; call 02 511 34 33 for a brochure.

Ticket prices vary from one event to another, even for the same venue. Philharmonic Society events are about €9-€60, with gala concerts such as the Queen Elizabeth finals costing up to double the usual price. At the Théâtre de la Monnaie expect to pay at least €10 and up to €50 for orchestra seats. Prices at other venues range from €4 to €40, but there are no strict guidelines. The tourist office, **TIB** (*see p303*), can furnish all necessary information, including addresses and phone numbers, for most events in the city, and sells tickets to many concerts. Book and record shop **Fnac** (*see p141*) also sells tickets to selected events in Brussels, Antwerp and even France.

Venues

For **DeSingel**, Antwerp's modern equivalent to the Palais des Beaux-Arts, *see p240*.

Conservatoire Royal de Musique

30 rue de la Régence, Upper Town (box office 02 507 82 00/24hr info in French & Flemish 02 507 84 44.) Métro Gare Centrale. **Open** *Box office* 1hr before performance. **Tickets** varies. **Credit** AmEx, DC, MC, V. **Map** p321 C5.
Smaller than the Palais des Beaux-Arts (*see below*) and slightly shabby, but also with great acoustics, the Conservatoire Royal de Musique's hall was partially designed by the French organ builder Cavaillé-Coll. The stage is too narrow for symphonic orchestras, but perfect for chamber formations and voice recitals. It is here that the preliminary rounds of the Queen Elizabeth competition are held – the most interesting part, according to contest connoisseurs. Tickets are also available up to ten days in advance from the Palais des Beaux-Arts.

Palais des Beaux-Arts

23 rue Ravenstein, Upper Town (box office 02 507 82 00/24hr info in French & Flemish 02 507 84 44). Métro Gare Centrale or Parc. **Open** *Box office*

11am-7pm Mon-Sat. *Phone bookings* 9am-7pm Mon-Sat. **Tickets** €10-€62. **Credit** AmEx, DC, MC, V. **Map** p319 C/D4.

Home of the National Orchestra, the Palais is also the seat of the Philharmonic Society. The entire complex, Brussels' most prestigious venue, is a fine example of art nouveau design. Acoustics in the splendid Salle Henri LeBoeuf were greatly improved for both musicians and the public by major renovation several years ago. The smaller, 400-seat chamber-music hall is excellent, though concerts here are rarer. The finals of the Queen Elizabeth competition are held here. *See also p216.*

Festival fever 1

A natural host to international music festivals, Belgium can always provide a reliable, discerning and free-spending audience. Geography helps too, with regular visitors coming across from neighbouring countries. The major festivals are world-class, well organised and well subsidised, with tickets kept at accessible prices. And the city has an extraordinary range of venues, from tiny baroque churches to internationally recognised concert halls.

The biggest classical music fest is the **Flanders Festival** (09 243 94 94/ www.festival-van-vlaanderen.be) which runs from May to November throughout Flanders and Brussels. It's now in its fourth decade, and still growing. The **Festival de Wallonie** (081 73 37 81/ www.festivaldewallonie.com), is the French community's equivalent, running between June and October. It stretches right into obscure parts of Wallonia, plus Brussels, with an emphasis on classical music, but also incorporating ethnic and jazz themes.

There's also **Ars Musica** (02 219 40 44/ www.arsmusica.be), a two-week festival of contemporary orchestral and vocal music in March. It's international by nature but with an emphasis on Belgian talent. **Midis-Minimes** (02 511 25 82/www.midis-minimes.be) is a Brussels institution, featuring a lunchtime classical concert every day in July and August, either at either **l'Eglise de Minimes** (*see p196*) or the **Conservatoire Royal de Musique** (*see p195*). Tickets are laughably cheap: €1.20 per concert or €25 for a pass to all of them.

Website **www.euro-festival.net** is an excellent generic resource for festivals across Europe.

Churches

Cathédrale des Sts Michel et Gudule

place St Gudule, Upper Town (02 217 83 45). Métro Gare Centrale or Parc. **Open** *Apr-Oct* 7am-7pm Mon-Fri; 7.30am-7pm Sat; 8am-7pm Sun. *Nov-Mar* 7am-6pm Mon-Fri; 7.30am-6pm Sat; 8am-6pm Sun. **Tickets** €12.50-€20. **No credit cards**. **Map** p319 D3.

Brussels' largest church: too large, in fact, to be acoustically ideal for music much more complicated than Gregorian chant. Nevertheless, it's the venue for quite a few major events, especially organ concerts on the excellent instrument high above the audience. The interior is just as grandiose as the exterior, and audiences of 1,000 or so help absorb some of the ten-second echo. Sunday-noon Masses feature special concerts during much of the year; evening concerts are rarer.

Chapelle Royale

Eglise Protestante, 5 Coudenberg, off 10 place Royale, Upper Town (02 673 05 81). Métro Gare Centrale. **Open & tickets** varies. **No credit cards**. **Map** p317 C4.

The favourite hall of many musicians, and a jewel both acoustically and architecturally. It's too small for anything larger than a baroque chamber orchestra, but ideal for authentic instruments. As maximum audience size is about 150, early booking is advised. It's also Brussels' best-heated church in winter. Concerts are held in the evening.

L'Eglise des St Jean et St Etienne aux Minimes

62 rue des Minimes, Lower Town (02 511 93 84). Bus 48. **Open** varies. **Tickets** €10-€25; sometimes free. **No credit cards**. **Map** p321 C5.

This high-baroque church, near the Sablon and Marolles quarter, has medium-quality acoustics but hosts a huge number of concerts. The Philharmonic Society produces some of its early music recitals here. Throughout much of the summer, the Midi-Minimes festival attracts a diverse crowd of tourists and locals on their lunch hours. During the rest of the year, on one Sunday morning a month, a mixed amateur/professional ensemble called La Chapelle des Minimes presents fine performances of Bach cantatas, as it has done for the past 20 years. The admission fee is voluntary, and the erudite programme notes are in four languages. It's best to arrive 30 minutes before the 10.30am starting time for these often standing-room-only events.

Occasional venues

Some interesting places – such as museums, chateaux or large townhouses – hold concerts sporadically. Catch a summer opera production at Château de La Hulpe (15 kilometres/ten miles south-east of Brussels), for example, and try to

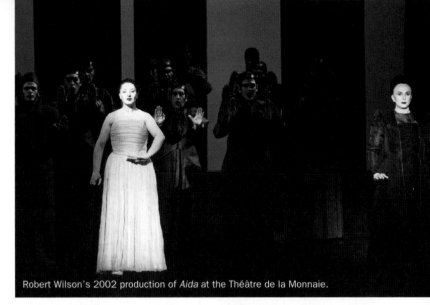

Robert Wilson's 2002 production of *Aida* at the Théâtre de la Monnaie.

recognise the setting from the film *The Music Teacher*. Also, many of Brussels' outlying *communes* have their own cultural centres, whose halls may be used for concerts.

One example is **Libretto**, a small hall behind an Ixelles townhouse (52 rue du Bailli; 03 646 97 35; tickets €10-€15). Even more unusual is **Skenegraphia**, organised by music-loving architects who produce concerts in different large homes of special architectural interest. Each concert's repertoire is deliberately matched to the style and epoch of its particular venue, making for events with lots of ambience. Call 02 375 51 47 for details; tickets cost €20 non-members, €15 members, €10 concessions.

Espace Senghor
366 chaussée de Wavre, Etterbeek (02 230 31 40). Métro Maelbeek/bus 59. **Open** *Box office* noon-2pm, 4-6pm Mon-Thur. **Tickets** €5-€12. **No credit cards. Map** p324 F5.
A former industrial building imaginatively renovated as a concert space. Worth a visit if only to admire the wrought-iron railings of bygone days, and appreciate the often unusual programming, with emphasis on innovative modern and didactic works. *See also p201.*

Hôtel Astoria
103 rue Royale, Upper Town (02 513 09 65/ automated reservations in French & Dutch 0900 28 877). Métro Parc or Botanique. **Open** *Concerts* 11am Sun. **Tickets** €8. **No credit cards. Map** p319 D3.
Enjoy magnificent turn-of-the-20th-century elegance in a working hotel that hosts Sunday brunch concerts. The small, opulent hall is ideal for chamber music – ambience guaranteed. There are also jazz concerts on Friday evenings (10-12.30pm) for which admission is free.

Hôtel de Ville – Salle Gothique
Grand' Place, Lower Town (tourist information 02 513 89 40). Pré-métro Bourse or Métro Gare Centrale. **Open** varies. **Tickets** usually free. **No credit cards. Map** p317 C3.
Although concerts here are rare, it's worth looking out for a performance, if only to savour the interior of the Grand' Place's most grandiose building. The Gothic Hall can accommodate a chamber orchestra and the acoustics are fine, although the ornate decor is almost a distraction.

Kaaitheater
20 square Sainctelette, St-Josse (02 201 59 59/ http://kaaitheater.vgc.be). Métro Yser. **Open** *Box office* 11am-6pm Tue-Fri. **Tickets** €12.50; €8.50 concessions. **Credit** MC, V. **Map** p318 B1.
Used mostly for Dutch-speaking theatre productions, this medium-sized hall occasionally features opera and contemporary music. Ictus is the resident ensemble. There's also a smaller studio at 81 rue Notre Dame du Sommeil. *See also p213.*

Musée d'Art Ancien
Auditorium, 3 rue de la Régence, Upper Town (02 508 32 11/02 512 82 47 for recording in French and Dutch with programmes for Concerts du midi). Métro Gare Centrale or Parc/tram 92, 93, 94. **Open** *Concerts* 12.30-1.30pm Wed. **Tickets** €5. **Credit** AmEx, DC, MC, V. **Map** p321 C4.
This museum has regular Wednesday lunchtime concerts, which can make a nice break during a tour of the exhibits. It has been encouraging musical events with themes, such as baroque concerts played on original instruments in the Rubens paintings hall.

Théâtre St-Michel
2 rue Père Devroye, Etterbeek (02 736 76 56). Métro Boileau. **Open** *Box office* 10am-1pm Mon-Fri. **Tickets** €7.50-€62.50. **Credit** AmEx, DC, MC, V.

Enjoy chamber concerts in a divine setting at the **Hôtel Astoria**. *See p197.*

This fairly large hall attached to one of Brussels' most important preparatory schools was the main replacement for the Palais des Beaux-Arts during its long closure for renovation. Although its acoustics are really more suitable for theatre, audiences and players appreciate its shape and generous volume.

UCL – Auditorium Lacroix

51 avenue Mounier, Woluwe-St-Lambert (02 764 41 28). Métro Alma. **Open** *Concerts* 1pm Tue. **Tickets** €6.20; €2.48 concessions. **No credit cards.**
An auditorium at the Université Catholique de Louvain for lectures and concerts, featuring interesting groups and high-quality programmes. Sandwiches are available before and after the Tuesday afternoon concerts.

Opera

For info on the **Vlaamse Opera** in Antwerp, *see p240.* Although run on a much smaller budget than its Brussels and Antwerp rivals, the **Opéra Royal de Wallonie** in Liège offers a chance to hear promising future stars in a little jewel of a hall.

Théâtre de la Monnaie

place de la Monnaie, 4 rue Léopold, Lower Town (02 229 12 11/www.lamonnaie.be). Métro/Pré-métro De Brouckère. **Open** *Box office* 11am-6pm Tue-Sat. **Tickets** €7.50-€75. **Credit** AmEx, DC, MC, V. **Map** p317 C3.
The national opera house is the jewel in the Brussels cultural crown, and soaks up the lion's share of arts subsidies. Its opulent interior reveals its glorious past; lavish attention to detail shows confidence in the future. The repertoire strives for a balance between contemporary works and innovative productions of the classics, with fine singers not yet famous enough for their prices to be out of reach. Current director Bernard Foccroulle, himself an organist, has had notable success with baroque

works played by period-instrument ensembles. The results are consistently first-class. Unfortunately, this means tickets are almost impossible to get hold of for many productions. Last-minute possibilities exist, but there are always more people than seats.

Rock, world & jazz

Brussels' central location means that hordes of acts feel obliged to include it in their European tours. Which means that – apart from lean periods such as January – there's no shortage of live shows to whet fans' appetites. Indeed, the city is the kind of place where you can be deafened by death-metal diehards, seduced by a free jazz maestro and captivated by an African rhythm section all in the space of the same weekend.

World-famous artistes such as Eminem and Tom Jones have recently played the city's best-known indoor venue, **Forest National**. The likes of Oasis and Iggy Pop, however, favour the slightly more intimate setting of **Ancienne Belgique**, a hip renovated theatre just a few minutes' stroll from the Grand' Place. Better again is the **Botanique**, a regular stomping ground of ex-Pixie Frank Black, where you have to walk through a luxuriant greenhouse to get to the main concert hall. If a sweaty moshpit is your natural habitat, then check out the **VK Club** or **Magasin 4**, both of which attract an array of ear-splitting left-field bands and the occasional cult legend.

LOCAL BANDS

The domestic music scene (*see p202* **The best Belgium has to offer ...**) is fragmented. For some reason, it seems to mirror the country's politics, with the francophone minority under-represented at its highest echelons. Virtually all the Belgian acts who have notched up respectable sales outside their own country come from a Dutch-speaking background – even those who ply their trade *en français.* Flame-headed **Axelle Red** regularly fills stadiums in France and has sold more than three million copies of her bubbly pop albums. While most of her lyrics are in French, she grew up in the Flemish province of Limburg.

In the field of rock, once dominant, now addled Antwerp outfit **dEUS** filled the music press in 2001 with rumours of their demise. Despite enjoying positive reviews across Europe, the post-grunge combo were disappointed that their 1999 album *The Ideal Crash* didn't catapult them into major-league success. Since playing sell-out end-of-millennium shows in Brussels, their members have devoted themselves to side projects (bassist Danny Mommens' band **Vive La Fête** offer a suitably sleazy tribute to Serge Gainsbourg). By the end of 2001, a new single and 'Best Of' compilation were released.

The most intriguing thing about dEUS's 'sabbatical' is how several of their compatriots emerged as ambassadors for Belgian music during it. **Hooverphonic**, Sint-Niklaas' leading

Even Lou Reed had fun here. *See p200.*

(OK, only) exponents of trip hop, have been described as a 'perfect' live act by US rawk bible *Rolling Stone*. Fellow Flemings **K's Choice** have also won healthy sales on the other side of the Atlantic with their FM-friendly ballads. And peroxide fiend Matthew Engelen – performing both under nom de plume **Praga Khan** and with his cohorts **Lords of Acid** – has thrilled hedonistic clubbers with his pulsating, sexually charged techno.

Meanwhile, Ghent quintet **Soulwax** sent decibel levels soaring when they appeared at many of Europe's largest festivals in recent years; **Das Pop** have established themselves as the Benelux answer to Britpop; and female a cappella trio **Laïs** have been hailed as 'angels' by no less a personage than Emmylou Harris.

One of Brussels' most famous sons is the alternately bawdy and romantic troubadour **Jacques Brel**. Nearly 25 years after he succumbed to lung cancer, Brel's spirit is kept alive today by bar room *chanteur*, Ostend's self-described European Cowboy **Arno Hintjens**.

INFORMATION AND TICKETS

For concert information, check the *What's On* section of the English-language *Bulletin*, or the French-language *Kiosque*. It's best to buy tickets direct from the venues, but tickets for many gigs are also available from **Fnac** (*see p141*) and online from **www.inthepocket.be**.

Rock venues

Ancienne Belgique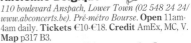

110 boulevard Anspach, Lower Town (02 548 24 24/ www.abconcerts.be). Pré-métro Bourse. **Open** 11am-4am daily. **Tickets** €10-€18. **Credit** AmEx, MC, V. **Map** p317 B3.

It may not be as well known as the Cavern or CBGBs, but this city-centre venue has a legendary status nonetheless. Belgium's most famous troubadour Jacques Brel put in many an electrifying performance on its stage. In more recent years, it has attracted acts as illustrious as Oasis, Iggy Pop, David Byrne, jazz great Herbie Hancock and James Brown's saxophonist extraordinaire Maceo Parker. Its main hall can hold about 2,000, but if you want a more intimate setting check out the upstairs club, where fresh talent is regularly showcased.

Botanique

236 rue Royale, St-Josse (02 226 12 11/reservations 02 218 37 32/www.botanique.be). Métro Botanique/ tram 92, 93, 94. **Open** 10am-10pm daily. **Tickets** around €13. **Credit** AmEx, MC, V. **Map** p319 D2.

This cultural centre is one of the most genteel venues in Europe. The main corridor is lined with luxuriant foliage and ponds. Incongruously perhaps, many of the acts playing here tend to revel in scruffy indie or grunge rock, with many stars of the US 'new country' scene also paying visits lately. Equipped

Ancienne Belgique: legendary. *See p199.*

with three separate theatres, it plays host to two of the central attractions on Brussels' cultural calendar: the Nuits Botanique rock festival and the Parcours *chanté* festival of francophone singing.

Cirque Royale

81 rue de l'Enseignement, Upper Town (02 218 20 15/02 218 37 32/www.cirque-royal.org). Métro Madou. **Open** & **tickets** varies; call for details. **Credit** MC, V. **Map** p319 D3.

Once an indoor circus, there is a feel of magic about this spherical auditorium with its high ceiling. It tends to draw spellbinding performances from even the most curmudgeonly of rock stars; top grouch Lou Reed was even spotted smiling at a show here.

Flanagan's

59 rue de l'Ecuyer, Lower Town (02 503 47 16). Métro/Pré-métro De Brouckère or Métro Gare Centrale. **Open** 10pm-1am Tue-Sun. **Tickets** around €7. **No credit cards. Map** p317 C3.

It might be situated in a neo-classical building but that description couldn't apply to the music performed by most of the acts here. Indie bands from Belgium and beyond are the staple diet, although many reggae gigs have been held recently. The Long Island Bar upstairs has a pool room – a convenient retreat if a show proves disappointing.

Forest National

rue Victor Rousseau, Forest (02 340 22 11/ www.forestnational.be). Tram 52/bus 48, 54. **Open** Box office 9am-6pm Mon-Fri; 11am-3pm Sat. **Tickets** €25-€37.50. **Credit** MC,V.

The biggest indoor venue in Brussels, this former bunker can accommodate 11,000. Unfortunately, it feels a bit like an aircraft hangar and acoustics can be so poor you sometimes wonder if gremlins have taken up residence in the sound system. Top names to appear in the past few years include Bob Dylan, Eminem and Robbie Williams.

Grain d'Orge

142 chaussée de Wavre, Ixelles (02 511 26 47). Métro Porte de Namur. **Open** 11am-3am Fri. **Tickets** free. **Credit** MC, V. **Map** p324 E5.

The ultimate spit-and-sawdust bar in Brussels, the Grain d'Orge hosts gigs every Friday night. Most of the acts tend to favour bluesy American rawk, and sport the kind of attire that was fashionable across the Atlantic about three decades ago.

Halles de Schaerbeek

22A rue Royale Ste-Marie, Schaerbeek (02 218 24 07/www.halles.be). Tram 92, 93, 94/bus 65, 66. **Open** varies; call for details. **Tickets** about €20. **Credit** AmEx, DC, MC, V. **Map** p322 E1.

While its Victorian architecture gives this spot a sense of grandeur, it can also be plagued by substandard sound. Ideally, all concerts should take place in its downstairs club. The trouble is that it is not big enough to hold all the punters clogging its main hall when big attractions, such as Beck and PJ Harvey, visit. *See also p216.*

Magasin 4

4 rue de Magasin, Lower Town (02 223 34 74. www.cyclone.be/magasin4). Métro Yser/tram 18. **Open** usually 8-10pm on gig nights. **Tickets** €6-€10. **No credit cards. Map** p318 B1.

Perhaps the only rock club in Brussels with the ambience of a sweaty New York venue in the late 1970s, Magasin 4 is gloriously ramshackle with spray-painted murals as the only decoration. Its regulars are still struggling to keep the spirit of punk alive, and the bands tend to be so uncompromising they'd consider record sales of more than 100 as a sell-out to commercialism.

La Tentation

28 rue de Laeken, Lower Town (02 537 45 47/ www.latentation.org). Métro/Pré-métro De Brouckère. **Open** gigs usually 7pm Fri, Sat. **Tickets** around €9. **No credit cards. Map** p318 B/C2.

This homely hangout is run as a cultural centre for the Galician community in Brussels. Not surprisingly then, music and dance from Spain's Celtic region is favoured. But it also boasts some rock and country shows, featuring the likes of Emmylou Harris and Tom Robinson of *Glad to be Gay* fame.

VK Club

76 rue de l'Ecole, Molenbeek (02 414 29 07/ www.vkconcerts.be). Métro Comte de Flandre/ bus 89. **Open** gigs usually 7.30pm. **Tickets** €10-€17. **No credit cards. Map** p318 A2.

The VK is located beside a chip shop well away from central Brussels. Sporting a glitter ball, it has an unmistakable student union feel. It tends to attract acts who sell slightly more than those gracing Magasin 4 (*see above*); alt rock heroes the Fall are regular visitors. It is also popular among the reggae and hip hop set, with acts such as Yellowman and the Black Eyed Peas making the odd appearance.

Folk & world venues

Brussels may have plenty of Irish pubs that are hugely popular with expats, but don't expect to hear an authentic bohdran drum. Their din has been all but drowned out in recent years by the roar of football on large TV screens. On the other hand, the large number of people in the city with origins outside Europe might explain why it's possible to catch the best musical acts from around the world. Award-winning a cappella outfit Zap Mama grew out of an African vocal workshop, and many clubs more thought of as jazz venues – **Music Village** and **Sounds** (for both, *see p203*) – now devote nights to Latin American music and salsa.

Auditorium 44

Passage 44, 44 boulevard du Jardin Botanique, Lower Town (02 218 56 30). Métro Botanique/tram 93, 94. **Open** varies; call for details. Closed July, Aug. **Tickets** varies. **Credit** DC, MC, V. **Map** p319 D2.
A 1960s utopia that almost became an urban nightmare: office blocks with an underground cinema (now closed), theatre and shopping gallery. The 800-seater auditorium occasionally puts on a folk or African music event, while the theatre is the venue for the annual International Festival of Fantasy, Thriller and Science Fiction Films (*see p166*).

Le Bizon Karperbrug

7 rue du Pont de la Carpe, Lower Town (02 502 46 99). Pré-métro Bourse. **Open** 6pm-late daily. **Tickets** free. **Map** p318 B3.
This cracking, *Cheers*-style bar is your best bet for some home-grown blues. Because of sound restrictions all musicians play unplugged sets. Sunday's '100% Pure Piano' begins early at 8pm, while the blues jam session on a Monday gets going at around 9pm, and Tuesday's acoustic blues acts don't strut their stuff till after 10pm. Friendly bar staff to boot.

La Bodega

30 rue de Birmingham, Molenbeek (02 410 04 49). Métro Gare de l'Ouest/bus 20, 58, 63, 89. **Open** 11.30am-late daily. **Tickets** free Fri, Sat; varies on other days. **No credit cards**.
Located in the ethnically diverse commune of Molenbeek, this Hispanic-run venue provides endless treats for Latin music aficionados. Flamenco and salsa are the preferred choices. As well as the sizzling sounds, there are some delectable Spanish wines and a much-used table football set.

Espace Senghor

366 chaussée de Wavre, Etterbeek (02 230 31 40). Métro Maelbeek/bus 59. **Open** Box office noon-2pm, 4-6pm Mon-Thur. **Tickets** €5-€12. **No credit cards. Map** p324 F5.
A decaying old theatre was heavily restored to become this modern venue, which regularly hosts world music concerts. The entrance is in a charming 19th-century pedestrian street near the place

Festival fever 2

As you might expect, most festivals take place in the summer. The **Brussels Jazz Marathon** (0900 00750/www.brussels jazzmarathon.be) hosts up to 400 musicians in cafés, clubs, restaurants and the open air, usually on the last weekend in May. It's hectic, it's colourful, it's a great event. The best way to enjoy it is to buy an all-embracing pass, which also entitles you to free transport between the various venues.

Couleur Café (02 672 49 12/www. couleurcafe.org) has become an important world music event, attracting thousands each year. Over a weekend in July, a series of villages springs up in the decaying splendour of the former customs depot Tour et Taxis. Music stages, food courts, shopping malls, it's all there.

Brosella (02 270 98 56/www.brosella.be) is a relaxed, free jazz and folk festival held on the second weekend of July and attracting a wide audience, from families to hippy hangovers.

Also free, **Klikende Munt** (02 513 82 90/http://beursschouwburg.vgc.be) in July, organised by the trendy Beursschouwburg, offers outdoor rock and avant-garde music, mostly in front of the opera house on place de la Monnaie and in rue Neuve, the pedestrianised shopping street.

Outside Brussels, **Rock Werchter** (0900 26060/www.rockwerchter.be) is one of the country's biggest rock festivals, which unfailingly features an impressive line-up of leading British, other European (mainly indie) and US bands in a muddy field near Leuven in June or July. Expect the likes of U2, Red Hot Chili Peppers and Oasis. Another major event is the **Audi Jazz Festival** (0900 00565/www.audijazz.be) with over 50 concerts staged across Belgium but centred on Brussels, from mid October to mid November. The music includes jazz, blues, avant-garde, world and hip hop. The star turn in 2001 was Herbie Hancock.

For online info, **www.agenda.be** is a short and to-the-point site that thumbnails events in Brussels, usually with links to festival sites. Also try **www.virtual-festivals.com/festivals/belgium/**, a thorough festival portal with links.

Belgium has to offer …

Arno

Ostend's gravel-voiced rock poet (*pictured*), honoured with a Chevalier des Arts et des Lettres from the state in 2002, and graffiti in the toilets of the Archiduc from way back when. In spring 2002 he released his 25th album in 25 years, *Arno Charles Ernest*, the usual mix of funk, *chanson française* and Belgian blues.

Starflam

An expansive rap crew from Liège, Starflam try to prove that hip hop can be just as arresting performed in French from a pretty town on the Meuse as by homeboys from the South Bronx.

PJDS

Ghent's answer to Scott Walker, Pieter-Jan De Smet ('PJDS') is influenced by both American crooners and French *chanson*. Has recently

collaborated with Arno's henchmen Geoffrey Burton (guitar) and Mirko Banovic (bass) on the stunning LP *Light Sleeper*.

Ozark Henry

Piet Goddaer is the son of acclaimed composer Norbert Goddaer, but performs under catchy Ozark Henry. An ex-rapper, he dabbled in reggae and trip hop before opting for gospel choirs and lush strings on well-received album *Birthmarks*.

Spencer the Rover

For some reason Koen Renders, formerly of cult legends Stormdaisy, chose to call his new band after a big shaggy dog. His poignant vocals have been compared with Neil Young and Roy Orbison. Koen Roenders' vocals, that is…

Miam Monster Miam

Effective one-man band Benjamin Schoos decided to keep his country's Surrealist tradition alive by naming an album *Hello Tank!*

Mauro

The latest incarnation of Mauro Pawlowski, frontman of the Evil Superstars, sadly no longer with us. His bandmates give free rein to his fascination with the cheesiest sounds of the 1970s.

El Tattoo del Tigre

A 30-piece Flemish collective that pays tribute to mambo pioneer Perez Prado by revisiting the rhythms of Havana dancehalls. They've mastered their music a lot better than their Spanish.

Jourdan. The atmosphere can be studious and the neighbourhood has little nightlife, but the choice of music is usually very good.

Salle de la Madeleine

14 rue Duquesnoy, Lower Town (02 511 97 32). Métro Gare Centrale. **Open & tickets** varies; call for details. **No credit cards. Map** p317 C3/4.
Best known for its collectible fairs, this venue in the city centre hosts occasional concerts by African artists such as Kofi and the long list of bands that have their genesis in the Zaiko Langa Langa family.

So What

37 rue du Vieux Marché aux Grains, Lower Town (02 513 63 93). Pré-métro Bourse. **Open** 11am-9pm Mon-Thur; 11am-late Fri, Sun. **Tickets** €2-€6. **No credit cards. Map** p318 B3.

This small atmospheric club plays host to a wide variety of acts, from soul and R&B to reggae on a Friday. On Sundays, resident Brazilian act Alvaro gets a pleasingly mixed crowd moving to their Latino rhythms. It can pack in as many as 200 pep-filled punters, so prepare to get hot.

Jazz venues

Brussels has welcomed many of the most famous names in jazz. The likes of Bobby Jaspar, René Thomas and Jacques Pelzer played with all the US greats in the 1960s. In recent years, the number of clubs catering to the jazz community may have fallen slightly, but notable new venues such as the **Music Village** and **L'Arts-O-Base** are testimony to the enthusiasm there is in Belgium for great jazz. Harmonica legend **Toots Thielemans** is a household name and at the age of 80 shows no sign of retiring, while sax player Steve Houben and pianists Michel Herr and Nathalie Lorier prove that the scene is still capable of producing notable talent.

Airport Sheraton Hotel

Brussels National Airport, Zaventem (02 725 10 00). Train to Zaventem. **Open** noon-3pm daily. *Jazz brunch* noon-3pm Sun. **Tickets** free. **Credit** AmEx, DC, MC, V.

Fitting its 'international' setting, the Sheraton welcomes jazz musicians from far and wide. The Sunday jazz brunch (€35) usually features fairly mid-stream bop, which suits the hour. The atrium is soundproofed, but keen plane-watchers can still see them float overhead. An unusual hangover cure.

L'Archiduc

6 rue Antoine Dansaert, Lower Town (02 512 06 52). Pré-métro Bourse. **Open** 4pm-4am daily. **Tickets** free-€10. **Credit** AmEx, DC, MC, V. **Map** p318 B3.

Built in the 1930s, this superb little bar (*see p127*) was for a long time a secretive after-hours club for jazz fans. Nat King Cole and others dropped by for an après-gig drink, and in his case to tinkle the ivories. Free Saturday gigs feature mainly local musicians; Sunday concerts (€10) bring in musicians from further afield. Both begin around 5pm. There are occasional other concerts for which it's advisable to book. You must ring the doorbell to enter.

L'Arts-O-Base

43 rue Ulens, Molenbeek (0475 79 07 05). Métro Yser. **Open** 8pm-late Tue, Wed, Fri, Sat. **Tickets** €5-€8; free Tue. **No credit cards**.

This new music club, snazzily furnished with jet-black tables, is rapidly becoming a magnet for the eclectic and ground-breaking in modern jazz. Its remit seems to be 'anything goes'. Wednesday night, when bands are booked in for a four-week stint, provides an opportunity for trying out new things. Saturday brings world music, and Tuesday's jam sessions are free.

Athanor Studio

Arlequin Hotel, 17-19 rue de la Fourche, Lower Town (02 514 16 15). Métro/Pré-métro De Brouckère. **Open** 9pm-late Thur-Sat. **Tickets** free-€7.50. **Credit** V. **Map** p317 C3.

Very much a nightclub venue, the Studio is located in the basement of the Arlequin Hotel (*see p43*). It attracts more alternative performers, and budding young things can work through new ideas at the music school, which runs on Wednesday nights (8-10pm) followed by a free jam session. Thursdays are free too, and when there isn't a band on the other nights, a guest DJ fills in. dEUS's Tom Barman likes to spin his choice discs here. Easy to get to, but note that the entrance is through the hotel.

Le Cercle

20-22 rue Ste-Anne, Upper Town (02 514 03 53). Tram 92, 93, 94. **Open** 7pm-late daily. **Tickets** €10. **No credit cards**. **Map** p317 C4.

A cosy little venue, down a quiet lane just off the swish Sablon, that hosts everything from stand-up comedians to poetry readings. The small theatre puts on the occasional jazz show, and something called the 'Wild Night', a crazy mixture of jazz and the spoken word.

Music Village

50 rue des Pierres, Lower Town (02 513 13 45). Pré-métro Bourse. **Open** 7pm-late Wed-Sat. **Tickets** €10-€20. **Credit** MC, V. **Map** p317 B3.

Opened in September 2000, the Music Village occupies two 17th-century buildings near the 'Grand' Place. The owners may have kept the 'Golden Spade' insignia from its previous existence as a warehouse, but this members-only club now welcomes some of the biggest names in Belgian jazz. Yearly membership costs €9; some hotels offer a welcome pass that waives this additional cost and gets you a bottle of bubbly for good measure. Inexpensive pastas and salads are served and it is advisable to book your table in advance. Wednesday is blues night, and Thursday is Latino – most of the latter night's acts have been Cuban to date, some with enough vim to stir dancing around the tables.

Le Nouveau Théâtre du Méridien

200 chaussée de la Hulpe, Overijse (02 672 38 20). Bus 95. **Open** gigs usually 9.30pm. **Tickets** €12.40-€17.40. **Credit** MC, V.

Although out of town – 30 minutes by bus from the city centre – the Meridien offers the chance to enjoy quality jazz in a picturesque setting by a lake. It attracts mostly Belgian musicians, but often brings together noted performers for a special one-off show. The location might explain the mostly well-heeled types tapping their feet in the seats. Advance booking is advisable.

Théâtre Marni

23-25 rue de Vergnies, Ixelles (02 217 48 00). Tram 81, 82. **Open** 8pm-midnight Tue-Sat. **Admission** €12.50. **No credit cards**. **Map** p324 E7.

For a week a month, this recently renovated theatre, a one-time bowling alley, promotes the best in Belgian and European jazz. Gigs take place in the main theatre or the entrance hall and begin at 8.30pm. It took over the business of the Travers jazz club, which closed in 2001, and continues its tradition of championing innovative new performers.

Sounds Jazz Club

28 rue de la Tulipe, Ixelles (02 512 92 50). Bus 54, 71. **Open** 8pm-4am Mon-Sat. **Admission** €2.50-€8; free Tue-Thur. **No credit cards**. **Map** p321 D5/6.

Very much the place to hear modern jazz, although Tuesday night is given over to New Orleans jazz and Saturday to 'big band'. The small stage even rumbles to the rhythms of salsa on Wednesdays. The Italian owners offer plenty of choice pasta dishes.

Sport & Fitness

From cycling to the beautiful game, Brussels has all the sporting bases covered.

City of beer, chips and chocolate, Brussels is an unlikely city for the sporting enthusiast. Nevertheless, the presence of so many expatriates means a well-organised network of non-native participatory sports, cricket being the prime example. The surrounding forests offer excellent possibilities for hiking, mountain biking and horse riding – and if cycling is your thing, you've come to the right country.

Cycling is a national obsession, and the one sporting discipline in which Belgium can claim a truly world-class hero. Grocer's son Eddy Merckx is still revered as the greatest natural cyclist the world has ever seen, winning the Tour de France five times. The sport also fits neatly into the country's flat topography and the nation's beery soul. Sunday rides are great social events, involving long liquid lunches and top-heavy picnics.

Today's world-class sporting contenders include tennis stars Justine Henin and Kim Clijsters (*see p208* **Complementary backhanders**), perhaps more recognisable, and certainly more photogenic, than billiards legend Raymond Ceulemans, whose province of Hainaut claims to produce 80 per cent of all the world's billiard balls. Judo is another non-mainstream sport in which the country has excelled recently, taking six medals in the past two Olympics, five of them by women. And, lest we forget, Belgium's very own Jean-Claude van Damme boasts a sporting pedigree, having once been a martial arts champion.

Behind the scenes, Jacques Rogge, president of the International Olympic Committee, is one of the most powerful men in world sport. Belgium has a distinguished Olympic past, having hosted the Games in Antwerp in 1920, when the Olympic oath was first uttered and the flag first unfurled. This was its most successful Games, with 14 golds. One was awarded for football, a decade before the first World Cup and the start of Belgium's love affair with the global game.

Sadly, the country is also known for the Heysel tragedy of 1985, in which 39 Juventus fans died at a European Cup Final. Fifteen years later, this same stadium, revamped and renamed the Roi Baudouin, successfully hosted the opening match of Euro 2000.

For fans who prefer to enjoy events from the safety of a TV screen, most Brussels' homes receive the BBC, plus neighbouring French,

Dutch and German stations. Radio listeners can pick up sports commentary from BBC Radio 4 and 5, and the World Service.

Information on sporting activities in Brussels and elsewhere in French-speaking Belgium is available from **ADEPS** (02 413 23 11/ www.cfwb.be), or from **BLOSO** (02 209 45 11) for the Flemish-speaking half. For English-speaking activities, the child-oriented **Brussels Sports Association** (02 354 11 14) is one-stop source for the myriad schools and clubs. For details of major sports events, contact the **Belgian Tourist Office** (*see p303*).

Spectator sports

With only a limited number of suitable venues, Brussels is hardly a world stage for spectator sports. The national stadium, Stade Roi Baudouin, hosts many of the major events, including the main athletics meetings, cycling races and the home games of Belgium's national football team.

Stade Roi Baudouin

Avenue du Marathon, Laeken (02 479 36 54). Métro Roi Baudouin. **Map** p326 A2.
Formerly the Heysel, Belgium's national stadium was a crumbling ruin when it closed after the appalling tragedy of 1985. Ten years later, it reopened as the Roi Baudouin, a 50,000-capacity all-seater with its own metro stop, new ticket office and a swish, spacious sports bar, Extra-Time. The four stands are colour-coded: *tribune* 1 (orange) houses the most expensive seats, 2 (green) and 4 (blue) are behind the goals and 3 (yellow) is along avenue des Athlètes by the metro stop.

Athletics

Two main events highlight the athletics calendar, one international, the other domestic. The prestigious **Ivo Van Damme Memorial** meeting is held at the Roi Baudouin towards the end of August. Named after the 800-metre runner who died shortly after his Olympic silver at the 1976 Games, this Grand Prix event draws a top field of international stars.

Earlier in the summer, in May or June, the popular **Brussels 20km Run** (*see p167*) attracts some 20,000 runners and twice as many spectators, who line the scenic route via the Royal Palace, rue Royale, avenues Louise and

The Belgians are cycling-mad – or is that mad to cycle?

Tervuren, through the Bois de la Cambre, starting and finishing at the esplanade du Cinquantenaire. Runners have to pay a €9 fee to participate; call 02 513 89 40 for details.

Cycling

Cycling is the national sport of Belgium, with national meets taking place all over the country from March to October. The main event is the **Tour of Flanders** (Ronde van Vlaanderen), a day-long race in which Europe's top riders tackle the steep and often cobbled hills of the Ardennes. Back in Brussels, the **Grand Prix Eddy Merckx** is a speed race held at the Roi Baudouin on the last Sunday in August; and some years the **Tour de France** takes a detour through the city. For full details, contact the Cycling Federation on 02 349 19 11.

In winter, cyclo-cross, the bastard son of classic cycling, sees hardy riders trek up steep hills and through thick mud on mountain bikes. The sport's top riders are either Belgian or based in the country.

Football

Belgium has a proud footballing tradition, dating back to the earliest international matches with its eternal rivals, France and Holland. Duty to this tradition saw Belgium board the *SS Conte-Verde*, joining three other European teams bound for the first World Cup in Montevideo in 1930. Sadly, another tradition was upheld when star forward Bernard Voorhoof drank so much beer on the ten-day journey he put on eight kilos and Belgium failed to score a single goal. Since then, the national side, 'the Red Devils' have appeared at most finals, including the upcoming event in June 2002, drawn with host Japan, Tunisia and Russia.

The domestic Jupiler League, divided into four divisions, has been dominated by Anderlecht, Brussels' major club and the most recognisable name in Belgian football. Although it has fan clubs all over the country, success, wealth and long-running corruption scandals ensure that the club is also the most loathed – especially in Flanders.

To watch a First Division match, you need to buy a Fan Card, obtained from any ticket office. Cards cost €12.50, valid for three seasons. To follow the league scene, the Belgian FA runs an extensive website at www.footbel. com. The daily sports supplement in *La Dernière Heure* has comprehensive coverage for French-speakers. The real heart of football in Brussels is the local scene, as personified by Molenbeek, Union Saint-Gilloise and a host of

Arts & Entertainment

Time Out Brussels Guide **205**

small clubs whose names colour league table charts on the walls of bars in the most obscure corners of the city.

RSC Anderlecht

Stade Constant Vanden Stock, 2 avenue Théo Verbeek, Anderlecht (02 522 15 39/02 522 94 00/ www.rsca.be). Métro St-Guidon. **Tickets** standing €6.20-€11; sitting €11-€19.80. **No credit cards.**

A stadium and treasury fit for top European challengers – but these days 'Les Mauves' are international flops. This wasn't always the case. Anderlecht won three European trophies from 1976 to 1983, but the last one was tainted with a bribery and blackmail scandal that had serious repercussions throughout the 1990s. At home, RSCA ceded their league crown to Club Bruges; abroad, they floundered. It is still the biggest club in the land, and the bars down Théo Verbeek are packed on match days. The home fans in *tribune* 4 can be raucous, but don't wear the blue and black of Bruges and you should be OK.

RWD Molenbeek

Stade Edmond Machtens, 61 rue Charles Malis, Molenbeek (02 411 99 00). Métro Beekkant then bus 85. **Tickets** standing €10-€15; sitting €12.50-€22.50. **No credit cards.**

RWDM, or *are-vay-day-emm*, are an amalgamation of the old Racing White and Daring clubs, merged in 1973. They yo-yo between divisions, but are always joined for their home games by a lively brass band who break out into *Brazil* and other numbers at rare moments of excitement. Fan Cards are necessary when RWDM dips its toes in the top flight.

Football fervour starts at the grassroots.

Royale Union Saint-Gilloise

Stade Joseph Marien, 223 chaussée de Bruxelles, St-Gilles (02 344 16 56). Tram 18, 52. **Tickets** standing €7.50; sitting €12.50-€25. **No credit cards.**

Union are an echo of Brussels' proud footballing past. Regular title winners between the wars (sepia team shots adorn many a bar wall around St-Gilles), Union now struggle before three-figure crowds in Division 3. Those wishing to join them are rewarded with a splendid club bar and a strange, romantic atmosphere at a ground hewn out of the Duden forest.

Horse racing/showjumping

Brussels' two major racecourses lie on the outskirts of town. **Boitsfort** (51 chaussée de la Hulpe; 02 660 87 38) has an all-weather flat track, while **Sterrebeek** (43 rue du Roy de Blicquy; 02 767 54 75) hosts trotting and flat racing. For further information, contact the Belgian Jockey Club on 02 672 72 48.

Horse racing's big day comes on a Friday in mid June, with the **Belgian Derby** in Ostend. There is also a major international showjumping competition at the Roi Baudouin each November. Phone the stadium for details.

Motor sport

The **Spa-Francorchamps Formula One** circuit, two-and-a-half hours from Brussels by train, has had a history as checkered as the final flag. The first race scheduled here, in August 1921, saw a field of only one competitor. Forty years later, this tricky course built into dense Ardennes forest was hosting motorbike races, a 24-hour event and the **Belgian Grand Prix** – still held at the end of August. The 14-kilometre circuit gained a reputation for danger, and security concerns forced it to close in 1970. A safer seven kilometre circuit was unveiled a year later, but its undulating course still features Eau Rouge, the most dramatic switchback kink the drivers have to take all season. Approached from a downhill swoop, drivers need to keep their nerve to shimmy through and sweep away uphill. Only the brave triumph. Bus 4 and 4A run the eight kilometres (five miles) from Spa train station to the track.

Many Belgians prefer the motorcross equivalent, the **Namur Grand Prix**, also held in August. Competitors zoom down streets and past monuments, including the hilltop citadel where Roman conquerors once trod. They also pass le Chalet du Monument bar, where Swede Hakan Carlqvist stopped for a beer on his victorious ride of 1988. Contact the Belgian Tourist Information Office (*see p303*) for further details.

If you want to act like a monkey, head to an indoor climbing wall.

Active sports/fitness

Expats swamp the sports courses, courts and pitches all over Brussels. Be advised that most tennis courts are available to club members only. Longer-term visitors have a wide choice of teams to join. Check the weekly *Bulletin* for details. Other sources of information include **www.expatsinbrussels.com**, the **British & Commonwealth Women's Club** (02 772 53 13), the **American Women's Club of Brussels** (02 358 47 53/www.awcb.org) and, for youngsters, the **Brussels Sports Association** (02 354 11 14).

Municipal sports centres are spread all around the city, many in the wooded eastern district of Woluwe-St-Pierre (head office 002 773 18 20). Bounded by forests and parkland, Brussels also offers ample opportunity for walking, jogging and cycling, most of it easily accessible by public transport.

Badminton

The British Badminton Club (www.brussels badminton.com) holds matches three times a week in Wezembeek-Oppem. Many fitness centres (*see p208*) also have badminton courts.

Billiards

Cercle Royal de Billard

Palais du Midi, 3 rue Vander Weyden, Lower Town (02 511 10 18). Pré-métro Anneessens. **Open** 2pm-midnight Tue, Fri; 2-7pm Sat. **No credit cards.** **Map** p320 B4.
Members can enjoy a quiet hour at the baize for €2.50 on the third floor of this sports complex. Membership is available on demand.

Bowling

Brussels has a handful of bowling alleys; the largest is listed below. For details of others, contact the Bowling Federation on 02 732 48 08.

Crosly Super Bowling

36 boulevard de l'Empereur, Lower Town (02 512 08 74). Métro Gare Centrale. **Open** 2pm-1am Mon-Thur; 2pm-2am Fri, Sat; 10am-1am Sun. **Admission** €2.50 per game. **Credit** MC, V. **Map** p317 C4.
Line up the pins on any of the 20 bowling lanes or sup beer at the late bar. Classic 1960s' building.

Climbing

Natural climbing is best undertaken in the Ardennes, near Namur. Closer to town, you can find man-made walls for climbers of all skill levels at the following venue:

Escalade New Rock

136 chaussée de Watermael, Auderghem (02 675 17 60). Métro Demey/bus 72, 96. **Open** noon-midnight Mon-Fri, Sun; noon-8pm Sat. **Admission** €7.50. **No credit cards.**
A large indoor climbing centre with an 18m (59ft) climbing wall. Harnesses hired for a nominal fee. Courses at all levels from beginners upwards.

Cricket

Cricket has a crooked history in Brussels, right from the few overs bowled on the eve of the Battle of Waterloo. Today there are two main expat associations, in Brussels (02 384 73 93) and Antwerp (03 239 74 03), with the 12 Stars Club (www.12stars.cricket.org), organising games and tours for teams of all ages.

Cycling

Tramlines and cobbled streets hinder the cyclist in Brussels. Beware crossing at junctions, when cars coming in from the right have right of way. A network of cycle lanes is expected to be brought in by 2003. On the outskirts, there are excellent cycle tracks in the Bois de la Cambre and the Forêt de Soignes. Belgian railways run a cheap and simple bike hire ('Train-Plus-Vélo') scheme, allowing you to pick up and drop off bikes at any of 20 stations. Bikes carry a €4

Arts & Entertainment

supplement per journey. Details on 02 555 25 25. For more cycling information, contact the Belgian Cycling Federation on 02 349 19 52/ www.kbwb-rlvb.be.

Pro-Vélo
15 rue de Londres, Ixelles (02 502 73 55/ www.provelo.org). Métro Trône. **Open** *July, Aug* 10am-6pm Mon-Fri; 1-7pm Sat, Sun. *Sept-June* 10am-6pm Mon-Fri. **No credit cards. Map** p321 E5.
Umbrella body of cycling organisations, which organises themed tours and hires out bikes at €12 per day, €20 per weekend.

Fitness centres

Of the myriad private centres in town, many specialise in particular areas, such as martial arts, squash, boxing and swimming. The most luxurious are to be found at the upmarket hotels. Here is a selection and their speciality:

American Gym
144 boulevard Général Jacques, Ixelles (02 640 59 92). Tram 23, 90. **Open** 10am-10pm Mon-Fri; 10am-3pm Sat; 10am-2pm Sun. **Admission** €45 per month. **Credit** MC, V.
Body building, boxing and kick-boxing.

Aspria
View Building, 26-38 rue de l'Industrie, EU Quarter (02 511 10 00/www.aspria.be). Métro Trône. **Open** 6.30am-10pm Mon-Fri; 9am-7pm Sat, Sun. **Admission** €15 per day. **Credit** MC, V. **Map** p324 E4.
Aspria is a spanking new fitness club in the heart of the EU Quarter, with a 21m swimming pool, gym, sauna and crèche.

Golden Club
33 place du Châtelain, Ixelles (02 538 19 06). Métro Louise then tram 93, 94. **Open** noon-10pm Mon-Fri; 10am-4pm Sat, Sun. **Admission** call for details. **Credit** AmEx, DC, MC, V.
The Golden Club's best-known former pupil is Jean-Claude van Damme – so, not surprisingly, it's big on muscle building and martial arts.

John Harris Fitness
Radisson SAS Hotel, 47 rue du Fossé-aux-Loups, Lower Town (02 219 82 54). Métro/Pré-métro De Brouckère. **Open** 6.30am-10pm Mon-Fri; 10am-7pm Sat, Sun. **Admission** €24.50 per day; €79 per month. **No credit cards. Map** p317 C2.
This fitness centre is small, high-powered, centrally located – and pricey.
Branch: Sheraton Hotel, 3 place Rogier, Lower Town (02 224 31 11).

Complementary backhanders

For reasons impossible to explain, Belgium has fathered not one but two genuine world-class tennis aces. Justine Henin and Kim Clijsters have also helped the Belgian public bond in a rare display of unity behind these teen idols – as dramatically shown in Belgium's Federation Cup victory in Madrid in November 2001, the nation's first major trophy in the sport.

There is no secret formula behind the mighty Belgian production line. The academy system, rooted in the regions, although hardly original, is seen as part of the girls' success. Now Henin and Clijsters are expected to haul serious silverware back to Belgium over the next few years. By the time they played each other in the quarter finals of the Australian Open in January 2002, Clijsters was fifth and Henin seventh in the world rankings.

Both owe much to the two national training centres: one near French-speaking Charleroi, where Henin trained from 14 and is still based; the other, near Flemish Antwerp, is key to Clijsters' progress. Individually, they could not have had more contrasting backgrounds, reflecting Belgium's cultural and linguistic fracture.

Clijsters, born in the Flemish town of Bilzen in 1983, has an obvious sporting pedigree. Her father, Leo, a Belgian international footballer and former Golden Boot winner, played for the Mechelen team that unexpectedly won the European Cup-Winners' Cup in 1988. Her mother, Els, had a promising gymnastic career that included a national junior championship. She seems to have inherited her father's chunky legs and her mother's agility. At the 2001 French Open, Clijsters became the first Belgian to reach a Grand Slam singles final, losing to Jennifer Capriati at the end of an epic 12-10 final set. She has since added an element of glamour to her image by stepping out with Australia's Lleyton Hewitt – a relationship that guarantees her local hero status in Australia.

Henin's career path has been defined by adversity and personal endeavour. Only the tennis has come easily for the gutsy and spirited 'Juju'. Born in Liège in 1982, the elfin blonde's poignant destiny was defined by one moment in 1992. As a nine-year-old, her mother, Françoise, took her to Roland Garros to watch the women's final between Steffi Graf, her favourite player, and

Winner's

13 rue Bonneels, St-Josse (02 280 02 70). Métro Madou. **Open** 9am-10pm Mon-Fri; 9am-8pm Sat, Sun. **Admission** €48 per month. **Credit** DC, MC, V. **Map** p322 F3.
More a functional multi-sports centre than a palace of body building. Comfortable and good prices. Climbing wall, squash and badminton courts, gym. **Branch:** 12 rue Général Thys, Ixelles (02 644 55 44).

Go-karting

Late-evening, infantile fun can be had here:

City Kart

5A square Emile des Grées du Lou, Forest (02 332 36 96/www.citykart.com). Bus 18, 52, 55. **Open** noon-11pm Mon-Fri; 9.30am-11pm Sat, Sun. **Admission** €10-€14 per 15mins. **No credit cards.**
A kilometre of karting track just across from Forest-Midi railway station.

Golf

Although there are many courses in Brussels' leafy outskirts, fees can be steep and greens for members. Some clubs are open to non-

members on weekdays. For full details, contact the Belgian Golf Federation (02 672 23 89/ www.golfbelgium.be).

Horse riding

The Forêt de Soignes and the Bois de la Cambre are the best options for a quiet trek. The Equestrian Federation (02 478 50 56) can provide full details of riding clubs.

Royal Etrier Belge

19 champ du Vert Chasseur, Uccle (02 374 28 60). Bus 41. **Open** 8am-7pm Tue-Sun. **Admission** €19 per lesson. **No credit cards.**
Trekking and English-language lessons in the Bois de la Cambre just south of Robinson Lake.

Ice skating

Ice skating is a traditional part of Christmas. Open-air skating used to take place right in the Grand' Place, but the rink was moved across to Ste Catherine for 2001. The admission price of €5, €2.50 for children, includes skate hire. The Tourist Office (*see p303*) will have details for upcoming yuletide venues.

Kim Clijsters (left) and **Justine Henin**.

Monica Seles. 'One day you will see me playing on that Centre Court,' she told her mother. Three years later her mother died from intestinal cancer, with the precocious promise unfulfilled.

It is a loss Henin still struggles to cope with, but at the time the 12-year-old waif was forced to grow up fast, taking charge of the household and her siblings. Life was hard. She turned to family friend Jean-Denis Lejeune as a surrogate father, but his daughter Julie was a victim of Belgian killer

Marc Dutroux in 1996. Her own father, José, brought up his children on a postman's salary in the pretty Ardennes village of Marloie, but they fell out in 2001 and now only talk on the phone. Even in one of her finest hours, the Wimbledon final of 2001, she played unaware that her grandfather had died hours earlier; the news was held back until after her defeat by Venus Williams.

Henin's success has been miraculously chiselled out of these tragic setbacks, and she uses them to fuel her desire and steely resolve. As someone who makes no excuses in defeat, she speaks eloquently but does not answer questions about her private life. She is also one of the smallest players on the circuit, at 166 centimetres (5 feet 4 inches) and 57 kilos (125 pounds). Her game is a sublime antidote to the Amazonian power merchants who have been dominating women's tennis. Henin is svelte, swift and smart enough to use her opponent's power to her own advantage.

And her divine one-handed backhand has enraptured all who have seen it. John McEnroe described it as 'the greatest backhand in the game, bar none'.

Arts & Entertainment

Patinoire de Forest

36 avenue du Globe, Forest (02 345 16 11).
Tram 18, 52/bus 48, 54. **Open** *Sept-May* 8.30am-
4.30pm Mon-Thur; 8am-4.30pm, 8-11pm Fri; 10am-
5.45pm Sat, Sun. Closed June-Aug. **Admission** €5;
skate hire €2.50. **No credit cards.**
This large outdoor rink is at the Forest National
entertainment complex.

Patinoire Poséidon

*4 avenue des Vaillants, Woluwe-St-Lambert (02 762
16 33). Métro Tomberg.* **Open** *Sept-Apr* noon-
midnight Mon, Tue; 10am-10pm Wed-Sat; 10am-
6.30pm Sun. Closed May-Aug. **Admission** €4.50;
skate hire €3. **No credit cards.**
Semi-covered, Olympic-sized rink in a sports centre.

Rollerblading & skateboarding

Brussels' rainy cobbled streets hardly make
for skate city – although there's plenty of rats
boarding down the Mont des Arts. The Bois
de la Cambre has a rollerskating rink, and its
paths are closed to cars and open to roller
bladers on Sundays.

Roller Park

300 quai de Biestebroeck, Anderlecht (02 522 59 15).
Métro Veeweyde then bus 49. **Open** 10am-10pm
Mon-Thur; 10am-midnight Fri, Sat; 10am-7pm Sun.
Admission €5; skate hire €2.50. **No credit cards.**
Offers rollerblading and skateboarding

Skiing

In winter, skiers flock to the Ardennes and its
70 small *stations*. Contact Ardennes Tourisme
(084 41 19 81) for details. There's online
information at www.idearts.com/magazine/
dossiers/ski/index.htm. In town, try:

Yeti Ski

Drève Olympique 11, Anderlecht (02 520 77 57/
http://yeti-snowboarders.netfirms.com). Tram 56/
bus 47. **Open** *Sept-Easter* 1-11pm Mon, Wed, Fri;
6-11pm Tue, Thur; 10am-8pm Sat, Sun. Closed
Easter-Aug. **Admission** €7.50 per hour; ski hire
€2.50. **Credit** MC, V.
A dry slope in the Parc de Neerpede, providing ski
hire and lessons, and snowboarding.

Squash

Most tennis clubs, and some sports and fitness
centres, have squash courts. Check with the
Squash Federation (03 286 58 03) for full details.

Liberty's Squash Club

1068 chaussée de Wavre, Auderghem (02 734 64 93).
Métro Hankar. **Open** 9am-midnight daily.
Admission € 7 per 30min. **Credit** MC.
Large squash centre with 16 courts. Membership
needed for phone bookings.

Swimming

Proper trunks and swimming hats – which can
be hired – are compulsory at Belgian pools.
Many fitness centres (*see p208*) also have
swimming facilities.

Centre Sportif de Woluwe-St-Pierre

2 avenue Salomé, Woluwe-St-Pierre (02 773 18 20).
Tram 39/bus 36. **Open** 8am-8pm Mon-Sat.
Admission €3. **No credit cards.**
Large leisure centre with an Olympic-sized pool,
warm tubs and waterslide, plus tennis, squash, bas-
ketball, a solarium and steam baths.

Océade

*Bruparck, avenue de Football, Laeken (02 478 43
20). Métro Heysel.* **Open** 10am-6pm Wed-Fri;
10am-10pm Sat, Sun (school holidays 10am-10pm
daily). **Admission** €12.50; €10 children over 1.5m.
Credit MC, V. **Map** p326 A2.
Impressive sports complex with everything to keep
kids noisily amused, including a wave machine and
water slides. Warm pools and saunas for adults.

Victor Boin

38 rue de la Perche, St-Gilles (02 539 06 15).
Pré-métro Horta/tram 18, 81. **Open** 8am-7pm
Mon-Fri; 9am-7pm Sat. **Admission** €1.70.
No credit cards. Map p320 A7.
Beautiful art deco pool with hydrotherapy and a
Turkish bath, reserved for women on Tuesdays and
Fridays, men the rest of the week.

Tennis

Members-only tennis clubs are filled with
networking expats. The Castle Club in
Wezenbeek-Oppem (02 731 68 20) is particularly
popular. Check with the Tennis Federation (02
513 29 20) for full details. Some sports centres –
such as the one in Woluwe-St-Pierre (*see above*
Swimming) – have courts rented by the hour.
Other venues include:

Tennis Club de Belgique

26 rue du Beau Site, Ixelles (02 648 80 35/
www.tennisclubdebelgique.be). Métro Louise then
tram 93, 94. **Open** To non-members *mid Apr-Aug*
7am-10pm Mon-Fri. **Admission** €12.40-€16.15 per
hour. **No credit cards. Map** p321 D7.
A well-heeled club with indoor courts that are hired
out on summer weekdays to non-members.
Coaching is available.

Wimbledon Tennis

*220 chaussée de Waterloo, Rhode-St-Genèse (02 358
35 23). Bus W.* **Open** 10am-12.45pm, 2.45-8pm Mon-
Fri; 9am-12.30pm, 1.30-6pm Sat, Sun. **Admission**
€20 per hour. **No credit cards.**
Racket sports complex with 19 outdoor tennis courts
and seven squash courts. Membership needed.

Theatre & Dance

The drama is decent, but it's the dance scene that's really dynamic.

A 2002 production of *Notre Pouchkine* at the **Théâtre National**. *See p213.*

In recent times, Brussels has become home to a diverse and international theatre and dance scene. The main producing houses are now supplemented with touring productions from all over the world. Brussels as a cultural melting-pot has become a reality.

In general, the theatre divides neatly into French and Flemish, though English is creeping in as an important ingredient to serve the international audience mix. Yet there is a state of flux; the two major publicly funded theatres – the Royal Flemish Theatre and the Théâtre National – are in temporary spaces while awaiting new homes. This has resulted in a blow to confidence in the scene, though some of the smaller theatres have taken advantage of displaced audiences.

What's on offer is the widest range of productions, from the most disturbingly avant-garde to the strictly traditional. The influences from Flanders are clearly apparent in the former, with work from the likes of Jan Decorte and Jos de Pauw reflecting a new multimedia/ mixed artform approach. The French-speaking theatre, while relying heavily on the classics, presents some astonishing new

work, particularly in the smaller producing theatres. Touring shows adds depth and colour to the overall picture, and most subsidised houses bring in international productions to supplement their own work. And it's not just nearby countries such as the UK, the Netherlands, France or Germany. Serious drama from North Africa represents the concerns of the large ethnic communities in Brussels, while dance theatre from the US and musical theatre from the Far East also appear.

Belgium continues to be a hotspot for dance, particularly in its contemporary and physical form (*see p217* **Dance demons**). Dance and theatre often go hand in hand, especially at major festivals such as the three-week Kunsten Festival des Arts (*see p218* **Festival fever 3**).

Going to the theatre in Brussels is a generally laid-back affair and, the classical theatres apart, is successful at attracting a young, enthusiastic audience. Ticket prices are cheap and most venues offer concessions to students, the unemployed, the over-60s and groups. It's worth bearing in mind that there is a definite theatre and dance season, from September to June, and most venues are closed in summer.

The beautifully preserved **Théâtre Royal du Parc**. *See p215.*

ENGLISH-LANGUAGE AND AMATEUR THEATRE

A regular programme of touring English-language theatre has been visiting Brussels in recent years, from one-person shows to the Royal Shakespeare Company. These are mostly organised by promoter/producer **Theatre Factory** (www.theatrefactory.com) in association with local venues. **Théâtre 140** presents regular offbeat productions from England, Wales and Australia; the **Théâtre National** hosts touring productions from the RSC; and the **Kaaitheater** brings in the likes of the Wooster Group from the US. For details of all three theatres, *see p213*.

However, the bulk of English-language theatre is provided by the numerous amateur groups in Brussels. They are organised mainly along national lines (English, Irish, American), but there is also a group dedicated to the plays of Shakespeare and various singing and musical outfits. Between them, they produce copious amounts of theatre ranging from café entertainment to main-stage productions. As one would expect, the quality varies greatly, though there has been a recent desire to push boundaries and escape the clutches of the predictable and safe.

Groups to look out for include the **American Theatre Company** (http://freespace.virgin.net/chez.burke); **English Comedy Club** (www.angelfire.com/nb/eccbrussels); **Irish**

Theatre Group (www.irishtheatregroup.be); and the **Brussels Shakespeare Society** (www.geocities.com/theatrebe/Shakespeare.html). Three of the groups have clubbed together to buy their own premises, the Warehouse, with a small 60-seater studio space.

TICKETS AND INFORMATION

It's usually best to book tickets in advance, although there is a turn-up-on-the-night culture. Ticket agencies and online bookings are becoming more popular, though you will pay a booking fee, and the smaller theatres may also charge a credit card commission. Try **Fnac** (premium rate 0900 00600/www.fnac.be), **TicketClic** (www.ticketclic.be) or **In the Pocket** (www.inthepocket.be). Their websites list a full agenda of events for which they hold tickets. For the best listings, try the *Bulletin* each Thursday or *Le Soir* each Wednesday. For online info, check **Cultural Agenda Belgium** (www.idearts.com/agenda/index.htm).

Theatre

Venues

Beursschouwburg

37 rue de la Caserne, Lower Town (02 513 82 90/ http://beursschouwburg.vgc.be). Pré-métro Anneessens. **Box office** 10am-6pm Mon-Fri. **Tickets** €7-€10. **No credit cards. Map** p320 A4.

A temporary home for this trendy and arty institution with its programme of modern dance, theatre and music. It also has a reputation as a place to party and there will be many who can't wait for the reopening, sometime in 2003, of the funky old premises opposite the Bourse. It's famous for its annual Klinkenmunde festival, which showcases Belgian comics across the language divide.

Kaaitheater

20 square Sainctelette, St-Josse (02 201 59 59/ http://kaaitheater.vgc.be). Métro Yser. **Box office** 11am-6pm *(July, Aug* 11am-5pm) Tue-Fri; 4-6pm Sat when performance. **Tickets** €12.50-€20; €8.50 concessions. **Credit** MC, V. **Map** p318 B1.

Another theatre, another change. What used to be the generic name for two performance spaces is now the name for the main house, while its little sister down the road is called the Kaaitheaterstudio. The programming is as radical as ever, with modern dance and theatre, avant-garde music and important visiting productions. The café at street level is as trendy as can be. *See also p197.*

Koninklijke Vlaamse Schouwburg

58 rue Delanoy, Molenbeek (02 412 70 40/ www.kvs.be). Métro Zwarte Vijvers/bus 89. **Box office** noon-6pm Tue-Sat. **Credit** AmEx, MC, V.

The Royal Flemish Theatre, known (mercifully) as the KVS, is currently housed in an old bottling plant, de Bottelarij. Its original space – an exquisite imitation baroque building on rue de Laeken, built in the 1880s – is undergoing radical and extensive renovation after years of indecisiveness. Once finished, hopefully in 2003, it will be one of Brussels' most glorious theatres. In the meantime, the KVS continues to serve up a mix of the old and the new in its strange and offbeat environment.

Théâtre des Martyrs

22 place des Martyrs, Lower Town (02 223 32 08/ www.europictures.com/martyrs/). Métro/Pré-métro De Brouckère or Rogier. **Box office** 11am-6pm Tue-Fri; 2-6pm Sat. **Tickets** €13.50; €7.50 concessions. **Credit** DC, MC, V. **Map** p317 C2.

Daniel Scahaise, artistic director of resident company Théâtre en Liberté, runs a tight ship in this glorious new theatre, which was reincarnated from the old Etoile cinema. The programme is based on new adaptations of the classics; *Antigone, King Lear,* Goethe, Balzac, Camus, the list goes on. In a brave new move, two other resident companies have joined to widen and deepen the programme. This is one of the most exciting theatre spaces in Brussels, hot and ultra-cool all at the same time.

Théâtre National

Le Palace, 85 boulevard Anspach, Lower Town (02 203 53 10/www.theatrenational.be). Pré-métro Bourse. **Box office** 11am-5.30pm Tue-Sat. **Tickets** €15; €7.50-€10 concessions. **Credit** DC, MC, V. **Map** p317 B3.

The National is a bit of a misnomer as it represents only the French-speaking community. Recently evicted from its now-demolished tower-block home, the National is in residence in a converted cinema as it awaits its promised new premises. Boss Philippe Van Kessel has come in for programming criticism and it has to be said that some strange decisions are made with visiting shows. But his own productions are beautifully crafted and no one can criticise his handling of the French classics.

Théâtre 140

140 avenue Eugéne Plasky, Schaerbeek (02 733 97 08/www.theatre140.be). Bus 29, 63. **Box office** noon-6pm Mon-Fri; Sat when a performance. **Tickets** around €13; €7.50 concessions. **Credit** MC, V. **Map** p323 H2/3.

Run by the indomitable Jo Dekmine for more than 30 years, this is a theatrical institution – as the fag-burned carpet bears witness, despite the place being a no-smoking zone for the past decade. The exciting programme includes physical and innovative theatre from both Belgium and abroad, aimed largely at a young audience. The after-show bar is worth a visit in its own right.

Théâtre de Poche

1A chemin de Gymnase, Ixelles (02 649 17 27/ http://poche.cediti.be). Tram 23, 90, 93, 94. **Box office** 9am-5.30pm Mon-Sat. **Tickets** €14; €7.50-€11 concessions. **No credit cards**.

This theatre has a fiercely loyal following, partly because of its programming (hard-hitting drama), but also because of its atmosphere. Founded more than 35 years ago by Roger Domani, it has proved to be a space that always pushes limits.

Théâtre du Rideau de Bruxelles

Palais des Beaux-Arts, 23 rue Ravenstein, Upper Town (02 507 82 00/www.rideaudebruxelles.be). Métro Gare Centrale or Parc. **Box office** 11am-7pm Mon-Sat. *Phone bookings* 9am-7pm Mon-Sat. **Tickets** €17; €7.50-€10 concessions. **Credit** AmEx, DC, MC, V. **Map** p319 D4.

Théâtre des Martyrs: leading light.

Arts & Entertainment

Le BOTANIQUE

Directeur Général
Georges Dumortier

Famous Festival
"Les nuits Botanique"

Concerts

Exhibitions

Theatre

INFOTICKETS : ++ 32 2 218 37 32
www.botanique.be
rue Royale 236 - 1210 Brussels - Belgium

The Rideau ('curtain') has been resident at the Palais des Beaux-Arts since 1943. Serving the French-speaking community, it aims to present the work of contemporary international writers. In this, it is rather successful and manages to get rights to English-language translations, even if they're still appearing in London's West End. Safe, solid, modern theatre, using top Belgian performers, but few surprises.

Théâtre Royal des Galeries

32 galerie de la Roi, Lower Town (02 512 04 07/ www.theatredesgaleries.be). Métro Gare Centrale. **Box office** noon-6pm Tue-Sat. **Tickets** €12-€23. **Credit** AmEx, DC, MC, V. **Map** p317 C3.

A beautiful little theatre set in the glass-covered shopping galleries. It's most famous for its annual revue, held in the New Year: local actors sing, dance, do funny turns and tell political jokes in a true vaudevillian way, and the local audience laps it up.

Théâtre Royal du Parc

3 rue de la Loi, Upper Town (02 505 30 30/ www.parc.belgonet.com). Métro Arts-Loi or Parc. **Box office** 11am-6pm Mon-Sat. **Tickets** €5-€22; €8 concessions. **Credit** MC, V. **Map** p319 D3.

Built in 1782, this little stunner of a building is arguably the most perfectly preserved theatre in western Europe, especially after its recent renovation. The programme had a reputation for hopelessly dated boulevard comedies, but now more modern productions are entering the repertoire. Whatever, the audience still tends to be of the dark suit and fur coat variety, which often offers more shock horror values than what is seen on stage.

Théâtre de la Toison d'Or

396 galeries de la Toison d'Or, Ixelles (02 510 05 10/www.theatredelatoisondor.be). Métro Porte de Namur. **Box office** 10am-4pm Mon; 10am-6pm Tue-Fri; 2-6pm Sat. **Tickets** €18; €10-€15 concessions. **Credit** AmEx, DC, MC, V. **Map** p321 D5.

Even though serious drama does creep in, this lively little theatre has a reputation for camp comedies and musicals based on such subject matter as Barbie and Ken or the Eurovision Song Contest. It's good for a laugh, even if you don't understand a word.

Théâtre du Toone

6 impasse Schuddeveld, off 21 rue des Petits Bouchers, Lower Town (02 511 71 37). Métro/ Pré-métro De Brouckère. **Box office** noon-midnight daily. **Tickets** €10; €7 concessions. **No credit cards. Map** p317 C3.

This tiny place is an absolute must-see, having been in the Toone family for seven generations. It remains a world-famous, world-class marionette theatre with productions in the Bruxellois dialect, including such classics as *The Three Musketeers* and *Cyrano*. They also drop in a version of Hamlet in 'Brussels English', whatever that may be. The dark, atmospheric bar is equally as famous and is open all day.

Théâtre Varia

78 rue du Sceptre, Ixelles (02 640 82 58/www.varia. be). Bus 34, 80. **Box office** 2.30-6.30pm Tue-Sat. **Tickets** €13-€16; €7.50-€10 concessions. **Credit** MC, V. **Map** p324 F6.

Firmly French in nature, Théâtre Varia presents work by young Belgians as well as translations of

Patrick Rogiers' *Vésale* by the **Théâtre National.** *See p213.*

international writers in the Mamet-Pinter genre. It also has a reputation as a dance venue. Anything that is likely to create a stir is welcome here.

Théâtre de la Vie

45 rue Traversière, St-Josse (02 219 60 06/ www.theatredelavie.be). Métro Botanique. **Box office** 1-4pm Mon-Fri. **Tickets** €5-€15. **No credit cards. Map** p322 E2.

Serious drama, serious audience, serious outlook. The programme here reflects the 'theatre of life' in its most disturbing, mystifying way. Hot topics at the moment are war, refugees and asylum. It's a tiny auditorium with only about 100 seats, so reservations are recommended for this mightily controversial theatrical hotspot.

Dance

Dance, by its nature, has its own language. This could be a reason why dance in Belgium has become a free-radical artform, breaking loose from all restraints and finding its own way through the multifarious layers of provincial Belgium and multilingual Brussels. Unlike theatre, with its inherent politics of language, dance can be whatever it wants; it can be all things to all people, whatever their background, wherever they find themselves in the great language divide. It's also fair to say that the geography of Belgium makes it a natural port of call for European dancers and choreographers, attracting the likes of Maurice Béjart who created his famous school in Brussels in 1960 and stayed until 1987.

When speaking of Belgian dance, read contemporary dance. The only truly classical company is the **Royal Ballet of Flanders** in Antwerp (www.koninklijkballetvanvlaanderen. be), which produces ballet and musical theatre of outstanding quality. Surprisingly there is no ballet in Brussels, which prefers to welcome visiting groups, both national and from abroad.

Venues

The **Kaaitheater** (*see p213*), or the Kaai, as it is known, is also an important dance venue, presenting international troupes and all kinds of dance at both its main house and its studio theatre down the road.

Chapelle des Brigittines

1 petite rue des Brigittines, Lower Town (02 506 43 00). Bus 20, 48. **Box office** 10am-6pm Mon-Fri. **Tickets** €8; €5 concessions. **No credit cards. Map** p317 B4.

The Chapelle is an extraordinary space, a decommissioned church taken back to its bare arches and pillars. The uncluttered performance space provides a perfect natural backdrop for atmospheric dance. It hosts Brussels' biggest summer dance festival.

Cirque Royal

81 rue de l'Enseignement, Upper Town (02 218 20 15/www.cirque-royal.org). Métro Madou. **Box office** 10.30am-6pm Mon-Sat. **Tickets** varies. **Credit** MC, V. **Map** p319 D3.

One of the biggest spaces in Brussels, which takes in the more commercial international touring shows, such as *Stomp* and the Chippendales.

Halles de Schaerbeek

22A rue Royale Ste-Marie, Schaerbeek (02 218 21 07/ www.halles.be). Tram 90, 92, 93, 94. **Box office** 2-6pm Mon-Fri. **Tickets** varies. **Credit** MC, V. **Map** p322 E1.

The magnificent ex-agricultural hall has become an important venue for artforms across the board. Its vast open space provides an opportunity for theatre and dance companies to go to town, as was witnessed in a recent dance show that recreated a deep, dark forest with six video screens buried within.

Palais des Beaux-Arts

23 rue Ravenstein, Upper Town (box office 02 507 82 00/24hr info in French & Flemish 02 507 84 44). Métro Gare Centrale or Parc. **Box office** 11am-7pm Mon-Sat. *Phone bookings* 9am-7pm Mon-Sat. **Tickets** €10-€15. **Credit** AmEx, DC, MC, V. **Map** p319 C/D4.

This veritable institution (*see p195*) has been trying to attract new, younger audiences. One way of doing this is to host occasional modern dance companies with Belgian choreographers, such as Wim Vandekeybus. The Palais swings wildly between doing lots, then doing little, but it's always worth keeping an eye on.

Théâtre de la Monnaie

place de la Monnaie, 4 rue Léopold, Lower Town (02 229 12 11/www.lamonnaie.be). Métro/Pré-métro De Brouckère. **Box office** 11am-5.30pm Tue-Sat. **Tickets** €7.50-€85; €7.50 concessions; all unsold seats 5mins before performance. **Credit** AmEx, DC, MC, V. **Map** p317 C3.

The Royal Opera is one of the few cultural institutions in Belgium to remain federal, thereby making it a place for cross-fertilisation of the arts. It is mainly an opera venue (*see p198*), but Belgian dance supremo Anne Teresa de Keersmaeker and her company Rosas (*see p217* **Dance demons**) are based here and often première works at the theatre before going on tour.

Théâtre les Tanneurs

75 rue des Tanneurs, Lower Town (02 512 17 84/ www.lestanneurs.be). Métro Porte de Hal or Gare du Midi. **Box office** 1hr before performance. **Tickets** €7.50. **No credit cards. Map** p320 B5.

In the heart of the Marolles, Les Tanneurs has got into the hearts of a loyal crowd. This is mainly because of its radical approach to theatre and dance, and its uncompromising belief in itself as part of the immediate community. Add to that Belgian dance goddess Michèle Noiret as resident choreographer and the little theatre's appeal starts to make sense.

Dance demons

Rosas perform *Rain*.

Belgium excels in modern dance; in fact, the influence of its dance-makers on the international stage is truly astounding for such a small country. The undisputed dancing queen is **Anne Teresa De Keersmaeker**, director of the **Rosas** company (www.rosas.be/Rosas), which is resident at La Monnaie, the Brussels opera house.

De Keersmaeker's sphere of influence is based on three pillars: to intensify the relationship between dance and music; to build a repertory; to launch a dance school (PARTS – *see p218*) to replace the void left after Béjart moved to Lausanne and disbanded his school. She has succeeded in all three, and won top awards in Belgium and internationally. It's no wonder the locals are proud and await each new production with fevered anticipation.

Equally admired is the company **Charleroi Danses/Plan K** (www.charleroi-danses.be), based at the Palais des Beaux-Arts in Charleroi and led by the legendary **Frédéric Flamand**. Now 50, Flamand's motto for his life's work is 'you make your own theatre'. His company is now among the top three subsidised arts companies in Wallonia, which only goes to show the esteem in which dance is held.

There are three other main players to look out for. **Michèle Noiret**, resident choreographer at Les Tanneurs (*see p216*), worked for years with Stockhausen who used her to develop a new codified body language.

While his influence remains, they were tortuous times and she has broken from his straitjacket by developing a freer, looser style, with her dancers often moving in silence. **Wim Vandekeybus** and his company **Ultima Vez** (www.ultimavez.com) are renowned for harsh, startling imagery with no compromise. His images are symbolic, surreal, sexual; they get under the skin and literally leave an audience stunned, and the Belgians seem to adore this raw earthiness.

Jan Fabre has become something of an enigma in Belgium. His reputation has soared as a notorious choreographer, theatre director and film-maker; his is a stark, primitive style and he has grabbed performance art by the throat to expose its inner cruelty. As a freelancer, he leaves his mark across the country from the Flanders Ballet (*Swan Lake*) to his collaborations with Jan Lauwers at **Needcompany** (www.needcompany.org).

In Belgium, dance is forever moving, re-evaluating and welcoming new influences. Film, video, specially commissioned music and sound, the use of actors and singers: all are brought in to a performance to extend the experience of dancer and audience alike. Meanwhile, numerous festivals (*see p218* **Festival fever 3**) give further opportunity for younger companies to showcase their individual styles and to contribute to the ever-invigorating, ever-regenerating Belgian dance scene.

Arts & Entertainment

Festival fever 3

Belgium is home to performing arts festivals too numerous to list here. From enigmatic one-day specials to high-profile, month-long super-fests, events successfully explore the most up-to-date and avant-garde work available on the world stage.

The biggest annual happening of them all is the **Kunsten Festival des Arts** (070 22 21 99/www.kunstenfestivaldesarts.be). Staged in May, in venues around Brussels, it is a truly international festival of mammoth proportions – but insists on placing big Belgian names, such as Josse de Pauw and Frank Decortes, firmly in the spotlight. **Festival Bellone-Brigittines** (02 506 43 00/www.bellone.be) is Brussels' biggest summer dance festival, filling an uncomfortable gap when theatres close in August. There is usually an annual theme, and performances take place in the sublime Chapelle des Brigittines (*see p216*). Note that the website only goes live nearer the time.

D'ici et d'ailleurs (02 538 90 20) brings contemporary dance, workshops and classes to Brussels between March and May, while **Summer in Antwerp** (03 224 8528/www.zomervanantwerpen.be) is unashamedly Flemish in nature and makes no bones about being aimed at Antwerpenaars. Every July the city bursts to life with circus, theatre, dance and street performance.

For events in Brussels, information is available from the **TIB**; for the rest of Belgium, from the **Belgian Tourist Office** (for both, *see p303*). Also check www.idearts.com/agenda/index.htm, which has a special festivals section. If it isn't listed there, it's likely it's not happening.

Classes & institutes

Centre de Danse Choreart
985 chaussée d'Alsemberg, Uccle (02 332 13 59/ www.choreart.be). Tram 55/bus 38, 41, 43.
The biggest dance school in Brussels, ranging from tots in tutus to chaps in trainers. The one-off membership fee is €7; a week of classes costs €93-€140.

Maison du Spectacle – La Bellone
46 rue de Flandre, Lower Town (02 513 33 33/ www.bellone.be). Métro Ste-Catherine. **Open** *Library* 10am-6pm Tue; 10am-5pm Thur; 2-5.30pm Fri. Closed July. **Map** p318 B2.

An essential reference point for theatre and dance, including an archive and library and hosting many government-supported arts organisations. It's worth visiting just to see the magnificent 18th-century house in the glass-covered courtyard.

PARTS
164 avenue Van Volxem, Forest (02 344 55 98/ www.rosas.be/Parts/index.html). Bus 50/tram 52.
The Performing Arts Research and Training Studios is a joint initiative of dance company Rosas and La Monnaie. Its director is choreographer Anne Teresa De Keersmaeker, who designed the artistic and pedagogical curriculum. The school offers a full-time training in contemporary dance, is international by design and the working language is English.

Vlaams Theater Instituut
19 square Sainctelette, St-Josse (02 201 09 06/ www.vti.be). Métro Yser. **Open** *Library* 2-6pm Mon-Fri. **Map** p318 B1.
The Flemish Theatre Institute is the resource centre for the Flemish theatre in Belgium. An archive, library, study centre and centre of research, the institute is regarded as the heartbeat of the Flemish theatre arts, including dance. It also publishes its own books and articles, some of which are in English or French translation.

La Bellone: stunning archive-cum-library.

Trips Out of Town

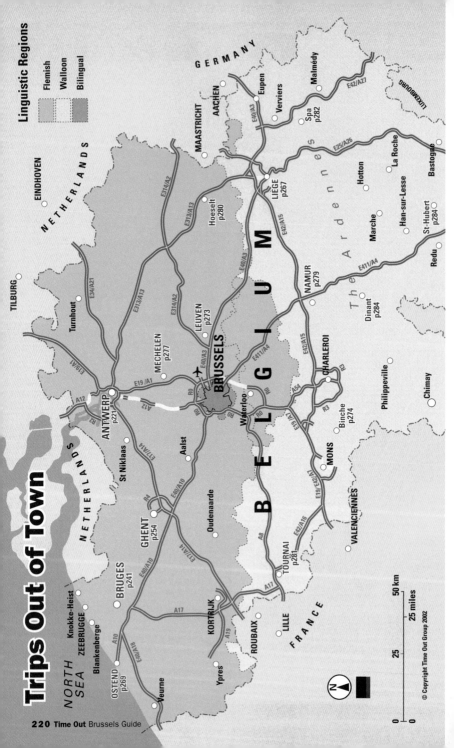

Trips Out of Town

Linguistic Regions

Flemish
Walloon
Bilingual

NORTH SEA

NETHERLANDS

GERMANY

LUXEMBOURG

FRANCE

BELGIUM

The Ardennes

EINDHOVEN

TILBURG

Turnhout

E34/A21

E314/A2

E313/A13

E19/A1

A12

ANTWERP
p221

St Niklaas

GHENT
p254

BRUGES
p241

Knokke-Heist
ZEEBRUGGE
Blankenberge

OSTEND
p269

Veurne

Ypres

KORTRIJK

ROUBAIX

LILLE

A19

A17

A10

E40/A18

E40/A10

E17/A14

R4

Oudenaarde

Aalst

A8

TOURNAI
p281

VALENCIENNES

E42/A16

E19/E42/A7

MONS

Binche
p274

Waterloo

BRUSSELS

R0

E40/A3

MECHELEN
p277

LEUVEN
p273

Hoeselt
p280

MAASTRICHT

AACHEN

Eupen

Verviers

Malmédy

E42/A27

Spa
p282

E25/A26

La Roche

Hotton

Han-sur-Lesse

St-Hubert
p284

Redu

Bastogne

Marche

Dinant
p284

NAMUR
p279

E411/A4

CHARLEROI

R3

R3

Philippeville

Chimay

LIÈGE
p267

E40/A3

E42/A15

E313/A13

E314/A2

E19/A1

E411/A4

R0

A54

E40/A3

LIÈGE
p267

E40/A3

50 km

25 miles

25

N

© Copyright Time Out Group 2002

Antwerp

The perfect destination for art lovers, fashionistas and diamond dealers.

Antwerp is firmly enjoying a second Golden Age. Not since the 16th century has the city, home to the second biggest port in Europe, enjoyed such appreciation. It's famous for its fashion; the number of high-profile home-grown designers is astounding for a city of 500,000. Then there's the huge diamond business; Antwerp is the world's hub for the uncut diamond industry. And, of course, its rich artistic and cultural heritage is evident in the historic centre and numerous museums.

The town started to develop as a significant trading city in the 12th century. As the rival port of Bruges silted up and the Flemish textile industry flourished, so Antwerp bloomed; by the mid 16th century the population was 100,000 and the city was the leading trading centre in Europe. The diamond industry was founded by Jews fleeing Portugal.

This era of prosperity came to a savage end with the Reformation and subsequent religious riots and repression; by 1589, the population had shrunk to 42,000. Although a brief period of recovery saw a cultural flowering, with Anthony Van Dyck, Jacob Jordaens and Pieter Paul Rubens working in the city, the death blow was dealt by the Treaty of Münster in 1648, closing off the River Scheldt to shipping.

Antwerp prospered again with the Industrial Revolution, to the extent that it ranked as the world's third largest port by the end of the 19th century. Being chosen as the venue for the World Fair in 1885, 1894 and 1930, and the Olympic Games in 1920, confirmed the city's major status. Although Antwerp suffered badly during the two world wars and the interim slump of the 1930s, it recovered again during the 1980s and 1990s.

These days, Antwerp's long-neglected southern side has sprung to life. The hip area around the fine arts and contemporary art museums, 't Zuid, is scattered with galleries and new nightclubs, restaurants and bars. Richard Rogers is designing the new Justitiepaleis (law courts), due to be completed in 2004. Other aspects of Antwerp life remain timeless – a Sunday walk by the River Scheldt or in one of the parks; the vibrant weekend markets and cafés near the Grote Markt; and the port around which the city grew and upon which much of its prosperity still depends. The nightlife beats Brussels too.

However, there's one huge black cloud that hovers over Antwerp as visitors soak up the city's multicultural richness. This is where the extreme-right Vlaams Blok draws the most votes; one in three Antwerp residents supported the party in elections in 2000. General hostility may not be overt – unless you try speaking French instead of English or Dutch. But the militant arm of Vlaams Blok wants Flanders to be a nation of white Flemings, with one race, one culture. A sobering thought while you're contemplating your next beer.

GETTING THERE

From Brussels there are four trains an hour from Gare du Nord, Gare Centrale or Gare du Midi. The journey takes 45 to 60 minutes.

Sightseeing

Note that all museums are closed on Mondays.

The Grote Markt & the cathedral

Antwerp's historical centre stretches all around the lovely **Grote Markt**, with its ornate guildhouses and 16th-century **Stadhuis** (Town Hall). In the centre of the market square is a 19th-century statue of **Brabo**, symbol of the city. According to legend, a giant called Druon Antigon cut off the hand of any sailor who could not pay the toll to sail on the River Scheldt. The giant carried on chopping off hands and terrifying sailors until he was defeated (and had his own hand chopped off) by a Roman, Silvius Brabo, who then became Duke of Brabant. The legend curiously fits the name of the city; with slight alteration, Antwerp translates as 'hand throwing' in Dutch.

The majestic **Onze Lieve Vrouwekathedraal** (Our Lady's Cathedral), the largest Gothic church in Belgium, is just off the square. Although a chapel was built here in the 13th century (there is evidence that there may have been an earlier church on the site), work on the cathedral itself began in the 14th century, before Antwerp's Golden Age. With trade and wealth steadily increasing over the succeeding centuries, ambitions for the cathedral grew and grandiose plans were drawn up to make it one of the most gigantic in Europe. The resulting construction was interrupted several times by fires and the city's

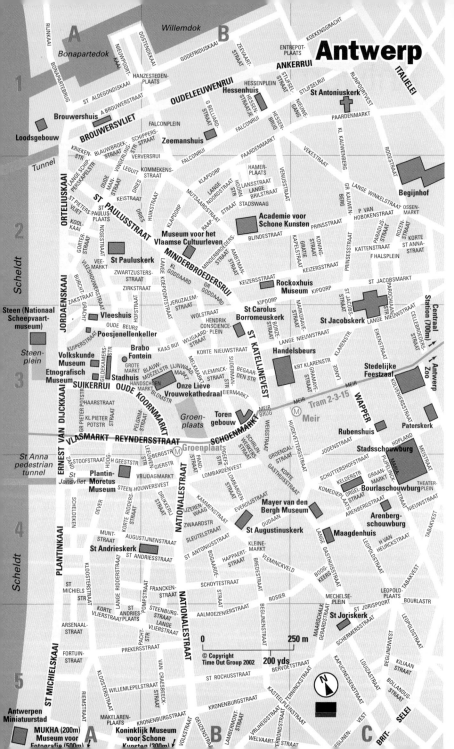

Rubenshuis: see how the old master lived. *See p226.*

changing fortunes; these same fires, iconoclastic fury and damage caused at the time of the French Revolution also resulted in the destruction of many of the cathedral's original features. A recent 25-year renovation, however, has restored much of the building's original splendour, and the white, light-filled interior now gleams.

The interior is adorned by a particularly rich collection of paintings and sculpture, the most celebrated of which are by the ubiquitous **Pieter Paul Rubens**. Many of his works in Antwerp are inspired by religion rather than Greek mythology, so those who are not great fans of the ample, sensuous ladies for which he is renowned may find themselves drawn to his work in his home town. There are four paintings by Rubens in the cathedral: *The Raising of the Cross*, *The Descent from the Cross*, *The Resurrection* and *The Assumption*. The last of these is located directly over the altar and can only be seen from a distance. Its dynamism and dazzling colours are self-evident, but it is difficult to appreciate the detail. The other paintings are more dramatic. *The Raising of the Cross* is a rich, emotional work. The real masterpiece, though, is *The Descent from the Cross*.

Glimpses of the earlier church can be seen beneath the choir, where parts of a Romanesque choir and some brick tombs are visible. Outside, the sole tower/spire rises 123 metres (404 feet) and would have been flanked by its twin had funds not dried up.

Onze Lieve Vrouwekathedraal

Handschoenmarkt (03 213 99 40/ www.dekathedraal.be). **Open** 10am-5pm Mon-Fri; 10am-3pm Sat; 1-4pm Sun. **Admission** €2; €1.50 concessions; free under-13s. **No credit cards**. **Map** p222 B3.

West of the Grote Markt

Just north-west of the Grote Markt, on Vleeshouwersstraat, is the **Vleeshuis** (Butchers' Hall), which was built as a guildhouse and meat market by the Butchers' Guild in 1503. It's a puzzling construction, in late Gothic style, with little turrets and walls that alternate red brick and white stone. Today the hall is used as a museum for archaeological finds, applied art and objects pertaining to local history. The labelling is only in Dutch.

Much of the area in the immediate vicinity of the Vleeshuis has been renovated, but the style of the new houses is insipid. The intention must have been to build in a manner that would not be at odds with the medieval and Renaissance architecture nearby. The policy is sound, but the end result makes you wish the city fathers had had the nerve for something more daring.

South of here, behind the Stadhuis, are two minor museums, the small but not uninteresting **Volkskunde Museum** (Folk Museum) and the **Etnografisch Museum** (Ethnography Museum). The latter has an excellent reputation. It's arranged on several floors (which would benefit from better

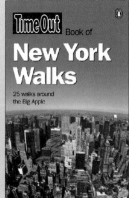

lighting), each representing a different part of the world. The top floor is generally reserved for temporary exhibitions. Documentation is in Dutch only.

A minute's walk west brings you to the river Scheldt and the **Steen**. This bulky castle once guarded the river and now houses the **Nationaal Scheepvaartmuseum** (National Maritime Museum). The Steen is almost as old as Antwerp itself and has become a symbol of the city. Built in 1200, it was originally part of the fortifications. Later it served as a prison, where inmates had to pay the guards for their stay. This meant that the wealthier prisoners lived in better conditions than poorer ones, regardless of the seriousness of their offences. For a while it served as a sawmill before being turned into a museum. Today you'll find an endearingly old-fashioned collection of maps, maritime objects and countless models of ships. Of more general interest are the old photos of Antwerp dock life. There is labelling in English. Real ships can be found in the outdoor section.

Spacious terraces by the castle allow for a quiet drink and pleasant stroll by the Scheldt.

Etnografisch Museum

19 Suikerrui (03 220 86 00/www.antwerpen.be/ cultuur/etnografisch_museum). **Open** 10am-5pm Tue-Sun. **Admission** €4; €2 concessions; free under-12s. **Credit** MC, V. **Map** p222 A3.

Steen (Nationaal Scheepvaartmuseum)

1 Steenplein (03 232 08 50/www.antwerpen.be/ cultuur/scheepvaartmuseum). **Open** 10am-5pm Tue-Sun. **Admission** €4; €2 concessions; free under-12s. **No credit cards. Map** p222 A3.

Vleeshuis

38-40 Vleeshouwersstraat (03 233 64 04/ www.antwerpen.be/cultuur/vleeshuis). **Open** 10am-5pm Tue-Sun. **Admission** €2.50; €1.50 concessions; free under-12s. Free Fri. **No credit cards. Map** p222 A3.

Volkskunde Museum

2-6 Gildekamerstraat (03 220 86 66/ www.antwerpen.be/cultuur/volkskundemuseum). **Open** 10am-5pm Tue-Sun. **Admission** €2.50; €1.25 concessions; free under-18s. **No credit cards. Map** p222 A3.

North of the Grote Markt

Between the Vleeshuis and the Napoleon Docks, near Verversrui, is what remains of the red-light district. Perhaps because it is so close to the historic centre, many of the prostitutes are being persuaded to move elsewhere. This seems a little harsh, especially since many women working in the red-light district helped save a slew of old masters when fire broke out in

1968 in **St Pauluskerk** (03 232 32 67; May-Sept 2-5pm daily; free). St Paulus' 16th-century exterior is in flamboyant Gothic style and is crowned with a late 17th-century baroque bell tower. The baroque interior contains some stunning Flemish masters (including Rubens, Jordaens, Van Dyck and David Teniers the Elder) and wonderfully carved wood panelling; there's also a new treasure room. The church stands on a lively square, not as neat, perhaps, as others in the centre, but somehow more integrated into city life.

North of here are the docks built by Napoleon in the early 19th century, but now practically at a standstill. Few ships remain and those that do are used for tours or leisure. Despite this, you will still be able to get a fair picture of what this part of the port must have been like in the 19th century. The port proper is further north and can be toured by boat (ask at the tourist office).

East of the Grote Markt

The narrow, tortuous streets behind the cathedral emerge at the baroque church of **St Carolus Borromeuskerk** (03 231 37 51; opening times vary – see schedule by door; free) on Hendrik Conscienceplein. On one side of this square – one of the prettiest in the city – stands the church, and opposite is the city library. Built for the Jesuits in the early 17th century, St Carolus is an exuberant, frothy monument to baroque excess. The façade is elaborate and ornate, with columns and statues. Rubens produced 39 widely praised ceiling paintings and three altarpieces for the church, only for the lot to go up in smoke during a fire in 1718.

Close by is the lovely Rockoxhuis Museum. Mayor Nicolaas Rockox was a friend of Rubens and his 17th-century townhouse is filled with period furnishings. It's more gallery than re-created home, though, and the main attraction is the small but perfectly formed art collection, which includes works by Matsys, Van Dyck and local boys Joachim Beuckelaer and Frans Snyders (who lived next door).

East of here on Lange Nieuwstraat is another church worth a visit: **St Jacobskerk**. As you walk towards it from a distance the church looks hefty and impressive, but the closer you get the more it seems to diminish. Little houses completely surround it, barely making space for the main and side entrances. The interior is decorated in heavy baroque style, reflecting the fact that this was a wealthy district of Antwerp and the parishioners made sure the church reflected their status. It is as Rubens' burial place that St Jacob's is best known. The artist painted the work that hangs over his tomb, *Our Lady Surrounded by Saints,*

Trips Out of Town

Master class

The Royal Museum of Fine Arts is the focal point of southern Antwerp, and a great place to get your teeth into some outstanding Flemish painting, from 1350 to the present.

Start with the 15th-century Flemish Primitives, including Jan van Eyck, Rogier van der Weyden, Dirk Bouts and Hans Memling. **Jan van Eyck** improved significantly on old oil painting techniques, moving away from the limitations of tempera – hence the glowing colours of his paintings. Look out for his unfinished picture of St Barbara. There are works from the same period by Simone Martini, Antonello da Messina and France's Jean Fouquet.

The 16th century is often considered a period of transition, probably because a number of different styles were developing at the same time. There are instances of mannerism in the work of **Bernard van Orley** (see his *Last Judgement* and *Seven Acts of Mercy*), while **Quentin Matsys** (see his *Entombment of Christ*) is clearly influenced by the Italian Renaissance. Note the use of colours and light, and the minute attention to detail. The influence of Michelangelo can be seen clearly in the work of **Frans Floris**, especially in his portrayal of the human body. The museum contains no original works by **Pieter Bruegel the Elder**, but there are several paintings by his school. These works, like those of Bruegel himself, are fascinating for their details of contemporary working-class life. Many are landscapes.

The most stunning section is the one devoted to the 17th century, with marvellous paintings by Rubens, Jordaens and Van Dyck. The **Rubens** works are mostly religious, though *Venus Frigida* is a notable exception. The idea that hunger and cold cool the fire of love is clearly reflected in the attitude of the goddess. *Adoration of the Magi* (*pictured*) is another impressive work. Theatrical, mobile and expressive, it is a beautiful depiction of baroque art. Lovers of historical detail should study *The Disbelief of St Thomas*. The painting was ordered by Nicolaas Rockox, mayor of Antwerp in Rubens' time, and the portraits on the side panels of the triptych are of Rockox and his wife.

Jacob Jordaens' compositions are less dramatic. The colours are darker and the movement less dynamic, but his subjects convey a great generosity and sensuality. The range of his subjects is also more varied. His themes are often joyous, sometimes even uproarious (see his famous *As the Old Sang, the Young Play Pipes*), apparently like the artist himself. **Anthony Van Dyck's** work is less vigorous and flamboyant than that of either Jordaens or Rubens. The emotion is more subdued and contained, but also more intimate. This can best be seen in works such as *Portrait of the Painter Marten Pepyn*. Van Dyck spent a lot of time in England, where he was the court painter of Charles I.

The 18th-century section seems a little drab in comparison to the preceding century. Many artists were happy to follow in Rubens' footsteps, and there was little innovation, apart from the growing importance of historical and flower painting. In the 19th century Belgian artists found fresh subject matter in their country's newly acquired independence, and several works in the museum depict significant historical events. Meanwhile, artists such as **Joseph Stevens** and **Constantin Meunier** were depicting scenes of daily life. Antwerp-born **Henri de Braekeleer** is an important figure of the 19th century, and the city is one of his recurrent themes. His realism is delicate and moving.

specifically for this purpose. St George is believed to be a self-portrait, while the Virgin is a portrait of Isabella Brant, Rubens' first wife. Mary Magdalene is a portrait of Hélène Fourment, his second wife.

Not far south of the church is one of the city's major tourist draws, the **Rubenshuis**, home to the artist for most of his life. With works displayed in the **Koninklijk Museum voor Schone Kunsten** (Museum of Fine Arts; *see above* **Master class**), as well as in several city churches, and with a whole souvenir industry dedicated to him, Pieter Paul Rubens

is unavoidable in Antwerp. Born in 1577, he began his career in the city, where he became an apprentice to several outstanding artists before travelling to Italy in 1600 to study the Italian masters. He bought this house in 1611, shortly after his return from Italy, and soon after being appointed city painter by Archduke Albrecht and Isabella.

It's wise to come early if you want to avoid the tour parties. Speed through the ugly modern ticket office outside the house and plunge into the wonderful interior. This is one of the few baroque buildings in Antwerp, which, in

The museum's extensive collection of paintings by **James Ensor** gives an overview of the artist's development. His first works, among them *Le Salon Bourgeois* and *La Mangeuse d'Huître*, are influenced by the French Impressionists and by Turner. His more disturbing and impressive works came later on, when his world becomes filled with skeletons, masks and puppets. These paintings are haunting, vivid and occasionally grotesque.

The works of **Rik Wouters**, exhibited in the same room, are less disturbing. Filled with sunlight, his colours are more those of Fauvism than of Impressionism. He is influenced by Cézanne, but his use of rich reds and blues puts one in mind of Matisse. Wouters was painting during World War I, when he saw active service and lost his sight. Strangely, his suffering rarely surfaces in his paintings and sculptures. Even *Rik au*

Bandeau Noir, though clearly sadder than the festive *La Repasseuse*, has a definite optimistic quality.

The modern section of the museum includes works by internationally renowned artists such as Modigliani and Chagall, and paintings by the Belgian Surrealists **René Magritte** and **Paul Delvaux**. There are sculptures by **Ossip Zadkine**, and elegant works by **George Minne**.

A section is also devoted to Flemish expressionism, the Cobra movement and the *groupe zero*.

Koninklijk Museum voor Schone Kunsten

1-9 Leopold de Waelplaats (03 238 78 09/ www.antwerpen.be/cultuur/kmska). **Open** 10am-5pm Tue-Sun. **Admission** €5; €4 concessions; free under-18s. Free Fri. **No credit cards**.

Rubens' time, and much to his regret, was predominantly Gothic. The house passed through several owners before the city of Antwerp bought it. It has been fully renovated and the garden entirely reconstructed. Much of the furniture dates from the 17th century but was not originally in the house.

Highlights include the semicircular gallery (based on the Pantheon in Rome) where Rubens displayed his collection of classical sculpture, and his spacious studio, overlooked by a mezzanine, where his work could be admired by potential buyers. Rubens was an exceptionally

prolific painter (knocking out around 2,500 works in his lifetime), chiefly because he didn't do all the painting himself. Canvases were mass-produced by staff in his workshop; he would direct proceedings and add the necessary key brushstrokes. With pupils such as Jordaens and Van Dyck, he could afford to limit the extent of his contribution to attentive supervision. The only disappointment in the house is that there aren't more Rubens paintings on display. Look out though for an endearing self-portrait (from c1630) and a later, more anxious-looking one in the studio.

Rockoxhuis Museum

12 Keizerstraat (03 201 92 50). **Open** 10am-5pm
Tue-Sun. **Admission** €2.50; €1.25 concessions; free
under-12s. Free Fri. **No credit cards. Map** p222 B2.

Rubenshuis

*9-11 Wapper (03 201 15 55/www.antwerpen.be/
cultuur/rubenshuis).* **Open** 10am-5pm Tue-Sun.
Admission €4; €2.50 concessions; free under-18s.
Free Fri. **No credit cards. Map** p222 C3.

St Jakobskerk

Lange Nieuwstraat (03 232 10 32). **Open** *Nov-Mar*
9am-noon Mon-Sat. *Apr-Oct* 2-5pm Mon-Sat.
Admission €2; €1.50 concessions. **No credit
cards. Map** p222 C2/3.

South of the Grote Markt

The south side of Antwerp is home to the
city's older residential districts and contains
many of its best museums. A few minutes'
walk south of the Grote Markt, close to the
appealing **Vrijdagmarkt** square, is the
Plantin-Moretus Museum, home of printing
pioneer Christophe Plantin. According to
legend, French-born bookbinder Christophe
Plantin was mistakenly injured in a brawl in
1555 and, with the hush money he was paid,
bought his first printing press. The business
he was to build in this immense 16th-century
house became the largest printing and
publishing concern in the Low Countries
(with 22 presses), and the house became a
magnet for intellectuals.

Plantin printed many of the greatest works
of his day, including an eight-volume polyglot
Bible. Here you can discover all the intricacies
and difficulties of printing, and examine the

Centraal Station. *See p230.*

huge presses, a beautiful proofreading room
and a foundry. If the technical aspects of
printing do not fascinate you, the house itself
probably will. There are some fine paintings,
Mercator maps, Plantin's Biblia Regia, one of
the rare Gutenberg Bibles and other invaluable
manuscripts. When Plantin died in 1579 the
business was taken over by his son-in-law Jan
Moretus and run by his family until 1865 when
the city authorities bought the ailing business.
In 1877 they converted it into a museum.

Equally enjoyable is the idiosyncratic **Mayer
Van den Bergh Museum**. A worthwhile five
or so minutes' walk south-east from the centre,
this thoroughly engaging display of the private
collection of Fritz Mayer Van den Bergh is
housed in a re-created 16th-century townhouse.
Purpose-built in 1904 by Mayer van den
Bergh's mother after the early death of her son
(aged 33), this immensely charming place
boasts as its prize exhibit Pieter Bruegel the
Elder's astonishing *Dulle Griet* ('Mad Meg'), a
Bosch-like allegory of a world turned upside
down. Look out also for a powerful crucifixion
triptych by Quentin Matsys, works by Bouts,
van Orley, Cranach and Mostaert and some
beautiful 15th-century carved wooden angels.

On the same street is the **Maagdenhuis**, a
one-time foundling hospital that now contains
a small art collection and, wait for it, Belgium's
largest collection of medieval porridge bowls.

The city's major museums are a few
kilometres further south (tram 8 from
Groenplaats). It's a journey that lovers of art
should make, especially to the **Koninklijk
Museum voor Schone Kunsten**, which is
outstanding – *see p226* **Master class**.
Antwerp is also where it's at for modern art.
Belgium's top artists, including Panamarenko
(*see p229*), choose Antwerp as their home, and
the city has a brash, optimistic attitude towards
encouraging new talent. The high-profile
contemporary art museum **MUHKA** (Museum
voor Hedendaagse Kunst van Antwerpen)
displays works from the 1970s onwards. The
focus is on temporary exhibitions, and the
strength of the museum lies in the way in
which space is used in the light-flooded, mostly
white-painted rooms. The result is a relaxed
atmosphere, ideal for contemplating works that
are not always effortlessly accessible.

Meanwhile, fashion-followers will adore
MoMu (ModeMuseum), the new museum
devoted to design, located in the beautiful late
19th-century ModeNatie complex. An ambitious
project that has dragged on for years, it is
finally due to open in autumn 2002. The
complex is home to the Flanders Fashion
Institute and the fashion department of the
Royal Academy of Fine Arts. Contemporary

fashion and a historic costume and lace collection are central to the project. It is far more than just a museum, with a trendy café-resto, library and workshops.

Photography buffs should head to the **Museum voor Fotografie**, currently under renovation – it will reopen in 2003. A new wing designed by architect Georges Baines contains large exhibition halls and houses the Antwerp Film Museum. The museum's photography collection is one of the most important in Europe, for equipment and images. It takes an interactive approach with workshops, temporary exhibitions, film performances and lectures – and there's a great café.

MoMu
9-12 Drukkerijstraat (entrance on Nationalestraat) (03 385 82 33/www.momu.be). **Open** 10am-6pm Tue, Wed, Fri-Sun; 10am-9pm Thur. **Admission** €5; €3 concessions. Free Fri. **No credit cards**.

Maagdenhuis
33 Lange Gasthuisstraat (03 223 56 10). **Open** 10am-5pm Mon, Wed-Fri; 1-5pm Sat, Sun. **Admission** €2.50. Free Fri. **No credit cards**. Map p222 C4.

Mayer Van den Bergh Museum
19 Lange Gasthuisstraat (03 232 42 37/ www.antwerpen.be/cultuur/museum_mvdb). **Open** 10am-5pm Tue-Sun. **Admission** €4; €2 concessions; free under-18s. **Credit** MC, V. Map p222 C4.

MUHKA
16-30 Leuvenstraat (03 238 59 60/www.muhka.be). **Open** 10am-5pm Tue-Sun. **Admission** €4; €2.50 concessions. **Credit** V.

Museum voor Fotografie
47 Waalsekaai (03 242 93 00/www.provant.be/ fotomuseum). **Open** 10am-5pm Tue-Sun. Closed until 2003. **Admission** free.

Plantin-Moretus Museum
22 Vrijdagmarkt (03 221 14 50/03 221 14 51/ www.antwerpen.be/cultuur/museum_plantinmoretus). **Open** 10am-5pm Tue-Sun. **Admission** €4; €2 concessions; free under-12s. Free Fri. **No credit cards**. Map p222 A4.

The left bank

South of the Steen, in St Jansvliet, is the entrance to the **St Anna pedestrian tunnel**, which connects right with left bank. Wooden escalators take you underground, then it's a ten-minute walk to the other side of the river. Antwerp was built mainly on the right bank of the Scheldt and the left bank is consequently not particularly lively. The 20th-century architect Le Corbusier had an ambitious plan to move all the administration buildings to the

Panamarenko

Antwerp is home to one of the most revered – and eccentric – contemporary artists. Panamarenko, visionary artist-technologist (his term), was born in the city in 1940, studied at the Antwerp Académie des Beaux-Arts (though he spent most of his time at the local science library or at the cinema) and has lived and worked there ever since. His first exhibition was at Antwerp's avant-garde Wide White Space Gallery in 1966, the year in which he adopted the pseudonym Panamarenko, supposedly an abbreviation of 'Pan American Airlines Company'. His name, like his artworks, reflects his life-long obsession with flight, space, energy and the force of gravity. More machines than sculptures, his creations are the bastard offspring of a bizarre marriage between science and art, engineering and aesthetics.

The early *Das Flugzeug* (1968) is typical: a hybrid helicopter-cum-aeroplane-cum-bicycle, it's huge and insect-like, both ungainly and incredibly delicate. It's a flying machine, but one that will never fly. As is the gallery-sized *Aeromodeller* (1969-71), a zeppelin made of transparent PVC with a battered, silver wickerwork gondola.

Whether racing cars, self-propulsion devices, pedalos, submarines or spaceships – the marvellously named *Bing of the Ferro Lusto* (1999) is straight out of the iconography of 1950s sci-fi comics – all Panamarenko's works have a home-made quality; it's part of their charm. More the product of the garden-shed inventor than the 21st-century scientist, held together by rivets and elastic bands and patched with tape, they exhibit a sense of humour that is hugely appealing.

Unfortunately, it's hard to find Panamarenko's work in his native city – but this will change at the end of June 2002 with the opening of the new **Antwerp Airship Building** (2 Karolgeertstraat; 03 216 30 47; June-Aug 10am-6pm Mon, Wed-Sun). Housed in a huge old electricity station near the ring road (take tram 10 or 24), it will be a workspace for Panamarenko in the winter, then open to the public in the summer to show his new creations. SMAK in Ghent (*see p257*) also has some major works, including the *Aeromodeller*, but they're not always on show.

left bank, thinking that this was the only way in which it might have a chance to develop. The project was turned down and the left bank never did pick up.

Nevertheless, the left bank can claim the only beach in Antwerp, the **St Anna Strand**. The original beach was dug up because of fears of pollution from the river, but in recent years Antwerpers have rediscovered the strand. The beach now gets packed out in fine weather, although, despite the reappearance of some fish in the river, it is still considered unsafe to swim in the Scheldt. The beach is a good 15 minutes' walk north once you reach the west bank.

Centraal Station, the diamond district & the Meir

Antwerp's striking **Centraal Station** stands about two kilometres east of the centre. Built in 1905 by Louis Delacenserie in iron and glass, with an impressive dome, majestic stairs and lashings of lavish gold decoration, it's a surprising and splendidly ostentatious construction. The extensive **Antwerp Zoo** is handily located bang next to the station. It's Belgium's major zoo, and one of Europe's oldest (opened in 1843). The original architecture is more impressive than the animals' living quarters; check out the giraffe house.

Antwerp's **diamond district** begins on Pelikaanstraat on the west side of the station. This predominantly Jewish area has the highest concentration of jewellers in the country. The Bourse aux Diamants in Pelikaanstraat is heavily guarded. The **Provinciaal Diamantmuseum** has moved from Lange Herentalsestraat to an impressive square facing Centraal Station. Visitors are taken on an interactive tour showing how rough diamonds become polished and end up as gorgeous jewellery. There are three floors of treasures to explore too. The run-down area itself glitters rather less than the stones in which it trades, and has a highly visible police presence.

The **Meir**, Antwerp's main shopping street, takes you from the station to the historic centre. Don't let the window displays cause you to miss more remarkable 19th-century buildings, such as the art deco **Boerentoren**, one of Europe's first skyscrapers. Just to the north, off the Meir, the **Handelsbeurs** (Stock Exchange) is on the site of one of the oldest stock exchanges in Europe. The original building was replaced in the 16th century; the current structure dates from 1872.

Further afield, it's well worth getting out to the splendid **Middleheim Open-air Sculpture Museum**. There are works by major sculptors from Rodin to the present day, including Belgian artists Panamarenko and Vermeiren. The biennial summer exhibition of international sculpture should not be missed; contact the tourist office for details.

Antwerp Zoo

26 Koningin Astridplein (03 202 45 40/ www.zooantwerpen.be). **Open** *July, Aug* 10am-7pm daily. *Sept-June* 10am-6pm daily. **Admission** €13; €8.50 concessions; free under-3s. **Credit** AmEx, MC, DC, V.

Middelheim Open-air Sculpture Museum

61 Middelheimlaan (03 828 13 50/ www.antwerpen.be/cultuur/museum_middelheim). **Open** *June, July* 10am-9pm Tue-Sun. *May, Aug* 10am-8pm Tue-Sun. *Apr, Sept* 10am-7pm Tue-Sun. *Oct-Mar* 10am-5pm Tue-Sun. **Admission** free. About 5km (3 miles) from the city centre. You can catch tram 7 or 15 then walk 1km; or bus 18 or 32; or – easiest of all – take a taxi.

Provinciaal Diamantmuseum

19-23 Koningin Astridplein (03 202 48 90/ www.diamantmuseum.be). **Open** *May-Oct* 10am-6pm daily. *Nov-Apr* 10am-7pm daily. **Admission** €5; €3 concessions; free under-18s. Free Fri. **Credit** MC, V.

Tourist information

For information on Antwerp's many churches, visit **www.topa.be**.

Toerisme Antwerpen

13 Grote Markt (03 232 01 03/fax 03 231 19 37/ www.visitantwerpen.be). **Open** 9am-6pm Mon-Sat; 9am-5pm Sun. **Map** p222 A3.
If you want information about Antwerp province, try the tourist office at 16 Koningin Elisabethlei (03 240 63 73/fax 03 240 63 83/www.tpa.be).

Accommodation

Finding somewhere to stay isn't usually a problem, though it's a good idea to book ahead for July and August. The tourist office (*see above*) offers a free accommodation booking service (by phone or in person), and often can get cheaper rates than you would directly from the hotel. Check its website for hotel details.

Astrid Park Plaza

7 Koningin Astridplein, 2018 Antwerp (03 203 12 73/fax 03 203 12 75/www.parkplazaww.com). **Rates** single €115; double €130. **Credit** AmEx, DC, MC, V.
A relatively recent addition to the square outside Centraal Station, the exterior of the Astrid Park Plaza has all the charm of a construction made out of Lego. Fortunately, the inside is much easier on the eye, and the view of the city from the Astrid Lounge

is certainly impressive. Among the many facilities are a pool, sauna and fitness room, a bar, café and restaurant, and Nintendos in all rooms.

Diamond Princess

2 St Laureiskaai (Bonapartedok), 2000 Antwerp (03 227 08 15/fax 03 227 16 77). **Rates** single €57; double €77-€114; suite €139. **Credit** AmEx, DC, MC, V. **Map** p222 A1.

This five-deck 'boatel' has 57 luxuriously furnished rooms, all with bathroom, phone, colour TV and minibar. There's also a restaurant (La Combuse), a 'beach deck' (terrace), bar, library and disco.

Greta Stevens – Miller's Dream

35 Molenstraat, 2018 Antwerp (03 259 15 90/ fax 03 259 15 99/http://users.pandora.be/molenaars droom). **Rates** *Mon-Thur, Sun* single €36; double €47. *Fri, Sat* single/double €59. **No credit cards**.

Greta Stevens' beautiful colonial-style house is located near the town park, just to the south of Britselei. The three spacious B&B rooms are decorated with modern art and all have a bathroom, TV and telephone. Two of the rooms look out on to an interior courtyard, while the third has a balcony overlooking the street. Non-smokers are preferred.

Hilton

Groenplaats, 2000 Antwerp (03 204 12 12/fax 03 204 12 13/www.hilton.com). **Rates** single/double €270-€295. **Credit** AmEx, DC, MC, V. **Map** p222 B3.

The sand-coloured Antwerp Hilton takes up nearly an entire side of this pleasant, busy square, a minute's walk from the Grote Markt. The hotel offers all the facilities and services associated with the chain (including a Nintendo in every room), but with a lot more charm than one normally expects.

Hotel Prinse

63 Keizerstraat, 2000 Antwerp (03 226 40 50/ fax 03 225 11 48/www.hotelprinse.be). **Rates** single €102; double €119; suite €137. **Credit** AmEx, DC, MC, V. **Map** p222 C2.

The historic exterior of this 16th-century private house hides a striking modern interior and a lovely courtyard. Not far from the main shopping and sightseeing area, the four-star hotel has 35 rooms (all en suite). Breakfast is included in the price.

Hotel Rubens

29 Oude Beurs, 2000 Antwerp (03 222 48 48/ fax 03 225 19 40/hotel.rubens@glo.be). **Rates** single €123-€155; double €185-€445. **Credit** AmEx, DC, MC, V. **Map** p222 A3.

Situated near the Grote Markt, the privately owned Rubens has its own parking, and all rooms come with a minibar, cable TV, phone and modem. There's nothing particularly special about the decor, but there's a lovely garden and, if it's space you're after, try the massive Presidential Suite.

Hotel Villa Mozart

3 Handschoenmarkt, 2000 Antwerp (03 231 30 31/ fax 03 231 56 85/www.wanadoo.be/villa.mozart). **Rates** *Mon-Thur* single €132; double €170;

suite €236-€268. *Fri-Sun* single €92; double €96; suite €199-€210. **Credit** AmEx, DC, MC, V. **Map** p222 A/B3.

The 25 luxury rooms and suites of the Villa Mozart are all decorated in Laura Ashley style and have a phone, radio and TV. Hotel services include a sauna, conference room, bar and babysitting.

New International Youth Hostel

256 Provinciestraat, 2018 Antwerp (03 230 05 22/ fax 03 281 09 33). **Rates** dorm €13; single €26; double €40-€50; quad €65-€77. **No credit cards**.

A ten-minute walk south of the station, this hostel has only 30 rooms so booking is essential. Rooms are for one, two, four or eight people; six have their own bathroom. There's also a TV room, bar and restaurant. Price includes breakfast.

'T Sandt

17 Zand, 2000 Antwerp (03 232 93 90/fax 03 232 56 13/www.hotels-belgium.com/antwerp/tsandt.htm). **Rates** *Mon-Thur* single €155; double €170; suite €205-€270. *Fri-Sun* single/double €130; suite €170-€220. **Credit** AmEx, DC, MC, V. **Map** p222 A4.

A one-time customs house, soap factory and fruit importing company office, now converted into an immensely classy hotel. All rooms in this neo-rococo 19th-century building by the Scheldt are suites (some are duplexes) and very spacious; each is decorated in a different style. An Italianate garden and a rooftop terrace bar are further attractions.

Vandepitte B&B

49 Britselei bte 6, 2000 Antwerp (tel/fax 03 288 66 95). **Rates** €55-€87. **No credit cards**. **Map** p222 C5.

It may be located at the top of an unprepossessing modern block on the busy inner ring road, a good ten- to -15-minute walk from the centre, but this is about the most elegant and stylish B&B you'll ever stay in. Two of the three rooms are relatively small (although one does have a bathroom to die for), but it's the penthouse that really steals the show – with black stone floors, a large terrace, views over Antwerp on two sides, a flash stereo, TV and video, ethnic art aplenty and bags of space. Breakfast is equally impressive.

Vlaamse Jeugdherberg op Sinjoorke

2 Eric Sasselaan, Antwerp (03 238 02 73/fax 03 248 19 32). **Rates** double €17.50-€20 per person; triple/quad €12.50-€15 per person. **Credit** MC, V.

For the seriously skint traveller, this hostel in a park has dead-cheap rooms, 3km (2 miles) from the city centre (tram 2 or bus 27). Showers and toilets are shared and there's a communal TV, table tennis and two conference rooms.

De Witte Lelie

16-18 Keizerstraat, 2000 Antwerp (03 226 19 66/ fax 03 234 00 19/www.dewittelelie.be). **Rates** single €170; double €225-€400; suite €235-€300. **Credit** AmEx, DC, MC, V. **Map** p222 C2.

An absolute stunner. The building may be 17th-century, but the interior, renovated in 1993, is utterly contemporary. Expect good-sized rooms, oceans of white, lashings of low-key luxury and a generous breakfast (included in the price). The hotel's position is perfect for exploring the trendy part of town.

Eating & drinking

Restaurants

Dock's Café
7 Jordaenskaai (03 226 63 30). **Open** noon-2.30pm, 6.30pm-midnight Mon-Fri; 6.30pm-midnight Sat; noon-2.30pm, 6-11pm Sun. **Main courses** €30-€35. **Credit** AmEx, DC, MC, V. **Map** p222 A2/3.
Close to the waterfront, a flamboyant interior and Mediterranean-style cuisine with plenty of fish dishes. Booking essential.

'T Fornuis
24 Reyndersstraat (03 233 62 70). **Open** noon-2pm, 7-9.30pm Mon-Fri. **Main courses** €100-€125. **Credit** AmEx, DC, MC, V. **Map** p222 A/B3.
Booking is advisable for this extremely popular two-storey corner restaurant. The interior is classic rustic Flemish, while the food is French-influenced but adapted to modern tastes. The clientele is business-oriented and owner and chef Johan Segers doesn't stick to a menu.

Grand Café Leroy
49 Kasteelpleinstraat (03 226 11 99). **Open** 11.30am-10.30pm Mon-Fri; 6-11.30pm Sat; 6-10.30pm Sun. **Main courses** €20-€40. **Credit** AmEx, DC, MC, V. **Map** p222 B/C5.

Sir Anthony Van Dyke. *See p234.*

This café offers an out-of-the-ordinary mix of fusion cuisine served at high speed. In summer, the attractive inner courtyard is a popular spot.

De Kaai
94 Rijnkaai, Hangar 26 (03 233 25 07). **Open** 10am-midnight daily. *Food served* noon-10pm daily. **Main courses** €30-€53. **Credit** MC, V. **Map** p222 A1.
A former dockside warehouse on the River Scheldt that is now a hip café-resto big on atmosphere rather than the food. The place truly comes in to its own when the tables are moved back and the dancing begins (after 11.30pm Thur-Sat). Passable pasta dishes and steaks are on the menu.

Kei Kei Oriental Canteen
34-36 Minderbroedersrui (03 213 22 26). **Open** 6-10pm Tue-Sat; noon-2pm, 6-10pm Fri. **Main courses** €11.50-€15.50. **Set menu** €22.50. **Credit** MC, V. **Map** p222 B2.
Kei Kei offers a range of noodle soups and fried or steamed rice dishes in a clean, minimalist environment, and takes in the cuisines of a number of Far Eastern countries. Clients tend to be young, trendy and health-conscious.

La Luna
177 Italiëlei (03 232 23 44). **Open** noon-2pm, 7-10pm Tue-Fri; 7-10pm Sat. **Main courses** €20-€25. **Credit** AmEx, DC, MC, V. **Map** p222 C1.
A fabulous hip interior, a joint effort by architect Jean de Meulder and fashion designer Jo Wyckmans, and fabulous food. An upmarket brasserie with simple cuisine and a vibrant ambience.

De Matelote
9 Haarstraat (03 231 32 07). **Open** noon-2pm, 7-10pm Mon-Fri; 7-10pm Sat. **Main courses** €75. **Credit** AmEx, DC, MC, V. **Map** p222 A3.
Near the Grote Markt, De Matelote ('the sailor') is a first-rate seafood restaurant. The fish is unfailingly fresh and of the best quality: it's nigh on impossible to make a poor choice.

Pottenbrug
38 Minderbroedersrui (03 231 51 47). **Open** noon-2pm, 6.30-10pm Tue-Thur; noon-2pm, 6.30-11pm Fri, Sat. **Main courses** €15-€18. **Credit** AmEx, MC, V. **Map** p222 B2.
A beautiful restaurant with an old-time Parisian bistro atmosphere, Pottenbrug has been serving simple yet classy food for more than two decades. Popular with artists and local workers, its cuisine is invariably fresh and tasty. Go at lunchtime for its excellent set menus.

Santatsu Yamayu
19 Ossenmarkt (03 234 09 49). **Open** noon-2pm, 6.30-10.30pm Tue-Sat; 6.30-10.30pm Sun. **Main courses** €25-€40. **Set menus** €43-€48. **Credit** AmEx, DC, MC, V. **Map** p222 C2.
A small but very good Japanese restaurant specialising in sushi and sashimi, but also serving soba and udon noodles. The excellent lunch menu offers a

Culture clubs

Without doubt, Antwerp is party city. The nightlife hub of Belgium has built its club scene on the thriving fashion and gay cultures, with a touch of Flemish ingenuity. Boldness rules. The vibe is far closer in feel to Amsterdam – or even London – than sleepy old Brussels. Twice a year, the city comes alive with **Antwerp Is Burning** (www.antwerpisburning.be), a one-night seven-club extravanganza, one entrance ticket allowing access to the free shuttle between venues. August in nearby Linkeroever sees **Clubland** (www.clubland-festival.be), an enormous event assembling six of Europe's biggest clubs (Berlin's Tresor, Amsterdam's Chemistry and so on) in an open field outside town. For the rest of the year, check out **www.noctis.com** for updated information. Also, **5 voor 12** (www.5voor12.com) stages major club events across Belgium, such as the irregular but kicking **Night Cruiser** at De Cinema (12 Lang Brilstraat; 03 226 49 63).

The two main areas in town for nightlife are t'Zuid, the former docklands south of the centre; and Schipperskwartier, the red-light district just north of town by the docks. The main club in the latter area – in fact, anywhere in Antwerp – is the **Café d'Anvers** (15 Verversrui; 03 226 38 70/www.cafe-d-anvers.be – pictured). More a legend than a club, the red-brick café was first a church, then a cinema, a warehouse and a ballroom before its transformation to a kicking deep house club in the early 1990s. They all started here: Koenie, Poltergeist, Steve Cop, Danny V and Pierre. Then came Cop's brother Kenneth, Smos & Baby B, Stéphanie and more recently Prinz or Isabel, the new rising name of the Belgian house scene. Expect uplifting house Thursday through Saturday, courtesy of the artistic direction of Ben Biets. The atmosphere is enhanced by omnipresent brick and iron, tanned wood, thick curtains, elegant armchairs, and a well-worn dancefloor towered over by a vertiginous ceiling.

Towards the docks, 200 metres along, is the Friday-only **Fill Collins** club (11-13 Lange Schipperskapelstraat; 03 213 05 55/www.fillcollinsclub.com). A huge place, decked out as if by a hedonist Captain Nemo, the Fill Collins is the brainchild of Peter Decuypere, also behind the Fuse in Brussels and I Love Techno. Built on the reputation of Studio Brussels' Jan van Biesen, these

days it's not about star names but solid resident DJs (Olivier Abbeloos, Deviera, Dee & Gee, percussive support by Felipe Cortez). On Saturdays, it hosts **Red & Blue** (www.redandblue.be), the biggest gay dance club in the Benelux (see p237). Just a little north is **Kaaiman** (57 Napelstraat; 0486 47 70 33/www.kaaiman.be), which attacts a regular alternative crowd to its simple drum 'n' bass and house parties.

Although the t'Zuid scene is considerably worse for the recent closure of Le Zillion (www.zillion.be), the **Club Geluk** (6 Luikstraat; www.clubgeluk.com) makes up for it with refined DJs Mo & Benoelie, Timaxx and Stéphanie playing house and breakbeats in a cellar done out '70s-style. In town, two steps from the railway station, there's the funk and R&B of **Club Flavers** (8 Anneessenstraat; 0495 456 512), featuring the DJ mastery of Twice and Master Lee.

Two clubs outside town are also worthy of note. The legendary **La Rocca** (384 Antwerpsesteenweg; 03 489 17 67/ www.larocca.be) in Lier, 15 kilometres (nine miles) south-east, attracts a more commercial crowd from Friday through Sunday. **Cherry Moon** (144 Gentsesteenweg; 09 349 01 38/ www.cherrymoon.be), 25 kilometres (15 miles) south-west in Lokeren, is a vast techno-trance club on Fridays and Saturdays.

Trips Out of Town

good choice of dishes. The look is sharply modern, with a bar and counter in the middle of the room. Reservations are recommended in the evening.

Sir Anthony Van Dyck
16 Oude Koornmarkt (03 231 61 70). **Open** sittings noon & 6.30pm Mon-Sat. **Main courses** €15-€21. **Set menu** €40. **Credit** AmEx, DC, MC, V. **Map** p222 A/B3.
A wonderful, exclusive restaurant, owned by an antiquarian and displaying impeccable taste. Note that the classic food is served at two sittings, but you can linger in the bar. Booking essential.

Spaghettiworld
66 Oude Koornmarkt (03 234 38 01). **Open** noon-3pm, 5-11pm Tue-Sun. **Main courses** €7.50-€12.50. **Credit** MC, V. **Map** p222 A/B3.
An artsy coffeehouse/restaurant/meeting place for Antwerp's bright young things. Acid house, trip hop and soul bubble out from the speakers as diners tuck into their pasta.

Table D'Anvers
43 Vlaamse Kaai (03 248 51 51). **Open** noon-2.30pm, 6-11pm Tue-Fri; 6-11pm Sat. **Main courses** €12.50-€20. **Set menus** €30-€42.50. **Credit** MC, V.
A classy restaurant in a former coffee warehouse with a fabulous healthy menu (it's rare to find plentiful helpings of veg) and a cool decor.

Ulcke Van Zurich
50 Oude Beurs (03 234 04 94). **Open** 6-11pm Mon, Wed-Sun. **Main courses** €12.50-€17.50. **Credit** AmEx, MC, V. **Map** p222 A3.
The happening restaurant for club kids, DJs and fashion victims. The menu is rib-sticking meat and fish to provide sustenance for the night ahead. Not many restaurants take their names from prostitutes who used to live on the premises: this one does.

De Varkenspoot
5 Armeduivelstraat (03 232 63 63). **Open** noon-2.30pm, 6-10pm Mon-Thur; noon-2.30pm, 6-11pm Fri, Sat. **Main courses** €15-€22. **Set menus** €18-€33.50. **Credit** AmEx, MC, V. **Map** p222 C4.
Near the Graanmarkt, De Varkenspoot ('the pig's trotter') offers traditional Belgian fare: fruits de mer, tenderloin and so on. The wine list features some excellent French, Chilean and Italian bottles.

Via Via
7 Pelgrimsstraat (03 226 52 42). **Open** 6-10.30pm Mon-Thur, Sun; 6-11pm Fri, Sat. **Main courses** €13.50-€18.50. **Set menu** €50. **Credit** AmEx, MC, V. **Map** p222 A3.
Excellent French-Italian dishes are served in a Roman villa-style interior, designed by students of the art academy.

Zuiderterras
37 Ernest Van Dijckkaai (03 234 12 75/ www.zuiderterras.be). **Open** 9am-midnight daily. **Main courses** €12.50-€23. **Credit** AmEx, DC, MC, V. **Map** p222 A3.

Designed by architect bOb Van Reeth, Zuidterras stands on the east bank of the Scheldt. The decor is a mix of metal fittings and black and white tiles, but with huge, heated windows on all sides it is the river that really dominates the place. Salads and seafood, and mussels in season, are the strong points. Zuidterras is also a good bet for afternoon coffee. In summer, the restaurant-cum-café spills out along the jetty, a lovely place to sit and watch the boats go by.

Cafés & bars

Café Au Lait
8 Oude Beurs (03 225 19 81). **Open** 6pm-late daily. **No credit cards. Map** p222 A3.
A *soi-disant* Afro-Belgian bar, with African-style paintings on the wall and a billiard table, Café Au Lait plays funk, R&B, soul and salsa. There's no dancefloor, but that's no deterrent to the young, lively crowd or, indeed, the management, who still book DJs on most week nights.

Café Hopper
2 Leopold de Waelstraat (03 248 49 33/ www.jazzinbelgium.org/clubs/hopper.htm). **Open** 10.30am-2/3am daily. **No credit cards**.
This bright, street-corner jazz café on the southern side of the city stages good concerts on week nights and Sunday afternoons. Music on the bill (check the website for details) ranges widely from post-bebop to modern contemporary jazz, stopping at most points between. Café Hopper is highly popular, particularly with artists.

Den Engel
3 Grote Markt (03 233 12 52). **Open** 9am-late daily. **No credit cards. Map** p222 A3.
On a corner of the Grote Markt, opposite the Stadhuis, Den Engel is your classic Antwerp café. Its customers transcend class and age barriers, even if it's just for the time it takes to drink a Bolleke. Everyone in town, and probably most of Belgium, has been here at least once. It's pretty much always open, day and night, and regulars mix comfortably with whoever happens to be passing.

L'Entrepôt du Congo
42 Vlaamsekaai (03 238 92 32). **Open** 8am-3am daily. **No credit cards**.
Located in the trendy southern part of Antwerp, this is a fave meeting place of java-drinking intellectuals and an interesting, disparate crowd of regulars and occasionals. Goods from Belgium's former colonial outpost were once stored here, and the café retains an elegant faded colonial look. The music tends to classical in the mornings, mellowing on to reggae and soul in the afternoons and evenings. You can eat too, and service is both friendly and efficient.

Grand Café Horta
Horta Complex, 2 Hopland (03 232 28 15). **Open** 9am-midnight daily. **Credit** AmEx, DC, MC, V. **Map** p222 C3.

Imbibe faded colonial grandeur at **L'Entrepôt du Congo**. *See p234.*

Built in 2000, this sleek café on several floors is 'decorated' with salvaged architectural features from one of art nouveau architect Victor Horta's greatest works, Maison du Peuple, a building that was criminally pulled down in Brussels in 1965. It serves brasserie-style food, drinks and afternoon teas.

Kleine Bourla

3 Kelderstraat (03 232 16 32/www.come.to/ kleinebourla&mares). **Open** 11am-1am Mon-Thur; 11am-2am Fri, Sat. **Credit** AmEx, DC, MC, V. **Map** p2227 C4.
Close to the Bourla theatre, the Kleine Bourla bar was beautifully renovated in 1999. Its interior, with wooden floor, dramatic carmine-red walls and a life-sized harlequin, is a treat.

Lombardia

78 Lombardenvest (03 233 68 19). **Open** 7am-6pm Mon-Sat. **No credit cards. Map** p222 B4.
Popular since the 1970s, this wacky fruit and vegetable juice bar serves wholesome sandwiches with vegetarian fillings on nutty brown bread. There's an outdoor terrace, which is open in summer, and a small healthfood shop inside.

De Muze

15 Melkmarkt (03 226 01 26). **Open** noon-4am daily. **No credit cards. Map** p222 B3.
Near Groenplaats, De Muze is a very popular two-storey jazz café. A lot of locals hang out here but it pulls in a fair number of tourists too. There are live concerts every day except Saturday.

De Vagant

25 Reyndersstraat (03 233 15 38/www.devagant.be). **Open** *Bar* 11am-late Mon-Sat; noon-late Sun. *Shop* 11am-6pm Mon, Wed-Sat. *Restaurant* 6pm-late Fri, Sat. **Credit** MC, V. **Map** p222 A/B3.
De Vagant is a typical Belgian pub, known for its extensive collection of *genevers* – there are more

than 200 different ones to choose from. It's part of a mini empire: the owner also has a restaurant and a shop of the same name in the street.

K Zeppos

78 Vleminckveld (03 231 17 89). **Open** 10am-late Mon-Fri; 11am-late Sat, Sun. **No credit cards. Map** p222 B4.
Immensely popular and youthful bar/diner on the south side of the centre. The decor is severly plain, but the staff and clientele are friendly and unoppressively trendy. The basic salads and pastas are supplemented by daily specials.

Clubs

For info on Antwerp's thriving club scene, *see p233* **Culture clubs**.

Gay clubs & bars

Atthis

27 Geuzenstraat (03 216 37 37). **Open** 8.30pm-2am Fri, Sat. **No credit cards. Map** p222 B5.
A women-only private club that's a little more refined than most lesbian clubs in Belgium. There's a video library and a lesbian centre that's run under the same name.

Boots

22 Van Aerdstraat (03 233 21 36). **Open** 10.30pm-5am Fri, Sat. **Admission** free. **No credit cards.**
Without a doubt the raunchiest, sleaziest bar in Belgium: tell someone that you're a regular here, and you immediately have a reputation to live up to. Rooms are designated for any sexual activity you could imagine (well, almost: no llamas yet) and the crowds are completely oblivious to anything but their own pleasure. There's a dress code, but you can change your clothes inside the bar.

Antwerp: fashion capital

In 1987, six fashion graduates of the classes of 1980 and 1981 from Antwerp's Royal Academy of Art showed their work at London Fashion Week. 'We never thought anyone would take designers with such unpronounceable names seriously,' says Dries Van Noten. They were in for a shock. Within a year, their well-crafted, thought-provoking and occasionally alarming collections were being hailed as revolutionary from Paris to Tokyo. They were branded the Antwerp Six, and Belgian fashion has never looked back.

Modegelanded, 2001's year-long fashion exhibition around the city, and the long-planned fashion museum **MoMu** (due to open in September 2002; *see p228*) confirm Antwerp as one of Europe's best spots for fashion cognoscenti – and the shops are fantastic. These days, you will even see groups of Japanese tourists being guided around the best-known boutiques. You can get a booklet (€3) containing five self-guided fashion walks from the city tourist office (*see p230*).

Most of the Antwerp Six are still major players globally. **Ann Demeulemeester** and **Dirk Bikkembergs** are the most alike from the group, sharing a strong military influence and a fondness for various shades of black. Bikkembergs' father was stationed as a soldier in Germany, where he is now based; the other five still live and work in Antwerp. He goes for more of a bondage feel, with lashings of leather and studs, but is also known for his gorgeous, often handmade shoes. Demeulemeester's clothes wear their ideas on their sleeves, and tend to suit pale waifs. Her muse? Patti Smith.

● **Where to buy**: Demeulemeester at her own shop (*see p238*); Bikkembergs at **Verso** (39 Huidevettersstraat; 03 226 92 92), **SN3** (*see p239*), **Stijl** in Brussels (*see p148*). Shoes by both at **Coccodrillo** (*see p238*).

Dries Van Noten is probably the most commercial of the bunch, with soft, rich clothing that recalls Romeo Gigli and Paul Smith. He is known for championing layering early on in his career: 'a result of Belgium's changeable weather'. Recent collections have been inspired by such diverse sources as the Bloomsbury Group, Romany gypsies and Indian market-places. Tom Cruise, Tina Turner, Isabella Rossellini and Sharleen Spiteri are all fans. Van Noten is so big in Japan that he designs separate collections for that market.

● **Where to buy**: **Het Modepaleis** (*see p238*); **Stijl** in Brussels (*see p148*); **L'Héroine** in Bruges (*see p253*).

The fashion-conscious clubber's favourite designer is **Walter Van Beirendonck**. He created the costumes for U2's 1998 Popmart tour; muscle-plated super-hero outfits that set off Bono's shades perfectly. He once had 60 shops in Japan but, after splitting from German backers Mustang in 1998, has radically scaled down his company. Van Beirendonck designs two collections: Wild & Lethal Trash (W&LT, pronounced Walt) and Aesthetic Terrorists. Recurring themes are extra-terrestrials and bio-technology; 'I'm fascinated with the possibilities of cloning,' he says.

Van Beirendonck has taught at the Academy since graduating and, along with fellow Sixer **Marina Yee**, has been the mentor for a new generation of Belgian designers. He also owns funky Antwerp store Walter with **Dirk Van Saene**, who has had much less of a media profile, but creates beautiful, romantic womenswear.

● **Where to buy**: **Walter** (*see p239*). Marina Yee only sells her designs for charity.

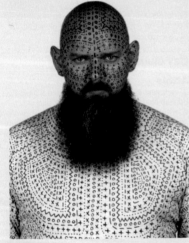

Walter Van Beirendonck...

... and his epnonymous shop.

Martin Margiela is the unofficial seventh member of the group (he graduated a year later). He has given just a handful of interviews, preferring to speak through his cerebral, avant-garde creations. Recent seasons have included outsized and distressed sweaters, cloven-toed boots and leather ponchos. All his clothes have a plain white label. In early 2002, he opened his first premises in Belgium, an unmarked shop in Brussels' rue Antoine Dansaert. He also designs womenswear for Hermès.

● **Where to buy**: **Louis** (*see p238*); **Martin Margiela** in Brussels (*see p147*); **Stijl** in Brussels (*see p148*); **Hermès** in Brussels (50 boulevard de Waterloo; 02 511 20 62).

In the past five years, a new wave of young Belgian designers – most of them Antwerp Academy graduates – has come through: Veronique Branquinho, Bernhard Willhelms, Jurgi Peersons, Angelo Figus and Olivier Theyskens, among others, have been feted in the international style press. Watch for one of the Belgian pack to take over a major fashion house before too long.

Hessenhuis

53 Falconrui (03 231 13 56). **Open** 10am-late daily. **No credit cards**. **Map** p222 B1.

By day, Hessenhuis serves as a tranquil cafeteria, but at night it becomes a popular pre-club venue, primarily attracting a gay audience. The interior is a combination of modern and rustic design. Two large chandeliers with fake electric candles add the necessary charm. On Sunday mornings breakfast is served. Near Boots (*see p235*) or Rubzz (*see below*).

Red & Blue

11-13 Lange Schipperskapelstraat (03 213 05 55). **Open** 11pm-late Fri; 11pm-7am Sat. **No credit cards**. **Map** p222 A2.

Every Saturday Red & Blue holds one of the biggest gay events in Belgium, which has Dutch punters flocking across the border. With dancers and special theme nights, this has become the best and most popular gay disco in Antwerp. Friday's club is open to all, not just gays.

Rubbzz

28 Guelinckxstraat (03 232 78 14/http://users. skynet.be/rubbzz/). **Open** 11pm-4am daily. **Admission** varies. **No credit cards**.

A variation on the Boots (*see p235*), though perhaps a bit less tough, and getting more popular. Resident DJs play on Friday and Saturday nights.

Shakespeare

24 Oude Koornmarkt (03 231 50 58). **Open** 10pm-late Fri, Sat. **No credit cards**. **Map** p222 A/B3.

Catering to a largely butch crowd, this small, dark pub is the oldest survivor in the Antwerp lesbian landscape. Music is a mix of rock, soul, house and disco; men are welcome if accompanied by a woman.

Shopping

Antwerp's role as one of the world's most celebrated fashion hubs (*see p236* **Antwerp: fashion capital**) has made it a shopper's paradise. Designer-led stores with a hip reputation to maintain open their pilot stores in Antwerp rather than Brussels. It is cooler, cleaner and has that buzz that other Belgian cities strive for but just don't pull off.

The main shopping drag with the usual blend of international chainstores is pedestrian street **Meir**. **Huidevetterstraat** to the south is more upbeat with some one-off boutiques, and things start to get interesting around **Schutterhofstraat**, where there are hip bathroom shops, contemporary jewellers and understated designer clothes shops. The avant-garde core of the city is the warren of streets closed to traffic and affectionately known as 'De Wilde Zee'. It includes upbeat **Kammenstraat** with kooky streetwear stores and record dives; **St Antoniusstraat**, where Walter Van Beirendonck hangs out; and **Nationalestraat**,

Trips Out of Town

Dries Van Noten's **Het Modepaleis**.

home to Dries Van Noten's temple of fashion. For food on the hoof make a beeline for nearby **Wiegstraat** or **Schrijnwerkersstraat**.

Antwerp also has a well-deserved reputation for its fine antiques shops, most of which can be found around **Lombardenvest** and **Steenhouwersvest** (south of Groenplaats).

All the shops below are closed on Sunday unless otherwise stated.

Fashion & accessories

Ann Demeulemeester
38 Verlatstraat (03 213 01 33). **Open** 11am-7pm Mon-Sat. **Credit** AmEx, DC, MC, V.
Ann Demeulemeester, star member of the Antwerp Six, has her minimalist shop in a different part of Antwerp to that of her contemporaries. It's opposite the Koninklijk Museum voor Schone Kunsten, south of the city.

Closing Date
15 Korte Gasthuisstraat (03 232 87 22). **Open** 11am-6.30pm Mon-Sat. **Credit** AmEx, DC, MC, V. **Map** p222 B4.
Clubbers with cash and eccentrics with panache gather here to pore over racks of clothes by Owen Gaster, Dsquared2 and Amaya Arzuaga.

Coccodrillo
9A/B Schuttershofstraat (03 233 20 93). **Open** 10am-6pm Mon-Sat. **Credit** AmEx, DC, MC, V. **Map** p222 C4.
The collections of Prada, Patrick Cox, Jil Sander, Ann Demeulemeester, Veronique Branquinho and Helmut Lang are among those represented at this heavy-hitting mecca of fashion footwear.

Erotische Verbeelding
10-12 Ijzerenwaag (03 226 89 50). **Open** 11am-6pm. **Credit** AmEx, MC, V. **Map** p222 B4.

This women-only store run by women stocks tame sex aids, tasteful-looking dildos, a smattering of S&M and slinky lingerie.

Fish & Chips
36-38 Kammenstraat (03 227 08 24/ www.fishandchips.be). **Open** 10am-6.30pm Mon-Sat. **Credit** AmEx, MC, V. **Map** p222 B4.
A chaotic store and legendary supplier to Antwerp's youth culture. DJs spin party music in a booth overhanging the ground floor, which is packed with shoes, hats and skatewear labels. A fruit and veg juice counter is upstairs.

Hit!
43 Kammenstraat (03 226 02 31). **Open** 10.30am-6.30pm Mon-Sat. **Credit** AmEx, MC, V. **Map** p222 B4.
Run by the former owners of Babe's Store, a Fish & Chips-style place a few doors down, this funky shop sells G-Star jeans and sports holdalls by Fred Perry.

Huis Boon
4 Lombardenvest (03 232 33 87/www.glovesboon.be). **Open** Sept-Feb 10am-6pm Mon-Sat. *Mar-Aug* 11am-6pm Mon-Sat. **Credit** AmEx, DC, MC, V. **Map** p222 B4.
A delightfully old-fashioned glove shop, with hundreds of different gloves for men and women, displayed on dark wooden shelves. Staff still soften the leather gloves by putting them on wooden hand models before you try them on.

Louis
2 Lombardenstraat (03 232 98 72). **Open** 10am-6pm Mon-Sat. **Credit** AmEx, MC, V. **Map** p222 B4.
This small boutique was one of the first to champion Belgian fashion (along with Stijl in Brussels), and is now a shrine for fashion-conscious Japs. Martin Margiela, Veronique Branquinho and Olivier Theyskens are the staple labels. The management recently changed, so here's hoping the stock doesn't.

Het Modepaleis
16 Nationalestraat (03 470 25 10). **Open** 10am-6.30pm Mon-Sat. **Credit** AmEx, DC, MC, V. **Map** p222 B4.
One of the designers who helped launch world interest in Flemish fashion, Dries Van Noten sells his own collections in this landmark building dating from 1881. The men's and women's floors are decorated with late 19th-century furniture, complemented by contemporary lighting and furnishings. Jewellery by Belgian duo Wouters & Hendrickx is also on sale.

Nadine Wijnants
26 Kloosterstraat (03 226 45 69). **Open** 11am-6pm Tue-Sat. **Credit** MC, V. **Map** p222 A4.
One of the top youngish jewellery designers in Belgium, Wijnants creates charming pieces with semi-precious stones and oxidised or sterling silver, bronze and gold plate. Incorporating influences that run from India to street-style, Wijnants always aims to make her collections affordable.
Branch: 14 Nationalestraat (03 231 75 15).

Naughty I

65-67 Kammenstraat (03 213 35 90). **Open**
11am-6.30pm Mon-Fri; 11am-7pm Sat. **Credit**
AmEx, MC, V. **Map** p222 B4.
Garish vintage stuff from the 1960s and '70s, a real
treat to browse through.

Nitya

9D Schuttershofstraat (03 213 07 37). **Open**
10am-6m Mon-Sat. **Credit** AmEx, MC, V.
Map p222 C4.
A luxury Indian label for women designed by a team
of international designers. The result is a superb
collection with an Asian twist: separates, suits and
shawls. The cotton and silk fabrics are from China,
suit cloths from France and the embroidery and
other hand-finishings are done in India.

SN3

46-48 Frankrijklei (03 231 08 20/www.sn3.be).
Open noon-6.30pm Mon; 10am-6.30pm Tue-Sat.
Credit AmEx, DC, MC, V.
Housed in a large former cinema, this designer bou-
tique carries the principal collections by the likes of
Chanel, Prada, Gucci and Dior. Despite a tradition
of being snobbish and a touch sterile (two floors of
streamlined plate glass and flattering soft lighting),
SN3 is nonetheless worth a visit.

Walter

10 St Antoniusstraat (03 213 26 44/www.walt.de).
Open 1-6pm Mon; 11am-6.30pm Tue-Sat. **Credit**
AmEx, DC, MC, V. **Map** p222 B4.
This creation by two of the original Antwerp Six
designers (Walter Van Beirendonck and Dirk Van
Saene) is an extraordinary and rather ambiguous
space, which comes on as a gallery as much as a
shop. Wendy houses, white boxes and even a massive recumbent teddy bear conceal a choice selection
of designer labels and Van B's collections Wild &
Lethal Trash and Aesthetic Terrorists. If any take

your fancy, you can pay at the Marc Newson-
designed cash desk, shaped like a UFO and suspended from the ceiling.

XSO

13-17 Eiermarkt (03 231 87 49). **Open** 10am-
12.30pm, 1-6pm Mon-Sat. **Credit** AmEx, DC, MC,
V. **Map** p222 B3.
Wrapping around a quiet courtyard in the centre of
town, this shop has a stunning decor, mixing
Japanese purity (white walls, slate floors) with
Italian flourishes. Which is appropriate as it stocks
clothes by Issey Miyake, Kenzo and Giorgio Armani

Food & confectionery

Goossens

31 Korte Gasthuisstraat (03 226 07 91). **Open**
7am-7pm Tue-Sat. **No credit cards.** **Map** p222 B4.
Founded in 1884, this small and popular traditional
bakery offers a good choice of pastries and cakes,
all displayed on metal racks.

Kashandel Vervloet

28 Wiegstraat (03 233 37 29). **Open** 8am-6pm
Mon-Sat. **No credit cards.** **Map** p222 B3.
Run by master cheese buyer Luc Wouters, who specialises in cheeses from Belgium: sheeps' milk from
the Ardennes, Herve Remoudou from a Liège farm
and Wouters' own, a hard goat's cheese.

Health & beauty

Aveda

28 Schuttershofstraat (03 232 78 97/
www.aveda.com). **Open** 10am-6.30pm Mon-Sat.
Credit AmEx, MC, V. **Map** p222 C4.
Stock up on natural skincare and hair products at
this shop, a success story of the 1990s, and no need
for any introduction.

Trips Out of Town

Soap

13 Plantinkaai (03 232 73 72). **Open** 9am-6.30pm
Mon-Thur; 9am-8pm Fri; 9am-6pm Sat. **Credit** MC,
V. **Map** p222 A4.

The salon in Belgium where the ultra-stylish get
their hair dyed, fried or laid to the side. The interior
features large paintings of Japanese superhero art
and milky fluorescent colours, and it has been the
backdrop for more than a few fashion shoots. Unlike
Brussels salons, everyone speaks fluent English.
Branch: Box 2 Korte Schytterskappelstraat
(03 213 10 13).

Home furnishings

Kloosterstraat is the place for antique and
bric-a-brac lovers to head.

Avant-Scène

3-5 Hopland (03 231 88 26). **Open** 11am-6pm
Tue-Sat. **Credit** MC, V. **Map** p222 C3.

Belgian design talent doesn't halt at fashion. A crop
of furniture designers are making a name for themselves on the international scene. You'll find pieces
here by the Van Severen brothers, Maarten and
Fabiaan, and by rising star Xavier Lust.

'T Koetshuis (Chelsea)

62 Kloosterstraat (03 248 33 42). **Open** noon-6pm
Tue-Sun. **No credit cards. Map** p222 A4.

This store's official name is Chelsea, but 't Koetshuis
('the carriage') is what you'll find written over the
front door. The art deco and art nouveau furnishings – large and small – are chosen and displayed
with care, so don't expect any bargains. On the first
floor there is a cosy, rustic café-bar.

Scapa World

26-30 Hopland Complex, Hopland (03 226 79 93).
Open 10am-6.30pm Mon-Sat. **Credit** AmEx, DC,
MC, V. **Map** p222 C3.

Ralph Lauren is the name that actually springs
immediately to mind upon entering this gleaming
homestore: Turkish, Irish and Austrian are a few of
the many cultures influencing the clothes and home
furnishings on display. Great household linen too.

Music & books

Mekanik Strip

*73 St Jacobsmarkt (03 234 23 47/
www.mekanikstrip.be).* **Open** 10am-6.30pm
Mon-Fri; 10am-6pm Sat. **Credit** AmEx, DC,
MC, V. **Map** p222 C2.

Mekanik Strip has more than 15 years of experience
in comics. It has a huge selection of English, French
and Dutch comics, plus magazines, books, videos,
posters, Tintin collectibles – and its own gallery.

Metrophone

47 Kammenstraat (03 231 18 65). **Open** 10am-6pm
Mon-Fri; 10am-6.30pm Sat. **Credit** AmEx, DC, MC,
V. **Map** p222 B4.

Girls with muso boyfriends (or vice versa) should
steer clear of this record shop, which stocks a mammoth amount of new and used vinyl and CDs: rock,
indie, dance and everything else. Guys, they might
just have that Swans bootleg you've spent years
searching for.

Toys

Sjokkel

4 Wijngaardstraat (03 234 28 27). **Open** 11am-
6pm Mon-Sat. **No credit cards. Map** p222 B3.

Set on two floors, this charming toyshop has a magical quality. As in every child's dream attic, there are
toys everywhere: wooden toys, beautiful Victorian
dolls, mechanical contraptions. Both kids and adults
will want to spend hours rummaging through it all.

Theatre, film & art

Kladaradatsch! Cartoon's (4-6 Kaasstraat;
03 232 96 32) in the historical city centre,
opposite the Steen, is both an attractive café
and an excellent alternative cinema.

DeSingel

25 Desguinlei (03 248 38 00). **Box office** 10am-
7pm Mon-Fri; 4-7pm Sat. **Tickets** €10-€40.
No credit cards.

Antwerp's modern equivalent to Brussels' Palais des
Beaux-Arts: an international centre for dance and
theatre in a huge concrete setting, with a consistently intelligent programme of events. The huge
Blue Hall can accommodate major philharmonic
orchestras, while the Red Hall is ideal for smaller
groups. Acoustics are excellent. Four international
companies are chosen each season, with the emphasis very much on innovation and originality.

Vlaamse Opera

3 Frankrijklei (03 233 66 85). **Box office** 11am-
5.45pm Tue-Sat. **Tickets** €7-€90. **Credit** AmEx,
DC, MC, V.

The Flemish Opera has also recently undergone a
radical overhaul, especially the orchestra, which is
now excellent. Productions are divided between the
newly revamped opera house in Ghent (3
Schouwburgstraat; 09 225 24 25) and the old but
acoustically splendid Antwerp Hall. As with the
Brussels opera, the emphasis is on quality rather
than big names and productions are usually thoroughly rehearsed. The management encourages
orchestra players to participate in weekday lunchtime chamber concerts in the foyer.

Zwarte Panther

70-74 Hoogstraat (03 233 13 45). **Open** 1.30-6pm
Thur-Sun. **No credit cards. Map** p222 A3/4.

This small, discreet gallery in the centre of town has
one of the best reputations in the country. It specialises in figurative art and is the best place in
Belgium for Art Brut.

Bruges

Too popular for its own good, especially with Brits, but still a beaut.

In 1995, the British writer and comedian Stephen Fry, distraught at reviews of his performance in a London play, disappeared. His family and friends feared the worst until, a week or so later, a British tourist in Bruges reported having seen him in the town. Had he truly wanted to escape, Fry could not have chosen a worse spot. Bruges (Brugge in Dutch) is constantly jam-packed with tourists ogling the gabled houses lining the canals – and most of them seem to be Brits.

Bruges attracts around two million tourists a year, easily the most popular destination for visitors to Belgium (even more so than Brussels). As well as canals, churches and museums galore, Bruges, like so many towns – Glasgow, Bilbao, Antwerp even – has decided to reinvent itself. European City of Culture for 2002, Bruges has a spanking new concert hall and international events by the bucketload (*see p251* **Culture city**).

The city owes a lot to the British. Until the 16th century, this was one of the most important trading posts in Europe, the hub of the wool, lace and diamond industries and home to the world's first stock exchange. But then the Zwin estuary, the city's link to the sea, began to silt up and, before long, the merchants and traders were packing their bags. As a result, Bruges went into hibernation for more

than 300 years, missing out on the Industrial Revolution and the prosperity of the rest of the country. But it was to have its revenge: in the early part of the 19th century, British souvenir hunters began visiting the town on their way to the battlefield at Waterloo. Many who passed through were seduced by its sleepy charm and decided to settle. By 1860, around 1,000 Brits were living in the city, running shops, tearooms and hotels. The word began to spread: here was a magical place that had remained unchanged for centuries.

As the British population in Bruges grew, so the former tourists had a greater stake in attracting more. Many French visitors came to the city after reading Georges Rodenbach's 1892 novella *Bruges-la-Morte*. Rodenbach's depiction of the city as desolate and dreamlike was seductive at the time. People commonly mistake Bruges for a medieval city; the reality is that much of it was renovated in this style to appeal to tourists.

GETTING THERE

From Brussels, there are two trains an hour (50 minutes) from Gare du Nord, Gare Centrale or Gare du Midi. The station is a ten- to 15-minute walk from the centre, or you take a taxi or bus.

Canals and bridges weave through the city.

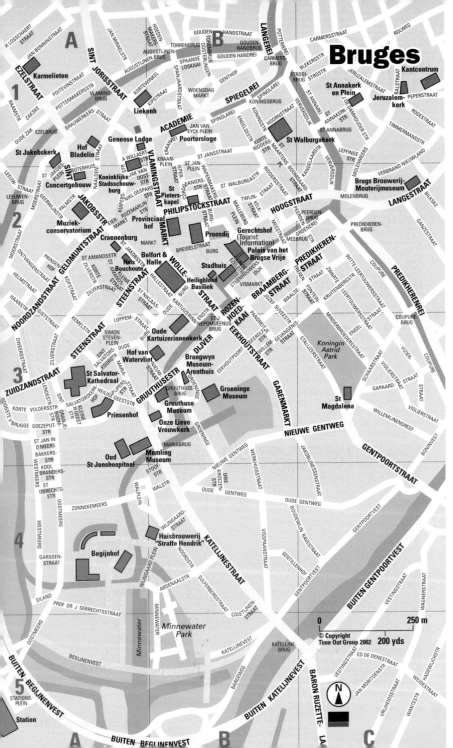

Sightseeing

The Markt & the Burg

The most enjoyable way to visit Bruges is on foot. It's compact, profoundly medieval and easy to get around – and anything must be better than one of those horse-drawn carriages.

The traditional starting point for any visit is the main square, the **Markt**. Its most striking monuments are the Cloth Hall, the Halle (covered market), and the **Belfort** (belfry), the finest in Belgium. Both the belfry and market are symbols of the civic pride and mercantile power of medieval Bruges; the view from the 80-metre (263-foot) belfry makes the climb – all 366 steps – worthwhile. Around the square are some of Bruges's finest old houses, including the stained-glass **Craenenburg**, where Emperor Maximilian was held prisoner by the people of Bruges. It's now a typical and popular Bruges café (*see p252*).

The statues at the centre of the square are of Jan Breydel and Pieter de Coninck, who led the people of Bruges against the French in the 'Brugse Metten' at the start of the 14th century. The statues were unveiled by King Léopold II, who is said to have spoken Dutch for the first time during the ceremony.

From here it's a very short walk to the **Burg**. This beautiful square was the site chosen by Baldwin I to build his castle in the ninth century. In its place, the **Stadhuis** (Town Hall), with its long, elaborate windows, statues and octagonal turrets, was built in a splendid and dizzying Gothic style in the 14th century. On the first floor is the lavish Gothic Hall. The ceiling is a swooping, vaulted stunner, while the walls are painted with scenes relating the history of the city, often with more verve than accuracy. The paintings are relatively recent additions, dating from the turn of the 20th century and have a certain Pre-Raphaelite/art nouveau romance to them. The **Tourist Information Office** (*see p247*) is housed in the ground floor of the same building.

On one corner of the Burg stands the Old Recorders' House, the **Paleis van het Brugse Vrije**, built in the 16th century and renovated in the 18th. The façade overlooking the canal is all that remains of the original structure; the rest is neo-classical in style. Inside the palace there's only one room that can be visited, with an impressive baroque chimney piece (1528) of black marble and oak by Lanceloot Blondeel, running almost the whole length of one wall.

The oldest building on the Burg, tucked away in a corner next to the Stadhuis, is the easily missed **Heiligbloed Basiliek** (Basilica of the Holy Blood). Its façade is one of the first examples of Italian Renaissance style in Flanders. The Lower Chapel was built in the 12th century in honour of St Basil, and is in a pure Romanesque style. Its refined sobriety is in surprising contrast to the generous interior of the Upper Chapel. Built in the 12th century, the chapel was first Romanesque, then Gothic, being heavily altered in the 19th century. The decorated wooden ceiling, many of the colourful frescoes, the marvellous stained-glass windows and globe-shaped pulpit all date from this time.

It is in the Upper Chapel that the crystal phial containing two drops of holy blood, stored in a silver tabernacle, is exhibited every Friday. This is one of the holiest relics of medieval Europe. The phial is supposed to have been given to Thierry d'Alsace by the Patriarch of Jerusalem during the Second Crusade. Legend has it that the blood contained in the phial liquefied every Friday, but the miracle apparently stopped in the 15th century.

The **Procession of the Holy Blood**, a major traditional event in Bruges, takes place every year on Ascension Day. The event commemorates the procession that accompanied Thierry d'Alsace when the holy phial was first brought to the city. Today, people dressed in rich costumes walk in a similar procession, enacting biblical scenes.

Belfort
Markt. **Open** 9.30am-5pm Tue-Sun. **Admission** €5; €3 concessions; free under-13s. **No credit cards. Map** p242 B2.

Heiligbloed Basiliek
13 Burg. **Open** *Apr-Sept* 9am-noon, 2-6pm daily. *Oct-Mar* 10am-noon, 2-4pm Mon, Tue, Thur-Sun; 10am-noon Wed. **Admission** €1.25. **No credit cards. Map** p242 B2.

Paleis van het Brugse Vrije
11A Burg (050 44 82 60). **Open** 9.30am-5pm Tue-Sun. **Admission** combination ticket with Stadhuis €2.50; €1.50 concessions; free under-13s. **No credit cards. Map** p242 B2.

Stadhuis
12 Burg (050 44 81 13). **Open** 9.30am-5pm Tue-Sun. **Admission** combination ticket with Paleis van het Brugse Vrije €2.50; €1.50 concessions; free under-13s. **No credit cards. Map** p242 B2.

Museums along the canal

From the Burg you can head south on to the **Vismarkt** (fish market), taking the narrow Blinde Ezelstraat (Alley of the Blind Donkey). The fish market still takes place here every morning from Tuesday to Saturday. The walk east from here by the canal, along the **Groenerei**, is one of the most popular in Bruges. The water, trees and pretty gabled houses – especially the Pelican House at No.8 – make it a favourite romantic spot. It is not, however, one of the most secluded ones, with a constant traffic of boats and pedestrians.

Just west of Vismarkt is Huidevettersplaats (Tanner's Square), which leads to the **Rozenhoedkaai**, one of the most photogenic locations in all Bruges. The view of the canal, bordered by fine buildings and trees, is a treat, as the hundreds of snappers around you will undoubtedly testify. The quay melds into another beautiful street, the **Dijver**. Along it is the splendid **Groeninge Museum** (*see p248* **Primitive passions**) and, nearby, the **Brangwyn Museum-Arentshuis**. Set in Arentspark, this is named after Bruges-born British painter and engraver Frank Brangwyn, whose works are shown in the museum. There is also glassware, china and brass and, opposite the main building, a collection of sledges once used to transport goods over the frozen canals.

Over the bridge from the Groeninge stands the **Gruuthuse Museum**. This extensive 15th-century mansion originally belonged to the powerful Gruuthuse family, who had a monopoly on the making of *gruut*, a mixture of dried flowers and plants used for brewing before hops came into fashion. Lodewijk van Gruuthuse was a diplomat, a patron of the arts, a chum of Edward IV of England, and a Knight of the Golden Fleece; he also invented a nastier version of the cannonball. His motto, 'Plus est en vous', is reproduced around the palace, which was bought by the city of Bruges and opened as a museum.

Lace-making has always been big in Bruges.

The furniture in the reception hall dates from the 16th, 17th and 18th centuries, as do the silverware and ceramics. The bust of Charles V, showing a young and candid emperor, is one of the most important pieces in the collection. Many of the other pieces are objects of daily life, some interesting, some curious – the beautiful collection of ancient musical instruments in the music cabinet is particularly noteworthy. The second floor is devoted almost entirely to lace. Lace-making is a Bruges tradition that dates back to the Middle Ages, when lace was made with imported linen, always by women and often in convents and in the *béguinages* (houses for lay sisters). In the 17th century, Bruges, Ghent, Brussels and Mechelen were quite unrivalled in the art of lace-making. Next door is the small **Arendts Garden**, containing four modern sculptures representing the Horsemen of the Apocalypse.

On the other side of the garden stands **Onze Lieve Vrouwkerk**, the Church of Our Lady, an imposing brick structure with a massive tower. As the front entrance is on a busy street, its solid architecture can be best appreciated from the garden. The church was built over three centuries and the combination of styles is not considered a happy one. Recent alterations, including some of the glass panels, divide up the structure and make it difficult to form a complete impression of the place.

The church is chiefly famed for its works of art. First and foremost among these is Michelangelo's *Madonna and Child*. The sculpture was ordered by the Piccolomini family for Siena Cathedral, but a Bruges merchant bought it when the Piccolomini family failed to pay up. The sculpture is an early work by the artist and one of the few to have left Italy during his lifetime. It is delicate and tender, subtly moving rather than powerful.

In the choir are the tombs of Charles the Bold and his daughter, Mary of Burgundy. Unlike her husband, Maximilian of Austria, Mary of Burgundy was loved by the people of Bruges. Tragically, she died young and beautiful after falling from a horse. Their joint mausoleum (overlooked by a giant altar painting of the crucifixion by Bernard van Orley) is both lavish and solemn. The golden brass glitters in the hazy light of the choir; a graceful brass sculpture of the princess lies over the heavily adorned base. The monument for Charles the Bold, made at a later date, is very similar in style. In 1979, the original tomb of Mary of Burgundy was among several that were dug up. These painted stone coffins are exhibited just below the monuments. Look out also for works by Pieter Pourbus and Gerard David.

What the tourists come for: Bruges' famous gabled houses.

Directly opposite the church is the medieval **St Janshospitaal**, which was still in use as a hospital as late as the 1970s. Visitors can look round a number of the old hospital rooms and admire some of the most puzzling surgical instruments you're ever likely to see.

Within the hospital's old chapel is the renovated **Memling Museum**, dedicated to the 15th-century painter Hans Memling. This is a small, remarkable collection of the Frankfurt-born artist, one of the most acclaimed of his day. Memling lived and studied in Bruges, where he created several pieces for the hospital, undertaking commissions for English poet John Donne and Italian banker Portinari. Memling's talent as a portrait artist and his hunger for detail are quite astonishing. Like all the Flemish Primitives, Memling believed that the material world was a product of divine creation, and that it was necessary to reproduce God's work as faithfully as possible. His use of colours is brilliant and scenes always carefully composed.

The Mystical Marriage of St Catherine is one of several similar works by Memling (another is in New York's Metropolitan Museum). In the central panel, Jesus, sitting on Mary's lap, is sliding a ring on St Catherine's finger. Although Memling's paintings are often said to be rather devoid of feeling, here the colours are vivid and passionate. The *Sibylla Sambetha* is believed to be a portrait of Marie Moreel, who commissioned many works from Memling. Also on display in the museum is a shrine made by Memling in 1489, which contains the relic of St Ursula. The

story of pagan martyr St Ursula and the 11,000 virgins was a popular legend; the shrine is shaped like a Gothic cathedral and decorated with scenes of the saint's life.

Brangwyn Museum-Arentshuis
16 Dijver (050 44 87 63). **Open** 9.30am-5pm Tue-Sun. **Admission** €2.50; €1.50 concessions; free under-13s. **Credit** AmEx, MC, V. **Map** p242 B3.

Gruuthuse Museum
17 Dijver (050 44 87 62). **Open** 9.30am-5pm Tue-Sun. **Admission** €5; €3 concessions; free under-13s. **Credit** AmEx, MC, V. **Map** p242 B3.

Memling Museum
38 Mariastraat (050 44 87 70). **Open** 9.30am-5pm Tue-Sun. **Admission** €7; €4 concessions; free under-13s. **Credit** AmEx, MC, V. **Map** p242 A/B3.

Onze Lieve Vrouwkerk
Mariastraat. **Open** 9.30am-12.30pm, 1.30-5pm Tue-Fri; 9.30am-12.30pm, 1.30-4pm Sat; 2.30-5pm Sun. **Admission** €2.50; €1.50 concessions; free under-13s. **No credit cards**. **Map** p242 B3.

Begijnhof & Minnewater Park

Coming out of St Janshospitaal, turn right on Katelijnestraat and walk towards the Begijnhof, taking any of the side streets on your right. The **Begijnhof**, founded in 1245 by Margaret of Constantinople, is one of the most charming locations in Bruges. A row of small white houses encircles an inner lawn, which in spring is completely covered with daffodils. Perhaps

Onze Lieve Vrouwkerk. *See p244*.

because of the colours, the silence or the nuns walking softly by, the atmosphere is calm and serene. There are no longer any *béguines* (lay sisterhoods) in Bruges; the last of them died around 1930. The women you see walking around the Begijnhof today are Benedictine nuns. It is possible to visit the church, and one of the houses is also open to visitors.

At the Begijnhof's southern entrance is the picturesque **Minnewater Park** (or Lac d'Amour), with swans, lawns and small houses. Before the Zwin silted up, barges and some ships would penetrate this far into the city. The 16th-century lock-keeper's house is still on the north side of the lake, next to the 1398 Watch Tower. The lake is named after a woman called Minna who, according to legend, fell in love with a man of whom her father disapproved. She fled from her father's house and hid in the woods around the lake. Unfortunately, her beloved was a little slow in finding her and Minna died in his arms. The heartbroken man still found enough strength in him to change the course of the water, bury Minna's body, and let the waters flow over the grave again.

Walking back to the Markt, you can pause to look at the massive **St Salvator-kathedraal**, surrounded by trees. Work on the cathedral

began in the tenth century, but after four fires and the Iconoclastic Riots nothing of that period has survived except the base of the tower. These incidents are also responsible for the varied and eclectic style of the interior. The choir dates from the 14th century, although part of the 13th-century construction survives. The painted columns, similar to those in the Upper Chapel of the Heiligbloed Basiliek, are a relatively recent addition, as are the stained-glass windows. There are several paintings by Van Orley in the right transept, but the lighting is bad and they are difficult to see.

St Salvator-kathedraal

St Salvatorskerkhof. **Open** 2-5.45pm Mon; 8.30-11.45am, 2-5.45pm Tue-Fri; 8.30-11.45am, 2-3.30pm Sat; 9-10.15am, 3-5.45pm Sun. **Admission** free. **Map** p242 A3.

Churches of St Anna

The area of St Anna, north-east of the Burg, is a poorer and more populated area of Bruges, and less visited by tourists. There are fewer shops and the bars are mostly frequented by locals, yet there's still charm aplenty.

Follow Hoogstraat east of the Burg and turn left on Vervedijk by the canal. The houses here are still very impressive. To your left you can see the Jesuit church of **St Walburga**, built between 1619 and 1641. It's a bright structure, with tall, solid, grey, Tuscan-style columns. The style is baroque and the dominant colours gold and white, yet the interior is more harmonious than overbearing and presents a refreshing change from other monuments in the city.

Cross the little bridge between the Vervedijk and St Annarei and you'll find yourself facing the 17th-century **St Annakerk en Plein**, a rather austere building from the outside, but with a luxurious interior.

Behind St Anna, on the corner of Peperstraat, is the curious **Jeruzalemkerk**, built by a rich family of Italian merchants and still belonging to its descendants. It's a small church, built on three levels, supposedly following the model of the Holy Sepulchre. Highlights include a crucifix decorated with bones and skulls over the altar, a copy of the tomb of Christ in the crypt and some fine stained glass. Next door is the **Kantcentrum**, the Lace Museum, a tourist attraction where women demonstrate the intricate skills of lace-making. Walking north on Balstraat brings you to the **Engels Klooster**, the English Convent and its church on Carmersstraat. Ring a bell to visit.

The houses in this part of town are far removed from the flamboyant style of the historical centre. This is no longer an open-air museum, but living, breathing Bruges, warts and all. Witnesses to more difficult times are the numerous **Maisons Dieu**. As Bruges's fortunes declined, people abandoned the city, leaving vast spaces in the centre completely uninhabited. Richer citizens took it upon themselves to build almshouses to shelter the poor and elderly. There are about 30 Maisons Dieu in Bruges, and some still fulfil their original role today. The entrance is usually marked by a small statue of the Virgin. Inside is a little courtyard and anything between three and 24 identical, modest but pretty little houses, each with its individual character. The lawns are usually carefully tended and surrounded with flowers.

Jeruzalemkerk

3A Peperstraat (050 33 00 72). **Open** 10am-noon, 2-6pm Mon-Fri; 10am-noon, 2-5pm Sat. **Admission** combination ticket with Kantcentrum €1.50; €1 concessions. **No credit cards.** Map p242 C1.

Kantcentrum

3A Peperstraat (050 33 00 72). **Open** 10am-noon, 2-6pm Mon-Fri; 10am-noon, 2-5pm Sat. **Admission** combination ticket with Jeruzalemkerk €1.50; €1 concessions. **No credit cards.** Map p242 C1.

St Annakerk en Plein

J De Damhouderstraat. **Open** *Apr-Sept* 10am-noon, 2-4pm Mon-Fri; 10am-noon Sat. Closed Oct-Apr. **Admission** free. Map p242 C1.

St Walburgakerk

Koningstraat & Hoornstraat. **Open** *June-Sept* 8-10pm daily. Closed Oct-Apr. **Admission** free. Map p242 B1.

The city walls

Little remains of the old city walls – only three of the original city gates and just one of the watchtowers. Instead, Bruges is now nearly entirely surrounded by a belt of parks and lawns. Walking around the entire perimeter can take a long time – it is easier to cycle. Look out for the three impressive windmills. Only one of the three is original; the other two were taken from nearby villages and brought to Bruges.

Tourist information

Toerisme Brugge

11 Burg (050 44 86 86/fax 050 44 86 00/ www.brugge.be). **Open** *Apr-Sept* 9.30am-6.30pm Mon-Fri; 10am-noon, 2-6.30pm Sat, Sun. *Oct-Mar* 9.30am-5pm Mon-Fri; 9.30am-1pm, 2-5.30pm Sat, Sun. Map p242 B2. The website is in Dutch, French, German and English.

Accommodation

For online info try **www.hotels-brugge.org**. The tourist information office also has an accommodation booking service.

Bauhaus

135-137 Langestraat, 8000 Bruges (050 34 10 93/ fax 050 33 41 80/www.bauhaus.be). **Open** 7pm-midnight Mon, Tue, Thur-Sun; 7pm-1am Wed. **Rates** €9.50-€11.77 per person. **Credit** AmEx, MC, V. Map p242 C2. This is one of Bruges's largest youth hostels, with 80 rooms sleeping two, three, four or eight. The decor is an eclectic mix of oriental, colonial and religious, with lots of mirrors and a giant clock hanging on the wall. There's also bike rental, a cyber café and a public bar that attracts an international set.

Charlie Rockets

19 Hoogstraat, 8000 Bruges (050 33 06 60/fax 050 33 66 74/www.charlierockets.com). **Open** 8am-4am daily. **Rates** €12-€37 per person. **Credit** MC, V. Map p242 B2. Just five minutes from the market square, Charlie Rockets combines two roles: popular youth hostel and Mexican/American bar-diner. Booking is essential and is only accepted by post or email.

Dieltiens B&B

40 Waalsestraat, 8000 Bruges (050 33 42 94/ http://users.skynet.be/dieltiens). **Rates** single €45-€50; double €50-€55. **No credit cards.** Map p242 B2. A very stylish B&B. Koen and Annemie Dieltiens' beautiful 18th-century mansion is in the heart of Bruges, two minutes' walk from the Markt and Burg. There are only three rooms, so book well in advance. The Dieltiens also rent a studio apartment in a small, recently renovated 17th-century house.

Gheeraert B&B

9 & 18 Ridderstraat, 8000 Bruges (050 33 56 27/ fax 050 34 52 01/http://users.skynet.be/brugge-gheeraert). **Rates** €45-€70. **No credit cards.** Map p242 B2. This exquisitely decorated townhouse, just a couple of minutes from the Burg, has three second-floor guest rooms. Two have fine views out over St Walburga's church, and all are decorated in a classy, pared-down style and hung with prints by Flemish masters. The breakfast is notable. You can also rent self-catering holiday flats.

Golden Tulip Hotel de' Medici

15 Potterierei, 8000 Bruges (050 33 98 33/fax 050 33 07 64/www.hoteldemedici.com). **Rates** single €91.81-€110; double €107.95-€131; suite €236. **Credit** AmEx, DC, MC, V. Map p242 B1. Although located near the historic centre, this is a modern hotel. The look of the interior is clinically efficient, but the rooms are spacious and comfortable; all have en suite bathrooms, TV, minibar, trouser press and hairdryer. There's also a recreation centre with sauna, steam bath, sun beds and a gym.

Trips Out of Town

Hotel Acacia

3A Korte Zilverstraat, 8000 Bruges (050 34 44 11/ fax 050 33 88 17/www.hotel-acacia.com). **Rates** single €113-€123; double €128-€138; suite €148-€208. **Credit** AmEx, DC, MC, V. **Map** p242 A2.
There has been a hotel on this spot since the 1430s. The original building was demolished in the 1960s, but was rebuilt 20 years later and is now part of the Best Western chain. Centrally located, it's got 48 rooms (all en suite), plus an indoor swimming pool, sauna and jacuzzi. No animals allowed.

Hotel Adornes

26 St Annarei, 8000 Bruges (050 34 13 36/ www.proximedia.com/web/adornes.html). **Rates** single €75-€95; double €80-€100. **Credit** AmEx, MC, V. **Map** p242 C1.
The Adornes is a cosy family hotel near St Annakerk en Plein and overlooking a canal; a good location for exploring Bruges's historic centre. The rooms are comfortable and stylishly decorated, and there is parking and a number of bicycles (available free of charge). Dogs are welcome.

Primitive passions

The Groeninge Museum represents one of Bruges's two heavyweight collections of paintings, and is worth setting aside an afternoon for. The biggest attraction are the **Flemish Primitives** – in particular, works by **Jan van Eyck**, who spent the last decade of his life in Bruges.

The booming commercial activity in Bruges in the 15th century was paralleled by a flourishing of the arts. Rich merchants ordered works from painters, as did many Italian bankers living in the city at the time. While Italian painting tended to glorify humanity, the Flemish masters remained more religious in their outlook, and medieval in their complexity and spirit. To best achieve texture and detail, oil and varnish would be applied in painstaking layers. Such was their technical virtuosity and strict attention to detail that Dürer came here to learn what he could from the Flemish Primitives.

No master illustrates the concept of Flemish 15th-century painting better than Jan van Eyck. The fine collection here allows the visitor to appreciate two fundamental aspects of his work: religious painting and portrait painting. Van Eyck's improvements in the technique of oil painting are visible to this day. The colours are not only longer lasting, but the malleability of the paints enabled him to achieve an unprecedented subtlety of clarity and hue.

The results can be seen in *Madonna with Canon George van der Paele* (*pictured*), which dominates Room 1. The realism of the work, the colours and textures, particularly of the clothes and carpet, are striking. The portraits of the Madonna and the canon are minutely detailed and, as ever with van Eyck, his use of light is strikingly realistic. In the same room, the *Portrait of Margareta van Eyck*, the artist's wife, is also typical of his style. Unlike many portraits by Italian artists, van Eyck's

works are not embellished. The artist paints people as they are, their faults reflections of the flaws in human nature. The accuracy of the portraits is emphasised by the elaborate and curious hats that the subjects often wear. Despite his sharp realism, van Eyck's work often conveys a sense of mystery and divinity, communicated by the stillness in a number of his paintings.

In Room 2, the *Portrait of Philippe Le Bon* is a good 15th-century copy of a work by the fervent **Rogier van der Weyden**, who combined the technique of Van Eyck with his own emotional and dramatic vision. **Hugo van der Goes**, like many of his contemporaries, was influenced by van Eyck. His realism is particularly noticeable in his reproduction of the physical world. For van der Goes, all objects had a strong symbolic import that was part of a higher reality. *The Death of Our Lady* in Room 3 is a work characterised by dramatic tension and strong religious feeling. The Italian banker Portinari, who was then living in Bruges, ordered a triptych from the artist for a church in Florence. The artist's composition, his use of colours and his minute reproduction of vases and flowers were all unlike the works to be found in Italy in the same period, and the triptych made a great impact on Renaissance artists.

The works of **Hans Memling** are clearly influenced by van der Weyden, although Memling shows a softer touch. The *Moreel Triptych* in Room 4, named after and commissioned by the Bruges *burgomester*, is one of his most impressive works. On one of the side panels is a portrait of Memling himself, and one of his five sons, while his wife and daughters are depicted on the other.

The last of the great Bruges artists was **Gerhard David**, who became the city painter after Memling's death. The *Baptism of Christ*, dating from the early 16th century, is one of

Hotel Jacobs

1 Baliestraat, 8000 Bruges (050 33 98 31/fax 050 33 56 94). **Rates** single €61-€70; double €70-€82. **Credit** AmEx, DC, MC, V.
More earthbound price-wise than Die Swaene (*see below*), this basic hotel has comfortable, practical rooms that are good value for money.

Hotel De Orangerie

10 Kartuizerinnenstraat, 8000 Bruges (050 34 16 49/ fax 050 33 30 16/www.hotelorangerie.com). **Rates** single €173-€222; double €198-€247; suite €272-€297. **Credit** AmEx, DC, MC, V. **Map** p242 B2/3.
This centrally located 15th-century convent, by a canal, has 20 rooms, all individually decorated by Antwerp interior designer Pieter Porters.

Hotel Die Swaene

3 Steenhouwersdijk, 8000 Bruges (050 34 27 98/ fax 050 33 66 74/www.dieswaene-hotel.com). **Rates** single €145-€230; double €170-€245; suite €320-€420. **Credit** AmEx, DC, MC, V. **Map** p242 B2.

his best works. The realism of the piece, evident in the background and plants, is the characteristic that unifies all Flemish 15th-century artists. David's brutally lifelike diptych *Judgement of Cambyses*, which combines a legend from the Ancient World and contemporary Bruges, is another famous piece displayed here. The work is said to symbolise the beheading of the city treasurer in 1488, so punished for opposing the imprisonment of Maximilian.

Hieronymus Bosch's *Final Judgement* is one of the best expressions of the artist's fantastic imagination. The work, where reality and fantasy combine, is a relatively small but enticingly detailed vision of apocalyptic hell. Two rooms of later works are housed in the Xavier Wing, formerly a 19th-century assembly hall. Not as immediately impressive as the 15th-century material, it features domestic and landscape views from the 17th, 18th and 19th centuries. A neo-classical section – including Joseph Suvée's unusual *Invention of the Art of Drawing* – can be found up the spiral staircase leading from Room 10.

The modern section, in Rooms 12-18, is back downstairs. Works by Paul Delvaux, René Magritte and James Ensor are the main attractions here, as well as a diverse selection of Flemish Pop Art.

Groeninge Museum

12 Dijver (050 44 87 11). **Open** 9.30am-5pm Tue-Sun. **Admission** €7; €4 concessions; free under-13s. **Credit** AmEx, MC, V. **Map** p242 B3.

Trips Out of Town

Right in the centre of the city, this 15th-century mansion next to a canal is wonderfully romantic – as close to Venice as you can get in Belgium. All 22 rooms are individually decorated and come in standard to superior deluxe versions. A candlelit restaurant, pool and sauna are further pluses.

Relais Oud-Huis Amsterdam

3 Spiegelrei, 8000 Bruges (050 34 18 10/fax 050 33 88 91/www.oha.be). **Rates** single €161-€173; double €198-€223; suite €223-€322. **Credit** AmEx, DC, MC, V. **Map** p242 B1.
A splendid hotel set in a beautifully renovated 17th-century house, overlooking one of the canals. With its carved wooden staircase, chandeliers, antique furniture and bare wooden beams, the opulent interior is quite staggering. There is a comfortable bar and a very pretty interior courtyard.

Romantik Pandhotel

16 Pandreitje, 8000 Bruges (050 34 06 66/fax 050 34 05 56/www.pandhotel.com). **Rates** single €111-€198; double €136-€223; suite €272-€297. **Credit** AmEx, DC, MC, V. **Map** p242 B3.
This charming, classy 23-room hotel located in a leafy, tranquil corner of Bruges occupies an 18th-century carriage house. Chris Vanhaecke, her family and staff offer a friendly welcome to guests.

Snuffel Travellers' Inn

47-49 Ezelstraat, 8000 Bruges (050 33 31 33/fax 050 33 32 50/www.snuffel.be). **Rates** €11-€13 per person. **Credit** AmEx, MC, V. **Map** p242 A1.
For bargain hunters, the Snuffel offers hostel-like accommodation in rooms sleeping four, six, eight or 12 people. Breakfast costs extra.

De Tuilerieën

7 Dijver, 8000 Bruges (050 34 36 91/ fax 050 34 04 00/www.hoteltuilerieen.com). **Rates** single €173-€222; double €198-€247; suite €310-€434. **Credit** AmEx, DC, MC, V. **Map** p242 B3.
An elegantly converted 15th-century mansion, this is the sister hotel of De Orangerie (*see p249*). The rooms are all decorated by trendy Pieter Porters, and there's a pool, sauna, jacuzzi and solarium.

Van Nevel

13 Carmersstraat, 8000 Bruges (050 34 68 60/ fax 050 34 76 16). **Rates** single €33-€40; double €40-€48. **Credit** MC, V. **Map** p242 C1.
Close to the church of St Anna (a ten-minute walk from the city centre) in a quiet part of Bruges, the Van Nevels rent two well-equipped rooms in a 16th-century house.

Het Wit Beertje

4 Witte Beerstraat, 8200 Bruges (050 45 08 88/ fax 050 45 08 80). **Rates** single €28.50; double €39.66. **No credit cards.**
At Jean-Pierre Defour's friendly 'Little White Bear' guesthouse all rooms are en suite and come with a telephone and TV. Prices include breakfast. It's about a ten-minute walk to both the centre of Bruges and the train station.

Eating & drinking

Bruges is packed with restaurants. All strive to attract tourists, some very obviously so by offering menus to suit different nationalities (English breakfasts, for instance), but most of them with tourist menus, consisting of several courses of either seafood or regional specialities. When they are in season you can eat mussels practically everywhere.

Restaurants

Aneth

1 Maria van Bourgondielaan (050 31 11 89). **Open** noon-2pm, 7-9pm Tue-Sat. **Main courses** from €30. **Set menus** €50-€73. **Credit** AmEx, DC, MC, V.
A gourmet fish restaurant with a good selection of fixed-price menus. Specialities include lobster with foie gras, and swordfish with baby vegetables.

De Belegde Boterham

5 Kleine St Amandstraat (050 34 91 31). **Open** noon-6pm Mon-Sat. **Main courses** €5-€10. **No credit cards.** **Map** p242 A2.
De Belegde Boterham serves salads, sandwiches and other simple dishes. Friendly and trendy rustic decor, with plain wooden tables for sharing. It's very busy around lunchtime and customers are mostly local workers.

Bistro De Schaar

2 Hooistraat (050 33 59 79). **Open** noon-2.30pm, 6-11pm Mon-Wed, Fri-Sun. **Main courses** €14.50-€17. **Credit** AmEx, DC, MC, V.
A little way out of the tourist centre (just off Predikherenrei), but all the better for it, this cracking little bistro offers a modern take on cosy rusticity and first-rate grills, as well as less traditional dishes of the day such as prawns in garlic and cheese-filled ravioli. Service is friendly.

Cafedraal

38 Zilverstraat (050 34 08 45). **Open** noon-2am Tue-Sat. *Food served* noon-2.30pm, 6-11pm Tue-Sat. **Main courses** €20-€35. **Credit** AmEx, MC, V. **Map** p242 A2.
A good brasserie in a 15th-century house with a church-like interior and a lovely terrace in summer.

Chagall

40 St Amandstraat (050 33 61 12). **Open** 11am-12.30am daily. **Main courses** €11.16-€18.50. **Credit** AmEx, DC, MC, V. **Map** p242 A2.
Chagall serves fine seafood in a relaxed enviroment. Specialities include scampi, eels and mussels; the shellfish come highly recommended.

De Hobbit

8 Kemelstraat (050 33 55 20/www.hobbitgrill.be). **Open** 6pm-1am daily. **Main courses** €13. **Set menus** €16-€58. **Credit** AmEx, MC, V. **Map** p242 A3.

A loyal yuppie and student following come to take advantage of the reasonably priced pasta, chicken and other standard fare, served at big round tables by candlelight.

De Karmeliet
19 Langestraat (050 33 82 59/www.resto.be/ karmeliet). **Open** noon-2pm, 7-10pm Tue-Sat. **Main courses** €30-€50. **Set menus** €50-€115. **Credit** AmEx, DC, MC, V. **Map** p242 C2.
De Karmeliet is a really wonderful restaurant with a three-star Michelin rating. Chef Geert van Hecke's favourite staples include rabbit, special breeds of chicken, truffles and scallops. Special menus cover

such themes at 'the flat country'. The decor is airy and contemporary and you can see the chef at work behind glass at the back of the dining room.

De Stove
4 Kleine St Amandstraat (050 33 78 35/ www.restaurantdestove.be). **Open** noon-1.45pm, 6.45-9.30pm Mon, Tue, Fri-Sun. **Main courses** €15.50-€23.30. **Set menus** €37-€52. **Credit** AmEx, DC, MC, V. **Map** p242 A2.
An elegant little restaurant, just off one of the main shopping streets, serving a variety of hearty meat and fish dishes. Its old-time decor, with an old stove and chimney, is simple and unpretentious.

Culture city

For the second time in as many years, a Belgian city has been chosen as a Cultural Capital of Europe. Praise indeed for such a small country, but no surprise to those in the know, those that recognise the artistic diversity of this nation. The beauty of Bruges gives the year-long programme, entitled Bruges 2002, a ready-made auditorium, whether events take place inside or out. And the city is not afraid to move forward, cherishing that for which it is famous, while livening it up with an injection of the new. Fireworks at the opening ceremony (*pictured*) meant proceedings started with a bang.

Something that marks out Bruges 2002 is its numerous civil engineering projects, which add exciting modern architecture to the ancient streets and skyline. The most important of these is the Concertgebouw, a world-class concert hall. Its red-brick light tower reflects the three famous Bruges spires and shows that the modern can mix admirably with the ancient.

Another project has finally fixed a bone of contention for residents. There has always been a gap in the ramparts surrounding the old town. Pedestrians and cyclists could never complete a full circuit until the arrival of Jürg Conzett's minimalist crossing, which still allows boats to pass up the canal. Further mixing the old with the new is another building on the Burg, right in the heart of romantic Bruges. What could be seen as controversial modern architecture is already applauded as a brilliant feat of ingenuity by Japanese designer Toyo Ito. A clean, transparent pavilion using water and glass is reached by a tiny bridge, literally linking the old and the new.

Youth-oriented events during the year include DJ workshops and techno parties; live performances bring out controversial names such as Jan Fabre and Jos de Pauw, and the visual arts make the most of both the Flemish masters and the utterly modern. Bruges 2002 has not only put together an outstanding programme of arts, events and exhibitions, it has ensured that its famous centre has a firm foot in the new millennium.

Bruges 2002
Culture Desk, Concertgebouw, 34 't Zand (070 22 33 02/www.brugge2002.be). **Admission** varies, but 3-day pass €25 for one person, €35 for two.

Trips Out of Town

Tanuki

1 Oude Gentweg (050 34 75 12/www.tanuki.be).
Open noon-2pm, 6.30-9.30pm Wed-Sun. **Main
courses** €15-€29. **Set menus** €45-€55. **Credit**
AmEx, MC, V. **Map** p242 B4.
If you need a break from hearty Belgian food,
Tanuki's oriental minimalism will be welcome.
Sushi and sashimi cost between €12 and €20; noodle
dishes are a reasonable €4 to €9.

In Den Wittekop

14 St Jacobstraat (050 33 20 59). **Open** *Café*
6pm-late Mon-Sat. *Restaurant* 6-11pm Mon-Sat.
Main courses €12.40-€21.70. **Credit** AmEx,
DC, MC, V. **Map** p242 A2.
Very close to the tourist centre, but an authentic
Bruges experience, this rustic bistro doles out earthy
Flemish grub, or you can just partake of one of the
many fine beers on offer.

Cafés & bars

Celtic Ireland

8 Burg (050 34 45 02). **Open** 10am-varies daily.
Main courses bistro €9.80-€14-80; restaurant
€12.40-€18. **Set menu** €42. **Credit** AmEx, MC, V.
Map p242 B2.
Celtic Ireland is a combination of pub and restaurant (Kells Room). The interior is adorned with
miniature manuscripts from the *Book of Kells* and
there are stunning stained-glass windows. Live
music every weekend.

Craenenburg

16 Markt (050 33 34 02). **Open** 7am-midnight
daily. **Main courses** €4.46-€9.67. **No credit
cards**. **Map** p242 A/B2.
Set on Bruges's main square, the house in which
Maximilian of Austria was held captive has now
become a typical Bruges café, with yellowed walls
and wooden tables and some fabulous stained
glass. Expect old favourites such as French onion
soup and salad niçoise.

Eetcafé de Vuyst

15 Simon Stevinplein (05 34 22 31). **Open** 10am-
9pm Mon, Wed-Sun. **Main courses** €12.90-€15.50.
Set menu €12.40-€18.60. **Credit** AmEx, DC, MC,
V. **Map** p242 A3.
This is a fun café-bar with newspapers plastered on
the walls and glass-topped tables containing original paintings. There are various *moules* options, as
well as salads, crêpes, croques and a three-course
lunch for €12.40.

De Garre

1 De Garre (050 34 10 29). **Open** noon-midnight
Mon-Thur; noon-1am Fri; 11am-1am Sat; 11am-
midnight Sun. **No credit cards**. **Map** p242 B2.
Right at the back of the shortest blind alley in
Bruges (off Breidelstraat), this bar sells a huge selection of Belgian beers. It's situated in a 16th-century
house, so expect wooden beams, brick walls and lots
of atmosphere.

De Medici Sorbetière

9 Geldmuntstraat (050 33 93 41). **Open** 8.30am-
4.30pm Mon, Wed-Fri; noon-4.30pm Tue; 8.30am-
7pm Sat; 3-6pm Sun. **Main courses** €7-€17.
Credit MC, V. **Map** p242 A2.
A tiny café that is usually packed out with people
hankering after their tarts, quiches and cakes. The
friendly staff also serve pasta dishes and omelettes.

Sukerbuyc

5 Katelijnestraat (050 33 08 87/www.sukerbuyc.com).
Open 8.30am-6.30pm daily. **No credit cards**.
Map p242 A3.
A tearoom-cum-chocolate shop where a hot chocolate is served as a dish of melted liquid to be stirred
into a mug of hot milk. Tea cakes and tarts are
served with huge dollops of cream and chocolates.

The Top

5 St Salvatorskerkhof (050 33 03 51). **Open** 6pm-
2am daily. **No credit cards**. **Map** p242 A3.
Probably the best bar in Bruges, formerly run by a
genial east Londoner, since taken over by local dance
music buff Karel Lievens. It still attracts expats,
acolytes from the local, less prestigious football club,
Cercle Brugge, and locals interested in decent dance
sounds until early hours.

De Versteende Nacht

11 Langestraat (050 34 32 93). **Open** 7pm-1am
Tue-Thur; 6pm-1am Fri, Sat. **No credit cards**.
Map p242 C2.
The manager is a real comic strip and jazz fan, and
it shows: there are comic books aplenty and the
walls are festooned with cartoons and jazz instru-
ments. There's a free jazz session/piano show on
Wednesday nights.

Trips Out of Town

Shopping

Look hard and you'll find that there's a lot more to Bruges than twee touristy shops specialising in lace, chocolates and overpriced antiques. The main shopping drag with the usual run of international chainstores is **Steenstraat**, which runs from the Markt to 't Zand. **Noordzandstraat** has a cluster of high fashion boutiques. **Wollestraat** has its share of touristic lace shops, but don't be misled; there are some gems too. Many shops are closed on Sundays.

Design

Callebert & O-Nivo
25 Wollestraat (050 33 50 61/www.callebert.be). **Open** 2-6pm Mon; 10am-noon, 2-6pm Tue-Sat; 3-6pm Sun. **Credit** AmEx, DC, MC, V. **Map** p242 B2.
An unexpected celebration of Belgian contemporary furnishings and design with four linked shops selling homeware objects and clothes by some of the best. It's great in summer because there is a small café with an attractive decked terrace with a view through three of the shopfronts. Check out B for ceramics by Pieter Stockman and architect bOb Van Reeth and furniture by internationally famed brothers the Van Severens. Callebert is good for Scandinavian glassware and cool cutlery.

Fifty Fifty
48 Katelijnestraat (050 34 69 87). **Open** 2-6.30pm Tue; 10am-4.30pm Wed-Sun. **Credit** AmEx, DC, MC, V. **Map** p242 B4.
Decorative American items from the 1950s, from large items (replica jukeboxes, fridges) to small ones (dolls). Good ideas for presents, even if you're not a big fan of the decade.

Fashion

L'Héroine
32 Noordzandstraat (050 33 56 57). **Open** 10am-6.30pm Mon-Sat. **Credit** AmEx, DC, MC, V. **Map** p242 A2.
Bruges is a resolutely romantic city and if a wedding is in the offing look no further than this gorgeous boutique with its second floor devoted to dresses by Belgian designers Mieke Cosyn, Kaat Tilley and Ann Huybens. Downstairs there is menswear by Dries Van Noten, womenswear by Martin Margiela and jewellery by Antwerp duo Wouters & Hendrix.

Joaquim Jofre
7 Vlaamingstraat (050 33 39 60). **Open** 9.30am-6.30pm Mon-Sat. **Credit** AmEx, DC, MC, V. **Map** p242 B2.
Come here and marvel at the art deco shop fittings imported from the owner's home country of Spain. The women's clothes are classic, well cut and beau-

tifully finished and there is also a good line-up of accessories, including hats. The shop is open on Sunday afternoons (2-6pm) in March and April.

Gifts

'T Apostellientje
11 Balstraat (050 33 78 60). **Open** 9.30am-6pm Mon-Sat; 10am-1pm Sun. **Credit** AmEx, DC, MC, V. **Map** p242 C1.
Be careful when you are buying lace as there is much on the market that is passed off as being authentic handmade Bruges handiwork when it's not. The genuine stuff is sold here by a mother (in the business for 20 years) and her daughter, who has written several books on lace.

The Bottle Shop
13 Wollestraat (050 34 99 80). **Open** *Summer* 9am-11pm daily. *Winter* 9am-7pm daily. **Credit** MC, V. **Map** p242 B2.
From the outside, it's easy to dismiss this shop as a tourist trap. But that would be a big mistake: it stocks 850 types of Belgian beer – Trappist brews, hard-to-find *gueuzes*, jars of *genever* and an astounding selection of mineral waters.

Soap Bar
21 Wollestraat (050 61 52 71). **Open** 9.30am-7pm daily. **Credit** AmEx, DC, MC, V. **Map** p242 B2.
The Soap Bar is remarkably similar to chainshop Lush – the same kind of decor, stock and presentation – with blocks of soap sold by the gram in weird and wonderful scents and colours. Under the same ownership as the Bottle Shop.

Music & books

De Reyghere
12 Markt (050 33 34 03). **Open** 10am-12.30pm, 1.30-7pm Mon-Sat; 2-6pm Sun. **Credit** AmEx, DC, MC, V. **Map** p242 A/B2.
Established in 1888, De Reyghere is a bookshop that specialises in international newspapers and travel guidebooks. You'll also find there is a large selection of foreign literature.

Rombaux
13 Mallebergplaats (050 33 25 75/www.rombaux.be). **Open** 9am-12.30pm, 2-6.30pm Mon-Fri; 9am-6pm Sat. **Credit** MC, V.
If you are a classical music lover this shop alone is almost worth a trip to Bruges. Rombaux has been owned by the same family for three generations (they started out by selling pianos; see 3 Kelkstraat round the corner). The CDs are catalogued by composer, country of concert or type. Rock and pop greats are stocked, but classical is the speciality. Enjoy the furnishings too, original turn-of-the-last-century portraits and chandeliers – the shop was once a private home. The back room has piles of sheet music in alphabetical order.

Trips Out of Town

Ghent

Small, friendly and bohemian, the capital of East Flanders is a must-see.

Wander down the platform underpass of Gent St Pieters train station on a late Friday afternoon, and you'll find students with bulging rucksacks cheerily bidding farewells in two languages before making their way home for the weekend to other parts of monolingual Wallonia or Flanders. Ghent is a friendly little place, less crowded than Bruges and lacking the attitude of Antwerp. In any other country it would be a major tourist attraction, but being quite quaint and fairly fashionable doesn't cut it when you're sandwiched between Bruges and Antwerp – so many put off Ghent until their next visit to Belgium. Don't make the same mistake: it's small enough to stroll round in a day and you'll soon be vowing to return.

Gent to the Flemings and Gand to the Walloons, the capital of East Flanders and Belgium's second port – it's on the banks of two rivers, the Leie and the Ketel – is 56 kilometres (35 miles) north-west of Brussels. It has almost as many canals, museums and paintings as Bruges and the bars, cafés and shops cramming its streets rival those in Antwerp, but Ghent has its own unmistakable atmosphere: young, bohemian, laid-back and just a little shy. The city has become more aware of its potential as a tourist destination in the past decade – the major attractions are now floodlit – but it still feels embarrassed at having to promote itself.

The city has had a rich, if erratic, history. In 1540, Charles the Great – who was born in Ghent – returned to the city in a rage after its citizens refused to pay higher taxes. Charles revoked the city's trading privileges and had the rebellion's ringleaders executed. He then forced 50 of the city's elders, dressed only in white shirts and with nooses around their necks, to beg for his mercy. Because of this, Ghent's residents are known as *stropdragers*, meaning noose-wearers.

But Ghent today feels very privileged. It may not be the commercial hub that it was in the Middle Ages – when the cloth trade saw it become the largest town in Western Europe – but there's still a lot of money here. The city is clean, airy and pedestrianised. It can be very chilled out during the day, not to say comatose, but its large student population makes sure the evenings burn long and brightly. The best time to visit is in the summer, when there's the

Kozzmozz and I Love Techno parties, plus the annual **Ten Days Of...** during the Geentse Feesten (*see p264* **Party on**).

GETTING THERE

It's a half-hour journey from Brussels; there are four fast trains an hour from Gare du Nord, Gare Centrale or Gare du Midi. From Gent St Pieters station take any one of five trams into town (1, 10, 21, 22 or 40; pay on board). If you arrive by car, follow the signs reading 'P-route'; this will take you through streets where you are allowed to park and, eventually, to a multi-storey car park.

Sightseeing

Ghent has the most listed buildings in Belgium, but the must-see attractions are the towers of **St Niklaaskerk**, the **Belfort** and **St Baafskathedraal** (and the view of the three of them together); the van Eycks' extraordinary painting *The Adoration of the Mystic Lamb*, which is in St Baafskathedraal; and the **Gravensteen castle**.

St Michielsbrug to St Baafskathedraal

The **St Michielsbrug** is a good place to start a tour of the city. One of the best views of the cathedral is from this bridge over the Leie, which overlooks the **Graslei** (Herb Quay) and **Korenlei** (Corn Quay). Both are lined with beautiful houses, most built during the Flemish Renaissance but some dating back as far as 1000. Just south of the bridge, on the west side of the river, is **St Michielskerk**, standing alongside the former Dominican monastery Het Pand, now part of the University of Ghent – the public are free to wander around. On the other side of the bridge stands **St Niklaaskerk**. This outstanding piece of Scheldt Gothic architecture was built in the 13th century. Its interior is dominated by a fantastically over-the-top baroque altarpiece.

Next door stands the **Stadhuis** (Town Hall), designed to be the largest town hall in Europe. Building began in 1518 but had to be halted because of religious strife and diminishing funds (the bickering contributed to that tantrum of Charles V's). Work resumed at the end of

The triple towers of Ghent: **St Niklaaskerk**, the **Belfort** and **St Baafskathedraal**.

the 16th century, and the result of this staggered construction is clearly visible. One part, decorated with countless statues, is in an ornate Gothic style, while the more sober section of the façade reflects post-Reformation taste. Check with the tourist office for information on guided tours.

Across the Botermarkt from the Stadhuis soars the **Belfort** (belfry), built in the 14th century (though later heavily restored). Its interior – containing a carillon and a bell museum – isn't exactly thrilling, but it's worth the entrance fee for the view over the city and the neighbouring cathedral. The **Tourist Office** (*see p257*) is also in the building.

Ghent's first cathedral was founded (as St Peter's) by the Brabant-born St Bavo in the seventh century. Built over six centuries, the current **St Baafskathedraal** is remarkable as much for its high and late Gothic style as for the works of art it contains. Laurent Delvaux's elaborate rococo pulpit, in oak and marble, is the first thing you see on entering,

and Pieter Paul Rubens' *Entry of St Bavo into the Monastery* is displayed in the north transept. But the cathedral's – and the city's – undisputed masterpiece is *The Adoration of the Mystic Lamb* by Hubert and Jan van Eyck. The painting is on show in the De Villa Chapel, which can become very crowded. It's worth the wait, though. The picture depicts a scene from the Apocalypse according to St John, but the colours are so bright and glistening that the painting seems to light up the whole chapel.

The 12th-century crypt is the oldest part of the cathedral. Although it contains tombs and the usual religious paraphernalia, it's more notable for its frescoes and for Justus van Gent's painting *The Calvary Scene*.

The area south and west of the cathedral contains Ghent's main shopping streets, including **Veldstraat** (running south from St Niklaaskerk), the most crowded but the least exciting, and the more interesting **Magaleinstraat** and **Koestraat**, which lie south of the Belfort.

Trips Out of Town

The suitably fortress-like **Gravensteen castle**.

Belfort

17A Botermarkt (tourist office 09 266 52 32).
Open *Easter-Oct* 10am-1pm, 2-4pm daily. Closed
Nov-Easter. **Admission** €2.48; free under-7s.
No credit cards. **Map** p258 B3.
Free guided tours between 1 May and 9 Sept.

St Baafskathedraal

St-Baafsplein (09 225 49 85). **Open** *Apr-Oct*
8.30am-6pm Mon-Sat; 1-6pm Sun. *Nov-Mar*
8.30am-5pm Mon-Sat; 1-5pm Sun. **Admission** free.
The Mystic Lamb **Open** *Apr-Oct* 9.30am-5pm
Mon-Sat; 1-5pm Sun. *Nov-Mar* 10.30am-noon,
2.30-4pm Mon-Sat; 2-5pm Sun. **Admission**: €2.48;
€1.24 concessions; free under-6s.

Gravensteen castle & around

Surrounded by water on the north-west edge
of the centre is the **Gravensteen castle**. Built
in 1180 by Philippe of Alsace, Count of Flanders,
on the site of the first count's original stronghold,
this is the only medieval fortress in Flanders.
The arrestingly grim structure lost its military
function centuries ago – it was subsequently
used as a mint, a court of justice and even a
cotton mill. It has a small collection of torture
instruments, which young boys will love.

Next door to the castle, on St Veerleplein, a
bas-relief Neptune towers over the entrance of
the **Vismarkt** (fish market), while across the
water stands the **Museum voor Sierkunst**

en **Vormgeving** (Museum of Decorative
Arts and Design). Located in an 18th-century
house, this superb collection includes beautiful
royal portraits set off by crystal chandeliers,
silk wall coverings and tapestries. The
furniture, mostly French, includes baroque,
rococo and Louis XVI pieces. A huge and
startlingly modern extension was added at the
back in 1992; the design part of the museum is
housed here, as well as temporary exhibitions.
There is a stunning collection of modern design,
including art nouveau pieces by Victor Horta,
Paul Hankar and Henri van de Velde.

Just east of the castle on the Kraanlei is the
quirky **Museum voor Volkskunde** (Folklore
Museum, also called the Het Huis van Alijn).
Occupying 18 almshouses, with a garden and
chapel, this museum is aimed primarily at
children, but parents will also enjoy it. It aims
to show life in Ghent in the 19th century: you
can see candlestick-makers, cloth-makers,
reconstructions of sweet shops, pubs and a
chemist's. The museum has been undergoing
major refurbishment for the past two years.

Patershol, the tangle of streets just north
of here, is packed with great restaurants and
bars. Market lovers should head back over the
Leie to the **Vrijdagmarkt**, a vast square that
used to be the focal point of political life and
quarrels in the Middle Ages and is still used

several days a week as a market-place; restaurants and bars line its sides. There are market stalls on many squares and markets most days of the week. There's a fruit and vegetable market in **Groentenmarkt** every morning (except Sunday), and a bird market in Vrijdagmarkt on Sunday mornings. You'll come across several excellent traditional bakeries and cheese shops in the area, and plenty of cafés and tearooms.

If you're a keen walker or are feeling energetic, you might want to venture outside the historical centre. The River Leie along **Lievekaai** and **St Antoniuskaai**, north of the castle, is a particularly charming walk.

Gravensteen

St-Veerleplein (09 225 93 06). Open Apr-Sept 9am-6pm daily. Oct-Mar 9am-5pm daily. **Admission** €4; free under-12s. **No credit cards. Map** p258 A2.

Museum voor Sierkunst en Vormgeving

5 Jan Breydelstraat (09 267 99 99/http://design.museum.gent.be). **Open** 10am-6pm Tue-Sun. **Admission** €2.50; €1.20 concessions; free under-12s. **Map** p258 A2.

Museum voor Volkskunde

65 Kraanlei (09 269 23 50/http://volkskunde.museum.gent.be/www.huisvanalijn.be). **Open** 11am-5pm Tue-Sun. **Admission** €2.50; €1.75 concessions; free under-12s. **No credit cards. Map** p258 B2.

The deep south

The area between St Pieters station and the city centre has three intriguing museums. Along the west side of the River Leie, the former Abdij (Abbey) van de Bijloke contains the **Bijlokemuseum**. The red-brick abbey was founded in the early 13th century and kept its religious function until it was closed down by the French in 1797. Its interior now provides a sympathetic home to a varied collection of furniture, religious sculpture, paintings, guild banners and Chinese porcelain. It's a low-key treat.

South of here, across the river (a five-minute walk from the train station; around 25 minutes from the centre) is the **Citadelpark**, laid out in the 1870s on the site of a Habsburg castle. Here you'll find the outstanding **SMAK** (Stedelijk Museum voor Actuele Kunst – Museum of Contemporary Art), which opened in 1999. Generally thought to be Flanders' finest collection of modern art, it boasts first-rate works by Francis Bacon, Joseph Beuys and David Hockney. There's also a good spread of minimal and conceptual art, with the 1960s particularly well represented with pieces by Christo, Warhol and Broodthaers.

Facing the SMAK is the **Museum voor Schone Kunsten** (Museum of Fine Arts). It's a bright, spacious and not overwhelmingly huge collection of paintings and sculptures from the 14th century to the first half of the 20th. Works by Hieronymus Bosch, the Elder and Younger Pieter Bruegels, Rubens and Van Dyck are all on show.

Bijlokemuseum

2 Godshuizenlaan (09 225 11 06). **Open** 10am-6pm Thur; 2-6pm Sun. **Admission** €2.48; €1.24 concessions; free under-12s. **No credit cards.**

Museum voor Schone Kunsten

3 Nicolaas de Liemaerckereplein, Citadelpark (09 222 17 03/www.finearts.museum.gent.be). **Open** 10am-6pm Tue-Sun. **Admission** €2.48; €1.24 concessions; free under-12s. **No credit cards.**

SMAK (Stedelijk Museum voor Actuele Kunst)

Citadelpark (09 221 17 03/www.smak.be). **Open** 10am-6pm Tue-Sun. **Admission** €4.96; €3.71 concessions; free under-12s. **Credit** AmEx, DC, MC, V.

Tourist information

City of Ghent Tourist Office

Belfort, 17A Botermarkt (09 266 52 32/www.gent.be). **Open** Apr-Oct 9.30am-6.30pm daily. Nov-Mar 9.30am-4.30pm daily. **Map** p258 B3. The useful and detailed website is also available in English and French.

Elaborate **St Baafskathedraal**. *See p255.*

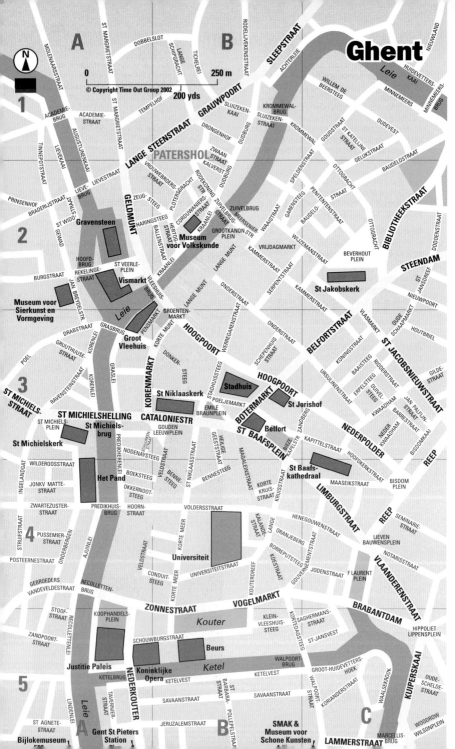

Accommodation

Ghent can provide a decent supply of
accommodation to suit all budgets – depending
on the time of year. At Christmas, Easter
and especially during the Gentse Feesten in
mid July (*see p264* **Party on**) you would be
wise to book at least a fortnight, if not a month,
in advance. To do this, you need to call the
tourist administration office (09 225 36
41/www.gent. be; 8.30am-noon, 1-4.30pm
Mon-Fri). They will check availability by
phone within your price range, then reserve
free of charge when you call them back 30
minutes later. Visitors to the office in town
(*see p257*) can have the English-speaking
staff reserve rooms for a €5 deposit, deducted
from the final bill.

The **Guild of Guesthouses in Ghent**
(www.bedandbreakfast-gent.be) has 34 families
who offer B&B accommodation, from a room
in a cosy private home to a self-contained suite
in a 17th-century cloister. Check the website
for a list with descriptions; the tourist office
also has an album of snapshots. Rates from
€20 for a room to €372 for a luxury suite.
There is also a B&B bureau, **Chambres
d'Amis** (09 238 4347/www.chambres@
pandora.be), which runs a 24-hour reservation
service. Doubles are charged at €45-€50 per
room, including breakfast.

Boatel
*29A Voorhoutkaai, 9000 Ghent (09 267 10 30/
fax 09 267 10 39/www.theboatel.com).* **Credit**
single €72-€87; double €95-€119. **Credit** AmEx,
DC, MC, V.
Ghent's first floating hotel. This former transport
boat, near Dampoort train station, ten minutes' walk
from town, has been converted into a seven-room
hotel, complete with original woodwork and port-
holes. Good breakfast too.

Brooderie
8 Jan Breydelstraat, 9000 Ghent (09 225 06 23).
Rates single €38; double €58-€63. **No credit
cards. Map** p258 A2.
Charming three-room B&B in the centre of Ghent,
in a pretty gabled house overlooking the canal. The
light-filled rooms are clean and fresh; toilets and
shower are shared. Brooderie is also a bakery with
a health food café that serves a vegetarian menu and
hearty brunch (open 8am-6pm Tue-Sun).

De Draecke Youth Hostel
*11 St Widostraat, 9000 Ghent (09 233 70 50/
www.vjh.be).* **Rates** €14.50-€22.50 per person.
Credit MC, V. **Map** p258 A2.
Located in a picturesque part of the centre, De
Draecke takes some beating if you're young and on
a tight budget. There are 106 beds in rooms that
sleep two to six people. All come with bathrooms.

Erasmus
*25 Poel, 9000 Ghent (09 224 21 95/09 225 75 91/
fax 09 233 42 41/hotel.erasmus@proximedia.be).*
Rates single €67-€79; double €96-€105; family
room €143. **Credit** AmEx, MC, V. **Map** p258 A3.
A cosy hotel, only five minutes' walk from the
medieval town centre. The owners have preserved
the authentic character of the 16th-century building
while providing the 11 well-furnished rooms with
every desirable modern comfort. The hotel lounge
is another plus point.

Hotel Adoma
*19 St Denijslaan, 9000 Ghent (09 222 65 50/
fax 09 245 09 37/www.hotel-adoma.be).* **Rates**
single €44-€49; double €55-€65; suite €75-€100.
Credit AmEx, DC, MC, V.
A bargain – and it has the advantage of being a
stone's throw from the station (a tram ride from the
centre). The rooms are comfy and all have phones
and TVs. There's also a car park.

Hotel Cour St Georges
*2 Botermarkt, 9000 Ghent (09 224 24 24/
fax 09 224 26 40/www.hotelbel.com/cour-st-
georges.htm).* **Rates** single €65-€75; double
€95-€105; suite €135-€145. **Credit** AmEx, DC,
MC, V. **Map** p258 B3.
Hotels don't come with much more of a historical
pedigree than the Cour St Georges, which is located
opposite the Stadhuis and near the Belfort. Boasting
origins from 1228, and Charles V and Napoleon
among former guests, the rooms aren't as characterful as they might be, but have all the mod cons.
Beware that the 'small room' fits the description. The
restaurant comes recommended.

Hotel Gravensteen
*35 Jan Breydelstraat, 9000 Ghent (09 225 11 50/
fax 09 225 18 50/www.gravensteen.be).* **Rates**
single €99; double €114. **Credit** AmEx, DC, MC, V.
Map p258 A2.
A beautiful hotel set in a 19th-century *hôtel partic-
ulier*. The Second Empire style is imposing and
impeccable; the elegant rooms are all equipped with
modern facilities. The hotel has a bar, sauna, conference room and private car park.

Hotel Sofitel
*63 Hoogpoort, 9000 Ghent (09 233 33 31/fax
09 233 11 02/www.sofitel.com).* **Rates** Mon-Thur
double €233; executive double €270; suite €394.
Fri-Sun double €147; executive double €233; suite
€270. **Credit** AmEx, DC, MC, V. **Map** p258 C3.
In the heart of the historic centre, the Ghent Sofitel
may not be the most charming place in town to lay
your head, but it does offer the full range of facilities, spacious rooms and efficient staff. There's a bar,
conference room, sauna, restaurant and car park.

La Maison de Claudine
*20 Pussemierstraat, 9000 Ghent (tel/fax 09 225
75 08/mobile 0495 443 130/maison.claudine@
newmail.net).* **Rates** €38-€50; double €62-€75.
No credit cards. Map p258 A4.

Some of Ghent's most beautiful buildings line the **Graslei**. *See p254.*

For a classy B&B with a whiff of the bohemian about it, 'La Maison' is hard to beat. Two luxury suites and one room (all no-smoking) are available. The largest suite is an enormous penthouse in the house's eaves, with a superbly comfortable bed and fine views over the towers of Ghent. The other suite is a self-contained former coach house, which looks out on to the walled garden. Every room has central heating, an en suite bathroom and a TV. Breakfast is a communal affair in the owner's high-ceilinged living room.

PoortAckere Monasterium

50-58 Oude Houtlei, 9000 Ghent (09 269 22 10/ fax 09 269 22 30/www.poortackere.com). **Rates** single €95.44; double €120.23. *Guesthouse* single €45.86; double €86.76. **Credit** AmEx, DC, MC, V. Not far from the centre, this renovated convent dates from 1278, and now houses a hotel, a restaurant and a concert venue, all arrayed around two lovely walled gardens. Some bedrooms are rather spartan, others are more luxurious, but all are fresh, clean and a welcome antidote to chain blandness.

Eating & drinking

Your impression of Ghent nightlife is likely to depend on the area of town you visit and the evening you happen to choose. The southern part of the city is certainly livelier and has the trendiest bars, largely because this is the student area and attracts a younger crowd. Most students, however, go home for the weekend and their big night out is usually Thursday. On Saturday the bars of the student area are still busy, but the crowd is older, calmer and somewhat smarter. You'll rarely have a problem getting a drink in the early hours around here.

The Patershol area, on the north side of the city's historical centre, also has plenty of restaurants and bars. With the canals and medieval streets, the atmosphere can be

magical in the evening. The streets are quieter than around St Pietersnieuwstraat and there is hardly any traffic at all. Patershol bars and restaurants tend to be rather elegant, and more subdued than in the student area.

Restaurants

If you're vegetarian, Ghent is one of the best cities to be in Belgium; elsewhere it can be tough finding non-meaty fare. Many pubs and bars (*see p262*) also serve food.

Le Baan Thai

57 Corduwanierstraat (09 233 21 41). **Open** 6.30-10pm Tue-Sat; noon-2pm, 6.30-10pm Sun. **Main courses** €10.65. **Set menu** €30. **Credit** AmEx, DC, MC, V. **Map** p258 B2. A pretty restaurant set back from the street and overlooking a courtyard, which serves excellent Thai food to eat in or take away. Booking essential.

Het Blauwe Huis

17 Drabstraat (09 233 10 05). **Open** noon-2pm, 7-10pm Tue-Fri; 7-10pm Sat, Sun. **Main courses** €15. **Set menu** €30. **Credit** AmEx, MC, V. **Map** p258 A3. Formerly known as Diavolo, Het Blauwe Huis is hard to miss: it's the only electric-blue townhouse on the block. The music and decor are the same as in its Diavolo days, but the once-inexpensive food is now more sophisticated and pricey French cuisine.

Brasserie Keizershof

47 Vrijdagmarkt (09 223 44 46). **Open** noon-2.30pm, 5.30-11pm Tue-Sat. **Main courses** €9. **Credit** V. **Map** p258 B2. A high-ceilinged, beautifully renovated restaurant in the centre of town. The wide-ranging menu has no shortage of traditional Ghent dishes, and also features fish, pastas, steaks and French standards. Prices are reasonable.

Brasserie the Moka

46 Koestraat (09 225 00 54). **Open** 11am-late
Mon-Sat. **Main courses** €34-€80. **Credit** AmEx,
DC, MC, V. **Map** p258 B4.
Generous quantities of traditional Belgian food. The
lunchtime specials are usually varied and good, and
local specialities such as the *waterzooi* and *carbon-
nade flamande* are worth trying.

'T Buikske Vol

17 Kraanlei (09 225 18 80). **Open** noon-2pm,
7-10pm Mon-Tue, Thur, Fri; 7-10pm Sat, Sun.
Main courses €15. **Set menus** €26. **Credit**
AmEx, MC, V. **Map** p258 B2.
The upmarket Buikske Vol is well regarded. The
open kitchen produces rather more daring dishes
than you'll find in many local restaurants, such as
wild rice risotto with prawns and shiitakes. Its speciality is fish *waterzooi*.

Chez Jean

3 Cataloniëstraat (09 223 30 40). **Open** noon-2pm,
7-10.30pm Wed-Sun. **Main courses** €15-20. **Credit**
AmEx, MC, V. **Map** p258 B3.
Chez Jean has a well-established reputation, and
deservedly so. The food is first-rate and, for the
quality, reasonably priced. Ghent specialities feature heavily, as do fish and shellfish dishes.

Georges

23-27 Donkersteeg (09 225 19 18). **Open** noon-
2.30pm, 6.30-9.30pm Wed-Sun. **Main courses**
€15-€20. **Credit** AmEx, DC, MC, V. **Map** p258 B3.
A father-and-son-run fish restaurant that has been
in the same family since 1924. Like most seafood
eateries, the prices are a tad steep – but the fish is
ultra fresh and expertly cooked. The scrupulously
clean fishmonger's next door, with its tanks of lobsters, is under the same ownership and a good
advertisement for eating at the restaurant.

Greenway

42 Nederkouter (09 269 07 69). **Open** 11am-9pm
Mon-Sat. **Main courses** €5.50. **Set menu** €8.50.
No credit cards. **Map** p258 A5.
Healthy and tasty vegetarian snacks are available
from what looks like an upmarket fast-food joint, but
the jazzy music and welcoming setting make you
feel anything but rushed. Choose from a range of
imaginative toasted sandwiches, rice and noodle
dishes and assorted drinks.

De Hel

81 Kraanlei (09 224 32 40). **Open** noon-2pm,
6-10pm Mon, Fri, Sun; 6-10pm Thur, Sat. **Credit**
AmEx, DC, MC, V. **Map** p258 B2.
In years past De Hel (Hell in English) had a devilish
decor to match its name. Nowadays, the design of
this cosy, wood-beamed restaurant changes regularly – with the exception of an old Chinese room
that can be booked for dinner. Flemish and French
cuisine is served – specialities include *waterzooi* and
eel dishes – although you might also find the likes
of goat curry on the menu.

'T Klokhuys

65 Corduwaniersstraat (09 223 42 41). **Open**
6-11pm Mon; noon-2.15pm, 6-11pm Tue-Sun.
Main courses €10-20. **Set menu** €23. **Credit**
AmEx, MC, V. **Map** p258 B2.
Green banquettes line the walls and dried hops
snake along the ceiling at rustic 't Klokhuys. Expect
a selection of local regional dishes – such as chicken
casserole, stewed eels in chervil sauce – with an
emphasis on seasonal produce. The Zeeland mussels are recommended.

De Kruik

5 Donkersteeg (09 225 71 01/www.dekruik.be).
Open 11.30am-2.30pm, 6-11pm Mon-Wed, Fri, Sat;
11.30am-2.30pm Sun. **Main courses** €15-€20.
Set menus €20-€37. **Credit** AmEx, DC, MC, V.
Map p258 B3.
This fine, peachy-pastely restaurant, just off the
Korenmarkt, offers accomplished renditions of the
traditional Ghent dishes, as well as good fish and
first-rate French cuisine. There's also a menu of the
month (aperitif, three-course meal, wine, coffee).

La Malcontenta

7-9 Haringsteeg (09 224 18 01). **Open** 6-11pm
Thur-Sun; reservations only Mon-Wed. **Main
courses** €15. **Set menu** €25. **Credit** AmEx,
DC, MC, V. **Map** p258 A/B2.
Don't be misled by the name of this restaurant: the
interior and staff may be a touch casual, but the
kitchen's keenly priced specialities from the Canary
Isles are a treat – try the seafood pancake or the
squid in spicy tomato sauce. Tapas cost €2-€10.

De Onvrije Schipper

7A Korenlei (09 233 60 45). **Open** 10am-1am Mon,
Tue, Thur-Sun. **Main courses** €6.25. **No credit
cards**. **Map** p258 A3.
This basement café, decorated in African style,
offers good breakfasts and a short but decent lunch
menu, plus jazz, blues, Afro or rock concerts every
Thursday evening. Food tends towards the exotic –
perhaps African or South American specialities.

Pablo's

2 Kleine Vismarkt (09 233 71 51). **Open** Sept-mid
May 6-11pm Tue-Thur; noon-3pm, 6pm-midnight Fri-
Sun. *Mid May-Aug* noon-3pm, 6-11pm Tue-Thur;
noon-3pm, 6pm-midnight Fri-Sun. **Main courses**
€12.50-€17. **Credit** AmEx, DC, MC, V. **Map** p258 A2.
A huge Mexican restaurant made to look like an
upmarket cantina, Pablo's is located directly over
the canal. You can eat tapas, chilli or empanadas, all
served to the sound of salsa. The crowd is young.

Pakhuis

4 Schuurkenstraat (09 223 55 55/www.pakhuis.be).
Open noon-2.30pm, 6.30pm-midnight Mon-Sat.
Main courses €6-€9.50. **Set menu** €20. **Credit**
AmEx, DC, MC, V. **Map** p258 A3.
This large renovated storage depot is worth visiting
as much for its unique architecture as its French-
Italian food: the cast-iron pillars, wrought-iron

Trips Out of Town

balustrades, parquet floor and imposing oak bar are mighty impressive. You can also just have a drink if you don't want to eat.

Raj

43 Kraanlei (09 234 34 59). **Open** noon-2.30pm, 6-11pm Tue-Sun. **Main courses** €10-€15. **Set menu** €20. **Credit** MC, V. **Map** p258 B2.

People from Brussels think nothing of coming here for an authentic Indian meal. The ambience is relaxed and you sit on benches with large cushions to rest your back against. A fabulous selection of spicy vegetable and meat dishes with all the accompaniments and good bread.

Tête à Tête

32-34 Jan Breydelstraat (09 233 95 00). **Open** 6.30-10pm Tue; noon-2.30pm, 6.30-10pm Wed-Sun. **Credit** AmEx, DC, MC, V. **Map** p258 A2.

Successful and expensive, Tête à Tête serves light and beautifully rendered French cuisine (*magret de canard* with green pepper sauce, bouillabaisse). The decor is equally splendid, with soft lighting, chrome and wood fittings, and a terrace overlooking the Gravensteen. Booking essential.

Wakame

32-34 Lostraat (09 221 87 35). **Open** 11.30am-2pm, 6-9pm Mon-Fri. **Main courses** €7. **Set menus** (Fri only) €13.30-€17. **No credit cards.**

If you're after a snack in a hurry, this is a useful vegetarian joint for a fast-food takeaway, either from a machine or at the counter.

Cafés & bars

Aba Jour

20 Oudburg (09 234 07 29). **Open** 11am-late daily. **No credit cards. Map** p258 B1/2.

Aba Jour is relaxed, chic but unsnobby, with an art deco bar, cane seats and tables (some overlooking the canal) and soft lighting. People come here to enjoy cocktails and chat, or a laid-back lunch.

Bar Bier

18 St Margrietstraat (09 223 45 93). **Open** 9am-noon, 1.30-6.30pm Tue, Wed; noon-10pm Thur, Fri; 10am-6pm Sat. **No credit cards.**

Bar Bier combines unisex hairdressing with drinking. Many students come to get their hair trimmed while supping a glass of beer. There are only three tables, so it's not a place to linger.

Damberd Jazz Café

19 Korenmarkt (09 329 53 37/www.damberd.be). **Open** 11am-late daily. **No credit cards. Map** p258 A3.

An impressive art nouveau live jazz venue on two floors, with comfortable seating. Like all good jazz bars, the ambience is friendly and very smoky and the crowd all ages. There are live jazz concerts every Monday (Jan-Mar) and Tuesday (Oct-Mar). When bands are not playing, the café's well-stocked music archive is used.

'T Galgenhuisje

5 Groentenmarkt (09 233 42 51). **Open** noon-late Tue-Sun. *Restaurant* noon-2pm, 6-10pm Tue-Sun. **Credit** (restaurant only) MC, V. **Map** p258 B3.

A diminutive pub since the late 17th century, 't Galgenhuisje means 'the gallows' – there are no prizes for guessing what stood near this spot in medieval times. There's also a restaurant in the 14th-century cellar, which majors in grilled meat and fish and local specialities.

Groot Vlees Huis

7 Groentenmarkt (09 223 23 24/www.grootvlees huis.be). **Open** Sept-June 10am-6pm Tue-Sun. *July, Aug* 10am-8pm Tue-Sun. **Credit** AmEx, DC, MC, V. **Map** p258 B3.

Groot Vlees Huis is essentially a centre to promote the best regional specialities from West Flanders, with a café serving formula breakfasts (from €6) and lunches (around €13.50). It's housed inside a centuries-old former covered meat market. A quite marvellous assortment of hams, cheese, beers and *genevers* can be enjoyed in the café or bought as souvenirs at the counter.

De Grote Avond

40 Huidevetterskaai (09 224 31 21). **Open** 6pm-late Tue-Sun. **No credit cards. Map** p258 C1.

Foliage cascades over the façade of this pub, cloaking a nostalgia-soaked interior. Old advertising posters and biscuit tins decorate the walls, while jazz, blues or classical music wafts over customers as they tuck into hearty meals – such as the speciality vegetable pie.

Hotsy Totsy

1 Hoogstraat (09 224 20 12). **Open** varies; phone for details. **No credit cards.**

The Hotsy Totsy jazz bar is a Ghent institution. It pulls in a varied crowd, including lawyers, politicians and media types who come to enjoy the strong drinks and jazz. Despite the intimidating wooden door and heavy curtains, it's not a private club. Hoogstraat is a continuation of St Michielsstraat (map p258 A3), on the west bank of the Leie.

Lazy River Jazz Club

5 Stadhuissteeg (09 222 23 01). **Open** varies; phone for details. **No credit cards. Map** p258 B3.

One of Ghent's best jazz venues is a popular place to finish off the evening with drinks and music. There are gigs every Friday evening.

'T Oud Clooster

5 Zwarte Zusterstraat (09 233 78 02). **Open** 6pm-late Mon-Fri; 7pm-late Sat. **No credit cards. Map** p258 A4.

This friendly pub draws in a mixed, relaxed crowd who come for a drink and conversation, or to nibble from the good, if not particularly extensive, restaurant menu. When you come to ask the bartender for a menu, don't be surprised if you're soon handed a Bible – just look inside…

Pink Flamingo's Lounge

55 Onderstraat (09 233 47 18). **Open** noon-midnight Mon-Wed; noon-3am Thur, Fri; 2pm-3am Sat; 2pm-midnight Sun. **No credit cards.** **Map** p258 B2.

This pub is well known for its collection of kitsch, which changes every three months. The place is packed with dolls, old records, cartoon books, religious figures and tat of every description. There's also a restaurant, open until 11pm.

Pole Pole

8 Lammerstraat (09 233 21 73). **Open** 6.30pm-4am Mon-Sat. **No credit cards.** **Map** p258 B2.

Pole pole means 'slowly slowly' in Swahili. The decor is African, with great masks and other wooden artefacts, the music is enticingly upbeat and the exotic cocktails and food are excellent value.

Rococo

57 Corduwanierstraat (09 224 30 35). **Open** 9pm-late Tue-Sun. **No credit cards.** **Map** p258 B2.

Located in Patershol, Rococo is one of Ghent's moodier clubs. Artists gather around candlelit tables and a piano sits in a corner, sometimes too tempting for the would-be *chanteur* who's had a few too many. There's also an outdoor café at the back.

De Tap en de Tepel

7 Gewad (09 223 90 00). **Open** 7pm-midnight Wed-Sat. **Credit** AmEx, MC, V. **Map** p258 A2.

An extraordinary cheese and wine bar, close to the Gravensteen. Low lighting and crackling fires contribute to an otherworldly atmosphere in which to sip a fine vintage and nibble from among the huge selection of cheese displayed on the 'altar of the holy cow', or sample one of the toothsome home-made quiches. Dog-haters stay away: the owners have quite a few.

Den Turk

3 Botermarkt (09 233 01 97). **Open** 11pm-late daily. **No credit cards.** **Map** p258 B3.

Dating all the way back to 1340, Den Turk is the oldest pub in Ghent, although you wouldn't know it from its distinctly ordinary decor. It hosts regular jazz (plus the odd dash of blues and flamenco) and you can munch on a sizeable choice of snacks while you enjoy the music.

'T Velootje

2-4 Kalversteeg (09 223 28 34). **Open** varies; phone for details. **No credit cards.** **Map** p258 B2.

One of the oldest brick houses in Ghent, partly built on the ruins of a Roman fortress, 't Velootje is not your average boozer. Its claustrophobic interior must be the most picturesque fire-risk in town, crammed as it is with an extraordinary mishmash of decorative paraphernalia, religious objets and a number of antique bicycles (including one, catalogued in the Louvre, that once belonged to a member of Napoleon III's cycling army). Look for the blue-and-white 'Pater Lieven' sign on the apricot-painted house and the pile of junk outside – you'll never find it otherwise.

Het Waterhuis aan de Bierkant

9 Groentenmarkt (09 225 06 80/www.waterhuis aandebierkant.be). **Open** 11am-2am Mon-Fri; 11am-3am Sat, Sun. **Credit** AmEx, MC, V. **Map** p258 B3.

A good stop for beer lovers, with an excellent range of brews (including 14 on draught, and all six Trappists), all described on the menu. Its riverside location makes it very popular, particularly during the warmer months when tables are put out on the terrace. Firmly on the tourist trail, however.

Clubs

The festive youth of Ghent do not go lightly into the night. Although much more parochial than Antwerp, the scene here is more lively – or certainly less world-weary – than in Brussels. Much of its development is thanks to **Kozzmozz** (www.kozzmozz.com), a techno organisation built on the enthusiasm of Mathias. Beginning with small boat parties of 500, through years of obstinate will and quality DJing, Kozzmozz now runs huge party nights at the 6,000-capacity **Kuipke Centre** outside town (Kozzmozz-Kuipke, Citadelpark; 09 242 81 50) and Star Wurz in the **Vooruit** (23 St Pietersnieuwstraat; www.vooruit.be), a beautiful old concert hall. This was also the last venue for the **Ten Days Of...** festival, a chance to see 50 of the world's top DJs in one week (*see p264* **Party on**).

In town, the most happening area is around the Oude Beestenmarkt. Here you'll find the small but enjoyable **Bardot** (No.8), with its theme nights of drum 'n' bass on Mondays and disco nouveau on Saturdays; **69** (No.4), run by the omnipotent Dewaele Brothers; and the more poppy **Video** (No.6). **Hoogport** is another happy stomping ground, with the world dance, drum 'n' bass and lounge of the basement **Sous-Sol** (No.41; 09 233 71 70), plus more mainstream music at **La Tropical** (No.12) and **Café Central** (No.32).

Overpoortstraat, although mainly packed with student bars, does contain **Decadence** (No.76/www.decadence.be), spinning progressive house and drum 'n' bass. The newest venue in town is the **Culture Club** (174 Afrikalaan; 09 267 64 41/www.culture club.be), playing a mixture of house and funk, in classy surroundings. Notoriously difficult to get in, we hear...

Shopping

Ghent is a great place to stroll around; the shopping district is compact and the centre of the city is essentially closed to traffic. The pace is slower than in Antwerp or Brussels

Trips Out of Town

Party on

'Good people of Ghent,' proclaims the mayor proudly from the podium on the main square, perhaps the only man in town still able to stand without wobbling. 'These last ten days have seen our fine town in the best festive spirit – and I am proud to announce that another Ghent Festival has passed off without arrest or incident.'

The mayor's 11th-day speech is as traditional as the ten days and ten nights of revelry preceding it. During **De Gentse Feesten** (www.gentsefeesten.be), in the third week of July, the whole town is transformed into a huge party zone; the bars are packed all night, there's wanton drinking on the streets and loud rock music booming from outdoor stages in the main squares. Ghent's narrow, cobbled streets are packed to the gills. And Ghent is a small town. After a long day's drinking into the night, any beered-up

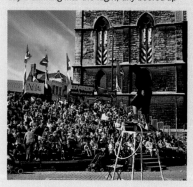

young Ghenter is bound to bump into the guy who ran off with his girlfriend, the history teacher he always hated, his boss at work. And yet... with everyone flat-faced drunk, nary a punch is thrown in anger, or rubbish bin overturned. Could any other townsfolk be as convivially trashed?

It all started in the 1970s when local folk singer Walter De Buck wanted to bring the good people of Ghent out on to the streets – and give artists from all over the country the opportunity to promote themselves to a wider, if inebriated, audience. Over 30 years, the festival has developed an international allure, not least thanks to the quality of DJs invited to play the famous Ten Days of Techno, now mysteriously renamed **Ten Days Of...** (03 226 49 63/www.5voor12.com). Launched in 1991, when guests included Jeff Mills, Carl Cox and Dave Clarke, Ten Days soon became a major draw on the international circuit. Moved to the expansive Vooruit venue in 2001, Goldie, Slam and Squarepusher were among the names posted on flyers around town.

But De Gentse isn't just an excuse for a ten-day rave. It also embraces one of the world's most famous street theatre festivals (*pictured*). You'll see bizarre chaps on stilts continually clacking past, there's a circus, a funfair on Vrijdagsmarkt, a puppet theatre, political debates, markets, free entrances to the museums, local crafts, an open-air cinema at Baudelo Park, street artists and, above all, music. Each main square becomes an open-air festival tent, with its own themed programme: the Korenmarkt is for Top 20

and the lack of crowds makes for a calmer shopping experience all round. **Veldstraat** is the main shopping drag with the usual line-up of international chainstores such as Zara, H&M and Fnac and department store Inno. Check out **Bennesteeg** for the city's most upscale fashion boutiques, and streets **Volder**, **St Niklaas** and **Magelein** for more quirky addresses. All the shops listed below are closed on Sundays.

Children's clothes & toys

Krokodil
5 Groot Kanonplein (09 233 22 76). **Open** 10am-6pm Mon-Sat. **Credit** AmEx, DC, MC, V. **Map** p258 B2.

Krokodil is a real winner: two floors of soft and wooden toys, puppets and board games. There are lots of beads, wooden ovens and doll's houses, and a large art and crafts section with big pencils, paints and chunky chalks.

Puzzles
6 Bennesteeg (09 223 17 88). **Open** 10am-1pm, 2-6pm Mon-Fri; 10am-6pm Sat. **Credit** MC, V. **Map** p258 B4.

You can find clothes by Ghent designer Catharina Bossaert elsewhere; she supplies many shops throughout Belgium, but this is her only dedicated store. The clothes, casual and practical, are for kids aged three to 14. Bossaert is an official licensee of comic-strip characters Quick & Flupke (Hergé) and Sachat by Philippe Geluck, and many of the items are tastefully emblazoned with their motifs.

Ghent

acts; Groentenmarkt has C&W and a little jazz; Beverout Plein by St Jakobskerk features the black drainpipe-trousered brigade, the alternative music acts (www.trefpuntvzw.be). The Vlasmarkt next door is the most popular hangout, with a mix of all types of music, dancing, assorted revelry and the constant rumour that local hit combo Soulwax have just turned up. They haven't – but you should.

De Verbeelding
121 Henegouwenstraat (09 225 21 48). **Open** 10am-6pm Mon-Sat. **Credit** AmEx, MC, V. **Map** p258 B/C4.
The entrance to De Verbeelding is through a large iron gate into a small courtyard with a fountain, pink walls and a frieze of little ceramic tiles. The shop itself is a delight with high ceilings, polished light wooden floors and cream walls, and stocks clothes by the likes of Paul Smith, Simple Kids, Dada and Lili Gaufrette. For babies, children and teens.

Collectibles

The Fallen Angels
29-31 Jan Breydelstraat (09 223 94 15/www.the-fallen-angels.com). **Open** 1-6pm Mon, Wed-Sat. **No credit cards. Map** p258 A2.

A wonderful place to browse for an original souvenir from the many boxes of vintage postcards of Ghent and other sights of Belgium. The shop also stocks antique toys. Next door the owner's daughter sells original posters and advertising signs.

Fashion & accessories

Ann Huybens
4 Trommelstraat, bottom of Kalversteeg (09 224 36 16). **Open** 1-6pm Tue-Sat. **Credit** V. **Map** p258 B2.
Huybens ready-to-wear wild wedding dresses are sold in all the best hip bridal shops, but this is her own boutique. Get fitted out for a made-to-measure gown or choose from a limited selection.

Christa Reniers
1A Bennesteeg (09 224 33 52). **Open** 1-6pm Wed-Fri; 11am-6pm Sat. **Credit** AmEx, MC, V. **Map** p258 B4.
Reniers is Belgium's top avant-garde jewellery designer; her only other shop-cum-atelier is in her home city Brussels. Reniers favours silver and platinum over gold, and most of her ring and necklace designs are inspired by plant and flower shapes.

Hot Couture
34 Gouvernementstraat (09 233 74 07/ www.hotcouture.be). **Open** 10am-6.30pm Mon-Sat. **Credit** AmEx, DC, MC, V. **Map** p258 B/C4.
The latest men's fashions and accessories by designers such as Dries van Noten, CP Company and Paul Smith. The shop, arranged in several rooms, has wooden floors, velvety armchairs and charming staff. Great for classy pampering.

Hydo
40 Mageleinstraat (09 233 06 37/www.hydo.be). **Open** 10.30am-6.30pm Mon-Sat. **Credit** AmEx, DC, MC, V. **Map** p258 B4.
In Mageleinstraat, one of Ghent's most charming shopping streets, Hydo sells designer handbags, wallets, briefcases, umbrellas and other accessories. The upmarket bags and belts include mostly Belgian labels by Scapa Interiors, Olivier Strelli, Emmy Wieleman, Xandres and Cat & Co.

Illmus
18 Jan Breydelstraat (09 233 40 90). **Open** 10am-12.30pm, 2-6.30pm Tue-Fri; 10am-6.30pm Sat. **Credit** AmEx, MC, V. **Map** p258 A2.
Upscale fashion labels include hard-to-find-in-Belgium Ghost, DKNY Jeans and Georges Rech for women, plus Paul Smith and Kenzo for men.

LenaLena
19 Bennesteeg (09 233 79 47/09 222 23 30/ www.lenalena.com). **Open** 12.30-6.30pm Mon; 10.30am-6.30pm Tue-Sat. **Credit** AmEx, DC, MC, V. **Map** p258 B4.
Miet Crabbé is the designer behind this label for fashion-conscious voluptuous women. One half of the shop has upscale decorative homeware by other Belgians, including Christophe Coppens.

Trips Out of Town

Movies

*5 St Pietersnieuwstraat (09 223 59 12/
www.movies.be).* **Open** 10am-6.30pm Mon-Thur;
10am-7pm Fri, Sat. **Credit** AmEx, DC, MC, V.
Looking for a cool T-shirt, pullover, jeans or shoes?
Since 1984, Movies has been the fashion point in
Ghent. You'll find high-quality designer fashion in
a pleasant and musical environment. Men's and
women's wear, young fashion and streetwear
includes Adidas, Fornari, G-Star, Schott and more.

Oona

12 Bennesteeg (09 224 21 13). **Open** 11am-6pm
Mon-Sat. **Credit** AmEx, DC, MC, V. **Map** p258 B4.
The concrete walls and minimalist interior at
Oona's complements the designer women's clothes
by the likes of Barbara Bui, Costume National,
Joseph and Martine Sitbon.

Het Oorcussen

7 Vrijdagmarkt (09 233 07 65). **Open** 1.30-6pm
Mon; 10.30am-6pm Tue-Sat. **Credit** AmEx, MC, V.
Map p258 B2.
This stylish boutique in a 16th-century house offers
exclusively Belgian designers: Dries Van Noten,
Dirk Bikkembergs, Ann Demeulemeester, AF
Vandevorst and Martin Margiela. There's also a
small collection of jewellery and accessories by
Wouters and Hendrix.

Orsacchino

7B Gouvernementstraat (09 223 08 47). **Open**
10.30am-6.30pm Mon, Wed-Sat. **Credit** MC, V.
Map p258 B/C4.
Sophisticated and daring lingerie, and bathing cos-
tumes for men and women. Men are restricted to
D&G, but woman can also pick from Joop, André
Sardá and Pain de Sucre.

Food & confectionery

Temmerman

79 Kraanlei (09 224 00 41). **Open** 11am-6pm
Tue-Sat. **No credit cards. Map** p258 B2.
Temmerman is a confectioner of great charm, with
an absolutely fabulous assortment of chocolates,
biscuits, sweets, edible sugared flowers, honey and
teas. Every type of sweet has a history attached and
the staff are most willing to tell you all about it.

Vishandel de Vis

48 Voldersstraat (09 224 32 28/www.devis.be).
Open 10am-6.30pm Mon; 9am-6.30pm Tue-Sat.
Credit MC, V. **Map** p258 B4.
A first-class food shop specialising in fish and all
kinds of seafood: the fresh variety on slabs, ready-
to-eat winkles and live oysters; freezer cabinets
stuffed with bags of shellfish and fish suppers; and
a *traiteur* with a wonderful selection of various
take-home-and-heat recipes.

Vve Tierenteijn-Verlent

3 Groentenmarkt (09 225 83 36). **Open** 8.30am-
6pm Mon-Sat. **No credit cards. Map** p258 B3.

This shop, with authentic fittings from when it first
opened in 1858, specialises in mustard. A huge vat
of mustard prepared according to a family recipe of
1790 stands in one corner, and can be bought by the
gram and put in various containers sold in the
shop. Other spices are sold, along with every type
of mustard seed imaginable.

Music, books & comics

De Kaft

*44 Kortrijksepoortstraat (09 225 50 34/
http://users.pandora.be/dekaft/home.html).*
Open 10am-6pm Mon-Sat. **No credit cards**.
This second-hand shop sells books, comics, vinyl,
CDs, posters, videos and computer software. It's
neat and tidy – not always the case with nearly-new
shops – so you should find what you're looking for.

Music Mania

*197 Bagattenstraat (09 225 68 15/www.music
maniarecords.com).* **Open** 11am-7pm Mon-Sat.
Credit MC, V.
Three floors of every type of music, although
drum 'n' bass, jungle, jazz and reggae are the specialities here. The shop used to be known for its
heavy metal selection, which is still very good.
Although no second-hand CDs are sold here, you
should find some bargains on the third floor.
Check out the vinyl as well.

De Poort

137 Nederkouter (09 225 31 28/www.depoort.com).
Open 7.30am-6pm Mon-Fri; 8am-6pm Sat.
No credit cards. Map p258 A5.
A relatively small shop, but with lots of mainly
French and Dutch comics, second-hand and newly
released. Publishers include Casterman, Lombard,
Dupuis and Big Ballon.

Walry

6 Zwijnaardsesteenweg (09 222 91 67). **Open**
10am-6pm Mon-Sat. **Credit** AmEx, MC.
There are three parts to Walry – one is a bookshop,
another is a newspaper shop and the third is a café.
The latter is usually rather quiet, making it an
excellent place to read.

Film

Every year, at the beginning of October,
Ghent hosts the increasingly important
Flanders International Film Festival
(www.filmfestival.be), which has been going
since 1973. Special programmes are shown
at the city's cinemas, prizes are awarded
and the odd celebrity pops by. Among
Ghent's best cinemas are **Decascoop** (12
Ter Platen; 09 265 06 00/www.kinepolis.be),
Sphinx (3 St Michielshelling; 09 225 60 86/
www.cinebel.com) and **Studio Skoop** (63
St Annaplein; 09 225 08 45).

Day Trips

Historic towns, seaside resorts, lovely country: all within an hour of Brussels.

Liège

If Bruges is the 'Venice of the North', Liège could stake a claim to being the Milan. A large number of Italian immigrants began arriving here after World War II to work in the coal mines, and their influence is partly responsible for the city's fire and flair: great nightlife, superb restaurants, fashionable shops and an infectious, devil-may-care atmosphere. It does have grim industrial estates and derelict factories, but persevere into the heart of the city and you'll find it also has a laid-back charm.

Although on the border of the Netherlands, the city is French-speaking. From the tenth century, it was ruled by powerful prince-bishops. Strife between the Church and the professionals drawn to the growing town led to a charter being laid out in 1361, creating an uneasy power-sharing between the two parties. The French Revolutionary armies ousted the last of the prince-bishops in 1794, just as the city was entering a period of prosperity as a leading coal and steel centre. But with the collapse of heavy industry, the city slumped, which accounts for the grunginess of some neighbourhoods.

Today, Liège is probably most famous for being the birthplace of Georges Simenon, the pipe-smoking novelist who created canny police detective Maigret. The writer was born in 1903 at 24 rue Léopold, a stone's throw from the district of Outremeuse where he grew up: the building is now a discount junk shop. (Opposite is now a nightlife must, the Maison du Pequet, pequet being a local type of gin with freshly squeezed fruit juices.)

There's plenty for Simenon fans to discover elsewhere in the city: the war memorial outside the Town Hall includes the name 'Arnold Maigret', from which the writer took his detective's name; it would last him through 75 novels. The church of St-Pholien, also in Outremeuse, is a slightly grislier landmark: a young cocaine addict was found hanged from its door handle in 1922. Was it suicide or murder? You'll have to read Simenon's 1931 thriller *Le pendu de Saint-Pholien* to find out.

The main railway station is two kilometres south of the centre in place Guillemins (there's a small information office here: 04 252 44 19;

The **Palais des Princes-Evêques**, Liège.

Oct-Mar 10am-noon, 1-4pm Mon-Sat; *Apr-Sept* 9.30am-12.30pm, 1-5pm Mon-Sat; 10am-12.30pm, 1-4pm Sun). It's a 25-minute walk to the historic heart of the city, the charmless place St-Lambert. Here you'll find the **Palais des Princes-Evêques**, the stately former home of the prince-bishops, dating from the 16th century but much altered in subsequent centuries. The Palais now serves as the court for Liège Province, and only the outer courtyard is usually accessible to the public.

The older part of the city lies east of here, in the shadow of the steep Montagne de Bueren, atop which stand the remains of the ramparts of the **Citadel**. It's a stiff climb, but your reward is a fabulous panorama of the city.

Need a break from museums? Liège has bars and restaurants aplenty.

Parallel to the bottom of the hill runs Feronstrée, the backbone of this part of Liège. Many of Liège's museums are either on or just off Feronstrée.

Housed in a 17th-century Minorite cloister, the **Musée de la Vie Wallonne** (Cour des Mineurs/Hors Château; 04 223 60 94; 10am-5pm Tue-Sat; 10am-4pm Sun; €2) is devoted to all things rustically Wallonian, while the nearby **Musée d'Art Religieux et d'Art Mosan** (rue Mère-Dieu, off Hors Château; 04 221 42 25; 11am-6pm Tue-Sat; 11am-4pm Sun; €2.50) displays a fine selection of locally produced religious art. More things local are celebrated in the **Musée de l'Art Wallon** (86 Feronstrée; 04 221 92 31; 1-6pm Tue-Sat; 11am-4.30pm Sun; €3), which boasts more than 3,000 paintings and sculptures, giving a sample of the best of Brussels and Wallonia. This is a must for lovers of Magritte and Delvaux.

A little further along Feronstrée are the delightfully presented 18th-century furniture and furnishings of the **Musée d'Ansembourg** (114 Feronstrée; 04 221 94 02; 1-6pm Tue-Sun; €2.50), while around the corner on the riverside are the immense collection of arms and armour of the **Musée d'Armes** (8 quai de Maestricht; 04 221 94 16; 10am-1pm, 2-5pm Mon, Wed-Sat; 10am-1pm Sun; €1.25) and the more appealing **Musée Curtius** (13 quai de Maestricht; 04 221

94 04; 10am-1pm, 2-5pm Mon, Wed-Sat; 10am-1pm Sun; €1.25). The latter displays decorative objects going back to the tenth century and some prehistoric artefacts, many with religious significance and in precious metals and stones, with a sumptuous 17th-century Renaissance palace as its backdrop.

The area south and west of place St-Lambert may not be as old as around Feronstrée, but its pedestrianised streets and multitude of bars, restaurants and shops make it more appealing. There are also plenty of churches. The **Cathédrale St-Paul** on place Cathédrale (8am-noon, 2-5pm daily; €4) was begun in the 14th century but not finished until the 19th. It's not that interesting outside, but inside are some vibrant 16th-century ceiling paintings and stained glass. South of the cathedral, close to avenue Maurice Destenay, is the church of **St-Jacques** (9am-noon, 1.30-5pm Mon-Sat; 9-10am Sun; free), founded in the 11th century. Only the western wing of the original church survives, with Gothic and Renaissance styles mingling in the rest of the church.

The most notable feature of **St-Denis** (9am-noon, 1.30-5pm Mon-Sat; 9-10am Sun; free), between the cathedral and place Lambert, is its immense 16th-century retable. West of here, on place Xavier Neujean, stands **St-Jean** (*June-Sept* 10am-noon, 2-5pm Mon-Wed, Fri,

Sat; 2-5pm Thur, Sun; *Oct-May* call 04 222 14 41 for reservations; free). Dating from the tenth century, it was modelled on Charlemagne's church at Aachen, although only the tower remains of the original structure.

A dominant figure in Liègeois lore is Tchantchès, a legendary character with a famously huge nose and a passion for fighting and drinking. He's most often encountered today in puppet form, and is celebrated in the **Musée Tchantchès** at 56 rue Surlet (04 342 75 75; 9am-4pm Mon-Thur; 9am-noon Fri, Sun; free). From October to Easter you should also be able to catch a puppet show here every Wednesday at 2.30pm and Sunday at 10.30am. Admission is €2.50 including the museum.

The other main attraction on this side of the river Meuse is further south, at 3 parc de Boverie the **Musée d'Art Moderne** (04 343 04 03; 1-6pm Tue-Sat; 11am-4.30pm Sun; €2.50). The museum holds a mixed bag of paintings, including works by Ensor, Chagall, Picasso, Magritte and Gauguin.

For entertainment, stroll around Le Carré ('the square'), a pedestrianised area roughly between the Theatre Royal and the cathedral. Its narrow streets are packed with cafés, clubs, bars and boutiques: start from the trendy rue du Pot d'Or and make your way out.

Where to eat

Liège is a place to eat well. Diagonally opposite the end of the rue du Pot d'Or is **Le Bruit Qui Court** (142 boulevard de la Sauvenière; 04 232 18 18; main courses €20), an elegant brasserie serving modern French cuisine in a former bank. Celebrity chef Robert Lesenne has several restaurants in the city: the flagship is **As Ouhès** (19-21 place du Marché; 04 223 32 25; main courses €16-€30), which serves local specialities such as *boulettes* (Liège's traditional meatballs) and mashed potato made with black pudding. Nearby is the tiny **L'Eurèye** (9 place du Marché; 04 223 28 13; closed Sun; main courses €8-€15), which also serves classic Liègois dishes. It's often full. Just up the road is **Le Bistrot d'en face** (8-10 rue de la Goffe; 04 223 15 84; mains €15), serving specialities for the slightly braver gourmet: ox snout and pig's ears are both on the menu.

For bars, rue Tête de Beouf is the place to start, although they are liberally sprinkled around the city. If you've had a long night, you could have a coffee and breakfast at **Café Lequet** (17 quai sur Meuse; 04 222 21 34), an old haunt of the Simenon family, which opens at 6am on Sundays. It's the perfect spot to greet a new day in passionate, mysterious, hard-living Liège.

Getting there

From Brussels, there are four trains an hour from Gare du Nord, Gare Centrale or Gare du Midi. Journey takes 65 minutes.

Tourist information

City of Liège Tourist Office
92 Féronstrée, 4000 Liège (04 221 92 21/fax 04 221 92 22/www.liege.be). **Open** 9am-6pm Mon-Fri; 10am-4pm Sat; 10am-2.30pm Sun.

Ostend & the Coast

Belgium's coastline may not be one of Europe's most exotic or sexiest destinations, but it has oodles of charm and quaint traditions. Sandy beaches that stretch for 67 kilometres (42 miles) along the North Sea, shallow bathing, wide paved promenades and a tram line that stops at 14 seaside resorts make an overnight or longer stay an appealing option. There are numerous watersports to enjoy, activities for children (*see p174*), excellent fish restaurants, art museums in Ostend, casinos, golf courses and more.

A simple ferry ride from England, Ostend was such a fashionable bathing spot for the Victorians that even the queen took a dip here in 1834. It was also one of the first places that allowed mixed bathing, strictly forbidden in France and England in the 19th century. While Ostend may never regain the glory of its belle époque when Léopold II took up residence in a simple house in Langestraat and Europe's bourgeoisie gambled in its casinos, it is busily remaking itself as a cultural, artistic and social centre.

One of the most charming sights to greet you when you arrive at the Belgian seaside is the little wooden beach cabins painted in bright colours. These date back to the bathing machines of the 1870s – little cabins on wheels pulled by horses down to the sea from which modestly clothed bathers would discreetly walk into the waves. Another tradition is to rent bikes, pedal cars and tandems and ride them along the beachside promenades on reserved lanes. Parents often sit at one of the many wind-sheltered cafés and watch while their kids cycle back and forth.

Belgium's coastline has suffered from tourism. At the beginning of the 20th century there were 5,000 hectares (12,355 acres) of sand dunes. Today, with the construction of villas and unsightly high-rise apartments, there are fewer than 1,000 hectares (2,470 acres) remaining. In contrast, the Dutch coast has scrupulously preserved its dunes, flora and fauna. However, there are pockets of charm to be found and plenty of things to seek out at Belgian resorts. The remaining dunes are now rigorously protected and at Zwin a vast area of dunes are the setting for a bird sanctuary.

Knokke-Heist, close to the Dutch border, is Belgium's most upscale resort. It is here that you'll find the smartest shops (open on Sundays), the poshest restaurants and most exclusive beach clubs. Less popular with young families, this is where body-beautiful youngsters come for watersports. The resort has a golf club with two 18-hole courses with a sand dune backdrop, and a chic tennis club. Nature reserve and bird sanctuary **Zwin** is nearby and is a lovely place to stroll, and there is a small butterfly park, well worth a visit. **Surfers Paradise** (13 Acacialaan; 050 61 59 60/www.surfersparadise.be), a glorified beach hut on Knokke-Heist seafront, is a good place to rent boards and hang out at the expensive juice bar. The **Royal Tennis Club du Zoute**

(7 Astridlaan; 050 60 28 60) is a regular tennis club by day and a nightclub venue by night on Fridays and Saturdays.

For food, try restaurant **Jean** (14 Sylvain Dupuisstraat; 050 61 49 57; closed Tue) for top-notch brasserie-style cuisine. Allow €30 per head. **'T Kantientje** (103 Lippenslaan; 050 60 54 11; €25 per head) offers excellent mussels. The **food market** (Gemeenteplein, near Lippensplein) on Wednesday and Saturday mornings is a must for ready-to-eat North Sea shrimps, *maatjes* (herrings) when in season or cooked lamb steaks. Five-star hotel **La Réserve** (160 Elisabethlaan; 050 61 06 06; double €260-€355) opens its luxury facilities to the public, including a swimming pool and health spa.

Take the coastal tram along the seafront if you want to check out some other resorts. **De Haan** has an unspoilt promenade with belle époque architecture, plenty of beautiful wooded dune walks and excellent bathing

The healing years

Arousal and Ostend are unlikely bedfellows. But one of the foxiest songs of all time, Marvin Gaye's multi-million-selling, Grammy-winning 'Sexual Healing', was written here, during an 18-month stay in the early 1980s. Most certainly, this damp Belgian coastal town floated Marvin's boat. What on earth was he doing here?

In 1980, Gaye was living in London. His career in freefall, he was spending the remains of his fortune on cocaine. In stepped Belgian promoter Freddy Cousaert. Cousaert had organised a promotional tour of Belgium for the young Cassius Clay, and was a huge fan of R&B, particularly Gaye. In London to find new acts, Cousaert had heard that Gaye was in town and sought him out. The two became fast friends, and the Belgian invited the singer, his 24-year-old Dutch girlfriend Eugenie Vis and his young son Bubby to his home town of Ostend. Seeking escape, Gaye agreed. On 15 February 1981, the trio boarded a Sealink ferry.

On arrival, Cousaert set Gaye up in an apartment overlooking the North Sea (Résidence Jane, 77 promenade King Albert). The Belgian ran a small hostel nearby with his wife; Gaye was a frequent visitor, soon becoming integrated into the family.

The singer began to recover: he ran on the beach in front of his flat, made friends with locals and was the subject of a half-hour

documentary, *Transit Ostende*, by Belgian director Richard Olivier. The film shows the singer playing darts in a fishermen's pub (since closed) and singing an extraordinary a cappella version of the Lord's Prayer in a church in Mariakerke, a small town nearby.

Some of Olivier's footage was used – without his permission, he claims – in the 1992 BBC documentary *Trouble Man*. The BBC film took on a cult status in England as a lost classic – it will be revived with a Universal release of the video and DVD in late 2002. The new version will also feature rare footage of Gaye performing in July 1981 at Ostend Casino.

The US also picked up on Gaye's strange exile. Music journalist David Ritz flew in from the States in March 1982. Gaye's outpourings during their long conversations became the central part of Ritz's keynote biography, *Divided Soul*. 'Gaye loved the calmness of Ostend,' says Ritz, 'it seemed to symbolise rebirth. But he was also frustrated by the bourgeois, provincial feel, and complained that he felt "like a raisin in a bowl of milk."'

The singer also spent hours wandering around James Ensor's house. 'Marvin was a big fan of Ensor,' says Ritz. 'I think the sexual ambiguity appealed to him.' Gaye particularly loved a self-portrait in which Ensor wore a woman's hat, as he was also partial to cross-dressing. One day, noticing

for children. **Blankenberge** is loved for its 1930s pier, Sea Life theme park, scary serpentarium and great watersports. While there, stop off at **Kreeftenput** (16 Oude Wenduinsesteenweg; 050 41 10 35; main courses €35). Live lobsters are kept on one side of an old hangar and cooked and served at tables on the other. Unspoilt **Zeebrugge** is another possibility and can now be reached by a direct train link from Bruges.

Ostend

Ostend is the most accessible and best-known of the Belgian resorts. In the early 1900s, it was considered the jewel of the coast. Money poured into the former fishing village when Léopold II was on a mission to turn it into the North Sea's most elegant resort. James Ensor also helped to bring Ostend international fame by painting some of his best-known works during a long stay. Two wars and property developers turned

it into what you see today, but it has many redeeming qualities. Ostend is essentially a working town all year round.

The first week of March is a good time to come for the macabre **Bal du Rat Mort** (Dead Rat's Ball), a carnival celebration that dates back to 1898. It includes a lantern-carrying parade, an evening party in the casino and a clog-throwing event. Another must in Ostend is to saunter along the **pier** and stop off at one of its tearooms. The French word for this type of walking is *flâner* – to stroll nonchalantly. It helps to be well dressed against the whipping winds.

In its golden era, Ostend had casinos and racecourses to rival Monte Carlo. But then the big gamblers left, and the casino was destroyed in World War II. A new one, **Casino Kursaal**, was built in 1950, and now doubles as a cultural centre and concert hall. Although said to have some of the best acoustics in the world, some consider it pretty ugly from the

a pornographic book in Gaye's apartment, Ritz told the singer that he needed 'sexual healing'. Gaye had been trying to fit lyrics to a backing track by his keyboard player Odell Brown. Taken with Ritz's phrase, he asked the journalist to help him out with the words. Recorded in the modest Katy studio in Ohain, near Waterloo, 'Sexual Healing' became Gaye's biggest hit.

In autumn 1982, Gaye heard that his mother was ill in the US, and rushed home. He told Cousaert he would return to Belgium in a couple of weeks, but it was not to be.

Instead, Gaye went on tour again, slipping back into hard drugs and gradually retreating into paranoia. On April Fool's Day 1984, after a petty argument, the singer's father shot him twice in the chest. Gaye would have celebrated his 45th birthday the next day.

Marvin Gaye's time on the Belgian coast seems to have been a moment of respite in a troubled life. 'Ostend was where he should have got it together,' is how Ritz puts it. Keyboard player Odell Brown agrees. 'I've never understood why he left Belgium,' he says. 'He was so happy there.'

Trips Out of Town

The wide beach at Ostend with the **Casino** in the distance. *See p271.*

outside. Inside, it's a different matter, with Delvaux frescoes in the gaming hall (though you have to play to see them).

Besides the casino, Ostend's other architectural gem is Girault's lovely covered **Galeries Royales**, completed in 1905 and a faint reminder of Léopold II's Ostend. Around 400 metres (438 yards) long, the galeries, which linked the Royal Chalet with the Wellington Racecourse, were designed to protect high society from the sun and rain during their walks. The **Thermae Palace**, now a four-star hotel, was built next to the galeries in the 1930s. In front of the galeries is an open-air swimming pool.

From the pier, it's a short walk to Ostend's cultural and social centre, an area loosely bordered by Christinastraat, Langestraat and Visserskaai. The tourist office is rather pretentiously calling part of this area Montmartre. That's going too far, but Ostend is a town associated with artists, including James Ensor, Léon Spilliaert and Constant Permeke.

An Ensor trail of 15 street panels features reproductions of his (often macabre) paintings, commemorating Ostend's beaches, souvenir shops, carnival masks and festivals – one of his most celebrated works is of the Bal du Rat Mort. Ensor's mother sold seashells by the seashore. The first two houses the family lived in have been knocked down (panels commemorate them), but, fortunately, Ensor's Aunt Mimi also went into the seashell business and he inherited her house. Today, it is the

Ensorhuis (27 Vlaanderenstraat; 059 50 33 37; *June-Sept* 10am-noon, 2-5pm Mon, Wed-Sun; *Oct-May* 2-5pm Sat, Sun; €2). Shells, stuffed swans and souvenirs are perfectly preserved in the old shop and a trademark skull wears a flowery hat.

Just below Ensorhuis in the Palais des Fêtes et de la Culture on Wapenplein (place d'Armes) is the **Museum voor Schone Kunsten** (Fine Arts Museum; 059 80 53 35; 10am-noon, 2-5pm Mon, Wed-Sun; €2), which has two rooms full of works by Ensor and a third room devoted to Spilliaert. The **tourist office** (*see p273*) is also here. The **Museum voor Moderne Kunst** (Museum of Modern Art; 11 Romestraat; 059 50 81 18; 10am-6pm Tue-Sun; €2.50) is devoted exclusively to 20th-century Belgian art, featuring such luminaries as Permeke, de Smet, Panamarenko and Van Hoeydoncke.

Where to eat & stay

At the coast you should definitely be eating fish. Try no-frills restaurant **Adelientje** (9 Bonenstraat; 059 70 13 67; closed Mon). The fish is cooked simply and portions are generous; count on €25 a head. Similarly priced is the teeny **Auteuil** (54 Albert I, on the promenade; 059 70 00 41; closed Thur, dinner Wed). Cheaper is **Stad Kortrijk**, where fresh fish and a limited menu are reasons for its success. Ostend is also known for its nightlife. **Jan's Café** at 60 Van Iseghemlaan (059 70 19 34) is arty and friendly, though it tends to shut by midnight. Langestraat is lined with bars and small dance clubs that have rather lenient door policies. The **Dôme** at No.15 (059 80 32 15) is one of the largest and raunchiest; it's open only on Fridays and Saturdays, from 10pm. Nearby, Visserplein is trendier and this is where you will find Ostend's concentration of gay bars.

If you fancy staying, the youth hostel **De Ploate** is bang in the centre at 82 Langestraat (059 80 52 97; bed and breakfast €14.90) and is modern and comfortable. Alternatively, the **Hotel Thevenet** (61 Koningsstraat; 059 70 10 35; double €47-€54) has clean rooms with showers and is a short walk from the beach.

Getting there

Many Belgians rent or own holiday places along the coast to which they escape at weekends during the hot, sticky summer months. Travelling on the motorway can be a miserable experience, especially at peak times, so the train is often the best option. From Brussels, there is one direct train an hour from Gare du Nord, Gare Centrale or Gare du Midi. The journey takes about 70 minutes. There's a direct connection to Knokke-Heist (90 minutes) or, if you're arriving by boat from Zeebrugge, it is only five kilometres (three miles).

Tourist information

Toerisme Oostende

2 Monacoplein, 8400 Ostend (059 70 11 99/fax 059 70 34 77/www.oostende.be). **Open** *June-Aug* 9am-7pm Mon-Sat; 10am-7pm Sun. *Sept-May* 10am-6pm Mon-Sat; 10am-5pm Sun.
Check out **www.visitflanders.be** for hotel details and upcoming events.

Leuven

A mere 30-minute train journey from Brussels, Leuven (Louvain in French) is a university city and student life adds a lively pulse, especially at night-time. There are plenty of cheery cafés, a fair share of good restaurants, cool shops and riverside walks to enjoy. Bicycles rule around the city centre, with many streets closed to cars and bike hire shops if you want to join in.

A good place to start exploring is around the **university**, one of the world's oldest Catholic universities (founded 1425) and mercifully spared from two bouts of bombing during the world wars. It was also the scene of fierce linguistic battles in the mid 1960s. After four years of fighting, the university was split; the Flemings stayed and a new campus was

built for francophones in Louvain-la-Neuve. It is hard to imagine the past as you stroll through its quiet, pleasant grounds and follow riverside walks or cool cycle paths.

The town centre (a five-minute walk from the train station along Bondgenotenlaan) is focused on **Grote Markt**. Here you'll find the city's architectural highlights. The impressive and elaborate **Stadhuis** (Town Hall), built between 1439 and 1469, is a masterpiece of Brabant late Gothic architecture. Its delicate pinnacles, towers and other intricate details have a fairy-tale harmony. It was supposed to outshine Brussels' town hall, back in the days when Leuven was prosperous from the cloth trade and was capital of Brabant. The original plan for statues in each of the 282 niches proved too ambitious, the money ran out and it wasn't until the mid 19th century that the majority of the niches were finally filled with non-medieval figures such as Napoleon and Belgian royalty.

The Town Hall faces Leuven's other major Gothic building, **St Pieterskerk** (016 22 69 06; 10am-5pm Mon-Sat; 2-5pm Sun; closed mid Dec-mid Jan; €5). The church has an unhappy past. Begun in the 1420s (on the site of a Romanesque basilica), it was intended to have three spires, the central one of which was to

The gigantic **Stadhuis** in Leuven.

be a lofty 170-metre (558-foot) high, but the marshy subsoil proved unable to support such a structure. Work lasted 70 years and the prematurely capped current towers mark the builders' insurmountable problem. And then the exterior was badly battered during both world wars. Yet once you're inside, Gothic harmony is re-established in the vertiginous nave. In the ambulatory there's a worthwhile small museum – the **Treasury of St Peter**, which contains a copy of Rogier van der Weyden's *Descent from the Cross* and two rare surviving triptychs from his apprentice Dirk Bouts, who was to become the city painter of Leuven.

Entrance to the museum costs €5, which also gets you into the **Museum Vander Kelen-Mertens** (6 Savoyestraat; 016 22 69 06; 10am-5pm Tue-Sat; 2-5pm Sun), near the **tourist office** (*see p276*). In mock-historical rooms, it contains an appealing miscellany of porcelain, ceramics, stained glass, sculpture (including pieces by Constantin Meunier) and paintings such as a *Holy Trinity* by van der Weyden.

Stroll south from St Pieterskirk along Naamsestraat to the superb baroque mid 17th-century **St Michielskerk**, then continue down to **Groot Begijnhof**, just off the street to the right. Founded around 1230, this gorgeous

Beer, bears and bathtubs

Let's face it, Belgium isn't all beer and roses. Belgium can be grey. Belgian villages, greyer still. We cannot claim otherwise. Grey, grey, grey. But some are only grey for only 364 days of the year. For one day – and if they're lucky, perhaps two or three days – certain villages will fiesta as madly as any Mexican on All Souls' Day. In the name of bizarre pagan ritual, irreligious religious festival or rites of fertility, entire villages go completely haywire, preferably in fancy dress, in order to celebrate some tradition or other.

Some don't even require tradition. Commercial exigence will do. Every August, **Dinant** stages its **Festival of the Bathtub**, in which locals outdo each other to decorate their bathtubs in the most bizarre way possible (the Eiffel Tower, a 2CV, and so on), and then steer them, without the thing sinking, down the River Meuse. The event, organised by local bar owners, is a blatant excuse to drink Dinant dry. More traditionally, in the same month, in **Zaffelare**, near Ghent, to commemorate the ridding of plague, the **Shooting of the Rats Festival** requires archers to aim at rats in cages 27 metres (88 feet) up. If hit, the cages shatter in mid-air, the rats fall to the ground and, while lying there, stunned, their throats are slit.

Also near Ghent, in the village of **Geeraardsbergen**, dignitaries undertake the **Live Fish Swallowing Festival**, aided by a goblet of wine – a drinking ceremony dating back five centuries. Another hamlet nearby gathers the locals around the village green, which is divided up into little squares. They then let a cow rampage around the grass while bets are made on which square Daisy will bless with the steaming **Ritual of the Cowpat**. Every rite and ritual, fête and

festival, is accompanied by copious amounts of beer and hearty local fare. A better day trip from Brussels would be hard to imagine.

Not surprisingly many events are centred around Lent and Shrove Tuesday. Belgian Mardi Gras, although working on the same indulgent principle of scoff and celebrate before the forty days of fast, often has a peculiar twist. The **Bear Carnival of Andenne** stays true to the legend of Charles Martel, grandson of Ste-Begge, who killed a terrifying bear with his hammer. Menfolk commanded by this year's Charles Martel tiptoe around the village before the Carnival King and Queen shower them in little bears thrown from the Town Hall balcony. (In **Ypres** it's toy cats – it used to be live ones – with a **Giant Cat Parade** taking place every three years in May, the next one being due in 2003.)

In **Olloy-sur-Viroin**, the evil-doing three-metre (ten-foot) tall 'Chebette' is punished by being burned to a crisp and thrown into the river, thus excluding him from the ritual mass eating of the omelette in the main square. Omelettes, in fact, feature as highly in Belgian Mardi Gras as pancakes do on kitchen ceilings in England. Less appetising, perhaps, is **Ostend**'s **Bal du Rat Mort**, the Dead Rat's Ball, which involves a grand finale in full rat costume at the Casino on the Saturday before Easter.

But the mother of all mardis, the party to end all parties, is in **Binche**. Considered the country's most prestigious carnival, its origins have been traced back to the 14th century. The present celebrations have their roots in an event that was organised in 1549 by Mary of Hungary, who ruled the region at the time. When her brother, Emperor Charles V, and son, Philip II of Spain, decided to visit, hospitable Magyar Mary threw a lavish party.

and extensive complex (with its 62 houses, ten convents, church and squares) was once home to lay sisterhoods (*béguines*), but is now mostly student accommodation.

If you want a change from culture, hot shops include **Profiel** (37 Mechelsestraat; 016 23 72 62) for cutting-edge womenswear by the likes of Ann Demeulemeester, Dries Van Noten and Kaat Tilley, together with less well-known and cheaper labels. Men have **Jonas** opposite (No.34; 016 23 41 04) for casual fashion by Antwerp Sixer Dirk Bikkembergs and Paul Smith. For tasteful wooden and soft toys for kids, visit fab **Krokodil** (14 Grote Markt;

016 29 23 74). Drop in at **Het Besloten Land** (16 Parijsstraat; 016 22 58 40) to soak up some Belgian comic-strip culture. The shop is piled high with titles in French, Dutch and English.

Time your visit for a Saturday morning and you'll catch the town's excellent **food market** on Brusselsestraat, where local farmers come to sell their produce. Cheese lovers should not miss **Elsen** (36 Mechelsestraat; 016 22 13 10), run by a professional cheese ripener who buys most of his specials from the food market outside Paris. It's a dream, and if you ask the owner nicely he'll show you the special ripening chambers.

During the festivities, which lasted several days, many of the courtiers, who had only recently been introduced to the joys of South America (particularly Peru), decided to dress up Inca-style. They donned flamboyant tri-coloured costumes and plumed hats, which remain the preserve of the Gilles (as the courtiers called themselves) to this day. A Gille can only be male, and the right to be a Gille is passed from father to son.

Although the villagers start preparing for **Carnival** with a series of balls and processions in January, the main three-day action kicks off the Sunday before Shrove Tuesday. The Gilles, clad in glorious costumes, open the spectacle with a parade at 3pm. For the rest of the day – and well into the night – the beating of drums resounds through the streets, as people dressed up in all manner

of costumes (frogs, astronauts) clink glasses. Monday is Children's Day – only they don fancy dress on this day – but everyone else continues to enjoy the celebration, which includes the playing of barrel organs in the streets and a firework display in the evening.

The highlight of the Carnival takes place on Shrove Tuesday, when all the Gilles dress up in the Inca costume of their ancestors and parade through the streets. Later in the day, more fireworks are followed by dancing well into the small hours.

Given the length of the celebration and long opening hours of all the bars in Binche during the festival, it's no surprise to learn that the English word 'binge' is derived from Binche.

For more information, contact the **Belgian Tourist Information Office**, 63 rue du Marché aux Herbes, Lower Town (02 504 03 90).

Trips Out of Town

Where to eat & stay

Time for beer or a spot of lunch? Make a beeline for the Oude Markt area, just south of the Grote Markt, and pick one of the many bars or cafés that line the square. **Café Komeet** (54 Oude Markt; 016 29 63 00) is a cool hangout that serves soups, sarnies and salads. Other, more studenty dives include the **Rock Café** and **Artmania**. In August, the square becomes the hub of outdoor rock festival Marktrock.

For eating, try Parijsstraat that runs parallel with the Oude Markt on the west side. There's a variety of restaurants here to suit most tastes and budgets. Top choices include the stylish **Kapsiki** at No.34 (016 20 45 87), which has several vegetarian options and main courses at €12-€17. Or try upmarket restaurant-traiteur **Il Pastaio** (016 23 09 02; closed Sun; main courses €13) at No.33. The fresh pasta is made in-house; try the sauce of scampi, tomatoes, basil and olive oil.

For quieter dining, consider **Ombre ou Soleil** (20 Muntstraat; 016 22 51 87; closed Sat lunch, Sun) where the menu focuses on Mediterranean simplicity and the ambience is relaxed. Sit in front of an open log fire in winter. A meal starts at around €20 per head. Or there's trendy **De Blauwe Zon** (28 Tiensestraat, 016 22 68 80; €22 per head) on five floors, with the kitchen serving modern fusion cuisine and wicked steaks. Finally, for a true gourmet experience and smart setting, go for **Belle Epoque** (94 Bondgenotenlaan; 016 22 33 89). In fair weather you can sit outside in the restaurant's pretty courtyard. Expect to pay from €50 per person.

If you want to extend your stay, try **Jeff's Guesthouse** at 2 Kortestraat (016 23 87 80; double €75-85). It's a hotel, a restaurant and a shop – all devoted to the Italian way of life. There are six rooms; some overlook the square. The shop is devoted to olives and their derivatives: oils, pasta sauces, beauty products and olive oil containers.

Getting there

From Brussels, there are five trains an hour from Gare du Nord, Gare Centrale or Gare du Midi. Journey takes 35 minutes.

Tourist information

Leuven Tourist Office

Stadhuis, 9 Grote Markt, 3000 Leuven (016 21 15 39/fax 016 21 15 49/www.leuven.be). **Open** *Mar-Oct* 9am-5pm Mon-Fri; 10am-1pm, 1.30-5pm Sat, Sun. *Nov-Apr* 9am-5pm Mon-Fri; 10am-1pm, 1.30-5pm Sat.

Mechelen's **Stadhuis** on the Grote Markt.

Mechelen

Mechelen – or Malines in French – is a sleepy little city. This was not always the case, as its rich collection of public buildings will testify. When Burgundian ruler Charles the Bold died in 1477, his widow Margaret of York moved to Mechelen with her grandchildren. One of them, Margaret of Austria, grew up to become regent of the Netherlands, moved back to the city and built up around herself one of the most celebrated courts of the day, attracting scholars and painters of the calibre of Erasmus and Dürer.

The golden age was short-lived. Margaret's successor moved the court back to Brussels in 1530, leading to a rapid decline in Mechelen's fortunes, evidence of which is the number of unfinished 16th-century buildings around the city. It is for these and other architectural treasures that Mechelen is worth a visit. It's an easy place to explore – and there's hardly anyone here in winter.

From the railway station, it's a 15-minute walk to the centre of town along Hendrik Conscienceplein. You end up in the **Grote Markt** – almost as impressive as those in Brussels and Antwerp – which is overlooked by the ornate **Stadhuis**, stuck on the left-hand end of the austere 14th-century **Cloth Hall**. One wing of the hall was demolished to accommodate the building, with the idea of gradually replacing the rest of the hall with something flashier. Rombout Keldermans the Younger began work on it in 1526, but eight years later, probably owing to financial difficulties, it was abandoned and remained in a state of dilapidation until the late 19th century when Keldermans' original plans were finally completed. Close by stands a modern statue of the doll **Op Signoorke**, Mechelen's mascot, being tossed in a blanket. In the rich tradition of weird Belgian festivals (*see p274* **Beer, bears and bathtubs**), the townsfolk parade through the streets every September, flinging a dummy into the air from a sheet.

Just west of the Grote Markt is Mechelen's artistic showpiece, **St Romboutskathedraal** (015 27 19 90; 9am-4.30pm daily; free). It was started in the 13th century in early Gothic style, but finished, following a fire in 1342, in late Gothic. The west tower should have been the tallest in the world at the time (it was planned to be 167 metres/548 feet), but the general plummeting of Mechelen's fortunes after 1530 put a stop to such lofty ambitions (the unfortunate Keldermans was in charge of this project, too). Still, the 97 metres (318 feet) that were built are immensely handsome (Louis XIV's great military engineer Vauban thought it the eighth wonder of the world).

Unfortunately, the cathedral has suffered severe subsidence problems and remains in danger of falling apart. The elegant interior soars upwards and is filled with light and Gothic purity (if you can ignore the later florid baroque additions). The painting to look out for is Van Dyck's *Crucifixion.*

North of the cathedral is a clutch of intriguing religious buildings. Walking up Wollemarkt brings you to the gabled 16th-century **Abdij van St Truiden** by a weed-choked canal. Almost opposite stands the Gothic **St Janskerk**, which contains a Rubens

triptych of the *Adoration of the Magi,* but is, alas, rarely open. St Jansstraat runs along the side of the church and leads to the prestigious **Koninklijk Beiardschool** on the corner, one of the world's leading schools of carillon playing (bells sounded from a keyboard).

Next door is the late Gothic, early 16th-century **Museum Hof van Busleyden** (015 20 20 04/015 29 40 37; 10am-5pm Tue-Sun; €2). Hieronymus van Busleyden was a lawyer and leading Flemish humanist who entertained the likes of Erasmus and Thomas More here. The latter was so impressed with the house that he wrote three poems about it. The house now contains an agreeably disparate – if not exactly thrilling – collection of paintings, bells and architectural bits and bobs.

If you head south-east from here, you come to Veemarkt, and the baroque **St Pieter en Pauluskerk** (*Apr-Oct* 1.30-5.30pm Tue-Sun; *Nov-Mar* 1.30-4.30pm Tue-Sun; free), next to the remains of the **Palace of Margaret of York**. The beautiful 16th-century **Palace of Margaret of Austria** is also here.

From Veemarkt, Befferstraat leads back to the Grote Markt. Running south-west from here, past the Gothic Schepenhuis, is Ijzerenleen. Just before the street crosses the River Dijle, Nauwstraat leads off to the right, curving round via Draabstraat to an iron bridge leading to Haverwerf. Here are three superb façades, the most remarkable of which is the curious **Duivelhuis** (built in 1519) at

The beautiful formal gardens of the **Palace of Margaret of Austria** in Mechelen.

No.23. Turn left here and walk along the river, looking out for **De Zalm**, a stunning Flemish Renaissance house with a gilded salmon over its entrance. Head down 't Plein on the right and finish up at the white sandstone church of **Onze-Lieve-Vrouw over de Dijle** (*Apr-Oct* 1.30-5.30pm Tue-Sun; *Nov-Mar* 1.30-4.30pm Tue-Sun; free). Started in the 15th century, it was not finished until the 17th, and the variety of styles in vogue during these 200 years (from Gothic to baroque) is evident. Inside hangs Rubens' *Miraculous Draught of Fishes*.

Where to eat & stay

There are plenty of bars and restaurants around the Wollemarkt, behind the cathedral, but they're mostly aimed at tourists. For a better selection, head for Nauwstraat and the Vismarkt, down by the river. The **Madrid** (4 Lange Schipstraat; 015 29 03 95) is opposite Nauwstraat and overlooks the river. It's not cheap (main courses €14-€20), but it is highly recommended – although the house speciality is tripe. Another option is the rustic **De Cirque** (8 Vismarkt; 015 20 77 80; closed Sun; main courses €10), which has a comfortable feel and an eclectic menu. Before your meal there, you could enjoy an aperitif on the terrace overlooking the river at the nearby **De Gouden Vis** in the Nauwstraat.

For fish, a good option is **'t Zeepaardje** (16 Vismarkt; 015 20 46 35; closed Mon), where you'll find loup de mer and sole meunière at €17.50. If you want a drink and a snack (there is also a restaurant at the back), try **Den Akker** (11 Nauwstraat; 015 33 10 78) or on the Grote Markt there's the trendy **Den Beer** at No.32-33. Alternatively, there's the **Borrel-babbel** (5 Nieuwwerk; 015 27 36 89), the smallest bar in Mechelen.

If you want somewhere to stay, head for the **Anker Brewery** (49 Guido Gezellelaan; 015 20 38 80; double €73), home to the famous

The bad boy of Belgian art

His depictions of women being molested by skeletons, nailed to crosses and pleasuring themselves made him one of the most scandalous figures of his time. He took two sisters for lovers. And he adored gardening.

Félicien Rops was one of the fathers of Belgian Symbolist art. Born in Namur in 1833, he started producing caricatures of prominent figures in high society and politics while at university in Brussels. The satirical magazine *Uylenspiegel* that he founded became an outlet for his lithographs, which soon brought him fame in Belgium's intellectual circles.

The rakish young artist became a regular visitor to Paris, where his remarkable graphic talent and technical advances in etching gained increasing acclaim. In 1864, he met Baudelaire in Namur and drew the frontispiece to *Epaves*, the collection of poems banned from appearing in *Les Fleurs du Mal*. Rops' motto – 'Autre ne veulx estre', or 'No desire to be otherwise' – must have been right up Baudelaire's street: the French poet described him as 'the only true artist' he met in Belgium.

He later lived in Paris (with two seamstress sisters) and worked for several novelists, becoming the city's highest-paid illustrator. He also travelled to Scandinavia, Spain, the US, Algeria and Hungary, looking for inspiration for his paintings.

Rops' reputation has only recently been rehabilitated. 'Twenty-five years ago, people were still burning his work,' says Thierry Zéno of the Fondation Félicien Rops. Today, Rops is rightly seen as a trail-blazer who paved the way for Magritte, Ensor and others to explore the darker side of the human soul. In this spirit, the Fondation Rops is converting the artist's former home in Mettet, outside Namur, into a residence for promising young artists. The *château* is occasionally open to the public, and you can see the bed Baudelaire slept in, and wander the grounds.

To see Rops' work, you have to go to Namur. Housed in a brick and stone building that once belonged to the artist's parents-in-law, the Félicien Rops Museum in the Old Town is currently undergoing restoration, but there's still enough to see, from early caricatures to mature landscape paintings to those fantastical, licentious engravings (hidden in drawers upstairs, with handles that are just too high for young arms to reach). The renovation means that the temporary exhibitions change fairly frequently, so call ahead to check what's on.

Félicien Rops Museum
12 rue Fumal (081 22 01 10/www.ciger.be/ rops). **Open** *July, Aug* 10am-6pm daily. *Sept-June* 10am-6pm Tue-Sun. **Admission** €2.48; €1.24 concessions.

Gouden Carolus (Golden Charles). It's an excellent place for a beer or an unpretentious meal, and it also has 22 rooms. It's about a ten-minute walk from the centre, just behind the Grande Béguinage.

Getting there

From Brussels, there are seven trains an hour from Gare du Nord, Gare Centrale or Gare du Midi. Journey takes 25 minutes.

Tourist information

Dienst Toerisme Stad Mechelen

Stadhuis, 21 Grote Markt, 2800 Mechelen (015 29 76 55/fax 015 29 76 53/www.mechelen.be). **Open** *Easter-Sept* 8am-6pm Mon-Fri; 9.30am-12.30pm, 1.30-5pm Sat, Sun. *Oct-Easter* 8am-6pm Mon-Fri; 10am-noon, 2-4.30pm Sat, Sun. From November to February, the office closes at 5pm during the week.

La Deche.

For more information on the occasional open days at the Château Thozée in Mettet, call 071 72 72 62 or visit www.fondationrops.org.

Namur

Some 60 kilometres (37 miles) south-east of Brussels, Namur is the capital of Wallonia – and one of its most intriguing towns. Tucked in a misty valley at the strategically significant juncture of the Sambre and Meuse rivers, it has had a lively history of successive invasions and struggles for control, producing what is now a major tourist draw, the mighty **Citadelle de Namur** (8 route Merveilleuse; 081 22 68 29; *Easter, June-Sept* 11am-6pm daily; closed rest of the year; €6).

Dominating the town from its rocky promontory, this site has been fortified for 2,000 years, although the Citadel's current appearance dates mainly from the period of Dutch rule between 1815 and 1830. Covering an area of around 80 hectares (200 acres), you need to leave a good couple of hours to explore it properly. Within the grounds are atmospheric underground passages, an audio-visual show, exhibitions on military history, a miniature train ride, a museum dedicated to the flora and fauna of Wallonia, an archaeological exhibition, Belgium's largest open-air theatre and various children's amusements. The most exhilarating way to reach it is via the *téléphérique* (cable car), which starts from near the Pont du Musée.

But there's much more to Namur than the Citadel. Its large university population ensures a rowdy nightlife, but during the day, most visitors tend to wander around museums, stroll through town and lounge in terrace cafés. Nobody seems in much of a hurry in Namur.

The **tourist office** (*see p280*) is just outside the station entrance, from which rue de Fer leads down to the centre around the chaotic place d'Armes. Just east of here is the superb **Trésor du Prieuré d'Oignies** (17 rue Julie Billiart; 081 23 03 42; 10am-noon, 2-5pm Tue-Sat; 2-5pm Sun; €1.50), a tiny but eminently worthwhile collection of exquisite early 13th-century gold and silver work by Brother Hugo d'Oignies.

Back on rue de Fer, housed within a fine 18th-century mansion, is the **Musée des Arts Anciens du Namurois** (24 rue de Fer; 081 22 00 65; 10am-6pm Tue-Sun; €1.24-€2.48), which includes fine examples of local metalwork, medieval sculptures and a variety of paintings – several by Henri Bles.

West of the place d'Armes, you'll find over-the-top baroque extravagance in the 17th-century church of **St Loup** on rue du Collège. Leading off this street is rue Fumal, home to the **Félicien Rops Museum** (*see left* **The bad boy of Belgian art**). Namur-born

Trips Out of Town

Fancy that

Much as England is the cradle of football, Belgium is the cradle of pigeon fancying. The world's first pigeon race took place near Hoeselt, a small village in Limburg. In 1828 a pastor put several pigeons in a basket, cycled to the nearby town of Tongeren and released them to see which would make it back first. Hoeselt is also near the German border, and pigeons were put to good use by the Allies in both world wars, relaying signals behind enemy lines. Many soldiers owed their lives to pigeons, whose role is honoured in memorials in both Brussels and Lille.

Nobody really knows why pigeons have a homing instinct, but they can fly thousands of kilometres at up to 75kph (46mph) before returning to the exact spot they set out from. They also have an affinity for human contact. Mike Tyson, Marlon Brando and Paul Newman have all kept pigeons, as did Darwin, Monet, Picasso and the prophet Mohammed.

Hoeselt is now home to the World Pigeon Center, the biggest pigeon loft on the planet, founded by Jean-Louis Jorissen and Jos Thoné. Thoné, a four-time winner of the world pigeon-racing championships, is boyishly enthusiastic about the sport. 'Fanciers all over the world look to Belgium,' he says. 'We're in the ideal spot.' The centre includes a restaurant (run by a Michelin-starred chef), shop and science labs, where scientists are currently developing pigeon passports, DNA certificates that will guarantee each bird's breeding.

The centre houses 2,000 pigeons, 200 of whose owners live in Japan and China. Prince Faisal of Saudi Arabia also keeps his birds here. If you want to take up the sport, you can register a pigeon for €50 a year. It gets its own space and is trained by Thoné and others for competitions. Wherever you are in the world, you can watch your bird live in its loft via webcam.

What's the attraction? 'We all wish we could fly,' is Thoné's theory. 'With a pigeon, you're a team, it's like it's flying in your place.'

World Pigeon Center

32 Industrielaan, Hoeselt (089 51 99 99/ www.wpc.be). **Open** *Guided tours* 3pm daily. *Restaurant* 11am-11pm daily.

artist Rops was notorious during his lifetime for his epicurean appetites, his fascination with the occult and the erotic nature of his drawings.

Where to eat & stay

For refreshment, the area west of the place d'Armes is your best bet. Those with deep pockets and a hunger to match should try out **La Petite Fugue** (5 place Chanoine Descamps; 081 23 13 20), an outstanding establishment where French cuisine rules. Main courses cost around €25 and a six-course gastronomic feast is €42. Across the square is the atmospheric **Fenêtre sur Cour** (café 6 place Chanoine Descamps; restaurant 35 rue des Présidents; 081 23 09 08) with its menu du marché at €23.

Also reasonably priced is the delightful (and typically Namurois) **Le Temps des Cerises** (22 rue des Brasseurs; 081 22 53 26; closed Mon, Tue, Sun) with its renowned *choucroute maison*. If you like Belgo-Italian fare, try **Roberto's** (15 rue de la Croix; 081 23 13 13). Finally, off the beaten track is **La Bonne Fourchette** (112-116 rue Notre Dame; 081 23 15 36) between the Citadel and the River Meuse.

If you only feel in need of a drink, try the cool **Extèrieure-Nuit** (6 place Chanoine Descamps) in front of the Fenêtre sur Cour or the more traditional **Métropole** (1 rue Emile Cuvelier) facing the theatre and offering more than 30 beers. Indeed, there are many small cafés and bars around the place du Théâtre. Alternatively, you can investigate the place du Marché aux Légumes, where you'll find several haunts including the **Piano Bar** (jazz, rock and R&B concerts most weekends). Another lively student bar is **Le Monde à l'Envers** (26 rue Lelièvre).

Should you be contemplating some time in the Ardennes, Namur's position in the foothills plus excellent transport links make it an ideal jumping-off point for venturing into the wilds. If you are making it your base for a night or two, try the 17th-century **Les Tanneurs de Namur** (13 rue de Tanneries; 081 24 00 24; rooms €60-€210) with two restaurants and a quiet location close to the centre. More affordable is **Le Parisien** (16 rue Emile Cuvelier; 081 22 63 79; rooms €41-€56).

Getting there

From Brussels there are two to five fast trains an hour from Gare Centrale. Journey takes one hour.

Tourist information

Maison du Tourisme de Namur

square Leopold, 5000 Namur (081 24 64 49/fax 081 74 99 29/www.namur.be). **Open** 9.30am-6pm daily.

Information Kiosk Grognon
1 avenue Baron Louis Huart (081 22 34 24).
Open Apr-Sept 9.30am-6pm daily. Closed Oct-Mar.
There are guided tours of the Old Town and the
Citadel from the kiosk daily during July and August.
There are also tours of the Old Town on Mondays
at 2.30pm in May, June and September.

Tournai

Tournai offers some of the charms of the
more famously picturesque Flemish towns,
without the accompanying tourist industry.

Although it's the second oldest city in
Belgium, it is the French that have most
influenced Tournai. Founded by Roman
soldiers, Tournai (Doornik in Dutch) was capital
of the Frankish Merovingian dynasty in the fifth
century. Handed over to the courts of Flanders
shortly after their demise, Tournai then spent
much of the Middle Ages as part of France.
Its citizens are among the few Walloons not
offended to be taken for French. Henry VIII
managed to occupy it for five years from 1513,
and had the cathedral painted with an English
rose gracing the fresco. After surviving World
War I virtually unscathed, much of Tournai was
destroyed by Allied bombing 25 years later.

The compact centre still has charm, and
the growing number of high-tech parks in
the suburbs promise better times. For the
moment, though, the town has the run-down
feel of much of Wallonia and is suffering from
the same economic problems.

The train station is located on the north-east
side of the centre. A 15-minute walk from place
Crombez along rue Royale and rue de l'Hôpital
Notre Dame takes you over the River Escaut
(Schelde in Dutch) to the city's architectural
highlight: the **Cathédrale Notre Dame** (069
84 34 69; 10.15 or 10.30am-12.30pm, 1.30-6pm
daily; €1). Frequently referred to as the finest
cathedral in the country (although the crowd of
jostling buildings surrounding it don't do it any
aesthetic favours), its five distinctive towers
dominate the city and crown the immense bulk
of its blue granite main body. The current
church is the third on the site and was largely
completed by the end of the 12th century.

The Porte Mantile, on place Paul Emile
Janson, is decorated with intriguing if rather
weathered Romanesque carvings, and there are
more fine carvings, dating from later periods,
on the west façade facing place de l'Evêché.
Once inside, the soaring proportions of the
light-bathed nave and the beautiful transepts
with their 16th-century stained glass are
the most arresting features. It's worth paying
the small entrance fee to see the Treasury,

which contains a host of religious artefacts
including superb reliquary shrines and *Ecce
Homo* by Quentin Matsys.

The south side of the cathedral overlooks
the Grand' Place. Here you'll find the ill-
proportioned 72-metre (236-foot) **Beffroi**,
the oldest belfry in Belgium. It was begun in
the late 12th century but has been much altered
and renovated since. Also on the Grand' Place is
the rather gloomy-looking **Halle aux Draps**;
only the façade of the early 17th-century
Renaissance cloth hall is original.

Tournai has plenty of museums; most are
closed on Tuesdays and take a two-hour
midday lunch break. The most prestigious
are the **Musée d'Histoire Naturelle** (Cour
d'honneur de l'Hôtel de Ville; 069 23 39 39; *Nov-
Mar* 10am-noon, 2-5pm Mon, Wed-Sat; 2-5pm
Sun; *Apr-Oct* 10am-1pm, 2-5.30pm Wed-Sun;
€2.50), which has a large collection of dioramas
and biotopes; and the **Musée des Beaux-
Arts** (1 rue St-Martin; 069 22 20 43; 10am-5pm
Mon, Wed-Sun; €3). Built by Victor Horta in the
1920s, in his later, streamlined art deco style,
this beautifully economical building is a fitting
location for the small but choice selection of
paintings by of Rubens, Monet and Van Gogh.
Lovers of the Flemish Primitives will find
themselves drawn to the exquisite works of
Tournai-born Rogier van der Weyden.

Tournai also boasts museums of tapestries,
archaeology, folklore and decorative arts. The
tourist office (*see p282*) supplies an excellent
sightseeing map.

Where to eat & stay

Tournai is stuffed to the gills with restaurants.
Take a wander from the cathedral down to
the river – quai du Marché au Poisson – and
you shouldn't be disappointed. **L'Eau à la
Bouche** (No. 8A-B; 069 22 77 20; closed Mon,
dinner Thur, lunch Sat) has a menu at €25 and
a vegetarian menu at €12.50 – the specialities
are pâté and game in season; **Le Giverny**
(No. 6; 069 22 44 64; closed Mon, lunch Sat,
dinner Sun) is recommended if you want to
splash out – main courses range from €19
to €40. It specialises in fish and game.

Nearer the cathedral, the best bet is **Le
Bistro de la Cathédrale** (15 rue Vieux
Marché aux Poteries; 069 21 03 79), where
you'll find the ubiquitous *lapin à la
tournaisienne* (rabbit cooked in beer with
prunes and raisins). Main courses usually cost
€10-€15. At weekends, an excellent choice is
the characterful **La Flambée** (4 rue Dame
Odile; 069 22 18 78), which has a set menu –
four courses and a half bottle of wine – for
€40. It's open Friday and Saturday evenings

(7-10pm), and Sunday lunchtimes (noon-2pm). For something lighter, home-made tarts, quiche and suchlike, try **La Tartine Quotidienne** at 3 rue de Paris (069 23 35 88; closed Sat, Sun, dinner Mon-Thur, Sat).

Bars equally cluster down by the river. There's the trendy **La Fabrique** (13B quai du Marché au Poisson) and the lively **L'Entracte** (7 rue de l'Hôpital Notre Dame; 069 22 61 20). Also worth investigating is the eclectic **Hangar** (6 rue de L'Arbalète), with its variety of DJs and occasional live concerts.

Accommodation in Tournai is tricky. The best option is likely to be the modern **D'Alcantara** (2 rue des Bouchers St-Jacques; 069 21 26 48; double from €83). Alternatively, there's the **Holiday Inn Garden Court** (2 place St-Pierre; 069 21 50 77; double €105-€117), housed in the converted fire station.

Getting there

From Brussels, there are one to three direct trains an hour from Gare du Nord, Gare Centrale or Gare du Midi. The journey takes 55 minutes.

Tourist information

Tournai Tourist Office

14 rue Vieux Marché aux Poteries, 7500 Tournai (069 22 20 45/www.tournai.be). **Open** *July-Sept* 8.30am-6pm Mon-Fri; 10am-1pm, 3-6pm Sat, Sun. *Apr-June* 8.30am-6pm Mon-Fri; 10am-noon, 3-6pm Sat; 2-6pm Sun. *Oct-Mar* 8.30am-5.30pm Mon-Fri; 10am-noon, 2-4pm Sat; 2-6pm Sun.

The Ardennes

The Ardennes spreads over three provinces in the south (Namur, Luxembourg, Liège) and the region is as popular as the coast for a weekend getaway for Belgians. This is an area of enormous charm, of gentle hills and valleys, rapid-flowing rivers and dark forests, grottoes and megalithic sites. It's touristy, but very relaxed, mercifully sparsely populated and has kept a calm, venerable atmosphere.

Typical to the Ardennes are old stone artisanal houses, beautiful abbeys and churches and immensely pretty medieval villages, dominated by imposing, crumbling castles.

The original spa

The little town of Spa in the Ardennes was the world's first health resort. Pliny the Elder knew of the healing properties of the sulphur-laden waters, and a resort was established in the 16th century, which attracted royalty, statesmen and aristocrats from all over Europe. Regular visitor Henry VIII, a martyr to his gout, swore by Spa. Peter the Great, Casanova, Fenimore Cooper, they all came here, to the main thermal baths in the centre of town, Les Thermes de Spa. The town gave its name to Bath Spa – and all those other spa towns around the world – as well as an eponymous brand of bottled mineral water.

But, after 500 years of communal use by the world's rich and infamous, the main thermal baths are going to be converted into a conference centre – after a brand-new leisure complex of baths, saunas and fitness rooms is built on a hillock overlooking the town centre.

Capable of attracting 150,000 visitors a year, the swanky new centre will be connected to the town centre by a cable car, swishing bathers to their destination in two minutes. The project is expected to be completed by late 2003. In the meantime, the old thermal baths still offer visitors a

huge range of health, beauty and relaxation cures, including post-natal treatment for mothers and newborns, mud treatment for arthritis, and water treatments for any number of ailments. It's not cheap – prices start at around €70 per day – but it is original.

Les Thermes de Spa

2 place Royale (087 77 25 60/ www.aqualis.be). **Open** 9am-12.30pm, 1.30-5pm Mon-Sat. Closed Jan.

Dinant, with the **Church of Notre Dame** and, above, the **Citadel**. *See p284.*

The Ardennes is steeped in history. This was the hunting grounds of some of Europe's most famous rulers: Godfrey de Bouillon, Charles V and Louis XIV. More recently, the Ardennes is where Germany's final desperate advance of World War II was stopped – memorials are found at all the battle sites. Visit the **Musée de la Bataille des Ardennes** in La Roche-en-Ardenne (084 41 17 25; 10am-6pm daily; €5.50) or the **American Historical Centre and Memorial** in Bastogne (061 21 14 13; *July, Aug* 9.30am-6pm daily; *May, June, Sept* 9.30am-5pm daily; *Feb-Apr, Oct-Dec* 10am-4.30pm daily; €7.50) This is where, on 22 December 1944, General McAuliffe famously said 'Nuts!' to the Nazis' demand for surrender (at least one café in the town is named Nuts).

Things to do

The Ardennes has something for everyone. Typical activities include:

Eating: Even within a country as gastronomically minded as Belgium, the Ardennes is still renowned for its food. It has wonderful local produce, including game, wild boar and pike, and a particular smoked ham, *jambon ardennois*.

Architecture: Almost every village in the Ardennes has a church or castle of note. The churches (some dating from the 11th century) are among the oldest in Belgium, while the castles reinforce the feudal atmosphere. Of particular note is Godfrey de Bouillon's 13th-century castle at **Bouillon** (061 46 62 57; €4), lit by torches at night in July and August. Opening hours: *July, Aug* 10am-7pm Mon, Thur; 10am-10pm Tue, Wed, Fri-Sun; closing times vary the rest of the year.

Adventure sports: The Ardennes is criss-crossed by rivers (Ourthe, Meuse, Semois), hills, valleys and rocks. This makes it perfect for all manner of sports including swimming, kayaking, rafting, trekking, mountain biking, rock climbing and skiing. For more information on such activitites, contact **Durbuy Adventure** (086 21 28 15/www.durbuy adventure.be) or **Bouillon** (061 25 68 78).

Grottoes: The Ardennes' river valleys lend themselves particularly well to the formation of grottoes. Stunning examples are found at **Han-sur-Lesse** (084 37 72 12; 10am-4pm/ 5.30pm daily, with a break for lunch; €10.30) and **Hotton**, where the 'Grotto of 1001 Nights' was discovered in 1958. It is celebrated for the variety in size and colour of its formations (084 46 60 46; *July, Aug* 10am-6pm daily; *Sept, Oct, Apr-June* 10am-5pm daily; *Nov-Mar* call 083 68 83 65 for reservations; €7).

Parcs à Gibiers: Wooded nature reserves, home to deer and wild boar, are found all over the Ardennes. The park at **Han-sur-Lesse**

(084 37 72 12; €7.80) is the largest and has rather more savage animals (lynx, bears, wolves) than the others. It's open the same hours as the grotto.

Festivals: The Ardennes has kept its traditions, and festivals and processions lend colour to villages throughout the year – *see p274* **Beer, bears and bathtubs**.

Dinant

Pretty Dinant is an easy getaway for the day. There's enough here to occupy yourself for a few hours or so – but probably not much longer than that. Its principal attraction is the **Citadel** (082 22 36 70; *Apr-Oct* 10am-6pm daily; *Nov-Mar* 10am-4pm daily; €5.20) in the main place Reine-Astrid. Included in the ticket price is the cable car journey; those of nervous disposition can climb the 400 steps. The site of many a fierce battle – including one in 1914, after which occupying Germans set light to the town and shot scores of locals – the Citadel has been converted into a museum depicting the conflict with the French, Dutch and Germans.

Another chairlift runs from rue en Rhée to the **Tour Mont Fat** (082 22 27 83; *Apr-Oct* 10.30am-7pm daily; €5), a family play park with panoramic views. Dinant's other main attraction is the Gothic **Church of Notre-Dame** (10.30am-6pm daily), which has paintings by local artist Antoine Wiertz. For a drink and a bite to eat, try **Le Sax** (13 place Reine-Astrid). Musical inventor Adolphe Sax came from Dinant, and his home at 35 rue Adolphe Sax features a suitable mural.

St-Hubert

It's difficult to get round the Ardennes without a car – railway stations are few and buses are infrequent. St-Hubert has the great advantage of being near a train station. Once there, you are in the middle of the Ardennes forest and can trek or cycle to most places.

St-Hubert is the spiritual centre of the province of Luxembourg and one of the finest towns in the Ardennes. It is dominated by the imposing **Basilique St Pierre-St Paul-St Hubert**, which has as many architectural styles as it has names: it was founded in the 11th century, rebuilt in the Flemish Gothic style in the 16th, and given a classical façade in the 18th. The interior is full of magnificent late Renaissance sculptures, tombs and paintings.

The town is named after St-Hubert, the seventh-century patron saint of hunters and butchers, and the European hunting capital. It is accordingly famous for its game restaurants. Though quiet and not renowned

for its nightlife, it has its share of festivals throughout the year: the first Sunday of September is the Festival for Hunters; the last Sunday is the Festival of the Brotherhood of Butchers. Throughout July, there are classical music concerts every night. It is also a place of pilgrimage: on the Monday before Pentecost, the Landesdorf pilgrimage reaches the town, while Pentecost itself sees the Ardennes pilgrimage. On 3 November, the Festival of St-Hubert provides folkloric processions, markets and solemn mass.

St-Hubert is surrounded by great natural beauty. Just two kilometres outside the town is **Parc à Gibiers** (061 25 68 17; 9am-6pm daily) where deer, stags and wild boar roam at will. A little further along the same road is the celebrated **Fourneau St-Michel**: the iron forge that was established by Dom Spirot, the last abbot of the Abbaye St-Hubert, in 1771. It still works. Here, also set in a valley, is a perfectly preserved pre-Industrial Revolution village of farms, small houses, granaries, printing house, church and schoolhouse. This is the **Musée de la Vie Rurale en Wallonie** (084 21 08 44; *July, Aug* 9am-6pm daily; *Sept-Nov, Mar-June* 9am-5pm daily; closed Dec-Feb; €2.50).

If you fancy overnighting it, try the **Hôtel Borquin** (6 place de l'Abbaye; 061 61 14 56; double €38.45). Right in the centre, facing the basilica, this is a modest, comfy hotel with a restaurant that serves excellent local produce.

To the west of St-Hubert is **Redu**, a village totally dedicated to books. Shops sell rare and precious books, while engravers, illustrators and binders have all set up shop here.

Getting there

From Brussels there is one train an hour to **Dinant** from Gare du Nord, Gare Centrale or Gare du Midi. Journey takes 90 minutes. To **Poix St-Hubert** (change at Jemelle), there is one train an hour from Gare Centrale; journey takes 2 hours 15 minutes. Then it's a six-kilometre (four-mile) bus journey to St-Hubert (12 buses a day; four a day at the weekend).

Tourist information

Dinant Tourist Office
8 avenue Cadoux, 5500 Dinant (082 22 28 70/ fax 082 22 77 88/www.dinant-tourisme.be). **Open** *June-Aug* 8am-6pm Mon-Fri; 9am-7pm Sat; 10am-6pm Sun. *Sept-May* 8.30am-6pm Mon-Fri; 9.30am-4pm Sat; 10.30am-2pm Sun.

St-Hubert Tourist Office
12 rue St-Gilles, 6870 St-Hubert (061 61 30 10/ fax 061 61 54 44/www.sthubert.be). **Open** 9am-6pm daily.

Directory

Directory

Getting Around

By air

Brussels' international airport is located at Zaventem, 14 kilometres (nine miles) north-east of the capital, with good road and rail connections to the centre. The airport information desk (7am-10pm daily) is in the check-in area. Hotel information with a phone link for reservations is in the arrivals section. Hotel shuttle buses run from level 0.

Transport and flight info, is at **www.brusselsairport.be**. For flight information, call **0900 70000**.

Airport parking

Airport Parc International (02 715 21 10) charges €12.27 or €24.66 (guarded) per day; **Car Hotel** (02 753 01 10/ www.carhotel.com) is cheaper (€11.20 per day) although the car park is a shuttle ride away.

Connections to the city

There is a frequent shuttle train service – **Airport City Express** (02 753 24 40) – from Zaventem to Gare du Nord, Gare Centrale and Gare du Midi. Second-class tickets cost €2, first-class €3.10. There are four trains an hour from 6am to midnight; journey time 20 minutes. Women travelling alone at night are best to disembark at Gare Centrale.

An hourly **bus** service to Gare du Nord operates from below the arrivals hall. The journey time is about 35 minutes. For information on local buses from the airport, call **De Lijn** on 02 526 28 28. There is an **Airport Express** which runs hourly to Antwerp

and costs €5.30 for a single ticket (for further details, call 02 511 90 30).

Taxis wait by the arrivals building and should display a yellow-and-blue licence. The fare from Zaventem to central Brussels should cost €26 – many accept credit cards. A rooftop indicator shows 1 or 2 for single or double tariff. Strictly speaking, the double tariff is only applicable outside the limits of the 19 *communes*. In practice, most drivers switch to double as soon as they're on a motorway. Autolux (orange-and-white aeroplane sticker) offer 25 per cent off for a return journey.

Car rental desks can be found in the arrivals hall and are open from 6.30am to 11pm. *See p289* **Car hire**.

Ryanair flies to what it calls Brussels South, a tiny airport 55 kilometres (34 miles) away in **Charleroi** (07 125 12 11/ www.charleroi-airport.com). There is little in the way of money-changing facilities or tourist information. A shuttle bus connecting with arrivals runs the ten-minute journey to Charleroi train station, where a half-hourly train (€6.60) takes 50 minutes to reach Brussels. Ryanair run a shuttle bus (€8.70) from Charleroi airport to the Wild Geese pub, 2-4 avenue Livingstone, by Maelbeek metro in the EU Quarter of Brussels. Journey time is 45 minutes.

By rail

Eurostar

There are **ten departures a day** (nine on Saturdays; eight on Sundays) from Brussels

Gare du Midi and London Waterloo, and the journey time is around **two hours 40 minutes**. Check in at least 20 minutes before departure. In the UK, Eurostar information and reservations are available from selected travel agents and rail stations. In Belgium, Eurostar tickets are available at travel agents and international ticket desks in mainline stations.

Waterloo International

Call centre 01233 617575/local rate charges for callers within the UK 08705 186186/www.eurostar.co.uk. **Open** *Call centre* 8am-9pm Mon-Fri; 8am-8pm Sat; 9am-5pm Sun. *Ticket office at Waterloo International* 4.15am-9.30pm Mon-Fri; 5am-9.30pm Sat; 6am-9.30pm Sun. **Credit** AmEx, DC, MC, V. Prices from London to Brussels start at £70 for a 'Weekend Day Return', although the best deal is probably the £79 'Leisure Apex 14' return ticket (must be booked at least 14 days in advance and you must stay over two nights or a Saturday night).

Gare du Midi

02 555 25 55/Eurostar 02 528 28 28/www.b-rail.be/internat/E/ booking/index.html. **Open** 8am-8pm Mon-Fri; 9am-5.30pm Sat, Sun. **Credit** MC, V. Adult prices from Brussels to London start at €85 ('Dayreturn Apex'). The 'Tourist 7' fare is €115; the 'Tourist' fare costs €150; the 'Tourist Flexi' is €185.

Le Shuttle

If you're driving to Brussels from the UK, Le Shuttle can transport you and your vehicle from Cheriton Park on the M20 near Folkestone to Coquelles near Calais in 35 minutes. There are good motorway connections to Brussels from there. Le Shuttle is a 24-hour service with up to four shuttles an hour from Folkestone. There are also facilities for

the disabled. Tickets can be
bought from a travel agent, Le
Shuttle or (with the exception
of Apex or promotional offers)
on arrival at the tolls. Hertz
and Le Shuttle have a Le Swap
rental system so that you can
drive a left-hand- and right-
hand-drive car in France and
the UK respectively.

Le Shuttle
UK 08705 353535/
www.Eurotunnel.co.uk. **Open** 8am-
8pm Mon-Fri; 8am-6pm Sat, Sun.
Credit AmEx, DC, MC, V.
A standard five-day return costs
£185. Single tickets cost £139.50
(overnight travel) or £159.50
(daytime travel), more at peak times.
If you're paying by credit card, the
card holder must be in the car.

By sea

Hoverspeed
0870 240 8070/08705 240241/
www.hoverspeed.co.uk. **Credit**
AmEx, DC, MC, V.
There are both hovercraft and seacat
(vehicle-carrying catamaran)
services between **Dover and
Calais**. In the peak season, there are
around 14 crossings daily and the
journey is 35 minutes by hovercraft
and 50 minutes by seacat. A
standard single fare for a car with
two passengers is £109-£139. The
seacat service between **Dover and
Ostend**, now the only sea crossing,
is a two-hour journey, and a standard
single ticket for a car with two
passengers is £109-£139.

By coach

Eurolines
01582 404511/08705 808080/
www.eurolines.com. **Open** 8am-
6.30pm Mon-Fri; 9am-5.30pm Sat.
Credit AmEx, DC, MC, V.
A return fare from London Victoria
to Brussels between 1 Apr 2002-31
March 2003 is £46 for adults, £42
for 13-25s and £23 for 4-12s (1 July-
31 Aug, 15 Dec-3 Jan £52 adult,
£47 youth, £26 child).

Eurolines (Brussels)
*80 rue de Progrès, St-Josse (02 274
13 50/02 201 11 40/www.eurolines.
com/belgium). Métro Gare du Nord.*
Open 9am-11pm daily. **Credit**
AmEx, DC, MC, V. **Map** p319 C1.
Eurolines buses depart from CCN
Gare du Nord (80 rue de Progrès).
There is also an office for ticket sales
at 50 place de Brouckère, Lower
Town (02 217 00 25).

Public transport

Brussels' cheap, integrated
public transport system is
made up of metro, rail, buses
and trams, with tickets
allowing any changes in town
for up to an hour.

Belgian railways

Léopold I was responsible
for bringing the railroad to
Belgium, the first in mainland
Europe. Société Nationale des
Transports Intercommunaux
(SNCB) runs a clean, efficient
system on 4,000 kilometres
(2,485 miles) of track.
  Brussels has three mainline
stations – **Gare Centrale**
(1km from the Grand' Place),
Gare du Midi (South Station)
and **Gare du Nord** (North
Station) – which are directly
linked. Two more minor
stations, Schuman and
Quartier Léopold, serve the
European institutions.
  Belgium is a small country
and most tourist spots are an
hour or so away by rail from
Brussels. Most trains are clean
and efficient. Rail travel is
good value with a variety of
special offers available. These
include the **Eurodomino**
pass, which provides unlimited
travel for periods of five or ten
days. Normal tickets, priced
per kilometre, can be bought

on board with a modest
supplement. For information
about Belgian railways, call
0891 516444 in the UK or,
in Belgium, **02 555 25 55**
(national) or **02 528 28 28**
(international).
  Brussels is at the hub of the
superb **Thalys** network of
high-speed trains (0900 10177/
www.thalys.com), connecting
Paris, Amsterdam, Cologne
and Geneva. The regular
service to Paris takes about
90 minutes and costs around
€50, to Amsterdam two-and-a-
half hours for around €75.
  Look up the excellent
website **www.b-rail.be/E** (in
English) for timetable details
and ticket prices (both national
and international), including a
range of cheap deals if you're
planning on making a number
of train journeys.
  Baggage facilities are
available at mainline railway
stations. Gare du Midi's left
luggage office is next to the
Eurostar terminal.

Metro, trams & buses

The efficient public transport
network in the capital is run by
STIB (Société des Transports
Intercommunaux de Bruxelles).
Transport maps and timetables
are available from STIB info
centres at Gare du Midi, Porte
de Namur and Rogier.

Pré-métro

Looking at a map of the Brussels metro, it looks as
though there's a metro line running from the Gare du Nord
south to the Gare du Midi and beyond. This is actually
an **underground tram line**, known as the **pré-métro**. The
underground stations are marked by the usual blue 'M'
signs used for all metro stations, and some, such as
De Brouckère, serve both metro trains and the pré-métro
underground trams. Don't be surprised, though, if you
descend into **Bourse** metro station and find no trains.
Anneessens and **Lemmonier** are the other central pré-métro
stations. In this guide we have indicated the pré-métro
stations by writing, for example, 'Pré-métro Bourse' or
Métro/Pré-métro De Brouckère'.

De Lijn (Flanders Public Transport Service)

02 526 28 20/www.delijn.be.
Open *Phone enquiries* 8.15am-4pm Mon-Fri.
Call the above number for info on services leaving from Brussels.

STIB

Sixth floor, 15 galerie de la Toison d'Or, Ixelles (02 515 20 00/ bus information 02 515 30 64/ www.stib.irisnet.be). Métro Porte de Namur. **Open** 8am-7pm Mon-Fri; 8am-4pm Sat. **Map** p321 D5.

TICKETS AND TRAVEL PASSES

Tickets are sold at metro and rail stations, on buses and trams, at a kiosk by the Bourse, at STIB information centres, and at many newsagents. A one-day **Tourist Passport** is available for €6 from the tourist information office in the Grand' Place and includes reductions on admission to museums. Points of sale for monthly passes are Métro Porte de Namur, Gare du Midi, the kiosk by the Bourse, SNCB stations and approved outlets. Tickets must be electronically stamped by the machines at metro stations and on trams and buses at the beginning of the journey. Controllers run random checks and can fine €55 for being without a validated ticket.

The most economical way of travelling for a few days is to buy a batch of ten tickets ('*une carte de dix trajets*') for €9. Five tickets cost €6.20, one costs €1.40 and a **one-day unlimited travel pass** is €3.60. Children under six can travel free if accompanied by an adult with a valid ticket. Public transport operates from 5.30am to midnight.

SIGNS AND LINES

Metro stations are indicated by a white letter 'M' on a blue background, while red-and-white signs mark tram and bus stops. Brussels is served by three lines and **pré-métro**

trams, which run through various underground sections (*see p287* **Pré-métro**). Métro **Line 1** is divided into Lines 1A and 1B. 1A runs from Roi Baudouin (close to the Atomium) to Hermann-Debroux. 1B goes from Bizet to Stockel. **Line 2** links Simonis to Clemenceau and mirrors the inner-city ring of boulevards above. The **pré-métro** line runs north–south, linking Gare du Nord to St-Gilles via Gare du Midi.

DISABLED TRAVEL

Public transport is not specially adapted for disabled passengers, but some trams have a low-level platform improve access slightly. A low-cost STIB minibus service (02 515 23 65) with vehicles equipped for wheelchairs is available to transport disabled travellers door-to-door. STIB has also installed facilities for blind passengers, such as braille information panels, in at least 12 of its metro stations.

For those travelling outside Brussels by train or on certain bus services, the disabled passenger pays and any accompanying person travels free. There are also reductions for the blind (call SNCB on 02 224 64 00 for details).

Taxis

Brussels' taxi drivers are notoriously shifty – watch the meter. Taxi ranks are situated outside mainline railway stations and at strategic locations such as Porte de Namur, place d'Espagne, the Bourse and De Brouckère. If you have a complaint to make against a taxi driver, record the registration number of the vehicle and inform the police.

The price per km should be €0.99, if the journey is inside the 19 *communes*.
Autolux *02 411 41 42*
Taxi Bleues *02 268 00 00*
Taxis Verts & Taxi Orange *02 349 49 49/www.taxisverts.be*

Driving

It's not easy driving around Belgium, and around Brussels in particular. Unless you're leaving the city, you really would be better off to take public transport or even walk.

Driving licences were issued to any adult over the counter at Post Offices in the 1960s, and mandatory tests were only introduced in 1974. This means that a scary percentage of the driving population of Belgium cannot drive – but carry on regardless. Although stiff penalties exist for drink driving, the law is routinely flouted. To say that bad driving was endemic would be an understatement.

Close examination of any Belgian vehicle may provide evidence of a further driving headache. Dents and scratches on the right-hand side show damage caused by the country's notorious 'priorité à droite' rule, the frequent reason for so many accidents. Motorists must give way to the right, even on a major road, except when marked otherwise. For example, a white sign with a yellow diamond on your road means cars from the right must stop for you.

Another factor to contend with is the aggressive behaviour of Belgian drivers, especially in rush hour and in tunnels. You would be best to avoid the main roads during the Great Escape, late afternoon on Fridays. In contrast to the sleek motorways, roads in town are also riddled with potholes. Remember also that trams have absolute right of way. Road rage could have been invented for Brussels.

A comprehensive tunnel system links major points in the city, making it possible to traverse Brussels without seeing the light of day. The inner ring is a pentagon of boulevards (marked with signs showing a blue ring on which the yellow dot is your current location). The secondary city ring was never completed and the outer ring has ended up as an elongated pear shape with a missing base, divided into an east and west motorway ring.

The speed limit on motorways is 120kph (74mph), on main roads 90kph (56mph) and in built-up areas 50kph (31mph). The wearing of seat belts is compulsory in both the front and the rear of the car.

Officially you need an international driver's licence, but police will usually accept a valid licence from your home country. If your car is towed, go to the nearest police station to get a document releasing it. Police may give you the document free of charge or demand a nominal fee, depending on the area of town. They will then give the address of the garage holding your car. Present the police letter there and pay another fee – the sum can vary – to get your vehicle back.

Driving with no traffic (a rare occurrence) and no stops, it takes about 30 minutes to Antwerp, 45 minutes to Ghent, 90 minutes to Liège And Bruges. Calais and Amsterdam are two-and-a-half hours away and Paris three hours. Destinations are indicated in two languages (but not in Flanders), so from Brussels, Antwerp is shown as Anvers/Antwerpen, Ghent Gand/Gent and Bruges Bruges/Brugge.

Major roads have phones along them. And immediate fines are commonplace if you are caught speeding and you don't happen to be Belgian.

Breakdown services

In the event of a breakdown, there are two national organisations to call:

Tourist Club Belgique (TCB)
24hr emergency service 070 344 777/enquiries 02 233 22 11; 8am-5pm Mon-Fri.

Royal Automobile Club de Belgique
24hr emergency service 078 152 000/enquiries 02 287 09 11; 8.30am-5pm Mon-Fri.

Car hire

To hire a car, you must have a full current driving licence (normally with a minimum of one year's experience) and carry a passport or an identity card. Many car hire companies also insist on a minimum age of 23. Car rental is expensive, with weekly rates beginning at about €350 with unlimited mileage. Day rates usually start at around €90, but it's worth shopping around. The major car hire companies can be found in the arrivals hall of Zaventem airport and at Gare du Midi. Their offices are generally open from 6.30am to 11pm. Hire rates at the airport can be steeper than those in town. Special all-inclusive weekend rates (Fri afternoon to Mon morning) are available from around €75.

Avis
107 rue Colonel Bourg, Schaerbeek (02 730 62 11/airport 02 720 09 44). Métro Diamant. **Open** 8am-6pm Mon-Fri; airport 6.30am-11.30pm daily. **Age requirement** over-23s only. **Credit** AmEx, DC, MC, V.

Budget
327B avenue Louise, Ixelles (02 646 51 30/airport 02 753 21 70). Métro Louise then tram 93, 94. **Open** 8am-6pm Mon-Fri; 9am-noon Sat. *Airport* 6.30am-11pm daily. **Age requirement** over-23s only. **Credit** AmEx, DC, MC, V.

Hertz
8 boulevard Maurice Lemonnier, Lower Town (02 513 2886/airport 02 720 60 44). Pré-métro Anneessens or Lemonnier. **Open** 7.30am-7pm Mon-Fri; 8am-2pm Sat; 8am-noon Sun. **Age requirement** over-25s only. **Credit** AmEx, DC, MC, V. **Map** p320 A/B4.

Repairs & services

The agents listed below should be able to help get you back on the road. Or check the Yellow Pages under 'Carrosseries (Reparations)-Autos/ Carrossierieherstellingen-Autos'.

Autocenter East NV 'Toyota'
438 chaussée de Louvain, Schaerbeek (02 725 12 00). Métro Meiser. **Open** *Office* 9am-7pm Mon-Fri; 10am-5pm Sat. *Maintenance/repair* 8am-5pm Mon-Thur; 8am-3pm Fri; 8am-noon Sat. **Credit** V. **Map** p323 H2.

BMW Brussels
22-38 rue du Magistrat, Ixelles (02 641 57 11). Métro Louise then tram 93, 94. **Open** 7.30am-6pm Mon-Fri; 10am-5pm Sat. **Credit** AmEx, DC, MC, V.

Rover Grand Garage St Michel
35-43 rue de l'Escadron, Etterbeek (02 732 46 00). Métro Thieffry. **Open** 8am-6pm Mon-Fri; 10am-5pm Sat. *Showroom* 8am-6pm Mon-Fri. **Credit** AmEx, DC, V.

Cycling

Cycling in the centre of Brussels is a daunting prospect. However, cycling out of town – eg along the route to Tervuren – is a scenic and relatively safe method of exploring the city's environs. Cycle lanes are designated by two broken white lines and are less secure than the cycle tracks, which are separated from the traffic.

Bike-In
02 245 25 06. Phone for details. If you want to explore further afield, SNCB operates a scheme whereby you can purchase a combined ticket for train journey and bike hire. A bike will be reserved for your collection on arrival at one of the 31 participating stations.

Pro-Velo
www.provelo.org. An action group working within the Brussels region to improve life for cyclists. They also hire bikes by the hour and day, and organise group tours; *see p167.*

Directory

Resources A-Z

Addresses

When addressing an envelope, write the house number after the street name and place the postcode before the city, as in the following example:

Monsieur Ledoux
avenue Louise 100
1050 Bruxelles

To avoid confusion between 7 and 1, always cross your 7s.

Age restrictions

In Belgium, you have to be 18 to drive vote or marry, and 16 to smoke and/or have sex.

Business services

Conferences

Espace Moselle

40 rue des Drapiers, Ixelles (02 502 65 45/fax 02 502 66 28). Métro Porte de Namur. **Open** 9am-6pm Mon-Fri. **No credit cards.** **Map** p321 C5.
Espace Moselle offers a renovated late 19th-century home with crystal chandeliers and high ceilings as a meeting venue. Food and cocktails can be arranged for up to 250 people. Parking available, as is a garden.

Management Centre Europe

118 rue de l'Aqueduc, Ixelles (02 543 21 00/fax 02 543 24 00). Métro Louise then tram 93, 94/bus 54, 81. **Open** 8.30am-6.30pm Mon-Thur; 8am-5.30pm Fri. **Credit** AmEx, DC, MC, V.
MCE is one of the top business management and training organisations in Europe, hosting a variety of large seminars and conferences. It also sets up training sessions and conferences specific to a client's request.

Palais des Congrès de Bruxelles

3 Coudenberg, Lower Town (02 515 13 11). Métro Gare Centrale. **Open** 8.30am-4.30pm Mon-Fri. **Credit** AmEx, DC, MC, V. **Map** p317 C4.
Near the Grand' Place, this must be one of the most convenient conference centres in Brussels. Its rooms can accommodate groups of ten for small meetings, or more than 1,200 people for large-scale events such as trade exhibitions.

Couriers

BTC Express

02 345 85 05/fax 02 346 42 25. **Open** 8am-5pm Mon-Fri. **No credit cards.**
Letters and packages can be picked up and dropped off anywhere around Brussels within the space of two hours for €8.70 plus VAT.

DHL

Customer service 02 715 50 50/ fax 02 721 45 88. **Open** 8am-9.30pm Mon-Fri; 9am-5pm Sat, Sun;. *Phone enquiries* 24hrs daily. **Credit** AmEx, DC, MC, V.
Pick-ups are handled through late afternoon in most parts of the city. Packages can be dropped off at the airport in Zaventem until 10pm.

FedEx

119 Airport Building, 1820 Melsbroek (toll free 0800 13555/ fax 02 752 72 80). **Open** 8am-7pm Mon-Fri. **Credit** AmEx, MC, V.
If you arrange a pick-up before 2.30pm, your package will reach the US the next day. This office, based by Brussels National Airport, cannot handle deliveries within Europe.

Office & equipment hire

New Telephone (Protel)

312 chaussée de Bruxelles, Ouderghem (02 354 60 98/fax 02 354 26 19). Bus W (Waterloo Centre stop). **Open** 9.30am-12.30pm, 2-6.30pm Mon-Sat. **Credit** AmEx, DC, MC, V.
New Telephone specialises in equipping offices with new phone systems, answerphones, voicemail, faxes and mobile phones. It also rents out photocopiers.

Papeterie IPL

635 chaussée de Waterloo, Ixelles (02 344 89 61/fax 02 343 17 51). Tram 90, 94. **Open** 9.30am-6.30pm Mon-Fri. **Credit** V.
This office supplies store sells all kinds of stationery, ranging from the serious to the downright silly. It is also happy to make up business cards for rates much lower than you'll find at the many printing shops around town.

Regus

6 rond-point Schuman, box 5, EU Quarter (02 234 7711/ www.regus.com). Métro Schuman. **Open** 8.30am-6pm Mon-Fri. **Map** p325 G4.
Reliable international company renting office space across Belgium.

Chambers of commerce

American Chamber of Commerce

Centre for American Studies, 50 avenue des Arts, Box 5, Upper Town (02 513 67 70/ www.amchambe). Métro Arts-Loi **Open** 9am-noon, 1-5pm Mon-Fri. **Map** p319 D4.

British Chamber of Commerce

15 rue d'Egmont, Ixelles (02 540 90 30/www.britcham.be). Métro Trône. **Open** 9am-5.30pm Mon-Fri. **Map** p321 D5.

Business libraries

Royal Library

4 boulevard de l'Empereur, Upper Town (02 519 523/www.kbr.be). **Open** 9am-12.30pm, 2-5pm Mon-Fri. **Map** p317 C4. *See also p295.*

Secretarial services

If you don't wish to use an employment agency, you can place a classified ad in the situations vacant section in the weekly *Bulletin.*

Manpower

523 avenue Louise, Ixelles (02 639 10 70/fax 02 639 10 71). Métro Louise. **Open** 8.30am-6pm Mon-Fri. **No credit cards.**
Can match up clients with secretaries who speak foreign languages. Rates vary according to requirements.

Vedior Gregg

Riverside Business Park, 55 boulevard International, Anderlecht (02 555 16 11/fax 02 555 16 16). Bus 78. **Open** 8am-6pm Mon-Fri. **No credit cards.**
With 90 offices, this is one of Belgium's largest employment agencies, with a whole range of positions. Rates for bilingual secretaries are €12-€15 an hour.

Translators

Also check the *Yellow Pages* under 'Traducteurs'.

Abetras

11 rue de l'Ecole Moderne, Anderlecht (02 520 22 22/02 520 15 84). Métro Clemenceau or Gare du Midi. **Open** *Phone enquiries* 24hrs daily. **No credit cards.**
Rents out microphones, receivers and booths. Provides interpreters for video conferences on an à la carte basis for €496 per day.

Customs

The following customs allowances apply to people bringing duty-free goods into Belgium from outside the EU.

● 200 cigarettes **or** 100 cigarillos **or** 50 cigars **or** 250g (8.82oz) tobacco;

● 2l still table wine **and** either 1l spirits/strong liqueurs (over 22% alcohol) **or** 2l fortified wine (under 22% alcohol)/sparkling wine/other liqueurs;

● 50g perfume;

● 250ml toilet water;

● 500g coffee **or** 200g coffee extracts/coffee essences;

● 100g tea **or** 40g tea extracts/essences;

● other goods for non-commercial use up to a maximum value of 7,300BF.

EU citizens over 17 are not required to make a customs declaration. That means you can bring as much duty-paid beer or wine as you can carry. There's also no limit to the amount of foreign currency that can be brought in or out of Belgium. For more information, call the

Belgian Administration of Customs & Excise (02 210 38 15; open 9-11.45am, 2-4pm Mon-Fri).

Electricity

The current used in Belgium is 220V AC. It works fine with British appliances (which run on 240V), but you'll either need to change the plug or buy an adapter. Both are available at most electrical goods shops, and airports. American appliances run on 110V. To use an American hairdryer in Belgium, you'll need to buy a converter, which can be pricey. Most good hotels should be equipped with hair dryers and be able to provide adapter plugs to fit appliances from most countries.

Embassies

It's certainly advisable to phone to check opening hours of the embassies listed below. Some situations may need an appointment. In emergencies it's worth ringing after hours; there may be staff on hand to deal with crises. For embassies or consulates not listed, check the *Yellow Pages*.

American Embassy

27 boulevard du Régent, Upper Town (02 508 21 11). Métro Arts-Loi. **Open** 9am-6pm Mon-Fri. **Map** p322 E4.

Australian Embassy

6-8 rue Guimard, EU Quarter (02 286 05 00). Métro Arts-Loi. **Open** 9am-12.30pm, 2-5pm Mon-Fri (visas morning only). **Map** p322 E4.

British Embassy

85 rue Arlon, EU Quarter (02 287 62 11). Métro Maelbeek. **Open** *Visas* 9.30am-noon Mon-Fri. *Passports* 9.30am-12.30pm, 2.30-4.30pm Mon-Fri. **Map** p324 E4.

Canadian Embassy

2 avenue de Tervuren, Etterbeek (02 741 06 11). Métro Merode. **Open** 9am-noon, 2-5pm Mon-Fri.

Irish Embassy

89 rue Froissart, EU Quarter (02 230 53 37). Métro Schuman. **Open** 10am-1pm Mon-Fri. **Map** p325 F4.

New Zealand Embassy

47-48 boulevard du Régent, Upper Town (02 512 10 40). Métro Arts-Loi. **Open** 9am-1pm, 2-5.30pm Mon-Fri. **Map** p322 E4.

Gay & lesbian

Help & information

Egalité

02 295 98 97/bernard.lonnoy@ ccc.eu.int. **Open** *Phone enquiries* 9am-noon, 1-6pm daily.
This ambitious organisation works tirelessly to improve the conditions for gays and lesbians employed in the various European Union institutions, with the ultimate aim of achieving full equality across the board in the workplace.

Infor Homo

100 avenue de l'Opale, Schaerbeek 1030 (02 733 10 24/ www.geocities.com/infor_homo). Métro Diamant. **Open** *Phone enquiries* 8-10pm Mon-Fri. **Map** p323 H3.
This laudable association offers help, advice and counselling and organises social events for men and women of all ages. Regular meetings are held in its friendly salon-café every Wednesday and Friday (8pm-midnight). It also publishes *Regard*, a bi-monthly magazine that is widely read around Belgium.

International Lesbian & Gay Association

81 rue du Marché au Charbon, Lower Town (02 502 24 71/ www.ilga.org). Pré-métro Bourse. **Open** by appointment.
The International Lesbian & Gay Association is a network of international bodies that campaigns vigorously for an end to global discrimination. The Brussels office is of particular importance because of its ability to lobby at European Parliament level.

Emergencies

Police **101**
Fire or ambulance **100**
Non-urgent medical advice **105** or **02 479 18 18** or **02 648 40 14**
Out-of-hours emergency dental help **02 426 10 26**

For advice on any other emergency, from the unusual to the mundane, call the 24-hour English-language **Community Help Service** (**CHS**) helpline on **02 648 40 14**. *See p294.*

Télégal

02 502 79 38. **Open** 8pm-midnight daily.
An anonymous helpline dealing with legal and social issues for the gay and lesbian community.

Health

Belgium enjoys an excellent healthcare system. You'll find the majority of doctors are fluent in English.

Accident & emergency

The following hospitals are able to provide 24-hour emergency assistance and offer consultations (but do call first for consultation hours). In the case of emergencies involving children, visit the **Hôpital Universitaire des Enfants** or the **Hôpital St-Pierre**.

Hôpital Brugmann

4 place van Geuchten, Laeken (02 477 20 10). Métro Houba-Brugmann.

Hôpital Erasme

808 route de Lennik, Anderlecht (02 555 31 11). Métro Veeweyde.

Hôpital St-Pierre

322 rue Haute, Lower Town (02 535 31 11). Métro Porte de Hal. **Map** p320 B5/6.

Hôpital Universitaire des Enfants Reine Fabiola

Paediatric emergency room: 15 avenue Jean Jacques Crocq, Jette (02 477 31 00/01). Métro Heysel. **Open** *Emergencies* 24hrs daily. *Consultations* 9-11.30am, 2-4.30pm Mon-Fri; 9am-noon Sat.

Hôpital Universitaire St-Luc

10 avenue d'Hippocrate, Woluwe-St-Lambert (02 764 11 11). Métro Alma.

Complementary & alternative medicine

Homeopathy is still considered alternative medicine in Belgium. Listed below is one practitioner in Brussels; call

the **Federation of Medical Homeopathy** on 02 206 37 73 for further information.

Dr Dany Dejonghe

2 De Robianostraat, Tervuren (02 767 56 57). Tram 44. **Open** *Appointments* 8-11am, 3-5pm Mon-Fri. *Medical information* 7-8pm Mon-Fri.

Contraception & abortion

Condoms are widely available and are sold at most supermarkets and pharmacies (although condom-vending machines are not widespread). Birth control pills can be bought at pharmacies with a doctor's prescription.

After years of stuggle, abortion is legal in Belgium. The mother can request it up to 12 weeks of pregnancy – thereafter, in case of foetal abnormality or of any health risks to the mother, the agreement of two independent doctors is required.

Dentists

Dental care in Belgium is of a high standard. The **Community Liaison Office** of the American Embassy (02 513 38 30 ext 2227) can provide a list of English-speaking dental practitioners, as can the **Community Help Service** helpline (02 648 40 14).

Doctors

Unusually perhaps, most doctors with private practices don't employ receptionists, preferring to handle the administration of payments and appointments themselves. You can walk in without an appointment during weekday office hours. If you are too sick to go in to the surgery, some doctors will make house calls. After hours, you can often reach your physician (or one on call) through an answering service.

Even if you're insured, expect to pay for your visit on the spot, either in cash or with a cheque. The same goes for pharmacies. Hang on to all medical receipts to claim reimbursement from your insurance company.

Hospitals

Outpatient clinics at private or university hospitals have an excellent reputation worldwide for their state-of-the-art technology, but often suffer from overcrowded waiting rooms and bureaucracy. Despite the drawbacks, they have a convenient concentration of specialists in one place, as well as laboratory and X-ray facilities on hand. For a list of hospitals, *see above* **Accident & emergency**.

Pharmacies

Pharmacies (*pharmacies/apotheeks*) in Belgium are clearly marked with a green cross. Most are open 9am-6pm/7pm Mon-Fri. Some also open on Saturday mornings or afternoons. When closed, each pharmacy should display a list of alternative pharmacies open after hours. *See also p164.*

STD, HIV & AIDs

Aide Info SIDA

02 514 29 65/02 511 45 29/ www.cromozone.be/ais/intro.htm. **Open** 6-9pm Mon-Fri.
Not just an anonymous helpline, but an organisation offering support and care for people with AIDS at home, in hospital and in prison.

Act Together

02 511 33 33.
An HIV/AIDS support group that organises referrals and runs a helpline on 02 512 05 05.

Act Up

145 rue Van Artevelde, Lower Town (02 512 02 02/www.actupb.org). Métro Anneessens. **Open** *Office* 2-5pm Tue, Sat.

Directory

Part of the international Act Up network, which campaigns aggressively for better research, recognition and treatment for people living with AIDS.

Women's clinics

La Famille Heureuse
4 place Quetelet, St-Josse (02 217 44 50). Métro Botanique. **Open** 9am-noon, 2-8pm Mon, Thur; 9am-5pm Tue, Wed; 9am-6pm Fri. *Drop-in visits* noon-3pm Wed. **Map** p322 E2.
One of the first women's clinics to open in Brussels (1962) and one of the most comprehensive. Services include contraceptive and psychological counselling, abortion, cervical smear tests and referrals. A visit with a doctor will set you back €16-€20.
Branches: St-Gilles (Brussels), Mons, Tournai & Verviers.

Aimer à l'ULB
38 avenue Jeanne, Ixelles (02 650 31 31). Tram 23, 90, 93, 94/bus 71. **Open** 9am-6.30pm Mon-Fri; 9.30am-12.30pm Sat.
Although located on the ULB campus, this bright and cheery clinic is open to all. The cost of medical visits is based on income, so if you're on a tight budget this is a good place to come for a check-up, prescription or cervical smear.

Helplines

Brussels' large foreign community has established an extensive network of support groups. Unless indicated in the listings, the groups below are for English speakers. More organisations will be listed at the back of the weekly *Bulletin.*

Community Help Service (CHS) Helpline
02 648 40 14/www.belgium-info. com/helpline/bel22.htm. **Open** *Phone enquiries* 24hrs daily.
A group of trained English-speaking volunteers can handle problems ranging from the critical to the mundane. They can also refer you to other specialists. There is no charge for callers. To make an appointment for a private face-to-face counselling session, call 02 647 67 80. The rates are determined by one's means.

Alcoholism

Alcoholics Anonymous
(02 537 82 24) offers daily

meetings in English or counselling by phone. **Al-Anon English-speaking Group** *(02 762 76 53/771 52 64)* gives phone counselling to friends and relatives of alcoholics. It holds meetings every Tuesday at 8pm at the International Cultural Affairs Center, 8 rue Amédée Lynen, St-Josse (métro Madou).

Rape/battered women

Amazone
10 rue du Méridien, St-Josse (02 229 38 00/www.amazone.be). Métro Botanique. **Open** 9am-6pm Mon-Fri. **Map** p322 E2.
Various women's groups – including La Coordination des Groupes Contre la Violence Faite aux Femmes – and a restaurant are housed here. The emphasis is on sexual equality, but it is also a gay-friendly centre.

Le Refuge (Collectif pour Femmes Battues)
02 647 00 12. **Open** 9am-7pm Mon-Fri; 9.30am-5pm Sat, Sun.
The Collective for Battered Women can be of help if you speak French. Otherwise try the CHS Helpline *(see above).*

SOS Viol
02 534 36 36. **Open** 9.30am-5.30pm Mon-Fri.
This is mainly a French-speaking support group for rape victims. A few staff members speak basic English. For after-hours assistance try the CHS Helpline *(see above).*

Poisons

Centre Antipoisons/ Antigifcentrum
Emergency 070 245 245/office 02 264 96 36. **Open** 24hrs daily.
A group of physicians man this free helpline. They will try to determine if someone has swallowed a poisonous substance and offer advice on what measures to take.

ID

Like many other European countries, Belgium has has an identity card system. As a visitor, you are also expected to carry photographic ID, such as your passport, with you at all times.

Insurance

As members of the European Union, both the UK and Ireland have reciprocal health agreements with Belgium. You'll need to apply for the necessary E111 form back home first. British citizens can get this by filling in the application form in leaflet SA30, available in Department of Social Security offices or at post offices. Try to get the E111 at least two weeks before you leave. Make sure you read the small print on the back of the form so you know how to obtain medical or dental treatment at a reduced charge.

The E111 doesn't cover all medical costs – for example, dental treatment – so it's wise to take out private insurance. Before shelling out money on health insurance, college students should check whether their university's medical plan already provides cover. A homeowner's policy may similarly cover holidays.

Non-EU citizens should take out full private insurance before they visit. Remember to keep all receipts for medicine or treatment that you have paid for. You'll need it to claim reimbursement from your insurance company once you're back home.

For long-term visitors, after six months of residence you are eligible for coverage under Belgium's basic health insurance system, the *mutuelle.* It allows you to recover a large chunk of doctors' and dentists' bills, and other costs. Regular payments are automatically deducted from your salary. For phone numbers look in the *Yellow Pages* under 'Mutualités/Ziekenfondsen'.

Internet

One of the best bets for hooking up to the internet in Belgium is Skynet (0800

98640/www.skynet.be). For internet cafés, *see below;* for websites, *see p308.*

Left luggage

Main train stations have left luggage offices, open 6am-midnight. Smaller stations have coin-operated lockers.

Libraires

Bibliothèque Royale de Belgique

4 boulevard de l'Empereur, Upper Town (02 519 53 11/www.kbr.be). Métro Gare Centrale or Parc/tram 92, 93, 94. **Open** 9am-8pm Mon-Fri; 9am-5pm Sat. **Map** p317 C4.
This is the state library, holding primarily everything published in Belgium, as well as foreign journals and publications. You need a membership card to consult the enormous collection of books here (it is possible to get day or week membership). Bring in a photograph, your identity card and €7.50 if you're a student (€15 non-students). As usual, books cannot be taken out. The computerised catalogue lists only books that were printed in Belgium after 1985. All other books

before then are still listed in the card catalogue. To consult the library's vast catalogue via the Internet, log on to www.kbr.be.

ULB (Université Libre de Bruxelles)

50 avenue Franklin Roosevelt, Ixelles (reception 02 650 47 00/audio-visual department 02 650 43 78). Tram 93, 94/bus 71. **Open** 8am-10pm Mon-Fri; 10am-5pm Sat. *English audio-visual section* 1.30-5.30pm Mon-Fri.
Although the ULB library is mainly intended for students at the university, it's also open to non-students for an annual fee. It holds a surprisingly large collection of materials in English in various media. ULB bought the materials from the British Council Resources Centre when it closed down.

Lost property

Report lost belongings to the nearest police inspector's office or police HQ on rue du Marché au Charbon (02 517 96 11). You must also ask for a certificate of loss for insurance purposes. If you lose your passport, contact your local embassy or consulate (*see*

p292 **Embassies**). Note that staff may be present after office hours to cope with any such emergency.

Air

If you've lost an item on a flight to Brussels, you need to contact your airline. SN and AVIA Partner are the handling agents that represent most of the major airlines.

AVIA Partner

02 723 07 07. **Open** *Phone enquiries* 6am-10pm daily. *In person* 6am-11pm daily.
AVIA Partner is the handling agent for British Airways, Air France, Air Belgium, Air Malta, United Airlines, KLM and Singapore Airlines.

SN Airlines

02 723 60 11. **Open** 24hrs daily.
Contact former Sabena airlines for any items left on its flights.

Airport

If you've misplaced something at the airport, try any of the lost and found numbers given

You've got mail

Internet cafés are the postes restantes of the modern age. Paris, Amsterdam, Munich or Rome – breeze into town and step into any number of venues, negotiate the whims of a foreign keyboard and you're away.

And in Brussels, capital of Europe? Well, there's the ubiquitous orange shopfront of an **easyEverything**, right on De Brouckère in the Lower Town (9-13 place De Brouckère; 02 211 08 20). It used to be open 24 hours a day, but – unlike branches in London, Paris and Amsterdam – Brussels' branch has been forced to close before midnight owing to rowdy custom. There's a bouncer on the door, truant officers tracing recalcitrant adolescents, and (where else but Brussels?) a Madame Pipi guarding the toilet door. It's ugly. Send for Stelios!

In the meantime, you trawl around the Grand' Place, the major boulevards, comb the Lower Town. Nada, zilch, sweet zipola. Where's the answer? It's simple. Which area has the most need and least computer

ownership? Yep, Matongé. Here, internet cafés are virtually a cottage industry. For the Turkish community, surfing has proved more profitable than kebabs. For owners of cut-price international call centres, it's another string to the telephone line.

One particular small patch, where **chaussée de Wavre** meets **rue de Dublin**, is lined with tiny centres. The Turkish **InterCall** (75 chaussée de Wavre) looks flash but its computers are slower than postmen and its service snotty. **Cyber Espace II** at 22 Dublin looks dingy, but it's cheap (scaled in €1.24 15-minute increments), fast and friendly. The unnamed venue two doors down is similarly functional and funky.

Perhaps best is the branch of the local **Visiotel** chain (59A chaussée de Wavre/www.visiotel.be; open 10am-10pm daily). It's clean, comfortable and cheap(ish), and there are seven other branches around town, so if you're in Schaerbeek or St-Gilles, you won't go without mail.

Directory

Poste encounters

Sod mussels. For that authentic Belgian experience, nothing beats a trip to the local post office. With Brussels bereft of corner *tabacs*, La Poste is the only place where you can get stamps, either from annoyingly temperamental machines outside – or from annoyingly temperamental clerks inside. The post office is also the place to pay bills, bank and conduct myriad mysterious activities often witnessed but rarely understood. Always keep packages at under 2 kilos (4.4lbs), otherwise you really will be here till doomsday.

You enter the great, granite edifice at De Brouckère – Brussels' central post office – nervously clutching your virgin letter, and first take your queue number from the dispenser. A glance over the long queue to the 12 windows reveals that all but ten are operating. Absenteeism at La Poste is twice the rate in local government. Bukowski would be proud.

When your number eventually comes up you slide your letter under the glass towards the butler-faced clerk. He shows you an array of stamp choices that all seem to require discussion. No wonder you had to wait

55 minutes. After showing you his stamp collection – and after much sage, diplomatic nodding on your part – for a letter overseas you are then asked the million-dollar question: '*Normalisé ou non-normalisé?*' To determine this, you need to measure your letter (refer to blueprint at http://pv.en.bpg. post.be/EN/private/default.asp). If it strays from the norm, either in height, width or thickness, suffers from drooping corners or is a shade too oblong, then your missive is *non-normalisé*.

For the standard letter, the question is a breeze. '*Normalisé.*' You are expected to slap on a blue 'A Prior' sticker – get a supply of them here if necessary. Your post is now normalised. That'll be 52¢. You wait an aeon for the computer – clack, clack, clack – to calculate change of 50¢ from the €1.02 you thoughtfully gave the clerk, he tears off the stamp of your choice (royal head or warbling bird?) and sticks it on himself. The deed is done. *Normalisé* to the UK two days; *non-normalisé* – same price – one week.

PS. La Poste have just introduced dinky new boutiques across town. Stamps available! Only in blocks of ten...

---

below. You'll find that there's usually somebody on duty who speaks English.

Belgian Police
Gendarmerie/Rijkswacht 02 715 62 11. **Open** 24hrs daily.
The lost property office is in the new main terminal on the departure level near border control. Although there's no office number, directions are indicated by overhead signs.

Airport Police
Police Aeroportuaire/Luchthaven-politie 02 753 70 00. **Open** 24hrs daily.
The airport police have their own building next to the Sheraton Hotel and opposite the departure hall.

Airport Authorities
Régie des Voies Aerienne/Regie der Luchtwegen 02 753 68 20. **Open** 8am-4.15pm Mon-Fri.
Anything not claimed at either of the police offices ends up here, in office 418 on the departure level, in the old part of the terminal building. Follow signs for F14 – the steps to the office are just by the entrance.

Rail

For articles left on a train, enquire at the nearest railway station or check with the main rail lost property office at the Gare du Nord (02 24 61 12).

Metro, buses & trams

STIB/MIVB
Porte de Namur, Ixelles (02 515 23 94). **Open** 9.30am-4pm Mon-Fri. **Map** p321 D5.
The STIB/MIVB lost property office is inside Porte de Namur metro station next to the Press Shop.

Media

Belgium has a decent-sized media sector of its own, but owing to the number of languages used in the country, its inhabitants are well attuned to competitors from

neighbouring countries. Most newsagents and kiosks in Brussels stock the leading papers and magazines from Britain, France, Germany, the Netherlands and elsewhere (including the US). But the local press is still surprisingly broad, and runs the gamut from the conservative (*De Standaard*) to the more outrageous (*Humo*, *Ché*).

Belgians are even more spoilt for choice when it comes to television. Cable TV has been widely available since the 1960s, and more than 90 per cent of households are hooked up to receive around 40 channels, many from overseas.

Newspapers

La Dernière Heure
www.dhnet.be

Popular right-leaning French-speaking tabloid, with an emphasis on grisly crime stories. But its sports coverage is undeniably the best.

L'Echo
www.echonet.be
Pre-eminent French-speaking business paper in Belgium, crammed with pie charts, balance sheets, share tips and takeover rumours. Dry, but comprehensive.

European Voice
www.european-voice.com
This weekly English-language news broadsheet specialises in the workings of the European Union. Although it's published by the Economist, the Voice is much less acerbic, approaching the status of in-house paper for the EU – it has a special distribution agreement with the institutions. It carries some incisive political interviews and in the past few years has become a little livelier, but one of its main draws is the large number of high-profile, mostly EU-linked, job ads.

Het Laaste Nieuws
www.hln.be
Once renowned as the traditionally liberal Flemish daily, Het Laaste Nieuws now allows itself to take an interest in the seamier side of life. Fun, if occasionally sensationalistic.

La Libre Belgique
www.lalibre.be
Very Catholic French-language daily. It has the distinction of being the only Francophone paper to have maintained its editorial independence during World War II. If you don't mind wading through moralising editorials and articles about the papacy, it's a better read than anything else you'll find in French.

Metro
http://metro.rug.be/
This free newspaper can be picked up in most metro stations in Brussels. It comes in French (green) and Dutch (blue) versions and is a good way to scan the day's events. Don't expect anything too deep, though.

De Morgen
www.demorgen.be
Once the staple of socialist workers, De Morgen has evolved into a more general left-wing Flemish daily, covering the arts, fashion and human interest as well as national and international news. It has a reputation for investigative journalism.

Le Soir
www.lesoir.be
The most widely read francophone daily. Its prose can be long-winded,

but this is an independent-minded, quality broadsheet. Wednesday's issue contains *MAD*, a cultural supplement with the week's key listings, and Friday's issue includes *Victor*, a glossy lifestyle magazine.

De Standaard
www.standaard.be
The biggest Dutch-speaking daily takes few risks, opting for a conservative Catholic angle on most issues. But there are some decent arts pieces to be found among the slightly flat news coverage.

Vlan
www.vlan.be
Thousands of ads from property to cars to jobs to junk appear in this paper every Sunday. Along the lines of *Loot* in the UK.

Magazines

The Bulletin
www.ackroyd.be
Brussels' only English-language weekly has been around since the 1960s. It contains in-depth features on some very Belgian phenomena, often written by prominent Brussels-based journalists, as well as articles of interest to English-speaking expats. However, its text-heavy black-and-white layout is looking increasingly dated. It comes with a pull-out supplement of arts and entertainment listings (including TV schedules), and also runs job and accommodation ads. A must for any anglophone spending time in the city.

Ché
www.che.be
Flashy lad-mag launched a couple of years ago, bringing pictures of scantily clad young women and features on cars, gadgets and fashion to loaded young Flemings.

Dag Allemaal
This Dutch-language TV and radio listings magazine also includes frothy celebrity interviews and glossy photo spreads.

Humo
www.humo.be
Originally a Flemish mag with TV listings, Humo has become an irreverent, ironic, intellectual and anarchistic publication, rather like a lefty student who never grew up. Music, film, politics and the arts all get a weekly going-over.

Kiosque
Pocket-sized, French-language monthly listings magazine. Cafés, bars, restaurants, clubs, films, exhibitions and more are covered.

La Libre Match
Recently launched joint venture between *Paris Match* and *La Libre Belgique*, providing all the usual investigative reporting and topless celebrities of the former, but with more of a focus on Belgium.

The Ticket
www.theticket.be
Pocket-sized arts and entertainment listings magazine in French and Dutch versions, available free from trendier shops, bars and clubs. Sometimes features bought-in interviews with celebrities and bands. Essential for clubbers and rock kids.

Le Vif-Express/Knack
These sister publications – the former in French, the latter in Dutch – are the country's only news magazines. Both come with upmarket supplementary magazines covering fashion, travel and lifestyle. *Knack* also includes *Focus*, a separate arts, entertainment and TV listings magazine.

Radio

To keep the American and British pop/rock music at bay, radio stations receiving subsidies must make at least 60 per cent of their music broadcasts in the language of the region from which the station is funded – a good way to pick up some linguistic tips. Bear in mind that frequencies for the same station differ in other parts of the country.

Bel RTL
104 MHz
News, music and games are the mainstay of this French-speaking station, which began as a spin-off from the TV channel RTL-TVi (*see p298*). Some star presenters continue to appear on both.

Bruxelles-Capitale
99.3 MHz
News station, available only in Brussels, which makes the most of the intimacy of its listener-base.

Musique 3
91.2 MHz
French-owned classical music station.

La Première
92.5 MHz
The French-language state-owned station now has a distinctly old-

fashioned air, but still schedules news programmes, political debates, game shows, sport and serials.

Radio Contact
102.2 MHz
The most visible radio station in Brussels. Its blue dolphin logo is on the back of every Renault Clio, its (never *quite* up-to-the-minute) pop output on the PA of every boutique.

Radio 21
93.2 MHz
Francophone pop-rock station that tends to play music that's neither new enough to be current nor old enough to be nostalgic. However, it's also the place to catch up on music that you're unlikely to hear anywhere else.

Studio Brussel
100.6 MHz
As hip as Brussels gets: this Flemish station makes anyone over the age of 20 feel decrepit, playing the latest singles by alternative rock and dance acts from both sides of the Atlantic, and occasionally dipping into 1980s and '90s indie obscurities. World music, reggae and jazz also get a spin.

VRT1
91.7 MHz
The most serious of the three Flemish state-owned radio stations, VRT1 features political discussions as well as classical music.

VRT2
93.7 MHz
The popular station in the Flemish state-owned VRT (formerly BRTN) triumvirate, generally concentrating on oldies and some Top 40 hits.

VRT3
89.5 MHz
High culture is this Flemish station's forte: you'll find profiles of composers, choral, chamber and classical concerts, and opera.

Television

Cable TV gives Belgians access to the likes of BBC1 and BBC2, CNN, CNBC and MTV, as well as a host of channels from Holland and France and a smattering from Germany, Spain, Portugal and Italy. The selection varies slightly from region to region.

Among the foreign channels, the best for English-speakers are the Dutch ones, which show films in their original language with subtitles; French channels usually dub. Canvas and Holland 1 often show British series. French-German channel Arte has fewer mainstream films and documentaries, often subtitled.

TV5 is a French-language channel shown all over the world, and is also strong on documentaries. Subscription channels such as Canal Plus are also available (in French or Dutch), offering the latest Hollywood blockbusters, high-profile sporting events and erotic films. Digital TV is not expected to be rolled out in Belgium for a few years yet – with so many homes having cable, it will be a tough sell.

These are the main Belgian channels:

AB3
This privately owned French-speaking channel launched in 2001, and aims to lure the youth market with its fast-moving schedule of cartoons, trashy thrillers and American soaps.

Kanaal 2
Sister station to VTM, showing mainly anglophone series and made-for-TV films. Broadcasts from 5pm to midnight.

RTBF
The state-run francophone station has retained respectability because of the lack of competition. It plays on two complementary channels. L'Une has a varied programme, including news, popular films and game shows; La Deux offers more cultural programming, with documentaries, cookery shows and undubbed films. Broadcasts from 6am to midnight.

RTL-TVi
The commercial French station is beginning to give state-owned TV a run for its money with its current affairs coverage. Otherwise, it's undemanding: soaps, sitcoms and talk shows. Its sister station, Club-RTL, shows cartoons and old movies. Both stations broadcast from noon till midnight.

Télé-Bruxelles/TV Brussel
Twin public-access French and Dutch stations covering local news with more streetwise flair than the state-owned and commercial stations.

Done on a shoestring budget, which makes it more compelling. Broadcasts from 6pm to 2am.

VRT
The Flemish version of RTBF, this state-owned station (formerly BRTN) is fighting a prolonged ratings war with the commercial channels – hence the number of soaps, serials and game shows. Even in its news coverage, VRT has lost its old dominance. Broadcasts from 6am to midnight.

VT4
This independently owned station started out in the early 1990s as a cultural alternative to the populist VTM and stodgy VRT. Unfortunately, its experiments with off-the-wall chat shows and would-be innovative series failed to attract sufficient ratings to justify costs, and it's since resorted to cheaper, largely American programming, with a plethora of soaps. Broadcasts from 7am to midnight.

VTM
This popular, privately owned station offers the best Flemish news coverage, as well as its own talk shows, soap operas and game shows. Broadcasts from 7am to midnight.

Money

On 1 January 2002 the euro became the official currency of Belgium. Foreign debit and credit cards can automatically be used to withdraw euros. At the time of going to press, €1 was worth about 60p, or 90¢.

Try to keep a few cent coins handy. They are constantly needed, whether for a public phone, supermarket trolley deposit, toilet fee or a tip.

Belgians tend to use cash for petty transactions, and debit cards (Bancontact or Mister Cash) for more expensive purchases. Although not as widely used, credit cards are fairly common, especially in restaurants, shops and hotels. ATMs are notoriously difficult to find – the one in Gare du Midi always has a long queue of people before it. Eurocheques are best avoided, since most banks charge a hefty fee for each one.

Banks & foreign exchange

Banks are the best places to exchange money. Generally they open from about 9am to between 3.30pm and 5pm on Monday to Friday. A few have half-days on Saturdays. It's wise to call and check opening times beforehand as hours can vary.

After banking hours you can change money and travellers' cheques at offices in the main train stations: Gare du Nord, Gare du Midi (7am-11pm daily) and Gare Centrale (8am-9pm daily), although they don't give advances on credit cards. However, several banks at the airport give cash advances on MasterCard (called Euro-Card in Belgium) or Visa, as well as convert currency. Most open early and close around 10pm. Banque Bruxelles Lambert (BBL), for example, opens daily from 7am to 9.45pm. Kredietbank also has a branch at the airport.

Also bear in mind that many credit cards, if members of the appropriate international network, will allow you to withdraw Belgian francs direct from most ATMs.

American Express has two branches in Brussels (though neither are very central), which issue travellers' cheques, replace lost or stolen cards, offer cash advances and even book flights for various fees.

American Express Gold Card Travel Service
10 rue de Genève, Evere (02 727 22 02/02 727 24 24). Bus 63. **Open** 8am-6pm Mon-Fri.

American Express Travel & Financial Services
100 boulevard du Souverain, Watermael-Boitsfort (02 676 26 26/ 24hr customer service 02 676 21 21). Métro Herrmann-Debroux. **Open** 9am-5pm Mon-Fri.

Lost/stolen credit cards

Report to the police and the 24-hour services listed below.

Diners Club
1 boulevard du Roi Albert II, Wemmel (02 206 95 11). Métro Roi Baudouin. **Open** 9am-5pm Mon-Fri. After hours, the above phone number handles calls 24 hours a day.

MasterCard (EuroCard)
24hr toll free 0800 150 96.

Visa International
24hr toll free 0800 18756.

Tax

In many shops, non-EU residents can request a Tax-Free cheque on purchases of more than €145. *See p141.*

Numbers

Dates are written as follows: day, month, year. When writing figures, Belgians use commas where Americans and Britons would use decimal points and vice versa: two thousand five hundred Euros is written as €2.500. Times are written according to the 24-hour clock. For example, 4pm is 16:00.

Opening times

Most banks open at 9am and close at between 3.30pm and 5pm. Some also close for lunch. Many offices close early on Friday, although this is not official. Generally, post offices are open 9am to 5pm; some remain open until 5.30pm or 6pm.

Although there is no official closing time, most shops open from 9am to 6pm. Some groceries and supermarkets stay open till 9pm. Big department stores open until 9pm on one day a week, usually Friday. There is also a chain of (mostly) 24-hour grocer-tobacconists called White Night.

Most museums are open 9am to 4pm Tuesday to Saturday, and sometimes on Sunday. They close on Mondays. Several are only open from Easter Sunday to September. It's wise to call the museum before visiting.

Police stations

For the police, call 101. The central police station in Brussels is at 30 rue du Marché au Charbon (02 279 79 79).

Postal services

Post offices are generally open 9am to 5pm Monday to Friday, but times can vary according to branch. If you need to post something urgently, try the central post office at the Centre Monnaie. Letters mailed to the UK and other EU countries usually take three days. Airmail to the US takes a week.

A letter weighing up to 20g costs 52¢ to any EU country. Mail to non-EU countries costs 84¢ airmail and 57¢ surface mail for letters up to 20g. Owing to the complexity of the postage system, it's best to buy stamps at a post office rather than from a vending machine. Price is determined by the size of the envelope. Stick to using Belgian envelopes, as non-standard sizes – even if different by only a fraction of an inch – can jack up the cost of postage. They *will* measure. *See p296* **Poste encounters**.

Central Post office
Centre Monnaie, place de Brouckère, Lower Town (02 226 21 11). **Open** 8am-7pm Mon-Fri; 9.30am-3pm Sat. **Map** p317 C2.

Sending packages

Packages up to 2kg (4.4lbs) can be mailed from any post office. Anything heavier should be taken to a post office at a railway station or the

Directory

airport. All packages weighing more than 20kg (44lbs) must be shipped. The exception is if you use **EMS Taxipost**, an express delivery service offered by the Belgian postal system. Its limit is 27kg (59.5 lbs). Taxipost guarantees delivery within 24-72 hours. It's cheaper but also a bit slower than other express delivery companies. Call your local branch for prices.

DHL International

02 715 50 50. **Open** 24hrs Mon-Sat. Can express deliver to most parts of the world. In the downtown area, pick-ups can be made until 7.30pm; in other areas, packages must be picked up earlier. Call a day in advance if you want to send something on Saturday.

Poste restante

Poste restante is available at the central post office at De Brouckère (*see p299*). For information, call 02 226 23 10.

Public toilets

Public toilets in Brussels, as is the case in most major cities, are not always very clean. Most restaurants don't mind you using their loos – though you are expected to cough up a few cents for the attendant. *See p137* **Madames Pipis**.

Religion

Many churches and synagogues hold services in English. There are several mosques in the city, but none of them has English services. For places away from the city centre, it is advisable to phone for directions.

Anglican & Episcopalian

All Saints' Church

Services held at *Centre Notre Dame d'Argenteuil, 563 chaussée de Louvain, Schaerbeek (02 384 35 56). Bus 558.* **Services** *English* 11.15am Sun. **Map** p323 H2.

Holy Trinity Church

29 rue Capitaine Crespel, Ixelles (02 511 71 83). Métro Louise. **Map** p321 C5.
The Holy Communion service in English is held at 8.30am and 10.30am on Sundays, and evening praise is at 7pm. The International Christian Fellowship is held by the church's African congregation at 2pm on Fridays.

Jewish

Beth Hillel Liberal Synagogue of Brussels

96 avenue de Kersbeek, Uccle (02 332 25 28). Tram 18, 52/bus 54. **Services** 8pm Fri; 10.30am Sat.
This liberal Jewish synagogue is led by an English-speaking rabbi, David Meier. Phone for directions.

Protestant

International Protestant Church

Services held at International School of Brussels, 19 mont des Chats (02 673 05 81). Bus 366. **Services** *English* 10am Sun (church school for children 9am Sun).

Presbyterian

St Andrew's Church of Scotland

181 chaussée de Vleurgat, Ixelles (02 649 02 19). Métro Louise/tram 93, 94. **Services** *English* 11am Sun. **Map** p324 E7.

Roman Catholic

Eglise St Nicolas

1 rue au Beurre, Lower Town (contact Rev Phillip Sandstrom on 02 743 09 78 for details). Pré-métro Bourse or Métro/Pré-métro De Brouckère. **Services** *Mass* 10am Sun. **Map** p317 C3.

St Anne's Church

10 place de la Ste Alliance, Uccle (0478 742673). Bus 43. **Services** *Mass in English* 5pm Sat; 10am, 1pm Sun.

Quaker

Quaker House (Quaker Council for European Affairs)

50 square Ambiorix (02 230 49 35). Métro Schuman. **Open** *Office*

9am-5pm Mon-Thur; 9am-4pm Fri. **Meetings** 11am Sun. **Map** p322 F3.

Safety

The number of violent crimes in Brussels is low compared with London or New York, but be vigilant against petty theft. Pickpockets and purse-snatchers are part of the city's landscape, especially in cinema auditoria and particularly in crowded areas.

As Brussels becomes more cosmopolitan and the population grows, it is slowly starting to gain the less desirable attributes of a big city, including increasing levels of street violence. Nowadays, a single woman hitch-hiking is a rare sight indeed. You'd be well advised to avoid being alone late at night in the city centre, and try to have at least your taxi fare on you in case you can't get a lift home. Under Belgian law you are required to have ID on you at all times. *See also p292* **Emergencies**.

Smoking

Smoking in confined public places is banned by law. This amounts to no smoking in railway stations (except on open-air platforms) and public buildings such as town halls and theatres. The law has had little effect on restaurants, though. Very few have non-smoking sections. Recently, some of the top hotels have initiated no-smoking rooms and floors.

Studying

Exchanges

Most universities have an office for exchange programmes, or at least their own branches of **Socrates** on campus. Listed below are the main offices.

AIESEC (Association Internationale d'Etudiants en Sciences Economiques et Sociales)

50 avenue Franklin Roosevelt, Ixelles (02 650 26 21/www.aiesec.org). Tram 93, 94/bus 71.
AIESEC has offices in most universities around the world and helps students in economics or social sciences find internships abroad during their final year. The organisation also contacts companies to set up 'job days'. This address is for ULB's branch of AIESEC.

Socrates & Youth

70 rue Montoyer, EU Quarter (02 233 01 11/www.socrates-youth.be). Métro Trône. **Open** 9am-1pm, 2-5.30pm Mon-Fri. **Map** p324 E4.
Socrates (previously called Erasmus) is the EU agency that sets up student exchanges throughout Europe. The grants are less than substantial, but the experience is well worth it. If you want to arrange an exchange with an institution that is not already a Socrates member, you can set up your own programme.

Language schools

Most *communes* offer language courses at reasonable prices and can be contacted for more details. The Chamber of Commerce and Industry also offers day and evening classes at VUB; contact it on 02 629 27 61 for more details.

Alliance Française

59 avenue de l'Emeraude, Schaerbeek (02 732 15 92/www.alliancefr.be). Tram 23, 90/bus 29, 63. **Open** 8.30am-7pm Mon-Thur; 8.30am-4pm Fri. **Map** p323 H2.
This bastion of French culture has group and private classes in French only. Classes include intensive one-month courses and twice-weekly evening classes.

Brussels Language Studies

8 rue du Marteau, EU Quarter (02 217 23 73). Métro Arts-Loi or Madou. **Open** 9am-7pm Mon-Thur; 9am-6pm Fri. **Map** p322 E3.
This well-reputed school teaches classes in virtually every language imaginable and is extremely flexible about meeting the needs of its students. Group classes number no more than five students.

Fondation 9

485 avenue Louise, Ixelles (02 627 52 52/www.ulb.ac.be/assoc/fondation9/). Tram 93, 94. **Open** 8am-7pm Mon-Fri; 9am-noon Sat.
The '9' refers to the nine languages of the European Union (before Spain and Portugal joined in 1986 – it really should be Fondation 13 by now). Anyway, sponsored by the Université Libre de Bruxelles (ULB), the Chamber of Commerce and the City of Brussels, Fondation 9 offers group classes of up to eight students in all the official EU languages.

Universities

Académie Royale des Beaux-Arts de Bruxelles

144 rue du Midi, Lower Town (02 511 04 91/www.brunette. brucity.be/aca/academie.htm). Pré-métro Anneessens. **Map** p318 B4.
The Royal Academy of Fine Art has four-year courses in weaving, illustration/comic strip art, advertising and design, but it is best known for its painting and sculpture programmes.

Boston University Brussels

8 font St-Landry, Neder-Over-Heembeek (02 650 21 11/www.bostonu.be). Tram 23 then bus 47.
Boston University set up its campus in Brussels in 1972 and joined with VUB (*see below*) to set up an English-language Masters of Science in Management (MSM) programme. In addition to the MSM course, the university offers an MS in Administrative Studies as well as several specialised graduate certificates.

Ecole Nationale Supérieure des Arts Visuels de la Cambre

21 Abbaye de la Cambre, Ixelles (02 648 96 19/www.lacambre.be). Tram 23, 90, 93, 94.
Brussels has two main art schools, this and the Beaux-Arts (*see above*), the former being more commercially oriented and perhaps the snootier of the two. Housed in a beautiful 13th-century abbey in Ixelles, La Cambre has courses in fine art as well as animation, printmaking and industrial design. But the school's fortes are architecture, graphic design and fashion. Courses are taught in French.

ICHEC (Institut Catholique des Hautes Etudes Commerciales)

2 boulevard Brand Whitlock, Woluwe-St-Lambert (02 739 37 11/www.ichec.be). Métro Montgomery/tram 23, 44, 81, 90.
Founded in 1934, ICHEC is rated as the second-best business school in Brussels, after Solvay, and its students tend to be of the BCBG (*bon chic bon genre* – smart set), old money variety. Course work is extremely demanding, with between 30 and 40 class hours per week and, as with ULB, only a quarter of the initial student intake end up bringing home a degree to *maman*.

Open University

38 avenue Emile Duray, Ixelles (02 644 33 72/73/www.open.ac.uk). Tram 23, 90, 93, 94.
The Open University caters mostly for working adults who want to get a degree but don't want or can't afford to quit their jobs. Students follow a course book and audio-visual materials at their own pace, and meet regularly with a tutor at study centres either in Brussels or Antwerp. BAs and BScs take anything from four to six years to complete, depending on the student's own study plan. Degrees are offered in the social sciences, technology, computing, mathematics, arts and sciences. There is also an MBA programme.

ULB (Université Libre de Bruxelles)

50 avenue Franklin Roosevelt, Ixelles (02 650 21 11/www.ulb.ac.be). Tram 93, 94/bus 71.
The Free University of Brussels was founded in 1834 by lawyer Theodore Verhaegen in order to counter the stagnant state of higher education in Brussels. At the time, the Catholic Church had a monopoly over the curricula of the country's three universities, and intellectual advancement proceeded along rigid lines. ULB began as an independent, liberal institution, although it did receive strong backing from masonic circles (whether this support compromises the university's independence remains a subject of controversy). Today, it is the largest university in Brussels, with more than 18,000 students, of whom roughly a third are foreigners. Solbosch, ULB's main campus, is home to most faculties – Philosophy and Letters, Social Sciences, Applied Sciences, Law and European Studies – with the exception of Medicine, which is located at Hôpital Erasme.

Directory

Solbosch is also home to the city's most prestigious business school, Solvay, which offers a tough five-year *grade d'ingénieur commercial* and a one-year MBA in English. Student life is scattered – most students live at home or in apartments around the city – although there are a number of student associations and clubs on the Solbosch Campus.

Vesalius College

32 boulevard du Triomphe, Ixelles (02 629 36 26/ www.vub.ac.be/VECO/aveco/ index.htm). Métro Hankar/ tram 23, 90.

Vesalius was created in 1987 as part of the VUB (*see below*) and in association with Boston University. Although it shares a campus with VUB (which issues Vesalius diplomas), the language of instruction is English and the style of education is decidedly American – selective admission, small classes and close faculty-student relationships – and American-style fees. Vesalius offers bachelor's degrees in the likes of economics, computer science, engineering (computer and electrical), English lit, business and human resources management. The student body is diverse, with over 50 nationalities represented, and student life is accordingly interesting.

VUB (Vrije Universiteit Brussel)

2 boulevard de la Plaine, Ixelles (02 629 21 11/library 02 629 25 05/www.vub.ac.be). Métro Petillon/ tram 23, 90.

In 1970, the Free University of Brussels split into two entities along linguistic lines, the French-speaking ULB and its Dutch-speaking counterpart, VUB. Each is funded by its respective community and educational policies are decided upon separately by the national parliament and by each of the communities' cultural councils. VUB today has an enrolment of roughly 8,000 students. Although most of the courses are taught in Dutch (with the exception of Vesalius College, *see above*), there are a number of English-language postgraduate degrees.

Telephones

Note that, when in Belgium, it is now necessary to dial area codes as well as phone numbers, even when you are dialling from the relevant area. Using the *Yellow* and *White Pages* in Brussels is a cinch, as both include an English index.

Making a call

To call overseas, dial 00 then the country code and number (Australia 61; Canada 1; France 33; Germany 49; Holland 31; Ireland 353; New Zealand 64; UK 44; USA 1). When in Belgium, dial the city code and number (Antwerp 03; Bruges 05; Brussels 02; Ghent 091; Liège 041). To call Belgium from abroad, dial the international code, then 32, and then 2 if you want Brussels.

International calls are expensive. Rates are a little lower on Sundays, holidays and between 8pm and 8am. But if you plan to stay in Belgium for an extended period, the best way to save on calls is to sign on with a discount call service such as **Kallback** (call 00 1 206 216 1200 in the US for more information). For a short-term stay, a calling card with **Sprint** or **AT&T** is recommended. Despite a surcharge for each call, rates are lower than Belgacom's.

A worthwhile service called **Phone Tone** can be accessed by dialling 077 777 777. You can then dial international numbers in many countries for a cheaper rate per minute.

Public phones

Public telephone booths are found at stations, post offices and other usual locations. There are several close to the Grand' Place, around place de Brouckère and the Bourse. Booths sporting European flags can be used for direct-dial international calls. Many public phones accept only prepaid electronic telephone cards – coin phones are quite rare. You can buy phone cards at post offices, stations, newsstands and some banks and supermarkets.

Useful numbers

(Fr = French; Fl = Flemish)

Operator assistance/ reverse-charge calls
1324 Fr, 1224 Fl.

Directory enquiries (domestic)
1307 Fr, 1207 Fl; **(international)**
1304 Fr; 1204 Fl (English spoken).

Telegrams
1325 Fr, 1225 Fl.

Time
1300 Fr, 1200 Fl.

Wake-up service
0800 51248.

Gas leaks
02 244 34 54; 02 512 05 06.

Poison control centre
02 345 45 45.

Mobile phones/pagers

Belgium is part of the growing European mobile telephone network called GSM. Telephones on this system work in most of western Europe and even beyond. You can rent GSM phones at the airport or from some car hire agencies. The rental fee is usually low but the cost per call is high. For a number of years Proximus was the only mobile phone network in Belgium, but it now has to fight it out with other players such as Mobistar and Orange.

Changing prices and packages mean that none of them can be singled out as giving the best value. Each have their own shops, but for an overview of the latest various deals, it's worth dropping into a store like Phonehouse (98 rue Neuve; 02 227 53 83).

Most pagers work simply: dial the pager number and after the recording punch in your phone number and end

Tourist information

TIB

Hôtel de Ville, Grand' Place, Lower Town (02 513 89 40/fax 02 514 45 38/ tourism.brussels@tib.be). Métro Gare Centrale or Pré-métro Bourse. **Open** *Mar-Nov* 9am-6pm daily. *Dec-Feb* 9am-6pm Mon-Sat.
Map p317 C3.
This cramped little office is conveniently located on the Grand' Place, in the heart of the capital. The English-speaking staff can offer tips on what to see in Brussels and how to go about it. They can also book rooms (or you could phone 02 513 74 84). The *Brussels Guide & Map* provides complete information on sights within walking distance of the city centre. There's also a telephone booking service for shows and concerts (0800 21221).

Belgian Tourist Information Office

63 rue du Marché aux Herbes, Lower Town (02 504 03 90/fax 02 504 02 70). Métro Gare Centrale or Pré-métro Bourse. **Open** *Nov-Apr* 9am-6pm Mon-Fri; 9am-1pm, 2-6pm Sat; 9am-1pm Sun. *May, June, Sept, Oct* 9am-6pm Mon-Fri; 9am-1pm, 2-6pm Sat, Sun. *July, Aug* 9am-7pm Mon-Fri; 9am-1pm, 2-7pm Sat, Sun.
Map p317 C3.
If you plan to make an excursion out of the city, this is the place to contact. The national tourist service, located in a handsome old building, provides information about the whole of Belgium. One of the most useful books it offers is the annual *Tourist Attractions Guide*, covering the whole country. The office is broken down into Flemish and French sections. If you're planning a trip to Bruges or a weekend on the coast, ask for the **Flanders Tourist Office**. It sells a useful brochure, *Le Pays Flamand de Vos Vacances*, which lists over 200 quick trip ideas in Flanders. For information about the French-speaking region, ask for the **Walloon Tourist Office**. It can advise on tourist attractions and has loads of info on accommodation. **Belsud Reservation** (02 504 02 80/fax 02 514 53 35) can book rooms and organise stays on farms and holiday camps.

with the # key. Some work beyond Belgium, extending to Holland and Luxembourg.

Faxes

You can find a working phone, buy a telecard or send a fax, telex or telegram at TT (*Telephone-Telegraphe/ Telefoon-Telegraaf*) centres. The one on 17 boulevard de l'Impératrice downtown opens daily from 7am to 10pm.

Time

Belgium is one hour ahead of Greenwich Mean Time, six hours ahead of US Eastern Standard Time and nine hours ahead of US Pacific Standard Time.

Tipping & VAT

Service and VAT are included in hotel and restaurant prices, though people will throw in

a few extra euros when service has been exceptional. At lower-price restaurants, round up the bill by a few cents. You shouldn't feel embarrassed – this is common practice. At mid-priced restaurants customers usually kick in up to five per cent extra. At first-class restaurants it's customary to add an extra ten per cent. Tips are also included in metered taxi fares, which are steep, although you'll often find that the devious Bruxellois cabbie will expect extra tips from foreigners. Brace yourself for additional charges for baggage, Sundays and night trips. And a grimace.
At cinemas and theatres, tipping the attendant 20¢ for a programme is expected. Although there's generally no charge for a public toilet, it's customary to leave either 10¢ and 20¢ for the women on duty. *See also p137* **Madames Pipis**.

Visas & immigration

All European Union and Swiss citizens need to show a national identity card or passport when they enter Belgium. Americans, Canadians, Australians, New Zealanders and Japanese need a valid passport. If entering as a tourist, you don't need a visa. For longer stays, *see p304* **Anyone for cards?**

Weights & measures

Belgium uses the metric system. Food items are priced by the kilogram. There are 1,000g (or 2.2lbs) in a kilo. *Une livre*, a pound, is a half-kilo or 500g. To convert kilometres into miles, multiply by 0.6. To convert centimetres to inches, divide by 2.54.

Directory

When to go

Climate

The Belgian climate is mild. Winters are very cold and damp, without much snow; summers are warm and often reasonably hot. Rain, however, is a force to be reckoned with all year round. The best line of defence in dealing with Brussels' fickle weather is always to bring an extra jumper or two and a collapsible umbrella. A sense of humour is also handy.

The biggest drawback to winter in Brussels is the shortness of the days. Much of the city stays at home or in cosy bars in the evening, since daylight only lasts from 8am to 5pm in December and January. The city starts to shake off the winter blues at Easter. Spring is officially welcomed as attractions open and activities, dormant during winter, start up again. In April and May, average temperatures range between 4°C (40°F) and 16°C (60°F). The

heat picks up in June and July, reaching the mid-20s°C (70s°F) and occasionally hitting the high 20s°C (80s°F). Everyone heads for the Ardennes or the coast, and in town the royals open their palaces to the public. September can be lovely. The flip side to sad, short, dark winter days is the seemingly endless days of summer in Brussels. It's not uncommon to sit out on a café terrace at 10pm with the sky still light. Autumn is often rainy, with temperatures usually around 10°C-16°C (50°F-60°F) during October.

Public holidays

The following are public holidays in Belgium: **New Year's Day** (1 Jan); **Easter Monday**; **Labour Day** (1 May); **Ascension Day** (6th Thur after Easter); **Pentecostal Whit Monday** (7th Mon after Easter; **Belgian National Day** (21 July); **Assumption** (15 Aug); **All Saints' Day** (1 Nov); **Armistice Day** (11 Nov); **Christmas Day** (25 Dec).

Although it is not an official holiday, banks and government offices usually close on **15 November** for King's Day. And as if the country didn't have enough holidays, the Belgians make a habit of tacking on more free days to make long weekends even longer. If a holiday falls on a Tuesday or Thursday, most offices, by tradition, will 'make the bridge' (*faire le pont/de brug maken*) and observe a four-day weekend. The longest of these 'bridges' is Easter, when many Belgians take the opportunity to embark on short trips across Europe.

As with everything in Belgium, the French and Flemish communities celebrate separate regional holidays. A day off on **11 July** marks the anniversary of the Battle of the Golden Spurs in 1302 for the Flemish region of Flanders, while a holiday on **27 September** commemorates the end of French-speaking Wallonia's revolution for independence from Holland in 1830. National Day, **21 July**, is a rare joint celebration.

Anyone for cards?

EU nationals, Americans, Canadians, Australians and New Zealanders do not need a visa to enter Belgium. Nor do they have to register upon entering – unless they wish to stick around for longer than three months, in which case they must embark on the complex and long-winded bureaucratic journey of registration.

This quest for the **Carte de Séjour** – a Belgian identity card measuring 12.5 centimetres by 9 centimetres, unable to fit into any wallet known to man – begins at the local council, or *commune*. Greater Brussels is composed of 27 such councils. To find your nearest one, look under 'Administrations Communes' of the *White Pages* telephone directory.

Documents required vary from *commune* to *commune* – phone ahead before your first visit. These local town halls are large,

imposing structures with intricate façades, marble staircases and a criminal overuse of perspex. After queuing for an application card, you must enter your details – typewritten. Having found a typewriter, the next day you head back, bringing with you the right papers, photographs, accommodation lease and employment details, administrative fee, and crossed fingers.

With the first paperwork submitted, you are invited back for an interview, after which you are given a temporary *carte*, valid for three months, and instructed to wait for the police. After a fortnight or so, Monsieur Plod arrives *chez vous* to check you live at your address, and you are invited back for your full, unfitting, five-year Carte de Séjour.

The whole process should take about three months, involving three visits, each of around three hours each – fingers crossed.

Resources A-Z

Working in Brussels

All British visitors need a valid passport to enter Belgium. The same goes for Swiss citizens and EU nationals, who can also use a valid national ID card. Visitors from the US, Australia, New Zealand and Japan need only a valid passport to stay for three months as a tourist (no visa is required).

If you wish to stay longer, you must participate in a maddening paper chase. For EU nationals, the process is fairly simple. You don't need to apply for a work permit, but you must register with the police. This involves a trip to the town hall of the *commune* in which you are living. Provide three photos, pay a nominal fee, have your fingerprints taken (not all *communes* insist on this), and you'll receive a three-month residence card. This is renewable for another three months. You're then eligible to receive an ID card valid for five years, should you wish to stay. *See also p304* **Anyone for cards?**

If you live or work in Belgium, you must carry your Belgian identity card (*carte d'identité/identiteitskaart*) with you at all times. If you don't have one, carry your passport. Belgian police have the right to stop you at any time to see proof of identity. If you can't produce it, they can hold you at a police station until your identity is proven, even if you haven't committed a crime.

Before starting work EU nationals should apply for forms Council Regulations 1408/71 and 574/72, which concern social security payments for those moving within the EU. For non-EU citizens the situation is trickier. Due to high unemployment, it's becoming more difficult to get work

permits (*permis de travail/werkvergunning*). The applicant must prove that no Belgian or other EU national can do the job. Your employer must apply for the permit on your behalf. You will also need to provide three photos, a certificate of good health and a copy of your work contract. Processing can take anything up to 12 weeks.

The type of permit you get depends on how long you are planning to stay in Belgium. Most people receive B permits, which are valid for one year and then must be renewed; they are not transferable from one employer to another. After three or four years with a B permit, one can apply for an A permit, which is valid indefinitely with any employer in any field.

Working illegally is not recommended. Unlike France, seasonal cash-in-hand work is thin on the ground. The national governments of each of the Benelux countries have made concerted efforts to crack down on illegal employment. Those caught by the authorities working illegally can be fined, jailed or even deported.

The only place where you're likely to find under-the-counter work is in the port city of Antwerp – and probably not Brussels, unless it involves the most menial and even dangerous of tasks.

Ministère de l'Emploiet du Travail
51 rue Belliard, EU Quarter (02 233 41 11/fax 02 233 44 88). Métro Maelbeek. **Open** 9am-noon, 2-4pm Mon-Fri. **Map** p324 E4.
Contact it for a work permit application form.

Women's groups & centres

International women's groups abound in Brussels – Canadian, American, South African, Sri Lankan, Swedish,

British – you name it, there will be one here. These groups organise charity events, excursions, social events and courses, and can be a very useful way to meet other women in Brussels.

The most comprehensive source of information on the activities of the myriad women's groups can be found in the weekly *Bulletin. See p297* **Media**.

For a more complete list of women's organisations around Brussels, consult the *Repertoire Francophone d'Adresses pour les Femmes*. It can be found at either the Université des Femmes (which compiled the directory) or at bookshop Artemys (8-10 galerie Bortier, rue Saint-Jean, Lower Town; 02 512 03 47; metro Gare Centrale).

A couple of the most popular women's groups for expatriates are the **American Women's Club of Brussels** (02 358 47 53) and the **British & Commonwealth Women's Club of Brussels** (02 772 53 13).

Amazone
10 rue du Méridien, St-Josse (02 229 38 00/restaurant 02 229 38 00). Métro Botanique or Madou/tram 92, 93, 94. **Open** 9am-6pm Mon-Fri. **Map** p322 E2.
Amazone was inaugurated in May 1995 with the triple ambition of supporting women's organisations, providing comprehensive information on women's issues to the public and offering a *point de rencontre* for women in Brussels. The centre is home to the following organisations: Université des Femmes, Sophia, Le Conseil des Femmes Francophones de Belgique, Nederlandstalige Vrouwenraad, Le Comité de Liaison des Femmes, Vrouwen Overleg Komitee, Stichting Vrouwen tegen Mishandeling, La Coordination des Groupes Contre la Violence Faite aux Femmes and finally La Coordination des Groupes Politiques des Femmes pour la Démocratie Paritaire. Described as 'gay-friendly' but not exclusively lesbian, Amazone also houses a restaurant for women and men, open for lunch. The cadre is bourgeois and the food is salad fare, but it's a handy place to make contacts.

Directory

Time Out Brussels Guide **305**

Languages

Although officially bilingual, Brussels is largely French-speaking. For this reason (and for simplicity's sake), we have usually referred to Brussels' streets, buildings and so on by their French name. In town, all street signs are given in both languages (as they are on our street maps, staring on p317).

French is also the language of Wallonia (the south), while Flemish, a dialect of Dutch, is the language of Flanders (the north). (The French, who consider the Belgians stupid, frown upon the easier Belgian numerical use of *septante*, *huitante* instead of the complicated French *soixante-dix* and *quatre-vingts*; the Flemings think that the Dutch spoken in Holland sounds like English.)

There is also a small German-speaking enclave in the east of the country. In the **Trips Out of Town** chapter (*see p219*) we use Dutch for place names in Flanders.

English is widely spoken in Brussels and Flanders, but attempts to speak French in Flanders will fall on deaf ears at best. At worst, it could earn you a punch on the nose. Simply put, the Flemings won't speak French and the French can't speak Dutch – but the issue is far more politically vexed than that. If you can't speak Dutch, use English if the following modest vocabulary doesn't stretch.

Words and phrases are listed below in **English**, then French, then *Dutch* – with pronunciation for the latter given afterwards in brackets.

Useful expressions

Good morning, hello bonjour *hallo* ('hullo'), *dag* ('daarg')
Good evening bonsoir *goedenavond* ('hoo-dun-aav-and')
Good night bon nuit *goedenacht* ('khoo-dun-acht'
Goodbye au revoir *tot ziens* ('tot zeens'), *dag* ('daarg')
How are you? comment allez vous? *hoe maakt u het?* ('hoo markt oo hut')
How's it going? ça va? *hoe gaat het?* ('woo hart hut')
OK d'accord *okay, in orde, goed* ('okay', 'in or-the', 'hoot')
Yes oui *ja* ('yah')
No non *nee* ('nay')
Please s'il vous plaît *alstublieft* ('als-too-bleeft')
Thank you/thanks merci *dank u* ('dank oo'), *bedankt* (bur-dankt')
Leave me alone laissez moi tranquille *laat me met rust* ('laat mu mat rust')
How much?/how many? combien? *hoeveel, wat kost?* ('hoo-vale waht cost?')
I would like… je voudrais… *ik wil graag?…* ('ick will hraak')
My name is… je m'appelle… *mijn naam is…* ('mine narm is')
Left/right gauche/droite *links/rechts* ('link-s'/'reckts')
Open/closed ouvert/fermé *open/gesloten* ('open'/'he-slo-tun')
Good/bad bon or bonne/mauvais or mauvaise *goed/slecht* ('hoot'/'sleckt')
Well/badly bien/mal *goed/slecht*
Stamp timbre *postzegel*
Toilet WC *toilet* ('twalet')
Do you know the way to…? est-ce que vous savez où se trouve…? *weet u de weg naar…?*

Language expressions

Do you speak English? parlez-vous anglais? *spreekt u Engels?* ('spraykt oo engels?')
I don't speak French/Dutch je ne parle français *ik spreek geen Nederlands* ('ick sprayk hain nay-der-lants')
Speak more slowly, please parlez plus lentement, s'il vous plaît *kunt u wat trager spreken, alstublieft?* ('kunt oo waht tra-her spray-cun, als-too-bleeft')
I don't understand je ne comprends pas *ik begrijp het niet* ('ick be-gripe hut neet')

Eating & drinking

I'd like to reserve a table… je voudrais réserver un table… *ik zou graag een tafel reserveren…* ('ick zoo hraak an ta-full ray-sir-va-run')
…for two people/at eight o'clock …pour deux personnes/

a vingt heures …*voor twee personen/ om acht uur* ('for tway per-sone-an'/'om acht oor')
Can I have the bill, please? l'addition, s'il vous plaît, *mag ik de rekening, alstublieft?* ('mach ick de ray-cun-ing, als-too-bleeft')
Two beers, please, deux bières, s'il vous plaît, *twee bieren/pilsjes/ pintjes, alstublieft* ('tway beer-an/pils-yes/pint-yes, als-too-bleeft')

Accommodation

Do you have a room… avez-vous une chambre… *heeft u een kamer…* ('hay-ft oo an kam-er')
…for this evening/for two people? pour ce soir/pour deux personnes? *voor vanavond/voor twee personen?* ('vor van-aav-and/vor tway per-sone-an')
Double bed un grand lit *een tweepersoonsbed* ('an tway per-sones-bed')
With bathroom/shower avec salle de bain/douche *met badkamer/ douche* ('mat bart camer'/'doosh')
Expensive/cheap cher/pas cher *duur/goedkoop* ('th-oor'/'hoot-cope')

Numbers

zero zéro *nul;* **1** un/une *een;* **2** deux *twee;* **3** trois *drie;* **4** quatre *vier;* **5** cinq *vijf;* **6** six *zes;* **7** sept *zeven;* **8** huit *acht;* **9** neuf *negen;* **10** dix *tien;* **11** onze *elf;* **12** douze *twaalf;* **13** treize *dertien;* **14** quatorze *veertien;* **15** quinze *vijftien;* **16** seize *zestien;* **17** dix-sept *zeventien;* **18** dix-huit *achttien;* **19** dix-neuf *negentien;* **20** vingt *twintig;* **30** trente *dertig;* **40** quarante *veertig;* **50** cinquante *vijftig;* **60** soixante *zestig;* **70** septante *seventig;* **80** huitante *tachtig;* **90** nonante *negentig;* **100** cent *honderd;* **thousand** mille *duizend;* **million** million *miljoen.*

Date & season

Monday lundi *maandag;* **Tuesday** mardi *dinsdag;* **Wednesday** mercredi *woensdag;* **Thursday** jeudi *donderdag;* **Friday** vendredi *vrijdag;* **Saturday** samedi *zaterdag;* **Sunday** dimanche *zondag.*
January janvier *januari;* **February** février, *februari;* **March** mars *maart;* **April** april *april;* **May** mai *mei;* **June** juin *juni;* **July** juillet *juli;* **August** août *augustus;* **September** septembre *september;* **October** octobre *oktober;* **November** novembre *november;* **December** décembre *december.*

Further Reference

Books

Fiction, drama & poetry

Baudelaire, Charles
Amoenitates Belgicae
Not Baudelaire's finest verse, but a scathing and often pertinent look at the Belgians and their culture. The poems are rarely published by themselves, but can be found in editions of Baudelaire's collected works.

Bertin, Eddy C
His collections are not available in English, but short stories by this Belgian writer do occasionally turn up in out-of-print horror anthologies.

Brontë, Charlotte
The Professor
Brontë's first novel was set in Brussels, and she struggled to find a publisher for it, even after the huge success of her later works.
Villette
Brussels was the model for the town of Villette in Brontë's final novel, based on her experience of teaching there.

Christie, Agatha
The Mysterious Affair at Styles
Allons, mes petits vol au vents…
Poirot's début.

Claus, Hugo
The Sorrow of Belgium
Milestone novel, set during the Nazi occupation, by a major Flemish-language novelist.

Conrad, Joseph
Heart of Darkness
Conrad's masterpiece has early scenes in a corrupt, cheerless Brussels, unnamed but clearly identifiable.

Hergé
The *Tintin* books
Belgium's most famous author needs no introduction.

Hollinghurst, Alan
The Folding Star
Fictional art history and sexual obsession in a dreary city in northern Belgium.

Martin, Stephen (ed)
Poetry of the First World War
A very fine anthology, with poems about the battlegrounds of Flanders.

Maeterlinck, Maurice, et al
An Anthology of Modern Belgian Theatre
This 1982 anthology features works by Maurice Maeterlinck, Fernand Crommelynck and Michel de Ghelderode.

Meades, Jonathan
Pompey
Portrait of Belgium's imperial escapades in the Congo.

Royle, Nicholas
Saxophone Dreams
Magical-realist adventures in the landscapes of Belgian Surrealist Paul Delvaux, including a role for Delvaux himself.

Sante, Luc
The Factory of Facts
Autobiographical account of growing up in Belgium in the '50s.

Simenon, Georges
Maigret's Revolver
Or just about any other title by the Liège-born master of the crime/detective fiction genre.

Thackeray, William Makepeace
Vanity Fair
The middle section describes the social scene in Brussels on the eve of Waterloo.

Yourcenar, Marguerite
Zeno of Bruges
The wanderings of an alchemist in late medieval Europe. Yourcenar was born in Brussels in 1903. Her other books include *Anna, Soror, Alexis* and *A Coin in Nine Hands*.

History & politics

Since Belgium did not exist until 1830, few books deal specifically with its history. Instead, the determined reader will have to search for books about Spain, Austria, the Netherlands, etc.

Glover, Michael
A New Guide to the Battlefields of Northern France and the Low Countries
Covers Waterloo as well as the World War I battlefields.

Kossman, EH
The Low Countries
Dull but informative history of Belgium 1780-1940.

Parker, Geoffrey
The Dutch Revolt
Excellent history of one of Belgium's most interesting periods, when the Spanish empire was crumbling in the 16th century.

Art & architecture

Meuris, Jacques
René Magritte
The world of the Surrealist painter, in words and pictures.

Rombout, Marc
Paul Delvaux
Excellent selection of colour plates, plus biographical text.

Shinomura, Junichi
Art Nouveau Architecture, Residential Masterpieces 1892-1911
The selection of photographs of the Musée Horta would be a fine addition to anyone's coffee table.

White, Christopher
Pieter Paul Rubens: Man and Artist
A lavishly illustrated look at the Antwerp-born artist.

Food & drink

Hellon, John
Brussels Fare
Recipes from Belgian restaurants.

Van Waerebeek, Ruth
Everybody Eats Well in Belgium
Beautifully designed cookbook.

Webb, Tim
Good Beer Guide to Belgium & Holland
Excellent guide for beer lovers from the Campaign for Real Ale (CAMRA).

Directory

Wynants, Pierre

Creative Belgian Cuisine
Anyone who has eaten at
Wynants' wonderful Comme Chez
Soi (*see p101*) will need no further
encouragement.

Travel

Bryson, Bill

Neither Here Nor There
Belgium and Brussels fill two
amusing, if predictable, chapters
of Bryson's European travels.

Pearson, Harry

A Tall Man in a Low Land
Entertaining and affectionate
travelogue.

Alles Moet Weg

Jan Verheyen's finest hour. A
cool road movie about a gay law
student gone crazy. Based on a
famous Flemish novel. 1996.

Au-Delà De Gibraltar

Interesting docu-drama about
a Belgian Arab's love for a
white French-speaking girl in
Brussels. Emotional, realistic
and hard at times. Most of the
actors were suburban residents.
Made in 2002.

Le Bal Masqué

Violent and suggestive look at
one of the most notorious crime
cases in Belgium. Controversial
and graphic. 1998.

Daens

Probably the finest Flemish
film. An epic drama starring
Jan Decleir as a priest who cared
for oppressed workers in a
19th-century mill town. Oscar-
nominated. 1993.

Falling

English-language film based on
a famous Flemish novel. Slated for
international release. Great
soundtrack by dance wizards
Praga Kahn. 2001.

Le Huitième Jour (The Eighth Day)

Touching drama by Jaco Van
Dormael about a businessman
who befriends a Down's syndrome
fugitive. Won best actor at
Cannes; Oscar nominee. 1996.

Gaston's War

An English-language co-
production about a war hero
in Spain. 1997.

Iedereen Beroemd (Everybody Famous)

Unusual take on the desire to
become famous. Great thriller
element too. Very Flemish, but
with universal humour. Oscar
nominee. 2000.

Ma Vie En Rose (My Life In Pink)

A young lad thinks he's a girl
trapped in boy's body. Golden
Globe nominee. 1997.

Man Bites Dog (C'est arrivé près de chez vous)

Rémy Belvaux's hilarious and
shocking cult classic about three
film students who follow a brutal
killer. 1992.

Le Mûr

Great TV movie about a wall
between the Flemish- and French-
speaking community in Brussels.
From the maker of *My Life In
Pink*. 1999.

Pauline & Paulette

A mentally handicapped 65-
year-old woman needs caring
for by her sisters. Cannes
winner. And a surprise box
office hit. 2001.

La Promesse

An excellent movie about
illegal immigrants in the town
of Liège, made by the Dardenne
Brothers. 1997.

Rosetta

A young girl struggles to find
work in Liège. A very bleak,
but gripping film by Luc and
Jean-Pierre Dardenne. Cannes
winner. 2000.

Team Spirit

Flemish remake of Dutch film
All Stars. Football comedy
with a lot of famous Flemish
personalities. 2000.

Toto the Hero (Toto le héros)

Director Jaco Van Dormael's
debut film, an uplifting offbeat
drama of jealousy and revenge.
Cannes winner. 1991.

**http://pespmc1.vub.
ac.be/Belgcul.html**
Excellent generic site, containing
everything you might want to
know about Belgium, plus news
services, how to cook *frites*, the
weather forecast and more.

**www.geographia.com/
belgium/**
A generic Belgium site, including
a good history section.

**www.70south.com/
resources/history/
belgium**
A nice little site about Belgium –
and the South Pole!

**www.antiques-
world.com**
A great generic site for antiques
shops and fairs.

**www.tiac.net/users/
tjd/bier/belgium.html**
Reams of info about Belgian beer,
including cookery recipes.

**http://frenchfood.
about.com/cs/belgian
cuisine**
Belgium cuisine with useful
onward links.

**http://vbdw.com/
vbdw**
The Belgian Experts Shop: food,
chocolate, beer and much more.

**www.belgianstyle.
com/mmguide**
Guide to the beers of Belgium.

**www.ebrusselshotels.
com**
Descriptions, reviews, prices and
pictures of the capital's hotels.

**http://belgium.fgov.
be/monarchie/en00.
htm**
Learn all about the royal family.

www.gaydar.co.uk
Gay site, with an ever-growing
Belgian room split into Brussels
and Belgium-Rest. Messaging is
instant and in real time.

www.gay.be
Local gay chat room, available in
French, Dutch and English.

Index

Numbers in **bold** indicate key information on a topic; *italics* indicate photographs.

a

Abbaye de la Cambre 86, 88
accommodation **39-54**
  see also p314
  accommodation index
  best hotels, the 44
  by area
    EU Quarter & Montgomery 50
    Grand' Place & around 41-43
    Ixelles 50-52
    Marolles & Gare du Midi 45
    Ste-Catherine & St-Géry 44-45
    St-Josse & Schaerbeek 49-50
    Uccle 52
    Upper Town 45-49
  cheap 43, 44-45, 49, 52
  deluxe 40-43, 45-47, 49, 50-52
  expensive 44, 47, 49
  moderate 43, 44, 45, 47, 52
  out of town
    Antwerp 230-232
    Bruges 247-250
    Ghent 259-260
addresses 291
Africalia Festival 189
African Brussels 87
age restrictions 291
Agora market 163
air, arriving by 286
Aix-La-Chappelle, Treaty of 15
Albert I, King 22
Albert II, King **25**, 26
Albrecht of Austria, Archduke **12**, 26
Alva, Duke of 11
Ancienne Belgique 198, **199**
Anderlecht 57, **92-95**, *93*
  market 163
  restaurants 119
Anderlecht, RSC 205, **206**
antiques 139
Antwerp 10, 11, 12, 22, 26, **221-240**
Antwerp Six 236-237
Antwerp Zoo 230
ARAU (Atelier de Recherche et d'Action) 30, 32, 34, 36, **38**, 59

Arc de Triomphe 18, 34, **82**, *82*
Arcadia 59
architecture **30-34**
  tours 38
Ardennes, the **282-284**
Arenberg Galeries 67, **182**
arriving in Brussels 286-287
Ars Musica **166**, 195, 196
art 72
Antwerp 240
  see also galleries *and* museums: art & applied arts
Art nouveau **35-38**
  architecture 31, **34**
arts & crafts and hobby shops 160
arts & entertainment **165-218**
  festivals 185, 189, **218**
Artvelde, Jacob van 7
Astrid, Parc 92
athletics 204-205
Atomium *30*, 31, 34, 59, **93**, **94**
Auber, Daniel 20
Auber, François-Esprit 68
Auden, WH 79
Austrian Netherlands 13
Autoworld 82, 83
avenue Louise 36, 84, 121, 138, **141**

b

babysitting 172-173
badminton 207
Baldwin II 7
bars **120-137**
  see also p314 bars index
  best 121
  by area
    EU Quarter & Etterbeek 133
    Grand' Place & around 121-127
    Ixelles 133-135
    Marolles & Gare du Midi 130-132
    Ste-Catherine 127
    St-Géry 127-130
    St-Gilles 135
    St-Josse & Schaerbeek 137
    Upper Town 132-133
    Woluwe-St-Pierre 137
  crawls 120, 123, 126-127, 130-131, 135
  gay & lesbian 190
  late night drinking 126-127
  out of town

Antwerp 234-235
  Bruges 252
  Ghent 262-267
Basilique du Sacré Coeur 94
Baudouin I, King **24**, **25**, 26
beaches 269-272
Beckett, Samuel 30
bed & breakfasts 52-54
beer 94-95, 120, **125**
Belgae, the **6**, 26
Belgian Grand Prix 206
Belgian Revolution 71
Belgian Tourist Information Office 64, **303**
Belgian Tourist Reservation Office 40
Belgian Worker's Party 21
Belle Alliance Inn 15
Bellone-Brigittines, Festival 218
Benelux Customs Union **25**, 26
Berlaymont 31, **32-33**, *33*, 34, 78
Berlaymont, Count 11
Berlin Declaration of 1885 21
Beursschouwburg 212-213
Bike Festival, Dring Dring 167
Bikkembergs, Dirk 236
billiards 207
Binche 274
bingo 128
Black Death 26
Blankenberge 174, **270**
Blücher, Marshal 14, 15
Bois de la Cambre 86, **91**, 174
books
  further reference 307-308
  shops 141-143
    comics 142-143
    gay & lesbian 193
    second-hand 143
Bosch, Hieronymus 9
Botanique *97*, 98, 198, **199-200**
Bouillon 283
Bourse 62
bowling 207
Brabançon Revolution **16**, 26
Brabo 221
Braekeleer, Henri de 226
Braems, Renaat 30
Braine l'Alleud 13
Brangwyn, Frank 244
Brel, Jaques 29, 67, **96-98**, *97*, 199

Brosella Jazz & Folk Festival **169**, 201
Bruegel the Elder, Pieter 64, 70, 72, 73, 226
Bruges **241-253**
Bruges 2002 251
Bruges-la-Morte 241
Bruparck 93, *172*, **173**
Brussels 2000 27, 28
Brussels, origins of name 7
Bruxelles, Parc de 71, 76, **90**, *91*
'Bruxellisation' 30
Buimard, Barnabé 33
buses 287-288
business services 291-292
Butte du Lion 14
Buyl, Adolph 31

c

Caesar, Julius **6**, 26
cafés *see* bars
cameras & electronics shops 143
Cantillon Brewery *see* Musée Bruxellois de la Gueuze
cars 288-289
Cartoon & Animation Festival 184
Cathédrale des Sts Michel et Gudule 31, 59, 71, *71*, **75**, 76, **196**
Catholicism 20-21
Cauchie, Paul 37
Cavell, Edith 22
Centre d'art contemporain 83, **189**
Centre Belge de la Bande Dessinée 30, 36, 59, **63**, 68, 173, *175*
Centre Monnaie 67
Ceulemans, Raymond 204
Chapelle Royale 196
Charbon *see* rue du Marché au Charbon
Charlemagne **7**, 26
Charleroi Danses/Plan K 217
Charles II 13
Charles of Austria, Archduke 14
Charles of France 7
Charles of Lorraine 15
Charles the Bald 7
Charles the Bold 244
Charles the Rash 9
Charles V, Emperor **10**, *11*, 26, 244, 254
Charles V, King 32, 73
Charles VI of Austria, Emperor 14
Charlier, Guillaume 79

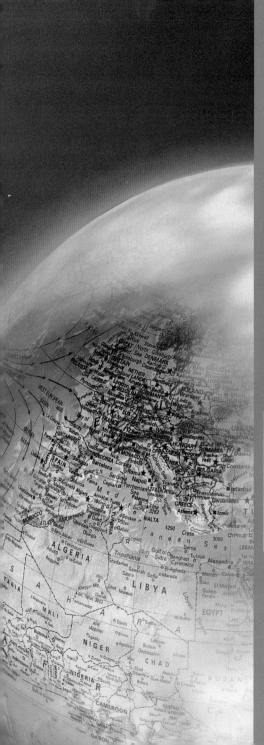

Maps

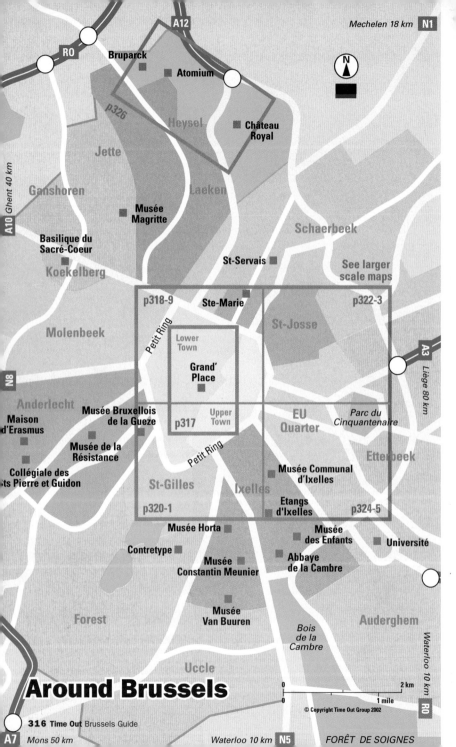

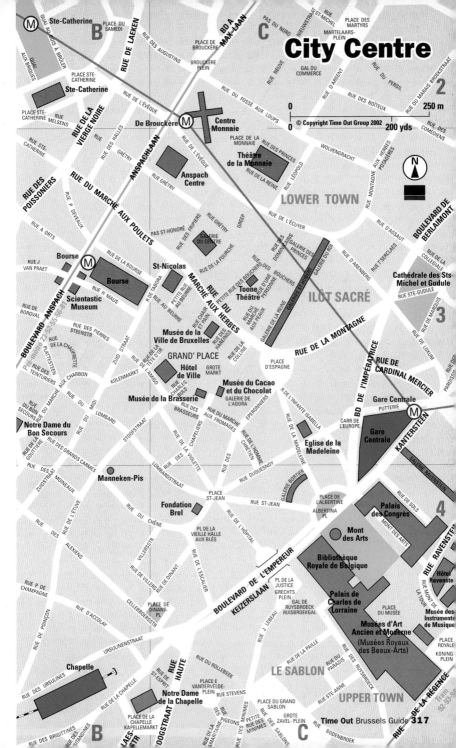

City Centre

LOWER TOWN

ÎLOT SACRÉ

UPPER TOWN

LE SABLON

GRAND' PLACE

0 — 250 m
0 — 200 yds
© Copyright Time Out Group 2002

Ste-Catherine
De Brouckère
Centre Monnaie
Théâtre de la Monnaie
Anspach Centre
Bourse
St-Nicolas
Scientastic Museum
Toone Théâtre
Cathédrale des Sts Michel et Gudule
Musée de la Ville de Bruxelles
Hôtel de Ville
Musée du Cacao et du Chocolat
Musée de la Brasserie
Gare Centrale
Notre Dame du Bon Secours
Eglise de la Madeleine
Manneken-Pis
Fondation Brel
Palais des Congrès
Mont des Arts
Bibliothèque Royale de Belgique
Palais de Charles de Lorraine
Musées d'Art Ancien et Moderne (Musées Royaux des Beaux-Arts)
Musée des Instruments de Musique
Hôtel Ravenste
Chapelle
Notre Dame de la Chapelle

Time Out Brussels Guide **317**

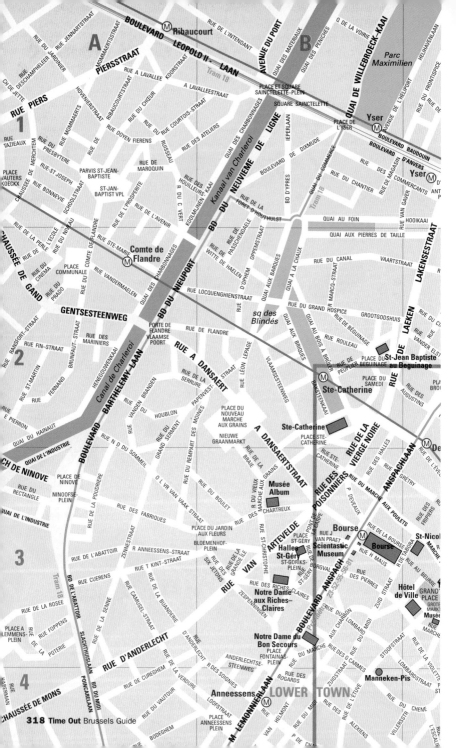

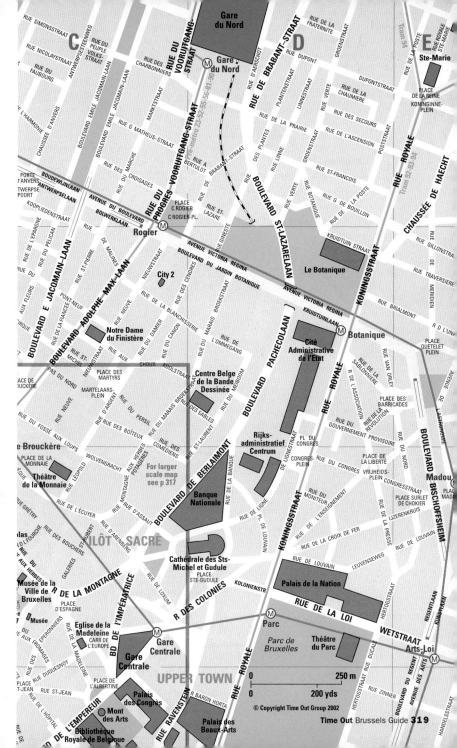

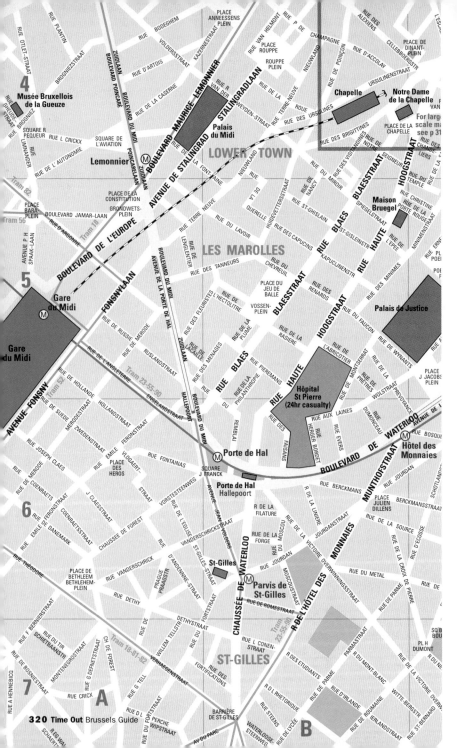

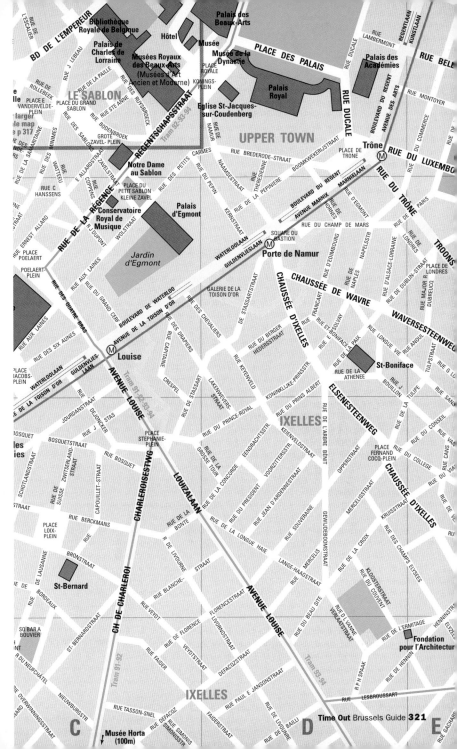

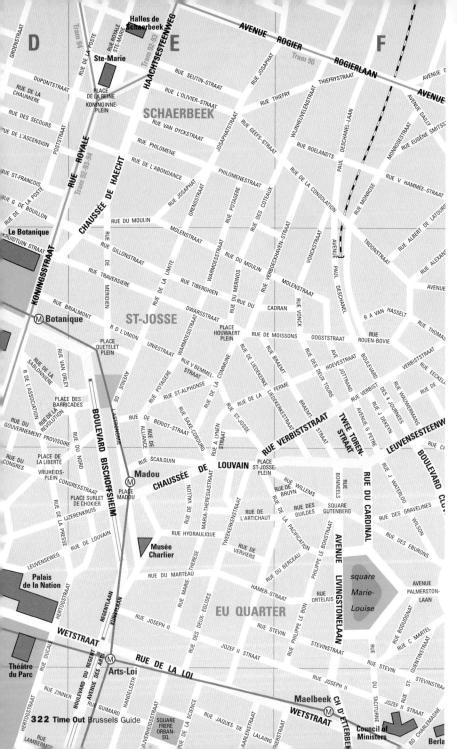

D

GROENSTRAAT

Tram 94

RUE DE LA POSTE

DUPONTSTRAAT

RUE DE LA
CHAUMIERE

RUE DES SECOURS

RUE DE L'ASCENSION

POSTSTRAAT

RUE ST-FRANÇOIS

RUE G. DE BOUILLON

RUE DE LA POSTE

Le Botanique
KRUIDTUIN STRAAT

KONINGSSTRAAT

RUE ROYALE
Tram 92-33-94

CHAUSSÉE DE HAECHT

M Botanique

RUE BRIALMONT

R D L'UNION

RUE DE LA
SABLONNIÈRE

R DE L'ASSOCIATION

PLACE DES
BARRICADES

RUE DE LA
REVOLUTION

RUE DU
GOUVERNEMENT PROVISOIRE

PLACE DE
LA LIBERTÉ

RUE DU
CONGRES

VRIJHEIDS-
PLEIN CONGRESSTRAAT

BOULEVARD BISCHOFSHEIM

PLACE SURLET
DE CHOKIER

RUE DE LA IJZERENKRUIS

RUE DE LA PRESSE

RUE DU NORD

Palais
de la Nation

HERTOGSTRAAT

LEUVENSEWEG

Théâtre
du Parc

RUE DUCALE

BOULEVARD DU REGENT

AVENUE DES ARTS

RUE ZINNER

RUE GUIMARD

RUE LAMBERMO

E

Halles de
Schaerbeek

RUE ROYALE
STE-MARIE

Ste-Marie

PLACE
DE LA REINE
KONINGINNE-
PLEIN

HAACHTSESTEENWEG
Tram 92-33

SCHAERBEEK

RUE SEUTIN-STRAAT

RUE L'OLIVIER-STRAAT

RUE VAN DYCKSTRAAT

RUE PHILOMENE

RUE DE L'ABONDANCE

RUE JOSAPHAT

GRENSSTRAAT

RUE DU MOULIN

MOLENSTRAAT

RUE GILLONSTRAAT

RUE
DE

RUE TRAVERSIERE

MERIDIEN

ST-JOSSE

PLACE
QUETELET
PLEIN

RUE DE LA LIMITE

AVENUE DE L'ASTRONOMIE

DWARSSTRAAT

WARMOESTRAAT

UNIESTRAAT

RUE POTAGERE

RUE ST-ALPHONSE

RUE DE BERIOT-STRAAT

RUE DE
L'ALLIANCE

RUE SCAILQUIN

Madou
PLACE
MADOU

CHAUSSÉE DE

RUE DE VALLON

MARIA-THERESIASTRAAT

RUE HYDRAULIQUE

Musée
Charlier

RUE DU MARTEAU

RUE MARIE-
THERESE

RUE DES DEUX EGLISES

EU QUARTER

WETSTRAAT

RUE DE LA LOI

M
Arts-Loi

SQUARE
FRERE
ORBAN-
SQ.

F

AVENUE ROGIER

ROGIERLAAN

AVENUE G

AVENUE

RUE JOSAPHAT

THIEFRYSTRAAT

RUE THIEFRY

WIJNHEUVELENSTRAAT

DESCHANEL-LAAN

PAUL

AVENUE DAILY

AVENUE EUGENE SMITSST

RUE SEUTIN-STRAAT

RUE GEEFS-STRAAT

JOSAPHATSTRAAT

PHILOMENESTRAAT

RUE DES COTEAUX

RUE DE LA CONSOLATION

RUE ROELANDTS

MONROSSTRAAT

RUE V HAMMÉE-STRAAT

RUE JOSAPHAT

RUE DU MOULIN

RUE POTAGERE

RUE DU RUE DU

CADRAN

PLACE
HOUWAERT
PLEIN

RUE DE MOISSONS

RUE V BEMMEL-
STRAAT

RUE DE LA COMMUNE

RUE DE LIEDEKERKE

LIEDEKERKESTRAAT

RUE A LYNEN
STRAAT

RUE ST-JOSSE

RUE SAXE-COBOURG

AVENUE

MONROSE

PAUL DESCHANEL

RUE MONROSE

TROONSTRAAT

RUE ALBERT DE LATOUR

RUE ALEXAN

AVENUE

R A VAN HASSELT

RUE THOMAS

RUE
ROUEN-BOVIE

OOGSTSTRAAT

AVE HOEVESTRAAT

RUE DES DEUX TOURS

BOULEVARD

JOTTRAND

RUE VERBIST

RUE DE LA
FERME

RUE BRAEM

BRAEM-
STRAAT

RUE VERBISTSTRAAT

TWEE TOREN-
STRAAT

STRAAT

VERBISTSTRAAT

RUE EECKELA

RUE DE

DES 4 JOURNEES

RUE WAUWERMANS

RUE J DEKEYN

AVENUE G PETRE

RUE J WATERLOO

LEUVENSESTEENW

BOULEVARD CLO

RUE CH

PLACE
ST-JOSSE-
PLEIN

LOUVAIN

RUE DE WILLEMS

RUE DE
BRUYN

RUE DES
GUILDES

SQUARE
GUTENBERG

RUE
BONNELS

RUE DU CARDINAL

RUE DES GRAVELINES

RUE DES EBURONS

WILSON

RUE DE
L'ARTICHAUT

TWEEKERKENSTRAAT

RUE DE
VERVIERS

RUE DE LA PACIFICATION

AVENUE LIVINGSTONELAAN

square
Marie-
Louise

AVENUE
PALMERSTON-
LAAN

RUE DU BERCEAU

PHILIPPE LE BONSTRAAT

HAMER-STRAAT

RUE
ORTELIUS

RUE STEVIN

RUE PHILIPPE LE BON

STEVINSTRAAT

RUE BODUOGNAT

RUE C MARTEL

RUE STEVIN

QUENTINSTRAAT

STEVINSTRAAT

JOZEF II STRAAT

RUE DES DEUX EGLISES

RUE JOSEPH II

JOZEF II STRAAT

RUE DE LA SCIENCE

RUE JAQUES DE LALAING

Maelbeek
M

WETSTRAAT

RUE JOSEPH II

DU

RUE ST-

CH D'ETTERBE

JOZEF II STRAAT

BD CHARLEMAGNE

Council of
Ministers

Berla

322 Time Out Brussels Guide

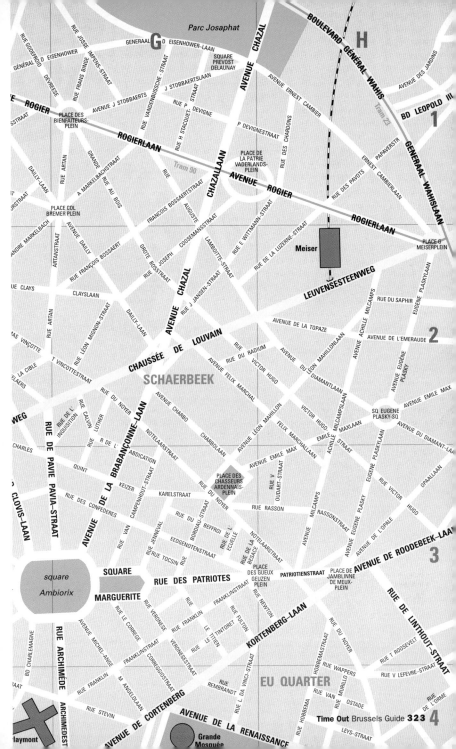

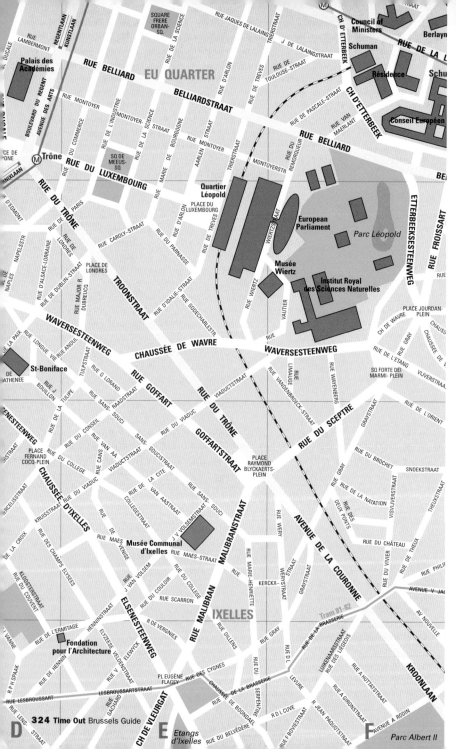

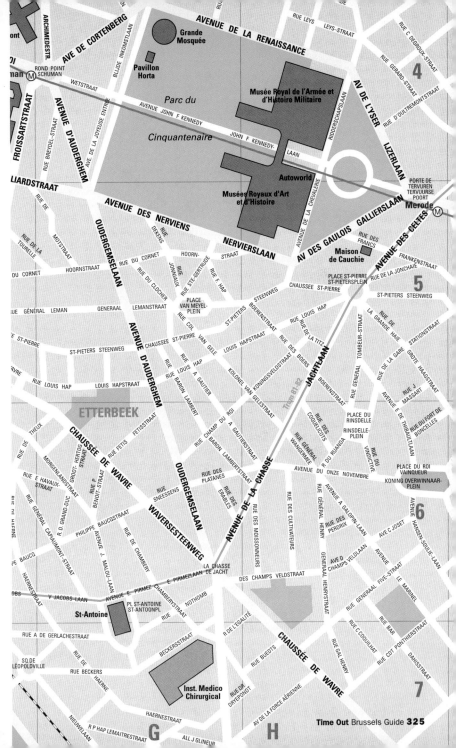

RUE LEYS LEYS—STRAAT

RUE C DEGROUX-STRAAT

AVENUE DE LA RENAISSANCE

RUE GERARD-STRAAT

Grande
Mosquée

Pavillon
Horta

Musée Royal de l'Armée et
d'Histoire Militaire

4

AVE DE CORTENBERG

ARCHIMEDESTR.

BLIDE INKOMSTLAAN

AVE DE LA JOYEUSE ENTRÉE

AVENUE JOHN F KENNEDY

Parc du

Cinquantenaire

JOHN F KENNEDY

JOHN F KENNEDY. LAAN

RIDDERSCHAPSLAAN

AV DE L'YSER

IJZERLAAN

ROND POINT
SCHUMAN

WETSTRAAT

RUE BREYDEL-STRAAT

AVENUE D'AUDERGHEM

FROISSARTSTRAAT

RUE D'OULTREMONTSTRAAT

PORTE DE
TERVUREN
TERVUURSE
POORT

Autoworld

Merode

LIARDSTRAAT

RUE DE

AVENUE DES NERVIENS

Musées Royaux d'Art
et d'Histoire

AVENUE DE LA CHEVALERIE

AV DES GAULOIS GALLIERSLAAN

AVENUE DES CELTES

RUE DE LA TOURELLE

RUE
MOTSTRAAT

RUE
DEKENS

NERVIERSLAAN

RUE DES
FRANCS

Maison
de Cauchie

FRANKENSTRAAT

DU CORNET

HOORNSTRAAT

RUE DU CORNET

OUDERGEMSELAAN

RUE STE-GERTRUDE

HOORN-
STRAAT

RUE F HAP

PLACE ST-PIERRE
ST-PIETERSPLEIN

CHAUSSÉE ST-PIERRE

ST-PIETERS STEENWEG

RUE DE LA JONCHAIE

5

RUE GÉNÉRAL LEMAN

GENERAAL LEMANSTRAAT

RUE DU CLOCHER

RUE
JONNIAUX

PLACE
VAN MEYEL-
PLEIN

RUE COL

STEENWEG

ST-PIETERS

BOERENSTRAAT

RUE DE LA TITZ

RUE LOUIS HAP

LA GRANDE HAIE

RUE DE
LA GRANDE HAIE

STATIONSTRAAT

STE ST-PIERRE

ST-PIETERS STEENWEG

AVENUE D'AUDERGHEM

CHAUSSÉE ST-PIERRE

VAN GELE

RUE HAP

LOUIS HAPSTRAAT

RUE DES BOERS

RUE GÉNÉRAL TOMBEUR-STRAAT

RUE DE LA GARE

GROTE HAAGSTRAAT

RUE J
MASSART

RUE LOUIS HAP

RUE LOUIS HAP

LOUIS HAPSTRAAT

RUE LOUIS A GAUTIER

KOLONEL VAN GELESTRAAT

KONINGSVELDSTRAAT

BOERENSTRAAT

JACHTLAAN

AVENUE E DE THIBAULTLAAN

RUE J DU FORT DE
BONCELLES

ETTERBEEK

AVENUE D'AUDERGHEM

RUE BARON LAMBERT

RUE CHAMP DU ROI

A GAUTIERSTRAAT

RUE BARON LAMBERTSTRAAT

RUE DES
COQUELICOTS

RUE GÉNÉRAL
WANGERMEE

RUE DU RUANDA

PLACE DU
RINSDELLE

RINSDELLE-
PLEIN

RUE DU
VINDICTIVE

PLACE DU ROI
VAINQUEUR

KONING OVERWINNAAR-
PLEIN

Tram B1-B2

RUE DE THEUX

CHAUSSÉE DE WAVRE

RUE FETIS

FETISSTRAAT

HERTOG-
STRAAT

GROOT-

RUE P
BENOIT-STRAAT

OUDERGEMSELAAN

RUE DES
PLATANES

RUE DES
ERABLES

AVENUE DE LA CHASSE

RUE DES MOISSONNEURS

RUE DES
CULTIVATEURS

AVENUE DU ONZE NOVEMBRE

AVENUE A GALOPIN-LAAN

RUE GÉNÉRAL HENRY

RUE DES
PERDRIX

AVE D
CHAMPS VELDLAAN

AVENUE

HANSEN-SOULIE-LAAN

6

RUE E HAVAUX-
STRAAT

MORGENLANDSTRAAT

RUE E HAVAUX-
STRAAT

R D GRAND-DUC

AVENUE J MALOU-LAAN

RUE
SNEESSENS

WAVERSESTEENWEG

AVENUE C JOSET

LE MARINEL

RUE DE HAERNE

RUE GÉNÉRAL CAPIAUMONT-STRAAT

PHILIPPE BAUCOSTRAAT

RUE DE CHAMBERY

LA CHASSE
DE JACHT

E. PIRMEZLAAN DE JACHT

DES CHAMPS VELDSTRAAT

AVENUE GÉNÉRAAL FIVE-STRAAT

RUE BAR

PE BAUCO

AVENUE E. PIRMEZ

CHAMBERYSTRAAT

NOTHOMB

JACOBS

V JACOBS-LAAN

PL ST-ANTOINE
ST-ANTOONPL

St-Antoine

RUE DE L'ÉGALITÉ

CHAUSSÉE DE WAVRE

RUE C CODULHAT

RUE COT PONTHIERSTRAAT

DAHISSTRAAT

RUE A DE GERLACHESTRAAT

RUE DE
HAERNE

BECKERSSTRAAT

RUE BUEDTS

RUE GAL HENRY

SQ DE
LÉOPOLDVILLE

RUE BECKERS

Inst. Medico
Chirurgical

RUE DE
DRYPDONDT

AV DE LA FORCE AÉRIENNE

7

NIEUWELAAN

HAERNESTRAAT

R P HAP LEMAITRESTRAAT

ALL J GLINEUR

G

H

Time Out Brussels Guide **325**

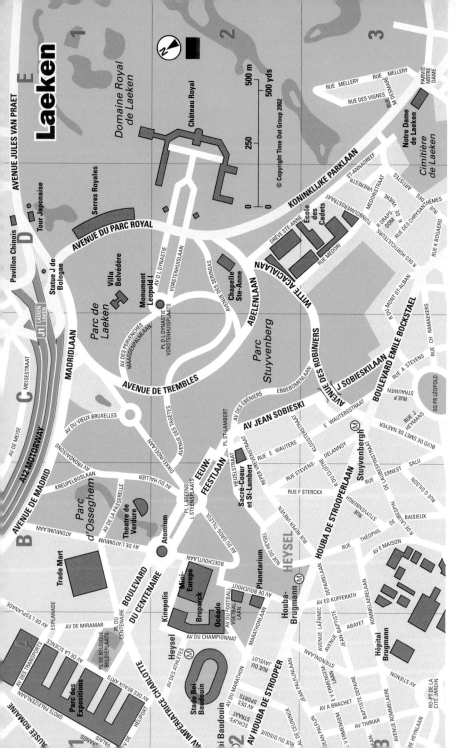

Street Index

Street Index

Lens, rue – p321/324 D7
Léopold II, bvd – p318 A/B1
Léopold III, bvd – p323 H1
Léopold, rue – p317/319 C3
Léopoldville, square de – p325 F6
Lepage, rue Léon – p318 B2
Lesbroussart, rue – p321/324 D/E7
Levure, rue de la – p324 F7
Leys, rue – p323/325 H4
Liberté, place de la – p319/322 D3
Liedekerke, rue de – p322 E/F2
Liégeois, rue des – p324 F7
Ligne, rue de – p319 D3
Limauge, rue – p324 F5
Limite – p322 E1/2
Limnander, rue – p320 A4
Linière, rue de la – p320 B6
Linné, rue – p319 D1
Linthout, rue de – p323 H3/4
Livingstone, ave – p322 F3/4
Livourne, rue de – p321 C6/D7
Locquenghien, rue – p318 A/B2
Loi, rue de la – p319/322/324
          D/E3/4/F4
Loix, place – p321 C6
Lombard, rue du – p317/318 B3/C4
Londres, place de – p321/324 E5
Londres, rue de – p321/324 D/E5
Longue Haie, rue de la – p321 D5
Longue Vie, rue – p321/324 D5
Lorand, rue Georges – p321/324 E5
Louise, ave – p321 C5/6/D6/7
Louvain, chaussée de – p322/323
          E3/F2/3/G/H2
Louvain, place de – p319 D3
Louvain, rue de – p319/322 D/E3
Loxum, rue de – p317/319 C3
Luther, rue – p323 G2/3
Luxembourg, place du – p324 E5
Luxembourg, rue du – p321/324
          D/E4/5
Luzerne, rue de la – p323 H1/2
Lycée, rue de – p320 B7
Lynen, rue Amédée – p322 E2

Madeleine, rue de la – p317/319 C3/4
Madou, place – p319/322 E3
Maes, rue – p321/324 E6
Magasin, rue de – p318 B1
Mahillon, ave Léon – p323 G2/3/H2
Malibran, rue – p324 E6/7
Malines, rue de – p319 C2
Malou, rue Jules – p325 G6
Marchal, ave Felix – p323 G2/H2/3
Marché aux Charbon, rue du –
          p317/318 B3
Marché aux Fromages, rue du –
          p317/318/319 C3
Marché aux Herbes, rue du –
          p317/319 C3
Marché aux Poulets, rue du –
          p317/318 B/C3
Marché, rue du – p319 C1
Marcq, Rue – p318 B2
Marguerite, square – p323 G3
Marie de Bourgogne, rue – p324 E4/5
Marie-Henriette, rue – p324 E6/7
Marie-Therese, rue – p322 E3
Marinel, ave le – p325 H6
Mariniers, rue des – p318 A2
Markelbach, rue Alexandre –
          p322/323 F2
Marnix, ave – p321/324 D5
Maroquin, rue de – p318 A1
Marquis, rue de – p317 C3
Marteau, rue du – p322 E3
Martel, rue Charles – p322 F3
Martyrs, place des – p317, 319 C2
Massart, rue Jean – p325 H5/6
Materiaux, quai des – p318 B1
Matheus, rue Georges – p319 C1
Maurice Lemonnier, bvd – p320 A/B4
Maus, rue Henri – p317/318 B3
Max, ave Emile – p323 H2/3/G3
Max, bvd Adolphe – p317/319 C2
Meeus, square de – p321/324 E4
Meiboom, rue du – p319 D2
Meiser, place Gen – p323 H2
Melsens, rue – p317 B2

Ménages, rue des – p320 A/B5
Mercelis, rue – p321/324 D6
Merchtem, chaussée de – p318 A1
Méridien, rue de – p319/322 E2
Mérinos, rue du – p322 E2
Mérode, rue de – p320 A5/6
Métal, rue du – p320 B6
Michel-Ange, ave – p323 G3/4
Midi, boulevard du – p318/320 A4-6/B6
Midi, rue du – p317/318 B3/4
Mignon, rue Léon – p323 G2
Milcamps, ave Achille – p323 H2/3
Minimes, petite rue des – p317 C4
Minimes, rue des – p317/320/321
          B5/C4-6
Miroir, rue du – p320 B4/5
Moineaux, rue des – p317 B4
Moissonneurs, rue des – p325 H6
Moissons, rue de – p322 E/F2
Mommaerts, rue – p318 A1
Moniteur, rue du – p319 D3
Monnaie, place de la – p317/319 C3
Monrose, rue – p322 F1
Mons, chaussée de – p318 A4
Mont de la Tour, rue – p317 C4
Mont des Arts – p317 C4
Montagne aux Herbes Potagères,
          rue – p317/319 C2/3
Montagne, rue de la – p317/319 C3
Mont-Blanc, rue du – p320 B7
Montoyer, rue – p321/324 E4
Montserrat, rue E – p320 B5
Moscou, rue du – p320 B6
Mot, rue de – p325 G5
Moulin, rue du – p319/322 E1/2/F2
Murillo, rue – p323/325 H4
Musée, place du – p317 C4

Namur, rue de – p321 D4/5
Nancy, rue de – p320 B4-5
Naples, rue de – p321/324 D5
Natation, rue de la – p324 F6
Nerviens, ave des – p325 G/H5
Neufchâtel, rue du – p320/321 C7
Neuve, rue – p317/319 C2
Neuvième de Ligne, bvd du – p318 B1
Newton, rue – p323 G/H3
Nicolay, rue – p319 C1
Nieuport, bvd du – p318 A2
Ninove, chaussée de – p318 A3
Ninove, place de – p318 A3
Niveau, rue du – p318 A1/2
Nord, passage du – p317/319 C2
Nord, rue du – p319/322 E2/3
Nothomb, rue – p325 G6
Notre Dame du Sommeil, rue – p318
          A2/3
Notre Seigneur, rue de – p320 B4
Nouveau Marché aux Grains, place
          du – p318 B2
Nouvelle, ave – p324/325 F6/7/G7
Noyer, rue du – p323/325 G2/3/H3/4

Olivier, rue l' – p322 E1
Ommegang, rue de l' – p319 D2
Onze Novembre, ave du – p325 H6
Opale, square de l' – p323 H3
Ophem, rue d' – p318 B2
Orient, rue de l' – p324/325 F6
Orley, rue Van – p319 D2
Orme, rue de l' – p323/325 H4
Ortelius, rue – p322 F3
Orts, rue Auguste – p317 B3
Otlet, rue – p318/320 A4
Oudart, rue V – p323 H3
Oultremont, rue d' – p325 H4

Pacheco, boulevard – p319 D2
Pacification, rue de – p322 E/F3
Paille, rue de la – p317/321 C4
Paix, rue de la – p321/324 D5
Palais, place des – p321 D4
Palmerston, ave – p322 F3
Paquot, rue Jean – p324 F7
Paradis, rue de – p317 C4
Parc, ave du – p320 A/B7
Paris, rue de – p321, 324 D/E5
Parme, rue de – p320 B6/7
Parnasse, rue de – p324 E5

Paroissiens, rue des – p317 C3
Pascale, rue de – p324 F4
Passchendaele, rue de – p318 B1/2
Patrie, place de la – p323 G/H1
Patriotes, rue des – p323 G3
Pavie, rue de – p323 F2/3
Pavots, rue des – p323 H1
Pélican, rue du – p319 C1/2
Péniches, quai des – p318 B1
Pépin, rue du – p321 C/D5
Pépinière, rue de la – p321 D4/5
Pequeur, square Robert – p320 A4
Perche, rue de la – p320 A7
Perdrix, rue des – p325 H6
Perle, rue de la – p318 A1/2
Persil, rue de – p317/319 C2
Petit Sablon, place du – p321 C5
Petits Carmes, rue des – p321 C/D4
Pètre, ave Georges – p322 F2
Peuple, rue du – p319 C1
Peuplier, rue de – p318 B2
Philanthropie, rue de la – p320 B5
Philippe le Bon, rue – p322 F3
Philomène, rue – p322 E1
Pieremans, rue – p320 B5
Pierres de Taille, quai aux – p319
Pierres, rue des – p317/318 B3
Pierron, rue Evariste – p318 A2
Piers, rue – p318 A1
Pigeons, rue des – p317 C4
Pirmez, ave Eudore – p325 G6
Plantes, rue des – p319 D1
Plantin, rue – p318/320 A4
Plasky, ave Eugène – p323 H2/3
Plasky, square Eugène – p323 H2
Platanes, rue des – p325 G6
Plume, rue de la – p320 B5
Poelaert, place – p320/321 C5
Poincaré, bvd – p320 A4
Poinçon, rue de – p317/320 B4
Poisonnier, rue des – p317 B3
Pont de la Carpe – p318 B3
Ponthier, rue Cdt – p325 H7
Pont-Neuf, rue du – p319 C2
Port, ave du – p318 B1
Porte de Hal, ave de – p320 A5
Porte de Tervuren – p325 H5
Porte Rouge, rue de la – p320 B5
Poste, rue de la – p319/322 D/E1
Potagère, rue – p322 E1-2
Poterie, rue de la – p318 A3
Poudrière, rue de la – p318 A3
Prado, rue du – p318 A2
Prague, rue de – p320 A6/7
Prairie, rue de la – p319 D1
Presbytère, rue du – p318 A1
Président, rue du – p321 D6
Presse, rue de la – p319/322 D3
Prêtres, rue de – p320 B5
Prévost Delaunay, square – p323 G1
Prévoyance, rue de la – p320 B5
Prince-Royal, rue de – p321 D5/6
Princes, galerie des – p317 C3
Princes, rue des – p317 C3
Prins Albert, rue de – p321 D5/6
Progrès, rue du – p319 C/D1
Prosperité, rue de l' – p318 A1
Putterie – p317 C3

Quatre Bras, rue des – p321 C5
Quatre Journées, bvd des – p322 F2
Querelle, rue de la – p320 B4/5
Quetelet, place – p319/322 E2
Quint, rue – p323 F/G3

Radium, rue du – p323 G/H2
Ransfort, rue – p318 A2
Rasière, rue de la – p320 B5
Rasson, rue – p323 G/H3
Ravenstein, galerie – p317 C4
Ravenstein, rue – p317/319/321
          C3/4
Rectangle, rue du – p318 A3
Régence, rue de la – p317/321 C4/5
Régent, bvd du – p319/321/322/324
          D4/5/E3/4
Reine, galerie de la – p317 C3
Reine, place de la – p319/322 E1
Reine, rue de la – p317 C3

Advertisers' Index

Pleas refer to the relevant pages for addresses
and telephone numbers

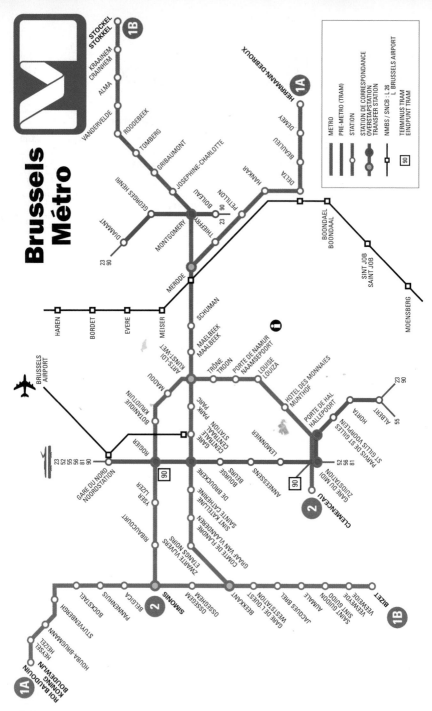

Brussels Métro

1B STOCKEL / STOKKEL
KRAAINEM / CRAINHEM
ALMA
VANDERVELDE
ROODEBEEK
TOMBERG
GRIBAUMONT
JOSEPHINE-CHARLOTTE
GEORGES HENRI
DIAMANT
MONTGOMERY
MERODE

BOILEAU
PETILLON
HANKAR
DELTA
90
23

1A HERMANN-DEBROUX
DEMEY
BEAULIEU

BOONDAEL / BOONDAAL
SINT JOB / SAINT JOB
MOENSBERG

HAREN
BORDET
EVERE
MEISER

SCHUMAN
MAELBEEK / MAELBEEK
ARTS-LOI / KUNST-WET
TRÔNE / TROON
PORTE DE NAMUR / NAAMSEPOORT
LOUISE / LOUIZA
HOTEL DES MONNAIES / MUNTHOF
PORTE DE HAL / HALLEPOORT
HORTA
ALBERT
23
90
55

LEMONNIER

MADOU
BOTANIQUE / KRUIDTUIN
GARE CENTRALE / CENTRAAL STATION
PARC / PARK
ANNEESSENS
PARVIS DE ST GILLES / ST GILLIS VOORPLEIN
GARE DU MIDI / ZUIDSTATION **2**
52
56
81

ROGIER
BOURSE / BEURS
DE BROUCKERE
SAINTE CATHERINE / SINT KATELIJNE
YSER / IJZER
90
90

BRUSSELS AIRPORT ✈
23
52
55
56
81
90

GARE DU NORD / NOORDSTATION

RIBAUCOURT
COMTE DE FLANDRE / GRAAF VAN VLAANDEREN
ETANGS NOIRS / ZWARTE VIJVERS
OSSEGHEM / OSSEGEM
BEEKKANT
BELGICA
PANNENHUIS
BOCKSTAEL
STUYVENBERGH
HOUBA-BRUGMANN
HEYSEL / HEIZEL
ROI BAUDOUIN / KONING BOUDEWIJN **1A**

SIMONIS **2**

GARE DE L'OUEST / WESTSTATION
JACQUES BREL
AUMALE
SAINT-GUIDON / SINT-GUIDO
VEEWEYDE
BIZET **1B**

CLEMENCEAU **2**

332 Time Out Brussels Guide